*Colonial
Chesapeake
Society*

Publication of this book has been supported by grants from the Maryland State Archives and Hall of Records Commission, the Maryland Humanities Council, and Historic St. Mary's City and St. Maries Citty Foundation.

Colonial Chesapeake Society

Published for
The Institute of
Early American
History and
Culture,
Williamsburg,
Virginia, by
The University
of North
Carolina Press
Chapel Hill &
London

Edited by

Lois Green Carr

Philip D. Morgan

and Jean B. Russo

The Institute of Early American History
and Culture
is sponsored jointly by
the College of William and Mary
and the Colonial Williamsburg Foundation.

Library of Congress Cataloging-in-Publication Data

Colonial Chesapeake society.

   Includes index.
   1. Chesapeake Bay Region (Md. and Va.)—History.
2. Maryland—History—Colonial period, ca. 1600–1775.
3. Virginia—History—Colonial period, ca. 1600–1775.
I. Carr, Lois Green. II. Morgan, Philip D. III. Russo,
Jean Burrell.
F187.C5C65   1988   975.5′18   88-4719
ISBN 0-8078-1800-3 (alk. paper)
ISBN 0-8078-4343-1 (pbk. alk.paper)

The paper in this book meets the
guidelines for permanence and durability
of the Committee on Production
Guidelines for Book Longevity of the
Council on Library Resources.

Printed in the United States of America

92 91   5 4 3 2

For Thad W. Tate

Contents

Preface

The Maryland State Archives is pleased to assist in the publication of this volume of papers drawn from the proceedings of two conferences held in 1984 in honor of Maryland's 350th Anniversary. The Institute of Early American History and Culture cosponsored both, one with the Johns Hopkins University, and the other with the Maryland State Archives as the Third Conference on Maryland History. The latter also was cosponsored by the St. Mary's City Commission, St. Mary's College of Maryland, and the Maryland Humanities Council.

The decade from 1974, when the First Conference on Maryland History was held in honor of retiring State Archivist Morris L. Radoff, to 1984 encompasses a remarkable renaissance in Chesapeake studies that continues to the present day. No other period since Herbert Baxter Adams's seminars at the Johns Hopkins University at the beginning of this century has witnessed such a ferment of interest in the history of our region. That such an interest should manifest itself again after seventy years of relative quiet is no accident. The Institute of Early American History and Culture, the Maryland Humanities Council, and the Maryland State Archives through their material support of scholarship, conferences, and publications have provided the setting and much of the stimulus. Today they are joined by the Department of History of the University of Maryland, which has undertaken a major new initiative in the promotion of graduate study in early American history.

In both Virginia and Maryland the archival resources provide a rich context for exploration of a wide range of topics, to which the following essays attest. In Virginia, the collections at Colonial Williamsburg and at the State Library in Richmond, to name but two, are a treasure trove of the highest order. In Maryland, the private papers of the Maryland Historical Society and the public records program of the State Archives begun by Dr. Morris Radoff and Gust Skordas in the late 1930s and continued unabated today in the context of a new state-of-the-art Hall of Records supply an unparalleled, readily accessible wealth of detail that even for the eighteenth century continues to grow with the discovery of exciting new sources. For example, the mother of an observer at a recent University of Maryland conference organized by John J. McCusker was so inspired by the new Hall of Records and the intellectual excitement generated by the conference that she promptly encouraged a relative to give his papers to the State Archives. Who could have imagined that one ledger would contain some of the earliest extant accounts for a storekeeper in Annapolis?

The successful study of history requires two essential ingredients: accessible records and carefully focused inquiry. Archivists can provide the former through sensible management of their collections and by supplying a hospitable environment within which scholars can work. Maryland is exceptionally fortunate in having good records and a government that cares about providing proper facilities for their preservation and use. By cooperating with such agencies as the Institute of Early American History and Culture and the Maryland Humanities Council in sponsoring conferences like those that produced this volume, and by supplying space for research fellows, we also have been able to offer an agreeable context for productive discussion and debate. But without the dogged determination of people like Thad Tate, Lois Carr, Jean Russo, and Phil Morgan to see the results published, collegial discussions of current research discoveries at the Archives and papers presented at conferences achieve little of permanence. Indeed, in large measure the credit for the burgeoning list of publications arising from the interest in seventeenth- and eighteenth-century Chesapeake society belongs to Thad Tate and Lois Green Carr, who have coerced into print more than one generation of aspiring scholars by their own example, and through countless hours of self-effacing suggestions for improvement.

To paraphrase Charles Dickens, there are not many places I find it more agreeable to revisit than some places to which I have never been. Dickens took delight in finding everything the same. "For, my acquaintance with those spots is of such long standing, and has ripened into an intimacy of so affectionate a nature, that I take particular interest in assuring myself that they are unchanged." Thanks to the editors of this volume and its other contributors, we can take pleasure in finding that everything in the early history of the Chesapeake is not what we thought it to have been, but is instead a world of mystery filled with expectations of discovering what we do not yet know.

Edward C. Papenfuse
Maryland State Archivist and
Commissioner of Land Patents

*Colonial
Chesapeake
Society*

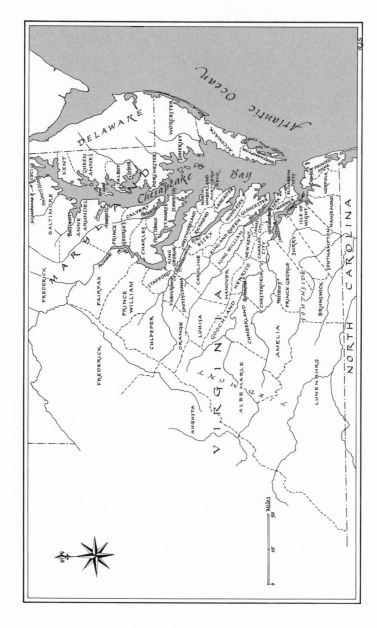

The Chesapeake, 1750

Drawn by Richard Stinely

Introduction

LIKE THE rivers that replenish the Bay, an out-
pouring of recent historical scholarship has enriched our understanding
of the early Chesapeake region. Fed by many springs, this historiography
has flowed through two major channels. The first, like a stream in spate,
dredges the unseen foundations that govern ordinary people's lives. How
long did people live? What proportion were able to marry and raise
families? Who prospered and why? How were property and power acquired and transferred to later generations? How did the thousands of
daily decisions of human beings affect the development of social, economic, and political structures and what constraints, in turn, did these
structures put on such decisions? The second channel, like rapids where
swirling waters and brilliant colors catch the eye, evokes the iridescent
surfaces rather than excavates the underlying foundations of colonial
Chesapeake society. What were the manners, customs, and social con-
ventions of the day? How did Chesapeake residents fashion their views of
the world? What cultural meaning can be extracted from the humble
activities—court day and cockfight, dance and dress, gambling and gestures—of ordinary people? How were the values of the great planters
bound up with their great houses, their horses, their planting and marketing of tobacco?

These two channels are not unique to Chesapeake historiography;
rather, they have guided much contemporary historical writing and, in the
smaller universe of early America, this has meant preeminently New
England history. Indeed, many of the questions asked of the Chesapeake
experience were pioneered in New England (and, before that, early modern England and France). A major consequence of New England's primacy was that it became the yardstick by which the Chesapeake and other
regions were measured. As the new Chesapeake research tumbled forth,
stark differences from the northern experience commanded most attention. Deviations could easily translate into deficiencies: unmarried servants rather than families; dying young rather than living old; the rigors of
tobacco cultivation rather than the more relaxed routines of subsistence
farming; scattering to the winds rather than settling down together; importing manufactured goods rather than making them; slave labor rather

than family labor; looking out for number one rather than for everyone. The Chesapeake, it could be argued, barely qualified as a society at all; rather, it seemed a Hobbesian nightmare.

Ironically, then, the first wave of the "new social history," which sought to understand the Chesapeake experience on its own terms, seemed to confirm New England as normative, the Chesapeake and other regions as deviant. However, as research broadened to other colonies, as some of the starker and more simplistic contrasts between Chesapeake and New England were moderated, and as we learned of yet more ways in which New England was exceptional, the Chesapeake gradually moved from the wings to center stage. The region now appears quite representative of a whole range of British colonial endeavors. If exploitation, materialism, and individualism, for instance, were some of the more prominent characteristics of British colonies, then certainly the Chesapeake held its own. Located roughly equidistant from Britain's most northerly and southerly Atlantic colonies, the Chesapeake may be said to represent the middle ground—in more ways than one. Containing both plantations and farms, an aristocracy and a broad yeomanry, a staple and a mixed agriculture, the Chesapeake was something of a hybrid, mixing elements from colonies both to the north and south of it. Indeed, perhaps the Chesapeake (certainly not New England) ought to be considered the norm against which to measure all other British American societies. If so, the Chesapeake will, in a sense, merely resume the central place that it occupied in the early modern Anglo-American world—the oldest, largest, most populous, economically valuable, and politically sophisticated region on the mainland.[1]

The deluge of recent scholarly work on the early Chesapeake, it must be acknowledged, has rarely pursued such comparative themes. More inwardly than outwardly directed, it has focused upon the dynamics, the internal evolution of its chosen society. Indeed, the introspective quality

1. New England's population (discounting Indians) was larger than that of the Chesapeake throughout most of the 17th century, but not generally thereafter. All the other characterizations are surely self-evident. For a provocative account of Chesapeake development, set within the context of British America, see Jack P. Greene, *Pursuits of Happiness: The Social Development of Early Modern British Colonies and the Formation of American Culture* (Chapel Hill, N.C., 1988). It is also notable that in 1774 net worth of free wealth holders in the Chesapeake was somewhere between the low levels achieved in New England and the extremely high levels achieved in the island colonies. See John J. McCusker and Russell R. Menard, *The Economy of British America, 1607–1789* (Chapel Hill, N.C., 1985), 61.

of much of this region's recent literature is quite striking; loving details seem to matter more than far-reaching generalizations. Yet lurking behind the welter of information are the rough outlines of a new chronology, based less on public events, more on deep changes in the social fabric. The broad lineaments of a Chesapeake social narrative are beginning to emerge. One of the purposes of the introduction, therefore, is to sketch this narrative, to provide a synthesis of present knowledge. Because other historiographical surveys exist, we concentrate largely on work completed in the last decade. Our second purpose is to identify a number of dominant themes in the essays in this volume, indicating what they have in common and locating them in the broader framework of recent scholarly work. Finally, we advance some suggestions about the directions that Chesapeake scholarship might take and end with a brief prospective agenda for future work.[2]

I

The seventeenth century, where the bulk of the new social history on the Chesapeake has concentrated, is now seen as

2. The best historiographical survey of the 17th-century literature, now a decade old, is Thad W. Tate, "The Seventeenth-Century Chesapeake and Its Modern Historians," in Tate and David L. Ammerman, eds., *The Chesapeake in the Seventeenth Century: Essays on Anglo-American Society* (Chapel Hill, N.C., 1979), 3–50. A more recent survey, primarily of monographs published during the past ten years, is Anita H. Rutman, "Still Planting the Seeds of Hope: The Recent Literature of the Early Chesapeake Region," *Virginia Magazine of History and Biography*, XCV (1987), 3–24. Two volumes in the History of the American Colonies series—Aubrey C. Land, *Colonial Maryland: A History* (Millwood, N.Y., 1981) and Warren M. Billings, John E. Selby, and Thad W. Tate, *Colonial Virginia: A History* (White Plains, N.Y., 1986)— provide good surveys. The latter, in particular, contains an excellent bibliographical essay. For a sweeping interpretation of Chesapeake society, see Allan Kulikoff, *Tobacco and Slaves: The Development of Southern Cultures in the Chesapeake, 1680–1800* (Chapel Hill, N.C., 1986). Our review of recent literature (1975–1987) reveals a total of 54 monographs (5 of which are in dissertation series), 4 essay collections, 12 documentary collections or editions (not counting the relevant "Great White Men" papers projects, on the grounds that these are about much more than the Chesapeake), 205 articles (excluding those later incorporated in monographs), and 52 noteworthy and unpublished dissertations. This is work that focuses exclusively or predominantly on the Chesapeake (there are, of course, pertinent general works that include much Chesapeake material). We will mention many, but certainly not all, of these particular and general works in the notes to this introduction.

something of a piece. Its historians have described a society disrupted by high mortality, excessive morbidity, imbalanced sex ratios, and a spartan material existence. They have emphasized the difficulties of establishing farms where the great majority of settlers had to start with nothing but freedom dues after spending many of their productive years as servants. They have seen impermanence woven into the very fabric of daily life, visible in everything from the houses in which people lived to the inability of many immigrants ever to become parents and of most parents ever to see their children reach majority. Fragility and insecurity have been the dominant catchwords.[3]

However, scholars have differed in assessing the consequences of these conditions. Some have stressed exploitation and instability—the pains of servitude, the parentless children without kin to assist them, the isolation of plantations, the frequent turnover that early death brought to political office, depriving inhabitants of secure and experienced leaders, the racial and class conflict. In the most compelling portrait of seventeenth-century Chesapeake life, Edmund Morgan has described a society barely managing to contain explosive social tensions. In his view, indentured servitude paved the way for slavery, and unmarried, landless ex-servants were a dangerous social element that helped make possible a number of late-seventeenth-century disorders, including Bacon's Rebellion, the largest and most violent colonial revolt of the century. Others have emphasized the development of the stabilizing institutions of church and local government, the creation of neighborhood networks of self-

3. Two collections of essays have been important in the dissemination of these views: the one by Tate and Ammerman previously mentioned, and the one edited by Aubrey C. Land, Lois Green Carr, and Edward C. Papenfuse, *Law, Society, and Politics in Early Maryland* (Baltimore, 1977), although the influence of a much earlier essay, Bernard Bailyn, "Politics and Social Structure in Virginia," in James Morton Smith, ed., *Seventeenth-Century America: Essays in Colonial History* (Chapel Hill, N.C., 1959), 90–115, cannot be overestimated. For recent work in the same vein, see Daniel Blake Smith, "Mortality and Family in the Colonial Chesapeake," *Journal of Interdisciplinary History*, VIII (1978), 403–427; Karen Ordahl Kupperman, "Apathy and Death in Early Jamestown," *Journal of American History*, LXVI (1979), 24–40; Cary Carson *et al.*, "Impermanent Architecture in the Southern American Colonies," *Winterthur Portfolio*, XVI (1981), 135–196; and Gloria L. Main, *Tobacco Colony: Life in Early Maryland, 1650–1720* (Princeton, N.J., 1982). For an account that stresses the 17th-century Chesapeake's dynamism and innovativeness from a geographical perspective, see Robert D. Mitchell, "American Origins and Regional Institutions: The Seventeenth-Century Chesapeake," Association of American Geographers, *Annals*, LXXIII (1983), 404–420.

help, the strong horizontal bonds among siblings, cousins, stepbrothers and stepsisters, the economic opportunity found in an expanding economy, and the upward political mobility in a society made fluid by high mortality. From this perspective, much of the seventeenth century was the age of the moderately successful small planter.[4]

How can we resolve these disagreements? As with many scholarly

4. Edmund S. Morgan, *American Slavery, American Freedom: The Ordeal of Colonial Virginia* (New York, 1975). The account of 17th-century Virginia in this study is far more subtle than many of its critics have noted. For instance, Morgan never denies the efforts to create social links—*vide* his pairing of the chapters "Living with Death" and "Settling Down," which cover the same years. For additional work that, in one way or another, supports or extends Morgan's views, see T. H. Breen, "Looking Out for Number One: The Cultural Limits on Public Policy in Early Virginia," in Breen, *Puritans and Adventurers: Change and Persistence in Early America* (New York, 1980), 106–126; T. H. Breen and Stephen Innes, *"Myne Owne Ground": Race and Freedom on Virginia's Eastern Shore, 1640–1676* (New York, 1980); and Joseph Douglas Deal III, "Race and Class in Colonial Virginia: Indians, Englishmen, and Africans on the Eastern Shore during the Seventeenth Century" (Ph.D. diss., University of Rochester, 1981). For work that generally emphasizes stability, see many of the essays cited in n. 3, above, and the community studies cited in n. 26, below, as well as Virginia Bernhard, "Poverty and the Social Order in Seventeenth-Century Virginia," *VMHB*, LXXXV (1977), 141–155; Lois Green Carr, "The Foundations of Social Order: Local Government in Colonial Maryland," in Bruce C. Daniels, ed., *Town and County: Essays on the Structure of Local Government in the American Colonies* (Middletown, Conn., 1978), 72–110; Russell R. Menard, Lois Green Carr, and Lorena S. Walsh, "A Small Planter's Profits: The Cole Estate and the Growth of the Early Chesapeake Economy," *William and Mary Quarterly*, 3d Ser., XL (1983), 171–196; Darrett B. Rutman and Anita H. Rutman, *A Place in Time: Middlesex County, Virginia, 1650–1750* (New York, 1984); Lois Green Carr, "Sources of Political Stability and Upheaval in Seventeenth-Century Maryland," *Maryland Historical Magazine*, LXXIX (1984), 44–70; and Jon Kukla, "Order and Chaos in Early America: Political and Social Stability in Pre-Restoration Virginia," *American Historical Review*, XC (1985), 275–298. There is also an interesting debate on the character of the law in early Virginia; cf. Warren M. Billings, "The Transfer of English Law to Virginia, 1606–1650," in K. R. Andrews, N. P. Canny, and P. E. H. Hair, eds., *The Westward Enterprise: English Activities in Ireland, the Atlantic, and America, 1480–1650* (Liverpool, 1978), 215–244, and "Pleading, Procedure, and Practice: The Meaning of Due Process of Law in Seventeenth-Century Virginia," *Journal of Southern History*, XLVII (1981), 569–584, with David Thomas Konig, " 'Dale's Laws' and the Non-Common Law Origins of Criminal Justice in Virginia," *American Journal of Legal History*, XXVI (1982), 354–375, and "Criminal Justice in the New World: English Anticipations and the Virginia Experience in the Sixteenth and Seventeenth Centuries," *ibid.*, forthcoming. John M. Murrin's research into jury trials throughout British America promises to illumine this subject.

debates, much can be attributed to where emphasis is placed—on desta-
bilizing social processes or stabilizing social institutions, on the many
exploited servants or the many small planters—but also to the difficulties
of drawing qualitative conclusions from quantitative evidence, and perhaps even to the personal temperaments of the respective historians.
Closer attention to variations across space and time may help resolve
seeming differences of interpretation. The disruptive forces in seventeenth-century Chesapeake society were strongest, of course, in the earliest years, and the stabilizing influences gradually exerted themselves as
the century proceeded. We need further analysis of how long the forces of
instability held sway and how quickly the countering networks of support
arose. It is notable, for instance, that the most sustained riposte to Edmund Morgan's vision of rampant individualism and harsh exploitation in
early Virginia is a study of the evolving web of associations in Middlesex
County, a frontier region settled in the *second* half of the seventeenth
century. By that time, older settlements were well established and the
nearest lifeline was not three thousand miles across an ocean. The con-
flicting views of the economic prospects of landless ex-servants in the late
seventeenth century may, in fact, both be correct—but for different parts
of the Chesapeake. In the oldest settled areas, economic fortunes may
have taken a turn for the worse well before Bacon's Rebellion, but in the
newer frontier areas (which would include parts of Maryland), economic
betterment may have been a reality far longer. Nevertheless,
prosopographical studies in both Maryland and Middlesex County have
revealed social networks that challenge the Hobbesian view of Chesapeake society. Further investigations of freedmen's careers, especially in
Virginia, will be necessary to clarify the issue.[5]

A major watershed in colonial Chesapeake history occurred around the

---

5. Rutman and Rutman, *A Place in Time*. For a perceptive view of the contrasting
interpretations of Bacon's Rebellion and Maryland's revolution of 1689, see John M.
Murrin's review of *Chesapeake in the Seventeenth Century*, ed. Tate and Ammerman, in
WMQ, 3d Ser., XXXVIII (1981), 115–121. The Rutmans' evidence that 24 Baco-
nians in Middlesex County were drawn from a full cross section of the local population hardly disproves Morgan's broader contentions. However, Lois Green Carr and
David William Jordan argue that there is little evidence that Morgan's disruptive
freedman was a factor in disorders in Maryland (*Maryland's Revolution of Government,
1689–1692* [Ithaca, N.Y., 1974], 192–193), and David T. Konig's work on the county
courts of 17th-century Virginia suggests that the small to middling landholder was the
chief promoter of discontent. For a stirring narrative, but eccentric interpretation, of
Bacon's Rebellion, see Stephen Saunders Webb, *1676: The End of American Indepen-*

turn of the century. One engine of change was economic, with consequences that reached into every sphere of Chesapeake life. Decades of rapid economic growth based on farm building came to an end in the late seventeenth century, although perhaps not so immediately on new frontiers. At the same time, the marketing of tobacco shifted from a supply-led operation, typical of the early development of a new product, to one led by demand. This process, combined with European wars that interrupted trade, ushered in a long period of stagnation and curtailed opportunity for the poor, at least in the older regions. Two major responses resulted. First, better-off planters, in particular, added wheat and other grains to their crops and produced cloth, leather, and metal products that earlier they had imported. Hence, local markets began to develop and over time the economy became more diversified and stable. Second, economic misfortune in the Chesapeake, combined with improving economic fortunes in England and more attractive opportunities in other British colonies, helped cut off the flow of white servants, prompting the momentous switch to black slave labor, a transformation that in turn was facilitated by the greater availability of African slaves in the late seventeenth century.

The turn to slavery had social as well as economic consequences. African slaves were an expensive investment, and initially only affluent planters could afford to purchase them, thereby generally increasing social distances. At the same time, however, slavery created a common bond among all free whites, regardless of position, and thus encouraged unity as well as stratification among whites. Slavery brought new and often frightening tensions to Chesapeake society. Unfortunately the institution also proved an effective way of repressing a large segment of the laboring population and thus contributed to the growing stability of the region. The implications of this "unthinking decision," not just for blacks, but for the society at large, were tragic.[6]

---

dence (New York, 1984). An excellent study of 17th-century Maryland politics is David W. Jordan, *Foundations of Representative Government in Maryland, 1632–1715* (New York, 1987).

6. Russell R. Menard, "The Tobacco Industry in the Chesapeake Colonies, 1617–1730: An Interpretation," *Research in Economic History*, V (1980), 109–177; McCusker and Menard, *Economy of British America*, chap. 6; Paul G. E. Clemens, *The Atlantic Economy and Colonial Maryland's Eastern Shore: From Tobacco to Grain* (Ithaca, N.Y., 1980); Lois Green Carr's essay in this volume; Russell R. Menard, "From Servants to

Another motor of change was demographic. Despite continuing high mortality rates, the number of native-born whites gradually outnumbered immigrants toward the end of the seventeenth century. The consequences of this transformation, like those in the economic sphere, were mixed. On the one hand, it mitigated the disruptive effects of unbalanced sex ratios, late marriages, short life expectancies, and absence of kin that were the experience of most seventeenth-century immigrants. On the other hand, a predominantly creole population sharply reduced social mobility as planters began to live long enough to see children come of age and step into inheritable family positions. Indeed, this period saw the emergence and consolidation of the great planter families, undoubtedly tied to earlier and hence longer marriages and perhaps increased longevity, as well as to the introduction of slavery and the contraction of opportunity for more humble inhabitants; the dynamic of this emergence deserves further study. These "first" families supplied the capital and entrepreneurial skills for frontier development and early diversification and provided much-needed political and social leadership.[7]

A third source of change may be labeled anglicization, to borrow a shorthand term much in vogue. In the late seventeenth century the Chesapeake, and many other colonial regions, became more closely inte-

---

Slaves: The Transformation of the Chesapeake Labor System," *Southern Studies*, XVI (1977), 355–390. It is certainly true that we need tobacco price series by region. For the impact of the shift from indentured servitude to slavery, see Morgan, *American Slavery, American Freedom*, 180–362, and Kulikoff, *Tobacco and Slaves*, 37–43 and *passim*. The phrase "unthinking decision" is from the title of chapter 2 of Winthrop D. Jordan, *White Over Black: American Attitudes toward the Negro, 1550–1812* (Chapel Hill, N.C., 1968).

7. See Kulikoff, *Tobacco and Slaves*, 42–43, for a review of the literature on the demographic transition, and Rutman and Rutman, *A Place in Time*, 76, for precise data. On the rise of a native-born elite, see David W. Jordan, "Political Stability and the Emergence of a Native Elite in Maryland," in Tate and Ammerman, eds., *Chesapeake in the Seventeenth Century*, 243–273; Carole Shammas, "English-Born and Creole Elites in Turn-of-the-Century Virginia," *ibid.*, 274–296; and Rutman and Rutman, *A Place in Time*, chap. 6. On the rise of the great planters, the work of Aubrey C. Land is still the place to begin: see *The Dulanys of Maryland: A Biographical Study of Daniel Dulany, the Elder (1685–1753) and Daniel Dulany, the Younger (1722–1797)* (Baltimore, 1955) and "Economic Base and Social Structure: The Northern Chesapeake in the Eighteenth Century," *Journal of Economic History*, XXV (1965), 639–654; and Clemens, *Atlantic Economy*, chap. 5. There is disagreement as to whether longevity increased. See Rutman, "Still Planting the Seeds of Hope," *VMHB*, XCV (1987), 7–9.

grated into a British Atlantic world. There is much to learn about exactly how this process occurred. Certainly the emerging gentry increasingly aspired to English norms of gentility. They built the model towns of Annapolis and Williamsburg while also gradually reconciling themselves to the lack of significant urban centers by extolling the virtues of country seats. Anglicization was further encouraged by the receding of the raw frontier and the stabilization of family life. Planters continued to give highest priority to capital investment, but now they paid more attention to creature comfort. Those who could afford to improved their houses and acquired consumer goods in greater profusion and variety. As more integrated members of the empire, the wealthier among Chesapeake residents gradually partook of the great explosion of consumption that swept England in the first half of the eighteenth century. To use T. H. Breen's phrase, this new world was "an empire of goods."[8]

8. The term *anglicization* is closely associated with the work of John M. Murrin, who pioneered the way in "Anglicizing an American Colony: The Transformation of Provincial Massachusetts" (Ph.D. diss., Yale University, 1966). For an excellent account of how the Atlantic shrank in the late 17th and early 18th centuries, see Ian K. Steele, *The English Atlantic, 1675–1740: An Exploration of Communication and Community* (New York, 1986). Studies of consumption, spurred in particular by Neil McKendrick, John Brewer, and J. H. Plumb, *The Birth of a Consumer Society: The Commercialization of Eighteenth-Century England* (London, 1982), are multiplying rapidly. For a most stimulating review of the literature, see T. H. Breen, "An Empire of Goods: The Anglicization of Colonial America, 1690–1776," *Journal of British Studies*, XXV (1986), 467–499. However, it should be noted that in the Chesapeake, at least, planters participated in this "empire" while putting a diminishing proportion of their estates into consumer goods. For detailed work on the Chesapeake, see Lois Green Carr and Lorena S. Walsh, "Changing Life Styles in Colonial St. Mary's County," Regional Economic History Research Center, *Working Papers*, I, no. 3 (1978), 72–118; Carr and Walsh, "Inventories and the Analysis of Wealth and Consumption Patterns in St. Mary's County, Maryland, 1658–1777," *Historical Methods*, XIII (1980), 81–104; Carole Shammas, "Consumer Behavior in Colonial America," *Social Science History*, VI (1982), 67–86 (see also Shammas, "The Domestic Environment in Early Modern England and America," *Journal of Social History*, XIV [1980], 3–24); Main, *Tobacco Colony*, chaps. 5–7; Lorena S. Walsh, "Urban Amenities and Rural Sufficiency: Living Standards and Consumer Behavior in the Colonial Chesapeake, 1643–1777," *Jour. Econ. Hist.*, XLIII (1983), 109–117; Lois Green Carr and Lorena S. Walsh, "Changing Life Styles and Consumer Behavior in the Colonial Chesapeake," in Cary Carson, Ronald Hoffman, and Peter J. Albert, eds., *Of Consuming Interests: The Style of Life in the Eighteenth Century* (Charlottesville, Va., forthcoming); and Cary Carson and Lorena S. Walsh, "The Material Life of the Early American Housewife," *Winterthur Portfolio* (forthcoming).

By the second quarter of the eighteenth century, then, the familiar contours of Chesapeake society were in place, and consolidation proceeded apace during the next few decades. From then until the Revolution was the "golden age" of Chesapeake society. A small and increasingly cosmopolitan planter elite dominated the society. The planter mansions that sprang up throughout the region were fitting monuments to this group's self-confidence and power. Below the elite existed a large number of middling planters and yeomen farmers, bound to the elite in many ways, not least by their shared status as landowners, tobacco planters, and slaveholders. The Chesapeake assumed the mantle of a stable, integrated social order. Local communities came together in ordered fashion in their county courts, militia musters, and parish churches. Politics tended to be placid, as the voters' representatives served their constituents with a skillful blend of public-spirited high-mindedness and oligarchic high-handedness.[9]

A fundamental prop of the golden era was an improved economy. The opening of the French market early in the eighteenth century brought renewed life to the tobacco industry, and growing diversification made the economy less dependent on a single crop. About 1750, economic growth began once more, this time tied to improving profits from exports. Oronoco tobacco prices soared. In some areas, vigorous growth rested on a rapid acceleration of the shift into wheat and corn for export, spurred by the opening of new markets in southern Europe and the expansion of old ones such as in the West Indies. The development of milling, iron production, and shipbuilding contributed to an increasingly diversified

9. We draw heavily here on Rhys Isaac, *The Transformation of Virginia, 1740–1790* (Chapel Hill, N.C., 1982), pt. 1, but for a more detailed rendering of the social structure, see Rutman and Rutman, *A Place in Time*, chaps. 5 and 8. On the gentry houses, see Daniel D. Reiff, *Small Georgian Houses in England and Virginia: Origins and Development through the 1750s* (London, 1986) and William M. S. Rasmussen, "Designers, Builders, and Architectural Traditions in Colonial Virginia," *VMHB*, XC (1982), 198–212. For the political order, one can still profit from Charles S. Sydnor, *Gentlemen Freeholders: Political Practices in Washington's Virginia* (Chapel Hill, N.C., 1952). Surprisingly, the literature on the "golden age" is much sparser than for earlier periods. Many of the best studies lose impetus in the early 18th century; thus, Morgan's study of colonial Virginia skates over the 18th century, Menard's detailed work on the Chesapeake economy halts about 1730, the Rutmans' thick description of Middlesex County thins out after about 1720. Among recent works, only Isaac and Kulikoff have written sustained, quite different, narratives. This era, therefore, offers many research opportunities. It does seem clear, however, that the inception of Maryland's "golden era" lagged somewhat behind that of Virginia's.

economy. A spectacular extension of credit sustained this economic expansion and helped make possible a large increase in the numbers and strength of independent colonial merchants that occurred after 1760. Scholars are not yet certain how far down the economic scale prosperity reached, but even some of the poor were undoubtedly enjoying material comforts unknown to their predecessors. On the other hand, opportunity for the poor to advance did not accompany economic growth, as had happened in the seventeenth century.[10]

In fact, the luster of this golden era was always tarnished. Most obviously, it rested on an extraordinarily high level of exploitation—particularly in the form of black slavery. Slavery in the Chesapeake was not the rigorous, regimented variety found in the Caribbean or even low country South Carolina, but it was nonetheless dependent, like all slave systems, on brute force. Chesapeake planters imported over 100,000 Africans

10. On the economy, see Jacob M. Price, *France and the Chesapeake: A History of the French Tobacco Monopoly, 1674–1791, and of Its Relationship to the British and American Tobacco Trades*, 2 vols. (Ann Arbor, Mich., 1973); Menard, "Tobacco Industry," *Research Econ. Hist.*, V (1980), 154–155; McCusker and Menard, *Economy of British America*, chaps. 3 and 6; and Kulikoff, *Tobacco and Slaves*, chaps. 3 and 4. On diversification, see Clemens, *Atlantic Economy*; David C. Klingaman, *Colonial Virginia's Coastwise and Grain Trade* (New York, 1975); Harold B. Gill, Jr., "Wheat Culture in Colonial Virginia," *Agricultural History*, LII (1978), 380–393; and Peter V. Bergstrom, *Markets and Merchants: Economic Diversification in Colonial Virginia, 1700–1775* (New York, 1985). For good summaries of the literature on ironmaking, shipbuilding, and so on, see Bernard Bailyn, *Voyagers to the West: A Passage in the Peopling of America on the Eve of the Revolution* (New York, 1986), 245–259, but see also Ronald L. Lewis, *Coal, Iron, and Slaves: Industrial Slavery in Maryland and Virginia, 1715–1865* (Westport, Conn., 1979) and Charles B. Dew, "David Ross and the Oxford Iron Works: A Study of Industrial Slavery in the Early Nineteenth-Century South," *WMQ*, 3d Ser., XXXI (1974), 189–224. On credit and merchants, Jacob M. Price is the unrivaled expert: see his "One Family's Empire: The Russell-Lee-Clark Connection in Maryland, Britain, and India, 1707–1857," *MHM*, LXXII (1977), 165–225; his edition of *Joshua Johnson's Letterbook, 1771–1774: Letters from a Merchant in London to His Partners in Maryland* (London, 1979); *Capital and Credit in British Overseas Trade: The View from the Chesapeake, 1700–1776* (Cambridge, Mass., 1980); and "The Last Phase of the Virginia-London Consignment Trade: James Buchanan & Co., 1758–1768," *WMQ*, 3d Ser., XLIII (1986), 64–98. See also John W. Tyler, "Foster Cunliffe and Sons: Liverpool Merchants in the Maryland Tobacco Trade, 1738–1765," *MHM*, LXXIII (1978), 246–277. As Price himself says, there is still much to learn about the independent merchants of the Chesapeake. For a later period, see Edward C. Papenfuse, *In Pursuit of Profit: The Annapolis Merchants in the Era of the American Revolution, 1763–1805* (Baltimore, 1975).

between 1700 and 1770, and the slave population grew by leaps and bounds from 13,000 to 250,000 in the same period. Turning from his books to beat his slaves, William Byrd II personified the bizarre coupling of Georgian elegance and primitive savagery that lay at the heart of the Chesapeake's gilded age. Nor was the exploitation directed wholly at blacks, for while the number of white servants arriving in the eighteenth-century Chesapeake subsided from the levels of the previous century, the region absorbed about 40,000 British convicts.[11]

Indeed, one might argue that the integrated, inclusive social order to which the Chesapeake gentry aspired was unraveling even as they stitched it together. The gap between rich and poor continued to grow. In some localities, tenants formed a third of households early in the century, rising to over half by the Revolution. Although tenancy should not be confused with poverty, many tenants were poor, as Gregory Stiverson has shown. Perhaps also gentry rule was less responsive to its constituents where large numbers of tenants abounded. Westward expansion, which took off in earnest in the second quarter of the eighteenth century, created a swath of more egalitarian and less ordered communities in the piedmont and the Shenandoah Valley. Consequently, the society as a whole appeared much less uniform. Moreover, fierce competitive impulses continued to course through the whole society, apparent in everything from the region's favorite pastimes—horse races, cockfights, and plain fisticuffs—to the restless one-upmanship of proud crop masters. Even the famed Chesapeake Enlightenment was somewhat lopsided in its accomplishments (excelling in politics, above all) and has certainly re-

11. On slavery, see Gerald W. Mullin, *Flight and Rebellion: Slave Resistance in Eighteenth-Century Virginia* (New York, 1972) and Kulikoff, *Tobacco and Slaves*, chaps. 8–10. African imports are calculated from information presented in Darold D. Wax, "Black Immigrants: The Slave Trade in Colonial Maryland," *MHM*, LXXIII (1978), 30–45; Walter Minchinton, Celia King, and Peter Waite, eds., *Virginia Slave-Trade Statistics, 1698–1775* (Richmond, Va., 1984); Susan Westbury, "Slaves of Colonial Virginia: Where They Came From," *WMQ*, 3d Ser., XLII (1985), 228–237; and Donald M. Sweig, "The Importation of African Slaves to the Potomac River, 1732–1772," *ibid.*, 507–524. For the size of the black population, see McCusker and Menard, *Economy of British America*, 136. On Byrd II, see Bernard Bailyn, *The Peopling of British North America: An Introduction* (New York, 1986), 118–119, and cf. Kenneth A. Lockridge, *The Diary, and Life, of William Byrd II of Virginia, 1674–1744* (Chapel Hill, N.C., 1987), 68–69, 113–116, 148. On convicts, see Kenneth Morgan, "The Organization of the Convict Trade to Maryland: Stevenson, Randolph & Cheston, 1768–1775," *WMQ*, 3d Ser., XLII (1985), 201–227, and A. Roger Ekirch, *Bound for America: The Transportation of British Convicts to the Colonies, 1718–1775* (Oxford, 1987), 116 and *passim*.

sisted a coherent and integrated interpretation by modern commentators.[12]

The golden age was also short-lived; high noon quickly became sunset. Some historians have detected elements of unease, even crisis, in Chesapeake society, particularly in Virginia, about midcentury. Perhaps there has been a tendency to search out problems in order to explain the coming revolution; nevertheless, listening to some thoughtful Chesapeake residents in the third quarter of the eighteenth century is to hear troubled voices, anxious at the directions their society was taking. They feared the effects of mounting debts, the chronic instability of the tobacco economy, the erosion of deference, the growing dissatisfaction with the administration of government and justice, the signs of youthful indolence and moral corruption. Rhys Isaac has argued that in Virginia the evangelicals helped to create a cultural crisis as Baptists and Methodists threatened the position of the established church and attacked the gentry's way of life. Of course despite these internal strains, the external crisis in imperial relations is still critical to any interpretation of the coming revolution, not just because Chesapeake political leaders seemed obsessive in their defense of constitutional rights and privileges, but because the crisis itself acted as a major source of tension among them. It is through the explication of these mutually reinforcing trends, their dynamic interaction, that the story of the spiral toward independence has to be told.[13]

12. On tenancy, see Gregory A. Stiverson, *Poverty in a Land of Plenty: Tenancy in Eighteenth-Century Maryland* (Baltimore, 1977) and Kulikoff, *Tobacco and Slaves*, 132–139. On westward expansion, see n. 14, below. On competitiveness, see T. H. Breen, "Horses and Gentlemen: The Cultural Significance of Gambling among the Gentry of Virginia," *WMQ*, 3d Ser., XXXIV (1977), 239–257; Breen, *Tobacco Culture: The Mentality of the Great Tidewater Planters on the Eve of Revolution* (Princeton, N.J., 1985), chap. 2; Isaac, *Transformation of Virginia*, 95–114; Nancy L. Struna, "The Formalizing of Sport and the Formation of an Elite: The Chesapeake Gentry, 1650–1720s," *Journal of Sport History*, XIII (1986), 212–234; Struna, "Sport and the Awareness of Leisure," in Carson, Hoffman, and Albert, eds., *Of Consuming Interests*; and Elliott J. Gorn, " 'Gouge and Bite, Pull Hair and Scratch': The Social Significance of Fighting in the Southern Backcountry," *AHR*, XC (1985), 18–43. On the Enlightenment, Richard Beale Davis's *Intellectual Life in the Colonial South, 1585–1763*, 3 vols. (Knoxville, Tenn., 1978) is a treasure store of information, but not really an integrated interpretation. Whether this reflects the book's limitations or the nature of the southern mind is a question worthy of further investigation.

13. It has not been told successfully as yet, with most of the interpretations being confined to essays, at least for Virginia. Gordon S. Wood was influential in the debate with his "Rhetoric and Reality in the American Revolution," *WMQ*, 3d Ser., XXIII

Did the extraordinary expansion of settlement that transformed the Chesapeake landscape, particularly in the third quarter of the eighteenth century, also contribute to the gentry's crisis of confidence? If the evangelicals were as important in provoking turmoil as Isaac has argued, then the crisis had sectional overtones, for evangelicalism was largely confined to the piedmont. Certainly, the society arising in the Virginia piedmont, western Maryland, and the Shenandoah Valley was ethnically more pluralistic, economically more diverse, socially more egalitarian, and politically more unstable than its tidewater counterpart. Nevertheless, these areas witnessed little overt sectional strife in the second half of the eighteenth century, in large part because of the responsiveness of gentry leaders to the needs of the new territories. Commercial agriculture penetrated the new regions remarkably quickly and joined them to the tidewater. As Robert Mitchell has shown, eastern planters rapidly moved into the Shenandoah Valley and transformed the region from an extension of Pennsylvania into a western extension of tidewater Virginia. It is not at all

---

(1966), 3–32. The most recent and provocative account is Breen, *Tobacco Culture*, but also see Jack P. Greene, "Society, Ideology, and Politics: An Analysis of the Political Culture of Mid-Eighteenth-Century Virginia," in Richard M. Jellison, ed., *Society, Freedom, and Conscience: The American Revolution in Virginia, Massachusetts, and New York* (New York, 1976), 14–76; Greene, " '*Virtus et Libertas*': Political Culture, Social Change, and the Origins of the American Revolution in Virginia, 1763–1766," in Jeffrey J. Crow and Larry E. Tise, eds., *The Southern Experience in the American Revolution* (Chapel Hill, N.C., 1978), 55–108; and Greene, "Character, Persona, and Authority: A Study of Alternative Styles of Political Leadership in Revolutionary Virginia," in W. Robert Higgins, ed., *The Revolutionary War in the South: Power, Conflict, and Leadership: Essays in Honor of John Richard Alden* (Durham, N.C., 1979), 3–42, as well as A. G. Roeber, *Faithful Magistrates and Republican Lawyers: Creators of Virginia Legal Culture, 1680–1810* (Chapel Hill, N.C., 1981); Isaac, *Transformation of Virginia*, pt. 2; and, for the most balanced account, Billings, Selby, and Tate, *Colonial Virginia*, chaps. 11–13. For a good review essay, see Herbert Sloan and Peter Onuf, "Politics, Culture, and the Revolution in Virginia: A Review of Recent Work," *VMHB*, XCI (1983), 259–284. It is surprising that so far Edmund Morgan is the only historian to address seriously the question of how slavery could be basic to the culture of a society whose leaders, at least in Virginia, promoted unprecedented equality for whites. For the coming of the Revolution in Maryland, see the classic by Charles Albro Barker, *The Background of the Revolution in Maryland* (New Haven, Conn., 1940); see also Ronald Hoffman, *A Spirit of Dissension: Economics, Politics, and the Revolution in Maryland* (Baltimore, 1973) and Jean Butenhoff Lee, "The Social Order of a Revolutionary People: Charles County, Maryland, 1733–86" (Ph.D. diss., University of Virginia, 1984).

clear, then, that westward expansion provided a source of great unease, although as Richard Beeman argues, Virginia piedmont society never came to mirror tidewater society, but instead emerged as sui generis—a middle-class, slave-based society.[14]

We have painted a portrait of colonial Chesapeake society with broad and exaggerated strokes. In brief compass, we have aimed to give shape to a complex process; inevitably, we have engaged in overschematization (though perhaps this is preferable to fragmentation). What impresses us, above all, is the dynamic quality of the region's evolution. From raw boomtown origins, Chesapeake society passed through almost a century of flux and fluidity before acquiring a real measure of stability and some of its most familiar features—slavery and a native-born elite who dominated their world from large plantations. The resulting golden age saw tremendous accomplishments, but it was also rather brittle and tenuous, reaching its peak early, in some parts becoming more unsettled and uneasy beginning about midcentury. Certainly the routines of everyday life were now considerably more comfortable and ordered than in the earlier period of flux. Nevertheless, the Chesapeake entered the Revolutionary War, if not in crisis, at least a society seriously disturbed.[15]

To look forward is to confront a number of ironies. One is simply that the Chesapeake region emerged from the war relatively unscathed. The region saw little of the internecine violence that wracked its neighbors. It was invaded, of course, but its loss of slaves was far less than, say, that experienced by the Lower South. Its economy did suffer more severely

14. Richard R. Beeman, *The Evolution of the Southern Backcountry: A Case Study of Lunenburg County, Virginia, 1746–1832* (Philadelphia, 1984); Robert D. Mitchell, *Commercialism and Frontier: Perspectives on the Early Shenandoah Valley* (Charlottesville, Va., 1977); Land, *Dulanys of Maryland*. For a not altogether persuasive attempt to see two factions—one committed to expansion and the other not—as central to the Revolution, see Marc Egnal, "The Origins of the Revolution in Virginia: A Reinterpretation," *WMQ*, 3d Ser., XXXVII (1980), 401–428. For the emergence of an alternative political culture to that of tidewater, see Albert H. Tillson, Jr., "The Militia and Popular Political Culture in the Upper Valley of Virginia, 1740–1775," *VMHB*, XCIV (1986), 285–306.

15. For different views on the need for, and value of, synthesis, see Bernard Bailyn, "The Challenge of Modern Historiography," *AHR*, LXXXVII (1982), 1–24; Jack P. Greene and J. R. Pole, eds., *Colonial British America: Essays in the New History of the Early Modern Era* (Baltimore, 1984), introduction; Rutman, "Still Planting the Seeds of Hope," *VMHB*, XCV (1987), 3–24; Thomas Bender, "Wholes and Parts: The Need for Synthesis in American History," *JAH*, LXXIII (1986), 120–136; and Eric H. Monkkonen, "The Dangers of Synthesis," *AHR*, XCI (1986), 1146–1157.

than that of the New England or Middle Atlantic states, since its prosperity was more dependent than theirs on staple exports. Yet this relative disadvantage could hardly explain why a region that long had been at the forefront of British mainland North America in creation of wealth gradually became an economic backwater. Perhaps the roots of this stagnation lie in the very success of the early Chesapeake economy, which discouraged flexibility and committed the region so heavily to agriculture.

A similar loss of vigor occurred on other fronts. Again, the irony is that the region whose leaders had led the independence movement, shaped the republican government, and provided the new nation's president for thirty-two of its first thirty-six years saw a gradual but inexorable diminution of its national influence. In Virginia, especially, by the early nineteenth century, many thoughtful men were already bemoaning the provincialism, the insularity, the backwardness of their region. Perhaps the kinetic energy that had characterized the early Chesapeake had been transferred—along with many of its residents and much of its cultural heritage—to the southwest. The essence of Chesapeake society may have flourished on the new frontier while the original cultural hearth ossified.[16]

16. This is very much a provisional characterization, for the war and early national years are underresearched. On the war, see Ronald Hoffman, Thad W. Tate, and Peter J. Albert, eds., *An Uncivil War: The Southern Backcountry during the American Revolution* (Charlottesville, Va., 1985), particularly the essays by Richard R. Beeman and Emory G. Evans, and Adele Hast, *Loyalism in Revolutionary Virginia: The Norfolk Area and the Eastern Shore* (Ann Arbor, Mich., 1982). On the Chesapeake (and national) economy in the late 18th and early 19th centuries, see McCusker and Menard, *Economy of British America*, 375–376; Ronald Hoffman, John J. McCusker, Russell R. Menard, and Peter J. Albert, eds., *The Economy of Early America: The Revolutionary Period, 1763–1790* (Charlottesville, Va., 1987); and for the most stimulating and provocative account, Thomas M. Doerflinger, *A Vigorous Spirit of Enterprise: Merchants and Economic Development in Revolutionary Philadelphia* (Chapel Hill, N.C., 1986), chap. 8. Indeed, Doerflinger suggests a critical distinction that we may have slighted in this attempt to generalize for the whole Chesapeake region, namely, the important one between Maryland's economic development with the rise of Baltimore and that of Virginia. The early national years may be most important for witnessing the gradual fragmentation of a single region, particularly the division between upper and lower Chesapeake. For just such a suggestion, see Richard S. Dunn, "Black Society in the Chesapeake, 1776–1810," in Ira Berlin and Ronald Hoffman, eds., *Slavery and Freedom in the Age of the American Revolution* (Charlottesville, Va., 1983), 49–82. This interpretation of the postwar years also draws heavily on Beeman, *Evolution of the Southern Backcountry*; the epilogue to Billings, Selby, and Tate, *Colonial Virginia*; the appropriate biographical studies cited in n. 44, below; and Daniel P.

II

The essays in this volume contribute to the emerging narrative and therefore have been organized in rough chronological order. However, they also speak to some major themes and we discuss them here in that context. First, several study transatlantic connections. That early America cannot be understood divorced from a European context is hardly a new idea, but as Bernard Bailyn has pointed out, what is novel is "the sense of large-scale systems of events operating over various areas. . . . Large-scale orbits developing through time have become visible, and within them patterns of filiation and derivation." Three essays approach this theme directly, while others too are aware of wider worlds, whether it be the role of artisans in societies far distant from the Chesapeake, or the more local relationship of piedmont periphery to tidewater core. Second, a number of essays explore a major focus of the new social history—the everyday concerns of ordinary folk, especially their material conditions, family life, and community development. Third, several examine the complexity and diversity of Chesapeake life as the frontier receded and communities settled down. Much work remains to be done on mapping the great elaboration of Chesapeake society that occurred in the eighteenth century. Many of the essays point the way, some by focusing on black-white relations, others by emphasizing regional variations, and yet others by exploring social and economic differentiation.[17]

The transatlantic connection, J. Frederick Fausz demonstrates, can be

Jordan, *Political Leadership in Jefferson's Virginia* (Charlottesville, Va., 1983). There are certainly alternative readings. Rhys Isaac argues that an integrated society c. 1740 became a polarized one in 1790, but perhaps he makes too little of the accommodations reached between gentry and evangelical cultures by the latter date. Similarly, Jan Lewis sees a gentry on the decline, withdrawing from public life, turning inward, and taking solace in their families, but the late colonial gentry were more ambivalent about public life and the immediate post-Revolutionary gentry more committed to it than Lewis acknowledges. Isaac and Lewis chart other developments—the rise of individualism and of romanticism, for example—which, in broad terms, make much sense. Whether they necessarily led to a less-integrated social order is another matter, however. See Isaac, *Transformation of Virginia*, and Jan Lewis, *The Pursuit of Happiness: Family and Values in Jefferson's Virginia* (Cambridge, 1983). Van Beck Hall is completing a study of the political economy of Virginia in the early national years that promises to advance our understanding.

17. Bailyn, "Challenge of Modern Historiography," *AHR*, LXXXVII (1982), 13.

readily applied to Indians. We all know that natives supported newcomers with corn; less well known, however, are the complex alliances among London merchants, Chesapeake entrepreneurs, and Indians that played a major role in the region's development from the 1620s to the 1650s. Fausz puts the Chesapeake Indians at center stage in a new way, not just as victims of white expansion or as neighbors both helpful and threatening, but as real players, equal partners in a north Atlantic enterprise, the fur trade. Fausz also ties the survival and expansion of the Virginia settlement to the ability of key leaders, after the 1622 massacre, to give up the ethnocentric English view of the Indians as savages who needed to be civilized and Christianized and to approach them instead as allies. This change of heart did not survive once the English were well established and the fur trade fell away, but by then such adaptive behavior was no longer required. Fausz locates the ruin of the trade, and the near collapse of Lord Baltimore's colony, in these competing transatlantic alliances that struggled for control of furs in the northern Chesapeake. One of the many contributions of his essay is the attention given to often obscure events in the public realm of both Virginia and Maryland—revealing the promise of writing social history with the politics left firmly in.[18]

Russell R. Menard studies transatlantic connections in the most direct way, by exploring the huge movement of people from Britain to the Chesapeake in the seventeenth century. Following Wesley F. Craven and David Galenson, he sees the migrants not as passive, but as active participants in the repeopling of the Chesapeake. They responded, he argues, to population trends (and their effect on the numbers of people looking for work), intensity of recruitment, and the relative attractiveness of possible destinations. Short-term fluctuations within these secular trends Menard relates to short-term movements in real wages in England and tobacco prices in the Chesapeake. He demonstrates that when tobacco prices were high and real wages low, Chesapeake planters wanted servants and potential servants in England were plentiful. When tobacco prices were low and real wages high, the opposite was true. Menard also reevaluates

18. The work of Jacob Price, already mentioned, on merchant alliances and that of Alison G. Olson, e.g., "The Virginia Merchants of London: A Study in Eighteenth-Century Interest-Group Politics," *WMQ*, 3d Ser., XL (1983), 363–388, point to the fruitfulness of this approach. There are obviously many other circles of influence spanning the ocean—from those interested in science to those in architectural design—that could be explored productively. Note the network of communications among dissenting congregations discussed in James Horn's essay in this volume.

the composition of the immigrant group, finding that a large proportion, perhaps the majority, came from the margins of British society and that over time this proportion increased. He does not return us to the views of Abbot Emerson Smith, undone by Mildred Campbell, but he finishes the critique, begun by Galenson, of her middle-class emigration.[19]

James Horn tackles the problem of what it meant in the daily lives of immigrants to leave England for the shores of the Chesapeake Bay. By careful examination of wills and inventories made during the second half of the seventeenth century, he contrasts the lives of men and women in the Vale of Berkeley in England, which supplied many immigrants, with those of settlers in St. Mary's County, Maryland. Horn's essay is the first systematic comparison of English and Chesapeake living standards, and some of his conclusions are surprising. Immigrants of all social levels experienced a much lower standard of comfort than they had enjoyed in England. In the Vale even very poor families lived on a par with planters of middling wealth in St. Mary's. Successful immigrants had traded domestic comfort for greater economic independence, supposing, as they evidently did, that they could not have improved their positions in England. In addition, while St. Mary's County was much less densely settled than the Vale, neighborly contacts assumed comparable importance in the new locale. Scattered settlement and the absence of kin were obstacles overcome. Continuities as well as changes characterized the lives of those who immigrated.[20]

19. For the works by Campbell, Craven, Galenson, and Smith referred to in this paragraph, see the footnotes to Menard's essay. The larger context of immigration to the New World has been recently mapped out in Bailyn, *Peopling of British America*. In *Voyagers to the West*, Bailyn explores in masterly detail British emigration on the eve of the American Revolution. We could do with more study of both bond and free immigration to the Chesapeake between the conclusion of Menard's essay and the opening of Bailyn's *Voyagers to the West*, i.e., c. 1700–1770. For previous forays, see David W. Galenson, *White Servitude in Colonial America: An Economic Analysis* (Cambridge, 1981); Audrey Lockhart, *Some Aspects of Emigration from Ireland to the North American Colonies between 1660 and 1775* (New York, 1976), especially appendix C; and Margaret M. R. Kellow, "Indentured Servitude in Eighteenth-Century Maryland," *Histoire Sociale*, XVII (1984), 229–255.

20. For essays that tend to view Chesapeake developments from a wider perspective, but without tying the particular and the general closely together, as Horn does so impressively, see David B. Quinn, ed., *Early Maryland in a Wider World* (Detroit, Mich., 1982). Perhaps the most interesting comparative work of recent times, building on the work of Quinn himself, is the Irish connection that Nicholas P. Canny has explored. See his "The Ideology of English Colonization: From Ireland to America,"

Horn's essay also addresses the theme of everyday life, a major focus of much recent social history, as well as of a number of other essays in this volume. Perhaps Horn's most interesting finding is that Englishmen of all wealth levels lived in smaller houses with much sparser furnishings when transplanted to the Chesapeake. Colonization is not always a forward movement, a positive leap ahead; it can, and often does, entail reversions—in this case, to a more primitive material culture. Early Chesapeake houses have been described as "gothic," and certainly architectural forms that were outmoded in England were revived in the Chesapeake because they were simple and could be constructed quickly. Archaeologists and architectural historians have found that buildings were not only small but also impermanent in seventeenth-century Maryland and Virginia. Many families even in the late seventeenth century lived in single- or double-roomed, dirt-floored, earthfast structures. Only five surviving homes and one church have been positively identified as dating from the seventeenth century. Apparently, high labor costs forced even well-to-do newcomers to build quickly and cheaply, and early death prevented planters from progressing to larger, better-built, more permanent houses.[21]

WMQ, 3d Ser., XXX (1973), 575–598, and "The Permissive Frontier: Social Control in English Settlements in Ireland and Virginia, 1550–1650," in Andrews, Canny, and Hair, eds., *Westward Enterprise*, 17–44. See also Ivor Noël Hume, *Martin's Hundred* (New York, 1982), which points out the parallels in the bawn-type palisaded enclosure between Wolstenholme Town and known Irish sites. For another kind of comparison, see Virginia Bernhard, "Bermuda and Virginia in the Seventeenth Century: A Comparative View," *Jour. Soc. Hist.*, XIX (1985), 57–70. Unlike Horn, who is skeptical of the influence of particular English regions on Chesapeake development, David Hackett Fischer, in a forthcoming study tentatively entitled *Albion's Sea*, attempts to trace Chesapeake folkways to the southwestern part of England. This work promises to provoke debate.

21. Carson *et al.*, "Impermanent Architecture," *Winterthur Portfolio*, XVI (1981), 135–196; Main, *Tobacco Colony*, chap. 4; Rutman and Rutman, *A Place in Time*, 69; Dell Upton, *Holy Things and Profane: Anglican Parish Churches in Colonial Virginia* (Cambridge, Mass., 1986); Garry Wheeler Stone, "Society, Housing, and Architecture in Early Maryland: John Lewger's St. John's" (Ph.D. diss., University of Pennsylvania, 1982). See also Henry Glassie, *Folk Housing in Middle Virginia: A Structural Analysis of Historic Artifacts* (Knoxville, Tenn., 1975); Dell Upton, "Toward a Permanence Theory of Vernacular Architecture: Early Tidewater Virginia as a Case Study," *Folklore Forum*, XII (1979), 173–196; Upton, "Vernacular Domestic Architecture in Eighteenth-Century Virginia," *Winterthur Portfolio*, XVII (1982), 95–119; Fraser D. Neiman, *The "Manner House" before Stratford (Discovering the Clifts Plantation)* (Stratford, Va., 1980); and William M. Kelso, *Kingsmill Plantations, 1619–1800: Archaeology*

Henry Miller explores another fundamental feature of everyday existence—diet. In this respect, Chesapeake inhabitants appear to have lived better than people who stayed in England. From archaeological analyses of bone refuse, Miller concludes that Chesapeake residents ate great amounts of fish, fowl, and meat. During the first half of the seventeenth century, the colonists relied heavily on wild animals, birds, and fish, sources of food not as available to the general population in England; thereafter, domestic animals formed the bulk of the settlers' meat consumption. This shift from early reliance on wild game to domestic animals owed less to resource depletion than to the entrepreneurial and familial priorities of the colonists. They valued cattle and hogs both for their sale value and for the increase that could provide an inheritance for children. Unlike Indians, who saw no advantage in raising domestic livestock when wild game was at hand, Englishmen saw no advantage in fishing and hunting once supplies of domestic livestock were adequate. Although there were variations by status, the poor as well as the wealthy enjoyed this protein-rich diet. These findings complement those of Robert Fogel and his students, who have discovered that British soldiers of the colonial wars were shorter by several inches than soldiers born in the colonies, including those in the South. This difference is surely related to nutrition, perhaps particularly to the fish and animal protein available to colonial inhabitants.[22]

A puzzling aspect of these findings, however, is that in the Chesapeake, so far as we now know, improved diet did not enable people to live longer than they did in England. We know, of course, that typhoid fever, dysentery, and malaria in large part account for the appalling mortality of the seventeenth century, but by the turn of the century most settlers had moved away from the dangerous areas and had built up resistance to unfamiliar diseases. However, between 1690 and 1775 life expectancy at birth in England generally ranged from about thirty-two to thirty-eight years, while in southern Maryland it probably never exceeded this range. Thus, by an index of well-being tied to nutrition, increased height, Chesapeake inhabitants outdid their English counterparts, but by another

---

of Country Life in Colonial Virginia (Orlando, Fla., 1984). Reversions to a more traditional past have, of course, figured in stories of New England—here is an interesting link between the regions.

22. Robert W. Fogel *et al.*, "Secular Changes in American and British Stature and Nutrition," *Jour. Interdisciplinary Hist.*, XIV (1983), 445–481.

index, life expectancy, they had not improved their lives. Perhaps the history of disease—with the introduction of yellow fever and a new, more virulent strain of malaria associated with African immigration—holds the key to this mystery.[23]

Demographic matters lead inevitably to questions about family. The literature on family life in the early Chesapeake has proliferated over the past decade. Part of the debate about the stability of the seventeenth-century Chesapeake has centered on the truncated, mixed character of families and what this meant to the participants. One emerging argument is that although some children were traumatized by the loss of parents and exploited by unscrupulous administrators of their estates, more found solace in a network of relatives and quasi relatives who came to their aid. For still others, local orphans' courts provided some relief. The changes in family life that accompanied the appearance of a native-born population have also been the subject of much discussion. Attention has focused on women, who both gained and lost position in the family polity. Husbands and fathers were more likely than before to favor children over wives in the distribution of property at death. With more children to endow and less land to distribute, however, fathers were also likelier to exclude daughters from land, while continuing to endow as many sons as possible with landed estates. On the other hand, women were more protected. They were less often orphaned at an early age and less likely to be widowed without children old enough to assist them. Their economic importance may have increased as home industries began to develop, and the disposable income women thus created may have helped to purchase the household amenities that were transforming everyday life. In the view of Daniel Blake Smith and Jan Lewis, the family itself began to change character after midcentury, at least among the wealthy, becoming more intimate, affectionate, and child-centered. Allan Kulikoff, by contrast,

23. On comparative life expectancy, see E. A. Wrigley and R. S. Schofield, *The Population History of England, 1541–1871: A Reconstruction* (Cambridge, Mass., 1981), 530; Kulikoff, *Tobacco and Slaves*, 62; and Rutman and Rutman, *A Place in Time: Explicatus*, chap. 4. On disease, see Darrett B. Rutman and Anita H. Rutman, "Of Agues and Fevers: Malaria in the Early Chesapeake," *WMQ*, 3d Ser., XXXIII (1976), 31–60; Carville V. Earle, "Environment, Disease, and Mortality in Early Virginia," in Tate and Ammerman, eds., *Chesapeake in the Seventeenth Century*, 96–125; and Jon Kukla, "Kentish Agues and American Distempers: The Transmission of Malaria from England to Virginia in the Seventeenth Century," *So. Studies*, XXV (1986), 135–147.

has argued that the patriarchal position of fathers and husbands and the strength of kinship networks beyond those of the nuclear family were the central developments of eighteenth-century family life.[24]

Jean Butenhoff Lee adds substantially to this picture by focusing on the role of inheritance in the period when demographic conditions had stabilized. In a complex analysis, she explores how family resources were used to provide for all members. Sons, as is well known, were more likely than daughters to receive land, but more of the slaves to work the land went to daughters than to sons, ensuring daughters' prospects for marriage and contributing vital labor to the plantation economy. Furthermore, sons often had to wait for full control of their land until their mothers died or remarried or until their sisters married. In short, Lee finds much less discrimination against daughters than traditionally has been argued. From the middle to the end of the eighteenth century, women were not as undervalued as some scholars have supposed.

Of particular interest is Lee's discussion of entails and life estates in land or slaves, whereby sons and daughters were restricted from dispos-

24. The 17th-century debate can be explored in Lorena S. Walsh, "'Till Death Us Do Part': Marriage and Family in Seventeenth-Century Maryland," in Tate and Ammerman, eds., *Chesapeake in the Seventeenth Century*, 126–152; Lois Green Carr and Russell R. Menard, "Immigration and Opportunity: The Freedman in Early Colonial Maryland," *ibid.*, 206–242; Lois Green Carr, "The Development of the Maryland Orphans' Court, 1654–1715," in Land, Carr, and Papenfuse, eds., *Law, Society, and Politics*, 41–62; and Rutman and Rutman, *A Place in Time*, chap. 4. On the changing roles of women in the late 17th century, see Lois Green Carr and Lorena S. Walsh, "The Planter's Wife: The Experience of White Women in Seventeenth-Century Maryland," *WMQ*, 3d Ser., XXXIV (1977), 542–571. The subject can then be followed in time via Lorena S. Walsh, "The Experiences and Status of Women in the Chesapeake, 1750–1775," in Walter J. Fraser, Jr., R. Frank Saunders, Jr., and Jon Wakelyn, eds., *The Web of Southern Social Relations: Women, Family, and Education* (Athens, Ga., 1985), 1–18; Joan R. Gundersen and Gwen Victor Gampel, "Married Women's Legal Status in Eighteenth-Century New York and Virginia," *WMQ*, 3d Ser., XXXIX (1982), 114–134; Linda E. Speth, "More Than Her 'Thirds': Wives and Widows in Colonial Virginia," in Speth and Alison Duncan Hirsch, *Women, Family, and Community in Colonial America: Two Perspectives* (New York, 1983), 5–41; Suzanne Lebsock, *The Free Women of Petersburg: Status and Culture in a Southern Town, 1784–1860* (New York, 1984); and Lebsock, "A Share of Honour": Virginia Women, 1600–1945* (Richmond, Va., 1987). On changing family character, see Michael Zuckerman, "William Byrd's Family," *Perspectives in American History*, XII (1979), 253–311; Daniel Blake Smith, *Inside the Great House: Planter Family Life in Eighteenth-Century Chesapeake Society* (Ithaca, N.Y., 1980); Isaac, *Transformation of Virginia*, 302–305; Lewis, *Pursuit of Happiness*; and Kulikoff, *Tobacco and Slaves*, pt. 2.

ing of the property bequeathed them. Such "lesser estates" were, in effect, protections for a daughter or daughter-in-law. They prevented her husband from selling the land or slaves she brought to her marriage or from inducing her to agree to sales of his land that would infringe on her dower rights. Some ambiguities of language make it impossible to be sure in all cases whether testators intended to establish entails. Nevertheless, Lee establishes that a considerable proportion of testators—admittedly, a minority of the decedent population, but probably a majority of the major property holders—devised at least some of their property with one form or another of limitation. Lee's is also one of the first analyses to differentiate the bequest practices of fathers and mothers.[25]

The formation of families and kin networks is, of course, vital to community life. Some of the most innovative work in early Chesapeake history explores the existence and character of local communities. Most influential has been Darrett Rutman and Anita Rutman's study of Middlesex County, Virginia, the best investigation of the texture of community life from frontier settlement onward. A number of doctoral dissertations scheduled for publication in the near future will make major contributions of a similar kind. Although a regional study, Allan Kulikoff's recent book, *Tobacco and Slaves*, incorporates an in-depth investigation of eighteenth-century Prince George's County, Maryland, in which he explores the development of community among blacks as well as whites. Several essays in this volume pursue community formation in newly settled areas. Horn, as we have seen, finds among the inhabitants of seventeenth-century St. Mary's County, Maryland, an interdependence not unlike that of the English Vale of Berkeley. Philip Morgan's essay, discussed below, traces the emergence of community among slaves transplanted to the Virginia piedmont. Two others—those by Lorena S. Walsh and Michael Graham—have the development of community networks as their central theme.[26]

25. For other recent work on inheritance in the Chesapeake, see Gail S. Terry, "Wives and Widows, Sons and Daughters: Testation Patterns in Baltimore County, Maryland, 1660–1759" (M.A. thesis, University of Maryland, 1983); Marylynn Salmon, *Women and the Law of Property in Early America* (Chapel Hill, N.C., 1986); and Lois Green Carr, "Inheritance in the Colonial Chesapeake," in Ronald Hoffman and Peter J. Albert, eds., *Women in the Era of the American Revolution* (Charlottesville, Va., forthcoming).

26. Dissertations that have community as a central theme include Michael L. Nicholls, "Origins of the Virginia Southside, 1703–1753: A Social and Economic Study" (College of William and Mary, 1972); Kevin Peter Kelly, "Economic and

Lorena Walsh describes the geographical and social boundaries of personal exchange that defined the possibilities of community. Using evidence from St. Clement's Manor in St. Mary's County, she shows how and why the English model of the manor that Lord Baltimore had promoted failed to take hold on the Chesapeake frontier. The justices of the county court offered competing institutional services, and the high turnover of inhabitants created by early death and the search for opportunity undermined a sense of place, social as well as geographical, that might have provided the "glue" to maintain a manorial organization. Nevertheless, the demise of the manor as an institution did not destroy "good neighborhood." Within the distances that walking, rowing, or horseback riding made convenient, people engaged in neighborly exchanges as the need arose. Drawing upon a wide range of information from seventeenth-century Maryland, Walsh demonstrates that no one could afford to distance himself entirely from such networks, lest he or she be excluded when cooperation was required. However, as the population became denser and people had greater choice of associates, social and religious differences began more and more to affect the boundaries of social intercourse.[27]

Michael Graham enlarges on this theme by exploring the effects of

Social Development of Seventeenth-Century Surry County, Virginia" (University of Washington, 1972); Lorena Seebach Walsh, "Charles County, Maryland, 1658–1705: A Study of Chesapeake Social and Political Structure" (Michigan State University, 1977); James Russell Perry, "The Formation of a Society on Virginia's Eastern Shore, 1615–1655" (The Johns Hopkins University, 1980); Gwenda Morgan, "The Hegemony of the Law: Richmond County, 1692–1776" (The Johns Hopkins University, 1981); John Thomas Schlotterbeck, "Plantation and Farm: Social and Economic Change in Orange and Greene Counties, Virginia, 1716 to 1860" (The Johns Hopkins University, 1980); James P. P. Horn, "Social and Economic Aspects of Local Society in England and the Chesapeake: A Comparative Study of the Vale of Berkeley, Gloucestershire, and the Lower Western Shore of Maryland, c. 1660–1700" (University of Sussex, 1982); and Lee, "Social Order of a Revolutionary People."

27. Perry's fine dissertation cited in the preceding note employs network analysis to trace the formation and nature of community on the Eastern Shore. His work shows the achievement of stability at a much earlier date than any other historian has yet demonstrated. On the other hand, his study is of landholders, the most stable members of the population. Moreover, perhaps the particular character of the Eastern Shore—its remoteness, its less than dynamic character—made it atypical. Rutman and Rutman, in *A Place in Time*, chap. 8, and earlier theoretical works cited therein, have pioneered this field.

religious differences on community. He shows how Quakers and Catholics alike utilized their experiences as dissenters in England to band into religious groups, thus fortifying the interdependence that shared religious convictions already encouraged. He argues that members of each group offered one another exceptional support that made them more prosperous than the population at large and also politically more influential, although the Quakers eventually withdrew from officeholding when they adopted strictures against taking oaths. The two groups had other distinctive social characteristics. Catholics contributed to social stability by incorporating unmarried men into their communities, and in different ways, both Catholics and Quakers gave women more power than they exercised elsewhere in the society. Graham argues that the opportunity to share religious rituals and experience attracted converts, especially in a society without public financing for churches and ministers. In a harsh environment, membership in religious communities eased hardships by creating identities for people as God's chosen and by supplying emotional and practical support. Graham's analysis reinforces a point that Horn makes: parish life in England had offered a form of community interaction that was absent in Maryland for settlers brought up in the Church of England. Catholic and Quaker communities helped mend a rent in the social fabric.[28]

The growing religious diversity of the Chesapeake region is but one way in which Chesapeake society underwent a vast social elaboration, a process that gained momentum as the eighteenth century wore on. We need to know much more about extensive growth. How did westward

28. There are many studies of religious groups in the Chesapeake, but they tend to be denomination oriented and rarely explore the broader community. David W. Jordan's work on Quakers—see "'Gods Candle' within Government: Quakers and Politics in Early Maryland," *WMQ*, 3d Ser., XXXIX (1982), 628–654, and "'The Miracle of This Age': Maryland's Experiment in Religious Toleration, 1649–1689," *Historian*, XLVII (1985), 338–359—and Rhys Isaac's on the Separate Baptists, in *Transformation of Virginia*, chap. 8, are notable exceptions. For other useful work, see Bartlett B. James, *The Labadist Colony in Maryland* (Baltimore, 1899); Kenneth L. Carroll, *Quakerism on the Eastern Shore* (Baltimore, 1970); Warren M. Billings, "A Quaker in Seventeenth-Century Virginia: Four Remonstrances by George Wilson," *WMQ*, 3d Ser., XXXIII (1976), 127–140; J. Stephen Kroll-Smith, "Transmitting a Revival Culture: The Organizational Dynamic of the Baptist Movement in Colonial Virginia, 1760–1777," *Jour. So. Hist.*, L (1984), 551–568; and John D. Krugler, "'With promise of Liberty in Religion': The Catholic Lords Baltimore and Toleration in Seventeenth-Century Maryland, 1634–1692," *MHM*, LXXIX (1984), 21–43.

settlement occur? What was the role of land speculation? In what ways did the new ethnic groups flooding the interior redraw the contours of Chesapeake society? We also need to know much more about intensive developments. How did the escalating cycles of international warfare affect civilian society? What were the roles of occupational groups like artisans, storekeepers, and tavernkeepers and professionals like ministers, physicians, and lawyers? What services did the rising number of towns provide? In sum, both the infrastructure and the extended structure of eighteenth-century Chesapeake society need investigation.[29]

A fundamental feature of the Chesapeake's diversity was its multiracial character. The relation between Indians and whites was, of course, important from the very beginnings of English settlement. Ethnohistorians,

29. For an excellent account of westward settlement and the role of land speculation in Virginia, see Mitchell, *Commercialism and Frontier*, chap. 3; needless to say this hardly exhausts the subject, particularly as we know little about piedmont expansion. A study that sheds much light on the subject for Maryland is Land, *Dulanys of Maryland*. For an account of western exploration, see Alan Vance Briceland, *Westward from Virginia: The Exploration of the Virginia-Carolina Frontier, 1650–1710* (Charlottesville, Va., 1987). Ethnicity is explored in Mitchell, *Commercialism and Frontier*, chap. 2 and *passim*, and touched on in Beeman, *Evolution of the Southern Backcountry*, 22–24 and *passim*, Dieter Cunz, *The Maryland Germans: A History* (Princeton, N.J., 1948), and Elizabeth Augusta Kessel, "Germans on the Maryland Frontier: A Social History of Frederick County, Maryland, 1730–1800" (Ph.D. diss., Rice University, 1981), but the presence of the Scotch-Irish has hardly been tapped. On artisans, see Carville V. Earle, *The Evolution of a Tidewater Settlement System: All Hallow's Parish, Maryland, 1650–1783* (Chicago, 1975); Jean Burrell Russo, "Free Workers in a Plantation Economy: Talbot County, Maryland, 1690–1759" (Ph.D. diss., The Johns Hopkins University, 1983); and Russo's essay in this volume. On storekeepers, see Rutman and Rutman, *A Place in Time*, chap. 7, and work in progress by Harold Gill of the Colonial Williamsburg Foundation. There is very little on tavernkeepers, except for Patricia Ann Gibbs, "Taverns in Tidewater Virginia, 1700–1774" (M.A. thesis, College of William and Mary, 1968) and a slender, general book by Kym S. Rice, *Early American Taverns: For the Entertainment of Friends and Strangers* (Chicago, 1983). Roeber, *Faithful Magistrates*, does not attempt a full social analysis of Virginia lawyers; for Maryland, see Alan Frederick Day, "A Social Study of Lawyers in Maryland, 1660–1775" (Ph.D. diss., The Johns Hopkins University, 1977). On ministers, see Joan R. Gundersen, "The Search for Good Men: Recruiting Ministers in Colonial Virginia," *Historical Magazine of the Protestant Episcopal Church*, XLVIII (1979), 453–464, and Carol Lee van Voorst, "The Anglican Clergy in Maryland, 1692–1776" (Ph.D. diss., Princeton University, 1978). On warfare, there is a 17th-century study—William L. Shea, *The Virginia Militia in the Seventeenth Century* (Baton Rouge, La., 1983)—but little on the 18th century; see John Ferling, "Soldiers for Virginia: Who Served in the French and Indian War?" *VMHB*, XCIV (1986), 307–328. An excellent book on land surveyors,

in particular, have taught us to look for cooperation and exchange as well as conflict between the two groups. Indeed, it is surely appropriate that the earliest English settlers, the Roanoke colonists, are now believed to have made their final home among the hospitable Chesapeaks in what would become tidewater Virginia. Frederick Fausz has written elsewhere on the military conflicts and accommodations that arose between Powhatans and Englishmen, but in his essay here he is most intrigued by the continuing possibilities for cooperation after the 1622 uprising. He may be right that had the fur trade survived the warfare between the white men of Maryland and Virginia, a prolonged era of interracial cooperation might have ensued, in which natives and newcomers shared a rich environment on equal terms. As we know all too well, however, tobacco, not furs, became the driving force of the Chesapeake economy, and Indians became obstacles, not allies, as whites relentlessly sought new lands. Even this process must not be assumed to have moved forward in unilinear fashion for, as James Merrell has shown so persuasively, intimate and cooperative contacts with whites were possible for some Chesapeake Indians throughout the century—as was their ability to maintain a measure of their cultural integrity. In the case of the Piscataways, economic continuities derived largely from their uninvolvement in the fur trade.[30]

---

which says much about the evolving social structure of Virginia, is Sarah S. Hughes, *Surveyors and Statesmen: Land Measuring in Colonial Virginia* (Richmond, Va., 1979). On urban development in general, see n. 33, below, but for artisans in one town late in the century, see Charles G. Steffen, *The Mechanics of Baltimore: Workers and Politics in the Age of Revolution, 1763–1812* (Urbana, Ill., 1984).

30. On the fate of the Roanoke refugees, see David Beers Quinn, *Set Fair for Roanoke: Voyages and Colonies, 1584–1606* (Chapel Hill, N.C., 1985), especially chap. 19. For a superb ethnohistorical approach (before the term even became fashionable), see Nancy Oestreich Lurie, "Indian Cultural Adjustment to European Civilization," in Smith, ed., *Seventeenth-Century America*, 33–60. For some of Fausz's other work, see his "Fighting 'Fire' with Firearms: The Anglo-Powhatan Arms Race in Early Virginia," *American Indian Culture and Research Journal*, III, no. 4 (1979), 33–50; "Patterns of Anglo-Indian Aggression and Accommodation along the Mid-Atlantic Coast, 1584–1634," in William W. Fitzhugh, ed., *Cultures in Contact: The Impact of European Contacts on Native American Cultural Institutions, A.D. 1000–1800* (Washington, D.C., 1985), 225–268; and "Middlemen in Peace and War: Virginia's Earliest Indian Interpreters, 1608–1632," *VMHB*, XCV (1987), 41–64. For work that stresses conflict, see Alden T. Vaughan, "'Expulsion of the Salvages': English Policy and the Virginia Massacre of 1622," *WMQ*, 3d Ser., XXXV (1978), 57–84; Francis Jennings, "Indians and Frontiers in Seventeenth-Century Maryland," in Quinn, ed., *Early*

Although a recent immigrant to Virginia could say in 1723 that he lived in an "Indian country," natives were fringe actors on the eighteenth-century Chesapeake's triracial stage; blacks played more central roles. Yet a marginal group also existed among blacks—those who were free. To date, we know most about this group in one small corner of the Chesapeake, the Eastern Shore of the seventeenth century. In that fluid world, as Timothy Breen and Stephen Innes have demonstrated, some blacks gained and maintained their freedom by acting as clients to white planter patrons, as rough equals to white servants, as friends to other blacks, and as loyal kin to their own families. In particular, they argue, the value Englishmen put on ownership of property underlay the social acceptance of blacks who managed to acquire land and possessions. Breen and Innes ascribe the decline of free black status toward the end of the century primarily to a disappearance of opportunity for all small planters.[31]

Douglas Deal explores the same free blacks in the same region, but creates a richer portrait of their family lives, pursues their histories well into the eighteenth century, and presents a more complex picture of their decline. Increasingly constricted by racial antipathy and by fears that their very existence threatened the whole institution of slavery, free blacks

---

Maryland, 216–241; and Bernard W. Sheehan, *Savagism and Civility: Indians and Englishmen in Colonial Virginia* (Cambridge, 1980). The most sophisticated recent study of a Chesapeake native group is James H. Merrell, "Cultural Continuity among the Piscataway Indians of Colonial Maryland," *WMQ*, 3d Ser., XXXVI (1979), 548–570. For a recent review essay that explores the literature, strongly argues the case for mutual acculturation, and rightly points up the little that is known of Indian-white relations after about 1630, see J. Frederick Fausz, "The Invasion of Virginia: Indians, Colonialism, and the Conquest of Cant—A Review Essay on Anglo-Indian Relations in the Chesapeake," *VMHB*, XCV (1987), 133–156.

31. Edgar Erskine Hume, ed., "A Colonial Scottish Jacobite Family: Establishment in Virginia of a Branch of the Humes of Wedderburn," *VMHB*, XXXVIII (1930), 110, 115. Ross M. Kimmel produced the first modern study of free blacks on the Eastern Shore, "Free Blacks in Seventeenth-Century Maryland," *MHM*, LXXI (1976), 19–25, which Breen and Innes made use of in *"Myne Owne Ground."* For another Eastern Shore study, see Thomas E. Davidson, "Free Blacks in Old Somerset County, 1745–1755," *MHM*, LXXX (1985), 151–156. The literature is sparse on free blacks in the rest of the Chesapeake, but see Michael L. Nicholls, "Passing Through This Troublesome World: Free Blacks in the Early Southside," *VMHB*, XCII (1984), 50–70. The fullest study, with wonderful cameo sketches of free blacks, is Deal, "Race and Class." Nicholls is now engaged on a large study of free blacks in Chesapeake towns. It should also be noted that we know little of the slaves on the Eastern Shore.

made valiant efforts to fend off reenslavement or its equivalent, lifetime servitude. They learned to use the courts to protect themselves but faced increasing limits on their legal ability to testify or otherwise enjoy the rights of free people. Despite such handicaps, a few did well as planters. But to be a property holder was not enough to confer status in an increasingly racist society. Deal argues that Breen and Innes oversimplify in stressing the ownership of property as the key to the blurring of racial boundaries in the mid-seventeenth century. The opportunity for blacks to acquire property did not entirely disappear, as the free black Azaricum Drighouse could attest; when he died in 1738, his movable property put him in the top third of wealth holders. What changed were the contours of the larger society, most particularly the rise of black slavery that degraded all blacks, whether they owned property or not.

Philip D. Morgan directs our attention to a particularly dynamic area of the Chesapeake in the eighteenth century—the rapidly growing piedmont region of Virginia. He focuses upon the slave population, although he also touches on the pockets of free blacks and even smaller numbers of Afro-Indians who lived in the area. His view of the world the slaves made falls somewhat between the two competing interpretations of black community life in the tidewater Chesapeake—one essentially stressing the favorable conditions for Afro-American community formation, the other the constraints. While emphasizing the obstacles slaves faced in establishing families and community networks, Morgan is impressed by the speed of Afro-American cultural formation in the piedmont. Creole slaves dominated the region, making adaptation for Africans a faster process than it had earlier been in the tidewater. He probes the distinctiveness of black life and black-white relations in the piedmont, but concludes that the region was primarily an extension of tidewater by the end of the eighteenth century.[32]

32. The optimistic interpretation can essentially be found in Kulikoff, *Tobacco and Slaves*, especially pt. 3, and the latter half of Russell R. Menard, "The Maryland Slave Population, 1658 to 1730: A Demographic Profile of Blacks in Four Counties," *WMQ*, 3d Ser., XXXII (1975), 29–54. For the more pessimistic interpretation, see Jean Butenhoff Lee, "The Problem of Slave Community in the Eighteenth-Century Chesapeake," *ibid.*, XLIII (1986), 333–361. Although Richard S. Dunn has not written at length on Chesapeake slavery, he takes the most balanced view, aided no doubt by his ability to make sustained comparisons with slavery in other parts of the British Atlantic world. See his "Masters, Servants, and Slaves in the Colonial Chesapeake and the Caribbean," in Quinn, ed., *Early Maryland*, 242–266; "Black Society in the Chesapeake," in Berlin and Hoffman, eds., *Slavery and Freedom*, 49–82; "Servants

The rapid settlement of the piedmont suggests a second major way in which Chesapeake society elaborated: it divided into subregions. Seventeenth-century Chesapeake colonists shared basic experiences as they adapted to the environment, cleared forests, and established farms, but with settlement, variations in resources created regional diversity in social and economic development. A considerable literature now exists on this subject. Jacob Price, Paul Clemens, and others have shown how variations in tobacco characteristics affected marketing patterns. Clemens has analyzed the shift from tobacco to grain on Maryland's upper Eastern Shore, and others have followed a similar transformation in parts of Virginia. Carville Earle and Ronald Hoffman have suggested some of the likely effects of these changes on social and economic structures: greater diversification into crafts, fewer extremes of wealth, and more urbanization in wheat areas than in those that concentrated on tobacco. Jacob Price has also tied urbanization to crop mix by correlating the ability to capture commercial services and urban growth. In the tobacco trade, such services remained in the hands of London merchants, whereas colonial merchants seized control of the trade in wheat and corn. Consequently, the Chesapeake proved inhospitable to towns before the middle of the eighteenth century; thereafter, two substantial urban centers, Baltimore and Norfolk, arose on the region's northern and southern flanks, where the export of grains had assumed primacy.[33]

---

and Slaves: The Recruitment and Employment of Labor," in Greene and Pole, eds., *Colonial British America*, 157–194, especially 177; and his continuing investigation into the differences between a Jamaican plantation and one in Virginia, a small part of which is reported in "A Tale of Two Plantations: Slave Life at Mesopotamia in Jamaica and Mount Airy in Virginia, 1799 to 1828," *WMQ*, 3d Ser., XXXIV (1977), 32–65. Philip Morgan compares 18th-century slave life in the Upper and Lower South in a forthcoming study.

33. For Price, Clemens, and other studies of diversification, see nn. 6 and 10, above. For the best general accounts of urban development, see Carville V. Earle and Ronald Hoffman, "Staple Crops and Urban Development in the Eighteenth-Century South," *Perspectives Am. Hist.*, X (1976), 5–78; Jacob M. Price, "Economic Function and the Growth of American Port Towns in the Eighteenth Century," *ibid.*, VIII (1974), 121–186; see also Lois Green Carr, "'The Metropolis of Maryland': A Comment on Town Development along the Tobacco Coast," *MHM*, LXIX (1974), 124–145. For more specific studies, see G. Terry Sharrer, "Flour Milling in the Growth of Baltimore, 1750–1830," *ibid.*, LXXI (1976), 322–333; David Curtis Skaggs, "John Semple and the Development of the Potomac Valley, 1750–1773," *VMHB*, XCII (1984), 282–308; and William H. Siener, "Charles Yates, the Grain

Lois Green Carr tests the proposition that crop mixes affected diversification into crafts. Of the six counties she studied, Talbot County on Maryland's upper Eastern Shore possessed soils most suitable for grains, and wheat became a major export crop by the middle of the eighteenth century. There, crafts and home industries especially flourished. By contrast, St. Mary's County, Maryland, which concentrated more completely on tobacco than any other locality studied, saw least diversification into crafts. Somerset County on Maryland's lower Eastern Shore, where soils were poor and planters had to maximize every resource, eventually diversified most of all.

Diversification into import replacements and new agricultural products, while varying in degree from place to place, occurred everywhere as the eighteenth century progressed and could lead in two directions: greater self-sufficiency or more local exchange. To date, historians have argued for greater self-sufficiency, especially on large plantations, where servants or slaves exercised a variety of skills. Carr opts for local exchange as the chief result on the grounds that few planters were fully diversified, but increasingly had skills and services to offer in a local market. This internal economic development provided a hedge against the price fluctuations of export crops, wheat and corn as well as tobacco. Such hedges strengthened the local economy. Imports did not diminish; rather, planters improved their ability to purchase them.[34]

Jean Russo explores self-sufficiency and local exchange from a different standpoint. She demonstrates that free craftsmen were an enduring element of Talbot County's economy. True, the kinds of crafts practiced were restricted in the face of cheap imports and a small market for expensive luxuries. But woodworkers, shoemakers, tailors, weavers, blacksmiths, bricklayers, and shipbuilders had all appeared by the 1690s and still flourished in the 1750s. Some servants and slaves possessed these skills, but only on very large plantations. Few planters owned enough adult male bound workers to put them to more than agricultural work, even if they had skills. Free, not bound, men dominated craft activity in this area, and they necessarily created networks of local exchange. Even the most diversified planters relied on neighborhood ser-

---

Trade, and Economic Development in Fredericksburg, Virginia, 1750–1810," *ibid.*, XCIII (1985), 409–426.

34. Earle, *Tidewater Settlement System*, chap. 5; Kulikoff, *Tobacco and Slaves*, 101; McCusker and Menard, *Economy of British America*, 127–128.

vices, which they in turn reciprocated. The self-sufficiency model implies a shortage of craftsmen, since many plantations show little craft activity. However, Russo's comparison of the density of craftsmen in Talbot and in several rural communities in England and New England indicates no such shortage. Carr's work demonstrates a degree of local variation, particularly in the value of investment in crafts, but Russo's essay suggests that minimum needs were met. While the amount of local exchange may have varied with the amount of craft activity, economic life was growing more complex in every Chesapeake area.[35]

III

This review of themes, together with the preceding narrative discussion, suggests some of the dominant lines of force in recent Chesapeake historiography. What should be the future agenda? At the risk of being presumptuous in a field that has generated its own momentum, we single out two broad directions as especially rewarding. They arise as much out of what Chesapeake historians are *not* doing as out of what they *are* beginning to do. We return to our basic division outlined earlier and offer one social and one cultural pointer that may prove useful as Chesapeake studies move forward. We will end by emphasizing the obvious: the relationship between society and culture, substructure and superstructure, cannot be understood simplistically or reductively. The two are in constant interplay, and the best histories of the Chesapeake region will aim at their fusion.

Our first suggestion concerns a difficulty that all colonial historians face in writing the social history of a region (but something that scholars of the Chesapeake have confronted more readily than others, because they have taken region seriously): how to encompass temporal *and* spatial change, linear *and* lateral developments. Our earlier survey of a Chesapeake social narrative rather tended to ignore this point. A more subtle and complex narrative must describe the timing of events not just in the core of the region, but also on its continually expanding periphery. The

35. Galenson argues for continued importation of skilled servants in the 18th century (*White Servitude*, 159–160). Bailyn finds considerable servant migration to Maryland, in particular between 1773 and 1776 (*Voyagers to the West*, esp. chaps. 5 and 6). Nonetheless, immigrant skilled servants represented only a small proportion of the labor pool.

progress of settlement—what Wilbur Cash once called the "roll of frontier upon frontier"—demands much more attention. Even in the seventeenth century, new settlements differed from those established earlier, as P. M. G. Harris's work on Maryland's lower Western Shore, the Rutmans' study of Middlesex, or Kevin Kelly's work on Surry ought to make clear. Settlements within the same county were significantly different, as Lorena Walsh tells us. Richard Beeman's study of Lunenburg County, Virginia, reveals marked variations in economic development and social organization between the well-settled tidewater and frontier areas like the southside. At any one time, then, Chesapeake historians are bringing to light major differences from area to area—variations, for example, in ethnic origins of settlers, in wealth distributions, in commitment to slavery, in crop mixes, in inheritance practices, in the tenures by which people held their land. A major task for the future is to determine when differences reflect regional variations in resources—including human resources—as opposed to varying dates of settlement and thus stages of development.[36]

But how should we characterize this developmental process? Surely, a simple cyclical model is inadequate. Each wave of settlement cannot be seen as simply repeating earlier stages of development, although important repetitions undoubtedly occurred. Philip Morgan's essay on piedmont expansion suggests that the model of a helix may be more appropriate, for later settlement processes could compress, skip almost entirely, perhaps even elongate, elements of earlier stages. Moreover, a continuous and expanding spiral encourages us to see regional core and periphery as constantly interacting. For example, as ex-servants emigrated from tidewater to the frontier, would they not blunt the edge of social tension in the older region? But if poor people grew numerous on the frontier, as Edmund Morgan argues happened in New Kent County in the third quarter of the seventeenth century, might not frontier tensions reverber-

---

36. W. J. Cash, *The Mind of the South* (New York, 1941), 4; P. M. G. Harris, "Integrating Interpretations of Local and Regionwide Change in the Study of Economic Development and Demographic Growth in the Colonial Chesapeake, 1630–1775," Regional Econ. Hist. Research Center, *Working Papers*, I, no. 3 (1978), 35–71; Rutman and Rutman, *A Place in Time*; Kevin P. Kelly, " 'In dispers'd Country Plantations': Settlement Patterns in Seventeenth-Century Surry County, Virginia," in Tate and Ammerman, eds., *Chesapeake in the Seventeenth Century*, 183–205; Walsh's essay in this volume; Beeman, *Evolution of the Southern Backcountry*. By contrast, it is striking how little of the literature on early New England takes a regional approach.

ate back upon older regions? This complex interplay and mutual inter-penetration of forces and influences between old and newly settled regions need much further explication. To take another example, the political skills of the third generation of the tidewater Virginia gentry (those who achieved majority in the second quarter of the eighteenth century) are well known, as is their failure to interest their sons in the same pursuits. What has been less appreciated perhaps is that a later political generation, even more glittering in its accomplishments—men like Patrick Henry, James Madison, James Monroe, and Thomas Jefferson—were from newer families, often located in the more dynamic interior. A generational *and* spatial analysis of elite formation and elite character in the eighteenth century would be instructive. Indeed, the complex patterning of regional variation and developmental processes needs to be worked out in much greater detail for many aspects of Chesapeake life.[37]

As historians attempt to map these overall patterns, they will have to be careful that their attempts do not conceal the dynamics of change. P. M. G. Harris has provided an excellent illustration of this potential pitfall in his discussion of an early hypothesis concerning the seventeenth-century

---

37. The phenomenon of continuous migration from settled areas to frontier regions is acknowledged or mentioned in almost all the detailed work on Chesapeake locales, but to date few have explored the matter with the attention the subject deserves. As Lorena Walsh points out in her essay in this volume, much depends on the size of the jurisdictional unit when measuring rates of persistence and mobility. For the best work, see Kulikoff, *Tobacco and Slaves*, 141–161; Kulikoff, "Uprooted Peoples: Black Migrants in the Age of the American Revolution, 1790–1820," in Berlin and Hoffman, eds., *Slavery and Freedom*, 143–171; Lorena S. Walsh, "Staying Put or Getting Out: Findings for Charles County, Maryland, 1650–1720," *WMQ*, 3d Ser., XLIV (1987), 89–103; and J. P. P. Horn, "Moving On in the New World: Migration and Out-Migration in the Seventeenth-Century Chesapeake," in Peter Clark and David Souden, eds., *Migration and Society in Early Modern England* (London, 1987), 172–212. See also Larry Dale Gragg, *Migration in Early America: The Virginia Quaker Experience* (Ann Arbor, Mich., 1980), and Georgia C. Villaflor and Kenneth L. Sokoloff, "Migration in Colonial America: Evidence from the Militia Muster Rolls," *Social Science Hist.*, VI (1982), 539–570. On tensions among the gentry in the late colonial era, see Isaac, *Transformation of Virginia*, chaps. 7, 9, and 10; the essays by Jack P. Greene cited in n. 13, above; and also an interesting essay, "Violence and Virtue in Virginia, 1766; or, The Importance of the Trivial," in Carl Bridenbaugh, *Early Americans* (New York, 1981), 188–212. Greene, in "Character, Persona, and Authority," briefly sketches the generations of Virginia's political leaders, although he does not mention the spatial aspect, with which he may disagree (Higgins, ed., *Revolutionary War in the South*, 4).

economic development of Maryland's lower Western Shore. Mean inventoried wealth in this area rose with the expansion of tobacco and leveled out with its stagnation, leading to the proposition that patterns of wealth accumulation were the effect of Chesapeake-wide movements of the tobacco economy. But breaking down wealth data by area of settlement, Harris overturned this putative relationship. The pattern was the product of a layering of settlement in which demographic processes and farm building, not the progress of tobacco, were the underlying causes of change. Profits from tobacco affected levels of wealth but not the overall pattern of accumulation. This approach requires the integration of broad regional patterns with comparative studies of properly selected small units. Historians can then better see how the daily lives and decisions of people in all their variety both contributed to, and were the product of, the interacting social, economic, and political structures and processes that historians undertake to study.[38]

A greater attention to temporal and spatial change may even reintroduce the importance of the public realm. In recent years, historians have treated the Chesapeake as a region, in which Maryland was at first a frontier. Such an approach has proved fruitful for understanding many social and economic processes, and the authors represented in this volume have generally followed it. Nevertheless, there were important intercolonial variations that should not be forgotten. A major difference was, of course, the religious complexion of the two colonies. For instance, in the seventeenth century, religious diversity and Catholic power in a predominantly Protestant population brought religious and political tensions to Maryland that did not exist in Virginia. Yet those tensions may have had some creative results. Powerful men in Virginia seem to have been particularly brutal toward servants and generally rapacious, whereas in Maryland they appear to have been more responsible and the courts more protective of servants. Possibly the political tensions that religious differences fostered made Maryland judges and other powerful officeholders more careful than their Virginia counterparts to avoid complaints of injustice. In the eighteenth century, a second difference may merit more investigation, for if evangelicalism proved threatening in Virginia with its long tradition of an established church, it was much less so in Maryland, a

38. Harris, "Integrating Interpretations," Regional Econ. Hist. Research Center, *Working Papers*, I, no. 3 (1978), 35–71; Russell R. Menard, P. M. G. Harris, and Lois Green Carr, "Opportunity and Inequality: The Distribution of Wealth on the Lower Western Shore of Maryland, 1638–1705," *MHM*, LXIX (1974), 169–184.

society long accustomed to religious diversity. Finally, in the early national years, a major difference arose between Maryland and Virginia in their commitment to slavery and in their numbers of free blacks, a difference that would have momentous consequences as the nineteenth century proceeded. Economic forces account for some of this difference, especially those that encouraged the rise of Baltimore, but the role of particular religious groups also proved vital. This intercolonial variation merits more research.[39]

Analyses of structures and processes, important as they are, can easily assume a rather desiccated air if the issue of culture is avoided. Herein resides the second line of development that will surely occupy, perhaps even preoccupy, historians of the Chesapeake in the future. Somewhat belatedly, scholars are exploring the mental world of the region's inhabitants. Their task will be much harder than that facing historians of early New England, for everything from sermons to gravestones, court records to political pamphlets, were produced in less profusion and less adequately preserved in the South. Nevertheless, with characteristic ingenu-

39. For religious and political tensions in Maryland, see Carr and Jordan, *Maryland's Revolution of Government*, and Carr, "Sources of Political Stability," *MHM*, LXXIX (1984), 44–70; for Virginia, see William H. Seiler, "The Anglican Church: A Basic Institution of Local Government in Colonial Virginia," in Daniels, ed., *Town and County*, 134–159. For rapaciousness and harsh treatment of servants, see Morgan, *American Slavery, American Freedom*, 126–129, 281–282, chaps. 10–12; Deal, "Race and Class," 117–128; and David T. Konig, "The Due Process Revolution in Virginia: The Ironic Progress of Legal Reform, 1660–1720" (paper presented at the annual meeting of the American Historical Association, Washington, D.C., 1987). For more responsible behavior in Maryland, see Carr, "Foundations of Social Order," in Daniels, ed., *Town and County*, 72–110; Lorena S. Walsh, "Servitude and Opportunity in Charles County, Maryland, 1658–1705," in Land, Carr, and Papenfuse, eds., *Law, Society, and Politics*, 111–133; and Carr and Menard, "Immigration and Opportunity," in Tate and Ammerman, eds., *Chesapeake in the Seventeenth Century*, 206–242. For an assessment of both views with respect to servants, see Main, *Tobacco Colony*, 114–115. On the growing divergence between upper and lower Chesapeake in terms of slavery and free blacks, see Dunn, "Black Society in the Chesapeake," in Berlin and Hoffman, eds., *Slavery and Freedom*, 49–82, although he does not fully explain it. For an interesting economic explanation, see Carville V. Earle, "A Staple Interpretation of Slavery and Free Labor," *Geographical Review*, LXVIII (1978), 51–65. For the religious view, see Kenneth L. Carroll, "Religious Influences on the Manumission of Slaves in Caroline, Dorchester, and Talbot Counties," *MHM*, LVI (1961), 176–197; Carroll, "Maryland Quakers and Slavery," *Quaker History*, LXXII (1983), 27–42; and Carroll, "An Eighteenth-Century Episcopalian Attack on Quaker and Methodist Manumission of Slaves," *MHM*, LXXX (1985), 139–150.

ity, historians of the Chesapeake are succeeding in wringing meaning from the most unlikely sources. While this is laudable, we urge a broadening of horizons and pose some larger issues that may be worth pursuing.

One is to take up the challenge that James Henretta and others have offered to economic and social historians. Henretta has criticized colonial historians for assuming a capitalist mentality in a society that in fact put more value on maintaining the lineal family and its place in the community than on individual entrepreneurial activity and profits. In addition, studies by Robert Mutch and others, based mostly on New England materials, have argued that local exchange in small communities was not based on a search for profits but on satisfying community needs. The essays in this volume do not address these issues, nor have other Chesapeake historians yet pursued them directly. In part, this may be because the questions Henretta posed seem to have so little relevance to the profit-conscious, market-oriented Chesapeake settlers. Nonetheless we believe there are issues worth pursuing.[40]

We need not set the questions in the dichotomous terms of Henretta. Planters certainly gave thought to the futures of their children and often their children's children, as Jean Lee's essay indicates, and neighbors certainly helped one another, as Lorena Walsh makes clear. Planters also bought and sold goods and services for profit in both local and international markets and enslaved a labor force that they then treated as property to be bought and sold. In sorting out these behaviors and tracking change over time, we need to determine how tightly keyed planters were to market values, especially in local transactions; how quickly planters changed inputs of land and labor in relation to market opportunities; and the degree to which men and women in the free population were dependent on work for wages and were thus less in charge of their lives than people who controlled some means of production and their own labor. We must explore further the extent to which men and women, by the terms of

---

40. James A. Henretta, "Families and Farms: *Mentalité* in Pre-industrial America," *WMQ*, 3d Ser., XXXV (1978), 3–32. The literature on this subject is now voluminous, and almost all directed at New England. See Michael Merrill, "Cash Is Good to Eat: Self-sufficiency and Exchange in the Rural Economy of the United States," *Radical History Review*, IV (1977), 42–72; Robert E. Mutch, "Yeoman and Merchant in Pre-industrial America: Eighteenth-Century Massachusetts as a Case Study," *Societas*, VII (1977), 279–302; and Mutch, "The Cutting Edge: Colonial America and the Debate about the Transition to Capitalism," *Theory and Society*, IX (1980), 847–863.

their gifts and wills, prevented later generations from disposing of property, and the degree to which such restrictions kept property in the lineal family. Further, we must examine the world of slaves. Did they exhibit more interest in family solidarity or community needs than in individual action? Answers to all these questions may vary by economic or social status; by area, depending on richness of natural resources or stages of demographic or economic development; and by cultural traditions, especially those of gender. Insofar as individuals controlled their own lives, attitudes toward risk may prove to be at the bottom of most decisions.[41]

Despite much innovative research over the past decade, we still do not know a great deal about the material culture of Chesapeake residents. Exactly what was the standard of living enjoyed by Chesapeake residents and how did it compare with that of other colonial regions and of England? How comfortably ordinary people live in day-to-day existence is a powerful measure of economic and political performance. For all social groups—bound or slave as well as free, female and male, young and old, poor and rich—scholars need to probe the adequacy of diet and shelter, the effects of disease, the quality of medical care, the opportunities to marry and establish families, and the availability, quality, and variety of consumer goods. How did the settlers view the landscape? If, as has been argued, they thought persistently in extractive terms, then here is another

41. Those who assume the market debate has little application to the Chesapeake should grapple with the opposing views of the Rutmans and members of the "Maryland school." Thus, the Rutmans have argued that Middlesex County planters were "innately conservative," more concerned with family and neighborhood than with the desire for self-aggrandizement (*A Place in Time*, 35, 70, and *passim*). Further, Charles Wetherell argues that planters responded to the simple imperative always to grow more tobacco, not to booms and busts in the international market for tobacco (" 'Boom and Bust' in the Colonial Chesapeake Economy," *Jour. Interdisciplinary Hist.*, XV [1984], 185–210). On the other hand, the work of Menard, Clemens, and others posits the international market as vital to understanding ordinary tobacco planters. Further, John J. McCusker has expressed surprise at the Rutmans' characterization. For McCusker, Chesapeake planters were risk takers, deeply interested in self-aggrandizement, "utility maximizers par excellence" (review of Rutman and Rutman, *A Place in Time*, in *JAH*, LXXII [1985], 129). Perhaps these protagonists are guilty of falling into the dichotomous trap laid by Henretta, but the vehemence of the opposing views indicates that we need more work on this subject. For good suggestions, see McCusker and Menard, *Economy of British America*, chap. 14. T. H. Breen favors the maximizing view of tobacco planters, yet cautions that the tobacco mentality was also bound up with honor and reputation (*Tobacco Culture*, 70 and *passim*). Breen also points up the importance of mapping local credit networks in the Chesapeake.

way of understanding the dominance of an exploitative mentality in the Chesapeake. Work on the household has documented a profound shift from communal spaces and utensils to more private, specialized rooms and to individual place settings, but it is now time to probe literary sources to explicate what this transformation meant to the participants. It is all very well to speak of the rise of individualism and privacy, but we need to ask what these changes meant to those who experienced them. Did attitudes toward personal hygiene, toward consumption, toward space itself change in the early Chesapeake? And what of people's attitudes toward work? Chesapeake inhabitants spent most of their waking hours at work, but it is rather remarkable that we know so little about the rhythms and routines of their daily rounds, and even less about their attitudes toward their central preoccupation. What was the work calendar of various crops and how did this affect social activities? Did attitudes toward time change in the early Chesapeake?[42]

42. On the quality of life, Main offers an excellent beginning for Maryland before 1720 (*Tobacco Colony*, chaps. 4–7). The needs are well laid out in Lorena S. Walsh, "Questions and Sources for Exploring the Standard of Living," *WMQ*, 3d Ser., XLV (1988), 116–123. There is no study of the Chesapeake landscape to match William Cronon, *Changes in the Land: Indians, Colonists, and the Ecology of New England* (New York, 1983), but for a perceptive beginning, see Thad W. Tate, "The Discovery and Development of the Southern Colonial Landscape: Six Commentators," American Antiquarian Society, *Proceedings*, XCIII (1984), 289–311, as well as Karen Ordahl Kupperman, "Fear of Hot Climates in the Anglo-American Colonial Experience," *WMQ*, 3d Ser., XLI (1984), 213–240, and Timothy Howard Silver, "A New Face on the Countryside: Indians and Colonists in the Southeastern Forest" (Ph.D. diss., College of William and Mary, 1985). The shift from communalism to privacy is a theme of importance in Isaac, *Transformation of Virginia*. For detailed studies documenting these changes, see the literature cited in n. 8, above. The subject of work is beginning to attract historians: see Morgan, *American Slavery, American Freedom*, 61–70, 77–91; Main, *Tobacco Colony*, 31–41, 128–134, 194–195; Kulikoff, *Tobacco and Slaves*, 178–180; Carole Shammas, "Black Women's Work and the Evolution of Plantation Society in Virginia," *Labor History*, XXVI (1985), 5–28; Lorena S. Walsh, "Land, Landlord, and Leaseholder: Estate Management and Tenant Fortunes in Southern Maryland, 1642–1820," *Agricultural Hist.*, LIX (1985), 373–396; Lois Green Carr and Lorena S. Walsh, "Economic Diversification and Labor Organization in the Chesapeake, 1650–1820," in Stephen Innes, ed., *Work and Labor in Early America* (Chapel Hill, N.C., 1988), 144–188; and Philip D. Morgan, "Task and Gang Systems: The Organization of Labor on New World Plantations," *ibid.*, 189–220. Lorena Walsh is also completing a large-scale study of plantation management in the Chesapeake to 1820, and Lois Carr, Russell Menard, and Lorena Walsh are preparing a book on agriculture and its work routines and social effects in the 17th century.

There are whole worlds of interior, subjective experiences that historians of the Chesapeake have hardly broached. As Russell Menard's essay demonstrates, immigrants have been counted and categorized, but what the ocean crossing meant for them is almost a complete mystery. Signatures and other measures have been tallied to arrive at approximate literacy rates, but the uses to which literacy was put and how this related to an oral culture await detailed exploration. We know a good deal about religious pluralism in the Chesapeake, but almost nothing about the world of wonders, of superstitions, of magic, of astrology that the region's settlers inhabited. Were there more Thomas Teackles, the Anglican minister on the Eastern Shore who seems to have been a defender of occult religious truth? Were there more Grace Sherwoods, the so-called "Virginia witch"? We know much about fertility and mortality but little about attitudes toward sexual behavior and toward death. We know much about the structure of slave life but little about Afro-American values and beliefs. What better way to understand community norms and values than through individuals deemed to have repudiated them? Few studies of crime, suicide, slander, and madness are available. In a useful survey of crime and law enforcement throughout British North America, Douglas Greenberg characterized the seventeenth-century Chesapeake as *the* most violent region. But can this generalization stand the test of further research? Finally, we need to consider the role of gender in all aspects of interior life, especially in power relations.[43]

Breen, *Tobacco Culture*, especially chap. 2, represents the most ambitious, if not altogether successful, attempt to link work and culture at the level of the great tidewater planters. For a study of one aspect of the "temporal horizon," see "Of Time and Nature: A Study of Persistent Values in Colonial Virginia," in Breen, *Puritans and Adventurers*, 164–196.

43. On literacy, see Kenneth A. Lockridge, *Literacy in Colonial New England: An Enquiry into the Social Context of Literacy in the Early Modern West* (New York, 1974) and Rutman and Rutman, *A Place in Time: Explicatus*, chap. 11, but also see David D. Hall, "Introduction: The Uses of Literacy in New England, 1600–1850," in William L. Joyce *et al.*, eds., *Printing and Society in Early America* (Worcester, Mass., 1983), 1–47, and Isaac, *Transformation of Virginia*, 121–131. On what Chesapeake residents were reading, see three recent studies: John Edgar Molnar, "Publication and Retail Book Advertisements in the *Virginia Gazette*, 1736–1780" (Ph.D. diss., University of Michigan, 1978); Cynthia Z. Stiverson and Gregory A. Stiverson, "The Colonial Retail Book Trade: Availability and Affordability of Reading Material in Mid-Eighteenth-Century Virginia," in Joyce *et al.*, eds., *Printing and Society*, 132–173; and Joseph F. Kett and Patricia A. McClung, "Book Culture in Post-Revolutionary Vir-

In the end, of course, interior experiences must be linked to external events. Culture and society, superstructure and substructure, private and public realms must come together. One way is to turn the spotlight onto key figures whose individual actions were shaped by, and in turn shaped, the course of events, thereby integrating interior worlds and external circumstances. A number of scholars are exploring this genre, one quite

ginia," Am. Antiq. Soc., *Procs.*, XCIV (1984), 97–147. The phrase "world of wonders" comes from an essay by David D. Hall in Hall and David Grayson Allen, eds., *Seventeenth-Century New England* (Boston, 1984), but see also Richard Beale Davis, "The Devil in Virginia in the Seventeenth Century," in Davis, *Literature and Society in Early Virginia, 1608–1840* (Baton Rouge, La., 1973), 14–42; Darrett B. Rutman, "The Evolution of Religious Life in Early Virginia," *Lex et Scientia*, XIV (1978), 190–240; and especially Jon Butler, "Magic, Astrology, and the Early American Religious Heritage, 1600–1760," *AHR*, LXXXIV (1979), 317–346. There is very little to report on attitudes toward sex or death, but for one attempt to explore sexual behavior, see Lee A. Gladwin, "Tobacco and Sex: Some Factors Affecting Non-Marital Sexual Behavior in Colonial Virginia," *Jour. Soc. Hist.*, XII (1978), 57–75. On slave values, see Mechal Sobel, *The World They Made Together: Black and White Values in Eighteenth-Century Virginia* (Princeton, N.J., 1987). On crime, Arthur P. Scott, *Criminal Law in Colonial Virginia* (Chicago, 1930); Raphael Semmes, *Crime and Punishment in Early Maryland* (Baltimore, 1938); and Hugh F. Rankin, *Criminal Trial Proceedings in the General Court of Colonial Virginia* (Williamsburg, Va., 1965) are still useful, but also see Douglas Greenberg, "Crime, Law Enforcement, and Social Control in Colonial America," *Am. Jour. Legal Hist.*, XXVI (1982), 293–325; Peter C. Hoffer, "Disorder and Deference: The Paradoxes of Criminal Justice in the Colonial Tidewater," in David J. Bodenhamer and James W. Ely, Jr., eds., *Ambivalent Legacy: A Legal History of the South* (Jackson, Miss., 1984), 187–201; Hoffer and William B. Scott, eds., *Criminal Proceedings in Colonial Virginia . . .* (Athens, Ga., 1984); Lois Green Carr, *County Government in Maryland, 1689–1709* (New York, 1986), 167–183, 193–285, and appendix 5; Gwenda Morgan, "Law and Social Change in Colonial Virginia: The Role of the Grand Jury in Richmond County, 1692–1776," *VMHB*, XCV (1987), 453–480; Morgan, "Hegemony of the Law"; and Ekirch, *Bound for America*, 167–193. The most useful recent data come from Rutman and Rutman, *A Place in Time*, where they suggest that offenses against person and property were no higher in Middlesex County from the late 17th century onward than in New England (p. 253). Philip J. Schwarz is completing a study of slave crime in Virginia from 1700 to 1860; see his "Gabriel's Challenge: Slaves and Crime in Late Eighteenth-Century Virginia," *VMHB*, XC (1982), 283–309. On slander, see Clara Ann Bowler, "Carted Whores and White Shrouded Apologies: Slander in the County Courts of Seventeenth-Century Virginia," *ibid.*, LXXXV (1977), 411–426, and especially Mary Beth Norton, "Gender and Defamation in Seventeenth-Century Maryland," *WMQ*, 3d Ser., XLIV (1987), 3–39. Norton is undertaking basic studies on the effect of gender on historical processes.

distinct from traditional biography: the career of Charles Carroll the Settler cannot be understood, Ronald Hoffman argues, apart from his native origins, a story that has implications for other immigrants to the Chesapeake; William Byrd II's story becomes, in Kenneth Lockridge's hands, that of a maturing personality, paralleling the maturity of his class in early-eighteenth-century Virginia; Rhys Isaac sensitively probes cantankerous Landon Carter as a way of exploring power and authority in late colonial Virginia, particularly the transformation from patriarchy to paternalism; Shomer Zwelling puts Robert Carter of Nomini Hall under the microscope as he moves from patriarch to mystic, a personal response to a more general challenge facing all Chesapeake gentlemen in the late eighteenth century; Charles Royster traces the impact of the Revolutionary War on the tragic career of Light-Horse Harry Lee; Drew McCoy explores how James Madison reconciled his republican idealism and his identity as a Virginian in the early national years; and Robert Dawidoff dissects John Randolph's despair at the degeneracy to which he thought early-nineteenth-century Virginia had succumbed. In general terms, this trend is a welcome antidote to the abstraction, the "facelessness" of much of the recent writing on the Chesapeake, but it is most compelling for its promise of telling rounded, comprehensive, whole stories.[44]

44. Ronald Hoffman, " 'Marylando-Hibernus': Charles Carroll the Settler, 1660–1720," *WMQ*, 3d Ser., XLV (1988), 207–220—this is just one installment of a much larger work on the Carroll family; Lockridge, *Diary, and Life, of William Byrd II* (see also Michael Greenberg, "William Byrd II and the World of the Market," *So. Studies*, XVI [1977], 429–456; Zuckerman, "William Byrd's Family," *Perspectives Am. Hist.*, XII [1979], 253–311; and Michael Zuckerman, "Fate, Flux, and Good Fellowship: An Early Virginia Design for the Dilemma of American Business," in Harold Issadore Sharlin, ed., *Business and Its Environment: Essays for Thomas C. Cochran* [Westport, Conn., 1983], 161–184); Rhys Isaac, "Communication and Control: Authority Metaphors and Power Contests on Colonel Landon Carter's Virginia Plantation, 1752–1778," in Sean Wilentz, ed., *Rites of Power: Symbolism, Ritual, and Politics since the Middle Ages* (Philadelphia, 1985), 275–302—another installment of a larger study (see also Jack P. Greene's introduction to his edition of *The Diary of Colonel Landon Carter of Sabine Hall, 1752–1778*, 2 vols. [Charlottesville, Va., 1965]; Dunn, "Masters, Servants, and Slaves," in Quinn, ed., *Early Maryland*, 242–266; and Philip Morgan, "Three Planters and Their Slaves: Perspectives on Slavery in Virginia, South Carolina, and Jamaica, 1750–1790," in Winthrop D. Jordan and Sheila L. Skemp, eds., *Race and Family in the Colonial South* [Jackson, Miss., 1987], 37–79); Shomer S. Zwelling, "Robert Carter's Journey: From Colonial Patriarch to New Nation Mystic," *American Quarterly*, XXXVIII (1986), 613–636; Charles Royster, *Light-Horse Harry Lee and the Legacy of the American Revolution* (New York, 1981); Drew McCoy, *The Last*

This is not to say that historians of the Chesapeake should focus upon idiosyncratic individuals rather than collective biography, on isolated figures rather than communities, on contingencies rather than central tendencies. Rather, the two ought to proceed hand in hand, even though ultimately the historian will always be more interested in wholes than in parts, aggregates rather than fractions. Rhys Isaac has pioneered another way to write integrated history of this kind. In the first part of *The Transformation of Virginia*, he has portrayed a society and a culture whole, although at the expense of showing us how it came into being. He discerns its social organization in church, home, elections, and court day and reads its values through the use of space, the pastimes, and the political theater of the day. In the future, it may be possible to go further by drawing upon the findings of literature specialists, art historians, museum curators, and archaeologists in order to delineate systematic relationships among an even greater variety of the region's artifacts— from furniture to folk songs, from poems to pottery, from games to gravestones—and meld them into one single, integrative history. As Isaac was well aware, reading a society whole means being aware of its constituent parts, particularly the relationship between genteel and vernacular cultures, patrician and plebeian worlds. It is in the explication of this encounter, at times antagonistic, at others cooperative, that the promise of an integrated cultural history will lie.[45]

---

of the Fathers: James Madison and the Republican Legacy (New York, forthcoming); Robert Dawidoff, *The Education of John Randolph* (New York, 1979). For other good work on individuals, see Richard R. Beeman, "Robert Munford and the Political Culture of Frontier Virginia," *Journal of American Studies*, XII (1978), 169–183; J. Frederick Fausz, "Opechancanough: Indian Resistance Leader," in David G. Sweet and Gary B. Nash, eds., *Struggle and Survival in Colonial America* (Berkeley, Calif., 1981), 21–37 (cf. Carl Bridenbaugh, "O-pe-chan-can-ough: A Native American Patriot," in Bridenbaugh, *Early Americans*, 5–49); Deal, "Race and Class"; and T. H. Breen, James H. Lewis, and Keith Schlesinger, "Motive for Murder: A Servant's Life in Virginia, 1678," *WMQ*, 3d Ser., XL (1983), 106–120. The recent editions of the writings of Capt. John Smith, Charles Willson Peale, and Benjamin Henry Latrobe, as well as those of George Washington, Thomas Jefferson, and James Madison, further facilitate this "individualizing" of Chesapeake history.

45. Isaac, *Transformation of Virginia*; Richard L. Bushman, "American High-Style and Vernacular Cultures," in Greene and Pole, eds., *Colonial British America*, 345–383. There have been attempts, not totally successful, to apply Isaac's insights to other aspects of Chesapeake life; see Upton, *Holy Things and Profane*, and Mark P. Leone, "Interpreting Ideology in Historical Archaeology: Using the Rules of Perspective in

Indeed the ultimate goal must be a fully integrated human history. The historian will draw upon all the sciences—from the demographics of population growth to the economics of accumulation, from the geology of social strata to the archaeology of gestures, from the cultural anthropology of celebrations to the social anthropology of networks, from the geometry of social relations to the calculus of human emotions. The arts will be equally inspiring—whether it be the use of *pointilliste* technique to create a series of exquisite miniatures, or the borrowing of poetic visions such as Ebenezer Cooke's "Sot-Weed Planters" clad in *"Scotch-cloth Blue / With neither Stockings, Hat, nor Shooe."* The aim will be to portray Chesapeake society in motion, as it cohered, transformed itself, and assumed new configurations. Ever broadening and deepening, these

---

the William Paca Garden in Annapolis, Maryland," in Daniel Miller and Christopher Tilley, eds., *Ideology, Power, and Prehistory* (Cambridge, 1984), 25–35. The best attempt at an archaeological overview of early America is James Deetz, *In Small Things Forgotten: The Archaeology of Early American Life* (Garden City, N.Y., 1977). Afro-American life is not totally closed to artifactual study; see John Michael Vlach, "Afro-American Domestic Artifacts in Eighteenth-Century Virginia," *Material Culture*, XIX (1987), 3–23. On the art of the Chesapeake, see Wayne Craven, "Virginia Portraits: Iconography, Style, and Social Context," *VMHB*, XCII (1984), 201–225, and Jessie Poesch, *The Art of the Old South: Painting, Sculpture, Architecture, and the Products of Craftsmen, 1560–1860* (New York, 1983). There has been a good deal of work on the literature of the early Chesapeake. Davis, *Intellectual Life*, has already been mentioned (see n. 12, above). For recent work, see J. A. Leo Lemay, *Men of Letters in Colonial Maryland* (Knoxville, Tenn., 1972); Robert D. Arner, "Westover and the Wilderness: William Byrd's Images of Virginia," *Southern Literary Journal*, VII, no. 2 (1975), 105–123; Edward H. Cohen, *Ebenezer Cooke: The Sot-Weed Canon* (Athens, Ga., 1975); Robert D. Arner, "Ebenezer Cooke: Satire in the Colonial South," *So. Lit. Jour.*, VIII, no. 1 (1975), 153–164; Arner, "The Quest for Freedom: Style and Meaning in Robert Beverley's *History and Present State of Virginia*," *ibid.*, VIII, no. 2 (1976), 79–98; Carl Dolmetsch, "William Byrd of Westover as an Augustan Poet," *Studies in the Literary Imagination*, IX, no. 2 (1976), 69–77; James R. Heintze, "Alexander Malcolm: Musician, Clergyman, and Schoolmaster," *MHM*, LXXIII (1978), 226–235; Ross Pudaloff, " 'A Certain Amount of Excellent English': The Secret Diaries of William Byrd," *So. Lit. Jour.*, XV, no. 1 (1982), 101–119; and David Curtis Skaggs, ed., *The Poetic Writings of Thomas Cradock, 1718–1770* (Newark, Del., 1983). For a rounded view of the significance of the Tuesday Club of Annapolis, see Elaine G. Breslaw, ed., *Records of the Tuesday Club of Annapolis, 1745–56* (Urbana, Ill., 1988); John Barry Talley, *Secular Music in Colonial Annapolis: The Tuesday Club, 1745–56* (Urbana, Ill., 1988); and Alexander Hamilton, *The History of the Tuesday Club of Annapolis*, ed. Robert Micklus (Chapel Hill, N.C., forthcoming). John Barth's *The Sot-Weed Factor* (New York, 1960) still provides a marvelous introduction to early Chesapeake life.

various streams of influence ought to flow together, reaching a confluence in a more comprehensive understanding of the early Chesapeake.
Numerous headstreams and tributaries, of which this volume represents
merely one, will feed the larger channel. Then we will see the region
whole.

J. Frederick Fausz

Merging and Emerging Worlds

Anglo-Indian Interest Groups and the Development of the Seventeenth-Century Chesapeake

> It is the glory of every Nation to enlarge them-
> selves, to encourage their own forraign attempts,
> and . . . to have . . . as many several commodities
> as they can attain to. . . .
> But alas, we Englishmen . . . vilifie, scandalize
> and cry down such parts of the unknown world,
> as have been . . . made flourishing, by the charge,
> hazzard and diligence of their own brethren, as if
> because removed from us, we either account
> them people of another world or enemies.
> —John Hammond, *Leah and Rachel* (1656)

TWO YEARS after the Powhatan Uprising of
1622 had nearly destroyed the Virginia colony, Gov. Sir Francis Wyatt
declared that "our first worke is expulsion of the Salvages to gaine the
free range of the countrey. . . for it is infinitely better to have no heathen
among us, who at best were but as thornes in our sides, then to be at
peace and league with them." However, even as he wrote those words,
Governor Wyatt was well aware that alliances with helpful distant Indian
groups would prove as decisive as aggression against hostile neighboring
tribes in assuring the survival and success of Virginia's English population. Only six months earlier, he had commanded unprecedentedly ambi-

Research for this essay was supported by a National Endowment for the Humanities
Fellowship for College Teachers (1982–1983), an American Association for State
and Local History Grant-in-Aid (1986), and Faculty Development Grants from St.
Mary's College of Maryland.

tious raids on the Piscataways of southern Maryland in order to protect the colonists' invaluable Patawomeke allies in their war with the Powhatans.[1]

Some three decades later, Virginians again gathered in Maryland waters to settle an important issue in Anglo-Indian relations. After a decade of waging separate wars on Lord Baltimore's colony, victorious Virginia commonwealthmen and leading chiefs of the "Nation and State of Sasquehanogh" concluded a significant, comprehensive treaty of "peace and league" in July 1652 in which they pledged their friendship until the "End of the World." For the Susquehannocks, the end of their Chesapeake world came only a quarter-century later, when reconciled Virginia and Maryland colonists who had benefited from a generation of peace under the terms of this treaty violently turned on them and destroyed their centuries-long influence in the region.[2]

Although most historians implicitly recognize that the early English Chesapeake emerged out of the confluence of two alien worlds, recent scholarship has not yet succeeded in restoring Indians to the center stage they occupied in the seventeenth century. Wesley Frank Craven's observation that "few historians have managed to convey a feeling for the full extent to which the Indian problem absorbed the energies and thought of the colonists" is still relevant almost forty years later. Despite the recent contributions of ethnohistory, most scholars continue to interpret Indians as incidental, rather than essential, to colonial Chesapeake history, often ignoring them altogether or at best regarding them only as a perplexing "problem" for white settlers. The recent proliferation of economic and demographic analyses of colonial societies has only exacerbated this interpretive imbalance. By deemphasizing the colonial leaders whose policies dealt with Indians, such accounts continue to obscure the influence that superbly adapted and strategically located native populations exerted on the actions and attitudes, the experiences and expectations, of all peoples in the early Chesapeake. This essay attempts a more realistic and

---

1. Gov. Sir Francis Wyatt to the earl of Southampton, summer? 1624, "Wyatt Documents," *William and Mary Quarterly*, 2d Ser., VI (1926), 118; Council in Virginia to Virginia Company, Jan. 30, 1623/24, Susan Myra Kingsbury, ed., *The Records of the Virginia Company of London*, 4 vols. (Washington, D.C., 1906–1935), IV, 450, hereafter cited as *Va. Co. Records*.

2. "Articles of Peace and freindship," July 5, 1652, William Hand Browne *et al.*, eds., *Archives of Maryland* (Baltimore, 1883–), III, 277–278, hereafter cited as *Md. Archives*.

balanced interpretation of Chesapeake development by identifying cooperative interethnic alliances and integrating their activities into the political and social history of the region.[3]

Colonists and Indians found a focus for mutual understanding in the
tidewater beaver trade, and the intercultural interest groups that grew
from it profoundly influenced the mid-seventeenth-century Chesapeake.
In a critical transition era between the Anglo-Indian wars in 1622 and
1675, tripartite alliances of fur-trading tribes, elite colonial entrepreneurs, and important London merchants found commodities and causes
that could potentially circumvent disruptive farmer expansionism and
reshape the political and economic future of the region. For the first and
last time in the tidewater Chesapeake, interethnic trade alliances gave
Englishmen intent on advancing their fortunes and Indians intent on
preserving their lands a common cause for excluding the growth of
intrusive colonial settlements. The early promise of these Anglo-Indian
interest groups indicated that the short-lived beaver trade, if given time to
mature under expert monopolists, might have obviated the large-scale
exploitation of slave labor and the massive dispossession of Indian lands
that became the southern frontier legacy. In the end, however, these
ambitious, innovative experiments in intercultural cooperation succeeded
only in promoting the intense competition that aborted the beaver boom

3. Wesley Frank Craven, *The Southern Colonies in the Seventeenth Century, 1607–
1689* (Baton Rouge, La., 1949), 173n; Thad W. Tate, "The Seventeenth-Century
Chesapeake and Its Modern Historians," in Thad W. Tate and David L. Ammerman, eds., *The Chesapeake in the Seventeenth Century: Essays on Anglo-American Society*
(Chapel Hill, N.C., 1979), 30–34; J. Frederick Fausz, "The Invasion of Virginia:
Indians, Colonialism, and the Conquest of Cant—A Review Essay on Anglo-Indian
Relations in the Chesapeake," *Virginia Magazine of History and Biography*, XCV
(1987), 133–156, esp. 133–140. The early inspiration for analyzing interethnic inter-
est groups derived from Bruce G. Trigger, *The Children of Aataentsic: A History of the
Huron People to 1660*, 2 vols. (Montreal, 1976), esp. I, 24–25. Although little attention
has been paid to transatlantic interest-group alliances involving Indians, scholars have
recently rediscovered important English colonial-homeland networks. E.g., see J. M.
Sosin, *English America and the Restoration Monarchy of Charles II: Transatlantic Politics,
Commerce, and Kinship* (Lincoln, Nebr., 1980); Alison G. Olson, "The Virginia Mer-
chants of London: A Study in Eighteenth-Century Interest-Group Politics," *WMQ*,
3d Ser., XL (1983), 363–388; Francis J. Bremer, "Increase Mather's Friends: The
Trans-Atlantic Congregational Network of the Seventeenth Century," American An-
tiquarian Society, *Proceedings*, XCIV, Pt. I (1984), 59–96; and David Cressy, *Coming
Over: Migration and Communication between England and New England in the Seventeenth
Century* (Cambridge, 1987).

and ultimately encouraged what they initially deferred—the emergence of a mature English tobacco coast inimical to Indian trappers, colonial traders, and beavers alike.

THE CHESAPEAKE'S first interethnic interest groups evolved gradually out of the mixed legacy of Anglo-Indian relations in Virginia between 1607 and 1630. Such alliances became possible only after Powhatan hostility made the colonists independent of inhibiting Virginia Company policies and became influential only after Susquehannock hospitality made the colonists aware of new commercial ventures with London merchants.

In the Virginia colony's first decade and a half, Englishmen suffered under a double dependency that precluded friendly relations with Indians, crippled local initiative in policy making, and jeopardized their very survival. Colonists depended on the distant Virginia Company for their legal status, financial support, and operational agenda, and on the neighboring Algonquians for food, farmlands, and security from attacks. Although the fifteen thousand or so Powhatans in 1607 were willing to share their "Corne, weomen and Country" with the English *tassantasses* ("strangers"), myopic company policies soon forced the colonists to alienate the Indians by depleting their food supplies and demanding their conversion to Christianity. Convinced of their cultural superiority and yet haunted by their total dependence on potential enemies for survival, the Jamestown colonists often procured Powhatan maize by coercion as a military necessity and rarely developed the kind of friendly trade relations that would "induce . . . Barbarous natures to a likeing and a mutuall society with us."[4]

Because the colonists threatened the Powhatans' cultural integrity without providing material incentives to encourage their trust or cooperation, Anglo-Indian relations based on "fear without love" frequently

4. Capt. John Smith, *A True Relation of Such Occurrences and Accidents of Noate as Hath Hapned in Virginia* . . . (London, 1608), in Philip L. Barbour, ed., *The Complete Works of Captain John Smith (1580–1631)*, 3 vols. (Chapel Hill, N.C., 1986), I, 67; Smith, *The Generall Historie of Virginia, New-England, and the Summer Isles* . . . (London, 1624), *ibid.*, II, 136–241, 323–329; Sir George Peckham, "A True Report . . ." (1583), in David Beers Quinn, ed., *Voyages and Colonising Enterprises of Sir Humphrey Gilbert*, 2 vols. (London, 1940), II, 452; Edmund S. Morgan, *American Slavery, American Freedom: The Ordeal of Colonial Virginia* (New York, 1975), 85–91; J. Frederick Fausz, "The Powhatan Uprising of 1622: A Historical Study of Ethnocentrism and Cultural Conflict" (Ph.D. diss., College of William and Mary, 1977), 228–250.

precipitated violent conflicts. Frustrated that Jamestown officials refused to accept his inferior furs or to pay for his maize, Wahunsonacock/Powhatan launched the First Anglo-Powhatan War (1609–1614) in the belief that the colonists' "comming hither is not for trade, but to invade my people, and possesse my Country." Emerging victorious from that devastating conflict, the English exploited the Powhatans as a conquered people, demanding their soils for the growing ranks of new tobacco farmers and their souls for the company's financially rewarding experiments in Christian conversion. Pressed to change their residence by officials in Jamestown and pressured to change their religion by officials in London, the Algonquians of tidewater Virginia faced different, but equally destructive, English policies.[5]

By 1621 the James River colonists were dispersed among dozens of seemingly safe plantation "islands," segregated from, and oblivious to, the sea of native neighbors surrounding them. Except for a few acculturated interpreters who crossed ethnic boundaries with ease and expertise, the vast majority of the colonists knew less about the Indian peoples and products in Virginia than had Capt. John Smith in 1608 or Capt. Samuel Argall in 1612. Complacent about the disruptive "antient quarrells" with the "trecherous" Powhatans, most colonists maintained their ethnocentric insularity and concentrated on their profitable tobacco fields.[6]

Company officials in London, however, ascribing their depleted treasury to the colonists' scandalous reputation for avarice and lack of commitment in anglicizing the Indians, challenged such complacency with aggressive reforms in Virginia society. Late in 1621, the Virginia Company dispatched a gentleman governor and new, well-connected councillors to carry out its idealistic and ambitious policies in the colony. Accompanying Gov. Sir Francis Wyatt to Jamestown were prominent kinsmen and gentry contacts from his native Kent, including the Reverend Haute Wyatt of Boxley, his younger brother; George Sandys, Esq., his uncle by marriage and the colony's new treasurer; Henry Fleet of Chatham, the

5. Smith, *Generall Historie*, in Barbour, ed., *Complete Works of Smith*, II, 195, 231–253; George Percy, " 'A Trewe Relacyon'—Virginia from 1609 to 1612," *Tyler's Quarterly Historical and Genealogical Magazine*, III (1922), 260–280; "A Breife Declaration of the Plantation of Virginia . . . by the Ancient Planters," H. R. McIlwaine, ed., *Journals of the House of Burgesses of Virginia, 1619–1658/59* (Richmond, Va., 1915), 35; J. Frederick Fausz, " 'Abundance of Blood . . . shed on both sides': England's First Indian War, 1609–1614" (forthcoming).

6. William J. Van Schreeven and George H. Reese, eds., *Proceedings of the General Assembly of Virginia . . . 1619* (Jamestown, Va., 1969), 33, 39, 43.

governor's second cousin; and young William Claiborne of Crayford Parish, the newly appointed surveyor general. Conventional wisdom dictated that men of such wealth and status, reputation and education, would promote the kind of social and political stability that the colony had not known since the regime of Gov. Lord De La Warr.[7]

The company's plans for a hopeful new beginning in Virginia were crushed only five months into Governor Wyatt's administration, however, when Opechancanough's brilliant and devastating uprising of March 22, 1622, claimed the lives of a fourth of the colonial population and produced a "sodayne alteration of the State of all thinges." Preoccupied with affairs in the company, court, and countinghouses across the Atlantic, the colonists were caught by surprise. The stunned survivors, recognizing how their ignorance of, and isolation from, local Indians had contributed to this tragedy, immediately directed their attention to the hidden dangers and unknown opportunities of this alien land.[8]

Thus, the Powhatan Uprising represented a crucial milestone in the acculturation of the Chesapeake colonists and created an atmosphere in which interethnic interest-group alliances could flourish for the first time. The Powhatans' failure to annihilate the colonists actually strengthened the English foothold in the Bay by encouraging the most aggressive and adaptive of the local leaders to seize power and seek revenge free of company interference. Rejecting the misguided policies and simplistic prejudices of the past, these colonial leaders sought a greater reliance on Indian friends and a better appreciation of Indian foes to strengthen their position. Ironically, the uprising that Opechancanough hoped would

7. Company instructions, July 24, 1621, *Va. Co. Records*, III, 468–491; Richard Beale Davis, *George Sandys, Poet Adventurer: A Study in Anglo-American Culture in the Seventeenth Century* (London, 1955), 112–117; Annie Lash Jester and Martha Woodroof Hiden, eds., *Adventurers of Purse and Person, Virginia, 1607–1625* (Princeton, N.J., 1956), 131–132, 172–173, 372–373.

8. "Discourse of the Old Company," April 1625, *Va. Co. Records*, IV, 524; Edward Waterhouse, *A Declaration of the State of the Colony and Affaires in Virginia. With a Relation of the Barbarous Massacre . . .* (London, 1622); J. Frederick Fausz, "Opechancanough: Indian Resistance Leader," in David G. Sweet and Gary B. Nash, eds., *Struggle and Survival in Colonial America* (Berkeley, Calif., 1981), 21–37; J. Frederick Fausz, "Patterns of Anglo-Indian Aggression and Accommodation along the Mid-Atlantic Coast, 1584–1634," in William W. Fitzhugh, ed., *Cultures in Contact: The Impact of European Contacts on Native American Cultural Institutions, A.D. 1000–1800* (Washington, D.C., 1985), 225–268.

reassert Powhatan supremacy led instead to an innovative reshaping of cultural allegiances by a new and dominant group of English frontiersmen.

"Plentifull in nothing but want & wanting nothing but plenty," the nine hundred or so colonists who survived the 1622 uprising had little choice but to rely on Governor Wyatt's decimated Council of State as "th'Instrument to make all this whole againe." With the Virginia Company bankrupt, discredited, and divided, and the court distracted with European affairs, authority to shape the colony's future descended upon the inexperienced governor and his new councillors. These surviving leaders were evenly divided between "men of Contemplation and discourse" (like Wyatt and Sandys, the Oxford-educated courtier-poets from Kent) and "men of action or experience" (such as Sir George Yeardley and Francis West, political and military veterans of earlier Virginia crises), and they derived their strength by unifying diverse talents under adverse conditions. This motley crew of poets and profiteers, scholars and soldiers, quickly developed into an effective, if unlikely, oligarchy based on their common acquisitive ambitions. By fairly distributing the bountiful spoils of office and considering it "ill nature or worse nurture, to desire contention" with their fellow oligarchs, Wyatt's councillors successfully merged public service with private gain and established the prototype for the seventeenth-century Virginia Council.[9]

9. Petition to Governor Wyatt and Council, Mar. 11, 1623/24, *Va. Co. Records*, IV, 468; [Robert Johnson], "An Answere to a Declaration of the Present State of Virginia," May 1623, *ibid.*, 141–142, 147; Capt. William Powell to Sir Edwin Sandys, Apr. 12, 1621, *ibid.*, III, 437; J. Frederick Fausz and Jon Kukla, "A Letter of Advice to the Governor of Virginia, 1624," *WMQ*, 3d Ser., XXXIV (1977), 104–129; H. R. McIlwaine, ed., *Minutes of the Council and General Court of Colonial Virginia*, 2d ed. (Richmond, Va., 1979), *passim*; Jon Kukla, "Order and Chaos in Early America: Political and Social Stability in Pre-Restoration Virginia," *American Historical Review*, XC (1985), 283–284; Fausz, "Powhatan Uprising," 447–463, 486–513. The ruling oligarchs under Wyatt constituted a unique transition group between Virginia councillors before 1622 and those under Gov. Sir William Berkeley after 1660. Bernard Bailyn identified these "tough, unsentimental, quick-tempered, crudely ambitious men" of the 1620s with a "common capacity to survive and flourish in frontier settlements," but he did not recognize the Powhatan Uprising as a key catalyst in providing a unifying experience for councillors of such different backgrounds ("Politics and Social Structure in Virginia," in James Morton Smith, ed., *Seventeenth-Century America: Essays in Colonial History* [Chapel Hill, N.C., 1959], 92–95). Although Edmund S. Morgan recognized the mixed heritage of these unlikely oligarchs,

The first task for Wyatt's oligarchs was to increase their individual power and stature in order to validate their positions and enforce their decisions. Whether gentry born or lowly, the successful councillors accomplished this through military command in the war with the Powhatans. The Indian uprising had placed hundreds of frightened, defenseless colonists under the councillors' control, and during the Second Anglo-Powhatan War (1622–1632), they assembled them into private armies to raid, trade, and farm for their personal benefit. Leading these highly mobile forces in lucrative raids against hostile Indians and in profitable trading expeditions with friendly allies, such as the Patawomekes and the Eastern Shore Accomacs, the Council warlords established new criteria for success in a dangerous frontier setting. Described as "Cheiftaines" by contemporary critics who compared their ruthless exploitation to the behavior of Powhatan *werowances*, Wyatt's councillors challenged the traditional belief that only high social status qualified men to govern by requiring military ability—not education, wealth, or pedigree—as the main criterion for leadership. Even the socially prominent Wyatt and Sandys were compelled to participate in the *rite de passage* of forest combat in order to prove that their capacity to command was consistent with their warrant to rule. This common initiation and shared danger under fire further unified Wyatt's councillors into a cohesive fraternity of leadership. Appropriately, the battlefield exploits of both the "men of Contemplation" and those "fitter for Action then advice" were immortalized in a mid-1620s Virginia ballad sung to the tune "All those that be good fellowes."[10]

Although successful military campaigning enhanced the councillors' reputations as guardians of public safety, raids against the Powhatans were also key sources of personal wealth and influence. Rejecting the holy war of genocide advocated by Londoners as too impractical and unprofitable, Virginia's leaders preferred to conduct modest harvest raids on nearby tribes so as not to interfere with tobacco production. These

---

his failure to distinguish between pre- and post-uprising developments obscured how the Indian war uniquely contributed to their wealth and power. "The First American Boom: Virginia 1618 to 1630," *WMQ*, 3d Ser., XXVIII (1971), 169–198.

10. Smith, *Generall Historie*, in Barbour, ed., *Complete Works of Smith*, II, 311, and "The Fourth Book" *passim*; Governor Wyatt's commission to Capt. Roger Smith, Apr. 13, 1622, *Va. Co. Records*, III, 609; George Sandys to John Ferrar, Apr. 11, 1623, *ibid.*, IV, 110–111; "Good Newes from Virginia, 1623," *WMQ*, 3d Ser., V (1948), 351–358.

"harshe visitts" and "feedfights" for appropriating Powhatan maize provided the councillor commanders with vast corn profits (often reaching
£1 sterling per bushel) and permitted their English servants to grow
tobacco exclusively. By never dealing a deathblow to the Powhatans,
Wyatt's warlords were assured of capital for financing other projects and a
continuing justification for exploiting servant labor under their "protection." With captured Powhatan maize keeping them alive, and fear of
Powhatan attacks keeping them in line, English laborers cultivated record
amounts of tobacco for the Council oligarchs throughout the 1620s, ever
increasing the power and profits of the "Lords of those Lands."[11]

By 1630 the brutal efficiency of Wyatt's wartime regime had transformed Virginia into a more prosperous, stable, and secure colony than
ever before. In only eight years, devastated James River settlements
emerged from the ashes of 1622, experiencing a fivefold increase in
population and a tenfold increase in tobacco exports. "Being thus . . . left
to themselves," Capt. John Smith observed of the colonists freed from
company control, "they have increased beyond expectation." Smith, the
prototypical self-made adventurer, seemed especially intrigued that the
councillors had turned Virginia into a paradise of possibilities for farsighted immigrants, reputedly enabling them to earn "more in one yeare,
than . . . by Piracie in seven."[12]

However, Smith was one of only a few Englishmen who truly appreciated frontier conditions or approved of the oligarchs' wartime ethics. To

11. Fausz and Kukla, "Letter of Advice," *WMQ*, 3d Ser., XXXIV (1977), 126–127;
Smith, *Generall Historie*, in Barbour, ed., *Complete Works of Smith*, II, 302, 310–321;
Council to Virginia Company, Jan. 20, 1622/23, *Va. Co. Records*, IV, 10; William Capps
to Dr. Thomas Wynston, Mar./Apr. 1622/23, *ibid.*, 37; "Breife Declaration," McIlwaine, ed., *Journals of Burgesses, 1619–1658/59*, 30, 32; "Good Newes from Virginia,"
WMQ, 3d Ser., V (1948), 355; Fausz, "Powhatan Uprising," 444–567 *passim*; Kukla,
"Order and Chaos," *AHR*, XC (1985), 283–285.

12. Capt. John Smith, *The True Travels, Adventures, and Observations of Captaine John
Smith* (London, 1630), in Barbour, ed., *Complete Works of Smith*, III, 215–218, 241;
Fausz, "Powhatan Uprising," 506–576. Virginia's rapid recovery during the 1620s
challenges the conclusion that this was an era of privation or instability. Cf. Bailyn,
"Politics and Social Structure," in Smith, ed., *Seventeenth-Century America*, 90, 94–
97; T. H. Breen, "Looking Out for Number One: The Cultural Limits on Public
Policy in Early Virginia," in *Puritans and Adventurers: Change and Persistence in Early
America* (New York, 1980), 106–126, esp. 109–111, 125–126; and Grace L. Chickering, "Founders of an Oligarchy: The Virginia Council, 1692–1722," in Bruce C.
Daniels, ed., *Power and Status: Officeholding in Colonial America* (Middletown, Conn.,
1986), 255.

the majority of London critics, the cynical, selfish behavior of Wyatt's councillors epitomized the corrupting influences of a sinister frontier savagism. The acculturative impact of woodland warfare seemed to be confirmed when Wyatt and Sandys, after only a brief tenure in America, bitterly denounced their close relatives and former patrons whenever local perspectives and Council colleagues were criticized. In 1624 Governor Wyatt wrote that "many things are Principles with us here that are disputed there as Problemes," having earlier suggested that an influential company director come to Virginia "that to his zeale he would add knowledge of this Contrey." Responding to homeland critics who considered Virginia society "odious or contemptible" because councillors assumed the independence and arrogance of kings, one of Wyatt's lieutenants eloquently justified the frontier philosophy of the 1620s: "[Although] itt is much to be desired, that either good men were commaunders or els that commaunders were good men . . . we are all by nature the sonnes of wrath: servinge . . . the spirrit that rules in the hartes of the disobedient."[13]

At the dawn of a new decade, three such "sonnes of wrath"—Councillors William Tucker, Samuel Mathews, and William Claiborne—emerged as the oligarchs best equipped to found the first interethnic interest-group alliances in the Chesapeake. As Indian raiders who had profited from the "peace of warres," they possessed the essential knowledge and the critical resources for exploiting the "wares of peace" as Indian traders. The tobacco boom of the 1620s was more a result of, than the reason for, their success, since the Powhatan war provided them with the monopoly on servants, ships, and political authority that launched their careers as merchant-planters. Combining their expertise in local affairs with a transatlantic network of key contacts, these aggressive opportunists made the "Wills and counsailes of Men of Trade" the dominant influence in the Chesapeake by 1630.[14]

13. Wyatt to Southampton, "Wyatt Documents," *WMQ*, 2d Ser., VI (1926), 120; Sir Francis Wyatt to George Wyatt, Apr. 4, 1623, *Va. Co. Records*, IV, 237; "Discourse of the Old Company," Apr. 1625, *ibid.*, 526; John Donne, *A Sermon upon the VIII Verse of the I. Chapter of the Acts of the Apostles* . . . (London, 1622), in Henry Alford, ed., *The Works of John Donne, D.D.* . . . , 6 vols. (London, 1839), VI, 229; Powell to Sandys, Apr. 12, 1621, *Va. Co. Records*, III, 437.

14. Samuel Purchas, "Virginia Verger: Or a Discourse Shewing the Benefits . . . of Virginia . . . " (1625), in *Hakluytus Posthumus, or Purchas His Pilgrimes*, 20 vols. (Glasgow, 1905–1907), XIX, 257 and *passim*; T. H. Breen, ed., "George Donne's

William Tucker, born into a Kentish-Dorset family prominent in New World colonization, was the prototypical wartime profiteer. Although he had arrived in Virginia in 1610 and survived the First Anglo-Powhatan War, Tucker achieved prominence only after the uprising of 1622 provided him with the opportunity to demonstrate his military skills, harvest Powhatan maize, amass servant labor, and sell goods from his Kecoughtan store at usurious prices. In 1622–1623 alone Tucker led eight raids on six different tribes from the James River to the Potomac. Co-commanding Wyatt's 1623 expedition against the Piscataways and the Nacotchtanks of Maryland, Tucker promoted the "setling of trade" with friendly tribes in the Potomac River basin. Tucker's able leadership was rewarded in 1624 with election to the House of Burgesses and in 1626 with appointment to the Council.[15]

Symbolizing the views and values of Virginia's elite frontiersmen that proved so baffling to Londoners, Tucker combined the roles of ruthless warlord, responsible for poisoning, shooting, and beheading several dozen Powhatan *werowances* at a fake peace parley, and respectable burgess, patriarch of an early triracial household shared with Algonquian and African Christians. As the powerful harbor master of the James River

---

'Virginia Reviewed': A 1638 Plan to Reform Colonial Society," *WMQ*, 3d Ser., XXX (1973), 460 and *passim*; John R. Pagan, "Trade and Politics in Virginia, 1625–1660" (B. Lit. thesis, Oxford University, 1975), chaps. 1–2 and appendix B, 157–159; Robert Brenner, "Commercial Change and Political Conflict: The Merchant Community in Civil War London" (Ph.D. diss., Princeton University, 1970), 50–100. In 1631 the Dutch visitor de Vries observed that Jamestown's merchant-councillors were "very hospitable, but they are not proper persons to trade with. You must look out when you trade with them, . . . or you will be struck in the tail; for if they can deceive any one, they account it among themselves a Roman action." Three decades later, Marylander George Alsop similarly contended that "the people of this place . . . are a more acute people . . . in matters of Trade and Commerce, then in any other place of the World. . . . [H]e that undertakes Merchants imployment for Mary-Land, must have more of Knave in him then Fool . . . carrying alwayes in his looks the Effigies of an Execution." David Peterson de Vries, "Voyages from Holland to America, A.D. 1632 to 1644" (1655), trans. Henry C. Murphy, New-York Historical Society, *Collections*, 2d Ser., III (1857), 127; George Alsop, *A Character of the Province of Maryland* (1666), in Clayton Colman Hall, ed., *Narratives of Early Maryland, 1633–1684* (New York, 1910), 379.

15. Alexander Brown, ed., *The Genesis of the United States*, 2 vols. (Boston, 1891), II, 1014; Michael Wickes, *The Tucker Family of Devon* (Bideford, Devon, 1984), 16–18, 31–33; Morgan, "First American Boom," *WMQ*, 3d Ser., XXVIII (1971), 190; Fausz, "Powhatan Uprising," 451, 496–505.

and brother-in-law of the London Puritan merchant Maurice Thomson, Tucker drew the old and new worlds of Englishmen closer together by his business connections and expertise in both.[16]

With similarly extensive interests and friendships, Councillor Samuel Mathews of London arrived in Virginia shortly before the Powhatan Uprising and quickly rose to prominence as an Indian raider and trader. By the time of his appointment to the first royal Council of State in 1625, Mathews's skill in stealing Indian maize was matched only by his success in exploiting large numbers of English laborers. A major exporter of tobacco (ten thousand pounds in 1630), land speculator, and husband to two wealthy widows, he established "Mathews Manor," near Newport News and Tucker's Kecoughtan, as a site of influence and affluence second only to Jamestown itself.[17]

Mathews's frontier acumen in Chesapeake Indian relations made him an indispensable contributor to the formation of interethnic alliances. He was one of the first colonists to sense the potential of a broad-based trade in the Bay, and in 1626 and 1629 his fellow councillors awarded him one-year monopolies on the maize and furs of the region. Promoting the public welfare in his search for personal profits, Mathews constructed a fort at Point Comfort and sponsored new plantations in the midst of hostile Indian territory. His 1626 plan for "winning . . . the Forrest" by means of an exorbitantly priced palisade connecting the James and York rivers initiated a fertile thirty-year friendship with co-author Claiborne. Maintaining key contacts with "notable combinations" of courtiers and London merchants, Mathews advanced the political and ideological, as well as commercial, agendas for Claiborne's formative interest-group alliance.[18]

As the youngest and longest lived of this triumvirate, William Claiborne learned valuable lessons from his associations with Tucker and Mathews and exerted a significant impact on events in the Chesapeake

16. Governor Wyatt to Council of State, Nov. 18, 1623, *Va. Co. Records*, IV, 399; commission to Tucker, Dec. 31, 1623, *ibid.*, 446, 450–451; "Musters of the Inhabitants in Virginia, 1624/25," in Jester and Hiden, eds., *Adventurers of Purse and Person*, 49; James H. Merrell, "Cultural Continuity among the Piscataway Indians of Colonial Maryland," *WMQ*, 3d Ser., XXXVI (1979), 554; Pagan, "Trade and Politics," 41–58.

17. "Musters, 1624/25," in Jester and Hiden, eds., *Adventurers of Purse and Person*, 38–39; Morgan, "First American Boom," *WMQ*, 3d Ser., XXVIII (1971), 188, 189n; Pagan, "Trade and Politics," appendix B, 157–159.

18. "A Proposition concerning the winning of the fforest," CO 1/3, fol. 28, Public Record Office, Kew; Jester and Hiden, eds., *Adventurers of Purse and Person*, 244–247.

for half a century. Raised to appreciate Kent's unique mixture of rural gentry values and London business ties, Claiborne was a kinsman of Capt. Nathaniel Butler, governor of Bermuda, and Maurice Thomson, England's "greatest colonial merchant of his day." In 1621 Claiborne, just out of Pembroke College, Cambridge, secured the lucrative post of Virginia surveyor, and by 1624 he had created the Jamestown suburb of "New Towne" to be the center of the colony's elite. Named to the first royal Council in 1625 and appointed secretary of state the following year, Claiborne collected and invested substantial fees from his many official posts. Like Tucker and Mathews, Claiborne benefited from the Second Anglo-Powhatan War, attaining the notice of courtiers by his 1626 proposal to build a defensive palisade and earning the respect of his fellow colonists in 1629 by commanding a daring and successful attack on Opechancanough's Pamunkey capital near present-day West Point.[19]

Although the eighty-five hundred pounds of tobacco he exported in 1630 ranked him among Virginia's top ten planters, Claiborne was the first of the oligarchs to substantially shift his attention to beaver trading in the northern Chesapeake. Favored with the Council's monopoly on captured Indian guides in 1626 and granted commissions of discovery and trade by four successive governors between 1627 and 1632, Claiborne made several exploratory voyages throughout the Bay before 1630 and came to know the native lands and languages north of the Potomac better than any colonist since his fellow Kentishman, Samuel Argall. By 1630 Claiborne became the first Englishman since John Smith to establish contacts with the important Susquehannock nation, located near the headwaters of the Chesapeake. Unlike that earlier encounter in 1608, however, Claiborne represented colonists who were most willing and able to join those beaver-rich Indians in a mutually beneficial trading alliance.[20]

In 1630 the Susquehannocks were ideally suited by location and incli-

19. Jester and Hiden, eds., *Adventurers of Purse and Person*, 131–135; Nathaniel C. Hale, *Virginia Venturer: A Historical Biography of William Claiborne, 1600–1677* (Richmond, Va., 1951), 50–57, 140–142 and *passim*; Edward C. Papenfuse et al., eds., *A Biographical Dictionary of the Maryland Legislature, 1635–1789*, 2 vols. (Baltimore, 1979), I, 221–222; Brenner, "Commercial Change and Political Conflict," 85 and *passim*.

20. McIlwaine, ed., *Minutes of Council*, I, 111, 147, 185; *Md. Archives*, V, 158–163; Pagan, "Trade and Politics," appendix B, 157–159; Hale, *Virginia Venturer*, 115–126. Claiborne's brother, a London hosier, traded in Virginia in 1627. Partial Calendar to London Port Books, 1982, shelf number C54A, 5–6, PRO, Chancery Lane.

nation to enter into a comprehensive partnership with the Virginians. Linked by water routes and ancient cultural ties to the League Iroquois to the north, the eight thousand or so Susquehannocks were the superior fur traders and dominant warriors in the entire Chesapeake region. From their well-fortified capital some thirty-five miles from the mouth of the Susquehanna River, the Susquehannocks ranged widely, trading with the allied Tockwoghs on the Eastern Shore and the allied Hurons along Lake Superior, and frequently warring with diverse rivals—the Mohawks, Lenni Lenape, and most of the tidewater Algonquians in the Chesapeake. However, despite their military prowess and access to prime pelts throughout the Middle Atlantic, the Susquehannocks were desperately seeking large quantities of European trade goods when Claiborne initiated his friendly contacts. Frustrated that the French and the Dutch favored rival tribes with their trade, the Susquehannocks embraced Claiborne as an English war chief with common enemies and welcomed his plan to establish a close, permanent trading base far removed from the heavily trafficked and bitterly contested fur territories to the north.[21]

Claiborne's encouraging first contacts with the Susquehannocks coincided with an intense and growing interest by London merchants in the profits of the beaver trade. The development of new felting processes in the late 1620s spurred a frantic exploitation of North American pelts to supply quickly expanding European hat markets. The beaver trade was already a "major industry" among the Hudson River Dutch, the St. Lawrence French, and New England Puritans when small-scale peripatetic traders, like Henry Fleet and his three brothers, initiated the quest for Chesapeake furs among the Potomac River Algonquians in the late 1620s.[22]

21. Smith, *Generall Historie*, in Barbour, ed., *Complete Works of Smith*, II, 170–172; Francis Jennings, "Susquehannock," in William C. Sturtevant, ed., *Handbook of North American Indians*, XV, Bruce G. Trigger, ed., *Northeast* (Washington, D.C., 1978), 362–364; Trigger, "Early Iroquoian Contacts with Europeans," *ibid.*, 344–356; Francis Jennings, "The Indian Trade of the Susquehanna Valley," American Philosophical Society, *Proceedings*, CX (1966), 406–424; Barry C. Kent, *Susquehanna's Indians* (Harrisburg, Pa., 1984), 5–48 and *passim*.

22. David B. Quinn, ed., *New American World: A Documentary History of North America to 1612*, 5 vols. (New York, 1979), III, 342 and chaps. 61–62; Quinn, *North America from Earliest Discovery to First Settlements: The Norse Voyages to 1612* (New York, 1977), 533–536 and chap. 19 *passim*; K. G. Davies, *The North Atlantic World in the Seventeenth Century* (Minneapolis, Minn., 1974), 168–178; Neal Salisbury, *Manitou and Providence: Indians, Europeans, and the Making of New England, 1500–1643* (New

The increasingly crowded and competitive Potomac trade that brought inferior pelts and disappointing returns to the Fleets, despite their expert knowledge of native languages and financing from London merchants, convinced Claiborne that only a well-managed monopoly of the Susquehannocks' superior beaver would permit the fur trade to realize its full potential in the Chesapeake. With the fortuitous collapse of the tobacco boom in 1630, Claiborne's entrepreneurial ambitions came closer to fulfillment. As tobacco prices plummeted to a few pence per pound while the value of a prime pelt rose to £1 sterling, London merchants searching for investment alternatives became as willing as colonial traders and Indian trappers to form cooperative commercial alliances. Men like Claiborne, Tucker, and Mathews logically emerged as the essential middlemen in such ventures because their dominant position in colonial government and local trade reassured overseas investors, while their control over Indian policy and settlement patterns convinced the Susquehannocks that neither English farmers nor Anglican missionaries would threaten their lands and lifeways.[23]

Considering that the Susquehannocks and the Claiborne clique were the most feared fighters and successful traders of their respective Chesapeake worlds, it was only natural that their alliance received financial backing from similarly daring and ambitious members of the London merchant community. Claiborne's proposals for a Chesapeake beaver trade appealed to a particularly aggressive group of influential entrepreneurs who had almost succeeded in conquering, and monopolizing the furs of, French Canada. Sir William Alexander, Viscount Stirling and

---

York, 1982), 55–60, 76–84, 144–154; Capt. Henry Fleet, "A Breife Journall of A voyage made in the Barque Warwick to Virginia and other partes of the Continent of America Anno 1631," Feb. 22, 1632/33, MS 688/19, fols. 3–4, 7, 11, Lambeth Palace Library; Raphael Semmes, *Captains and Mariners of Early Maryland* (Baltimore, 1937), 84–95. For contemporaneous English beaver-trading enterprises to the north, see Bernard Bailyn, *The New England Merchants in the Seventeenth Century* (Cambridge, Mass., 1955), and Stephen Innes, *Labor in a New Land: Economy and Society in Seventeenth-Century Springfield* (Princeton, N.J., 1983). A rare price list for Chesapeake pelts and furs, c. 1621, is in E[dward] W[illiams], *Virginia: More Especially the South Part Thereof, Richly and Truly Valued . . .* (1650), in Peter Force, comp., *Tracts and Other Papers, Relating Principally to the Origin, Settlement, and Progress of the Colonies in North America*, 4 vols., III (Washington, D.C., 1844), no. 11, 51–52.

23. Russell R. Menard, "A Note on Chesapeake Tobacco Prices, 1618–1660," *VMHB*, LXXXIV (1976), 404–407; Brenner, "Commercial Change and Political Conflict," 61, 70, 75–76, 82–83, 96.

secretary of state for Scotland, and the Puritan merchant William Cloberry helped fund the controversial seizures by Sir David Kirke and his
family of Port Royal, Tadoussac, and Quebec between 1627 and 1629,
while Maurice Thomson interloped in the Canadian fur trade through a
separate business syndicate. However, these bold imperialists had barely
begun to profit from their foothold in North America's most bountiful
beaver region when Charles I agreed to restore Canada to the French in
exchange for the long-deferred payment of his wife's dowry. Embittered
by the selfish caprice of the king and facing burdensome civil suits and
the possibility of criminal prosecution, Alexander, Cloberry, and Thomson gladly supported Virginia's safer beaver monopoly administered by
familiar frontier oligarchs of proven abilities. On May 16, 1631, Alexander issued Claiborne a royal trading license under the privy seal of
Scotland in the hopes that the Virginia-Susquehannock trade alliance
would weaken the French in Canada while inspiring cooperation among
all the British colonies in the northeast, including his own Nova Scotia
proprietary. Cloberry, who had financed Henry Fleet's Potomac River
beaver trade in 1627, organized the joint-stock association of investors
that funded Claiborne's trade in order to add the more marketable furs of
the northern Chesapeake to his already extensive transatlantic mercantile
interests. Thomson, who had resided in Virginia between 1617 and 1626
and remained a major tobacco exporter and land speculator there, invested in Claiborne's enterprise to further solidify the strong familial and
business connections between Jamestown and London. More than most
homeland investors, Thomson maintained strong personal ties to the
Chesapeake through his kinsman, Claiborne, and his sister and three
younger brothers living with Tucker at Kecoughtan.[24]

24. W. Noel Sainsbury *et al.*, eds., *Calendar of State Papers, Colonial Series* (London,
1860–), *America and West Indies, 1574–1660*, 96, 103, 106, 112, 117, 129–131, 204,
219, 415; "A breife declaration what beaver skins Captaine David Kirke and his
Company broughte from Canada in the yeare 1629," CO 1/6, fols. 26–27; Sir
William Alexander and David Kirke, "petition to Lords Commissioners for his Majesties Navie and Admiralty of England," Feb. 26, 1630/31, *ibid.*, fol. 7; "A note of all
suche things as the Company hath in Canada and the nomber of men," n.d., *ibid.*, fol.
99; royal trading license to Claiborne, May 16, 1631, *ibid.*, fols. 116–117; Charles
Rogers, ed., *The Earle of Stirling's Register of Royal Letters, Relative to the Affairs of
Scotland and Nova Scotia from 1615 to 1635*, 2 vols. (Edinburgh, 1884), I, xv–xlvii, 265,
II, 702; Brenner, "Commercial Change and Political Conflict," 100–108; Trigger,
Children of Aataentsic, II, 455–462; Pagan, "Trade and Politics," 41–58; "Musters,
1624/25," in Jester and Hiden, eds., *Adventurers of Purse and Person*, 49.

In August 1631 the Claiborne-Virginia-Susquehannock-London Puritan interest-group alliance, the Chesapeake's first ambitious attempt to bridge cultures and link continents by means of a business venture, began its operations when Claiborne landed settlers and supplies on the trading base of Kent Island. Lying some one hundred and fifty miles north of Jamestown and roughly seventy-five miles south of the Susquehannocks' capital, Kent Island was ideally situated to attract "the trade of Beavers and ffurs which the ffrench now wholly enjoy in the Grand Lake of Canada." From this secure base, experienced traders recruited from Accomack County (where Claiborne was justice of the peace) set out in small vessels each spring to collect the Susquehannocks' winter beaver pelts. These nearly defenseless colonists depended entirely upon the goodwill of the Susquehannocks for their survival and success. Since the exchange of commodities was conducted in the language of the Susquehannocks, Claiborne initially hired Thomas Savage of Accomack County, Virginia's most experienced and reliable interpreter, to accompany his men, but by 1634, a black Kent Islander had mastered the Iroquoian dialect and resided with the Susquehannocks on a regular basis.[25]

The Susquehannock trade had a most promising beginning. Over the equivalent of three and a half complete trading seasons, Claiborne grossed some £4,000 sterling on seventy-five hundred pounds of beaver pelts, while his extensive support personnel on Kent Island contributed another £700 from the sale of farm products. However, Claiborne soon discovered the inherent problems in conducting a transatlantic business. Because of the erratic delivery of indentured servants and appropriate trade goods from his London partners, Claiborne was forced to pay high wages to skilled traders and free laborers and excessive prices for supplementary trade goods from other Virginians. Although Tucker's store in Kecoughtan supplied some of Claiborne's needs, the endemic scarcity of quality trade goods for discerning customers like the Susquehannocks all too quickly put the Kent Island enterprise into the red. While Claiborne apparently pleased the Susquehannocks with the commodities he sent them, he was rarely able to purchase more than half of their available pelts in any one season. Despite their growing fears that better-supplied enemies like the Mohawks could soon eclipse their power, the Susquehan-

25. *Md. Archives*, III, 65–66; Erich Isaac, "Kent Island, Part I: The Period of Settlement," *Maryland Historical Magazine*, LII (1957), 93–119; Hale, *Virginia Venturer*, chap. 8; J. Frederick Fausz, "Middlemen in Peace and War: Virginia's Earliest Indian Interpreters, 1608–1632," *VMHB*, XCV (1987), 61–62.

nocks displayed a long-term loyalty to Claiborne that was inexplicable in purely economic terms.[26]

Although Kent Island was destined to fail as a business venture, the financial losses were inconsequential compared to the symbolic and strategic importance of the enterprise. Many in Jamestown and London, "carryed with a great forwardnes to seeke trade abroad," regarded the Virginia-Susquehannock trade alliance as the ultimate example of private entrepreneurship serving the public's greater good. With its residents represented in the House of Burgesses and served by the first Anglican ministers north of the James River, Kent Island symbolized the ambitious expansion of Virginia's empire and confirmed the colonists' impressive prosperity and progress in Indian relations since the 1622 uprising. While neither Claiborne nor the Susquehannocks expected to remain exclusive trading partners if their commercial needs were not satisfied, events from the mid-1630s to the mid-1650s demonstrated, in fact, that their alliance depended more on mutual friendship and common interests than on profits alone. As the essential intermediary who could identify with both the beaver dams along the Susquehanna and the boardrooms along the Thames, Claiborne uniquely exploited the mysterious intangible of personal loyalty among men of two cultures that gave Kent Island its ultimate symbolic significance.[27]

Ironically, the vast promise of the Kent Island fur trade doomed it as a commercial experiment. The interest it initially generated as Virginia's first outpost of empire in the northern Chesapeake encouraged envious competitors who would ultimately ruin any prospects for profits. The

26. "An accompt of disbursements . . . at the Isle of Kent in Virginia" (Nov. 1639), *Md. Hist. Mag.*, XXVIII (1933), 26–43, 172–195; "Claiborne vs. Clobery et als. in the High Court of Admiralty," *ibid.*, XXVII (1932), 99–107, 208–210, 345; testimony of Kent Island traders, 1639–1640, *Md. Archives*, V, 189–226; J. Frederick Fausz, " 'To Draw Thither the Trade of Beavers': The Strategic Significance of the English Fur Trade in the Chesapeake, 1620–1660," in Bruce G. Trigger, Toby Morantz, and Louise Dechêne, eds., *Le Castor Fait Tout: Selected Papers of the Fifth North American Fur Trade Conference, 1985* (Montreal, 1987), table: "Balance Sheet on the Kent Island Enterprise, 1631–1637," 60; J. Frederick Fausz, "Present at the 'Creation': The Chesapeake World That Greeted the Maryland Colonists," *Md. Hist. Mag.*, LXXIX (1984), table 1.

27. "The humble Representation and Petition of your Majesties Commissioners for the Plantation of Virginia," May 24, 1631, CO 1/6, fols. 80–81; Virginia Council to Lords Commissioners, Dec. 22, 1631, Virginia MSS, Best-U269c5, Kent County Archives Office, Maidstone; Virginia Council to Privy Council, Mar. 6, 1631/32, *ibid.*, Best-U269c.

economic incentives that induced Virginians to develop more-enlightened principles of ethnic toleration in their dealings with the Susquehannocks attracted Marylanders to the Chesapeake and promoted bitter commercial conflicts among countrymen that exacerbated age-old religious prejudices and divisive new political ideologies. Thus, long after its failure as a business enterprise, Kent Island endured as a symbol of Anglo-Indian cooperation and a source of intercolonial struggles over issues of sovereignty and hegemony.

Claiborne planted the seeds of his own destruction by providing an appealing entrepreneurial model for Maryland colonists to follow. In the midst of Claiborne's most fertile explorations in the Bay, Sir George Calvert, first Baron Baltimore, unexpectedly arrived at Jamestown in November 1629 and unwittingly initiated decades of competition and conflict between Virginia and Maryland. Frustrated with the escalating warfare between the Canadian French and the Kirkes, Calvert abandoned his colony in Newfoundland and visited Virginia as a preliminary step to seeking a southern proprietary. The haste with which Councillors Claiborne and Mathews harried Calvert's "Romishe" company out of Virginia and with which Claiborne subsequently procured his royal license "to trade and traffique ... [where] there is not allready a patent graunted to others" suggests a concern over Calvert's knowledge of, and interest in, the potential of the northern Chesapeake. Claiborne's successful exploitation of his trading license after 1631 provided all the encouragement that the Calverts needed to seek a charter for Maryland and to procure the necessary investors. In drafting the strong proprietary charter that finally passed the seals on June 20, 1632, Lord Baltimore took advantage of the Susquehannocks' preference not to have English traders living in their midst and laid claim to all lands between Delaware Bay and the Potomac River "not yet cultivated and planted." In lining up investors for their new colony, the Calverts made effective use of exaggerated rumors that Chesapeake beaver pelts could generate profits of 3,000 percent and the belief that "furres alone will largely requite ... [the] adventure" in the first year of settlement. With the Jesuits most interested in a lucrative trade that would also give them access to potential Indian converts, Lord Baltimore's supporters formed a joint-stock association for furs long before the first colonist arrived in Maryland.[28]

28. George [Lord] Baltimore to Charles I, Aug. 19, 1629, *Md. Archives*, III, 15–16; Virginia Council to Privy Council, Nov. 30, 1629, *ibid.*, 16–17; king's commission to Claiborne, May 16, 1631, *ibid.*, 20; Sainsbury *et al.*, eds., *Cal. State Papers, 1574–*

Because the Chesapeake beaver trade had become such an entrepreneurial preoccupation after 1630, similarities in economic goals, more than differences in religion, explain the origins of the quarter-century of conflict between Virginia and Maryland. Given the beavers' dependence on abundant freshwater streams and sufficiently cold winters to produce the finest pelts, the Indian trappers' dependence on a scarce and easily depleted beaver population to purchase European commodities, the colonial traders' dependence on well-managed monopolies of territories and trappers to procure marketable furs, and the colonies' dependence on traders to provide capital and to promote stability in Indian relations, the Chesapeake's first fur frontier quickly developed into a fierce and bloody battle zone. With so many variables and so much at stake, the only winner in the beaver wars of the Bay would be the person who controlled the Susquehannock territories of the northern Chesapeake—the sole source of prime pelts in the coastal plain.[29]

The crisis that Charles I precipitated in 1632 when he turned over two-thirds of Chesapeake Bay to Cecil Calvert, second Baron Baltimore (1605–1675), and returned Canada to the French had all the territorial and religious ramifications of the Quebec Act in 1774. In curtailing the profitable expansionism of prominent Puritan entrepreneurs in England and crown colonists in Virginia, the king alienated key constituencies that would plague him and his favorites throughout the 1630s and 1640s. By crushing the peaking expectations of the Claiborne clique, Charles's granting of the Maryland charter provided a new scapegoat for Virginia's "sonnes of wrath" to unite against just as the war with the Powhatans was ending. Outraged that the "bloud and estate" they had sacrificed since

---

1660, 96; charter of Maryland, June 20, 1632, in Hall, ed., *Narratives of Early Maryland*, 101; Thomas Birch, comp., *The Court and Times of Charles the First*, 2 vols. (London, 1848), II, 52–55, 60, 229–230; John D. Krugler, ed., *To Live Like Princes: "A Short Treatise . . . by Robert Wintour"* (Baltimore, 1976), 36; [Andrew White?], *A Declaration of the Lord Baltimore's Plantation in Maryland . . .* (London, 1633), 4; Thomas M. Coakley, "George Calvert and Newfoundland: 'The Sad Face of Winter,'" *Md. Hist. Mag.*, LXXI (1976), 12–15; R. J. Lahey, "The Role of Religion in Lord Baltimore's Colonial Enterprise," *ibid.*, LXXII (1977), 506–511.

29. On the prime beaver habitats in eastern North America, see Trigger, *Children of Aataentsic*, I, 229, 350–353, II, 618–625; Fausz, "English Fur Trade," in Trigger, Morantz, and Dechêne, eds., *Le Castor Fait Tout*, 42–71 *passim*. The beaver trade, like coastal fisheries, was an "open-access resource" especially vulnerable to frantic overharvesting of animals because of frequent interloping. See Philip D. Curtin, *Cross-Cultural Trade in World History* (Cambridge, 1984), 209–229.

1622 in promoting Virginia's development were now illegally negated by royal favoritism, the "Cheiftaines" of Jamestown felt "bound in duty . . . to Maintaine the Rights and Privileges" of their colony against the "Imperial Power" of Lord Baltimore. Fearing an influx of "Aliens, Savages or Enemies of the Kingdome" into the Chesapeake, Claiborne and Mathews solicited the support of key allies in England in seeking "no less then the subjection of Maryland." Wyatt and former members of the defunct Virginia Company protested the abrogation of Virginia's ancient boundaries in the expectation of reviving their charter, while Cloberry, Thomson, and other Kent Island investors lobbied vigorously against Maryland competitors in the fur trade. Despite extensive opposition to the emigration of English Catholics to America and protests to prevent inexperienced colonists from disrupting the delicate state of Anglo-Indian relations in the Chesapeake, however, the settlement of Maryland went forward with key courtier support (see tables 1 and 2).[30]

With the inherent contradiction between Claiborne's royal trading license and Calvert's royal charter, the evenly divided support of influential privy councillors for Virginia's and Maryland's claims to Kent Island, and the inability of the English courts to resolve the issues expeditiously, colonial competitors in the Chesapeake depended upon strategic Indian alliances and coercive measures to outmaneuver their rivals in the fur trade. The intense competition for Indian support commenced when the first Calvert colonists arrived in the region in February 1634. The first Marylanders "expected to finde [the Salvages] as our English ill wishers would make them," and the Claiborne clique obliged with an appropriately hostile reception. Vowing to drive out the new arrivals even if he had

30. [William Claiborne], "Declaration shewing the illegality and unlawfull proceedings of the Patent of Maryland," CO 1/39, fols. 166–168 (also see *Md. Archives,* V, 175–181); Virginia Council of State, Mar. 14, 1634, *Md. Archives,* III, 32–33; "A Breviate of Captaine Claiborne's Petition to his Majestie. May 1631–April 1635," *ibid.,* 32; "Considerations upon the Patent to the Lord Baltimore," June 20, 1632, *ibid.,* 17–19; Gov. John Harvey to Secretary of State Sir Francis Windebank, July 14, 1635, *ibid.,* 39; petition of Claiborne, Sir John Wolstenholme, and others to Privy Council, Nov. 1633, *ibid.,* 24–25; Sir John Wolstenholme to Sir William Beacher, Aug. 16, 1633, CO 1/6, fol. 209. Claiborne's authorship of the "Declaration" against the Maryland charter is substantiated by internal evidence and by its inclusion, along with other original documents dealing with his claims to Kent Island, in the packet of materials he submitted for royal review in March 1677 (see n. 60, below). His arguments were expanded and published anonymously in 1655 as *Virginia and Maryland, or the Lord Baltamore's Printed Case Uncased and Answered . . .* (see n. 52, below).

to do it "with the Indians in a canoa," Claiborne was promptly arrested by the Virginia governor, Sir John Harvey, for "animating, practizing and conspiring wth the Indians to supplant" the Marylanders. While Harvey reported "almost all against me in whatever I propose . . . concern[ing] Maryland" and feared the "many Letters and secrett intelligences" from England in support of Claiborne, Kent Islanders sought to make good the threats of their imprisoned commander. In April 1634 a contingent of Claiborne's traders attempted to convince the Susquehannocks to attack a Maryland vessel that had sailed into the Susquehanna River. Although the Indians refused, explaining that those "English had never harmed them, neither would they fight soe neare home," this first Maryland trading expedition to the Susquehannocks did experience "a little falling out with them" and returned to St. Mary's City less optimistic about the prospects for a quick fortune in furs. Shortly thereafter, some Virginian(s) circulated a malicious rumor among the Potomac River Algonquians identifying the Marylanders as the dreaded "Waspaines" (Spaniards), who were hated throughout the region. Only a high-level parley in June 1634, attended by leading *werowances* and the governors of Virginia and Maryland, restored the Indians' confidence in, and contacts with, their new English neighbors at St. Mary's City.[31]

Threatened by such determined hostility, the Marylanders organized their own interethnic interest-group alliance to promote local Indian trade and to provide protection from Claiborne and the Susquehannocks. Composed of Calvert family members, joint-stock investors, colonial officials, Jesuit priests, and assorted Potomac River fur traders, this alliance of necessity depended most critically upon the interest, skills, and loyalty of the nearby Piscataways of southern Maryland. As overlords of a

31. Andrew White, S.J., "A Briefe Relation of the Voyage unto Maryland" (1634), in Hall, ed., *Narratives of Early Maryland*, 34; Capt. Thomas Yong to Sir Toby Matthew, 1634, *ibid.*, 53–61; Governor Harvey to Secretary Windebank, Dec. 16, 1634, *Md. Archives*, III, 30; Cyprian Thorowgood, "A relation of a voyage . . . to the head of the baye" (Apr. 1634), fol. 1, doc. 7, Young Collection, Enoch Pratt Free Library, Baltimore, Md.; parley proceedings at Patuxent, June 20, 1634, CO 1/39, fols. 120–121 (*Md. Archives*, V, 164–167). While Charles I vacillated in his support of the rival claimants (see correspondence, *Md. Archives*, III, 22, 27, 29), his two secretaries of state, Sir John Coke (Protestant, pro-Virginia) and Sir Francis Windebank (Catholic, pro-Maryland), and his colonial advisory boards, the Dorset Commission, May 1631–Dec. 1633, on which Wyatt served (pro-Virginia), and Archbishop Laud's Commission for Foreign Plantations, Apr. 1634–1641 (pro-Maryland), consistently acted along partisan lines (see *ibid.*, 25–44).

relatively weak, and recently battered, Algonquian confederacy of some five to seven thousand persons, the Piscataways readily agreed to a military and commercial alliance with the Marylanders that would pit them against, while protecting them from, their strong traditional enemies from the Susquehanna, Potomac, and James rivers. Having already suffered devastating raids by the two groups that the Calverts now feared, the Piscataways needed the goods and the goodwill of the Maryland colonists if they were to cope with the military threats, and better furs, of their beaver-rich rivals. To ensure that the hospitable Piscataways continued to remain "glad of our company," Gov. Leonard Calvert hired the veteran Virginia fur trader Henry Fleet to help the Maryland colonists "conforme ... to the Customes of [the] Countrey" and thus avoid the bloody blunders that disrupted Jamestown's early years. Buttressed by skilled frontiersmen like Fleet, who pursued the fur trade under Maryland's protection in defiance of hostile Virginia councillors, and the Jesuits, who would soon convert many of the local Algonquians to Catholicism, the Calvert alliance with the Piscataways produced the Chesapeake's first instance of long-term interethnic harmony among adjoining Anglo-Indian populations.[32]

However, the Calvert-Maryland-Piscataway-English Catholic interest-group alliance was handicapped from the outset by two factors— investor impatience at the failure to procure sufficient beaver profits to match their expectations, and the absence of a strong colonial middleman able to centralize and coordinate all aspects of the transatlantic association. Because Maryland's Indian interest group functioned as a defensive military alliance as well as a business partnership, weakness in one area promoted disaster in the other. When they were not directly threatened by their adversaries, Maryland colonists often offended the Piscataways by seeking better beaver pelts from other tribes; but when such trade incurred the wrath of outside competitors, the lack of intercultural unity jeopardized the collective security of all. In crisis situations, the Calvert alliance suffered by not having a skilled intermediary such as Claiborne who could win support in London by his knowledge of frontier conditions.

In their first year of settlement, Maryland's fur entrepreneurs watched

32. White, "Briefe Relation," in Hall, ed., *Narratives of Early Maryland*, 42; [John Lewger and Jerome Hawley], *A Relation of Maryland* (1635), *ibid.*, 90, 71–77; Semmes, *Captains and Mariners*, 87–88; Merrell, "Cultural Continuity," *WMQ*, 3d Ser., XXXVI (1979), 554–557; Fausz, "Present at the 'Creation,'" *Md. Hist. Mag.*,

impatiently as Kent Island's trade thrived while theirs foundered. The Piscataways were predominantly "deer Indians" who had allegedly learned to cure beaver pelts from Virginia traders only in the late 1620s, and environmental factors dictated that they could never match the quantity or quality of Susquehannock pelts. A Jesuit observed that the Piscataways were frustrated in trying to obtain necessary trade goods because "English merchants . . . exchange cloath for nought but beaver, which every one could not get." Although a small-scale Potomac River trade continued for decades, establishing beaver pelts and native shell beads (*peake* and *roanoke*) as important currency in the local economy, Maryland's major fur investors suffered consistent and significant financial losses from the beginning.[33]

When the returns from the beaver trade proved so disappointing, neither the Lord Proprietor in England nor his appointees in America were equipped to reconcile the disparate demands of the Maryland allies. Governor Calvert tried unsuccessfully to balance the opportunistic desires of headstrong colonial neighbors with the sometimes idealistic expectations of a distant proprietor who did not fully appreciate local conditions or his brother's loyalty. Councillor Thomas Cornwallis, Maryland's leading entrepreneur and top military commander, came closest to the model of the Virginia oligarchs, but his pursuit of self-interest often conflicted with Lord Baltimore's policies and the public's greater good. With an absentee proprietor almost constantly preoccupied with defending his charter at home and his trusted appointees focused on making their own fortunes, Maryland and the Calvert alliance suffered from leaders who were divided by duties, distance, and individual distractions.[34]

However, the various components of the Calvert interest group did at

---

LXXIX (1984), 7–20; Christian F. Feest, "Nanticoke and Neighboring Tribes," in Trigger, ed., *Handbook of North American Indians: Northeast*, 240–252.

33. Fleet, "Breife Journall," MS 688/19, fols. 7–10; White, "Briefe Relation," in Hall, ed., *Narratives of Early Maryland*, 44; Fausz, "Present at the 'Creation,'" *Md. Hist. Mag.*, LXXIX (1984), 18–20; Garry Wheeler Stone, "Society, Housing, and Architecture in Early Maryland: John Lewger's St. John's" (Ph.D. diss., University of Pennsylvania, 1982), 26–30.

34. Russell R. Menard, "Economy and Society in Early Colonial Maryland" (Ph.D. diss., University of Iowa, 1975), chap. 3, 135–141; Stone, "Society, Housing, and Architecture," 26–33, 43–46; Papenfuse *et al.*, eds., *Biographical Dictionary*, I, 190, 234–235.

least temporarily unite on one critical course of action—the destruction of Claiborne's Kent Island enterprise, which all viewed as a common threat. Virginia's strategic base in the Bay assumed greater importance as the Potomac fur trade languished and Lord Baltimore's control over his colonists grew tenuous. The Piscataways, who were jealous of Susquehannock pelts, as well as English investors who were desperate for them, supported aggressive efforts to eliminate all impediments to Maryland's sovereignty and success. Cecil Calvert's skill as a London lobbyist and the weight of his legal title to Kent Island began to erode the confidence and support of Claiborne's homeland investors soon after 1634, delaying supply ships and forcing Claiborne to cover the mounting deficits out of his own pocket. Lord Baltimore's friends in England, notably Secretary of State Sir Francis Windebank, also gained Governor Harvey's loyalty despite the strong objections of the Virginia councillors. Having alienated the powerful oligarchs of Jamestown in 1632 by supporting Fleet's fur trade and in 1634 by arresting Claiborne, Governor Harvey in spring 1635 boldly enforced Governor Calvert's prohibition against Virginians trading in Maryland waters. No sooner was this policy announced than Fleet, acting as an agent for Maryland, seized one of Claiborne's pinnaces along the Patuxent River and confiscated a cache of valuable Kent Island trade goods, which were allegedly "better liked" by local Indians than Lord Baltimore's merchandise.[35]

Claiborne's violent and reckless response to these provocations damaged him far more than his enemies. On April 23, and again on May 10, 1635, well-armed ships from Kent Island found and fought Maryland vessels under Cornwallis's command near the mouth of the Pocomoke River along the Eastern Shore. Only five days after several Virginians were killed or wounded in the first battle with their "cruell neighbors," the Claiborne-Mathews Council faction forcibly expelled Governor Harvey from office, charging him with "Treason, for . . . betray[ing] theyr Forte into the hands of theyr enemies of Marylande." Following this bloodless coup, the united councillors "with one Consent" approved a

35. "Instructions to the Colonists by Lord Baltimore," Nov. 1633, in Hall, ed., *Narratives of Early Maryland*, 19; Yong to Matthew, 1634, *ibid*., 56–57; "An accompt of disbursements," *Md. Hist. Mag.*, XXVIII (1933), 26–43, 172–195; testimony of captured Kent Island traders, Thomas Smith and Henry Ewbank (Apr. 1635), *The Calvert Papers* (Baltimore, 1889), I, 141–149; Harvey to Windebank, Dec. 16, 1634, *Md. Archives*, III, 30; Edward D. Neill, *The Founders of Maryland* . . . (Albany, N.Y., 1876), 15–16, 33–37.

return to the "olde forme of government" that the oligarchs had enjoyed under Wyatt in the 1620s. Shipping Harvey off to England with threats to shoot him if he dared return, Claiborne's supporters vowed to "wring [Maryland] out of the hands both of the Indians and Christians . . . [and to] become Lords of that Country."[36]

Although the "thrusting out" of Governor Harvey kept Kent Island under Claiborne's control for two more years, the councillors' rough treatment of a royal appointee and their dire threats against a noble patentee constituted the kind of frontier vigilantism that most alarmed officials in London. In responding to such rebelliousness, King Charles had little choice but to uphold law and the royal prerogative by sending Governor Harvey back to his post in Virginia. Upon his return in January 1637, Harvey arrested Mathews and other prominent conspirators, dispatching them to trial in England, and deprived Claiborne of his many offices and seat on the Council. Lord Baltimore, who lobbied the Privy Council to punish the "Prime actors in the late Mutenye," used the opportunity that these disruptive events provided to place supporters such as Jerome Hawley and Robert Evelyn, Jr., on the Virginia Council, and even petitioned friendly courtiers to appoint him as Harvey's successor. Now seeing Claiborne as a business liability, Cloberry in early 1637 replaced him as commander of Kent Island with another Maryland supporter, George Evelyn. Exploiting this momentum for the Maryland cause, Governor Calvert and Commander Cornwallis invaded Kent Island in February 1638 and confiscated property worth an estimated £10,000 sterling in an elaborate double cross of both Claiborne and Cloberry. In March, Maryland officials ordered the execution of notable Kent Island "rebels" and attainted Claiborne for the capital crimes of piracy, murder, "seditious acts against the dignity, government and domi-

36. Samuel Mathews to Sir John Wolstenholme, May 25, 1635, *Md. Archives*, III, 33–37; William Claiborne to Secretary Coke, May 23, 1635, *ibid.*, 30–32; Harvey to Windebank, July 1635, *ibid.*, 38–39; Gov. John West to Lords Commissioners for Plantations, Mar. 28, 1636, *ibid.*, 40–41; Sainsbury *et al.*, eds., *Cal. State Papers, 1574–1660*, 214, 221; J. Mills Thornton III, "The Thrusting Out of Governor Harvey: A Seventeenth-Century Rebellion," *VMHB*, LXXVI (1968), 11–26. Mathews was described as the "patron of disorder" and the "strength and sinewes" of "this faction . . . soe fast linked and united" to "notable combinations" of London allies. Much of his influence derived from his (second) marriage to the daughter of Sir Thomas Hinton, M.P. 1620–1626, whose son was a gentleman of the king's Privy Chamber and a potential successor to Harvey. Yong to Matthew, 1634, in Hall, ed., *Narratives of Early Maryland*, 58–60.

nation of the Lord Proprietarie," and "sondry mischievous machinations" with the Susquehannocks. Following these triumphs of Calvert militancy, Archbishop Laud's Commission for Foreign Plantations finally ruled on April 4, 1638, that Kent Island did indeed belong to Lord Baltimore by charter right.[37]

Despite this apparent shift in the balance of power, however, Claiborne was neither as weak in defeat nor the Calverts as strong in victory as it appeared. What the resilient, defiant Claiborne knew intimately and Lord Baltimore never learned was that transatlantic interest-group alliances depended first and foremost upon the unswerving loyalty of Indian partners. Even after Claiborne was rendered nearly powerless and penniless, the Susquehannocks still "exceedingly seemed to love" their old ally and refused to abandon him in hard times. In spring 1637, when Maryland's invasion of Kent Island seemed imminent, the Susquehannocks gave Claiborne Palmer's Island at the mouth of the Susquehanna River and sent warriors to clear the land for settlement. Several Kent Islanders had lived on Claiborne's private trading base for almost a year when the Maryland militia invaded and "utterly ruined and laid void" Palmer's Island, renaming it "Fort Conquest." Such aggression backfired, because the Susquehannocks, who "would sooner trade with Claiborne then with any other" and who objected to battles waged "soe neare [their] home," refused to supply pelts to the Marylanders, despite their earnest solicitations. Instead, when Claiborne began a five-year exile from the Chesapeake in summer 1637, the Susquehannocks elected to transport their furs many miles to Peter Minuit's Swedish trade station just established at Fort Christina (Wilmington, Delaware).[38]

---

37. "Lord Baltimore's Memorial," Dec. 22, 1635, *Md. Archives*, III, 40; order of the Privy Council, July 2, 1635, *ibid.*, 37–38; Lord Baltimore to Secretary Windebank, Feb. 25, 1636/37, *ibid.*, 41–42; Memorial of Lord Baltimore to Secretary Windebank, Mar. 1637, *ibid.*, 42–43; Act of Attainder, Mar. 24, 1637/38, *ibid.*, I, 23–24; George Evelyn's commission as commander of Kent Island, Dec. 30, 1637, *ibid.*, III, 59; Maryland Council, order for expedition to Kent Island, Feb. 12, 1637/38, *ibid.*, 64; "Claiborne vs. Clobery," *Md. Hist. Mag.*, XXVII (1932), 21–23, 193–198, 208–211; Hale, *Virginia Venturer*, 210–227; Richard L. Morton, *Colonial Virginia*, 2 vols. (Chapel Hill, N.C., 1960), I, 140–143.

38. Testimony of Claiborne traders, 1640, *Md. Archives*, V, 189, 213–214, 226, 231–232; order of Maryland Council, May 28, 1639, *ibid.*, III, 85; order of Governor Calvert, July 10, 1641, *ibid.*, 98–99; [Claiborne], "Declaration," *ibid.*, V, 177, 181; Governor Calvert to Lord Baltimore, Apr. 25, 1638, *Calvert Papers*, I, 183; Francis Jennings, *The Ambiguous Iroquois Empire: The Covenant Chain Confederation of Indian*

Ironically, the Maryland Assembly in 1639 declared the Indian trade "the main and cheif encouragement" of the Lord Proprietor and his colonists just when the hostile Susquehannock reaction to Claiborne's downfall caused beaver pelts to be most elusive and divisive for the residents of St. Mary's City. The brief unity of the Calvert allies in defeating Claiborne quickly disintegrated over the distribution of the limited spoils of victory. Seemingly secure in the northern Chesapeake after 1638, Lord Baltimore betrayed his staunchest supporters by announcing new policies that implied his total control of the Bay beaver trade and violated provisions of the original joint-stock association for furs. In vocal opposition to this evident disloyalty, some of Cecil Calvert's oldest allies declared that there was "noe commoditye [so profitable as furs] to be gott by planting" and bitterly complained that "if your lordship canne but have the trade of Beaver and Corne to your self, the plantation is not much to be regarded." Convinced that Lord Baltimore's desire to be "mainteyned in splendor" as "princes are" had precipitated his "oprestion" of them, major fur investors predicted a "fateall difference aboute the [Indian] Trade" that would cause them "toe desert the Place."[39]

While Fleet and other traders did abandon Maryland in favor of the unregulated frontier of Virginia's Northern Neck, Lord Baltimore was forced to grant concessions to the more important of his angry colonists. The Lord Proprietor agreed to let Governor Calvert and Captain Cornwallis monopolize the largest share of the fur trade, and he attempted to appease his Jesuit critics in 1639 by allowing them to establish their first missions among the local Algonquians. This latter concession was most

Tribes with English Colonies from Its Beginnings to the Lancaster Treaty of 1744 (New York, 1984), 116–119; C. A. Weslager and A. R. Dunlap, *Dutch Explorers, Traders, and Settlers in the Delaware Valley, 1609–1664* (Philadelphia, 1961), chap. 6.

39. "An Act for Trade with the Indians," 1639, *Md. Archives*, I, 42–43; Andrew White to Lord Baltimore, Feb. 20, 1638/39, *Calvert Papers*, I, 204; Thomas Copley (Philip Fisher, S.J.) to Lord Baltimore, Apr. 3, 1638, *ibid.*, 160–161; Thomas Cornwallis to Lord Baltimore, Apr. 16, 1638, *ibid.*, 175–179. Cornwallis, the "most uncontionable Extortioner," contemplated "fetching the Truck and carrying what beaver I could get from and toe Virginia without bayting at St. Maryes" (*ibid.*, 178). Evidently Lord Baltimore's placeman on the Virginia Council, Treasurer Jerome Hawley, had the same idea. Shortly before his death in 1638, Hawley in effect renounced his allegiance to the Calverts by seeking "his owne . . . trade with the Sasquehannoughs which he might conceive better hopes to advance by its depenice on Virginia then Maryland." *Ibid.*, 188.

significant, for as more and more Marylanders abandoned the fur trade in favor of cultivating tobacco, Jesuit missionaries had a disproportional amount of access to, and influence among, the neighboring Piscataways. By 1642, the priests had established several strategic mission outposts in the region, converted important *werowances* to Catholicism, claimed thousands of acres of land as direct gifts from friendly Indians, and continued to sponsor fur trading expeditions. With their newfound influence, the Jesuits persistently challenged proprietary authority in matters of religious policy, Indian relations, and land allocation. Thoroughly alienated from this once-strong source of spiritual and financial support, Lord Baltimore, like previous London critics of Virginia, blamed such rebelliousness on the detrimental influences of the Chesapeake frontier. By 1642 he was convinced that the Jesuits "designe my destruction" and predicted a conspiracy "among the English to bring their ends about [or] they will endeavour to doe it by the Indians within a verie short time by arming them etc."[40]

Ironically, an Indian war did engulf Maryland in 1642 that ultimately threatened the position and power of the Jesuits as well as the Lord Proprietor. For a decade after 1642, a variety of enemies old and new attacked the Calvert alliance, increasing dissension among, and desertions of, its leading members. Across the Atlantic, the onset of the Irish rebellion in 1641 threatened Lord Baltimore's lands and revenues, while the English Civil War further curtailed his royal patronage and courtier support. In the Chesapeake, the cumulative hostility of Susquehannocks, Virginians, and parliamentary enemies threatened Maryland's sovereignty and survivability well into the 1650s.

The single link to these seemingly unrelated occurrences that again altered the balance of power in the Chesapeake was the Calverts' old nemesis, Claiborne. After a five-year absence, Claiborne returned to Virginia in 1643 a more determined and powerful antagonist than ever, fully prepared to take advantage of transatlantic events in exacting his revenge on Lord Baltimore. During his exile, Claiborne had joined the Providence Island Company and become a trusted partner of leading

40. Lord Baltimore to Governor Calvert, Nov. 23, 1642, *Calvert Papers*, I, 217; John Lewger to Lord Baltimore, Jan. 5, 1638/39, *ibid.*, 197–198; extracts from Jesuit letters for 1639–1642, in Hall, ed., *Narratives of Early Maryland*, 124–140; *Md. Archives*, III, 63, 104, 140, 145, 258–259, IV, 34–36, 42, 138; Stone, "Society, Housing, and Architecture," 27–30; James Axtell, "White Legend: The Jesuit Missions in Maryland," *Md. Hist. Mag.*, LXXXI (1986), 1–7.

Puritan entrepreneurs, such as Maurice Thomson and the earl of Warwick, and of parliamentary radicals, such as John Pym and John Hampden. When these men gained power and prominence in the war with the Stuarts, Claiborne seized the opportunity to link his personal goals in Chesapeake affairs to the larger Anglo-American struggle over political and religious ideology. Exploiting an expanded circle of interethnic allies and associates, Claiborne became the friend of every Maryland enemy, making their cause, his cause, and their triumphs, his triumphs. Although Claiborne did not coordinate every move of a united conspiracy, he was linked with, and benefited from, all the crises that befell the Calverts between 1642 and 1658.[41]

Maryland's decade of invasions began in summer 1642 when the Susquehannocks attacked Piscataway villages along the Potomac, twice sacked Jesuit storehouses along the Patuxent, and killed several settlers only eight miles from St. Mary's City. Intermittently raiding their old enemies for ten years, the Susquehannocks in 1648 dealt a damaging blow to the Calvert-Piscataway alliance when they captured the "King of Pawtomeck . . . and expelled his and eight other Indian Nations in Maryland, civilized and subject to the English Crown." In the decade following the fall of Kent Island, the Susquehannocks experienced volatile changes in their life-style, as their booming trade with the Swedes made them more affluent—and more dependent—than ever before. Even though they were now armed with "great quantities of Gunns, Powder and shot," the Susquehannocks faced a future of uncertainty, with Iroquois aggressions increasing and available supplies of beaver dwindling. The impressive new capital that the Susquehannocks built near present-day Colum-

---

41. Hale, *Virginia Venturer*, 227–237, chap. 12 *passim*; Arthur Percival Newton, *The Colonising Activities of the English Puritans: The Last Phase of the Elizabethan Struggle with Spain* (New Haven, Conn., 1914), 59, 251, 267, 270, 315. In his pathbreaking study of Puritan interest groups, Newton contended that the "leaders of the parliamentary opposition acquired their power of working harmoniously together in the joint schemes of colonisation" (*ibid.*, 2). The first settlers landed on Providence Island (Santa Catalina, off the Nicaraguan coast) in May 1631. The company granted Claiborne "Rich Island" (Roatán, off the Honduran coast) in June 1638, and his colonists remained there until Spanish raiders expelled them in 1642 (*ibid.*, 267). Contemporaneous with the Kent Island enterprise, the Providence Island Company was similarly an important "link between the anti-papist zeal of the 1580s and the aggressive Protestant imperialism of the 1650s." Angus Calder, *Revolutionary Empire: The Rise of the English-Speaking Empires from the Fifteenth Century to the 1780s* (New York, 1981), 198 and chap. 4 *passim*.

bia, Pennsylvania, in the mid-1640s seemed to symbolize power and permanence, with a massive palisade enclosing thirteen acres and housing about three thousand people. In fact, recent "purple rash" epidemics of scarlet fever or typhus or both had decimated their ranks, and they had largely abandoned the self-sufficient manufacture of fur clothing, pottery utensils, and traditional weapons. Increasingly dependent upon supplies of European products to maintain their status, comfort, and security, the Susquehannocks, with or without the urging of Claiborne or their Swedish suppliers, may have attacked Maryland to obtain the valuable trade goods that still circulated in the Potomac.[42]

Maryland's rather pathetic response to the Susquehannock raids revealed the fatal flaws in the Calvert alliance that other enemies would soon exploit. In September 1642 officials assembled a large expeditionary force at a "fruitless expence" of more than fifty-six hundred pounds of tobacco—fruitless because the refusal of the Kent Islanders to campaign against their former trading partners prevented any hostile action, "to the great disgrace & disrepute of our nation among the Indians our neighbors and dependants." Refused assistance by the Virginia Council, vacillating and factionalized Maryland councillors finally dispatched at least one retaliatory expedition against the Susquehannocks in summer 1643. An English source reported the success of Cornwallis's fifty-three militiamen in killing twenty-nine Indians out of a war party of two hundred and fifty while losing only four men, but Swedish accounts claimed that the Susquehannocks devastated a second Maryland force, capturing two cannon and torturing to death some fifteen colonists. In contrast to Virginia's brutally efficient response to Opechancanough's second uprising in 1644–1646, Maryland's confused and contradictory Indian policies dangerously exposed the colony to new aggressions. The fatal impotence of the Calvert-Piscataway alliance was demonstrated in June 1644, when

42. Jesuit letter of 1642, in Hall, ed., *Narratives of Early Maryland*, 136, 138; *Md. Archives*, I, 196–198, III, 106, 116–117, 119–121, 126, 130, 137–138, 146–151; [Sir Edmund Plowden], *A Description of the Province of New Albion* (1648), in Force, comp., *Tracts*, II, no. 7, 19, 24; Kent, *Susquehanna's Indians*, 22, 36–39, 171–172, 243, 292, 350–360, 364, 367, 371, 408; Arthur A. Futer, "The Strickler Site," in John Witthoft and W. Fred Kinsey III, eds., *Susquehannock Miscellany* (Harrisburg, Pa., 1959), 136–147. On the epidemics that ravaged the Susquehannocks in the late 1630s, see Henry F. Dobyns, *Their Number Become Thinned: Native American Population Dynamics in Eastern North America* (Knoxville, Tenn., 1983), 15, 22, 325n–327n, and Helen Hornbeck Tanner, ed., *Atlas of Great Lakes Indian History* (Norman, Okla., 1987), 169, map 32, "Epidemics among Indians c. 1630–1880," 170–171.

Councillor John Lewger solicited the services of the alienated Fleet to parley with the Susquehannocks and granted him complete discretion to "truce wth them" or "kill them." Before Councillor Giles Brent rescinded the order and suspended Lewger, Fleet was instructed to procure "as much as you can gett of the armes & other goods lost or left in our last march upon them [the Susquehannocks], at least the two feild peices" and to "terrifie our [Piscataway] confederates . . . from leaguing or treating with the common enemy . . . against our liking or consent."[43]

While the Susquehannock crisis revealed a critical disunity that made "common enemies" hard to identify for some Calvert supporters, a coalition of English adversaries old and new all too quickly pounced upon the wounded Maryland prey. Councillor Claiborne, restored to his powerful offices following the second governorship of Sir Francis Wyatt (1639–1641) and appointed Virginia's first major general of militia with the onset of the Third Anglo-Powhatan War, again emerged as the most dangerous enemy of the Calverts. In autumn 1644 he risked capture and execution to foment discontent on Kent Island, and in 1646 he returned, expecting to launch a rebellion with Virginia militiamen he diverted from the Pamunkey campaign. Although Governor Calvert moved swiftly to defend Kent Island against that "pretender to the said Lands," while Gov. Sir William Berkeley of Virginia sternly prohibited "intermiddl[ing]" in Maryland affairs, Claiborne could afford to wait for others to do his dirty work in an enlarged offensive against Lord Baltimore. Between Claiborne's daring forays to the northern Chesapeake, Capt. Richard Ingle in February 1645 invaded Maryland with armed adventurers from Virginia and letters of marque from Parliament, seeking to destroy the Calverts' alleged "tyrannical power against the Protestants." This captain of the ship *Reformation* from Gravesend, Kent, was a Chesapeake factor for Maurice Thomson, and the "plundering time" he initiated against the colonists of southern Maryland represented both his personal revenge for earlier mistreatment by Calvert councillors and the intention of London Puritan merchants to ruin the Stuart-tainted Lord Baltimore. Condemned as an enemy of the parliamentary cause because he had agreed to collect customs revenues for Charles I in 1644, the Lord Proprietor was in dire political and financial straits even before Ingle's invasion and

43. *Md. Archives*, III, 116–121, 148–151, IV, 128–129, 136, 248; [Plowden], *Description of New Albion*, in Force, comp., *Tracts*, II, no. 7, 19, 24; reports of Johan Printz (1644), John Rising (1655), and Peter Lindeström (1654–1656), cited in Jennings, *Ambiguous Iroquois Empire*, 120n; Robert Beverley, *The History and Present State of Virginia* (1705), ed. Louis B. Wright (Chapel Hill, N.C., 1947), 59–63.

occupation of his troubled colony. Cecil Calvert was nearly bankrupt from personally funding the Maryland enterprise in the absence of a successful fur trade, and the bitter wars in Ireland and England after 1641 threatened his lands and tested his loyalties as a Catholic peer. Many of Calvert's most influential supporters on both sides of the Atlantic had either died or left office by the time of Ingle's attack, and the Kirke family's recent appropriation of Calvert's Newfoundland colony portended the fate of Maryland in the hands of aggressive Protestant adventurers.[44]

By 1646 the beleaguered Maryland colony contained fewer English residents than it had at its founding a dozen years before, and Lord Baltimore's constricted circle of Catholic support forced him to rely upon Protestant Virginia associates of Claiborne in a desperate effort to strengthen his province and save his charter in the face of powerful London critics. In 1646 Governor Calvert returned from exile at Jamestown to oust Ingle's brigands with the unexpected assistance of Virginia Puritan mercenaries from south of the James River. Their leader was Col.

44. "Report from the Committee of Forraigne Plantations concerning Maryland, Nov. 28, 1645," *Md. Archives*, III, 164; Richard Ingle's petition to Parliament, Feb. 24, 1645/46, *ibid.*, 165; "Petition of the London merchants trading to the Plantations, Feb. 8, 1646/47," *ibid.*, 181 (also see *ibid.*, 161, 162, 170, 176, IV, 435–436, 455, 458–459); "Acts, Orders and Resolutions of the General Assembly of Virginia at Sessions of March 1643–1646," *VMHB*, XXIII (1915), 229–230; McIlwaine, ed., *Minutes of Council*, 503; Hale, *Virginia Venturer*, 248–251; Kukla, "Order and Chaos," *AHR*, XC (1985), 289–291; Russell R. Menard, "Maryland's 'Time of Troubles': Sources of Political Disorder in Early St. Mary's," *Md. Hist. Mag.*, LXXVI (1981), 128–130, 136–140; Lahey, "Role of Religion," *ibid.*, LXXII (1977), 506, 511; Calder, *Revolutionary Empire*, chap. 4 *passim*. Lord Baltimore's 1644 "Oxford Agreement" to collect customs revenues in the Chesapeake for Charles I (Hall, ed., *Narratives of Early Maryland*, 228–230) directly challenged Maurice Thomson and associates, who were in charge of the customs farm. Before the House of Commons could rule on their August 1644 petition, they dispatched Ingle to take revenge on Maryland as "their agent," with the obvious approval of the earl of Warwick, governor-in-chief of all American plantations since 1643, and Claiborne, who made much of Calvert's complicity with the king in his 1655 pamphlet (see n. 30, above). Pagan, "Trade and Politics," 110–115.

The financial and public relations nightmares facing Lord Baltimore were reflected in Plowden's 1648 report that "Maryland . . . was in war both with the Sasquehannocks, and all the Eastern Bay Indians, and a Civill war between some revolters, protestants, assisted by 50 plundered Virginians, by whom M. Leonard Calvert . . . was taken prisoner and expelled: and the Isle of Kent taken from him also by Captain Clayborn." *Description of New Albion*, in Force, comp., *Tracts*, II, no. 7, 6.

Richard Bennett, Claiborne's fellow councillor from an influential London merchant family with close ties to Maurice Thomson. Persecuted by
the Anglican orthodoxy of Governor Berkeley, Bennett's Nansemond and
Norfolk Puritans constituted the largest, most cohesive military force
available for hire in the Chesapeake. Even after Governor Calvert's death
in June 1647, these mercenaries remained in St. Mary's County still
awaiting payment from a government in disarray. To remedy the lack of
leadership, Lord Baltimore in August 1648 appointed the merchant-
planter William Stone of Northampton County, Virginia, to be Maryland's
new, and first Protestant, governor. Like Bennett, Stone came from a
prominent London merchant family connected with Thomson, began his
colonial career in 1628 during the era of the Wyatt warlords, and had ties
to religious nonconformity. Like Bennett, too, Stone was a close Claiborne associate, having served with him as justice of the peace on the
Accomack County Court. With the assistance of Bennett's southside
Puritan community, Stone made good on his promise to Lord Baltimore
to "procure five hundred People of British or Irish discent to . . . reside
within . . . Maryland," settling hundreds of Virginia émigrés along the
Severn and Patuxent rivers between 1648 and 1650.[45]

By appointing Protestant relatives of prominent London critics to offices in Maryland and encouraging Puritan immigration to make the
province seem less exclusively a haven for "Papists and Enemyes" of
Parliament, Cecil Calvert saved his province from imminent destruction
in the late 1640s, but those risky strategies provided only a temporary
reprieve. Either out of total ignorance or supreme courage, Lord Baltimore admitted dangerous political enemies into Maryland's inner circle
and, in effect, placed a dagger in Claiborne's hands aimed directly at the
heart of his province. Both before and after 1646, Colonel Bennett was
considered one of the Chesapeake's most intense Puritan ideologues and
parliamentary supporters, while Governor Stone had served as Ingle's
attorney and business agent on an Eastern Shore teeming with independent Virginia beaver traders. The political collaboration between Bennett

---

45. *Md. Archives*, I, 209, 217, 226–227, 238–239, 269, 270, III, 201–209, IV, 321,
344, 358, 369, 410, 432; Susie M. Ames, ed., *County Court Records of Accomack-
Northampton, Virginia, 1632–1640* (Washington, D.C., 1954), xxx–xxxi, xlvi; Ames,
ed., *County Court Records of Accomack-Northampton, Virginia, 1640–1645* (Charlottesville, Va., 1973), xii–xiii; Papenfuse *et al.*, eds., *Biographical Dictionary*, I, 129 (Bennett), II, 788–789 (Stone); Russell R. Menard, "Population, Economy, and Society in
Seventeenth-Century Maryland," *Md. Hist. Mag.*, LXXIX (1984), 71, 81.

and Claiborne and the polite compliance of Stone that subsequently displaced proprietary authority in Maryland revealed the strength of fundamental loyalties and personal friendships. Neither Lord Baltimore's conscientious policy of religious toleration nor liberal extensions of political rights could ever quite divert his most dedicated Virginia enemies from their original objective. As a pro-Calvert supporter keenly observed of the contest for Maryland by Claiborne and his allies, "It was not religion, it was not punctilios they stood upon, it was that sweete, that rich, that large Country they aimed at."[46]

By 1650 Claiborne's ever-enlarging interest-group connections dominated strategic positions of power on both sides of the Atlantic, giving him all the leverage he needed to take revenge on Lord Baltimore and to redirect the course of Chesapeake history. The several hundred Virginia Puritan émigrés living at Providence (Anne Arundel County) and along the Patuxent River constituted about half of Maryland's population and exerted enough political influence in the assembly to modify the religious toleration statute of 1649 and to elect one of their delegates as speaker of the house in 1650–1651. At Chicacoan, a short sail from St. Mary's City on the Potomac's southern shore, independent fur traders like Fleet, disgruntled former Marylanders like Giles and Margaret Brent, and land speculators like Mathews and Claiborne himself had transformed Virginia's fast-growing Northern Neck into a haven for anti-Calvert refugees. And far to the north, Kent Islanders were more rebellious than usual in anticipation of Maryland's ultimate downfall. In England, Claiborne's connections had defeated and executed Charles I and now occupied key positions in the Puritan Commonwealth. Maurice Thomson played an important role in passing the first navigation acts in 1650–1651, which legitimized monopolistic centralization to exclude foreign competition that the beaver traders had long advocated. A younger brother, Col. George Thomson, who had lived at Tucker's Kecoughtan home and served with Claiborne in the Powhatan war of the 1620s and

46. Richard Ingle to Capt. William Stone, Apr. 4, 1644, in Ames, ed., *County Records of Accomack-Northampton, 1640–1645*, 388–389; receipt of Richard Ingle for tobacco sold by Stone, *ibid.*, 437; depositions against Stone, Maryland Provincial Court, Nov. 1650, *Md. Archives*, X, 156–157; Morton, *Colonial Virginia*, I, 151–153, 174, 218, 225; John Hammond, *Leah and Rachel, or, the Two Fruitfull Sisters Virginia and Mary-land . . .* (1656), in Hall, ed., *Narratives of Early Maryland*, 304. Also see Lord Baltimore's own summary and interpretation of events in this period, dated Aug. 26, 1649, *Md. Archives*, I, 262–272.

with Cromwell in the Civil War, chaired the Commonwealth's Committee on Admiralty Affairs. In September 1651, he obtained authorization from the Council of State for Claiborne, Bennett, and Thomas Stegge (another Thomson factor) to "reduce all the plantations within the Bay of Chespiak to their due obedience" to the new political order.[47]

Buoyed by the victories and innovations of the new Puritan republic, Claiborne's impressive interest-group alliance prepared for a climactic offensive of colonial consolidation in the Chesapeake. Sharing the persistent dream of English expansionists from the Reverend Richard Hakluyt to Oliver Cromwell, the Claiborne clique ultimately envisioned an integrated Protestant empire in America, centralized by policies and diversified by products, strong enough to eliminate all rivals, both foreign and domestic. United against the restrictive, shortsighted policies of Charles I, the traditional preferments of ancient trading companies and peer proprietors, and Catholic colonies everywhere, this transatlantic entrepreneurial network viewed the conquest of Maryland as the symbolic elimination of all evil. Testing the effectiveness of centralized imperial administration from London and the loyalty of local agents along the Chesapeake frontier, Claiborne's final campaign against the Calverts represented the first phase of England's new policy of colonial consolidation.[48]

47. [Claiborne], *Virginia and Maryland*, in Hall, ed., *Narratives of Early Maryland*, 206–211, 218–221; John Langford, *Refutation of Babylons Fall* (1655), *ibid.*, 256; Northern Neck land patents (1640s–1650s), in Nell Marion Nugent, comp., *Cavaliers and Pioneers: Abstracts of Virginia Land Patents and Grants*, I, *1623–1666* (Richmond, Va., 1934), 151–226 *passim*; Papenfuse *et al.*, eds., *Biographical Dictionary*, I, 161–162 (the Brents); Hale, *Virginia Venturer*, 240, 263–266, 292–294; Sainsbury *et al.*, eds., *Cal. State Papers, 1574–1660*, 343, 360–361; "Instructions . . . for the Reduceing of Virginia" (Sept. 26, 1651), *Md. Archives*, III, 265–266; *Dictionary of National Biography*, s.v. "Thomson, George"; McIlwaine, ed., *Minutes of Council*, 193; Menard, "Maryland's 'Time of Troubles,'" *Md. Hist. Mag.*, LXXVI (1981), 128–130; Charles M. Andrews, *The Colonial Period of American History*, 4 vols. (New Haven, Conn., 1934–1938), IV, 43n; Jon Kukla, *Speakers and Clerks of the Virginia House of Burgesses, 1643–1776* (Richmond, Va., 1981), 35–37; Kukla, "Order and Chaos," *AHR*, XC (1985), 292–293.

48. [Claiborne], *Virginia and Maryland*, in Hall, ed., *Narratives of Early Maryland*, 187–230; Calder, *Revolutionary Empire*, 198, 211–215, 223–239; Andrews, *Colonial Period*, IV, 33–46, 50–57; Robert Brenner, "The Civil War Politics of London's Merchant Community," *Past and Present*, LVIII (1973), 77 and *passim*; Joyce Oldham Appleby, *Economic Thought and Ideology in Seventeenth-Century England* (Princeton, N.J., 1978), 73, 81, 99, 103, and chap. 5; J. E. Farnell, "The Navigation Act of 1651,

On March 12, 1652, parliamentary commissioners Claiborne and Bennett, at the head of a Commonwealth fleet, accepted the bloodless capitulation of Governor Berkeley's government, after promising to abrogate the Maryland charter and allow Virginians to "enjoy the antient bounds and lymitts granted by . . . former Kings." Two weeks later, they similarly "reduced" the government of the "Catholic tyrants" at St. Mary's City, encountering no armed resistance. At Jamestown, Bennett, the new governor, and Claiborne, the secretary of state, appointed the first Virginia Council of the century that was composed exclusively of military oligarchs and officers, while in Maryland, the commissioners appointed only loyal Virginia Protestants to high provincial office (see table 3).[49]

This unified administration of the Chesapeake brought immediate, albeit temporary, stability to the region. On July 5, 1652, Virginia Puritan émigrés, Claiborne's newest English allies, concluded the first comprehensive treaty with the Susquehannocks, Claiborne's oldest Indian friends. Amid "tokens of freindship mutually given, received and accepted on both sides," these intercultural negotiators with a common patron accomplished in only a few days what had eluded the Calverts since 1634. In this treaty, Sawahegeh, "the Treasurer," ceded vast territories along both shores of the northern Chesapeake to "the English Nation"—not Maryland—"Exepting the Ile of Kent and Palmers Ilands which belong to Captaine Clayborne." In return, the colonists acknowledged an end to the ten-year Indian war, recognized the "Nation and State of Sasquehanogh," made plans to revive the beaver trade, and guaranteed the Susquehannocks a safe southern border as they prepared to renew hostilities with their traditional Iroquois enemies to the north.[50]

Despite this impressive beginning, the spring and summer of 1652 brought only a brief, final moment of victory and vindication for the

----

the First Dutch War, and the London Merchant Community," *Economic History Review*, 2d Ser., XVI (1964), 440–446, 454; Sosin, *English America*, chap. 1.

49. Articles of surrender (Virginia), Mar. 12, 1652, McIlwaine, ed., *Journals of Burgesses, 1619–1658/59*, 79–81; "reduction of Maryland," Mar. 29, 1652, *Md. Archives*, III, 271–272; John R. Pagan, "Dutch Maritime and Commercial Activity in Mid-Seventeenth-Century Virginia," *VMHB*, XC (1982), 495; Hale, *Virginia Venturer*, 273–285.

50. Provincial Court proceedings, June 28, 1652, *Md. Archives*, III, 275–277; "Articles of Peace and freindshipp . . . agreed upon the 5th day of July 1652," *ibid.*, 277–278; Jennings, *Ambiguous Iroquois Empire*, 121–122.

Claiborne-Virginia-Susquehannock-London Puritan alliance. Although Claiborne seemed in a better position to influence the future of the Chesapeake than any one man ever had been or ever would be again, the appearance of ultimate triumph soon proved deceptive. The Susquehannocks and English commonwealthmen on both sides of the Atlantic attained the peak of their influence in 1652; but beginning in that year, each group embarked upon two decades of destructive warfare with cultural cousins and commercial competitors—the English with the Dutch and the Susquehannocks with the Senecas—that precluded the expansion of their power. Ironically, these trade wars in the mid-Atlantic colonies destroyed coastal beaver pelts as a source of profit—and thus conflict—long before the bloodshed ceased in the 1670s. The demise of that trade, coupled with the Puritans' abortive administration in England, removed prime incentives for the Claiborne interest-group alliance to enlarge its authority.[51]

Throughout the Chesapeake, the power of the old oligarchs waned when they realized the depth of local opposition to their monopolistic and militaristic designs. In Maryland, the Puritans' rigorous denial of religious freedom and political rights to Anglicans and Catholics finally prompted former Governor Stone into action, resulting in the bloody Battle of the Severn on Sunday, March 25, 1655. This shocking sabbath-day clash between pro-Calvert forces of the Virginia Protestant governor and anti-Calvert forces of the Virginia Protestant commissioners was a confrontation between colonial countrymen unprecedented in magnitude or malignity. Such destructive zealotry perhaps encouraged Claiborne to publish the pamphlet *Virginia and Maryland, or the Lord Baltamore's Printed Case Uncased and Answered* (London, 1655), justifying his aggressions against the Calverts, and may have ultimately encouraged Cromwell's government to restore the province to the more moderate and tolerant control of the Calverts. With the oversight of London officials, Lord

---

51. Kent, *Susquehanna's Indians*, 39–47; Jennings, *Ambiguous Iroquois Empire*, chaps. 6–7; Pagan, "Dutch Maritime and Commercial Activity," *VMHB*, XC (1982), 495–501; Trigger, *Children of Aataentsic*, II, 792–796. Significantly, the demise of the tidewater beaver trade was symbolized in 1652 when Claiborne, Fleet, Abraham Wood (Mathews's former servant), and Francis Yeardley (son of Sir George) became pioneers in the predominantly piedmont deer trade to the west and south of the James River. McIlwaine, ed., *Journals of Burgesses, 1619–1658/59*, 85; Alexander S. Salley, Jr., ed., *Narratives of Early Carolina, 1650–1708* (New York, 1911), 25–29; Hale, *Virginia Venturer*, 291–292.

Baltimore's claims in the Chesapeake were ratified by a treaty between Virginia and Maryland in 1657. By 1660, following the Calvert restoration in Maryland and the Stuart restoration in England, several of the leading Virginia Puritan émigrés grew disillusioned with fanatical armageddons between the Old Babylon and the New Jerusalem and became pacifistic Quakers.[52]

Although the goals of Bennett and Claiborne helped precipitate civil war in an already destabilized Maryland colony, the parliamentary commissioners conscientiously refused to permit such fratricidal violence among their fellow colonists in Virginia, thus preserving the traditional harmony of the Council. In an atmosphere of political moderation that allowed the temporarily victorious and the temporarily vanquished to live in peace on their plantations as they shuffled in and out of power between the 1640s and the 1660s, ideological rigidity could not and did not long survive.

In a contest of practical political manipulators, the deposed governor, Sir William Berkeley, was more than a match for Claiborne, Bennett, and the two Samuel Mathews. For a decade before 1652, the indefatigable Virginia royalist had masterfully maneuvered to undermine local support for the old oligarchs while they were preoccupied with expanding their power base in London and expelling the Calverts from Maryland. Unlike his beloved sovereign at home, Berkeley succeeded in thwarting revolutionary change in Virginia by identifying with popular concerns and demonstrating how his adversaries' selfish interests did not represent the public's greater good. For instance, while General Claiborne had his militiamen on a self-indulgent crusade to Kent Island in 1646, Berkeley personally captured Opechancanough to end the Third Anglo-Powhatan

52. "Acts and orders of a Generall Assembly holden for the Province of Maryland at Patuxent," Oct. 20, 1654, *Md. Archives*, I, 339–356; instructions from the Lord Proprietor, Oct. 23, 1656, *ibid.*, III, 324–327; petition of Lord Baltimore to the Lord Protector, Jan. 22, 1656/57, *ibid.*, 331; articles of agreement between the Lord Proprietary and Richard Bennett, Nov. 30, 1657, *ibid.*, 332–334; Leonard Strong, *Babylon's Fall in Maryland* . . . (1655), in Hall, ed., *Narratives of Early Maryland*, 236–246; *The Journal of George Fox* (1694), *ibid.*, 398–402; Lois Green Carr, "Sources of Political Stability and Upheaval in Seventeenth-Century Maryland," *Md. Hist. Mag.*, LXXIX (1984), 57–58. Also working in Lord Baltimore's favor with Cromwell's regime was Charles II's Feb. 16, 1649/50 condemnation of Cecil Calvert for "adher-[ing] to the Rebells of England, and admit[ting] all kinde of Schismaticks, and Sectaries . . . into . . . Maryland." *The Lord Baltemore's Case* (1653), in Hall, ed., *Narratives of Early Maryland*, 179–180.

War, thus earning hero's acclaim and beating the old frontier warlords at their own game. Similarly, Berkeley's strong stands against the importation of Puritan ministers from New England, the fanaticism of Bennett's disruptive southside Puritans, and Ingle's depredations against the Calverts in Maryland revealed his consistent commitment to public safety, political stability, Anglican orthodoxy, and governmental legitimacy when such ideals were under attack in the critical decade of the 1640s. Confronting some of the same Council oligarchs who had ousted Harvey, Berkeley curtailed their power through the support of the House of Burgesses in a new bicameral legislature. In convincing a coalition of county officials and small farmers that the Claiborne faction represented political elitism, economic opportunism, and religious extremism inimical to the interests of most Virginians, Berkeley wrote that "we can onely feare the Londoners who . . . would take away the liberty of our consciences, and tongues, and our right of . . . selling our goods to whom we please."[53]

By stressing the association of the Claiborne councillors with London's ruthless regicides and meddlesome mercantilists, Berkeley deprived his adversaries of critical support from the many Virginians who never felt personally oppressed by the Stuart kings, the Anglican church, Dutch traders, or Calvert "tyranny." Becoming a self-fulfilling prophecy, Berkeley's alienation of the old oligarchs from local loyalties forced them into an even greater dependence upon interest-group allies in London— supporters who were increasingly tainted with popular perceptions of political authoritarianism and personal avarice as the 1650s evolved. Realizing that the homeland allies they enlisted to defeat the Calverts had cost them the approval of their original constituency, the Claiborne councillors eschewed the fanatical coercion that bloodied battlefields in England and Maryland and reasserted Virginia's traditional resentment of outside political interference.[54]

53. Governor Berkeley, speech to the assembly, Mar. 1651, McIlwaine, ed., *Journals of Burgesses, 1619–1658/59*, 76 (also see *ibid.*, 66–78); *Md. Archives*, III, 171–172, 188–189; Kukla, "Order and Chaos," *AHR*, XC (1985), 289–291, 293, 296; Pagan, "Trade and Politics," 133–151.

54. Morton, *Colonial Virginia*, I, 174–189; Hale, *Virginia Venturer*, 298–309. For the Claiborne clique's innovations in Indian relations during their tenure in office, see Wilcomb E. Washburn, *Virginia under Charles I and Cromwell, 1625–1660*, Jamestown 350th Anniversary Booklet, no. 7 (Williamsburg, Va., 1957), 50–56. Ironically, parlia-

IN THE evolution of the English Chesapeake, from tiny, tenuous outposts in a strange land of powerful native nations to expansive, triracial societies embracing the lands of defeated peoples, Anglo-Indian interest-group alliances made the mid-seventeenth century one of the most fertile periods of intercultural adjustment and adaptation. Among the many new relationships that developed from merging worlds of alien lifeways, commercial partnerships held the most promise for peaceful interethnic cooperation because they recognized the essential contributions of all inhabitants, of whatever race or culture, in exploiting the resources of the region they shared. Although colonists and Indians formed mutually dependent relationships in order to preserve their viability and independence, their participation in London's growing global economy eventually ensnared them all in an enveloping process of increased subordination and subservience. The initial interest, eventual investment, and ultimate interference of Londoners in Chesapeake affairs advanced under Stuarts and Cromwellians alike and survived long after the trappers and traders had vanished.

The demise of the tidewater beaver trade forever altered the goals and perceptions of the Chesapeake's inhabitants, as Anglo-Indian alliances became less economically attractive and thus increasingly irrelevant to the majority of farming colonists after 1660. Although key characteristics of Claiborne's first interethnic interest group were perpetuated in the piedmont deer trade and the Anglo-Iroquoian Covenant Chain diplomacy of the eighteenth century, the thousands of English immigrants who followed the paths of colonial traders onto the lands of native trappers had little appreciation of, or sympathy for, an earlier, Indian-dominated Chesapeake world. The nine hundred English settlers who remained in the Chesapeake after the Powhatan Uprising of 1622 increased to twenty-five thousand colonists by 1660 and to some sixty thousand by 1680, thanks largely to the relative safety from Indian attacks that interethnic alliances helped promote. Focused on a single agricultural staple,

---

mentary commonwealthmen in Claiborne's home shire of Kent had a similar experience: "It was the paradox of Cromwell's regime that in one sense its very measure of success was the cause of its own downfall. If it was based upon the victory of the nation-state over the county community, it also, in the end, created that longing apparent in all parts of the country to return to older forms of society and government whose genius was essentially provincial and local." Alan Everitt, *The Community of Kent and the Great Rebellion, 1640–1660* (Leicester, 1966), 17 and chap. 1 *passim*.

this growing throng of land-hungry tobacco farmers quickly dispossessed the Indians who had been steadily depopulated and demoralized by decades of combat in the beaver wars.[55]

In the absence of the economic incentives that had stimulated intercultural cooperation and intercolonial conflict, Virginians and Marylanders after the Restoration increasingly reasserted their common heritage as brethren of an allegedly superior race and culture, disdaining the faceless, now useless, mass of "savages" they saw as hindrances to expansion. In September 1675, a combined force of one thousand Virginia and Maryland militiamen, some descended from rival traders who had brutalized one another decades before to gain the prized pelts of the Susquehannocks, launched a joint attack on the remnants of that Indian nation. After serving as loyal trading partners of the Virginians into the 1650s and as loyal military allies of the Marylanders after 1660, the once-mighty Susquehannocks had exhausted their beaver pelts and sacrificed all but a handful of warriors in their battles with the Mohawks and Senecas when the colonists turned on them. Leaving their Susquehanna homeland to reside along the Potomac near their old Piscataway adversaries, the Susquehannocks discovered too late the lethal prejudices of gentlemen farmers, among them George Washington's Protestant grandfather and Giles Brent's Catholic son, who *would* "fight soe neare home."[56]

Contributing as ever to the evolution of the Chesapeake, the Susquehannocks, who had for decades sheltered Englishmen from Iroquois raids, now gave the colonists a final, fleeting taste of frontier terror. In 1675–1676, Susquehannock vengeance in Virginia challenged the quiet complacency of Governor Berkeley's last years in office and triggered the

55. Jennings, *Ambiguous Iroquois Empire*, 136–142; Trigger, ed., *Handbook of North American Indians: Northeast*, 240–270; Menard, "Population, Economy, and Society," *Md. Hist. Mag.*, LXXIX (1984), 71–91; Stephen R. Potter, "The Dissolution of the Machoatick, Cekacawon, and Wighcomoco Indians," Northumberland County Historical Society, *Bulletin*, XIII (1976), 4–33; Daniel K. Richter and James H. Merrell, eds., *Beyond the Covenant Chain: The Iroquois and Their Neighbors in Indian North America, 1600–1800* (Syracuse, N.Y., 1987); Alan Vance Briceland, *Westward from Virginia: The Exploration of the Virginia-Carolina Frontier, 1650–1710* (Charlottesville, Va., 1987).

56. Kent, *Susquehanna's Indians*, 45–50; Jennings, *Ambiguous Iroquois Empire*, 133–141; Alice L. L. Ferguson, "The Susquehannock Fort on Piscataway Creek," *Md. Hist. Mag.*, XXXVI (1941), 1–9; Morgan, *American Slavery, American Freedom*, 250–252; Morton, *Colonial Virginia*, I, 227–234.

unprecedented devastations of Bacon's Rebellion. The converging crises of Indian war and civil war shattered the Council harmony that had largely endured for half a century and prompted a reassessment of the discredited policies of the Wyatt warlords. Since 1660 Berkeley had repudiated the self-made "sonnes of wrath" of the 1620s–1640s and patronized a new, genteel Council oligarchy of wealthy, well-educated planters. But the Susquehannock offensive revealed that the frontier training and military talents of Claiborne's generation had been abandoned one Indian uprising too early. When most of Berkeley's inexperienced councillors proved incapable of defending Virginia's citizens, young Nathaniel Bacon became the champion of a terrified people totally baffled by Indian behavior (see table 4).[57]

Each in his own way, Berkeley and Bacon crudely caricatured the Council warlords of the 1620s. While the governor and leading councillors followed their example by trading in Indian furs, they allegedly permitted these self-interested commercial ventures to compromise the public's safety. Physically prevented from repeating his battlefield heroics of thirty years before, Berkeley saw young Bacon usurp his role in unifying the citizenry through the catharsis of frontier combat. However, the demagogic opportunism and dangerous vigilantism of Bacon, as he indiscriminately slaughtered "Friends or Foes [just] Soe they be Indians," also distorted the values of those earlier colonial "Cheiftaines," who had respected the difference between native allies and adversaries and always resisted the temptation to unleash their forces on fellow Virginians.[58]

In precipitating the bloody conflicts of 1675–1677, the Susquehannocks again contributed to the creation of a new era in the ever-changing

57. "Virginias Deploured Condition" (1676), in *Aspinwall Papers* (Massachusetts Historical Society, *Collections*, 4th Ser., X [Boston, 1871]), 161–187; Wilcomb E. Washburn, *The Governor and the Rebel: A History of Bacon's Rebellion in Virginia* (Chapel Hill, N.C., 1957), chaps. 2–4; Morgan, *American Slavery, American Freedom*, 252–270; Kukla, "Order and Chaos," *AHR*, XC (1985), 293–295. Of the Virginia Council sitting in 1676, Berkeley was the only member from 1660; 10 of 17 councillors had been appointed since 1670, and 7 of them only in 1675.

58. "A True Narrative of the Late Rebellion in Virginia by the Royal Commissioners" (1677), in Charles M. Andrews, ed., *Narratives of the Insurrections, 1675–1690* (New York, 1915), 123; Bacon's "Declaration of the People," July 30, 1676, quoted in Washburn, *Governor and the Rebel*, 70–72, and with which he takes issue, 25–30 (see also chap. 3); Stephen Saunders Webb, *1676: The End of American Independence* (New York, 1984), 13–14, 28–30, 38–44, 71–72, 160–161.

English Chesapeake—an era marking the end of Indian and Council dominance. After 1677, no Indian group native to the region would possess the population, the power, or the products to influence key events in the coastal plain, which gave rise to the colonists' collective amnesia about the significant contributions of Indians in the formative years of "white society." The passing of the powerful Indian societies enabled genteel colonial "first families" to develop and perpetuate their economic and social dominance in safety, but in their climactic contribution to Chesapeake affairs, the Susquehannocks ensured that Virginia's Council oligarchs would also enter the new era with diminished political influence. Having attracted London investments to a Virginia riding the crest of expansionistic independence in 1630, the Susquehannocks attracted London intervention to a Virginia incapable of governing itself in 1676. The arrival of reform-minded commissioners accompanied by an English fleet recalled the abortive mission of Bennett and Claiborne a quarter-century before and reflected London's now-unchallenged supremacy in matters of transatlantic trade, Indian policy, and territorial expansion.[59]

It was quite fitting that William Claiborne, the aged, infirm, and last surviving of the old oligarchs, ended a half-century of life in the Chesapeake just as a London-dominated world of new race relations was emerging. Having known a generation of councillors less affected and affluent but more effective and influential, Claiborne lived to witness the downfall of Berkeley as well as Bacon and the mindless slaughter of both his Susquehannock allies and his Pamunkey enemies. The arrival of another English fleet in Virginia and the recent death of Cecil Calvert perhaps stimulated Claiborne's nostalgic memories of the power he once had and the ambitions he once held. As if to acknowledge Virginia's near-total dependence on England, the old parliamentary commissioner requested the new royal commissioners to deliver a petition to Whitehall when they returned home. Dated March 13, 1677, and accompanied by

59. Semmes, *Captains and Mariners*, chap. 20; Beverley, *History of Virginia*, ed. Wright, 85–93; Sosin, *English America*, 191–207; Stephen Saunders Webb, *The Governors-General: The English Army and the Definition of the Empire, 1569–1681* (Chapel Hill, N.C., 1979), 451–453, 458–459, and chap. 7; Webb, *1676*, 163, 409–416; Bailyn, "Politics and Social Structure," in Smith, ed., *Seventeenth-Century America*, 111–115; Carole Shammas, "English-Born and Creole Elites in Turn-of-the-Century Virginia," in Tate and Ammerman, eds., *Chesapeake in the Seventeenth Century*, 289–296.

dozens of original documents spanning fifty years of Chesapeake events, Claiborne's petition humbly asked Charles II to finally return to him that focus of daring dreams and countless conflicts—the "Island of Kent in Maryland."[60]

60. "Petition of Coll. William Claiborne A Poore Old Servant of Your Majesties Father and Grandfather," CO 1/39, fol. 110; "Petition to His Majesties Commissioners for the Settlement of Virginia in these troublesom times of Rebellion and Generall disturbance," Mar. 13, 1676/77, *ibid.*, fol. 112. These petitions are grouped with supporting documents (fols. 110–168) that chronicle Claiborne's activities back to the 1620s, which the old councillor and secretary doubtless used in composing his polemics against Lord Baltimore.

TABLE I. *William Claiborne's English Connections, 1621–1660*

William Claiborne (1600–1677)
of Kent, Kent Island, and New Kent County
Virginia Councillor, 1624–1637, 1643–1661; Secretary of State,
1626–1634, 1652–1661; Treasurer, 1642–1650; Major General of
Militia, 1644–1646; Parliamentary Commissioner, 1651–1660;
Deputy Governor, 1652–1660

THE VIRGINIA-LONDON INTEREST GROUP, 1621–1642

Old Virginia Oligarchs	*London Merchant Clique*
Sir Francis Wyatt (1588–1644)*	Sir John Wolstenholme
governor, 1621–1626, 1639–	(1562–1639)
1642	Virginia Company merchant;
George Sandys, Esq.	lobbyist
(1578–1644)*	Sir Edwin Sandys (1561–1629)*
Virginia treasurer, 1621–1626;	Virginia Company director,
poet-courtier; Virginia lobbyist	1618–1624; Member of
Sir George Yeardley	Parliament, 1603–1625
(1588–1627)	Sir John Coke (1563–1644)
governor, 1618–1621, 1627;	secretary of state, 1625–1639
councillor	Sir William Alexander
John West (1590–1659)	(1567–1640)
governor, 1635–1637;	secretary of state for Scotland;
councillor; brother to Lord De	earl of Stirling; proprietor of
La Warr	Nova Scotia
Samuel Mathews, Sr. (d. 1658)	Sir John Zouch (d. 1639)
councillor; merchant; lobbyist	Puritan member, Dorset
William Tucker	Commission
(c. 1589–1640?)*	Maurice Thomson (b. 1604)*
councillor; merchant	merchant; Puritan lobbyist
William Stone	Thomas Stone
(c. 1603–c. 1660)	merchant; partner of Thomson;
governor of Maryland, 1648–	uncle of William Stone
1657; J.P., sheriff, Accomack	William Cloberry
County	merchant; Puritan lobbyist

TABLE I. *(continued)*

Old Virginia Oligarchs	*London Merchant Clique*
Thomas Stegge (d. 1652)	Edward Bennett (d. 1664)
councillor; Thomson factor	merchant; Puritan lobbyist;
Richard Bennett	uncle of Richard Bennett
(c. 1608–1675)	
governor, 1652–1655;	
councillor; leader of southside	
Puritans	

THE CHESAPEAKE-LONDON PURITAN
COMMONWEALTHMEN, 1642–1660

Chesapeake Commonwealthmen	*London Commonwealthmen*
Col. Richard Bennett	Maurice Thomson*
(c. 1608–1675)	lobbyist for first navigation acts,
governor, 1652–1655;	1650–1651
parliamentary commissioner,	George Thomson (1604–
1652–1660; merchant	1669?)*
Col. Thomas Stegge (d. 1652)	chair of Admiralty Committee
parliamentary commissioner,	Col. Samuel Mathews, Sr.
1652; speaker, House of	(d. 1658)
Burgesses, 1643	Virginia agent in London,
Edward Digges (c. 1621–1676)*	1652–1657
governor, 1655–1656;	2d earl of Warwick (1587–1658)
councillor	governor-in-chief of all colonies
Col. Samuel Mathews, Jr.	
(d. 1660)	
governor, 1656–1660;	
councillor	

* Indicates members with Kentish connections through birth or residency.

TABLE 2. *Cecil Calvert's English Connections, 1630–1660*

Cecil Calvert, 2d Baron Baltimore (1605–1675)
    of Kent, London, Yorkshire, and Ireland
    First Lord Proprietor of Maryland, 1634–1675

Thomas Wentworth, 1st earl of Strafford (1593–1641) Yorkshire friend of Sir George Calvert and executor of his will; M.P., lord lieutenant of Ireland; Charles I's principal adviser, 1639–1641.	Attainted by Parliament for "cumulative treason." Executed May 12, 1641.
Sir Thomas Arundell, 1st Baron Arundell of Wardour (1560–1639) Cecil's father-in-law; Catholic count of the Holy Roman Empire; sponsored the 1605 Weymouth expedition to New England.	
William Peaseley, Esq., of Drury Lane, London Cecil's brother-in-law; Maryland's business agent.	
Sir Toby Matthew (1577–1659) Catholic courtier; diplomat.	
Sir Francis Windebank (1582–1646) Pro-Catholic secretary of state, 1632–1640; close adviser to Charles I on Calverts' behalf.	Forced into exile by Parliament in 1640 due to Catholic sympathies.
Leonard Calvert (1606–1647) Cecil's younger brother; first Maryland governor, 1633–1647.	
Thomas Cornwallis (1605–1676), of Norfolk Maryland commissioner, 1633–1637; councillor, 1637–1642, 1657; chief military commander and leading investor, merchant, and entrepreneur.	Backed Jesuits against Calvert; impeached in 1644; resettled permanently in England, 1659.

TABLE 2. *(continued)*

John Lewger (1602–1665), of London Maryland councillor, 1637–1644, 1647–1648; provincial secretary, 1637–1648; attorney general, 1644–1648.	Anti-Jesuit Calvert loyalist; left colony, 1648, and converted to Catholicism; Calvert's chaplain.
Giles Brent (1600–c. 1672), of Gloucestershire Maryland councillor, 1638–1644, 1647–1649; treasurer, 1639–1643; acting governor, 1643–1644; commander of Kent Island, 1640–1642.	Contentious councillor; charged with disloyalty to Calvert, 1645; emigrated to Virginia, 1649.
Jerome Hawley (1590–1638), of Middlesex Maryland commissioner, 1633–1637; councillor, 1637–1638; Virginia treasurer, 1637–1638.	Placed on Virginia Council to further Calverts' interests but did not.
Sir John Harvey (d. 1646), of London Governor of Virginia, 1630–1635, 1637–1639.	Supported Calvert cause; deposed by Council, 1635.
George Evelyn (d. after 1649), of London Agent of Cloberry & Company, Kent Island investor, 1636; commander of Kent Island, 1637–1638.	Helped take Kent Island; resettled in England, 1638.
Robert Evelyn (d. 1649), of London Agent of the crown, 1634–1635; captain of militia, 1637–1642; Virginia councillor and surveyor, 1637.	Supported Calvert takeover of Kent Island; left Maryland, 1642.
The Jesuit Fathers Substantial investors in the Maryland enterprise, 1632–1635, and leading intermediaries between the colonists and the Piscataways after 1639.	Challenged Calvert on issues of church and state and land rights.

TABLE 3. *The Contest for Maryland, 1650–1658*

Claiborne Supporters

Richard Bennett
(c. 1608–1675)
   Nansemond Puritan and Virginia councillor who led mercenary army to return Leonard Calvert to power, 1646, and settled Virginia Puritans in Maryland, 1648–1650; BUT becomes parliamentary commissioner who, with Claiborne, overthrows proprietary government and rules Virginia, 1652–1655.
Robert Brooke (1602–1655), of London
   Protestant Maryland councillor and manor lord, 1650–1652; became councillor under parliamentary commissioners, 1652–1654.
Col. Francis Yeardley
(c. 1624–1655)
   Virginia Protestant, father-in-law of Chandler, son of Sir George Yeardley; named councillor and colonel by parliamentary commissioners, 1652–1653; burgess and colonel in Virginia, 1653.
Capt. Richard Preston
(c. 1618–1670)
   Virginia Puritan émigré; parliamentary councillor, 1652–1658; commander of North Patuxent Puritans; became the "Great Quaker" by 1660.

Calvert Supporters

William Stone
(c. 1603–c. 1660)
   Accomack Protestant merchant-planter affiliated with Claiborne, Capt. Richard Ingle, and powerful London merchants; BUT becomes governor of Maryland, 1648–1656, and ultimately leads proprietary forces against Virginia Puritan émigrés in Battle of the Severn, 1655.
Thomas Hatton (d. 1655)
   Protestant Maryland councillor, 1648–1652; killed at Battle of the Severn fighting for proprietary cause, 1655.
Job Chandler (d. 1659)
   Accomack Protestant, son-in-law of Yeardley; named to Maryland Council to mollify criticism of LB by London merchant brother; remained loyal proprietary supporter.
Capt. John Price (c. 1607–1661)
   Protestant Maryland councillor, 1648–1655; supported LB and fought for proprietor in Battle of the Severn, 1655.
William Eltonhead
(1616–1655)
   Protestant Maryland councillor and manor lord, 1649–1655; captured in Battle of the Severn and executed as loyal Calvert supporter, 1655.

TABLE 3. *(continued)*

Claiborne Supporters

Capt. William Fuller
(d. by 1695)
  Virginia Puritan émigré; parliamentary councillor, 1654–1658; signed Susquehannock Treaty, 1652; converted to Quakerism by 1657.
Edward Lloyd (c. 1620–1696)
  Virginia Puritan émigré, brother of London merchant; parliamentary councillor, 1654–1658; commander of Providence Puritans; signed Susquehannock Treaty, 1652.
Thomas Marsh
(c. 1615–c. 1656)
  Virginia Puritan émigré; parliamentary councillor, 1655; signed Susquehannock Treaty, 1652; mortally wounded in Battle of the Severn, 1655.
Leonard Strong (d. by 1659)
  Parliamentary councillor, 1654–1655, and London lobbyist for Providence Puritans; antiproprietary pamphleteer; Quaker convert in late 1650s.

Calvert Supporters

John Langford
(c. 1595–d. after 1666)
  Catholic friend and agent of LB; Maryland councillor, 1642–1643; surveyor general, 1642–1648; wrote 1655 pamphlet in defense of LB against the Puritans.
Dr. Luke Barber (d. 1668)
  Protestant Maryland councillor, 1656–1660; deputy governor, 1657–1658; as former physician to Cromwell, allegedly reported to him on abuses of Puritan regime in Maryland.
John Hammond (d. 1663)
  Resident of both Virginia and Maryland in mid-17th century; pro-proprietary pamphleteer, author of *Leah and Rachel* (1656).

TABLE 4. *The Virginia Council of State, Representative Years*

1625	1652	1676
Sir Francis Wyatt Governor	Col. Richard Bennett Governor	Sir William Berkeley Governor
Capt. Francis West	Col. John West	Col. Nathaniel Bacon
Sir George Yeardley	Col. Argoll Yeardley	Col. Philip Ludwell
George Sandys, Esq.	Col. Thomas Pettus	Col. Thomas Beale
William Claiborne	Col. William Claiborne	Henry Corbin, Esq.
Capt. Samuel Mathews	Col. Samuel Mathews, Sr.	Col. Thomas Swann
Abraham Peirsey		Thomas Ballard, Esq.
Capt. Roger Smith	Col. Samuel Mathews, Jr.	Sir Henry Chicheley (April 1670)
Capt. Ralph Hamor		
Capt. Isaac Maddison	Col. Humphrey Higginson	Edward Digges, Esq. (April 1670)
Capt. John Harvey*		
Capt. John Martin*	Col. George Ludlow	Col. Joseph Bridger (November 1673)
	Col. Nathaniel Littleton	
	Col. William Barnett	James Bray, Esq. (March 1675)
	Capt. Bridges Freeman	
	Capt. Thomas Harwood	Lt. Col. William Cole (March 1675)
	Maj. William Taylor	Nathaniel Bacon (March 1675)
	Capt. Francis Eppes	
	Lt. Col. John Cheesman	Ralph Wormley, Esq. (March 1676)
		Rowland Place, Esq. (March 1676)
		Thomas Bowler, Esq. (March 1676)
		Col. William Spencer (March 1676)

* Appointed, did not serve.
Dates indicate month and year of first appointment.

Russell R. Menard   British Migration to the Chesapeake Colonies in the Seventeenth Century

MIGRATION, Bernard Bailyn notes, will play a major role in a new synthesis of early American history, a comprehensive perspective capable of integrating the explosion of scholarship produced during the past quarter-century into a coherent whole. The details of that new perspective have yet to be worked out, but its central theme is clear enough. As a field of inquiry, early America is being detached from the national historiographic tradition, from the view of the subject as the colonial background to the United States, and reinterpreted within the context of the early modern era as an aspect of that global process in which Old World peoples once largely isolated from one another were brought together through the militant expansion of Europe to form a New World. One way to approach the task, Bailyn argues, is through a focus on migration, "the movement of people outward from their original centers of habitation—the centrifugal *Völkerwanderungen* that involved an un-traceable multitude of local, small-scale exoduses and colonizations, the continuous creation of new frontiers and ever-widening circumferences, the complex intermingling of peoples in the expanding border areas," which culminated in the massive shift of Africans and Europeans to the Western Hemisphere.[1]

This emerging synthesis gives new urgency to the study of migration. Despite the recent interest in colonial population history and the appear-ance of some major new work, the movement of Europeans across the Atlantic remains poorly understood.[2] Making sense of the repeopling of

1. Bailyn, *The Peopling of British North America: An Introduction* (New York, 1986), 4–5. Such a reinterpretation was the intent if not the result of Jack P. Greene and J. R. Pole, eds., *Colonial British America: Essays in the New History of the Early Modern Era* (Baltimore, 1984).

2. Recent work on early American population history and on migration to the colonies is surveyed in John J. McCusker and Russell R. Menard, *The Economy of British America, 1607–1789* (Chapel Hill, N.C., 1985), 211–235; Jim Potter, "Demo-graphic Development and Family Structure," in Greene and Pole, eds., *Colonial*

British America and fixing the place of the colonies in early modern history demand better estimates of the number of migrants, improved descriptions of temporal patterns over both the short and long term, more-precise knowledge of the types of people attracted to the colonies, and more-penetrating analysis of the network of choices that led some to leave home for the New World.

This essay addresses those needs for the Chesapeake colonies during the seventeenth century. It opens with an effort to measure the number of immigrants before 1700, moves on to a description of changes over time in the volume of migration, and concludes with a discussion of the characteristics of the immigrants, their age, gender, place of origin, and social status. The essay places movement to the tobacco coast within a broad context of British migration patterns in which colonies competed with each other and with places in England, elsewhere in the British Isles, and in Europe for workers. And it argues that the process can be understood if it is assumed that migrants made choices among alternative destinations in an attempt, as Ravenstein's seventh law of migration has it, to "better themselves in material respects."[3]

How Many Immigrants?

Reliable, direct measures of the number of migrants to the Chesapeake colonies are not available, but historians have often used colonial land records to generate estimates.[4] Since land grants were tied to immigration through the headright system in both Maryland

---

British America, 123–156; and Richard S. Dunn, "Servants and Slaves: The Recruitment and Employment of Labor," *ibid.*, 157–194. The major study of migration published since those surveys is Bernard Bailyn, *Voyagers to the West: A Passage in the Peopling of America on the Eve of the Revolution* (New York, 1986).

3. E. G. Ravenstein, "The Laws of Migration," Royal Statistical Society, *Transactions*, XLVIII (1885), 167–235.

4. For efforts to use the Virginia headright records to measure migration, see Wesley Frank Craven, *White, Red, and Black: The Seventeenth-Century Virginian* (Charlottesville, Va., 1971), 1–37, and Terry L. Anderson and Robert Paul Thomas, "The Growth of Population and Labor Force in the Seventeenth-Century Chesapeake," *Explorations in Economic History*, XV (1978), 290–312. For commentary on those efforts, see Edmund S. Morgan, "Headrights and Head Counts: A Review Article," *Virginia Magazine of History and Biography*, LXXX (1972), 361–371; Russell R. Menard, "Immigration to the Chesapeake Colonies in the Seventeenth Century: A

and Virginia, such records should serve as a guide to migration. Unfortunately, the Virginia headright records are too flawed to be useful: the system was abused and the record keeping casual. Many fictitious settlers appear in the lists of headrights, immigrants are often recorded more than once, some people are listed who were not immigrants, and many immigrants are not entered. In Maryland, by contrast, the abuses that plagued Virginia's system were avoided and the records more carefully kept. Most important, it is possible to estimate the number of duplications and omissions and thus determine the approximate relationship between headright entries and the volume of migration. The Maryland headright records indicate that between 23,500 and 40,000 whites migrated to the colony between its founding in 1634 and the abolition of the headright system in 1681. The mean of the upper and lower bound figures, just under 32,000, provides a "best estimate."[5]

These figures can be used to generate a range for migration to the Chesapeake colonies as a whole. Given the white population of Maryland in 1680 of 18,500, the ratio of migrants to total population increase between 1634 and 1680 was 1.27 for the low estimate and 2.16 for the high. The Chesapeake white population increased by 50,700 during the period, from 4,900 in 1634 to 55,600 in 1680, indicating a migration range of 64,400 to 109,500. An estimate for Virginia can be calculated by subtracting the Maryland figures from those for the entire region. The results are summarized in table 1. The "best" series is simply a mean of the high and low estimates.[6]

Recently, H. A. Gemery estimated migration from Britain to the Americas by another method. His results provide an independent check on the figures in table 1. Net migration can be calculated as a residual, as that portion of a region's population change not the consequence of reproductive change. Given total population at both ends of an interval

---

Review Essay," *Maryland Historical Magazine*, LXVIII (1973), 323–329; and Menard, "The Growth of Population in the Chesapeake Colonies: A Comment," *Explorations Econ. Hist.*, XVIII (1981), 399–410.

5. For more detail on the construction of these estimates, see Russell R. Menard, "Immigrants and Their Increase: The Process of Population Growth in Early Colonial Maryland," in Aubrey C. Land, Lois Green Carr, and Edward C. Papenfuse, eds., *Law, Society, and Politics in Early Maryland* (Baltimore, 1977), 89–90.

6. For Chesapeake population estimates, see Russell R. Menard, "The Tobacco Industry in the Chesapeake Colonies, 1617–1730: An Interpretation," *Research in Economic History*, V (1980), 157–161.

TABLE I. *Estimated European Migration to Maryland and Virginia,*
1607–1700 (in Thousands)

| | Maryland | | | Virginia | | | Chesapeake | | |
	Low	High	Best	Low	High	Best	Low	High	Best
1607–1624						6.0			6.0
1625–1633				2.0	4.0	3.0	2.0	4.0	3.0
1634–1680	23.5	40.0	31.8	40.9	69.5	55.2	64.4	109.5	87.0
1681–1700			10.8			16.4			27.2
1607–1700	34.3	50.8	42.6	65.3	95.9	80.6	99.6	146.7	123.2

and the rate of reproduction, determining net migration is a straightforward calculation. Gemery used population figures provided by Stella Sutherland and Edmund Morgan, derived rates of passage and seasoning mortality and rates of natural increase from scanty demographic evidence, and calculated that 87,100 people left Britain for the southern colonies between 1630 and 1680, precisely the midpoint of the range in table 1. I have made several adjustments to Gemery's procedure. These reduced the result substantially, to 72,000 immigrants for the period 1630 to 1680. Still, the figure is well within the range of table 1 and within 15 percent of the "preferred" migration estimate (see table 3, below).[7]

These estimates can be extended to cover the entire seventeenth century. Approximately 6,000 Europeans migrated to Virginia between 1607 and the dissolution of the Virginia Company in 1624. Another 2,000 to 4,000 immigrants arrived from the mid-1620s to the mid-1630s.[8] Gemery's procedure, modified as above, yields 27,200 immigrants between 1680 and 1700. Adding these to the totals for 1634–1680 produces a range for the seventeenth century of 100,000 to 150,000 immigrants (see table 1).

How reliable are these figures? They almost certainly capture the range of possibilities, for the assumptions used in the critical period from 1634 to 1680, when the bulk of the migrants arrived, are extreme. However, the range is large, and although my guess is that the actual number falls

7. Gemery, "Emigration from the British Isles to the New World, 1630–1700: Inferences from Colonial Populations," *ibid.*, 179–231.

8. Craven, *White, Red, and Black*, 3; Irene W. D. Hecht, "The Virginia Colony, 1607–1640: A Study in Frontier Growth" (Ph.D. diss., University of Washington, 1969), 68, 70–71, 79.

near the midpoint, additional research is needed before it can be reduced with any confidence. Nevertheless, in a field as primitive as Chesapeake population history, ball park numbers are useful.

Secular Trends and Short-Term Movements

Between 100,000 and 150,000 Europeans, then, the vast majority of them English, came to the tobacco coast during the seventeenth century. How was the migration distributed over time? Were there shifts in the long-term trend? Were short-term movements patterned or merely random fluctuations around a mean? What accounted for the temporal patterns? This section addresses such questions, attempting to describe and explain secular and short-term changes in the number of migrants.

The Maryland land records are again a good starting point. In an effort to measure the temporal pattern of immigration I drew a small sample of just over eight hundred names from the headright entries and grouped them by date of arrival. Table 2 uses this distribution to generate a range of migration estimates by decade for Maryland. The low estimate assumes that because of double counting and fictitious settlers the headrights overstate immigration by 6 percent, the high that they understate immigration by 62.5 percent. Again, the preferred series is simply a mean of the high and low estimates. The number of immigrants to Maryland, these data indicate, increased rapidly at a rate of 10 percent a year from the 1630s before levelling out in the 1660s. A more finely graded annual series suggests that the turning point was reached in 1664.[9]

Can this pattern stand for that of the Chesapeake colonies as a whole? Not necessarily, for during the first few decades of its history, Maryland was the Chesapeake frontier, with rates of population growth and, doubtless, rates of immigration much higher than those of Virginia. The typicality of the Maryland series can be tested by using Gemery's method to generate immigration estimates by decade for the entire region (see table 3). These also show a rapid increase to the 1650s, although the rate of growth is much slower than in the Maryland figures and there is an actual decline in the 1640s. But growth did not end in the 1660s: instead,

9. For more detail on this sample, see Russell R. Menard, "Economy and Society in Early Colonial Maryland" (Ph.D. diss., University of Iowa, 1975), 156.

TABLE 2. *Estimated European Migration to Maryland, 1634–1680*

	Headrights in Sample		Low	High	Preferred
	No.	%	Estimate	Estimate	Estimate
1634–1640	17	2.1	494	840	667
1641–1650	46	5.8	1,363	2,320	1,842
1651–1660	116	14.5	3,408	5,800	4,604
1661–1670	308	38.5	9,048	15,400	12,224
1671–1680	313	39.1	9,188	15,640	12,414
Total	800		23,501	40,000	31,751

the number of immigrants rose to the 1670s, although at a much reduced and decelerating pace.

Unfortunately, there is little evidence that will help in choosing between the patterns. It is clear that the decline in the 1640s reflects the depression that continued until near the end of that decade rather than a secular shift. And there is other evidence that the number of indentured servants brought to Virginia followed the Maryland pattern, reaching a peak in the early 1660s and then stabilizing.[10] These data suggest that immigration to the region as a whole followed the pattern described by the Maryland headright records, but that those records greatly exaggerate the rate of increase. That is, the number of new settlers arriving in the Chesapeake colonies increased from the 1630s to the early 1660s at a slower pace than that of table 2 and then leveled out. However, until new sources are discovered or old ones made to yield more-certain results, the pattern will remain elusive. Given current information, the most that can be said is that the number of migrants to the tobacco coast increased from the 1630s to about 1660, and then either stagnated or continued to grow but at a much reduced and decelerating rate.

There is less uncertainty about the last two decades of the seventeenth century. As table 3 indicates and evidence from probate and county court records confirms, European migration declined sharply after 1680. In all probability, this decline continued into the eighteenth century as immi-

10. Russell R. Menard, "From Servants to Slaves: The Transformation of the Chesapeake Labor System," *Southern Studies*, XVI (1977), 355–390.

TABLE 3. *Estimated European Migration to British America and to Maryland and Virginia, 1630–1700 (in Thousands)*

	British America	Maryland and Virginia
1630–1640	39.7	8.9 (22.4%)
1640–1650	68.5	7.8 (11.4%)
1650–1660	60.2	16.2 (26.9%)
1660–1670	48.2	18.7 (38.7%)
1670–1680	45.2	20.5 (45.3%)
1680–1690	40.7	13.3 (32.6%)
1690–1700	40.1	13.9 (34.7%)

Sources: These estimates were generated by the procedure described by Henry A. Gemery, "Emigration from the British Isles to the New World, 1630–1700: Inferences from Colonial Populations," *Research in Economic History,* V (1980), 179–231, adjusted in three ways. First, I treated Maryland and Virginia as a separate region, whereas Gemery reported estimates for the southern colonies as a whole. Second, in order to measure arrivals in America rather than departures from Britain, I removed Gemery's estimate of passage mortality from the calculations. Third, I used the estimates of population reported in John J. McCusker and Russell R. Menard, *The Economy of British America, 1607–1789* (Chapel Hill, N.C., 1985), 103, 136, 154, 172, 203, and (for the West Indies in 1630 and 1640) in Richard S. Dunn, *Sugar and Slaves: The Rise of the Planter Class in the English West Indies* (Chapel Hill, N.C., 1972), 54–55.

gration rapidly became a minor source of population growth among European Americans in the Chesapeake colonies.[11]

Why these changes in long-term trends? Why, that is, did the number of immigrants to the Chesapeake increase rapidly during the first half of the seventeenth century, level out or grow much more slowly in the 1660s and 1670s, and then decline after 1680? We can approach the question by placing migration to the colonies in context and then looking at some of the processes that shaped movement to the tobacco coast. Since inden-

11. David Galenson offers a series of migration estimates for the Chesapeake colonies in the 18th century based on inferences from population size and vital rates. See *White Servitude in Colonial America: An Economic Analysis* (Cambridge, 1981), 212–218. See also Henry A. Gemery, "European Emigration to North America, 1700–1820: Numbers and Quasi-Numbers," *Perspectives in American History,* n.s., I (1984), 283–342, and Russell R. Menard, "Migration, Ethnicity, and the Rise of an Atlantic Economy: The Repeopling of British America, 1600–1790," forthcoming in a volume of essays on European migration to the Americas to be published by the Immigration History Research Center at the University of Minnesota.

tured servants dominated the British-Chesapeake migration stream, accounting for at least 70 percent of the total, the analysis will focus on their behavior, although free immigrants may have responded to the same incentives.

Migration is often studied as a single stream between sending and receiving regions. This wrenches the process out of context and artificially closes options. In so narrow a framework, potential migrants have a single choice: they can move to the destination under study or stay at home. Consider, however, the options facing a young English man or woman of the seventeenth century who could not find work at home or who hoped for greater opportunities than were foreseeable there. Maryland and Virginia were not the only possibilities. Servants could sign on for the West Indies, New England, Pennsylvania, or the Carolinas. They could move elsewhere in Britain and they could try Ireland or the European continent. Young men could join the army or the navy. Those from a village could move to a provincial town. And there was always London, the colonies' major competitor for immigrants. Moving to the New World should be put within a broad context of English migratory patterns in which colonies competed with each other and with places in England and elsewhere for new recruits.[12]

How would a migrant choose among this array of possibilities? Some were desperate and left England as a last resort without much thought for the future beyond the certainty of work. Francis Haires, for example, "a miserable wandering boy" of sixteen, "his father and mother and all friends dead," was apparently near the end of his rope when he indentured himself for the colonies. For others, like William Croppin of Devon, "a lusty young man about 26 years old and verrie desirous to go oversea," long-term opportunity was a primary consideration.[13] Migrants would be especially interested in life expectancies, wage rates, job opportunities, access to land and credit, the costs of starting a farm or entering a trade, and the like. They were doubtless also influenced by working conditions, climate, proximity to friends, kin, or coreligionists, and by the possibility of return should their new home not meet their expectations. Servants

12. The utility of thinking about movement to the colonies within the context of English migration patterns, now a common theme in the literature, was first stressed by E. E. Rich, "The Population of Elizabethan England," *Economic History Review*, 2d Ser., II (1950), 263–264.

13. John Wareing, "Migration to London and Transatlantic Emigration of Indentured Servants, 1683–1775," *Journal of Historical Geography*, VII (1981), 358n.

could not weigh the variables with statistical precision, but their decisions were not uninformed. There was a folk wisdom available—that a region was a charnel house, that the work was hard or easy, the masters abusive or kind, spouses scarce or plentiful, wages high or low, land easy to come by or impossible to obtain. There were stories of people who had done well or poorly in the various possible destinations. And, for those willing to ask, information could be gathered from scores of people who knew something or at least had opinions about conditions elsewhere: recruiting agents, merchants, mariners, travelers, the local squire or minister, and so forth. Such information was not necessarily accurate or up-to-date, but it at least provided some guidance for making a decision to move.[14]

It has been argued that such considerations were irrelevant to the young men and women who moved to the colonies under indenture. Gary Nash, for example, maintains that servants "were not making the choices, for power in the commercial transaction that brought bound labor across the Atlantic resided in the hands of the supplier and the buyer."[15] Similarly, James Horn contends that "the servant's individual desires played little part in determining where he eventually ended up. Instead, it was the trading community that was responsible for directing and regulating emigration in response to the needs of the colonies."[16] While there were instances of outright coercion and while uneducated rural youths must have been at a disadvantage in negotiations with shrewd, experienced merchants, servants were not simply passive victims of a process beyond their control. The best evidence on the issue is provided by David Galenson's analysis of indenture contracts. Older servants with skills and work experience who could read and write served shorter terms than younger, unskilled, inexperienced, and illiterate boys and girls. Further, servants clearly discriminated among destinations. Those who went to

14. Michael J. Greenwood, "Research on Internal Migration in the United States: A Survey," *Journal of Economic Literature,* XIII (1975), 397–433, summarizes work on the theory of migration. We know very little about the information on the American colonies available to people considering migration, although David Cressy, *Coming Over: Migration and Communication between England and New England in the Seventeenth Century* (Cambridge, 1987), 1–36, 213–234, shows that a good deal can be learned about the issue.

15. Nash, *The Urban Crucible: Social Change, Political Consciousness, and the Origins of the American Revolution* (Cambridge, Mass., 1979), 111.

16. Horn, "Servant Emigration to the Chesapeake in the Seventeenth Century," in Thad W. Tate and David L. Ammerman, eds., *The Chesapeake in the Seventeenth Century: Essays on Anglo-American Society* (Chapel Hill, N.C., 1979), 92.

the West Indies, where death rates were high and opportunities slender, were compensated with shorter terms than those who went to the mainland. The variations in the length of term were not trivial. Among servants who left London in the 1680s, for example, those who could write their names signed on for a term seven months shorter on average than those who could not; those who went to Maryland served nine months more than those in Barbados. Given a typical term of five or six years, these were substantial differences. The patterns make sense only if it is assumed that the migration was voluntary and that servants struck bargains and made choices among the competing destinations.[17]

There is evidence of a second type that will permit a test of the proposition that the choices of servants did little to shape the volume of migration to the colonies. If servants made the decision, one would expect that they would pay close attention to employment opportunities and incomes at home and that the size of the migrant stream would be inversely related to English real wages. If, on the other hand, the choices of merchants and planters regulated the volume of migration, there should be little relationship between real wages and the number of migrants. A comparison of annual fluctuations in the number of indentured servants who left Bristol in the seventeenth century with an English real-wage index shows a strong inverse relationship. Servants left in greater numbers when wages were low, powerful evidence that they made the decision to move.[18] This is not to say that variations in planter demand had no impact on the volume of migration. Indeed, it was critical, particu-

17. Galenson, *White Servitude*, 102–113.

18. Specifically, a regression on the total number of servants leaving Bristol during the years 1654–1680 and 1684–1685 yielded the following result: Total migrants per year = 366 - .66 real-wage index, R^2 = .44. The equation is significant at the .001 level, meaning that there is little chance that the association is random. The data on the number of migrants are from Galenson, *White Servitude*, 220–221, 224–225, except for 1684 and 1685, which are from Abbot Emerson Smith, *Colonists in Bondage: White Servitude and Convict Labor in America, 1607–1776* (Chapel Hill, N.C., 1947), 309. The real-wage index is from E. A. Wrigley and R. S. Schofield, *The Population History of England, 1541–1871: A Reconstruction* (Cambridge, Mass., 1981), 642–643, which relies on Henry Phelps Brown and Sheila V. Hopkins, *A Perspective of Wages and Prices* (London, 1981). The Phelps Brown and Hopkins data are drawn largely from London and the southeast of England, and one might wonder at the wisdom of using that index to interpret migration from Bristol and the southwest. While it seems likely that a real-wage index drawn from greater Bristol would yield an even stronger correlation, the regression results suggest that extensive migration within England had created a fairly well integrated national labor market by the second half of the 17th century. The major problem with the Phelps Brown and

larly in the short run, as differences in demand determined the distribution of the total number of migrants between Britain and America among the several colonies. However, it is clear that any effort to explain migration must pay close attention to the choices made by potential servants.

These considerations suggest that three factors regulated the size of the English-Chesapeake migration stream: the intensity of the recruiting effort; the size of the potential migrant group; and the attractiveness of the tobacco coast relative to other potential destinations both at home and abroad. Intensity of recruitment will not submit to measurement, although it is likely, particularly over the short run as merchants and planters responded to changes in the tobacco market, that this was a powerful influence. The size of the migrant pool and the relative attractiveness of the Chesapeake can be measured, however: during the seventeenth century both changed in ways that tended first to increase and later to reduce the number of servants willing to try their luck in tobacco.

The size of the migrant group in seventeenth-century England was a function of total population, an assertion that must be qualified by a recognition that the probability of migration varied by age, sex, and class (young men of the popular classes in their late teens and early twenties predominated) and that the propensity to migrate varied with time. Nevertheless, changes in the rate of population growth can provide a rough index to changes in the size of the migrant group. Recent estimates by Wrigley and Schofield describe a steady increase from 4.1 million in 1600 to 5.3 million in the 1650s. England's population declined slowly over the next thirty years, to about 4.9 million, its level in 1630, before beginning to grow again, slowly at first, more rapidly toward the middle decades of the eighteenth century.[19] If movement to the Chesapeake was a function

---

Hopkins real-wage index for this analysis is not its regional bias but rather its "stickiness." They deliberately selected evidence tending to dampen short-term fluctuations in wages. Again, I suspect that a more volatile index would produce a stronger correlation. The Phelps Brown and Hopkins index is assessed in Peter H. Lindert, "English Population, Wages, and Prices: 1541–1913," *Journal of Interdisciplinary History*, XV (1985), 618; David Loschky, "Seven Centuries of Real Income per Wage Earner Reconsidered," *Economica*, LVII (1980), 459–465; Donald Woodward, "Wage Rates and Living Standards in Pre-industrial England," *Past and Present*, XCI (1981), 29, 45; and D. M. Palliser, "Tawney's Century: Brave New World or Malthusian Trap?" *Econ. Hist. Rev.*, 2d Ser., XXXV (1982), 349–351. Further evidence on the connection between wages and migration is presented below, in table 5.

19. Wrigley and Schofield, *Population History of England*, 528–529.

of English population alone, one would expect the rate of immigration to increase during the first half of the seventeenth century and then to decline.

Work on parish registers suggests that the timing of changes in the growth rate of the migrant group fits the pattern of movement to the tobacco coast with great precision. Aggregation of baptisms and burials indicates a shift from high to low in the growth rate of English population, in large part the result of a sharp fall in the birthrate, in the mid-1640s. This finds support in the Wrigley-Schofield estimates of the size of the various age groups in England's population. They report that the number of people age fifteen to twenty-four, the range that contains the great majority of servants, peaked at 960,000 in 1661 and then fell precipitously, by nearly 17 percent, over the next twenty years. Other things being equal, a decline in the birthrate in the mid-1640s would lead to a reduction in the population of potential migrants and, therefore, of the number of servants bound for the Chesapeake, roughly twenty years later, in the mid-1660s.[20]

Other things were not equal, but instead reinforced the impact of changes in the number of potential migrants, tending first to increase and later to reduce the attractiveness of the Chesapeake relative to other destinations. In part, this reflected the pattern of population growth. Despite the demographic decline of the late seventeenth century, the number of city dwellers in England grew rapidly, from roughly 680,000 in 1670 to 850,000 in 1700. Given the high death rates of early modern towns, most of this growth was achieved through migration. Rapidly growing towns competed with the colonies for migrants and offered potential servants an attractive domestic alternative to crossing the Atlantic.[21] It was also a function of improving living standards, employment

20. For evidence of a fall in the English birthrate in the mid-1640s, see *ibid.*, 528, 532; E. A. Wrigley, "Family Limitation in Pre-industrial England," *Econ. Hist. Rev.*, 2d Ser., XIX (1966), 82–109, esp. 106; Michael Drake, "An Elementary Exercise in Parish Register Demography," *ibid.*, XIX (1962), 438–441; and Peter Laslett and Karla Oosterveen, "Long Term Trends in Bastardy in England: A Study of the Illegitimacy Figures in the Parish Registers and in the Reports of the Registrar General, 1561–1960," *Population Studies*, XXVII (1973), 267.

21. E. Anthony Wrigley, "Urban Growth and Agricultural Change: England and the Continent in the Early Modern Period," *Journal of Interdisciplinary History*, XV (1985), 688; David Souden, "Migrants and the Population Structure of Later Seventeenth-Century Provincial Cities and Market Towns," in Peter Clark, ed., *The Transformation of English Provincial Towns, 1600–1800* (London, 1984), 133–168.

opportunities, and wage rates, gains related to the rapid pace of urbanization. During the sixteenth and early seventeenth centuries, English real wages fell as a growing number of workers competed for employment. Falling real wages made movement to the colonies increasingly attractive. Relieved of the pressure of a rapidly growing work force, real wages rose across the last half of the seventeenth century. The pattern is difficult to interpret, but the increase seems to have started about 1640 and then occurred in two upward steps, the first in the 1650s, the second about 1680, both followed by long periods of relative stability. Rising real wages worked both to reduce the size of the migrating population and, for those who still chose to move, to increase the attractiveness of destinations within England.[22]

This hypothesis is supported by two types of evidence. First, Wrigley and Schofield estimate that England's net loss to migration rose from about 1 per 1,000 per year in the 1620s to a peak of over 2.4 in the 1650s and then fell sharply to below 0.8 per 1,000 in the 1680s.[23] Second, recent work reports a decline in both the intensity and scale of migration within England during the last half of the seventeenth century: after 1660 fewer Englishmen moved than earlier, while those who still did so tended to travel much shorter distances.[24]

Within the Chesapeake colonies, the course of opportunity for ex-servants may have helped shape the pattern of migration. The chances that a young man who completed servitude along the Bay would achieve a comfortable position in society were high to about 1660 and then declined, a decline that was especially sharp after 1680, when former servants often left the region in search of better prospects elsewhere. Clearly, had adequate information been available, the chances of success in the colonies would have encouraged immigration until the 1660s and subsequently discouraged it. However, the information available to prospective servants was not that precise, and it is unclear whether even the most sophisticated and knowledgeable Englishmen, let alone young workers, knew that the tobacco coast was no longer a good poor man's country in the late seventeenth century.[25]

22. On the course of real wages in England, see the work cited in n. 18, above.

23. *Population History of England*, 219.

24. Peter Clark, "Migration in England during the Late Seventeenth and Early Eighteenth Centuries," *Past and Present*, LXXXIII (May 1979), 57–90.

25. On the course of opportunity in the Chesapeake colonies, see Russell R. Menard, "From Servant to Freeholder: Status Mobility and Property Accumula-

Perhaps more important than the course of opportunity within the Chesapeake colonies was the changing attractiveness of other regions in British America. During the 1630s, poor English youths who decided to cross the Atlantic could choose among three destinations, but in the 1640s sugar and disease gave the West Indies a bad reputation and the failure of New England to find a staple crop prevented the growth of a lively demand for servants. These developments narrowed the options and focused the greatest part of the English transatlantic migratory stream on the tobacco coast. After 1680, the opening up of Pennsylvania and the beginnings of rapid development in the Carolinas ended this near monopoly and diverted migrants away from Maryland and Virginia. In sum, changes in the size of the British American migration stream and in the share of all migrants attracted to the Chesapeake colonies combined first to increase and later to reduce the number of servants bound for the tobacco coast.[26]

The relative impact of these two processes—the changing number of migrants from Britain to the Americas and their distribution among the several colonies—on immigration to the Chesapeake region is suggested by table 3. These data suggest that migration from Britain to the Americas increased from 1630 to 1650 and then declined. A similar pattern appears in recent estimates of net migration from England: these also

---

tion in Seventeenth-Century Maryland," *William and Mary Quarterly*, 3d Ser., XXX (1973), 37–64; Lois Green Carr and Russell R. Menard, "Immigration and Opportunity: The Freedman in Early Colonial Maryland," in Tate and Ammerman, eds., *Chesapeake in the Seventeenth Century*, 206–242; and Lorena S. Walsh, "Servitude and Opportunity in Charles County, Maryland, 1658–1705," in Land, Carr, and Papenfuse, eds., *Law, Society, and Politics*, 111–133. On the failure of knowledgeable Englishmen to perceive the decline, see the report of the Board of Trade prepared in late 1697 on which of the several American colonies offered the best opportunities for ex-soldiers. CO 324/6, fols. 196–203, Public Record Office.

26. Craven, *White, Red, and Black*, 29, noted the concentration of British American migration on the Chesapeake colonies after 1640. On the movement of English servants to Pennsylvania, see Gary B. Nash, *Quakers and Politics: Pennsylvania, 1681–1726* (Princeton, N.J., 1968), 50. On the rise of South Carolina as a competitor for servants, see Peter H. Wood, *Black Majority: Negroes in Colonial South Carolina from 1670 through the Stono Rebellion* (New York, 1974), and Russell R. Menard, "The Africanization of the Lowcountry Labor Force, 1670–1730," in Winthrop D. Jordan and Sheila L. Skemp, eds., *Race and Family in the Colonial South* (Jackson, Miss., 1987), 81–108.

TABLE 4. *Share of Indentured Servants Migrating from Bristol Who Went to Maryland and Virginia, 1654–1686*

| | Maryland and Virginia | | |
	No.	%	Total
1654–1659	797	35.1	2,272
1660–1669	2,504	56.3	4,445
1670–1679	1,557	65.1	2,394
1680–1686	152	24.4	622
Total	5,011	51.5	9,733

Source: Abbot Emerson Smith, *Colonists in Bondage: White Servitude and Convict Labor in America, 1607–1776* (Chapel Hill, N.C., 1947), 309.

Note: Those whose destinations were not recorded are excluded from the table.

describe a steady rise from 1620 to a peak in the 1650s and a fairly steep decline thereafter.[27] Initially, the share captured by Maryland and Virginia was small, less than a quarter of the total, but it grew after midcentury until, by the 1670s, more than 40 percent of all white immigrants to the colonies were bound for the Chesapeake. The region's share declined thereafter, to about a third for the last two decades of the seventeenth century. Table 4 presents less comprehensive but more reliable data on the destinations of servants who left Bristol between 1654 and 1686. It also shows the share to Maryland and Virginia rising steadily from the 1650s to the 1670s before falling off sharply in the 1680s.

The pattern becomes more complex if we consider movement from England to all possible destinations and assess the full array of options. How many English men and women moved to outposts of the empire in other parts of the world? How many chose Europe, particularly Holland? How many migrated to Ireland? Contemporaries, concerned with England's "want of people" in the latter half of the seventeenth century, thought Ireland a major destination. "Ireland takes many away," Henry Blunt reported in 1669; some two hundred thousand had been so "wasted," Carew Reynel estimated, as many as had "gone to planta-

27. Wrigley and Schofield, *Population History of England*, 528.

tions."[28] While direct measurement of the size of those migrations is impossible, the issue can be approached indirectly by comparing the Wrigley-Schofield estimates of English net migration to Gemery's estimates of migration to the colonies. Admittedly, this compares apples to oranges, but it should at least indicate rough orders of magnitude. This suggests that more than half of England's emigrants chose Ireland, Europe, or some other outpost before 1660, but that thereafter they concentrated on the Americas, until, by the 1680s, migration to the American colonies actually exceeded net migration from England. However, America's growing dominance of the migration stream proved insufficient to offset those processes tending to reduce movement to the tobacco coast in the late seventeenth century.[29]

Planters and merchants were not passive in the face of these changes. Indeed, recruiting agents were a critical link in the process and could, by varying the intensity of their efforts, shape both the volume and direction of migration. During the seventeenth century, their efforts were usually successful in the short run, and as a consequence, the supply of new servants brought to the Chesapeake proved sensitive to short-term shifts in planter demand. Over the long run, shifts in the composition of the servant group suggest some more permanent adjustment in recruiting practices as merchants cast their nets more widely in search of migrants. In the middle decades of the seventeenth century, recruiters apparently focused on young men in their late teens and early twenties from the middling ranks of English families, men who possessed some skills and work experience. After 1660, however, as their numbers dwindled and their prospects at home improved, fewer such men moved to Maryland and Virginia. Recruiters met the shortfall by drawing more heavily on other groups in Britain's population—convicts, homeless orphans, poor laborers, residents of England's Celtic fringe (especially the Irish), and perhaps women. Despite these efforts it proved impossible to overcome the powerful secular processes—a stagnant English population, greater opportunities at home, and the increasing pull of other colonies—tending to diminish the ability of tobacco planters to attract willing workers. During the last decades of the seventeenth century merchants were

28. Joan Thirsk and J. P. Cooper, eds., *Seventeenth-Century Economic Documents* (Oxford, 1972), 71; Reynel, *The True English Interest* (London, 1674), 59.

29. Wrigley and Schofield, *Population History of England*, 219; Gemery, "Emigration from the British Isles," *Research Econ. Hist.*, V (1980).

unable to meet growing demands for indentured labor without driving the cost of servants beyond what planters were willing to pay. The result was a major transformation of the Chesapeake work force as merchants tapped new sources of indentured servants and planters turned increasingly to African slaves as their principal source of unfree labor.[30]

SECULAR TRENDS in migration from Britain to the Chesapeake were punctuated by sharp short-term fluctuations in which the number of servants entering the work force rose rapidly, increasing severalfold from one year to the next, and then fell with equal speed. Some of this movement was doubtless random, reflecting imperfections in the organization of trade and the flow of information as well as temporary disruptions of life in England. However, the fluctuations are too sharp and too much a regular feature of the movement of servants to dismiss as mere chance variations about a trend.

In attempting to account for the short-term patterns of European migration to the Chesapeake, W. F. Craven emphasized the individual migrant's choice and chastised historians for treating indentured servants as mere commodities whose movement was regulated by the labor market. This led Craven to focus on conditions in England—bad harvests, political unrest, religious persecution—that could produce a decision to emigrate and on the opportunities that might lead an emigrant to choose the Chesapeake. In particular, Craven believed that there was a significant correlation between English harvest cycles and immigration: bad harvests encouraged migration, good harvests did not. However, Craven admitted that the correlation was weak and noted, by way of explanation, that there are examples in history of "migrations sustained over a significant period of time by their own momentum."[31]

The correlation is stronger than Craven suspected, particularly if his hypothesis is recast to take account of the options available to potential

30. See below, and Menard, "From Servants to Slaves," *So. Studies*, XVI (1977). Recent scholarship on the rise of slavery in the Chesapeake is ably summarized by Allan Kulikoff, *Tobacco and Slaves: The Development of Southern Cultures in the Chesapeake, 1680–1800* (Chapel Hill, N.C., 1986), 37–43.

31. *White, Red, and Black*, 20–21. Horn, "Servant Emigration," in Tate and Ammerman, eds., *Chesapeake in the Seventeenth Century*, 86, and Bailyn, *Peopling of British North America*, 27, also argue that short-term fluctuations in the rate of emigration were directly related to grain prices.

migrants and to measure more precisely their prospects at home. Grain prices had an impact on those prospects, but they were not the only determinant. A real-wage index that captures the incomes prospective migrants would receive if they stayed in England and the prices they would pay for all the goods and services they needed to buy is a more comprehensive measure. It seems likely that migration would be more highly correlated with real wages than with grain prices. Further, while a focus on real wages is essential to an analysis of migration, some attention must be paid to various "pull" factors. Servants, who made up the vast majority of immigrants to Maryland and Virginia, were certainly pushed to move when times were hard, but they also viewed migration as an opportunity to improve their prospects. To the merchant who financed the migration and to the planters who purchased their terms, on the other hand, servants were major investments. Thus, it is likely that short-term fluctuations in movement to the Chesapeake responded both to prospects in England and to assessments by merchants and planters of the possibility of turning a profit in tobacco.

Statistical analysis confirms this hypothesis. Table 5 reports the results of regression equations that assess the impact of the price of tobacco and of English real wages on annual fluctuations in the number of servants who had arrived in the colonies without indenture between 1680 and 1712. Among the servants brought to seven county courts to have their age judged and their term of service set, the relationships ran in the predicted direction, and in five of the seven counties the relationship was statistically significant and powerful, with the combined impact of real wages and tobacco prices accounting for 38 to 53 percent of the variation in the number of servants.[32] The number of migrants fluctuated directly with tobacco prices, inversely with real wages. When tobacco prices were low and wages high, few servants came to the Chesapeake; when tobacco was high and wages depressed, migration boomed. Short-term changes in the number of servants arriving along the Bay were not mere chance variations. Rather they reflected an intersection of planter demand for labor and the informed choices of young English men and women that

32. The two counties where the results were not significant may be the exceptions that prove the rule. Prince George's County, Maryland, was founded in 1696 and simply yielded too few observations for an adequate test. York County, Virginia, was one of the first regions along the Bay to invest heavily in slavery, and servants were only a minor part of the work force there after 1680.

joined to produce a patterned migration stream closely tied to the rhythms of an integrated Atlantic economy.[33]

Who Immigrated?

Though they are an essential first step, rough estimates of the number of European migrants and descriptions of long-term changes and short-term fluctuations in its pace only begin the history of Chesapeake immigration. Such a history demands an answer to further questions: Who immigrated? Were they mostly indentured servants or did free settlers make up a substantial share? Where did immigrants come from? How old were they? What proportions were men and what women? What position in society did they occupy when they left? Why did they leave? How was movement to the Chesapeake shaped by patterns of migration within England? While it is unlikely that most of these questions can ever be answered with precision, the data will support some suggestions and a few useful generalizations.

The evidence has an unusual bias: more is known about men and women who reached the tobacco coast as servants than about the more prosperous settlers who could at least pay their own passage. For individuals this is often not true, especially for prominent founders of enduring and distinguished families about whom genealogists have unearthed a great deal. It is true in the aggregate, however, for most seventeenth-century records are legal documents and the long-term contracts and complex transactions surrounding indentured servitude commanded the attention of government officials more frequently than the simple booking of a passage by a free immigrant. It is thus possible to generalize more broadly and accurately about servants than free settlers. The Maryland headright records do contain some information about free immigrants, but they must be used with caution because of the possibility of distortion due to internal migration. Many of the colonists who claimed headrights by virtue of immigrating at their own expense were from Virginia. Some had been born along the tobacco coast, although given the demographic

33. See, for similar arguments, Paul G. E. Clemens, *The Atlantic Economy and Colonial Maryland's Eastern Shore: From Tobacco to Grain* (Ithaca, N.Y., 1980), 47–57, and David Souden, "English Indentured Servants and the Transatlantic Colonial Economy," in Shula Marks and Peter Richardson, eds., *International Labour Migration: Historical Perspectives* (London, 1984), 19–33.

TABLE 5. *Relationship of Real Wages and Tobacco Prices to the Number of Servants Registered per Year in Several Chesapeake County Courts, 1680–1712*

	b*	r	t
1. Charles Co., Md.			
Real Wage Index	−.30	−.42	−2.09
Tobacco Prices	.49	.56	3.38
$R^2 = .40$			
$F = 10.0, N = 33$			
2. Somerset Co., Md.			
Real Wage Index	−.21	−.32	−1.20
Tobacco Prices	.53	.58	2.96
$R^2 = .38$			
$F = 6.1, N = 23$			
3. Talbot Co., Md.			
Real Wage Index	−.62	−.71	−3.54
Tobacco Prices	.18	.49	1.04
$R^2 = .53$			
$F = 11.4, N = 23$			
4. Lancaster Co., Va.			
Real Wage Index	−.50	−.57	−3.19
Tobacco Prices	.32	.45	2.14
$R^2 = .42$			
$F = 10.0, N = 31$			
5. Northumberland Co., Va.			
Real Wage Index	−.51	−.64	−3.32
Tobacco Prices	.36	.54	2.34
$R^2 = .52$			
$F = 12.8, N = 27$			
6. York Co., Va.			
Real Wage Index	−.03	−.09	−.12
Tobacco Prices	.18	.18	.82
$R^2 = .04$			
$F = 0.4, N = 27$			

TABLE 5. *(continued)*

	b*	r	t
7. Prince George's Co., Md.			
Real Wage Index	−.24	−.32	−1.03
Tobacco Prices	.33	.39	1.42
$R^2 = .21$			
$F = 2.0, N = 18$			

Sources: This table reports the results of ordinary least squares regression equations in which the number of servants whose terms of service were set in each county court is the dependent variable and English real wages and Chesapeake tobacco prices are the independent variables. The equations were estimated using SPSS. Norman Nie *et al.*, *SPSS: Statistical Package for the Social Sciences*, 2d ed. (New York, 1975), 320–367, describes the procedure and provides an introduction to the interpretation of the statistics it yields. Real wages are from E. A. Wrigley and R. S. Schofield, *The Population History of England, 1541–1871: A Reconstruction* (Cambridge, Mass., 1981), 642–643. Tobacco prices are from Russell R. Menard, "The Tobacco Industry in the Chesapeake Colonies, 1617–1730: An Interpretation," *Research in Economic History*, V (1980), 159–160. The number of servants was compiled from the county court records at the Maryland State Archives, Annapolis, and the Virginia State Library, Richmond.

characteristics of the region their numbers were probably small. Others changed their status, arriving as servants, completing their terms in Virginia, and moving to Maryland, where they entered the record as free men and women.[34] Despite this limitation, the sample drawn from headright entries yields some information about free immigrants (table 6).

Single men were the largest group among free immigrants in the headright sample. Half the free settlers were adult males, and 71 of those 122 free men were single, 49 married, and 2 widowers. The sex ratio among free adult immigrants was 239.2. Almost all the women who were free when they moved to Maryland were also married; only 2 of the 51 free women were single when they arrived. Despite the large proportion of single men, the majority of free immigrants (69.3 percent) came to Maryland as members of families. There were 51 family units in the sample, 49 headed by men who arrived with a wife and two by widowers with children. There were only 65 children in those families, and the average of 1.27 children per family suggests that most couples were

34. For examples of ex-servants who moved to Maryland, see the biographies of the early settlers in Clayton Torrence, *Old Somerset on the Eastern Shore of Maryland: A Study in Foundations and Founders* (Richmond, Va., 1935).

TABLE 6. *Characteristics of Free Immigrants to Maryland, 1634–1681*

Date of Arrival	Total Migrants	Total Free	Men	Women	Children	Families
1634–1645	20	3	3	0	0	0
1646–1652	77	51	27	14	10	14
1653–1657	32	4	4	0	0	0
1658–1667	263	116	50	24	42	24
1668–1681	414	64	38	13	13	13
Total	806	238	122	51	65	51

Source: A sample of headright entries drawn from the patent records at the Maryland State Archives, Annapolis, as described in Russell R. Menard, "Economy and Society in Early Colonial Maryland" (Ph.D. diss., University of Iowa, 1975), 156.

young and had been married only a short time before moving to the Chesapeake.[35]

It is impossible to be precise about the social position free immigrants occupied in England. All groups from the "common sort" through the gentry were represented, although in what proportions it is difficult to say. Individuals are often firmly identified with a specific status or occupation, but the critical linking information is too dependent upon accident—particularly on a genealogist's pursuit of ancestry—to warrant generalization until a systematic survey is conducted. Perhaps the most that can be said is that a majority of free immigrants were from yeoman and artisan families, that minor English merchants attracted to the Chesapeake by trade were a small but important element, and that historians have exaggerated both the number and significance of immigrants with gentry backgrounds. The gentry played a major role in the early histories of both colonies, but after 1625 in Virginia and 1645 in Maryland, men from landed families were replaced as the most prominent immigrants by men with mercantile backgrounds.[36]

35. This is supported by some specific information on the age of arrival of an admittedly special group. Free male immigrants who held major office in Maryland during the 17th century were 28.5 years old on average when they reached the colony; 69% were between 20 and 34, while only 12% (14 of 119) were 40 or more. Menard, "Economy and Society," 221.

36. Menard, "Economy and Society," chaps. 2 and 5; Bernard Bailyn, "Politics

The scanty information on free immigrants to the Chesapeake suggests that they resembled free settlers who moved to other regions of British America in the seventeenth century.[37] Further, they were a substantial proportion of the migrant group for only a brief period. Overall, free immigrants made up 30 percent of the headright sample, but they are concentrated in the 1650s and 1660s, with few arriving before 1645 or after 1667. Perhaps such settlers were part of a small but still significant migrant stream that left England for the Americas, a stream flowing to New England during the 1630s and to the Middle Colonies in the last third of the century. As intolerance and subsistence agriculture diminished New England's attractiveness before alternative destinations opened, this group of people saw in the Chesapeake colonies and in tobacco their best opportunity for a better life in the New World.

On the other hand, the headright sample may greatly exaggerate the proportion of free immigrants and distort the temporal pattern of their arrival. The majority of free immigrants arrived between 1646 and 1652 and between 1658 and 1667, both periods of substantial migration from Virginia to Maryland. Since some of the settlers from Virginia had arrived as servants and completed their terms before crossing the Potomac, the figure of 30 percent exaggerates the proportion of free immigrants. Before 1645, in the mid-1650s, and after 1667, when there is less evidence of internal migration, fewer than 15 percent of the people in the headright sample were free, a figure that perhaps more closely represents the composition of the European immigrant group in the entire Chesapeake region during the seventeenth century. In any case it is clear that the vast majority of immigrants—at least 70 percent and the proportion may have reached 85 percent—arrived as servants bound by some form of contract to serve long enough to pay their passage and earn a profit for all involved in the transaction, recruiting agent, merchant, shipowner, factor, and planter.

---

and Social Structure in Virginia," in James Morton Smith, ed., *Seventeenth-Century America: Essays in Colonial History* (Chapel Hill, N.C., 1959), 90–115.

37. For recent work on free immigrants to other colonial regions in the 17th century, see T. H. Breen and Stephen Foster, "Moving to the New World: The Character of Early Massachusetts Immigration," *WMQ*, 3d Ser., XXX (1973), 189–222; Anthony Salerno, "The Social Background of Seventeenth-Century Emigration to America," *Journal of British Studies*, XIX (1979), 31–52; Virginia DeJohn Anderson, "Migrants and Motives: Religion and the Settlement of New England, 1630–1640," *New England Quarterly*, LVIII (1985), 339–383; and Nash, *Quakers and Politics*, 48–56.

Most who came as servants (indeed, most who came) were English, although most countries in Western Europe contributed a few settlers. The only substantial groups of non-English colonists came from Scotland, Ireland, and Wales, the latter two perhaps accounting for a larger proportion than is usually recognized. In particular, the number of Irish servants rose sharply in the 1680s and by the turn of the century enough had arrived to arouse fears of popery in the more paranoid English colonial officials.[38] Even allowing maximum estimates for settlers from other places, however, the migration remains overwhelmingly English. Most of the Scots, Irish, and Welsh servants, furthermore, spoke English and were thus at least partially anglicized before moving to the colonies.

Firm measures of where within England most Chesapeake immigrants originated are difficult to obtain. The lists of emigrants from Bristol, London, and Liverpool demonstrate that all English and Welsh counties were represented, but these can be misleading if used to determine proportions from the various regions. Colonists left England from ports near their homes; recruiting agents worked close to the point of departure. Thus, the Bristol list is dominated by settlers from the southwest of England and southern Wales, the London list by immigrants from the Home Counties, the Liverpool list by servants from Lancashire, Cheshire, and northern Wales.[39]

However, if we can determine the proportions of servants who sailed to the Chesapeake from the several English ports, we can turn to advantage the importance of proximity in an immigrant's choice of a port from which to sail. The Maryland headright records afford such an opportunity. Beginning in 1668 and continuing until Lord Baltimore abolished the system in 1681, ship captains regularly claimed headrights for all passen-

38. On the increase of Irish servants, see Margaret Kellow, "Indentured Servitude in Eighteenth-Century Maryland," *Histoire Sociale/Social History*, XVII (1984), 236–237. On the importance of Welsh immigration, see Mildred Campbell's discussion of the geographic origins of servants leaving Bristol in "Social Origins of Some Early Americans," in Smith, ed., *Seventeenth-Century America*, 78. Roughly a quarter of the immigrants who left Liverpool for the Chesapeake from 1697 to 1707 were Welsh (compiled from Elizabeth French, *List of Emigrants to America from Liverpool, 1697–1707* [Baltimore, 1962]). See also the general discussion of geographic origins in Craven, *White, Red, and Black*, 1–2.

39. Campbell, "Social Origins," in Smith, ed., *Seventeenth-Century America*, 78–79; David Souden, " 'Rogues, whores, and vagabonds': Indentured Servant Emigrants to North America, and the Case of Mid-Seventeenth-Century Bristol," *Social History*, III (1978), 28–34; Horn, "Servant Emigration," in Tate and Ammerman, eds., *Chesapeake in the Seventeenth Century*, 66–74.

gers and reported their ship's home port and date of arrival in the colony (table 7). Assuming no variation in the propensity of captains from the various ports to claim headrights, 61 percent of the servants from Britain arriving in Maryland between 1668 and 1681 sailed from London, 20 percent from Bristol and other southwestern ports, 10 percent from Liverpool and Chester in the northwest, and 9 percent from the northeastern ports of York, Hull, and Newcastle. Given the evidence of the significance of proximity, it seems safe to conclude that London and the Home Counties supplied more servants than any other region in England, with the West Country a distant second. London's dominance requires some qualification, however, for some immigrants who listed London as their residence had moved there from distant parts of the kingdom before deciding to try their luck in tobacco.[40]

It may be more than a coincidence that London's share of the servant trade between 1668 and 1681 was roughly the same as its share of the tobacco trade. Perhaps ports regularly exported servants in direct relation to their imports of tobacco. If that was the case, London was the primary port of departure throughout the early colonial period and most migrants came from the southeast of England. Given this assumption, 80 to 90 percent of the servants who went to the Chesapeake before the 1640s sailed from London. London's share dropped to 60 percent with Bristol's rise as a tobacco port at midcentury, and remained there through the seventeenth century. Bristol and the southwestern regions were the second most important source of Chesapeake servants until the late 1670s, when Liverpool's growing share of the tobacco trade made northwestern England and northern Wales major recruiting grounds for Maryland and Virginia planters.[41]

Recently completed detailed studies of the geographic origins of servants who appear on several immigrant lists for London, Bristol, and Liverpool are helpful in understanding the dynamics of transatlantic

40. Campbell, "Social Origins," in Smith, ed., *Seventeenth-Century America*, 78–79; Horn, "Servant Emigration," in Tate and Ammerman, eds., *Chesapeake in the Seventeenth Century*, 73; Wareing, "Migration to London," *Jour. Hist. Geography*, VII (1981), 360–364.

41. Jacob M. Price, *France and the Chesapeake: A History of the French Tobacco Monopoly, 1674–1791, and of Its Relationship to the British and American Tobacco Trades* (Ann Arbor, Mich., 1973); Paul G. E. Clemens, "The Rise of Liverpool, 1665–1750," *Econ. Hist. Rev.*, 2d Ser., XXIX (1976), 211–225. London's changing share of the tobacco trade can be followed in U.S. Bureau of the Census, *Historical Statistics of the United States, Colonial Times to 1970* (Washington, D.C., 1975), II, Ser. Z 441–472, pp. 1190–1191.

TABLE 7. *Servants Arriving in Maryland by Port of Departure, 1668–1681*

	London	Bristol, Southwest	Liverpool, Northwest	Northeast	Total England	Scotland Ireland
1668	198	193		23	414	
1669	148	60		104	312	
1670	128	62		72	262	14
1671	93	27		17	137	
1672	121	79		28	228	
1673	99	82	20		201	
1674	140	129		37	306	
1675	187	52	103	29	371	
1676	205	59			264	
1677	379	15	53		447	
1678	460	19	11	34	524	113
1679	212	12	102	26	352	72
1680	128	7	69	9	213	20
1681	10	9	58		77	
Total	2,508	805	416	379	4,108	219

Source: Patents, Libers 11–22, WC2, Maryland State Archives, Annapolis.

Note: Bristol and Southwest includes Bristol (694), Falmouth (37), Salisbury (8), Weymouth (16), Bideford (34), Plymouth (7), and Poole (9). Liverpool and Northwest includes Liverpool (363) and Chester (53). Northeast includes York (119), Hull (110), and Newcastle (150). Scotland and Ireland includes Scotland (14), Waterford (117), and Youghal (88).

migration.[42] By paying close attention to distance traveled and possible routes taken and by comparing the behavior of those who sailed for the Americas with those who left their homes but stayed in England, it is possible to suggest that indentured servants were but a subset of British migrants. We still know too little about patterns of movement within Britain, but it is clear that "a remarkable fluidity of the labour force was a great antiquity," while "the picture of a mobile country population in-

42. Souden, "'Rogues, whores, and vagabonds,'" *Soc. Hist.*, III (1978); Horn, "Servant Emigration," in Tate and Ammerman, eds., *Chesapeake in the Seventeenth Century*, 66–74; Wareing, "Migration to London," *Jour. Hist. Geography*, VII (1981), 367–374.

creasingly engaged in the process of moving for the purpose of improving their condition, above all seeking their fortune in the towns, is now firmly established."[43] Indeed, country-to-town migration within Britain dwarfed movement from Britain to America: during the seventeenth century London alone was the destination of at least twice as many people as left England for the Americas.[44] For many, migration from country to town turned out to be the first step in a much longer, although perhaps not essentially different, move. Young men and women, already detached from the ties of family and birthplace, sufficiently ambitious and venturesome to test a city's opportunities, now with readier access to news of the Americas, were fertile recruiting ground for colonial merchants, especially if those opportunities seemed, upon closer inspection, less than promising.

The importance of proximity to a port of departure and the tendency of transatlantic migration to merge with and extend patterns of movement within England, when combined with the evidence that the number of migrants fluctuated directly with the price of tobacco, suggests that the opportunity to find passage was critical to the decision to move to the Chesapeake colonies. Young English men and women contemplating migration were presented with a wide variety of choices. They could try the tobacco coast, but if they were far from a port or if the merchants were uninterested, one of the other options was likely to prevail. If, on the other hand, young men and women were anxious to move at a time when tobacco merchants were actively seeking servants, it is easy to understand why they might end up in Maryland or Virginia, enticed by the opportunities vividly described by a recruiting agent, particularly if they lived (perhaps because an earlier move had brought them) near one of the major tobacco ports.

Migration to the Americas, then, "was a bulging out, an extension, of domestic mobility patterns into overseas territories." By the seventeenth century a fairly integrated national labor market had developed in England. Focused on London but with secondary centers in the major provincial cities, that network linked urban England into a tightly knit economy, tied the major towns to the capital city, and reached deeply into

43. J. D. Chambers, *Population, Economy, and Society in Pre-industrial England* (London, 1972), 45.

44. John Patten, "Rural-Urban Migration in Pre-industrial England," University of Oxford, School of Geography, *Research Papers*, VI (1973) provides a useful summary of research, as does Bailyn, *Peopling of British North America*, 20–32.

the countryside, extending work opportunities and wage rates to farms and villages scattered across the nation. Rural and village youths responded to the demands of the labor market, hitting the road in search of work and better prospects. Once on the road, detached from home and family, they became candidates for migration overseas in a process that made the Americas generally and the Chesapeake tobacco fields in particular "an annex to the labor markets" of early modern England.[45]

For understanding immigrants and immigration, the social origins of indentured servants are of more interest than their geographic origins. A misleading stereotype long dominated the perceptions of historians. As Craven noted, it presented the servant "as a person recruited chiefly from the lower levels of English society, and especially from the class of laborers, whose lot at the time was far from being a happy one; as very often a criminal or at best a rogue or vagabond; and as an individual so young as to have been an easy victim of the more unscrupulous methods employed by the recruiting agents."[46] "Rogues, vagabonds, whores, cheats, and rabble of all descriptions," A. E. Smith called them, "raked from the gutter and kicked out of the country."[47]

Doubtless many servants fell into one or another of these categories, but more systematic evidence suggests that such persons were not typical. An analysis by Mildred Campbell of seventeenth-century lists of servants who immigrated with contracts overstates the case in arguing that 80 percent or more came from middling social groups—yeomen, husbandmen, tradesmen, and artisans. Nevertheless, her work demonstrates that the proportion of such people was sizable.[48] David Galenson has argued that it was no more than half, the others being laborers or life-cycle servants—that is, young, unmarried, and unskilled men and women who hired out by the year as live-in servants to farmers and artisans.[49] Though they may not have been the "middling sort," such people certainly were not "raked from the gutter."

This more recent picture of the composition of the immigrant servant group requires further modification because an element is missing. Only

45. Bailyn, *Peopling of British North America*, 28.
46. *White, Red, and Black*, 5.
47. *Colonists in Bondage*, 3.
48. "Social Origins," in Smith, ed., *Seventeenth-Century America*.
49. "'Middling People' or 'Common Sort'? The Social Origins of Some Early Americans Reexamined," *WMQ*, 3d Ser., XXXV (1978), 499–524. On life-cycle servants in England, see Ann Kussmaul, *Servants in Husbandry in Early Modern England* (Cambridge, 1981).

servants with contracts are recorded in the lists that Campbell and Galenson studied, but many servants (a recent estimate suggests 40 percent)
arrived in the Chesapeake colonies without contracts and served according to local custom.[50] There were systematic differences between the two
groups. Servants by custom were younger, about sixteen years of age on
average when they immigrated, in contrast to servants with contracts, who
were usually in their late teens and early twenties.[51] Servants by custom
also served longer terms than those who arrived with indentures, even if
age is held constant, perhaps reflecting that, from the planter's perspective, they were less productive than those with written contracts.[52] Probably they were also less often skilled, more likely to be illiterate, of lower
social origins, more often without living parents or guardians to look out
for their interests, easier marks for an unscrupulous "crimp," and generally less sophisticated about labor relations and opportunities in the New
World.[53] Servants by custom perhaps had usually been life-cycle servants
in England. Since in England the terms of their arrangements were
ordinarily regulated by law and custom instead of written contract, life-
cycle servants may not have thought it extraordinary to move to the
colonies without indentures.

When these servants by custom are added to Galenson's estimate of
those who came from below middling status, we have a substantial revision of both Campbell and Galenson. This is not to suggest that we move
back to the view of A. E. Smith—that is a caricature. But it is clear that
many, perhaps the majority, who came, both with indentures and without,
lived near the margin of British society.

Despite the difficulty of precise generalization about the social origins
of servants, there is evidence that the proportion of those of low position
increased in the late seventeenth and early eighteenth centuries.[54] The

50. Walsh, "Servitude and Opportunity," in Land, Carr, and Papenfuse, eds., *Law,
Society, and Politics,* 129.

51. This difference emerges from a comparison of the ages of servants by custom
with the ages of indentured servants as reported by Horn, "Servant Emigration," in
Tate and Ammerman, eds., *Chesapeake in the Seventeenth Century,* 61–62, and Galenson, *White Servitude,* 26–33.

52. David Galenson, "British Servants and the Colonial Indenture System in the
Eighteenth Century," *Journal of Southern History,* XLIV (1978), 59–66.

53. Lorena S. Walsh, "Charles County, Maryland, 1658–1705: A Study of Chesapeake Social and Political Structure" (Ph.D. diss., Michigan State University, 1977),
156–162.

54. Souden, "English Indentured Servants," in Marks and Richardson, eds., *International Labour Migration,* 26–27, argues a contrary position, claiming that the pro-

growth of Irish immigration after 1680 implies such a change, as do the beginnings of large-scale convict importations in 1718.[55] Further support for the proposition is provided by evidence on the occupations of servants: among those bound for the Chesapeake from Bristol during the 1650s and early 1660s, roughly half reported occupations implying some degree of skill and prior work experience, a proportion that had fallen to less than a quarter by the mid-1680s.[56]

Evidence on the ages of servants also suggests a rise in the proportion from the margins of English society.[57] Throughout the seventeenth century most servants were young adults, with the great majority between sixteen and twenty-five at arrival. But age distributions for males reveal a sharp decline, particularly at the end of the century. In the 1630s, roughly 5 percent of the male servants were under sixteen, a proportion that reached perhaps 15 percent in the 1680s and 40 percent in the 1690s. The decline in age suggests a fall in social status. Parents, by this argument, would be reluctant to send young children to the New World unless providing for them at home was difficult. The frequent references in the immigrant lists to servants sixteen years old and under as poor, friendless, or orphaned support this hypothesis.[58]

---

portion of higher-status immigrants was inversely related to the volume of migration and that as the volume declined in the late 17th century their proportion rose. I suspect that he is correct for the short term, but efforts to relate shifts in the sex ratio and the average age of migrants (using the data described in table 5, above) to changes in volume produced no significant results. Galenson reports that servants leaving London in the 18th century were more often skilled than had been the case earlier (*White Servitude*, 51–64). However, as he notes, indentured servitude by that time played a much different role in the colonial economy than it had in the 17th century. See, in this context, Gloria L. Main's suggestion that there was a "bifurcation" of servants around 1700 "into a skilled or managerial elite on the one hand and common field workers on the other" (*Tobacco Colony: Life in Early Maryland, 1650–1720* [Princeton, N.J., 1982], 106). See also Kellow, "Indentured Servitude," *Histoire Sociale*, XVII (1984).

55. On convicts, see Smith, *Colonists in Bondage*, 189–203; Frederick Hall Schmidt, "British Convict Servant Labor in Colonial Virginia" (Ph.D. diss., College of William and Mary, 1976); and A. Roger Ekirch, *Bound for America: The Transportation of British Convicts to the Colonies, 1718–1775* (Oxford, 1987).

56. Galenson, *White Servitude*, 93.

57. These comments are based on Horn, "Servant Emigration," in Tate and Ammerman, eds., *Chesapeake in the Seventeenth Century*, 61–62, and Galenson, *White Servitude*, 26–33.

58. See, for examples, C.D.P. Nicholson, ed., *Some Early Emigrants to America* (Baltimore, 1965), 22, 32, 47, 58, 67, 73, 76, 77, 78, 79, 83, 92, and Michael Ghirelli,

One of the most striking characteristics of the immigrant group—and one more firmly rooted in evidence than generalization about social origins—was the preponderance of males. The proportion of women was very low in the 1630s, about six men to every woman, and while it improved markedly over the century, it was still two and a half to one among those who arrived around 1700. During the heaviest period of immigration to Maryland and Virginia, from the late 1640s to the late 1670s, men outnumbered women by about three to one among new arrivals.[59]

What is important here is the decline in the sex ratio, which with the increased proportion of servants from low social origins, may be related to secular trends in the number of men from middling families who moved from England to the Americas. As the number of such men declined after midcentury merchants may have countered the shortfall by recruiting more vigorously among other groups—women, orphans, convicts, Irish, poor laborers, and, most important, Africans—in order to prevent a labor shortage.[60] With respect to women, however, this hypothesis implies that males and females were interchangeable in the work force, and there is evidence that such was not the case. In the Chesapeake colonies, attitudes surrounding the gender division of labor may have limited the employment of white women (but not black) in the tobacco fields.[61] There are, moreover, other explanations for the increasing proportion of women. It may have had to do with supply. The decline in the intensity and scale of movement within England following the Restoration was confined to males: women moved as often and as far after 1660 as before. If emi-

---

A List of Emigrants from England to America, 1682–1692 (Baltimore, 1968), 3, 5, 11, 16, 18, 19, 30, 32, 39.

59. Evidence on sex ratios among migrants is summarized in Menard, "Immigrants and Their Increase," in Land, Carr, and Papenfuse, eds., *Law, Society, and Politics*, 96, and in Horn, "Servant Emigration," in Tate and Ammerman, eds., *Chesapeake in the Seventeenth Century*, 63.

60. For a similar shift in the age-gender profile among slaves delivered to the West Indies (rising prices and falling supplies of adult males leading to growth in the proportion of women and children), see David Galenson, "The Slave Trade to the English West Indies, 1673–1724," *Econ. Hist. Rev.*, 2d Ser., XXXII (1979), 241–249. See also David Eltis, "Fluctuations in the Age and Sex Ratios of Slaves in the Nineteenth-Century Transatlantic Slave Traffic," *Slavery and Abolition*, VII (1986), 257–272.

61. Lois Green Carr and Lorena S. Walsh, "The Planter's Wife: The Experience of White Women in Seventeenth-Century Maryland," *WMQ*, 3d Ser., XXXIV (1977), 547.

grants were drawn largely from internal migrants, the proportion of women in the population at risk to move to the Chesapeake grew in the late seventeenth century.[62] Despite the failure of England's population to rise, the absolute numbers of women willing to migrate may have grown due to a sharp upswing in the age at first marriage that swelled the ranks of single females in their early twenties—the usual age at which women left for the Chesapeake.[63] Alternatively, demand for women servants in the Chesapeake may have increased after 1650, not only to supplement a dwindling supply of male field workers but also to serve the growing subsistence sector of the economy in which the work of women was central.[64] While the evidence is not adequate to choose among these three hypotheses, what is available suggests that growth in demand for female servants to work in subsistence production was a principal dynamic behind the increasing proportion of women.[65]

It might be argued that the decline in the social origins of servants meant that an ever smaller portion actively chose emigration expecting to improve their long-term prospects, that more and more were simply pushed out, fleeing an inhospitable English economy in hopeless desperation. Perhaps, but there is evidence to the contrary. For one thing, the number of desperately poor people who wandered about England eking out a meager living by casual labor, petty theft, and begging—those whom Peter Clark calls "subsistence migrants"—fell off sharply after 1660.[66] For another, the data summarized in table 5 show that even the least-favored servants—the boys and girls who left for the Chesapeake without indenture to serve by custom—responded to changes in the English labor

62. Clark, "Migration in England," *Past and Present*, LXXXIII (1979), 69–73; Souden, "Migrants and the Population Structure," in Clark, ed., *Transformation of English Provincial Towns*, 147–148.

63. Wrigley, "Family Limitation in Pre-industrial England," *Econ. Hist. Rev.*, 2d Ser., XIX (1966), 87.

64. On the growth of the subsistence sector, see Russell R. Menard, Lois Green Carr, and Lorena S. Walsh, "A Small Planter's Profits: The Cole Estate and the Growth of the Early Chesapeake Economy," *WMQ*, 3d Ser., XL (1983), 171–196.

65. Two bits of evidence are worth considering here. The first is that the relative prices of male and female servants seem not to have changed in the 17th century, suggesting that it was not a rise in the supply of women servants that accounts for the fall in the sex ratio. The second is that in the regression analysis discussed above, in table 5, there was no relationship between the migration of female servants and the price of tobacco, suggesting that women were not wanted to work in the export sector.

66. Clark, "Migration in England," *Past and Present*, LXXXIII (1979).

market. Certainly there were people who were desperately poor in late Stuart England, but there were fewer of them than before the Restoration, their conditions were improving, their options greater. Moving to the New World under indenture was one of those options, a decision often taken within severe constraints and under considerable pressure, but a choice nonetheless.

Conclusion

Motivation is perhaps the most elusive question relating to immigration. We can agree with Governor Berkeley that servants came to the colonies with the "hope of bettering their condition in a Growing Country," and with those contemporaries and historians who mention such "push" factors as bad harvests, unemployment, personal tragedy, lack of opportunity, and religious or political persecution in accounting for the decision to migrate.[67] However, such a listing of factors is imprecise; it is impossible to rank ambition, curiosity, religious-political fervor, and disenchantment with life at home in any order of importance. Individuals left for a variety of motives, some idealistic, others practical, some simple, others complex, many perhaps contradictory and imperfectly understood by the migrants themselves.

Despite the complexity of motives, a straightforward economic approach that focuses on the changing numbers of potential migrants, fluctuations in the demand for labor, the opportunities to find passage, and the relative attractiveness of competing destinations accounts for the major temporal patterns in migration to the Chesapeake colonies: a secular increase in the number of migrants followed by stagnation and eventual decline; a tendency of servant migration to move directly with tobacco prices and inversely with real wages over the short run; shifts in the geographic origins of servants within Britain as the fortunes of major ports rose or declined; falling sex ratios; and a growing diversity of the immigrant group as the proportions of servants from low social origins increased. Such an approach does not treat indentured servants as mere commodities in an international labor market, for it assumes both initiative and freedom on the part of servants, that they could make choices in

67. Quoted in Thomas J. Wertenbaker, *The Planters of Colonial Virginia* (Princeton, N.J., 1922), 34.

response to perceived opportunities on the basis of information available to them. And it directs attention to the process of choice, to why potential migrants chose to move or stay and how those who moved selected destinations from among the various possibilities. To the extent that this is successful in explaining observed patterns, it implies that the incentives were primarily economic and that those who moved to Maryland and Virginia did so in large part because they thought migration promised greater opportunities and a more comfortable life than staying at home.

James Horn

Adapting to a New World
A Comparative Study of Local Society in England and Maryland, 1650–1700

THE MAJORITY of men and women who lived in Maryland and Virginia during the seventeenth century were born and raised in England. Most spent their childhood and early teens in rural and urban communities of southern and central England, specifically London, the Home Counties, and the Bristol region. Participants in a rich and variegated culture at local and national levels, they brought to the Chesapeake attitudes acquired during a formative period in their lives in their native country. Chesapeake society was part of English society, an offshoot of the parent culture.[1]

This view logically implies that English traditions and norms had considerable importance in shaping immigrant society along the tobacco coast in the seventeenth century despite the radically different conditions that settlers encountered. Obvious questions come to mind: What did immigrants make of their new environment? How did their new way of life compare to that of contemporaries in England? How successful were they in re-creating aspects of life they had left behind? To what extent did

I would like to thank Lois Green Carr, Philip Morgan, and Lorena S. Walsh for their helpful suggestions.

1. For the demography of the 17th-century Chesapeake, see Russell R. Menard, "Immigrants and Their Increase: The Process of Population Growth in Early Colonial Maryland," in Aubrey C. Land, Lois Green Carr, and Edward C. Papenfuse, eds., *Law, Society, and Politics in Early Maryland* (Baltimore, 1977), 88–110; Gloria L. Main, *Tobacco Colony: Life in Early Maryland, 1650–1720* (Princeton, N.J., 1982), 9–16; Robert D. Mitchell, "American Origins and Regional Institutions: The Seventeenth-Century Chesapeake," Association of American Geographers, *Annals*, LXXIII (1983), 404–420; P. M. G. Harris, "Integrating Interpretations of Local and Regionwide Change in the Study of Economic Development and Demographic Growth in the Colonial Chesapeake, 1630–1775," Regional Economic History Research Center, *Working Papers*, I, no. 3 (1978), 35–72; and John J. McCusker and Russell R. Menard, *The Economy of British America, 1607–1789* (Chapel Hill, N.C.,

the pattern of immigration and the environment encourage the early development of a Chesapeake subculture?[2]

This study compares everyday rural life in England and the Chesapeake during the second half of the seventeenth century, concentrating on local society in the Vale of Berkeley, Gloucestershire, and the lower Western Shore of Maryland. Detailed consideration is given, first, to standards of living, focusing on the domestic environment; and second, to the formal and informal structures that underpinned local communities: officeholding, the church, debt-credit networks, kinship, and friendship. Together these aspects of daily life illustrate the difficulties and achievements of English men and women in adapting to their new home "beyond the Seas."

I

The reasons why the Vale of Berkeley and the lower Western Shore of Maryland were chosen for this comparative study should be explained. A direct comparative analysis along the lines of those for England and New England is out of the question at the present

1985), 227–229. For the origins of English indentured servants, see James Horn, "Servant Emigration to the Chesapeake in the Seventeenth Century," in Thad W. Tate and David L. Ammerman, eds., *The Chesapeake in the Seventeenth Century: Essays on Anglo-American Society* (Chapel Hill, N.C., 1979), 51–95; David Souden, " 'Rogues, whores, and vagabonds': Indentured Servant Emigrants to North America, and the Case of Mid-Seventeenth-Century Bristol," *Social History*, III (1978), 23–41; Anthony Salerno, "The Social Background of Seventeenth-Century Emigration to America," *Journal of British Studies*, XIX (1979), 31–52; and John Wareing, "Migration to London and Transatlantic Emigration of Indentured Servants, 1683–1775," *Journal of Historical Geography*, VII (1981), 356–378.

2. The question of the transferal of English culture (or elements of it) from one locality to another is extremely complex and has received remarkably little attention from historians. Just how one measures it, or even describes it, is still an open issue. See A. L. Kroeber and Clyde Kluckhohn, *Culture: A Critical Review of Concepts and Definitions* (New York, 1963); T. H. Breen, *Puritans and Adventurers: Change and Persistence in Early America* (New York, 1980), chaps. 1, 4, 6, 9; and Breen, "Creative Adaptations: Peoples and Cultures," in Jack P. Greene and J. R. Pole, eds., *Colonial British America: Essays in the New History of the Early Modern Era* (Baltimore, 1984), 195–232.

time.[3] There is not yet sufficient information to link the social origins of emigrants from the mother country to the subsequent development of particular communities in the Chesapeake. Consequently this essay undertakes an indirect comparison between two areas not necessarily related by a common group of immigrants.

Two characteristics of the Vale of Berkeley make it suitable for such a comparative study. Relative to other rural areas the Vale provided large numbers of emigrants to Virginia and Maryland in the seventeenth century, and it is typical of one of the main types of community from which colonists emigrated, that is, a wood-pasture region in the southern half of England. The Vale's association with the tobacco coast began early. Between 1619 and 1620 about a hundred people from the area were transported to Berkeley Hundred on the James River. The project was not a success; only nineteen persons were alive by the summer of 1622 and the enterprise soon ended.[4] However, this failure did not discourage others from emigrating later in the century. Of the 113 indentured servants from Gloucestershire who emigrated via Bristol to the Chesapeake during the years 1654–1661 and 1684–1686, 25 were from the Vale. An additional 48 servants from the area emigrated to the West Indies during the same period. Since the places of origin of servants were not recorded in the

---

3. Sumner Chilton Powell, *Puritan Village: The Formation of a New England Town* (Middletown, Conn., 1963). See T. H. Breen and Stephen Foster, "Moving to the New World: The Character of Early Massachusetts Immigration," *William and Mary Quarterly*, 3d Ser., XXX (1973), 189–222; John J. Waters, "Hingham, Massachusetts, 1631–1661: An East Anglian Oligarchy in the New World," *Journal of Social History*, I (1968), 351–370; T. H. Breen, "Persistent Localism: English Social Change and the Shaping of New England Institutions," *WMQ*, 3d Ser., XXXII (1975), 3–28; and David Grayson Allen, *In English Ways: The Movement of Societies and the Transferal of English Local Law and Custom to Massachusetts Bay in the Seventeenth Century* (Chapel Hill, N.C., 1981).

4. Horn, "Servant Emigration," in Tate and Ammerman, eds., *Chesapeake in the Seventeenth Century*; Salerno, "Social Background of Seventeenth-Century Emigration," *Jour. British Studies*, XIX (1979); Souden, " 'Rogues, whores, and vagabonds,' " *Soc. Hist.*, III (1978). On Berkeley Hundred, see Wesley Frank Craven, *The Southern Colonies in the Seventeenth Century, 1607–1689* (Baton Rouge, La., 1949), 161–162; Joan Thirsk, "Projects for Gentlemen, Jobs for the Poor: Mutual Aid in the Vale of Tewkesbury," in Patrick McGrath and John Cannon, eds., *Essays in Bristol and Gloucestershire History: The Centenary Volume of the Bristol and Gloucestershire Archaeological Society* ([Bristol], 1976), 147–169; and Eric Gethyn-Jones, *George Thorpe and the Berkeley Company: A Gloucestershire Enterprise in Virginia* (Gloucester, 1982).

Bristol registers for most of the peak period of emigration to Maryland and Virginia (1660s and 1670s), we can surmise that at least another hundred left the Vale between 1662 and 1683.[5]

No attempt is made here to trace the distinctive characteristics of a Vale of Berkeley subculture in the Chesapeake. As a consequence of the pattern of emigration from England and the nature of the environment encountered, English provincial subcultures apparently failed to establish themselves in, or at least exerted no lasting influence on, Virginia and Maryland society. Certain regions supplied more emigrants than others, of course, and in the first half of the century doubtless many settlements along the tobacco coast had a decidedly southern or southeastern English flavor. Nevertheless, provincial subcultures did not have the same impact in the Chesapeake as in New England.[6]

Neither is the Vale of Berkeley conceived as a microcosm of English society in toto. Society in the region was influenced by the general political, socioeconomic, and cultural changes that affected other parts of England in the seventeenth century, but the Vale does not, nor could, represent the totality of experience of English local communities.[7] On the

5. The Bristol list is contained in four manuscript volumes: "Servants to forraign plantations, 1654–1663," Bristol Record Office (hereafter BRO) 04220 (1); "Servants to forraign plantacons, 1663–1679," BRO 04220 (2); "Actions and Apprentices," BRO 04355 (6); "Actions and Apprentices," BRO 04356 (1). The list has been partially transcribed by N. Dermott Harding and R. Hargreaves-Mawdsley, eds., *Bristol and America: A Record of the First Settlers in the Colonies of North America, 1654–1685* (London, 1929). A more recent and accurate transcript has been made by Noel Currer-Briggs, ed., "Indentured Servants from Bristol to America, 1654–1686" (unpubl. MS). I am grateful to Mr. Currer-Briggs for allowing me to use his transcript.

6. Breen, *Puritans and Adventurers*, xii–xiv, 72–79, 168–169; Breen, "Creative Adaptations," in Greene and Pole, eds., *Colonial British America*, 195–232.

7. During the last two decades British regional historians have become increasingly sensitive to local variation in demographic, social, and economic structures. See Joan Thirsk, *The Rural Economy of England: Collected Essays* (London, 1984), chaps. 11, 15, 16; Thirsk, ed., *The Agrarian History of England and Wales*, IV, *1500–1640* (London, 1967), and *ibid.*, V, *1640–1750* (Cambridge, 1984–1985), 2 vols.; David Underdown, *Revel, Riot, and Rebellion: Popular Politics and Culture in England, 1603–1660* (Oxford, 1985), chap. 4; Alan Everitt, *Change in the Provinces: The Seventeenth Century* (Leicester, 1969); Margaret Spufford, *Contrasting Communities: English Villagers in the Sixteenth and Seventeenth Centuries* (London, 1974); Alan Everitt, "River and Wold," *Jour. Historical Geography*, III (1977), 1–19; Peter Clark, "Migration in England during the Late Seventeenth and Early Eighteenth Centuries," *Past and Present*, LXXXIII (1979), 57–90; Keith Wrightson and David Levine, *Poverty and Piety in an English*

other hand, the Vale shared a range of characteristics with other wood-pasture areas (*pays*) in southern and central England. The Conclusions drawn from the analysis of society in the Vale can therefore be placed in the wider context of woodland parishes in other parts of Bristol's hinterland.[8]

SEVERAL CONSIDERATIONS dictated the choice of the lower Western Shore of Maryland. It was a region in the mainstream of Chesapeake development; sufficient sources survive to undertake a local study parallel to that of the Vale of Berkeley; and the area is one of the most intensely studied in the seventeenth-century tidewater.[9] During the middle decades of the century the region experienced rapid population increase as immigrants poured in from London, Bristol, and other outports. Again, no claim is made that the area represents the entire range of regional variation in the early Chesapeake. Virginia and Maryland historians are aware of significant local differences in economic and social structure along the tobacco coast. However, while it is important not to overlook these variations, there can be little doubt that society along the lower Western Shore also had much in common with that of other major tobacco-producing areas in terms of environment, economic base, and social development.[10] Further investigation of other parts of Maryland

---

Village: Terling, 1525–1700 (New York, 1979); and E. A. Wrigley and R. S. Schofield, *The Population History of England: A Reconstruction, 1541–1871* (Cambridge, Mass., 1981).

8. See Alan Everitt, "Country, County, and Town: Patterns of Regional Evolution in England," Royal Historical Society, *Transactions*, 5th Ser., XXIX (1979), and Underdown, *Revel, Riot, and Rebellion*, chaps. 3 and 4. General similarities include an emphasis on pasture farming, the existence of important rural manufactures and by-employments, a relatively open and mobile society, scattered settlement, high population density, widespread poverty, and the prevalence of dissent.

9. St. Mary's City Commission. I would like to thank Lois Green Carr and Lorena S. Walsh for their generous assistance with the Maryland material and for permission to use unpublished research generated by the following grants to the commission: National Science Foundation grants GS32272, RO6228-72-468, and RO10585-74-267.

10. See, for example, Harris, "Integrating Interpretations," Regional Econ. Hist. Research Center, *Working Papers*, I, no. 3 (1978); Edmund S. Morgan, *American Slavery, American Freedom: The Ordeal of Colonial Virginia* (New York, 1975), 227–230, 410–431; Main, *Tobacco Colony*, chaps. 2 and 3; and Paul G. E. Clemens, *The Atlantic Economy and Colonial Maryland's Eastern Shore: From Tobacco to Grain* (Ithaca, N.Y., 1980). The distinctive features of lower Western Shore society were therefore given less attention than the general socioeconomic characteristics it shared with other parts

and Virginia will help refine the conclusions drawn in this study, but should not invalidate the central thesis put forward.[11]

II

Situated along the eastern bank of the River Severn, the Vale of Berkeley extends for about fifteen miles midway between Gloucester and Bristol (see figure 1). The area was predominantly a dairy-farming district in the seventeenth century and specialized in the production of high-quality cheeses for the local market, Bristol, and London. It was a particularly fertile region, having "such abundance of pasture for kyne and oxen, as sufficeth the greedines of those beasts, and the couvetousnes of their owners." A traveler passing along the old Roman road to Gloucester would have been impressed by the extensive grasslands, the "lowe and fat grounds," where large herds of milch cows were put out to graze.[12] Although much of the area was enclosed, there

---

of the tidewater. See Mitchell, "American Origins," Assoc. Am. Geographers, *Annals*, LXXIII (1983), for similarities and differences between Maryland and Virginia.

11. Studies of living standards and local communities in other Chesapeake counties tend to confirm the results presented below. Lois Green Carr and Lorena S. Walsh, "Changing Life Styles and Consumer Behavior in the Colonial Chesapeake" (conference paper presented at "The Social World of Britain and America, 1600–1820," Williamsburg, Va., 1985) deals with St. Mary's, Somerset, and Anne Arundel counties in Maryland and York County in Virginia, 1634 to 1777. See also Walsh, " 'A Culture of Rude Sufficiency': Life Styles in Maryland's Western Shore between 1658 and 1720" (paper presented at the annual meeting of the Society for Historical Archaeology, Nashville, Tenn., 1979); Walsh, "Urban Amenities and Rural Sufficiency: Living Standards and Consumer Behavior in the Colonial Chesapeake, 1643–1777," *Journal of Economic History*, XLIII (1983), 109–117; and Main, *Tobacco Colony*, chaps. 4–7. On community, see Darrett B. and Anita H. Rutman, *A Place in Time: Middlesex County, Virginia, 1650–1750* (New York, 1984), esp. chap. 4; Lois Green Carr, "Sources of Political Stability and Upheaval in Seventeenth-Century Maryland," *Maryland Historical Magazine*, LXXIX (1984), 45–46; James Russell Perry, "The Formation of a Society on Virginia's Eastern Shore, 1615–1655" (Ph.D. diss., Johns Hopkins University, 1980), chaps. 2–4; and Kevin P. Kelly, " 'In dispers'd Country Plantations': Settlement Patterns in Seventeenth-Century Surry County, Virginia," in Tate and Ammerman, eds., *Chesapeake in the Seventeenth Century*, 183–205.

12. For general descriptions of the region, see Lewis Wiltshire, *The Vale of Berkeley* (London, 1954); Frank Walker, *The Bristol Region* (London, 1972), 3–51; and British

were still pockets of common land, generally on marginal soils, where villagers raised cattle and sheep. Availability of commons was vital to smallholders, who earned a living partly from farming and partly from the woolen industry.[13]

Between 25 and 35 percent of adult males were engaged wholly in agricultural occupations compared to nearly 50 percent for the entire county. At least two-thirds of the Vale's population were therefore not employed primarily in farming, and the majority worked in the woolen industry. A number of parishes, especially along the Cotswolds Edge, were important centers of broadcloth manufacture and formed part of the cloth-producing region that stretched in an arc from Wells and Shepton Mallet in east Somerset, through Wiltshire, to the escarpment bordering the vales of Gloucester and Berkeley. Over 40 percent of adult males were employed in the woolen industry in the early part of the century,[14] and despite decline in later years it remained a principal support of the local economy. In seventeenth-century terms, the Vale of Berkeley was a major industrial region.

Society was open, fluid, and characterized by large inequalities in the distribution of wealth. At the pinnacle of the social hierarchy were the Lords Berkeley: peers of the realm, the greatest landowners in the region, and representatives of one of the oldest and most distinguished families in England. Family prestige and wealth were symbolized by the massive

---

Regional Geology, *Bristol and Gloucester District* (London, 1968), 1, 5, 41–83 *passim.* The area encompasses 15 parishes: Berkeley (with Hill), Cam, Charfield, Cromhall, Dursley, Frampton-on-Severn, Kingswood (situated in a detached part of Wiltshire), North Nibley, Rockhampton, Slimbridge, Stinchcombe, Thornbury, Tortworth, Tytherington, and Wotton-under-Edge. John Smyth, *A Description of the Hundred of Berkeley, in the County of Gloucester and of Its Inhabitants,* vol. III of *The Berkeley Manuscripts,* ed. Sir John Maclean (Gloucester, 1885), 4.

13. Dr. Smith, "An Account of the Husbandry Used in Some Parts of Glostershire," Classified Papers, X, pt. 3, no. 31, fols. 397–398, Royal Society Archives, London; William Marshall, *The Rural Economy of Gloucestershire,* 2 vols. (Gloucester, 1789), II, 86; Daniel Defoe, *A Tour through the Whole Island of Great Britain,* ed. Pat Rogers ([Harmondsworth, Eng.], 1971), 364; Smyth, *Hundred of Berkeley,* 327–328, 331.

14. John Smyth, *Men and Armour for Gloucestershire in 1608,* ed. Sir John Maclean (London, 1902), *passim;* J. de L. Mann, *The Cloth Industry in the West of England from 1640 to 1880* (Oxford, 1971), xi; R. Perry, "The Gloucestershire Woollen Industry, 1100–1690," *Bristol and Gloucestershire Archaeological Society,* LXVI (1945), 49–137.

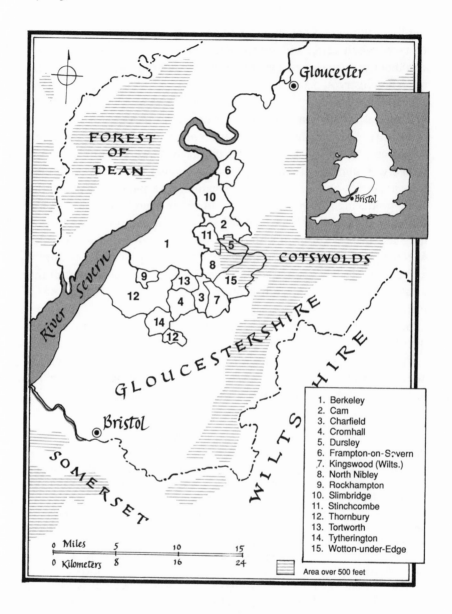

FIGURE 1. *The Vale of Berkeley*

Drawn by Richard Stinely

presence of Berkeley Castle, dominating the landscape, where the Berkeleys had lived since the twelfth century.[15]

About forty families made up the Vale's squirearchy, most of whom owned petty manors or were large freeholders. Land, let rather than farmed, was the basis of their wealth, and monopoly of local office the basis of their power. They did not form a "Venetian oligarchy," however; their ranks were open to those who could afford to pay the entry fee. Clothiers and mercers, among the wealthiest men in Gloucestershire, were frequently accepted into the gentry. "It was no extraordinary thing," Daniel Defoe remarked, "to have clothiers in that country worth, from ten thousand, to forty thousand pounds a man, and many of the great families, who now pass for gentry . . . have been originally raised from, and built up by this truly noble manufacture."[16] The richest groups in society—gentry, clothiers, and large farmers—made up between 10 and 15 percent of the region's householders in the second half of the seventeenth century (see tables 1 and 2).[17]

Below them a broad range of men and women of middling status (worth between £50 and £250 in personalty at death), who engaged in farming, rural trades, food and drink processing, and small-scale manufacturing, composed just under a third of the Vale's population. The yeomanry formed the core of this group. At the top end of the wealth spectrum their life-style was virtually indistinguishable from that of the lesser gentry, while at the bottom they differed little from husbandmen. Ownership of their farms, however, set them apart from most of the region's inhabitants; the large amounts of capital required to buy land and

15. James P. P. Horn, "The Distribution of Wealth in the Vale of Berkeley, Gloucestershire, 1660–1700," *Southern History*, III (1981), 81–109. On the Lords Berkeley, see H. P. R. Finberg, "Three Studies in Family History: Berkeley of Berkeley," in Finberg, ed., *Gloucestershire Studies* (Leicester, 1957), and Lawrence Stone, *Family and Fortune: Studies in Aristocratic Finance in the Sixteenth and Seventeenth Centuries* (Oxford, 1973), 243–267.

16. The heralds' visitation of 1683 mentioned 14 families as having legitimate coats of arms, but this would be a rather strict definition since at least another 30 families resident in the Vale between 1660 and 1700 were considered gentry by their contemporaries. T. Fitz-Roy Fenwick and W. C. Metcalfe, eds., *The Visitation of the County of Gloucester . . . [1682–1683]* (Exeter, 1884); Defoe, *Tour through Great Britain*, 262.

17. The extent of poverty in the Vale was not exceptional. Hearth tax returns reveal that 31% of householders in rural Kent and approximately one-third in Devon and Leicestershire were too poor to be taxed in the 1660s and 1670s. L. A. Clarkson, *The Pre-industrial Economy in England, 1500–1750* (London, 1971), 233–234.

TABLE 1. *Distribution of Personal Wealth in the Vale of Berkeley,*
1660–1699 (in Percents)

Decade	£0–£9	£10–£49	£50–£99	£100–£249	£250+
1660–1669	5.0	32.5	23.8	22.5	16.3
1670–1679	9.2	34.8	24.1	20.6	11.3
1680–1689	4.8	30.3	23.6	24.7	16.6
1690–1699	9.9	32.6	18.8	24.7	14.1
1660–1699 (*N*=983)	7.0	31.8	22.2	23.9	15.1

Sources: Probate Inventories, 1660–1699, Consistory Court Journal, 1668–1676, Will Act Book, 1678–1681, Wills, 1660–1699, Register of Administrations, 1677–1683, Register of Wills and Administrations, 1683–1704, Accounts of Administrations, 1684–1699, Gloucestershire Record Office; Prerogative Court of Canterbury Inventories, PROB 4 and 5, Public Record Office.

stock were beyond the means of most men. The majority of people at the bottom end of the middling range (£50 to £99) earned a living by working small holdings, by providing goods and services to the local community, or both. There was sometimes no clear division between them and those at "the Feet of the Body Politique," but in general, the possession of a skill, a little land, or age and experience placed lesser householders above the ranks of the poor.[18]

If these estimates of the size of rich and middling wealth categories are correct, then about 60 percent of the Vale's householders (worth less than £50) lived below or near the poverty line. Not all of them were paupers. As Charles Wilson says, "the collective title by which the least fortunate of the lower orders of society were known—'the Poor'—did not mean that they were all destitute. It meant that they had little or nothing to save them from destitution when times were bad or as they grew old: that a proportion of them was therefore always destitute, another proportion potentially destitute." Parish records reveal that the hard core of the poor were persons too old, young, or sick to work and consequently completely dependent on parish relief. They rarely formed more than a small mi-

18. Horn, "Distribution of Wealth," *So. Hist.*, III (1981).

TABLE 2. *Distribution of Personal Wealth in the Vale of Berkeley, 1660–1699, Adjusted to Include the Poor*

Assumption A: 50% Poor (1664 hearth tax returns indicate that 50% of households were exempt)

£0–£49	£50–£99	£100–£249	£250+
69.4%	11.1%	12.0%	7.5%

Assumption B: 33.3% Poor (1672 hearth tax)

£0–£49	£50–£99	£100–£249	£250+
59.2%	14.8%	15.9%	10.0%

Sources: E179/247/16, 13, 14, Public Record Office; Probate Inventories, 1660–1699, Consistory Court Journal, 1668–1676, Will Act Book, 1678–1681, Wills, 1660–1699, Register of Administrations, 1677–1683, Register of Wills and Administrations, 1683–1704, Accounts of Administrations, 1684–1699, Gloucestershire Record Office; Prerogative Court of Canterbury Inventories, PROB 4 and 5, PRO.

Note: The proportions of different wealth categories itemized in table 1 have been adjusted here to include the poor who did not go through probate. If, as indicated by the 1664 hearth tax returns, 50% of householders were officially paupers, then the adjusted wealth categories conform to Assumption A. More likely, about a third of householders lived at subsistence level (1672 hearth tax returns), hence the preferred estimates under Assumption B. See James P. P. Horn, "The Distribution of Wealth in the Vale of Berkeley, Gloucestershire, 1660–1700," *Southern History*, III (1981), 81–109.

nority of the disadvantaged. Far more numerous were those who, for one reason or another, were ineligible for relief: men and women "haveing no worke" because of temporary unemployment or chronic underemployment.[19]

HOW DO the social origins of emigrants to the Chesapeake fit into this general picture? Twenty-five servants left the Vale via Bristol in the second half of the 1650s, early 1660s, and mid-1680s. Three-quarters

19. Charles Wilson, *England's Apprenticeship, 1603–1763* (London, 1965), 17; P. 193, OV 2/1 (Kingswood), Gloucestershire Record Office, hereafter GRO; "A Booke of actes, rates and monuments of the parish of Cam in the country of Gloucestershire . . . ," Berkeley MSS, General Ser., no. 95, 50. I would like to thank the Trustees of the Berkeley Estate for allowing me to use these records, held in the muniment room of Berkeley Castle.

were male, and judging by their length of indenture (six years or more), at least a third were in their teens. The majority conformed to the typical profile of servants of this period: young, single, and poor. Of the males six were described as yeomen (probably sons of yeomen), two as laborers, and two as textile workers. Five of the women servants were spinsters and one a widow. They came from nine of the fifteen parishes in the region, but nearly half were from the two largest parishes and market towns, Berkeley and Thornbury.[20]

Clues about why people emigrated and the links that existed between the Chesapeake and the Vale of Berkeley can be gained from a variety of sources. The evidence is fragmentary but suggestive. Stephen and Jesse Trotman of North Nibley were indentured to Richard Nelme, "planter," in October 1654. It appears that Nelme had emigrated from Nibley to Northumberland County, Virginia, a few years before and wanted to engage servants from his former home. Stephen and Jesse may have been known to him personally since Nibley was not a large parish; Nelme may have been fulfilling an earlier promise to provide work for them in the Chesapeake.[21]

Poverty was clearly an important factor encouraging people to move.[22]

20. Currer-Briggs, ed., "Indentured Servants"; Horn, "Servant Emigration," in Tate and Ammerman, eds., *Chesapeake in the Seventeenth Century*, 56–74; David W. Galenson, *White Servitude in Colonial America: An Economic Analysis* (Cambridge, Mass., 1981). Of the 25 servants who emigrated to the Chesapeake between 1654 and 1680, 11 were from Berkeley and Thornbury. Of 48 who emigrated to the West Indies, 23 were from these two market towns.

21. See the entry for Stephen and Jesse Trotman, Oct. 14, 1654, bound for four and seven years respectively to Richard Nelme of Nibley, planter (Currer-Briggs, ed., "Indentured Servants"). For Nelme, see Nell Marion Nugent, comp., *Cavaliers and Pioneers: Abstracts of Virginia Land Patents and Grants*, 2 vols. (Richmond, Va., 1934, 1977), I, *1623–1666*, 269, 459. Richard Nelme may have been related to the Christopher Nelme, shoemaker, who emigrated to Virginia in 1619 as a member of the ill-fated Berkeley venture. That Nelme might have known the Trotmans is, of course, entirely speculative, but it is a possibility given that the Nelmes and the Trotmans were important families in the region.

22. For the importance of subsistence migration, see Peter Clark, "The Migrant in Kentish Towns, 1580–1640," in Peter Clark and Paul Slack, eds., *Crisis and Order in English Towns, 1500–1700: Essays in Urban History* (London, 1972), 117–163; Souden, "'Rogues, whores, and vagabonds,'" *Soc. Hist.*, III (1978); E. G. Ravenstein, "The Laws of Migration," Royal Statistical Society, *Transactions*, XLVIII (1885), 167–235; and Paul A. Slack, "Vagrants and Vagrancy in England, 1598–1664," *Economic History Review*, 2d Ser., XXVII (1974), 360–379.

Alice Jennings, a spinster from Berkeley, left Bristol for the Chesapeake in the summer of 1657. She was possibly related to Thomas Jennings of the same parish, who died in 1670 worth only £12 12s. 6d. Similarly, Alice Hurne, also of Berkeley, who emigrated two years later, was probably a relation of either Thomas or John Hurne (or both) who appear in the court rolls of the late 1660s as smallholders of the parish. The most convincing evidence of the relationship between poverty and emigration, however, concerns Thomas Harding of Thornbury, a recipient of parish alms in the early 1670s. In 1672 the overseers of the poor accounts show £1 11s. "paid for Linen and woolen & other necessarys for Thomas Harding when he was going to Virginia." He appears in the Bristol register of servants under an entry for November 1672 bound for four years' service in Virginia, and he may well have ended up in Lower Norfolk County.[23]

A final connection between the Vale and the Chesapeake involves the development of dissent in the mid-seventeenth century. After the Restoration, cloth-producing towns such as Wotton-under-Edge, Cam, Dursley, and Stinchcombe established themselves as local centers of nonconformity. Thornbury became associated with Quakerism from the mid-1650s and was probably the birthplace of Thomas Thurston, the "renegade Maryland Quaker," who emigrated to New England in 1656 and to Maryland two years later. Dissenting congregations created a network of communications by which news of brethren in the colonies could be channeled and their work supported. Although nonconformists were only a small proportion of the Vale's total population, the influence of religious issues should not be underestimated when considering the emigration of the 1650s and 1660s.[24]

23. Probate inventory, Thomas Jennings, 1670, GRO; "Rentals of Different Manors, 1667," Berkeley MSS, Unbound Books, 50 (manor of Ham). For Harding, see P. 330, OV 2/7, GRO; Currer-Briggs, ed., "Indentured Servants," entry for Thomas Harding, Nov. 2, 1672; and Nugent, comp., *Cavaliers and Pioneers*, II, *1666–1695*, 168, 185.

24. D2052, GRO; Kenneth L. Carroll, "Thomas Thurston, Renegade Maryland Quaker," *Md. Hist. Mag.*, LXII (1967), 170–192; Carroll, "Quakerism on the Eastern Shore of Virginia," *Virginia Magazine of History and Biography*, LXXIV (1966), 170–171; Russell Mortimer, ed., *Minute Book of the Men's Meeting of the Society of Friends in Bristol, 1667–1686* ([Gateshead, Durham], 1971). Religious factors encouraging emigration to the Chesapeake have tended to be overlooked in recent years because of the emphasis given to general social and economic developments in English society. See,

III

English immigrants arriving in the Chesapeake in the middle decades of the seventeenth century would have been struck initially by the features of their new environment that so obviously differed from the one they had left behind in England: the intricate maze of waterways; the vast tracts of unbroken forest; the hot, humid summers; the "strange" native population; the novel seasonal rhythms of life and labor imposed by plantation agriculture; the absence of towns and manufactures; the social mix of English people from different regions of the parent society; the high incidence of death and disease; and the larger numbers of males than females.[25] Before considering living standards and local community in the Chesapeake, it is worth outlining some of the salient features of society as it developed along the tobacco coast in the second half of the century.

Social structure differed from that in England in several important respects. Entire sections of English society were missing. There was little in the Chesapeake to attract men of established fortune in the mother country, despite the efforts of promotional writers to convince them otherwise. In numerical terms, apart from a brief flurry during the early

---

however, Mildred Campbell, "Social Origins of Some Early Americans," in James Morton Smith, ed., *Seventeenth-Century America: Essays in Colonial History* (Chapel Hill, N.C., 1959), 63–89.

25. Arthur P. Middleton, *Tobacco Coast: A Maritime History of Chesapeake Bay in the Colonial Era* (Newport News, Va., 1953), chap. 2; Morgan, *American Slavery, American Freedom*, chaps. 3–14; Main, *Tobacco Colony*, chap. 1; the essays by Menard, Carr, Walsh, Earle, Clemens, Rutman and Rutman, and Jordan in Land, Carr, and Papenfuse, eds., *Law, Society, and Politics*, and in Tate and Ammerman, eds., *Chesapeake in the Seventeenth Century*; Karen Ordahl Kupperman, *Settling with the Indians: The Meeting of English and Indian Cultures in America, 1580–1640* (Totowa, N.J., 1980); James Axtell, *The European and the Indian: Essays in the Ethnohistory of Colonial North America* (New York, 1981), chaps. 3 and 10; Rutman and Rutman, *A Place in Time*; Karen Ordahl Kupperman, "Fear of Hot Climates in the Anglo-American Colonial Experience," *WMQ*, 3d Ser., XLI (1984), 213–240; Lorena S. Walsh and Russell R. Menard, "Death in the Chesapeake: Two Life Tables for Men in Early Colonial Maryland," *Md. Hist. Mag.*, LXIX (1974), 211–227; Darrett B. and Anita H. Rutman, "Of Agues and Fevers: Malaria in the Early Chesapeake," *WMQ*, 3d Ser., XXXIII (1976), 31–60; Daniel Blake Smith, "Mortality and Family in the Colonial Chesapeake," *Journal of Interdisciplinary History*, VIII (1978), 403–427; Carr, "Sources of Political Stability and Upheaval," *Md. Hist. Mag.*, LXXIX (1984); Lois Green Carr and Lorena S. Walsh, "The Planter's Wife: The Experience of White Women in Seventeenth-Century Maryland," *WMQ*, 3d Ser., XXXIV (1977), 542–571.

years of settlement, the gentry and aristocracy did not play an important role in colonizing the tobacco coast. Further, lacking towns and industry and with a relatively small and dispersed population, the Chesapeake did not require the range of specialist trades and crafts to be found in the Vale of Berkeley and elsewhere in England. Consequently, as Lorena Walsh has pointed out, social status associated with most Old World occupations was not transferred to the New World.[26]

Nevertheless, if several important determinants of social status were missing in the Chesapeake one of fundamental significance remained: wealth. The absence of highborn gentry and aristocracy does not imply that Maryland or Virginia society was "middle class" or egalitarian in the second half of the seventeenth century. As in England, those with the greatest estates were judged the best qualified to govern. Political power followed economic power. The absence of a traditional ruling class weakened social cohesion and hierarchy, but the firmly established concept that political authority and wealth were natural partners helped to offset this problem.[27]

Second, the pattern of landholding in the Chesapeake was significantly different from that in England. Along the lower Western Shore of Maryland manorial organization "proved an anachronism in an area which quickly came to be peopled largely by freeholders." With a few exceptions tracts called manors were manors in name only.[28] As a result of the

26. Bernard Bailyn, "Politics and Social Structure in Virginia," in Smith, ed., *Seventeenth-Century America*, 90–115; Aubrey C. Land, "Economic Behavior in a Planting Society: The Eighteenth-Century Chesapeake," *Journal of Southern History*, XXXIII (1967), 469–485; Land, "Economic Base and Social Structure: The Northern Chesapeake in the Eighteenth Century," *Jour. Econ. Hist.*, XXV (1965), 639–654; William A. Reavis, "The Maryland Gentry and Social Mobility, 1637–1676," *WMQ*, 3d Ser., XIV (1957), 421; Lorena S. Walsh, "Charles County, Maryland, 1658–1705: A Study of Chesapeake Social and Political Structure" (Ph.D. diss., Michigan State University, 1977), 365–378.

27. Russell R. Menard, P. M. G. Harris, and Lois Green Carr, "Opportunity and Inequality: The Distribution of Wealth on the Lower Western Shore of Maryland, 1638–1705," *Md. Hist. Mag.*, LXIX (1974), 169–184; Keith Wrightson, "Aspects of Social Differentiation in Rural England, c. 1580–1660," *Journal of Peasant Studies*, V (1977), 35; David W. Jordan, "Political Stability and the Emergence of a Native Elite in Maryland," in Tate and Ammerman, eds., *Chesapeake in the Seventeenth Century*, 243–273; Russell R. Menard, "Economy and Society in Early Colonial Maryland" (Ph.D. diss., University of Iowa, 1975), 431–433, 435; Walsh, "Charles County," 442, 444.

28. Donnell MacClure Owings, "Private Manors: An Edited List," *Md. Hist. Mag.*, XXXIII (1938), 307–309.

abundance of land, holdings tended to be on average much larger than in England. In St. Mary's and Charles counties, 1659–1705, the mean size of tracts was between 450 and 600 acres, while the median was between 200 and 300 acres. Men with holdings as large as this in the Vale of Berkeley would have ranked among the landowning elite. On the other hand, land was very much cheaper in Maryland. An estate of 200 or 300 acres would have cost several thousand pounds in the Vale during the second half of the seventeenth century, whereas in the Chesapeake it could be had at the price of importing five or six persons, probably around £50.[29]

Early pamphlet literature that extolled the virtues of moving to Maryland and Virginia laid great stress on the availability of cheap, fertile land.[30] An opportunity to become landowners was extremely attractive to men inculcated with the symbolic as well as the economic value of landownership in the Old World.[31] Poor men who had little chance of ever acquiring more than a few acres in England might eventually find themselves in possession of several hundred in the Chesapeake. At least this was the ideal.[32] If the abundance of land made its social and economic value proportionately less along the tobacco coast than in England, nevertheless the individual satisfaction of working one's own land (for subsistence if not always for profit) must have been considerable.[33]

Finally, reference should be made to the newness of Chesapeake so-

29. Menard, "Economy and Society," 242; Clayton Colman Hall, ed., *Narratives of Early Maryland, 1633–1684* (New York, 1910), 91–92; Clemens, *Atlantic Economy*, 71.

30. Hall, ed., *Narratives of Early Maryland*, 6–10, 81, 298, 343–345, 358.

31. R. Colebrook Harris, "The Simplification of Europe Overseas," Assoc. Am. Geographers, *Annals*, LXVII (1977), 469–483; Harris, "The Extension of France into Rural Canada," in James R. Gibson, ed., *European Settlement and Development in North America: Essays on Geographical Change in Honour and Memory of Andrew Hill Clark* (Toronto, 1978), 29.

32. Lorena S. Walsh, "Servitude and Opportunity in Charles County, Maryland, 1658–1705," in Land, Carr, and Papenfuse, eds., *Law, Society, and Politics*, 111–133; Russell R. Menard, "From Servant to Freeholder: Status Mobility and Property Accumulation in Seventeenth-Century Maryland," *WMQ*, 3d Ser., XXX (1973), 37–64; Menard, "Economy and Society," chaps. 8 and 9; Lois Green Carr and Russell R. Menard, "Immigration and Opportunity: The Freedman in Early Colonial Maryland," in Tate and Ammerman, eds., *Chesapeake in the Seventeenth Century*, 206–242.

33. Main, *Tobacco Colony*, 97. The desire to establish themselves on their own land encouraged many poor freedmen to move out of Maryland in the last decade of the 17th century and restricted the growth of a landless laboring class.

ciety. John Smyth of Nibley recounted with pride in 1639 that the Lords Berkeley had governed the Vale since "shortly after William the Conqueror daies, (if not in his time)." Other families known to Smyth had owned land in the area for three or four centuries. "Ancient usage" sanctioned traditional ways of doing things. Inhabitants of the Vale had a common heritage—their own dialect, folklore, and local customs—which defined them as "naturall bred hundredors."[34] This sense of local tradition was missing in the early Chesapeake, where high rates of mobility and mortality maintained a rapid turnover of people in the newly developing communities of the tidewater. Demographic disruption was probably the most serious problem faced by English settlers in trying to put down roots in their new environment.[35]

Some aspects of Chesapeake society would have been more familiar. English men and women who moved to the New World encountered levels of poverty similar to those in rural areas of England. Not only did the great majority of immigrants arrive with little or no capital, but also many of those who eventually made it into the ranks of householders, and who began accumulating possessions, were cut short by early death.[36] Poverty in the Chesapeake, therefore, resulted from the pattern of immigration and high mortality rates as well as the falling price of tobacco in the last quarter of the century. Along the lower Western Shore of Mary-

34. Smyth, *Hundred of Berkeley*, 7. The Harvey family of Berkeley had resided in the parish since the 16th century; the Goughs since the 13th; and the Freames since the late 15th. The Selewins of Slimbridge had held their land "from the time of King Edward the first, (if not long before)" (*ibid.*, 117, 221, 219, 248). These examples could be multiplied. *Ibid.*, 4, 10, 22–23, 30.

35. Menard, "Immigrants and Their Increase," in Land, Carr, and Papenfuse, eds., *Law, Society, and Politics*; Walsh and Menard, "Death in the Chesapeake," *Md. Hist. Mag.*, LXIX (1974); Darrett B. and Anita H. Rutman, " 'Now-Wives and Sons-in-Law': Parental Death in a Seventeenth-Century Virginia County," in Tate and Ammerman, eds., *Chesapeake in the Seventeenth Century*, 153–182; Lorena S. Walsh, " 'Till Death Us Do Part': Marriage and Family in Seventeenth-Century Maryland," *ibid.*, 126–152; Smith, "Mortality and Family," *Jour. Interdisciplinary Hist.*, VIII (1978).

36. For wealth by life cycle, see Menard, Harris, and Carr, "Opportunity and Inequality," *Md. Hist. Mag.*, LXIX (1974), 176–178. In the Vale of Berkeley, too, younger decedents were generally less wealthy than older decedents; see James P. P. Horn, "Social and Economic Aspects of Local Society in England and the Chesapeake: A Comparative Study of the Vale of Berkeley, Gloucestershire, and the Lower Western Shore of Maryland, c. 1660–1700" (D. Phil. diss., University of Sussex, 1982), table 3.10, 129.

TABLE 3. *Distribution of Personal Wealth on the Lower Western Shore of Maryland, 1638–1705*

Total Estate Value	1638–1642		1658–1665		1683–1687		1658–1705	
(pounds sterling)	No.	%	No.	%	No.	%	No.	%
£0–£9	3	12.0	9	9.8	23	9.4	168	9.5
£10–£49	14	56.0	45	48.9	105	42.9	738	41.7
£50–£99	3	12.0	16	17.4	53	21.6	353	20.0
£100–£249	3	12.0	15	16.3	35	14.3	303	17.1
£250+	2	8.0	7	7.6	29	11.8	206	11.7
Total	25	100.0	92	100.0	245	100.0	1,768	100.0

Sources: Inventories for 1638–1642 are in William Hand Browne *et al.*, eds., *Archives of Maryland* (Baltimore, 1883–), IV, 30–33, 43–49, 73–113. Figures for 1658–1705 were computed from data supplied by the St. Mary's City Commission, Annapolis, Maryland.

land during Menard's "age of the small planter," in the late 1650s and 1660s, nearly 10 percent of those who went through probate had less than £10 in personal goods and almost 60 percent had less than £50 (see table 3). Even allowing that £50 is too much to describe someone as poor in Maryland, between 36 and 39 percent of probated decedents had less than £30.[37] In a study of six Maryland counties on the Western and Eastern shores between 1656 and 1696 Gloria Main found that 40 percent of decedents had less than £35 and about half had less than £50. It is likely that similar, or higher, proportions were to be found in parts of Virginia in the second half of the seventeenth century. Edmund Morgan cites a Virginian's estimate in the early 1660s that three-quarters of the planters "were so poor they would have to become servants to the others." This is an exaggeration, but it is a clear indication of the growing awareness of the high incidence of poverty, and its attendant problems, along the tobacco coast.[38]

37. Menard, Harris, and Carr, "Opportunity and Inequality," *Md. Hist. Mag.*, LXIX (1974). Percentages by wealth group were computed from data supplied by the St. Mary's City Commission. The figures were not deflated, because Maryland prices (as reflected in inventories) are constant before 1700.

38. Main, *Tobacco Colony*, table 2, 5, 60; Morgan, *American Slavery, American Freedom*, 225; W. Noel Sainsbury *et al.*, eds., *Calendar of State Papers, Colonial Series* (London, 1860–), *America and West Indies, 1677–1680*, 568–569, *1681–1685*, 47.

IV

The domestic environment had an enormous influence on the texture of everyday life in England and in the colonies; consequently standards of living, as revealed by probate records, suggest one facet of the gains and losses involved in settling in the Chesapeake. Slightly under five hundred inventories for the period 1660 to 1700 were used in the study of the Vale of Berkeley, which represents about 30 percent of all adult male decedents. Inventory coverage was much higher in Maryland during the second half of the seventeenth century, accounting for about 60–70 percent.[39] People at all levels of society in the Vale and other parts of England were less likely to go to the expense and trouble of having inventories drawn up for their kin, friends, or debtors. In particular, the "poorer sort" are not recorded in English probate records with anywhere near the same frequency as in Maryland.[40] This is a serious drawback when comparing wealth distribution in the two societies (because of the different nature of the probated populations), but it is less of a problem in the following analysis because sufficient inventories have survived to furnish a reliable indication of the living standards of the poor in both societies.[41]

39. Inventory coverage in the Vale of Berkeley was calculated by dividing the number of inventories by the number of deceased adult males per annum. In the case of the parish of Berkeley, the largest parish of the area, each inventoried decedent was checked off against entries in the burial registers. For a description of the procedures of probate in England, see Francis W. Steer, ed., *Farm and Cottage Inventories of Mid-Essex, 1635–1749*, 2d ed. (London, 1969), 4–8, and Richard Burn, *Ecclesiastical Law*, 2 vols. (London, 1763), II, 645–647, 651–652. The Maryland inventory figure is based on Menard, Harris, and Carr, "Opportunity and Inequality," *Md. Hist. Mag.*, LXIX (1974), 174–176, and Russell R. Menard, "The Comprehensiveness of Probate Inventories in St. Mary's County, Maryland, 1658 to 1777: A Preliminary Report," MS, St. Mary's City Commission, Annapolis, Md., 1976.

40. When calculating wealth distribution, hearth tax returns provide a more reliable guide to the extent of poverty in mid-17th-century England than probate inventories. The greater need to protect the estates of orphans and kin in the Chesapeake owing to the much higher turnover of population encouraged the Maryland Prerogative Court to supervise the accounting of estates with greater efficiency than most church courts in England. See Lois Green Carr, "The Development of the Maryland Orphan's Court, 1654–1715," in Land, Carr, and Papenfuse, eds., *Law, Society, and Politics*, 41–62.

41. To what extent do living standards represented by inventories from the Vale of Berkeley reflect the social origins of Chesapeake immigrants? Doubtless a proportion

MANY ENGLISH IMMIGRANTS from the Vale, and elsewhere, would have been profoundly dismayed by the primitive standard of housing common throughout the Chesapeake. Gloria Main estimates that two-thirds of householders in Maryland lived in dwellings of three rooms or less, and even among the top third it was rare to find houses of more than six rooms. In general, houses were notable for their "smallness" and for the "inconsequential nature of the construction methods and materials."[42] Walsh comments that the most significant features of seventeenth-century housing were "the small size and the relatively undifferentiated use of space within. Food preparation, cooking, eating, sleeping, sewing, reading, recreation, and craft activities were all carried on in one or two small rooms."[43] Another significant feature was the impermanence of Maryland dwellings. Houses were not expected to last long, perhaps no more than ten years. Cheap local materials, the demands of tobacco culture, and the ravages of the climate all contributed to the short life-span of housing in the Chesapeake.[44]

It has been suggested that despite their small size and crudeness of construction, Maryland dwellings were similar to those commonly inhabited by farm laborers and rural poor in England.[45] This is an exaggeration. Although little is known about impermanent vernacular buildings in

---

of indentured servants from the Bristol region came from a stratum of society below that of the poor described in inventories. They may have been squatters living in shacks on wastelands, on commons, or in forests, or they may have come from the poorer quarters of Bristol and neighboring large towns. Recent research, however, has shown that servants were from a broad spectrum of society, including significant numbers from farming backgrounds and skilled and semiskilled trades, as well as common laborers. It is likely therefore that the majority of servants would have been familiar with the description of housing and household goods presented in this study, not necessarily because they shared in this material culture at all levels but because they were surrounded by the physical reminders of this culture in their native communities.

42. Cary Carson *et al.*, "Impermanent Architecture in the Southern American Colonies," *Winterthur Portfolio*, XVI (1981), 135–196; Cary Carson and Lorena S. Walsh, "The Material Life of the Early American Housewife," *ibid.*, forthcoming; Main, *Tobacco Colony*, chap. 4 (quotation on p. 153); James Horn, "The Bare Necessities: Standards of Living in England and the Chesapeake, 1650–1700," *Historical Archaeology*, forthcoming.

43. Walsh, "Charles County," 251.

44. Carson *et al.*, "Impermanent Architecture," *Winterthur Portfolio*, XVI (1981); Walsh, "Charles County," 248, 252, 254.

45. Main, *Tobacco Colony*, 154–155, 254.

seventeenth-century England,[46] it is unlikely that more than a small proportion of the laboring classes or parish poor inhabited shacks and hovels associated with marginal areas.[47] There is little direct evidence of such humble structures in the Vale of Berkeley. People at the very bottom of the economic scale (worth less than £10 at death) lived in houses or lodgings of between two and five rooms; the mean was 3.3.[48] Two-thirds of the wealth group above the very poor, those worth between £10 and £50 (N = 57), lived in houses of five or more rooms. Thus persons who occupied an intermediate position between modest comfort and poverty in the Vale of Berkeley inhabited dwellings usually associated with the upper reaches of Chesapeake society. The most common type of dwelling found in the Vale was not the one- or two-room cottage but houses of between four and six rooms.[49]

Further up the social scale housing became more elaborate. The dwellings of middling and rich householders (£100–£250 and £250 +) had on average seven to ten rooms respectively. Many had similar layouts to smaller structures with the addition of a parlor, cellar, or whitehouse, as well as extra lofts. The gentry in the Vale most commonly lived in houses of eight to fifteen rooms, while the county elite invested in the

46. J. H. Bettey, "Seventeenth-Century Squatters' Dwellings: Some Documentary Evidence," *Vernacular Architecture*, XIII (1982), 28–30. See also Eric Mercer, *English Vernacular Houses: A Study of Traditional Farmhouses and Cottages* (London, 1975), chap. 2; Alan Everitt, "Farm Labourers," in Thirsk, ed., *Agrarian History of England and Wales*, IV, *1500–1640*, 442–445; J. T. Smith, "The Evolution of the Peasant House to the Late Seventeenth Century: The Evidence of Buildings," *Journal of the British Archaeological Association*, 3d Ser., XXXIII (1970), 122–146; Linda J. Hall, *The Rural Houses of North Avon and South Gloucestershire, 1400–1720* (Bristol, 1983); and N. W. Alcock, "The Great Rebuilding and Its Later Stages," *Vernacular Arch.*, XIV (1983), table 1, 47.

47. A survey of the manor of Urchfont, Wiltshire, for 1639 lists 33 cottages erected on the manorial waste since 1606. The largest cottage was 12 by 16 feet, and the smallest were 8 by 10 feet; most were 10 by 12 or 10 by 14 feet. They were probably constructed of lathe and plaster over a timber frame with a thatched roof. These dwellings were meant only as temporary refuges; they were not expected to last more than a few years. Bettey, "Seventeenth-Century Squatters' Dwellings," *Vernacular Arch.*, XIII (1983), 28, 30.

48. Only 10 of the 42 inventories in this group describe the dwelling or lodging of the decedent: 4 mention two rooms, 2 mention three rooms, 1 mentions four rooms, and 3 mention five rooms. Probate inventories, 1660–1700, GRO.

49. Decedents worth between £10 and £100 comprised the majority of the Vale of Berkeley's population. Most of them lived in dwellings of four to six rooms.

building and rebuilding of mansions, ornamental gardens, and parks carefully illustrated in Robert Atkyns's history of Gloucestershire.[50]

In short, the primitive nature of Chesapeake housing was not entirely unknown in England. Some impoverished inhabitants of forests, wastes, and other marginal areas may have lived in equally crude dwellings. More to the point, however, is the prevalence of these rudimentary structures among even relatively affluent Chesapeake planters. To put it differently, two-thirds of Maryland planters lived in dwellings of a type usually found only among the poorest sections of English society.[51]

Evidence from St. Mary's County, Maryland, suggests that the low standards of living indicated by Chesapeake housing were matched by equally low standards in domestic furnishing.[52] Barbara and Cary Carson have described the living standards of the poorer householders as "remarkably, almost unimaginably, primitive. . . . Equipment of any kind was so scarce that we must look to aboriginal cultures to find modern analogies that even approximate these pre-consumer living conditions of the seventeenth century."[53] Two examples highlight the difference between the Vale of Berkeley and St. Mary's County.

John Nelme, a yeoman of Berkeley, died in August 1697. At the time of

50. Excluding those of the gentry, the average number of rooms in the dwellings of the £100–£249 group was 7.3 compared to 9.1 of the £250+ group. See also John S. Moore, ed., *The Goods and Chattels of Our Forefathers: Frampton Cotterell and District Probate Inventories, 1539–1804* (London, 1976), table 12, 36. Extra rooms, then, do not always imply extra comfort. Larger dwellings might simply have had more storage space.

The houses of the social elite seem to have varied a great deal. Hezekiah Hewett and Timothy Hacker, described in their inventories as gentlemen, lived in dwellings with only 4 and 5 rooms respectively. At the other end of the scale, Smalcombe Court, owned by the Smyth family of North Nibley, had at least 27 rooms. The seats of the county gentry are represented in considerable detail in the engravings of Atkyns, *The Ancient and Present State of Glostershire* (London, 1712).

51. The figure is taken from Main, *Tobacco Colony*, 153.

52. Evidence from other Chesapeake counties bears out this conclusion; see Carr and Walsh, "Changing Life Styles and Consumer Behavior"; Walsh, "'Culture of Rude Sufficiency'"; Horn, "Social and Economic Aspects of Local Society," chap. 4 (for Lancaster and Northumberland, Virginia, 1650–1700); and Horn, "Bare Necessities," *Hist. Arch.*, forthcoming.

53. Barbara Carson and Cary Carson, "Styles and Standards of Living in Southern Maryland, 1670–1752" (paper presented at the annual meeting of the Southern Historical Association, Atlanta, Ga., 1976), 17.

his death his personal estate was valued at £65 13s., close to the median for all decedents from the Vale who died between 1660 and 1700. His house had six rooms: a parlor, hall, kitchen, and three chambers. In the parlor were a long table and frame with a carpet, five stools, and an old side table. One of Nelme's prized possessions stood in the hall: a clock valued at 13s. 4d. Food preparation and cooking were carried out in the kitchen, where Nelme kept his cooking equipment, tableware, and pewter. He may have occasionally eaten in the kitchen, seated at an old table. Upstairs, in the chamber over the hall, was a flock bed with a bedstead and bedding. In the best chamber stood a feather bed with bedstead, bolster, blankets, and rug. The room was furnished also with a chest, press, table, and wainscot chair, and was the only chamber that could be heated. The third chamber was more frugally furnished with a flock bed and bedstead.[54]

Nelme was fortunate in possessing a clock; not many inhabitants of the Vale at any wealth level did so. But in other respects the standard of living suggested by his household goods was similar to hundreds of other small farmers and artisans of the region.[55] It was a standard that offered few luxuries but provided the basic necessities of life.

ADAM HEAD emigrated to Maryland as a servant in 1659. He lived a long life by Chesapeake standards and died in 1698 worth £67 8s. No details are given in his inventory about his house, but it was probably the same as those inhabited by the vast majority of Maryland planters: about twenty feet long by sixteen wide and made entirely of wood. His household possessions were meager. He owned two feather beds and one flock bed with bedding, but no bedsteads. Other furniture was nonexistent. Possibly his old chest and "a parcell of old Sidr Caske" served as rudimentary tables and chairs. Cooking equipment was limited to two old iron

54. Probate inventory, John Nelme, 1697/152, GRO (the median for all decedents is £69 12s. od.). Nelme's arrangement of rooms was probably typical.

55. Published collections of inventories from Dorset, Devon, the area around Frampton Cotterell in Gloucestershire, and Essex suggest that this standard of living was common throughout southern England. See Robert Machin, ed., *Probate Inventories and Manorial Excepts of Chetnole, Leigh, and Yetminster [Dorset]* (Bristol, 1976); Margaret Cash, ed., *Devon Inventories of the Sixteenth and Seventeenth Centuries* (Torquay, 1966); Moore, ed., *Goods and Chattels*; and Steer, ed., *Farm and Cottage Inventories*.

pots and an "old Ketle." Apart from "a parcell of old pewter," an old gun, and some books, this was the sum total of his worldly goods.[56]

Nor was Head unusual in owning so little. Among the poorer planters (worth less than £10 in personalty at death) virtually all householders were without bedsteads and only two-thirds owned a proper mattress (see table 4). Those without bedding probably slept on piles of rags or straw. Over 70 percent were without purpose-made seating; they made do by using upturned barrels, pails, chests, and logs, or by simply squatting on the floor. Other common domestic furniture—tables, cupboards, benches, and forms—was almost entirely missing. Although it is possible to detect a slight improvement in the standard of living of householders who died with estates worth between £10 and £50, the largest single group of decedents in St. Mary's County in the second half of the seventeenth century, the primitiveness of domestic conditions is nevertheless striking.[57] Half the sample lacked any seating and between 70 and 80 percent were without bedsteads. Tables were to be found in about a third of households, but other furniture was much less common. As in the case of decedents worth less than £10, cooking equipment was limited in the main to an iron pot or two for boiling mush and stew and a couple of old frying pans. Between a half and two-thirds of householders owned pewter plates and dishes; the remainder used the more humble treenware. As one might expect, luxury items, with the important exception of books, were completely absent.[58]

The first substantial improvement in living conditions in St. Mary's County occurred among decedents worth between £100 and £250 at death (see table 4). At this level most people could, if they chose, sit at a table to eat their meals and sleep in beds raised off the floor on bedsteads. The great majority owned sheets as well as table linen. Furnishings were more varied. For the first time there were significant numbers of house-

56. St. Mary's City Commission, biographical files, no. 1273. Head lived 40 years in Maryland, which suggests that he died in his late fifties or early sixties. Since most men died in their early to mid-forties, Head would have been considered an old man at the time of his death. St. Mary's City Commission transcripts of St. Mary's County inventories.

57. See Carson and Carson, "Styles and Standards of Living," table 2, for similar conclusions.

58. See table 4, above; Carr and Walsh, "Changing Life Styles and Consumer Behavior"; Walsh, " 'Culture of Rude Sufficiency' "; and Main, *Tobacco Colony*, chaps. 4–7.

holders owning cupboards and chests of drawers. The incidence of non-essential items steadily increased in this group: warming pans, lighting equipment, chamber pots, books, plate, jewelry, and timepieces all became more common. Diet also appears to have been more varied. Most householders owned boiling, frying, and roasting implements, and a few had specialized utensils for preparing sauces, pastries, and fish. Almost everyone ate meals from pewter dishes, and there is more evidence of the use of knives at table.

These improvements continued among the economic elite (persons worth over £250). Ordinary furniture was present in almost every household and in greater numbers than among lower wealth groups. Elaborate case furniture—cupboards, clothespresses, writing desks, and chests of drawers—were more commonly found in the houses of the rich. Furniture was also more valuable. Capt. Joshua Doyne, who died in St. Mary's County in 1698 worth nearly £500, owned two beds with their bedsteads and "furniture" valued at £13 and a chest of drawers worth £1 10s.[59] The average value of beds, bedding, and bedsteads of all wealth groups, 1658–1705, was between £2 and £2 10s.[60] Other ordinary furniture was usually valued at between a few shillings and a pound.[61] As in England, the wealthy acquired furniture for display as well as comfort.[62]

Substantial wealth brought a greater variety of food, more comfort in dining and sleeping arrangements, and also a larger level of investment in nonessential items, particularly plate. However, despite notable differences in living standards between rich and poor planters, historians of the seventeenth-century Chesapeake have tended to stress the essential similarity of the domestic environment. "All in all," the Carsons have commented, "there was a decided sameness about material life in southern Maryland in the seventeenth century." Lorena Walsh agrees. "While families in higher wealth levels enjoyed a greater degree of comfort than did poorer households, until the end of the period [1720] most did not use personal possessions to create a markedly different way of living from

59. St. Mary's County inventories, no. 1315.

60. Mean values of beds were as follows: feather beds (N = 28), £2.75; flock beds (N = 12), £1.46; cattail beds (N = 7), £0.76; all beds (N = 62), £2.13.

61. Tables were usually valued at 2s. to 5s. (N = 29); chairs and stools at 1s. (chairs, N = 31, stools, N = 4); bedsteads at 5s. (N = 23); cupboards, clothespresses, and chests of drawers from a few shillings to over one pound (N = 22).

62. See, for example, the inventory of James Bowling, who died in 1694 worth £688. St. Mary's County inventories, no. 1067.

TABLE 4. *Distribution of Household Equipment by Wealth Group in St. Mary's County, Maryland, 1658–1699 (in Percents)*

Household Items	£0–£9 (N=15)	£10–£49 (N=134)	£50–£99 (N=98)	£100–£249 (N=67)	£250+ (N=58)
Boiling utensils	86.7	86.6	94.4	95.5	94.8
Frying utensils	53.3	53.7	64.0	67.2	72.4
Roasting utensils	6.7	24.6	44.9	73.1	77.6
Other cooking utensils	6.7	0.7	7.9	13.4	34.5
Brass	20.0	30.6	62.9	82.1	89.7
Pewter	53.3	70.9	89.9	95.5	94.8
Ironware	73.3	82.1	91.0	94.0	94.8
Earthenware and stoneware	13.3	35.1	49.4	64.2	75.9
Fine ceramics	0.0	0.0	0.0	0.0	5.2
Glassware	0.0	0.7	4.5	4.5	29.3
Knives	0.0	0.7	2.2	16.4	22.4
Forks	0.0	0.0	0.0	1.5	5.2
Spoons	26.7	29.9	23.6	29.9	44.8
Tables	6.7	34.3	52.8	88.1	89.7
Chairs	26.7	28.4	52.8	82.1	94.8
Benches and forms	0.0	11.2	32.6	41.8	34.5
Stools	0.0	9.7	10.1	22.4	31.0
Settles	0.0	0.0	0.0	0.0	1.7
Couches	6.7	9.7	30.3	38.8	34.5
No seats	73.3	55.2	30.3	10.4	1.7
Table linen	6.7	25.4	46.1	74.6	94.8
Household linen	33.3	36.6	64.0	83.6	96.6
Beds	66.7	87.3	97.8	98.5	98.3
Bedsteads	6.7	21.6	40.4	61.2	77.6
Sheets	20.0	20.1	43.8	67.2	93.1
Curtains and valances	6.7	11.2	28.1	49.3	72.4
Warming pans	0.0	5.2	20.2	35.8	62.1

TABLE 4. *(continued)*

Household Items	£0–£9 (N=15)	£10–£49 (N=134)	£50–£99 (N=98)	£100–£249 (N=67)	£250+ (N=58)
Cupboards	0.0	9.0	12.4	31.3	37.9
Clothespresses	0.0	0.0	0.0	0.0	12.1
Sideboards	0.0	0.0	1.1	3.0	5.2
Chests of drawers	0.0	0.0	6.7	11.9	36.2
Desks	0.0	2.2	3.4	9.0	15.5
Chests, trunks, and coffers	80.0	82.8	78.7	98.5	96.6
Lighting	20.0	26.9	48.3	61.2	75.9
Chamber pots and close-stools	0.0	10.4	15.7	34.3	48.3
Pictures	0.0	0.7	6.7	10.4	17.2
Books	26.7	17.2	39.3	52.2	51.7
Plate and jewelry	0.0	0.7	12.4	22.4	74.1
Clocks and watches	0.0	0.0	0.0	10.4	22.4

Source: St. Mary's City Commission transcripts of St. Mary's County inventories, 1658–1699.

their poorer neighbors."[63] Certainly the contrast in the domestic environment between the Vale of Berkeley and the tidewater is far more striking than that between different wealth groups in Maryland.

EVEN THE very poor in the Vale of Berkeley (worth less than £10) had a standard of living comparable to planters of middling wealth in the Chesapeake. Although beds and bedding at this level were cheap and unsophisticated, virtually everyone owned at least a bed, and over 80 percent had bedsteads. Most of the very poor possessed tables and seats. Over four-fifths had a table or table-board and two-thirds owned some kind of seating, most commonly in the form of chairs and stools (see table 5). Among the lower-middling wealth groups, £10–£49 and £50–

63. Carson and Carson, "Styles and Standards of Living," 17; Walsh, " 'Culture of Rude Sufficiency,' " 7–8. Barbara Carson has subsequently amended this view in "Living Habits in Seventeenth-Century Maryland" (paper presented at the Third Hall of Records Conference, "Maryland, A Product of Two Worlds," St. Mary's City, Md., 1984).

£99, ordinary domestic furniture was universal. Sideboards, presses, and chests of drawers were also to be found in their households and there was a greater readiness to invest in luxury goods. Nearly 10 percent of house-holders in the £10–£49 category and over 21 percent of the £50–£99 category possessed plate and jewelry. As householders accumulated a little wealth there was more to spare for nonessential items.

Above the lower-middling groups there was a steady, but not spectacular, rise in living standards. The proportion of middling to rich decedents (£100–£249 and £250 plus) owning the various forms of furniture item-ized in table 5 rose across the two wealth groups, but in most cases the increase was only a few percentage points. Houses of the rich were distinguished by the presence of more elaborate and expensive furnish-ings as well as by more of the ordinary types of furniture. Luxury goods were to be found in many households. Of the £100–£249 group nearly 28 percent owned plate and jewelry compared to 55 percent of the £250 plus group. Plate and jewelry were not only used for display purposes, they also provided a means of investing cash in goods that would not depreci-ate in value. Nearly half of the £250 group owned warming pans and nearly a quarter had chamber pots or close-stools. Sanitary conditions were further improved by the ubiquitous presence of household linen: sheets, tablecloths, napkins, and towels.

English men and women arriving in the Chesapeake during the seven-teenth century must have experienced considerable problems in adjusting to living conditions that were considerably lower than usual in English society. Modest wealth in Maryland (and Virginia) brought a degree of economic independence, the satisfaction of working for oneself, and landownership, but it does not appear to have brought domestic com-fort.[64] Housing was generally far more primitive along the tobacco coast than in southern and central England. In most dwellings there simply was not enough space for much furniture. Rooms served such a variety of purposes that furnishings had to be kept to a minimum or be sufficiently

64. See Main's comparison of living standards in 17th-century Maryland and Friesia, which confirms this conclusion (*Tobacco Colony*, 255–258). One area where living standards may have been better than in England was diet (see Henry M. Miller, "An Archaeological Perspective on the Evolution of Diet in the Colonial Chesapeake, 1620–1745," in this volume). Sarah F. McMahon comes to different conclusions with respect to 17th-century New England. "A Comfortable Subsistence: The Changing Composition of Diet in Rural New England, 1620–1840," *WMQ*, 3d Ser., XLII (1985), 26–65.

flexible (that is, capable of being stored away) to meet this demand. The lack of skilled craftsmen and housewrights, the abundance of timber, and the nature of plantation agriculture encouraged the development of a Chesapeake vernacular architecture characterized by "transience" or "impermanence." In England dwellings were more substantial, larger, and more complex. This in itself constituted an important difference in standards of living between the two societies.[65]

Not only were essential items of furniture such as tables, seats, beds, and bedsteads often missing from the households of many planters, but also there was an important qualitative difference in furnishings. In English inventories it is very rare for items to be described as "new" or "old" but in the Chesapeake the term "old" is commonly used. William Johnson's goods were described in 1662 as follows: "1 old brass kettle, 1 little iron pot (old), 1 little skillet full of holes, 6 old plates, 2 old pewter dishes, old pewter, 2 old corn barrels, 2 old frying pans . . . 1 old feather bed, 3 old leather chairs, 1 old trunk, 1 broken glass and trash." Similarly, nearly every item described in Thomas Nicholl's inventory or the inventory of Jacob Morris, both of St. Mary's County, is termed "old."[66]

Appraisers in Maryland and Virginia often valued items that were broken or worn out. Many of the household possessions of Capt. William Brocas of Lancaster County, who died in 1655, were described in these terms: "a parcel of old hangings, very thin and much worn," "a parcel of old Chayres, being 7, most of them Unusefull," "an old broken Cort Cupboard," "1 old rotten couch bedstead," and so on.[67] Cooking utensils and other metalwares are commonly described as "broken," "split," "crackt," or "full of holes." In the Chesapeake, old, broken, and worn goods still retained a certain value because it was sometimes cheaper to mend them, or use them for something else, than to buy new goods. Poverty was therefore reflected not only by the absence of essential furniture but also in the often poor condition of the limited range of items that were owned.

This appallingly low standard of living was the result of a combination of factors: the relatively short lives that many immigrants lived, the

65. Compare, for example, the dwellings described in Carson *et al.*, "Impermanent Architecture," *Winterthur Portfolio*, XVI (1981), with those itemized in Hall, *Rural Houses of North Avon*. See also Horn, "Bare Necessities," *Hist. Arch.*, forthcoming.

66. St. Mary's County inventories, nos. 22, 2032, 2041.

67. Lancaster County, Virginia, Deeds, Etc., No. 1, 1652–1657, 202–204, No. 2, 1654–1666, 40.

TABLE 5. *Distribution of Household Items by Wealth Group in the Vale of Berkeley, 1660–1699 (in Percents)*

Household Items	£0–£9 (N=37)	£10–£49 (N=155)	£50–£99 (N=103)	£100–£249 (N=111)	£250+ (N=74)
Boiling utensils	73.0	63.9	62.2	67.6	59.5
Frying utensils	10.8	23.2	12.6	14.4	13.5
Roasting utensils	29.7	63.2	73.8	77.5	81.1
Other cooking utensils	0.0	3.9	2.9	5.4	9.5
Brass	81.1	94.8	98.1	99.1	98.6
Pewter	83.8	96.1	98.1	96.4	98.6
Ironware	37.8	80.0	92.2	92.8	95.9
Earthenware and stoneware	0.0	9.7	8.7	11.7	14.9
Fine ceramics	0.0	0.0	0.0	0.0	0.0
Glassware	0.0	2.6	1.0	2.7	8.1
Knives	0.0	0.0	0.0	0.0	2.7
Forks	0.0	0.0	0.0	0.0	0.0
Spoons	2.7	4.5	1.9	7.2	4.1
Tables and tableboards	81.1	92.3	95.1	97.3	95.9
Table frames	35.1	52.3	48.5	61.3	62.2
Chairs	40.5	79.4	86.4	86.5	98.6
Benches and forms	40.5	63.2	77.7	74.8	71.6
Stools	24.3	61.3	62.1	78.4	85.1
Settles	10.8	21.9	22.3	27.0	43.2
Couches	0.0	0.0	0.0	0.9	5.4
Other seats	0.0	0.0	0.0	0.0	5.4
No seats	35.1	6.5	2.9	0.0	0.0
Table linen	8.1	40.6	49.5	60.4	73.0
Household linen	29.7	74.2	75.7	84.7	95.9
Beds	97.3	100.0	100.0	100.0	100.0
Bedsteads	81.1	94.2	95.1	95.5	100.0

TABLE 5. *(continued)*

Household Items	£0–£9 (N=37)	£10–£49 (N=155)	£50–£99 (N=103)	£100–£249 (N=111)	£250+ (N=74)
Sheets	29.7	47.1	45.6	40.5	54.1
Curtains and valances	0.0	13.5	23.3	27.9	40.5
Warming pans	5.4	23.9	31.1	38.7	44.6
Cupboards	29.7	33.5	40.8	37.8	39.2
Clothespresses	0.0	20.6	33.0	29.7	47.3
Sideboards	10.8	29.0	28.2	38.7	51.4
Chests of drawers	0.0	1.3	1.9	14.4	24.3
Desks	5.4	5.8	4.9	10.8	6.2
Chests, trunks, and coffers	81.1	92.3	92.2	88.3	100.0
Lighting	2.7	29.0	36.9	40.5	47.3
Chamber pots and close-stools	5.4	13.5	15.5	17.1	24.3
Pictures	0.0	0.0	0.0	1.8	4.1
Books	5.4	20.6	22.3	26.1	37.8
Plate and jewelry	0.0	9.7	21.4	27.9	55.4
Clocks and watches	0.0	1.9	6.8	13.5	28.4

Sources: Probate Inventories, 1660–1699, Gloucestershire Record Office; Prerogative Court of Canterbury Inventories, PROB 4 and 5, Public Record Office.

increasingly unfavorable economic conditions of the last third of the century, and the dependence on English merchants for manufactured goods.[68] Most poor settlers made do with crudely constructed homemade

68. Menard, Harris, and Carr, "Opportunity and Inequality," *Md. Hist. Mag.*, LXIX (1974); Menard, "Immigrants and Their Increase," in Land, Carr, and Papenfuse, eds., *Land, Society, and Politics*; Menard, "The Tobacco Industry in the Chesapeake Colonies, 1617–1730: An Interpretation," *Research in Economic History*, V (1980), 109–177.

items or "surrogate furniture" such as boxes, barrels, tubs, and chests. "Making do" in this way became a feature of everyday life, as far as the domestic environment was concerned, for many planters of lower and middling wealth in the second half of the seventeenth century.[69]

V

American historians, according to Darrett Rutman, "have waxed eloquent over the community orientation of the New Englanders and used that community orientation as a touch-phrase to distinguish New England from other regions where . . . community is discerned as much diminished or totally absent." Whereas the New England town is "the epitome of community," settlers in other colonies, particularly in the South, have been pictured as leading "hard, lonely lives on scattered farms and plantations, without community."[70] The characterization of the Chesapeake as lacking community is not merely a figment of the imagination of modern historians applying New England norms to the southern colonies. It derives in large part from contemporary criticisms. Besides constant complaints about the lack of towns, commentators were at pains to point out the dispersed nature of settlement: plantations strung out along rivers and creeks separated from one another by large areas of unbroken forest.[71] John Clayton, for example, described Virginia in 1688 as "thinly inhabited; the Living solitary and unsociable." An earlier pamphlet lamented "the great want of Christian Neighbourhood" as a consequence of settlers' "dispersed manner of Planting themselves."[72] Implicit was a contrast not with New England

69. Main uses the phrase "throwaway houses" (*Tobacco Colony*, 153). The same could be said of the "furniture."

70. Darrett B. Rutman, "The Social Web: A Prospectus for the Study of the Early American Community," in William L. O'Neill, ed., *Insights and Parallels: Problems and Issues of American Social History* (Minneapolis, Minn., 1973), 58–59.

71. Durand of Dauphiné, *A Frenchman in Virginia: Being the Memoirs of a Huguenot Refugee in 1686*, trans. Fairfax Harrison ([Richmond, Va.], 1923), 22–23; "Part of a Letter from the Rev. Mr. Hugh Jones to the Rev. Dr. Benjamin Woodroof, F.R.S., concerning several observables in Maryland," Jan. 23, 1698 [1699], LBC II (2), 250, Royal Society Archives, London; Kelly, " 'In dispers'd Country Plantations,' " in Tate and Ammerman, eds., *Chesapeake in the Seventeenth Century*; Walsh, "Charles County," 9–10.

72. Peter Force, comp., *Tracts and Other Papers, Relating Principally to the Origin,*

townships but with the hierarchy of English communities: village, town, and city. Implicit also was the belief that a society lacking community would necessarily lack order, discipline, and good government.

To what extent is it possible to detect the development of local communities in the early Chesapeake? What were their form and function? Did community ties at the local level help settlers overcome some of the everyday problems that they faced in their new environment? In what ways were local communities similar to or different from those in the mother country?

In making a comparison between local society in the Vale of Berkeley and in St. Mary's County a number of points strike one immediately. Population density in the Vale was at least twenty times greater than that of St. Mary's County during most of the second half of the seventeenth century. In 1675 the entire population of the county, about 2,200 persons, would have fit comfortably into the parish of Berkeley.[73] Half the emigrants from the Vale came from parishes with market towns: Berkeley, Thornbury, and Wotton-under-Edge. Maryland's only town was St. Mary's City, described in 1678 as consisting of "not above thirty houses, and those at considerable distances from each other."[74] Urban communities, such as contemporary Englishmen would have recognized, did not exist in Maryland or anywhere in the Chesapeake in the seventeenth century.[75]

IT IS possible to get some idea of the extent and function of the local community in the Vale of Berkeley by examining selected examples of

---

Settlement, and Progress of the Colonies in North America, 4 vols. (Washington, D.C., 1836–1846), III, no. 12, 21, no. 15, 5.

73. Population density in the Vale of Berkeley was about 130 persons per square mile in the second half of the 17th century compared to 6–7 persons per square mile in St. Mary's County. The population of Berkeley hovered around 2,000 to 2,500 inhabitants in the 17th century despite the high mortality rates of the four decades after the Restoration. See Horn, "Distribution of Wealth," *So. Hist.*, III (1981), and also P. 230 (Berkeley parish registers), GRO.

74. Sainsbury *et al.*, eds., *Calendar of State Papers, Col. Ser., America and West Indies, 1677–1680*, no. 633, 226.

75. John C. Rainbolt, "The Absence of Towns in Seventeenth-Century Virginia," *Jour. So. Hist.*, XXXV (1969), 343–360; "Part of a Letter from the Rev. Mr. Hugh Jones," LBC II (2), 253; Durand of Dauphiné, *A Frenchman in Virginia*, trans. Harrison, 90.

TABLE 6. *Place of Residence of Witnesses of Wills in the Vale of Berkeley,*
1661–1675

	No.	%
Same parish as decedent	99	59.6
Different parish	24	14.5
Unknown	43	25.9
Total	166	100.0

Sources: Wills, 1661–1675 (*N* = 63), Gloucestershire Record Office; biographical file for Vale of Berkeley compiled by the author.

social, economic, and political interaction: the places of residence of witnesses of wills and appraisers of inventories, debt-credit networks, and the role of parochial administration.[76] Table 6 shows that nearly 60 percent of witnesses of wills who could be traced were from the same parish as the testator. Only 14.5 percent were known to have come from different parishes, and in most cases these adjoined that of the decedent.[77] John Wimboll, a clothworker from Kingswood, witnessed the will of Susan Walford in 1669. "This deponent," he stated, "Liveing neare to the dwelling house of the sd. Susan Walford was sent for . . . to be a witness to . . . Susan Walford her will." In 1671 Thomas Vidler of Cromhall witnessed the nuncupative will of his "neere neighbour" Edward Goodman. And similarly, Thomas Payne of North Nibley visited his neighbor Thomas Croome "when he was sick," whereat Croome "declared his will in his presence."[78] Witnessing, and in some cases writing, a will was a task expected of friends and neighbors.

76. Jeremy Boissevain and J. Clyde Mitchell, eds., *Network Analysis: Studies in Human Interaction* (The Hague, 1973), vii–xiii, 3–35; Alan Macfarlane, Sarah Harrison, and Charles Jardine, *Reconstructing Historical Communities* (London, 1977), 10–11; Richard R. Beeman, "The New Social History and the Search for 'Community' in Colonial America," *American Quarterly*, XXIX (1977), 422–443; Darrett B. Rutman, "Community Study," *Historical Methods*, XIII (1980), 29–41; Horn, "Social and Economic Aspects of Local Society," chap. 6.

77. Wills, 1660–1700, GRO. The large proportion of unknowns is a reflection of the fact that the witnessing of wills was not a socially prestigious task and that even relatively humble persons such as servants were called to perform this service.

78. Gloucester Diocesan Registers, Nov. 26, 1669 (vol. 219), May 26, 1671 (vol. 221), Nov. 18, 1679 (vol. 232), GRO.

TABLE 7. *Place of Residence of Appraisers of Probate Inventories in the Vale of Berkeley, 1661–1665*

	No.	%
Same parish as decedent	120	79.5
Different parish	12	7.9
Unknown	19	12.6
Total	151	100.0

Sources: Probate Inventories, 1661–1665 (*N* = 52), Gloucestershire Record Office; biographical file for Vale of Berkeley compiled by the author.

Appraising inventories was also a duty commonly expected of neighbors, although mostly restricted to householders and in all cases to men. As table 7 shows, 79.5 percent of appraisers were local men from the same parish as the decedent. In large parishes, such as Berkeley, it was usual for appraisers to come from the same tithing.[79] It appears that the parish unit exerted a strong influence on the patterns of interaction. Individuals living on the borders of parishes were more likely to call upon the services of a fellow parishioner than upon a person from a neighboring community.

Debt-credit networks in the Vale confirm the local nature of interaction. Just over 70 percent of debtors during the 1660s and 1680s lived in the same, or neighboring, parish as their creditors. Thus the majority of creditors rarely lived more than a few miles from those who owed them money.[80] These findings conform to those of Wrightson and Levine for Terling, Essex, where only 16 percent of debts were contracted with persons outside the village. "Clearly financial aid of this kind was most commonly sought and found among neighbors."[81] This is a matter of some consequence, since as B. A. Holderness says, it does not appear that English rural society experienced the development of a "cadre of professional money-lenders" who monopolized the provision of credit.[82]

79. At least 58% of appraisers of Berkeley were from the same tithing as the decedent.

80. Of all inventories from 1660–1700, 55.9% mention either debts receivable or payable. Horn, "Social and Economic Aspects of Local Society," 317–326.

81. Wrightson and Levine, *Poverty and Piety*, 100.

82. B. A. Holderness, "Credit in English Rural Society before the Nineteenth

Village society was also spared the potentially disruptive influence of its credit facilities being dominated by a small group of outsiders. Instead, relationships between debtors and creditors gave coherence to the local community, even if those relationships were sometimes strained.

Reasons for the influence of the parish on the development of local community in the Vale of Berkeley are not hard to find. Despite the growth of dissent in the region after 1660, the Anglican church still retained enormous importance in the lives of most people. The vast majority were baptized, married, and buried in their local church. It served as a focus for social gatherings, festivities, and religious instruction, as well as a source of information about local and national events.[83] The parish was the principal unit of local government below county level, of far greater importance than the manor or hundred.[84] Successive Tudor and Stuart legislation had endowed the parish with extensive administrative powers. By the early seventeenth century it was the primary welfare agency in English society; everyone had a duty to contribute toward the upkeep of those who could no longer support themselves. Through its various officers the parish was in many respects of everyday life self-governing. If only a small proportion of people actually took part in the running of local affairs—probably about one in five male householders—nevertheless decisions taken by the vestry, churchwardens, and overseers of the poor affected the entire community.[85]

Century, with Special Reference to the Period 1650–1720," *Agricultural History Review*, XXIV (1976), 109.

83. Sidney and Beatrice Webb, *English Local Government from the Revolution to the Municipal Corporations Act: The Parish and the County* (London, 1906), Book II; W. E. Tate, *The Parish Chest: A Study of the Records of Parochial Administration in England* (Cambridge, 1946); Wrightson and Levine, *Poverty and Piety*, chaps. 4–6; Spufford, *Contrasting Communities*, chaps. 8–9; Christopher Hill, *Society and Puritanism in Pre-Revolutionary England* (London, 1964), 259–297.

84. Geoffrey W. Oxley, *Poor Relief in England and Wales, 1601–1834* (Newton Abbot, Devon, 1974), chap. 2; Tim Wales, "Poverty, Poor Relief, and the Life-Cycle: Some Evidence from Seventeenth-Century Norfolk," in Richard M. Smith, ed., *Land, Kinship, and Life-Cycle* (Cambridge, 1984), 351–404; Sidney and Beatrice Webb, *English Local Government: English Poor Law History*, pt. 1, *The Old Poor Law* (London, 1927); Dorothy Marshall, *The English Poor in the Eighteenth Century: A Study in Social and Administrative History* (London, 1926); John Pound, *Poverty and Vagrancy in Tudor England* (London, 1971), chap. 4; E. M. Leonard, *The Early History of English Poor Relief* (Cambridge, 1900).

85. The adult male population was between 3,600 and 4,200 in the second half of

The weight of evidence suggests that the geographical extent of the local community in the Vale was about four or five miles in radius. This area generally conformed to that of the parish or, in the case of large parishes, tithing. Particularly in the former, the community was given coherence not only by the everyday informal social and economic exchanges between people living in the same locality, but also by the church and the various duties and obligations associated with the administration of the parish. Since settlement tended to be dispersed, within the local community there existed smaller units, neighborhoods, that consisted typically of one or two dozen families living no more than a few miles from each other. North Nibley, for example, had eleven neighborhoods, or hamlets, while Berkeley was made up of a conglomeration of at least twenty different subunits in the form of chapelries, tithings, and farmsteads.[86] The neighborhood provided the locus for the most frequent and intimate relationships: visiting sick friends, loaning money or goods, spending leisure time together. In parish and neighborhood alike the role of friends and neighbors was crucial because of the relative unimportance of kin. Local community in the Vale of Berkeley, like Terling in Essex, appears to have been "little structured by ties of kinship. Its most functionally important social bond was that of neighborliness."[87]

I F K I N were relatively unimportant in giving coherence to local communities in the Vale of Berkeley, this was all the more the case in the immigrant-dominated society of seventeenth-century Maryland. The nature of immigration to the Chesapeake militated against the early development of extensive kinship networks. Family immigration was unusual; most people arrived singly as servants. High mortality rates restricted the evolution of kinship networks, and consequently, as Walsh points out, "few men and women had any kin living in Maryland, much less nearby."[88]

---

the 17th century, and the total number of officeholders was around 750, or between 17.9% and 20.8% of the total.

86. Atkyns, *Ancient and Present State of Glostershire*, 304, 139–141, 251–252, 363–364; Smyth, *Hundred of Berkeley*, passim.

87. Wrightson and Levine, *Poverty and Piety*, 109.

88. Menard, "Immigrants and Their Increase," in Land, Carr, and Papenfuse, eds., *Law, Society, and Politics*; Horn, "Servant Emigration," in Tate and Ammerman, eds., *Chesapeake in the Seventeenth Century*; Souden, " 'Rogues, whores, and vagabonds,' " *Soc. Hist.*, III (1978); Galenson, *White Servitude*; Walsh, "Charles County," 303.

In these circumstances the role of friends and neighbors in providing support and companionship was undoubtedly more critical than in England. Local communities developed early in the Chesapeake. Population density was much lower and settlement far more dispersed than in the Vale of Berkeley, but nevertheless people were not completely isolated from one another. Settlers clustered in neighborhoods near creeks and streams or around earlier settlements.[89] In the early 1660s on St. Clement's Manor, St. Mary's County, the typical household was within two and a half miles of fifteen other households, and within five to six miles of about twenty-five. Ten years later these numbers had risen to twenty-five and sixty respectively.[90] As in Surry County, Virginia, distances between neighbors "were short and easily covered by foot."[91]

In general terms, friends and neighbors in St. Mary's County fulfilled the same functions as their counterparts in England. As in the Vale of Berkeley the vital tasks of witnessing wills and appraising estates were done mostly by local people. At least two-thirds of appraisers, 1658–1675, were from the same manor or hundred as the decedent. Excluding unknowns the figure rises to 80 percent.[92] When William Harrington died in 1698 his inventory was "made before Thomas Cooke and Robert Croomes Two of the Neighbourhood."[93] Over 85 percent of witnesses of wills whose residence could be traced were from the same locality as the testator.[94] On a less formal level, neighbors, particularly women, frequently paid each other calls. Durand of Dauphiné, traveling in Virginia in 1686, commented that the women "spend most of their time visiting one another."[95]

89. Walsh, "Charles County," 294; Rutman and Rutman, *A Place in Time*, chaps. 2 and 3; Perry, "Formation of a Society," chap. 1; Kelly, " 'In dispers'd Country Plantations,' " in Tate and Ammerman, eds., *Chesapeake in the Seventeenth Century*; Lorena S. Walsh, "Community Networks in the Early Chesapeake," in this volume.

90. Carr, "Sources of Political Stability and Upheaval," *Md. Hist. Mag.*, LXXIX (1984), 45.

91. Kelly, " 'In dispers'd Country Plantations,' " in Tate and Ammerman, eds., *Chesapeake in the Seventeenth Century*, 203.

92. The sample consisted of 102 inventories and 200 appraisers. Of the latter, 65.5% were from the same manor or hundred as the decedent; 8.5% were from a neighboring manor or hundred; 7.0% were from other hundreds; and 19.0% from residences that could not be traced.

93. St. Mary's County inventories, no. 1278.

94. A sample of 50 wills from St. Mary's County, 1658–1705, gave 157 witnesses (141 males and 16 females). A third of the witnesses (53) could not be traced.

95. Durand of Dauphiné, *A Frenchman in Virginia*, trans. Harrison, 96–97.

Local economic exchanges reinforced the social links. Forty-six men and women from St. Clement's Manor who died between 1658 and 1705 owed money at death to 321 creditors. Of these, 52.6 percent lived in the same or neighboring hundred as the debtor; 19.3 percent lived in other hundreds in the county; 4.9 percent in other parts of Maryland or in England; and 23.1 percent could not be traced. Leaving out the unknowns the percentages are 68.4, 25.1, and 6.5 respectively.[96] Probably about 60 percent of debts were therefore generated within the local community (or within five miles), a figure slightly lower than that for the Vale of Berkeley.

The range and nature of social contacts within and beyond the manor have been analyzed by Lorena Walsh and Russell Menard for a number of residents in the second half of the seventeenth century.[97] Four examples, representing poor, middling, and wealthy planters, will serve to illustrate the pattern of local interaction.

Vincent Mansfield died in 1687 worth about £18. He was a longtime resident of the community and possibly the younger son of the John Mansfield who died in 1660. Twenty-four "points of interaction" have been traced for the course of his life. Obviously this represents an absolute minimum since it is impossible to chart the myriad of everyday associations that went unrecorded. Nevertheless, the more important events in his life stood a good chance of being recorded, and the range of contacts gives at least a rough impression of the social world of a small planter.[98]

Most notable is the restricted geographical extent of his world. Eighty-three percent of his contacts were within five miles of his plantation on Foster's Neck, and all of these were fellow residents of the manor. Nearly half were in easy walking distance, that is to say, less than two miles away. The nature of his contacts varied considerably. He was related through marriage to two of his neighbors, Richard Foster and John Tennison; served on a number of manor court juries; appraised the estates of a couple of neighbors; worked for a local big planter; entered into a debt

96. St. Mary's County inventories, 1658–1705; St. Mary's City Commission debt files.

97. I am indebted to Lorena S. Walsh and Russell R. Menard for permission to use their unpublished research on St. Clement's Manor.

98. Maps that illustrate the range of interaction of Mansfield and other residents of St. Clement's Manor are available at the Maryland State Archives, Annapolis, and belong to the St. Mary's City Commission.

with a resident merchant. His few excursions beyond the manor involved him in fighting Indians at Susquehanna Fort in 1676 and acting as an Indian interpreter at a Council meeting in St. Mary's City.

Peter Mills, a middling planter-cum-carpenter, lived on the manor between 1653 and 1667 before moving to Newtown Hundred, where he eventually died in 1685. Like Mansfield, the range of his social world was very limited: 89 percent of his contacts were within five miles of his residence. Again, these took the form of routine tasks such as serving as a juror on the manor court, witnessing wills, appraising estates, and loaning money. Interestingly, although he spent most of his life in Newtown Hundred he appears to have maintained close ties with neighbors of his former residence at Mills Birch on St. Clement's Manor.[99]

Large planters, such as William Brittaine and Luke Gardiner, present a different pattern of interaction. In both cases the pull of ties beyond the locality was much stronger than with Mills or Mansfield. Only about half the contacts of either man fell within a five-mile radius of his home. The main reason for this was that both men were frequently called away from the community to serve in public offices. They also had more extensive kinship and friendship networks than their less wealthy neighbors. Even so, both had important and close ties with the locality where they lived. Brittaine's residence at Little Bretton's developed as a focal point of the area, especially after a Roman Catholic church was built there in the early 1660s. Luke Gardiner, too, was intimately involved in the affairs of St. Clement's Manor as his many disputes with neighbors testify.

IN MARYLAND informal, rather than formal, ties tended to give the local community coherence and link it to the wider society. The absence of a parochial administration and an established church meant that the most important agency of local government was at county level.[100] Since the populations of most counties in Maryland during the second half of the seventeenth century did not exceed those of the larger parishes in the Vale of Berkeley, this lack is not so striking as first appears. However, in view of the greater distances involved in Maryland, local community was

99. Possibly he kept his plantation on the manor after moving to Newtown Hundred.

100. Lois Green Carr, "County Government in Maryland, 1689–1708" (Ph.D. diss., Harvard University, 1968); Carr, "The Foundations of Social Order: Local Government in Colonial Maryland," in Bruce C. Daniels, ed., *Town and County: Essays on the Structure of Local Government in the American Colonies* (Middletown,

not synonymous with local government. Residents of local communities such as St. Clement's Manor had to send their representatives to the seat of government, St. Mary's City, to ensure that their wishes were heard. The absence of parish administration necessitated the county court absorbing the duties usually attached to the vestry. Thus few decisions concerning the local community were made by a group of men *all* resident in the community itself. Poor relief, the care of orphans, the maintenance of highways, taxation, and various other aspects of local administration were matters decided at county level.[101] Local government was largely external to the local community in Maryland (unlike Virginia) as far as the decision-making process was concerned.

Despite the lack of administrative and religious institutions that would have reinforced the sense of community at the local level in Maryland, it is nevertheless impressive, considering the problems posed by the environment, that English settlers were able to re-create some aspects of community life as they had experienced it in the mother country. Demographic disruption and low population density were not so severe as to prevent family formation or the development of small clusters of households in neighborhoods. In both societies friends and neighbors, rather than kin, provided company and recreation, lent money, helped in periods of crisis, and carried out various official duties. They, not kin, were crucial to the existence of the community. The geographical range of links between individuals appears to have been about the same in the two societies: five miles with respect to the local community and one or two miles in the case of neighborhoods. Daily contact was difficult beyond these limits, whether in the Vale of Berkeley or southern Maryland. Thus

---

Conn., 1978), 72–110; Robert Wheeler, "The County Court in Colonial Virginia," *ibid.*, 111–133; Walsh, "Charles County," chap. 4; Carr, "Sources of Political Stability and Upheaval," *Md. Hist. Mag.*, LXXIX (1984), 44–70. See also Walsh, "Community Networks," and Michael Graham, "Meetinghouse and Chapel: Religion and Community in Seventeenth-Century Maryland," in this volume.

101. Carr, "Foundations of Social Order," in Daniels, ed., *Town and County*; Carr, "Sources of Political Stability and Upheaval," *Md. Hist. Mag.*, LXXIX (1984); Walsh, "Charles County," chap. 4. For a comparison with Virginia, see Wheeler, "County Court in Colonial Virginia," in Daniels, ed., *Town and County*; William H. Seiler, "The Anglican Church: A Basic Institution of Local Government in Colonial Virginia," *ibid.*, 134–159; C. G. Chamberlayne, ed., *The Vestry Book of Christ Church Parish, Middlesex County, Virginia, 1663–1767* (Richmond, Va., 1927); and Rutman and Rutman, *A Place in Time.*

in stressing the myriad of informal ties, which acted as a form of social cement within the community, a much stronger impression is gained of the similarities and continuities between everyday life in rural England and in the Chesapeake.

VI

Emigration to the New World involved many sacrifices. Most immigrants would never again see their native country, old friends, and kin. A significant proportion died young, within the first two years of arrival. Those who survived seasoning had a life-span ten years shorter on average than adults in England. Owing to the relative shortage of women, and because most immigrants arrived as servants, many men were denied the opportunity to marry or married late. Parents rarely survived to see their children attain adulthood. Consequently, early Chesapeake society took on a transient quality.[102]

In trying to put down roots in their new society settlers therefore faced considerable problems. The two aspects of everyday life examined in this essay illustrate their difficulties and achievements. In general they were unable to re-create a standard of domestic comfort that would have been considered usual in most parts of central and southern England. Housing was far more primitive and furnishings either entirely missing, old, or worn out. Immigrants, such as those from the Vale of Berkeley, would have had to adjust to a standard of living found only among the poorest levels of English society. Yet, in other respects colonists had more success. Chesapeake society did not consist of scattered, isolated plantations completely cut off from one another. During the second half of the seventeenth century, communities, focused on old centers of settlement or natural features, began to coalesce throughout the tobacco coast. The local community provided the same sort of support to individuals as in

102. Walsh and Menard, "Death in the Chesapeake," *Md. Hist. Mag.*, LXIX (1974); Walsh, " 'Till Death Us Do Part,' " in Tate and Ammerman, eds., *Chesapeake in the Seventeenth Century*; Rutman and Rutman, " 'Now-Wives and Sons-in-Law,' " *ibid.*; Menard, "Immigrants and Their Increase," in Land, Carr, and Papenfuse, eds., *Law, Society, and Politics*; J. P. P. Horn, "Moving On in the New World: Migration and Out-Migration in the Seventeenth-Century Chesapeake," in Peter Clark and David Souden, eds., *Migration and Society in Early Modern England* (London, 1987), 172–212.

England. Similarities in terms of geographical extent and function are striking. Thus English attitudes and expectations, as far as daily life in the locality was concerned, appear to have been adopted and adapted to suit the new conditions in the Chesapeake.

There can be little doubt that the environment and the nature of English immigration played a crucial role in the development of Chesapeake society and caused it to be different in many respects from that of England.[103] However, in recognizing these differences it is vital not to lose sight of the continuities between life in the two societies and the part played by English traditions and values in helping to shape colonial society. In this sense Chesapeake society was emphatically a product of two worlds.

103. Walsh, "Charles County," 7.

Henry M.   An Archaeological
Miller   Perspective on the
             Evolution of Diet in the
             Colonial Chesapeake,
             1620–1745

IN RECENT DECADES, the story of everyday
life has increasingly assumed center stage in history. The focus of historians has shifted from prominent figures and great public events to underlying cultural, economic, and social processes. One area of concentration
is the material conditions of life. Diet is critical to any such investigation.
Subsistence was a direct indicator of living standards and of the health
and mortality of settlers. It must also be central to any attempt to recover
the style of life of Chesapeake colonists.

Although historical documents provide information on the types of
livestock, the crops, and some of the preserved foods that were used by
the colonists, such documents do not permit an evaluation of the total
diet. They do not provide, for example, precise data on the relative
importance of various types of domestic animals nor do they measure the
significance of wild foods. Fortunately, archaeological research can, because excavators retrieve the actual remains of foods eaten by the early
settlers. When archaeological information is used in concert with historical data, a richer and more comprehensive understanding of the colonial
diet is obtained.

This essay presents the results of the first large-scale analysis of animal
remains from sites in the Chesapeake region. Using archaeological sam-

Many individuals provided assistance with this research, but the following persons
deserve special thanks: Keith Egloff, Charles Fithian, Susan Hanna, William Kelso,
Julia King, Nick Luckketti, Fraser Neiman, James O'Connor, Alain Outlaw, Merry
Outlaw, Garry Wheeler Stone, and Lorena Walsh. Joanne Bowen Gaynor and Michael Barber generously permitted use of their faunal reports on the Clifts and the
Maine sites. Finally, Lois Green Carr has contributed with her advice, enthusiasm,
and openness to new research perspectives.

ples dated between c. 1620 and c. 1745, the analysis provides an initial assessment of how the diet changed during the colonization of the tidewater Chesapeake.[1] Meat is the appropriate focus of this investigation because it was a central element of the traditional British diet and because meat consumption carried a high cultural value. Indeed, it has been argued that in Britain "the standard of living was judged to a considerable extent by the amount of meat eaten";[2] in all likelihood, early settlers brought these cultural attitudes to the Chesapeake. Although plants were also of great importance in the colonial diet, their role is more difficult to evaluate. Except for corn and beans, references to plants are rare in documents from the region, and there are few archaeological data currently available.

What evidence about the meat diet does the historical record provide? Although much information can be gleaned from letters, travelers' observations, and other accounts, these records are generally impressionistic. Colonial estate inventories provide the best source of quantifiable data. Examined here are a group of inventories from St. Mary's County, Maryland, drawn from two periods, 1638–1705 and 1720–1740.[3] Such a long sample period should reflect the full range of subsistence changes associated with colonization.

The presence, and more particularly the distribution, of livestock in seventeenth-century inventories is one clue to the composition of the Chesapeake diet. As figure 1 reveals, the proportion of households possessing cattle increased dramatically between the 1640s and the 1660s.

---

1. This article is based upon my dissertation, *Colonization and Subsistence Change on the Seventeenth-Century Chesapeake Frontier* (Michigan State University, 1984). The term *colonization*, as used here, does not refer only to the short-term phenomenon of establishing settlements. It is defined more broadly as a cultural process by which immigrant peoples slowly adapt to the new physical and social environment encountered on a frontier. See Stephen I. Thompson, *Pioneer Colonization: A Cross-Cultural View* (Reading, Mass., 1973).

2. J. C. Drummond and Anne Wilbraham, *The Englishman's Food: A History of Five Centuries of English Diet* (London, 1958), 102.

3. This group of inventories has served as the basis for several previous studies, including Russell R. Menard, P. M. G. Harris, and Lois Green Carr, "Opportunity and Inequality: The Distribution of Wealth on the Lower Western Shore of Maryland, 1638–1705," *Maryland Historical Magazine*, LXIX (1974), 169–184, and Lois Green Carr and Lorena S. Walsh, "Changing Life Styles in Colonial St. Mary's County," Regional Economic History Research Center, *Working Papers*, I, no. 3 (1978), 72–118.

Swine ownership, which was universal in the 1640s, declined significantly in the early 1660s but rose again later in the decade.[4] Throughout the rest of the century about eight out of ten estates possessed swine, whereas cattle ownership was almost universal. Sheep were rare during the first decades of settlement, but their appearance in inventories increased markedly during the 1680s and the 1690s. In short, livestock composition apparently changed significantly over the course of the century, which should be reflected in the archaeological record.

Because preserved foods were specifically intended for consumption, they provide more-direct evidence of colonial diet than does livestock. A study of probate inventories in Massachusetts has revealed the significance and changing proportions of vegetables and dairy products in the diet of New England colonists.[5] Regrettably, such an analysis is not possible in the Chesapeake because the region's estate appraisers seldom noted either dairy products or preserved plants other than grains and legumes. Appraisers often exempted a year's provisions for the family from inventories, and they almost never listed perishables. Nevertheless, Chesapeake inventories do contain some relevant data about this part of the settlers' diet.

Of the 765 household inventories examined, two-thirds do not refer to any preserved foods. Foods listed in the remaining third of the estates are summarized in table 1. Preserved meat is noted occasionally, pork twice as often as beef. Lamb, mutton, and veal never appear, probably because these meats were consumed only when fresh. The rarity of beef is surprising since nearly every household owned cattle after the first decades of settlement. Probably most beef was also eaten fresh, an idea supported, as we shall see, by the archaeological findings. Dairy equipment such as milk pans, cheese vats, and butter pots are referred to increasingly over

4. Although the reasons for the drop in swine ownership in the early 1660s are still unclear, the other downward fluctuations in livestock can be explained. The decline of cattle and swine in the early 1670s is related to a major plague that killed thousands of animals (Wesley Frank Craven, *The Southern Colonies in the Seventeenth Century, 1607–1689* [Baton Rouge, La., 1949], 376). In the late 1690s, severe cold weather claimed thousands of swine and cattle. William Hand Browne et al., eds., *Archives of Maryland* (Baltimore, 1883–), XX, 269–270.

5. Sarah F. McMahon, "A Comfortable Subsistence: The Changing Composition of Diet in Rural New England, 1620–1840," *William and Mary Quarterly*, 3d Ser., XLII (1985), 26–65.

FIGURE I. *Livestock Holdings in St. Mary's County, Maryland, 1638–1705*

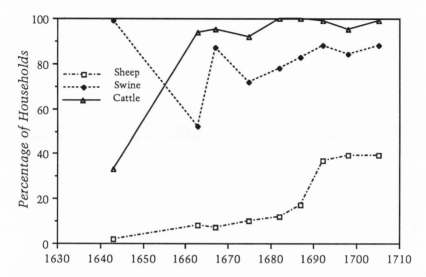

time, an indication that planters' wives processed milk for family use. However, dairy products are seldom mentioned, probably because milk, cream, and uncured cheeses were too perishable to inventory and making butter was very time consuming. Cured cheese and cheese presses are rarely listed.

Inventories almost never mention wild food. Preserved fish appears only twice in the 765 inventories. A seventeenth-century estate lists forty pounds of "Salt Fish," but it may have been imported since the household was that of a merchant. The other inventory, taken in 1733, includes a supply of seventy-five pounds of salt fish. No meat from wild game is recorded in any inventory, although animal skins are sometimes listed.

Grains are the most frequently mentioned food. Maize, or "Indian Corn," is the most common, occurring in 80 percent of those that specify food items. European grains are much less frequently noted, but of these, wheat and oats predominate. Beans are the second most commonly listed foodstuff, with peas occasionally mentioned. Wheat and legumes appear in increasing frequencies over time. The only other vegetables ever mentioned are pumpkins, in two 1640s inventories, and pickles, in a 1727 inventory. Sweeteners (sugar, molasses, and honey) are sometimes listed.

TABLE I. *St. Mary's County, Maryland, Inventories with Specific Foods (in Percents)*

	No.	Meat	Corn	Wheat	Other Grains	Beans/ Peas	Sweet- eners
1638–1647	17	5.8	88.0	0	5.8	5.8	17.6
1660s	18	11.1	72.2	11.0	5.5	11.1	16.6
1670s	22	36.0	77.0	9.0	4.5	13.6	18.1
1680s	41	19.5	80.0	29.0	21.9	19.5	9.7
1690s	15	26.6	93.0	26.6	20.0	26.6	11.1
1720s	38	23.6	73.6	44.7	10.5	26.3	31.9
1730–1745	60	43.3	76.6	36.6	1.6	40.0	18.0

Source: St. Mary's City Commission inventory file for St. Mary's County.

Apple cider is the only fruit product identified in these documents.[6] Other records provide some evidence that a few traditional European vegetables (cabbages, carrots, and onions, for example) were grown, along with New World plants such as squash, but in the absence of inventory listings, no quantifiable data are available to estimate their importance.[7] Thus, while corn and beans apparently were mainstays of

6. The sample of household inventories includes 334 from the period 1638–1705 and 431 from 1720–1745. In the 17th-century group, 218 (65.26%) lack food, beverages, or sweeteners. This percentage is even higher in the 18th-century sample, where 312 inventories (72.38%) lack foodstuffs. In the 17th-century sample, 13 list preserved pork but only 6 list beef. The 18th-century inventories reveal a similar pattern with 24 listings of pork and 12 references to beef. In each period, 7 households had unspecified meat on hand.

7. Thomas Glover, *An Account of Virginia . . .* (Oxford, 1904; orig. publ. 1676), 16. Most travelers were not impressed with the colonists' kitchen gardens. In 1679, a Dutch visitor reported that "a few vegetables are planted, but they are of the coarsest kinds and are cultivated in the coarsest manner, without knowledge or care" (*Journal of Jasper Danckaerts, 1679–1680*, ed. Bartlett Burleigh James and J. Franklin Jameson [New York, 1913], 134). A Swiss visitor at the beginning of the 18th century shared this view and noted that "the inhabitants pay little attention to garden plants, except lettuce." W. J. Hinke, trans. and ed., "Report of the Journey of Francis Louis Michel from Berne, Switzerland, to Virginia, October 2, 1701–December 1, 1702," *Virginia Magazine of History and Biography*, XXIV (1916), 32.

the vegetable diet, the importance of garden products and wild plants must remain an open question.[8]

To summarize, the inventories suggest that the meat diet did change during the seventeenth century. Swine were apparently more available than cattle during the early decades, and sheep were rare. In the second half of the century, cattle became far more numerous and sheep became more common on plantations. While fresh beef must have been widely available, pork is more frequently listed as a preserved meat.[9] In households with dairying equipment, milk, uncured cheese, and perhaps a little butter must have been a regular part of the diet.

Another perspective on colonial subsistence is provided by animal remains from twenty-four separate households on seventeen sites in tidewater Maryland and Virginia. These sites are concentrated in two areas—the lower Potomac River, especially around St. Mary's City, and the James River, particularly near Jamestown. For purposes of analysis, the samples are divided into three time periods: 1620–1660; 1660–1700; and 1700–1745. Most of these sites were plantations, although a sample from an ordinary is also included (see appendix 1). All the faunal samples come from well-dated sealed deposits. They are dated to a short time range, usually plus or minus ten years, on the basis of the associated artifacts and stratigraphic evidence.[10]

WHAT DO the animal bones from the earliest sites reveal about diet during the first decades of settlement? One of the most striking features is

8. The study of plant remains from sites will provide more information on this subject. Traces of corn, beans, squash, peach seeds, walnut shells, and hickory-nut fragments have been identified in 17th-century deposits so far, but the analysis of floral and pollen samples is just beginning. Eventually, enough data will be collected to identify the plants consumed and estimate their relative importance.

9. Evidence for higher beef consumption has been found in the analysis of the Robert Cole Account by Lois Green Carr. This yearly guardian account of the Cole estate covers the period 1662–1673 and permits a yearly reconstruction of the live-stock slaughtered on one Maryland plantation. It indicates that beef formed a larger portion of the diet than pork. Lois Green Carr, "Livestock Increase and Its Implications for Diet in the Seventeenth-Century Chesapeake," MS, St. Mary's City Commission, 1982.

10. Summary data on each of these sites are presented in appendix 1. A brief discussion of the analytic methods used in the study of animal remains is provided in appendix 2.

the variety of species, indicating that the colonists ate a diversity of animals. Some were domestic animals, especially cattle, swine, and chickens, but the bones of wild animals were found on every early site and in greater abundance than the remains of the domestic species. Indeed, the variety of wild resources exploited is exceptional and includes many animals not considered edible today. The largest wild beast consistently eaten was the white-tailed deer, but smaller mammals such as raccoons, gray and fox squirrels, and opossums were also popular. People ate a diversity of wildfowl, including land-oriented birds such as quails and turkeys and waterfowl such as Canada geese, canvasback, mallard, and redhead ducks, blue- and green-winged teals, loons, coots, and even double-crested cormorants.

The waters of the Chesapeake yielded an abundance of seafood that became a standard element of the early colonial diet. Popular types of fish included black drum, red drum, sheepshead, striped bass, white perch, catfish, sturgeon, and longnose gar. Colonists also commonly ate oysters, blue crabs, and aquatic turtles. Archaeologists have recovered the remains of snapping turtles, cooters, diamondback terrapins, and even Atlantic loggerheads. Most numerous, however, are fragments of the common box turtle, which could have been easily collected in the forests and along the streams of the Chesapeake region.

Evaluation of the relative significance of each of these species in the diet can be accomplished by determining the number of animals present and estimating the amount of meat they provided. This complex procedure, conducted for all sites, is revealing. Domestic animals were clearly of great importance from the early decades of settlement, but surprisingly it is beef, not pork, that accounts for the majority of the meat. Traditionally, historians have assigned to swine the central role in the colonial diet,[11] as the earliest inventories also suggest, but this was true at only one site—the Maine. Tenants of the Virginia Company occupied this dwelling, the earliest site in the study, from c. 1618 to c. 1626. Swine account for nearly 40 percent of the estimated meat here while cattle make up only 25 percent of the total.[12] But at the other early sites, beef dominates. This finding challenges a basic assumption about the early American diet.

11. The idea that pork was the major meat has long been accepted. See Richard Osborn Cummings, *The American and His Food: A History of Food Habits in the United States* (Chicago, 1940), and Craven, *Southern Colonies*, 212.

12. In the earliest sample, excluding the Maine site, beef accounts for an average of 48% of the estimated meat (range 41% to 57%). Pork averages 21.7% of the meat

Sheep bones are rare on the early sites, a finding that corresponds to information obtained from inventories. This sparsity of sheep remains stands in sharp contrast to bone assemblages from Britain, in which sheep usually predominate. Contemporary accounts suggest that predators, especially wolves, were a major problem in the early Chesapeake.[13] Archaeologists discovered dramatic evidence of such predation at the St. John's site in St. Mary's City, where they uncovered a sheep burial dating to the 1640s. Most of the hind quarters of this animal are missing, and the nature of the surviving bones suggests that she was killed and partially eaten by wolves.[14] Careful shepherding might have warded off wolves, but in a labor-short frontier economy that emphasized a cash crop, manpower could not be spared to protect vulnerable livestock.

Wild animals made a major contribution to the diet during the early decades of settlement, accounting for as much as 40 percent of the meat. While usage varied between households, wild species consistently provided from one-quarter to one-third of the meat eaten. This is a major finding, for until now it has not been possible to estimate the overall significance of wild meats in seventeenth-century subsistence.

Nearly every household consumed deer, small mammals, wildfowl, and turtles, but the use of fish was less uniform. This variation is directly

---

(range 11% to 35%). Not only is the Maine sample the earliest in the study, but it was occupied during and after the 1622 massacre. This event probably had a significant impact upon the food available to the tenants. For a discussion of food shortages at this time, see Edmund S. Morgan, *American Slavery, American Freedom: The Ordeal of Colonial Virginia* (New York, 1975), 102–105.

13. Among the British faunal studies are Barbara Noddle, "The Animal Bones," in *Excavations in Medieval Southampton, 1953–1969*, ed. Colin Platt *et al.* (Leicester, 1975), I, 332–340; R. E. Chaplin and Linda Barnetson, "The Animal Bones," in "Excavations at St. Mary's Street, Edinburgh," *Post-Medieval Archaeology*, XIV (1980), 157–184; and Philip Armitage, "The Faunal Remains," in "Excavations at Aldgate, 1974," *ibid.*, XVIII (1984), 131–145. The prevalence of predators in the Chesapeake is indicated by legislation authorizing wolf bounties in both colonies, as well as by statements in Glover, *Account of Virginia*, 19, and in *The Reverend John Clayton, A Parson with a Scientific Mind: His Scientific Papers and Other Related Papers*, ed. Edmund Berkeley *et al.* (Charlottesville, Va., 1965), 106.

14. This sheep was a pregnant ewe, found with the remains of two lambs still within her. She was probably one of a flock given to Lord Baltimore by Richard Kemp of Virginia in 1638 and kept at St. John's by John Lewger. He wrote in 1641 that several of the flock had been killed by wolves. Browne *et al.*, eds., *Archives of Maryland*, IV, 277–278.

related to water salinity in the Chesapeake Bay. Marine species, such as the drums, are found only in high-salinity waters while other species, such as the catfish, occupy low-saline and fresh waters. Consequently, the location of plantations determined the types of fish colonists could eat. This is significant because of the prominence of fish in the diet of the people living along the Chesapeake Bay and lower sections of the rivers. There planters concentrated upon bottom-dwelling fish such as sheepsheads and drums, which were large, abundant, and easy to procure. One seventeenth-century observer noted that "a planter does oftentimes take a dozen or fourteen [sheepshead] in an hours time, with hook and line."[15] In contrast, settlers in the low-saline water zones, such as those near Jamestown, ate catfish, white perch, and other small species, but overall, fish appear to have been less important in their diet. These colonists had regular access to only one large species, the sturgeon. Not surprisingly, they exploited it far more intensively than did planters dwelling nearer the Chesapeake Bay.

How was the consumption of these animals distributed over the year? Did the colonists enjoy a reasonably uniform diet from month to month or was it highly seasonal in character? Seasonal variations can be identified through analysis of trash deposits that date to the same general period and were filled over a relatively brief time span. The presence or absence of various seasonal indicators such as crab, migratory waterfowl, and fish, together with stratigraphic evidence, permits us to estimate the season of deposition.

Study of these discrete deposits from sites in Virginia and Maryland reveals striking differences in bone content and the estimated meat frequencies. Some pits contain mostly wild or domestic bones while other deposits yield a mixture of both. Table 2 shows how bone frequencies varied between five different pits at one of the sites studied, Kingsmill Tenement, occupied between c. 1625 and c. 1650.

An examination of seasonal indicators reveals that these trash deposits were created at different times of the year. This evidence suggests that the annual subsistence cycle of the early colonists was as follows. In the winter and early spring, settlers relied upon domestic beef and pork, much of it probably fresh, along with some deer, raccoons, and oysters. Colonists also hunted migratory waterfowl. As spring gave way to summer, colonists relied more on wild resources. Although deer and small

15. Glover, *Account of Virginia*, 5.

TABLE 2. *Composition of Animal Bones in Trash Pits at the Kingsmill Tenement Site (in Percents)*

	Pit A	Pit B	Pit C	Pit D	Pit E
Mammal	97.30	83.74	12.14	67.88	100.00
Bird	1.67	7.88	24.80	2.65	0
Fish	0.46	4.43	54.70	15.56	0
Turtle	0.55	3.94	8.35	13.90	0
	99.98	99.99	99.99	99.99	100.00
No. of bones	1,077	203	261	302	148
Estimated deposition period	Late Fall/ Winter	Early Spring	Late Spring/ Summer	Summer/ Early Fall	Winter

mammals remained important, fish became especially prominent. In the summer, domestic species, particularly cattle, contributed significantly less to the diet than during the early spring. Heavy usage of wild animals continued into autumn, when migratory waterfowl again provided food. In November or December, with cold weather, colonists shifted back to domestic meats. This was the traditional time for slaughter of livestock in Britain, a practice that apparently continued in the Chesapeake. During this portion of the year, deer was the only wild animal of major significance consumed, although the colonists ate some waterfowl and perhaps an occasional raccoon.

Given this general dietary pattern, were there any differences in meat consumption between the homes of poor to middling planters and the elite? The archaeological data suggest significant variations. At the two known tenant sites—the Maine and Kingsmill Tenement—swine compose 39 percent and 36 percent, respectively, of the total estimated meat. At the home of a middling planter at Bennett Farm and on the elite sites of the Calvert House and St. John's in St. Mary's City, however, pork accounts for less than 20 percent of the total meat. Beef makes up the largest proportion of the meat at all sites except the Maine, but tenant households consumed more pork than other households.

Exploitation of deer also distinguishes the wealthiest homes from the others. This animal accounts for 31 percent of the total meat at St. John's (the highest figure for any site) and makes up nearly 25 percent of the meat at the residence of Maryland's first governor, Leonard Calvert. In comparison, venison accounts for 7 percent of the meat at Kingsmill Tenement and only 6 percent at Bennett Farm. A likely explanation is that John Lewger, who lived at St. John's, Leonard Calvert, and other wealthy planters in early Maryland and Virginia had the means to employ professional hunters.[16] Venison, a meat consumed only occasionally by the elite in Britain, could thus serve as a mainstay in the diet of these colonists. Tenants or small planters, on the other hand, did not have the economic means to hire a hunter in the labor-starved early Chesapeake and, even if they owned guns, probably lacked the time to systematically hunt deer.

In summary, domestic animals were of importance in the early diet, but so were a variety of wild species. The colonists tended to exploit a wide diversity of animals in a seasonal pattern with a subsistence strategy that was highly eclectic. That they utilized a range of resources instead of concentrating on a few species is not surprising. A reliance upon many different foods provides greater nutritional security in an unfamiliar environment, where the failure of one resource can be compensated for by exploiting others.[17]

DID SUCH a dietary pattern continue into the late seventeenth century? With the development of a more stable society, a larger human population, and a likely depletion of some natural resources, it seems improbable that subsistence practices continued unaltered. Archaeological data from later sites confirm this hypothesis.

Two related trends are apparent: the growing importance of domestic mammals in the diet and the decline in consumption of wild animals. On sites from the 1660–1700 period, cattle account for a larger portion of the bones and beef increases to 65 percent of the estimated meat, compared to 44 percent in the first part of the century. Swine remain about the same in importance, but sheep begin to appear consistently and account for a

16. Browne *et al.*, eds., *Archives of Maryland*, III, 143; "Lower Norfolk County Records, 1636–1646," *VMHB*, XL (1932), 136; Raphael Semmes, *Captains and Mariners of Early Maryland* (Baltimore, 1937), 12.

17. See Charles E. Cleland, "The Focal-Diffuse Model: An Evolutionary Perspective on Prehistoric Cultural Adaptations in the Eastern United States," *Mid-Continental Journal of Archaeology*, I (1976), 57–67.

larger portion of the meat than during the early decades. Inventory analysis suggested this increase in food from cattle and sheep, and the faunal remains confirm it. Domestic fowl occur in low but persistent frequencies at all sites.

At the same time, colonists were eating fewer wild animals. Most planters still ate deer, small mammals, and waterfowl during this period, but wild foods in total account for about 10 percent of the meat consumed. The findings indicate that deer hunting was no longer as important for wealthy households, perhaps reflecting the depletion of deer populations.[18] The same fish species remained part of the diet but were less significant. Fish bone, as a proportion of the total bone recovered, declines from an average of 35 percent in the early period to 20 percent in the second half of the century. Overall, there is less variation among these samples than appeared in the pre-1660 sites, suggesting greater uniformity in the meat diet throughout the Chesapeake region.

Despite this apparent uniformity, the procedure of combining data from all sites to look at general trends may conceal important differences related to wealth. Indeed, greater variation between sites through time can be predicted, since social stratification became more pronounced, opportunity declined for middling and small planters, and resources became less available.

Two sites quite suitable for testing this proposition have been excavated along the James River, just downstream from Jamestown. Both were occupied during the second half of the seventeenth century, and the archaeological samples date to that period. Pettus Plantation was the home of a major planter and member of the Virginia elite.[19] The excavated foundations indicate a very large house with a ground-floor area of some 2,500 square feet. Artifacts found on the site include many elegant and specialized ceramics, among them Chinese porcelain. One-half mile

18. There are few data on wildlife depletion in the colonial Chesapeake. Hugh Jones wrote in 1724, "Their venison in the lower parts of the country is not so plentiful as it has been, though there be enough and tolerably good; but in the frontier counties they abound with venison, wild turkies, etc." (Hugh Jones, *The Present State of Virginia*, ed. Richard L. Morton [Chapel Hill, N.C., 1956], 79). Hunting may have reduced the deer population. On the other hand, the shifting-field agricultural method used by planters probably tended to increase the numbers of deer because it created an ideal deer habitat. Further study of the colonists' impact on wildlife is needed.

19. For further discussion of these sites, see William M. Kelso, *Kingsmill Plantations, 1619–1800: Archaeology of Country Life in Colonial Virginia* (Orlando, Fla., 1984).

away lies the site of Utopia. Tenants apparently occupied this house, on land owned by Thomas Pettus. The building had a ground-floor area one-fifth the size of the Pettus house. Artifacts include plain locally made earthenware, few specialized vessels, and no porcelain. Clearly, there were pronounced differences between these sites in the status of the occupants, the architectural remains, and the domestic artifacts.

Species found at each site are similar, among them cattle, swine, sheep, chickens, turkeys, deer, raccoons, opossums, and cooter turtles. More fish were found at Utopia, suggesting that this resource may have been of somewhat greater importance there. Otherwise, the two samples are remarkably comparable. The frequencies of bones from the major species at the sites are also very much alike. Swine bones are slightly more abundant at Pettus, but not significantly.

Bone counts do not necessarily indicate dietary significance, however. While cattle and squirrel bones may occur in equal numbers, one cow would obviously provide several hundred times the meat of a squirrel. To overcome this problem, the number of individual animals present and the meat available from each species were calculated. The results, presented in figure 2, reveal nearly identical patterns; most of the meat is beef and just over one-quarter of the total is pork. Sheep and wild animals are only of minor importance.

This striking similarity in bone and meat frequencies is unexpected, given the other differences known to exist between these sites. Was there a difference in the quality of cuts consumed? To investigate this question, the bones from cattle and swine were divided into high- and low-quality meat cuts and the frequencies determined. The results show that for cattle, high-quality meat bones dominate at both sites. Only a small amount of variation occurs between the samples of swine bones. Also, the ages of the slaughtered livestock are quite similar. Hence, this aspect of the faunal record reveals that the residents of each site consumed meats of similar quality.

Comparison of bone samples from other late-seventeenth-century sites also reveals a lack of variation comparable to that found at Pettus and Utopia. Only one site displays a significant difference. Faunal materials from the first decades of occupation (c. 1670–1690) at the Clifts Plantation in Westmoreland County, Virginia, indicate a diet composed of 48 percent beef, 36 percent pork, and 15 percent wild meat. While this was also a tenant home, it is not directly comparable with Utopia. Clifts was a new plantation, and the bone deposit accumulated while that area was being actively settled for the first time. Utopia, in contrast, was apparently

FIGURE 2. *Meat Frequencies from the Pettus and Utopia Sites*

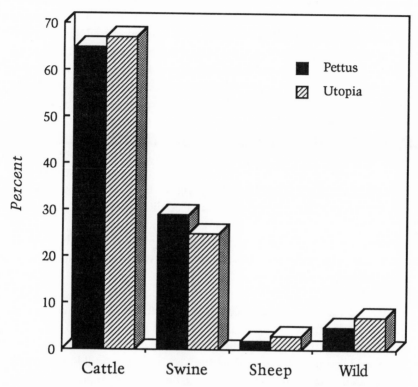

a well-established household in the longest-settled portion of the Virginia colony. This difference in cultural setting, especially the stage in the colonization process, makes comparison of these sites difficult. The Clifts residents were almost certainly involved in the process of herd development, and this probably influenced their decisions concerning resources to utilize as food.

With this exception, the available data suggest that late-seventeenth-century plantations in the settled areas shared a remarkably uniform meat diet. Independent planters, whatever their wealth status, seem to have had sufficient resources to maintain comparable meat diets. Obviously, there were distinctions in food preparation and dining style between these homes, as revealed by the equipment listed in inventories, but they nevertheless shared the basic ingredients of the meat diet.

None of these samples, however, are from the poorest households or from slave or servant quarters. Few such sites have even been located. Some limited data from the William Drummond site near Jamestown imply pronounced differences between the diets of planters and those of their servants and slaves. Two wells dating to about 1700 were excavated, and one, directly adjacent to the main structure, yielded high-quality artifacts clearly deriving from that building. The other well, located next to an outbuilding, probably a servant quarter, contained no high-quality objects. Bones from these deposits suggest that the occupants of the main house enjoyed a diet composed primarily of beef, especially high-quality cuts, supplemented with pork, mutton, and venison. Residents of the outbuilding consumed beef and pork in nearly equal ratios, but much of the beef came from low-quality cuts. They supplemented their diet with a few small mammals such as opossums. Such differences are not surprising, especially given the rapid increase in social distance that occurred between planters and their laborers during the late seventeenth and early eighteenth centuries. The most pronounced differences in meat diet will probably not be found between plantations, but within them. This is an important subject, but much additional archaeological research is necessary before we can adequately describe the diets of the poorest segments of Chesapeake society.

BONES FROM sites occupied during the first half of the eighteenth century testify that these trends in subsistence continued. Cattle and swine remained the central elements of the meat diet, while the harvesting of wild resources continued to diminish. Colonists still hunted a few deer, as well as small mammals and birds, but strikingly reduced their fish consumption.

Bone samples taken from all sites clearly express these trends. Table 3 displays the proportions of mammal and fish bone at all sites by period, with the standard deviations. The growing importance of mammals is apparent, as is the dramatic decline in fish. Fish make up only a tiny portion of the eighteenth-century samples. This trend in fish consumption was apparently widespread, for even though the sites are from various portions of the Chesapeake, little variation exists among the eighteenth-century bone samples. People still ate fish, but it was much less important to the diet than during the first half century of colonization.[20]

Data from individual trash pits illustrate the decline in consumption of

20. It must be emphasized that the decline in fish bone does not mean the colonists stopped consuming seafood. Oysters, crabs, and fish continued to be eaten in the 18th century, as attested by numerous historical documents and archaeological data. However, compared to the heavy usage of fish in the 17th century, this food source became much less significant. An alternative explanation, that disposal practices changed, has

TABLE 3. *Mean Frequencies and Standard Deviations (S.D.) of Mammal and Fish Bone from All Sites*

		Mammal	Fish
1620–1660	Mean	57.2%	35.0%
	S.D.	23.1	24.5
1660–1700	Mean	74.4%	20.0%
	S.D.	15.3	14.8
1700–1745	Mean	85.3%	4.5%
	S.D.	14.4	6.7

wild game and the increasing uniformity in the samples. Marked seasonal variations in resource usage characterized the diet during the first decades of settlement. This was clearly expressed in the changing proportions of wild meats represented by bones in deposits made during different seasons of the year. As figure 3 indicates, this variation essentially disappeared by the eighteenth century. The proportions of wild meat in later deposits reveal a steep overall decline in wild meat frequency from the early period along with greatly reduced variation between the samples.

Examination of each of the eighteenth-century samples reveals remarkably uniform meat proportions. Beef makes up about two-thirds of the estimated meat, while pork accounts for one-quarter.[21] The only exception is the faunal collection from the Deacon tenant site in St. Mary's City. Although no specific historical data identify the occupants of this site, it is known that William Deacon, the grandee of the neighborhood, owned the land and the structure. Artifacts found in association with the faunal remains indicate that the occupants were probably tenants of low to middling economic status.

Less than half of the total estimated meat in this sample is beef and one-third is pork. While the contribution of sheep is not significantly

---

little support. There is no evidence for this in other aspects of the faunal record, and it seems unlikely that the planters suddenly changed their agricultural practices and began using bones for fertilizer about 1700. Fish bone is still present in deposits throughout the region, but is just not abundant.

21. Except for the Deacon tenant site, the average beef frequency at the post-1700 sites is 64% of the total estimated meat (range 60% to 69%). For pork, the average is 25.7% (range 22% to 28%).

FIGURE 3. *Estimated Frequency of Wild Meat in Trash Pits*

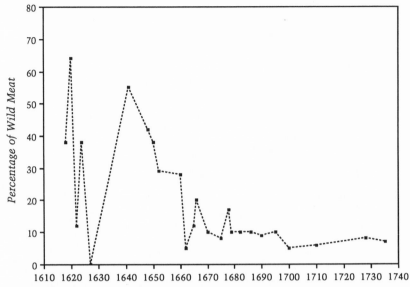

Note: Plot point represents median of estimated period of deposition.

different from that found on the other sites, the proportion of chicken bones and meat is larger. The Deacon site also shows the largest variety of mammal species (eighteen), one of the highest frequencies of wild meat (9.5 percent), and the greatest number of fish species (eight) of any sample from this period. On the other hand, it is the only colonial site in the entire study without deer bones.

Clearly, the faunal pattern at the Deacon site differs from the other post-1700 samples. Its chief characteristics are higher pork and chicken consumption, lower beef usage, and greater exploitation of wild resources, except for deer. This faunal pattern could be a reflection of limited economic means. The Deacon site is the only poor tenant site studied from this period. During the early eighteenth century, tenancy was no longer a temporary stop for planters on the road to economic advancement. For many, it was becoming a permanent status, especially in the long-settled areas.[22] As population density rose, grazing and pastureland became less available, and landowners probably utilized much of the pastureland for their own herds. Tenants were most likely restricted

22. Russell R. Menard, "Economy and Society in Early Colonial Maryland" (Ph.D. diss., University of Iowa, 1975), 425–431; Gregory A. Stiverson, *Poverty in a Land of Plenty: Tenancy in Eighteenth-Century Maryland* (Baltimore, 1977).

in the number of cattle they could keep and thus focused more upon swine and chickens, which required less land.

THE EVIDENCE presented here reveals that dramatic changes took place in the Chesapeake diet over the course of the first century of settlement. The major trends can be summarized as follows. There was an initial heavy reliance upon wild-meat sources, especially deer and fish, which dwindled to insignificance over time. Two domestic species— cattle and swine—had a central and increasingly important role. Sheep were of minor importance, although they became more abundant over time. There was a growing uniformity in the meat diet and less seasonal variation. The most pronounced wealth-related differences in the meat diet occurred during the early decades of the seventeenth century, though the eighteenth century also saw increasing disparity between wealth groups.

By its very nature, the process of colonization involves dynamic change. Colonization requires the selection of the most appropriate responses to a new environmental setting. The dramatic shifts in the dietary habits of the Chesapeake settlers are but one illustration of this more general phenomenon. The colonists' reliance upon the natural environment for food diminished greatly between 1650 and 1700. In both Virginia and Maryland, the same sequence of changes occurred, although the timing apparently varied according to the length of settlement in an area. But why did the usage of wild resources decline so conspicuously throughout the Chesapeake and the meat diet become so focused upon cattle and swine?

From a theoretical perspective, the changes are a predictable evolutionary response to increasing population size, a maturing culture, and decreasing natural resources. However, while the human population did increase and colonial culture did become more complex, wild resources in general were not depleted. Deer and turkeys were probably reduced in numbers through hunting, but there is no evidence that fish or waterfowl were overexploited. Most of these species migrated into the Chesapeake area and were not susceptible to overharvesting, except on a very temporary and localized basis. Yet despite continued abundance, harvesting of birds and especially of fish declined significantly through time.

Of greater relevance than resource depletion may have been the low market value attached to wild game. Domestic livestock, in contrast, were of real economic worth. Cattle could be sold on the hoof and swine marketed as barreled pork. In the unpredictable tobacco market of the

late seventeenth and early eighteenth centuries, livestock may have provided an important economic buffer for planters against low prices and
poor crops.[23] At the same time, livestock herds multiplied, thereby yielding a form of interest. Domestic animals thus provided a good means of
transferring wealth to children.

Moreover, colonial subsistence emphasized two hardy animals that
essentially cared for themselves in the Chesapeake environment. By the
second half of the seventeenth century, livestock herds were large and
breeding stock were not difficult to obtain. Because planters practiced a
woodland-pasture form of husbandry that required minimal labor and
facilities, only the absence of available land could have been a potential
problem.[24] Yet, even a small plantation of 100 acres contained plenty of
wooded or fallow land to permit livestock to graze, and given the absence
of fenced property boundaries, the actual foraging area was much larger.
With such an efficient adaptation, planters could easily produce sufficient
meat, a conclusion that is borne out by the lack of variation found between the elite and tenant samples in the late seventeenth century. Support also comes from the observations of travelers such as Durand of
Dauphiné, a Frenchman in Virginia in 1686. "As to cattle raised for food,
however rapidly they may multiply, their number is kept down, for there is
not a house so poor that they do not salt an ox, a cow and five or six large
hogs."[25] Only with higher human densities in the later eighteenth century

23. The economic significance of cattle is briefly discussed in Morgan, *American
Slavery, American Freedom*, 138–139. The export of meats to the West Indies probably
increased during the second half of the 17th century and certainly did so in the 18th
century. Exports included live animals and barreled meats. Marketing of a few barrels
of meat from plantations might have occurred periodically, but this does not appear to
have seriously distorted the faunal samples used here. On the sites, all portions of the
cattle and swine skeletons have been recovered and many of the bones display cut and
burn marks or have been broken into small pieces, indicative of consumption, not just
butchery. Even if meat was exported from a site, most of the bone would have gone
with it. Data from shipwrecks indicate that meats were often barreled with the bone;
even swine skulls have been recovered from wrecks. Hence, the faunal evidence does
indicate an actual increase in the consumption of domestic animals through time.

24. Evidence for this method of animal husbandry includes numerous references,
in inventories from Maryland and Virginia, to animals "In the Woods." Also see
Durand of Dauphiné, *A Huguenot Exile in Virginia; or, Voyages of a Frenchman Exiled for
His Religion* . . . , ed. Gilbert Chinard (New York, 1934), 123; *The Reverend John
Clayton*, ed. Berkeley *et al.*, 87–88; and Robert Beverley, *The History and Present State
of Virginia*, ed. Louis B. Wright (Chapel Hill, N.C., 1947), 203, 318.

25. Durand of Dauphiné, *Huguenot Exile*, ed. Chinard, 123.

would land and other resources become sufficiently limited to restrict livestock ownership.

It is clear that diet in the seventeenth-century Chesapeake differed markedly from that in England. Sheep predominate in archaeological collections from Britain but are not common on Chesapeake sites, even by the early eighteenth century. As a consequence, pork and beef apparently made up a greater proportion of the diet in the Chesapeake than they did in Britain. At the same time, the colonists consumed a greater variety of wild animals.

An extremely important yet elusive subject not addressed thus far is how much meat the colonists ate each year. Unfortunately, precisely estimating quantity is a difficult, if not impossible, task for all studies of past human diets. However, the Chesapeake sites have produced large numbers of bones, representing thousands of pounds of meat, and there is no evidence for the consumption of what the English considered "starvation foods," such as horses, snakes, or frogs.[26] Meat was apparently readily available.

This makes it unlikely that protein deficiency diseases such as pellagra or beriberi occurred in the seventeenth-century Chesapeake. Both require a considerable period of severe dietary deprivation before becoming a problem. Even the most wretched slave could have occasionally snared small animals, fished, or collected turtles and oysters from the bountiful lands and waters of the Chesapeake.

The abundance of game, readily acquired seafood, and many domestic animals all imply that settlers easily obtained meat and consumed it in large quantities. Indeed, it is likely that the colonists ate more meat than did their relatives in Britain. A comparison of inventories from Britain with those from the Chesapeake by James Horn indicates that the New World did not offer, in terms of material goods, a superior standard of living.[27] However, the evidence presented here suggests that New World immigration offered the advantage of a superior diet. Improved nutrition may well explain why, by the mid-eighteenth century, colonial soldiers were significantly taller than British and European troops.[28]

26. Frederick J. Simoons, *Eat Not This Flesh: Food Avoidances in the Old World* (Madison, Wis., 1961). During the starving time of 1609, the colonists were forced to eat "Doggs, Catts, ratts, Snakes, Toadstooles, horse hides and what nott." Lyon Gardiner Tyler, ed., *Narratives of Early Virginia, 1606–1625* (New York, 1907), 423.

27. James Horn, "Adapting to a New World: A Comparative Study of Local Society in England and Maryland, 1650–1700," in this volume.

28. Robert W. Fogel *et al.*, "Secular Changes in American and British Stature and

The subject of diet bears on many aspects of life. This analysis of animal remains from sites in the Chesapeake expands our understanding of one facet of the early American diet and points out new areas for study. Exploring colonial life, discovering why it changed, and learning how the

Nutrition," *Journal of Interdisciplinary History*, XIV (1983), 445–481.

APPENDIX I. *Archaeological Sites Utilized in This Study*

Sites	Date	Location	Site Type
Period 1 (1620–1660)			
The Maine	1618–1626	Near Jamestown	Plantation/Tenant
Kingsmill Tenement	1625–1650	Near Jamestown	Plantation/Tenant
St. John's I	1638–1660	St. Mary's City	Plantation
Calvert House	1645–1655	St. Mary's City	Plantation
Bennett Farm I	1645–1660	Lower Chesapeake	Plantation
Chancellor's Point	1640–1665	St. Mary's City	Plantation/Industrial
Period 2 (1660–1700)			
Will's Cove	1650–1680	Lower James	Plantation
Drummond I	1650–1680	Near Jamestown	Plantation
Bennett Farm II	1670–1700	Lower Chesapeake	Plantation
Smith's Townland	1670–1685	St. Mary's City	Lawyer's Lodging
Clifts I	1670–1685	Lower Potomac	Plantation/Tenant
Country's House	1680–1690	St. Mary's City	Ordinary
Pettus	1660–1700	Near Jamestown	Plantation
Utopia	1660–1710	Near Jamestown	Plantation/Tenant
Drummond II	1680–1710	Near Jamestown	Plantation
Van Sweringen	1680–1700	St. Mary's City	Dwelling/Inn
Period 3 (1700–1745)			
St. John's II	1700–1720	St. Mary's City	Plantation
Clifts III	1705–1720	Lower Potomac	Plantation/Tenant
Clifts IV	1720–1730	Lower Potomac	Plantation/Tenant
Drummond III	1720–1740	Near Jamestown	Plantation
Bray	1725–1745	Near Jamestown	Plantation
John Hicks	1721–1740	St. Mary's City	Plantation
Deacon's Tenant	1730–1745	St. Mary's City	Plantation/Tenant
Pope's Creek	1720–1750	Lower Potomac	Plantation

VRCA = Virginia Research Center for Archaeology
Neiman = Fraser D. Neiman, Robert E. Lee Memorial Association
HSMC = Historic St. Mary's City
Barka = Norman Barka, College of William and Mary

early settlers adapted to the New World is an exciting, yet difficult, task. The primary sources, historical and archaeological records, are both incomplete and offer different perspectives on the vanished world of the early colonists. By combining these independent, yet complementary, data sources, we may achieve a more comprehensive and perceptive view of colonial America.

Economic Position	Site Excavator	
Low/Middle	VRCA	1975
Middle	VRCA	1973–1974
High	HSMC	1972–1975
High	HSMC	1982
Middle	VRCA	1978
Middle	HSMC	1973
Middle	VRCA	1979
High	VRCA	1977–1980
Middle	VRCA	1978
High	HSMC	1981–1983
Middle	Neiman	1978–1979
Middle	HSMC	1982
High	VRCA	1972–1973
Low/Middle	VRCA	1972–1974
Middle/High	VRCA	1977–1980
High	HSMC	1977–1979
Middle	HSMC	1972–1975
Middle/High	Neiman	1978–1979
Middle/High	Neiman	1978–1979
Middle	VRCA	1977–1980
High	VRCA	1974
High	HSMC	1969
Low/Middle	HSMC	1977–1979
High	Barka	1974–1975

APPENDIX 2. *Methods of Analysis*

This study utilizes many samples, all of which were analyzed with the same standard procedures. Temporal control is obtained by studying only bones found in cellars, wells, pits, or other features that have been sealed since the time of deposition. In effect, these are time capsules. Dating of these deposits is based upon the associated artifacts, stratigraphic evidence, and pertinent historical data. Because of the temporal resolution obtainable with archaeological materials, time estimates are in decade intervals such as c. 1700, plus or minus ten years. For sites inhabited for long periods, the samples were separated into occupation phases to account for changes in household position, economics, and cultural setting.

All bone samples were found mixed with domestic trash, such as discarded pottery, tobacco pipes, and glass. Most of the bones are broken or display cut marks, and some have been burned. Taken together, these facts indicate that the bone deposits derive from domestic activities.

It is unlikely that many of these bones are from animals whose meat was marketed. Commercial butchery produces distinctive bone assemblages, mostly skull and foot bones, and such assemblages are rare on Chesapeake sites. According to data from shipwrecks, bones from most parts of the skeleton were included with barreled meats. Deboning large amounts of meat requires substantial effort, an unnecessary labor expenditure. Hence, while some bones in these samples could be from marketed animals, the evidence suggests that these deposits are primarily the result of domestic activities.

After selection of the bone samples, all materials from a deposit are sorted. Identifiable elements are first grouped by class (mammal, fish, bird), size, and type of bone. Each bone is then identified to a genus or species by comparison with modern skeletons of known animals. This procedure reveals the types of animals present and the frequencies of bones from each. While bone counts have analytic value, they permit only limited inference about the diet since a squirrel bone is considered equal to that of a cow.

To correct for this, the minimum number of individuals of each species represented in a bone collection is next calculated. This involves dividing the bones from each species into specific elements (femur, scapula, etc.) and sorting them into left and right sides. Then, the bone of a species with the largest number of specimens of the same side indicates the Minimum Number of Individuals (M.N.I.). This rough count is refined by considering the size of the bones, the ages of the individuals, and where possible, the sex. The result is an M.N.I. count for each species in a particular deposit or, at a broader scale, on the entire site.

These counts are then converted into estimates of the available meat to compensate for the size differences between species and to understand better their economic significance. For each type of animal, an estimate of the average amount of edible meat obtained from an individual is used. The meat weight estimates are further refined by determining the number of immature and mature individuals and adjusting the values accordingly. These weights are based upon modern laboratory measurements and historical data regarding the size of animals in the past. For colonial livestock, documents suggest that the animals were smaller than the modern improved breeds and this is confirmed by the size of the bones. Average weights used for mature domestic animals are: cattle, 400 pounds; swine, 100 pounds; and sheep, 35 pounds. The result of these steps is an available meat estimate for each species. Calculating the proportion of the total meat contributed by each species provides a measure of the relative significance of the animals in the diet and the overall subsistence pattern at a site.

Lorena S. Walsh

Community Networks in the Early Chesapeake

WHAT DID community and neighborhood mean to a seventeenth-century planter and his family? Indeed, is this a question worth asking? We have so often equated "community" with New England's closed, corporate, homogeneous, and cohesive "peaceable kingdoms" that the disparate, demographically disrupted, politically unstable, widely scattered settlements of the seventeenth-century Chesapeake have sometimes come to stand for nothing less than its antithesis. In all places and times rural communities have a certain elusive quality, since they often lack both central focus and clear exterior bounds.[1] Those of the seventeenth-century Chesapeake are particularly hard to define, as population densities remained relatively low, settlement patterns extremely diffuse, and in most instances not so much as a hamlet or village crossroads appears to provide a starting point in the search for a self-recognizing social unit. Thus any study of Chesapeake communities must rely on different sources from those used by scholars of New England, and the unit of study becomes the rural neighborhood rather than the town. The character, as well as the arena, of collective economic and social action that emerges also differs. But difference does not in itself prove the absence of some notion of community.

In Virginia and Maryland, settlers selected choice patches of land all along the large rivers emptying into Chesapeake Bay and by the 1670s had established farms on many major tributaries and on some minor creeks. Planters kept to the waterside with good reason. Rivers and creeks provided abundant sources of food. More important, they also "afforded a commodious Road for Shipping at every Man's Door."[2] In the seventeenth century the transatlantic trade was organized around direct bar-

---

1. See, for example, George A. Hillery, Jr., "Definitions of Community: Areas of Agreement," *Rural Sociology*, XX (1955), 111–123; Walter L. Slocum and Herman M. Case, "Are Neighborhoods Meaningful Social Groups Throughout Rural America?" *ibid.*, XVIII (1953), 52–59; and Selz C. Mayo, "Testing Criteria of Rural Locality Groups," *ibid.*, XIV (1949), 317–325.

2. Robert Beverley, *The History and Present State of Virginia*, ed. Louis B. Wright (Chapel Hill, N.C., 1947), 57.

gaining between English shipmasters and factors, who brought goods and servants to the Chesapeake in return for tobacco, and individual planters, who produced it. Ships stopped at landings along the rivers, and the captains then sent sloops to collect tobacco and to deliver goods where the ships themselves could not go.[3] Because tobacco was both too bulky and too fragile to transport easily on land, water access—even if only for a raft—was essential to profitable production of the staple.

The character of the tidewater soils also encouraged planters to cling to the rivers, for it was along their banks that the land best suited for tobacco cultivation lay. Inland soils were less adapted to the staple, and some areas were not particularly conducive to any kind of agriculture, some too sandy, some too gravelly, others subject to drought, and still others too steeply sloped to support intensive farming.[4] The result was a pattern of settlement broadly but thinly scattered along the edges of the waterways.

In Maryland, the normal administrative unit, the county, was simply too large to be coterminous with community, if by community we mean to include a group of people who engage in frequent collective action. A close reading of county court proceedings makes clear that the only collective action many county residents had in common was their periodic attendance at meetings of the county court and subsequent implementation of decisions made there. The records make equally clear, however, that among the persons present, there were groups of individuals who did share not only a way of life but also collective economic and social action.[5]

3. Lois Green Carr, " 'The Metropolis of Maryland': A Comment on Town Development along the Tobacco Coast," *Maryland Historical Magazine*, LXIX (1974), 124–145; Russell R. Menard, "Economy and Society in Early Colonial Maryland" (Ph.D. diss., University of Iowa, 1975), chap. 2; and Arthur Pierce Middleton, *Tobacco Coast: A Maritime History of Chesapeake Bay in the Colonial Era* (Newport News, Va., 1953).

4. Reports of modern soil conditions can be found in the U.S. Department of Agriculture Soil Conservation Service county level soil surveys. Augustin Herrman's 1670 map of Virginia and Maryland documents the concentration of farms along rivers and creeks. It is reproduced in Edward C. Papenfuse and Joseph M. Coale III, *The Hammond–Harwood House Atlas of Historical Maps of Maryland, 1608–1908* (Baltimore, 1982), 12–15.

5. Darrett B. Rutman's "The Social Web: A Prospectus for the Study of the Early American Community," in William L. O'Neill, ed., *Insights and Parallels: Problems and Issues of American Social History* (Minneapolis, Minn., 1973), 57–89, is an excellent discussion of the problems of locating and defining the nature of community in 17th-century America. The article also serves as an introduction to some of the recent

Only by painstaking reconstruction of the content and geography of individual associations can we identify and begin to understand the scope and functions of seventeenth-century Chesapeake communities.

The first part of this essay is based in large part on a study of St. Clement's Manor and associated Basford Manor, a 12,500-acre tract located in northern St. Mary's County between St. Clement's Bay and the Wicomico River. An assemblage of local records, including those of a manor court and two collections of private papers, makes St. Clement's Manor one of the few places where, for a brief time, a Maryland neighborhood can be fairly fully reconstituted. But even here documentation for human interaction is limited.[6] The second section of the essay draws on a general understanding of economic and political organization in seventeenth-century Maryland, illustrated by documented neighborly exchanges from a variety of contexts.

SOCIAL ORGANIZATION in the Chesapeake was much more diffuse than in New England. In a region where there were no towns and where the settlers shared no common, intense religious purpose, one would hardly expect to find anything approaching a closed, corporate, village-centered community of the New England type.[7] Conversely, the

---

sociological and anthropological literature on small communities. A second perceptive discussion of the study and interpretation of early communities is Richard R. Beeman, "The New Social History and the Search for 'Community' in Colonial America," *American Quarterly*, XXIX (1977), 422–443.

6. St. Clement's Manor court records are published in William Hand Browne *et al.*, eds., *Archives of Maryland* (Baltimore, 1883–), LIII, 627–637, hereafter cited as *Md. Archives*. Private papers include the Carroll-Maccubbin Papers, MS 219, Maryland Historical Society, Baltimore, and the McWilliams Papers, Manuscript Division, Graduate Library, Georgetown University, Washington, D.C. An 11-year farm account of a St. Clement's resident, found in Testamentary Proceedings, VI, 118–147, Maryland State Archives, Annapolis, is analyzed in Russell R. Menard, Lois Green Carr, and Lorena S. Walsh, "A Small Planter's Profits: The Cole Estate and the Growth of the Early Chesapeake Economy," *William and Mary Quarterly*, 3d Ser., XL (1983), 171–196. Compared to the volume of material surviving for other small geographic subdivisions of 17th- and early 18th-century Chesapeake counties, this is a rich cache indeed. However, even the best of sources are exceedingly limited. The manor court records for the years 1659–1672, for example, occupy only 10½ printed pages in the *Archives*, and much of this consists of lists of manor residents. Even with the addition of all other available evidence, we are hardly in a position to assess the quality of community life on the manor.

7. One thinks especially of Kenneth A. Lockridge, *A New England Town, the First Hundred Years: Dedham, Massachusetts, 1636–1736* (New York, 1970). See also Sum-

absence of these two ingredients does not in itself prove the other extreme—that Chesapeake settlers were merely a collection of "aggressive, competitive, highly individualistic" men and women "without strong communal bonds or any unifying ideology."[8] The peculiarities of local geography, of a staple-producing economy, and of a hierarchal social structure explain in part the settlers' relationships with one another. But more qualitative evidence also suggests that these rural folk forged meaningful associations based on something more than pure happenstance. St. Clement's Manor, perhaps the best organized and certainly the most long-lived of any manor in Maryland, provides an excellent place for probing the character and strength of community networks.[9]

Just as proprietary land policy affected settlement patterns and the pace of land acquisition in Maryland as a whole, so the policies of individual manor owners and other major investors affected the histories of particular localities. The decisions of Thomas Gerrard, the lord of the manor, for a time more closely shaped the physical and to some extent the social and economic world of settlers on St. Clement's Manor than would have been the case with families who took up freehold farms from the proprietor.[10] When Gerrard began developing his estate on St. Clement's in

---

ner Chilton Powell, *Puritan Village: The Formation of a New England Town* (Middletown, Conn., 1963); John Demos, *A Little Commonwealth: Family Life in Plymouth Colony* (New York, 1970); Philip J. Greven, Jr., *Four Generations: Population, Land, and Family in Colonial Andover, Massachusetts* (Ithaca, N.Y., 1970); and Michael Zuckerman, *Peaceable Kingdoms: New England Towns in the Eighteenth Century* (New York, 1970).

8. T. H. Breen and Stephen Innes, *"Myne Owne Ground": Race and Freedom on Virginia's Eastern Shore, 1640–1676* (New York, 1980), 67, 56. Cf. T. H. Breen, "Looking Out for Number One: The Cultural Limits on Public Policy in Early Virginia," in Breen, *Puritans and Adventurers: Change and Persistence in Early America* (New York, 1980), 106–126. Edmund S. Morgan, *American Slavery, American Freedom: The Ordeal of Colonial Virginia* (New York, 1975), suggests a similar interpretation. For an opposing view, see Lois Green Carr, "Sources of Political Stability and Upheaval in Seventeenth-Century Maryland," *Md. Hist. Mag.*, LXXIX (1984), 44–70.

9. Another Maryland manor community, St. Thomas's in Charles County, is examined in Lorena S. Walsh, "Land, Landlord, and Leaseholder: Estate Management and Tenant Fortunes in Southern Maryland, 1642–1820," *Agricultural History*, LIX (1985), 373–396.

10. One may want to compare Gerrard's role with the more effective patron-client relationships that were instrumental in the development of certain types of New England towns as described in Stephen Innes, *Labor in a New Land: Economy and Society in Seventeenth-Century Springfield* (Princeton, N.J., 1983).

1641, he was in effect planting a tiny colony on the outer fringes of prior settlement. Like Maryland's first settlers at St. Mary's City, Gerrard started farming on or near lands previously cleared and seated by the Indians, a tract that contained some of the more fertile lands on the manor. He built a "manor house" on the home plantation, Mattapany, and designated this farm demesne land.

After the manner of contemporary English landlords, Gerrard probably hoped to build a small empire based on dependent tenants, but in fact he began developing his estate with indentured servants, for there were few free men in the colony willing either to work as laborers or to rent farms. In 1642 only three free men had taken up leaseholds on Gerrard's land. However, he commanded the service of up to twenty indentured servants. These laborers were first employed in clearing land, raising corn and tobacco, constructing buildings on the manor farm, planting orchards, and caring for growing herds of cattle and hogs. Subsequently they set up quarters on outlying tracts on St. Clement's and adjacent Basford Manor and at Westwood farther north. By buying many servants, Gerrard added to his landholdings while benefiting from their labor. He was entitled to 1,000 acres in 1638, acquired 6,000 acres more by 1642, and added an additional 7,200 acres by 1651 using headrights obtained from transporting his family and numerous servants as well as a few rights purchased from others. Political offices—manor lord, Indian agent, justice of the peace, and provincial councillor—followed on the heels of Gerrard's economic rise.[11]

From the beginning, settlers in the St. Clement's area looked to the manor house at Mattapany to provide protection, direction, and legal services. In addition, during the initial years of settlement, ordinary planters depended heavily on large investors for credit, supplies, and marketing facilities. Should the settlers be unable to feed themselves, usually only those with large resources could obtain corn from the Indians. Even in good years, only those with many bound laborers produced surplus grain. The big men too owned most of the cattle in the colony, and ordinary settlers could not start herds of their own unless they arranged to buy a cow from a large landowner on credit. Finally, until English traders

11. The material presented here is expanded and documented in Lois Green Carr, Russell R. Menard, and Lorena S. Walsh, "Robert Cole's World," manuscript in preparation. Basford Manor was entitled to a separate manor court, but Gerrard administered it as a part of St. Clement's and required Basford freeholders and leaseholders to attend the St. Clement's court.

became familiar with the new settlement, small planters had to depend on their larger neighbors, most of whom already had contacts in the English mercantile community, to secure shipping for their tobacco and to provide introductions to ship captains.[12]

In the 1650s the growing flow of immigrants to the Maryland colony included a number of free men of moderate substance, some of whom arrived with young families. The Roman Catholics among them may have been particularly attracted to the settlements on the Potomac because of the Jesuit mission just across St. Clement's Bay at Newtown, the presence of other Catholics already settled in the area, and because Gerrard himself was a Catholic. There was as yet no church building, but missionary priests apparently conducted masses in the homes of various Catholic families.[13]

The arrival of these additional settlers offered Thomas Gerrard new and probably very welcome options for advancing his estate. In 1652, a full ten years after seating his manor, Gerrard had apparently attracted only four tenant farmers. Most of his rich domain remained undeveloped, yielding no income from rents. He had had to bear the full cost of what improvements had been made, through the purchase of servants, and he still owed money borrowed from his brother-in-law in 1640. The manor community still consisted of little more than Gerrard's own household and servant quarters.

In 1652 Gerrard commenced a different development strategy by selling off parts of his manors as freeholds rather than retaining all for leasing, thus sacrificing potential future revenues for immediate profit. By 1661 Gerrard had sold nine freeholds of 300 to 800 acres each, six of them to Catholic families. By the late 1650s Gerrard had had some success in attracting tenants as well; there were sixteen by 1661. Most were his own former servants or those of other nearby landowners. Having not yet accumulated enough capital to purchase land, they had to begin careers as planters by renting farms and housing.

Surviving manor court records for 1659–1661 allow us to reconstruct

12. Garry Wheeler Stone, "Society, Housing, and Architecture in Early Maryland: John Lewger's St. John's" (Ph.D. diss., University of Pennsylvania, 1982), chap. 2; Menard, "Economy and Society," chap. 2.

13. The early Maryland Roman Catholic community is perceptively described in Michael James Graham, "Lord Baltimore's Pious Enterprise: Toleration and Community in Colonial Maryland, 1634–1724" (Ph.D. diss., University of Michigan, 1983), chap. 3.

the St. Clement's community as it existed about twenty years after initial settlement. In 1661, nine householders owned freeholds, sixteen held leases, and an additional nineteen ex-servants and free immigrants worked as laborers or sharecroppers while boarding with one of the householders.

This small group of settlers lived on individual farms scattered along the sides of rivers and creeks (see map 1). Each tract had convenient access to the water for shipping the crop, and each had patches of good tobacco and corn land. In 1660 there were still fewer than two households per square mile on the manor. However, while the settlers chose not to live in close physical proximity to one another, informal neighborhood networks did spring up quickly. On the frontier, neighboring families relied heavily on each other for aid in time of sickness or in case of Indian alarms, for help with heavy work, for borrowing back and forth when supplies ran low or the proper tools were lacking, and simply for conversation or sharing important personal and family events. Whether the individuals knew their neighbors very well, whether nearby householders had arrived several years before or on the same ship, or whether one family liked or thoroughly detested a neighboring family was largely immaterial. Some amount of cooperation—whether warmly supportive or grudgingly extended—was essential to survival. Since the settlers did not arrive in organized groups, chance to a large degree determined who one's neighbor might be.

However, St. Clement's residents were not content to let chance define all their relationships. More-structured institutions soon followed. It was probably in the early 1650s that the manor court was fully organized and regularly convened. For the initial ten years or so, Gerrard could deal with his few tenants on an individual basis rather than in a formal meeting and had no need to hire a manor steward. But with the establishment of more households, disputes over ill-defined boundaries, transfers of land, and roving livestock arose, and occasional petty thefts and fights occurred. In addition, most of the new farmsteads lay too far from Gerrard's manor house for convenient access or constant personal administration. Hence the residents began to meet in formal courts, and Gerrard hired a steward to help with management of the manor.

The Roman Catholics in the area also set about organizing a church, desiring to "repayre on Sundays and other Holy dayes appoynted & Commanded by holy Church to serve Almighty God & heare divine Service." In 1661 they "unanimously agreed amongst themselves" to

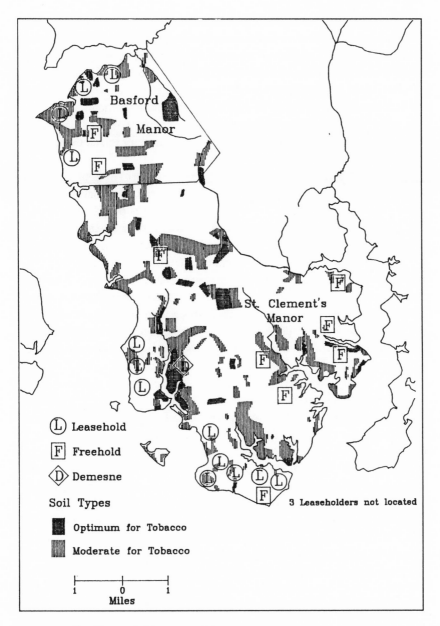

MAP I. *St. Clement's Manor c. 1660*

The maps in this essay were drawn by the Cartographic Services Laboratory, Department of Geography, University of Maryland.

build a chapel and prepare a graveyard. They selected a site on Newtown Neck, just across St. Clement's Bay, as the most convenient. Families supported the new church by paying voluntary taxes and by helping to build the chapel. Local Catholics also wanted parochial education for their children. A bequest by one parishioner in 1653 for a schoolmaster's salary and support for poor scholars led the Jesuits to open a school on Newtown Neck. Nearby residents boarded students who otherwise lived too far away to attend school regularly. Others cared for the cattle belonging to the school estate.[14]

Transplanted English social structure also gave form to the local community. Elements of the highly stratified society that Lord Baltimore had planned were visible on St. Clement's Manor in the 1660s. At the top was the lord of the manor, who sought to exercise the social as well as the economic dimensions of his position and who enforced his legal feudal prerogatives. However, the nine manor freeholders also occupied a responsible and privileged niche in the manor community. Most were free immigrants and family men, and by 1660 three were burgesses and justices of the peace. The freeholders' status and independence tended to set limits upon how far Thomas Gerrard might go in enforcing his feudal privileges. In contrast to the freeholders, the sixteen men who leased land on St. Clement's Manor stood several rungs lower in the official hierarchy. They had not arrived with the same advantages of status and resources with which most of the freeholders began, and they lacked the independence that landowning permitted. Luke Gardiner, for example, one of the most prominent manor freeholders and a justice of the St. Mary's County Court, refused to attend the manor court and was regularly fined for failing to do fealty to his lord. But other freeholders—including both men of somewhat less substance and those closely related by blood or marriage to Gerrard—as well as the leaseholders did attend so long as the manor court provided needed services. Indentured servants were at the bottom of the social hierarchy. They had no say in local government and they were subject to the control and discipline of the householders who had bought their term of service.

When manor courts were convened, residents were concerned primarily with establishing boundaries, regularizing land transfers, and set-

14. *Md. Archives*, XLI, 531, XLIX, 19–20; Wills, I, 44, Md. State Archives. Aside from individual bequests to priests and occasional payments to the church mentioned in estate accounts, there is little additional surviving evidence about the early organization of this church.

tling disputes among themselves. For example, Gerrard, according to one resident, "most Commonly sold and others bought land from him without Survey by Instruments bounding by guess from heads of Creeks to heads of Creeks or other parts as they agreed and Sometimes by Paths some times mentioning Courses & Distances and Sometimes not."[15] It was up to manor court juries to sort out the resulting confusion. The court also shut down Humphrey Willey's unlicensed "tippling house" when it became the scene of a drunken brawl, fined local Indians who had pilfered some of the settlers' goods, and ordered two families to stop sheltering a destitute couple whom Gerrard had not authorized to live on the manor. When Samuel Harris beat up John Mansell with a stick, when Clove Mace's wife threw her husband out of his own house in the course of a heated domestic argument, when Joshua Lee set his dogs on John Hoskin's straying hogs, and when John Tennison's horses damaged John Blakiston's cornfield, the court intervened.[16]

That the settlers' initial effort to structure local society in the New World should have included traditional English manorial institutions is hardly surprising. Familiar custom and proprietary vision gained reinforcement from uncertain frontier conditions that at first tended to magnify the role of the great landowner and forced most residents to cooperate closely to preserve order and to provide mutual aid and security. However, conditions unique to the New World, most particularly the wide availability of land, combined with continued population growth and the appearance of a greater degree of social stability, soon rendered Maryland manors obsolete, although St. Clement's Manor court lasted longer than the others.[17]

15. Deposition of Samuel Williamson, in *Mason v. Cheseldyne*, 1722, St. Mary's County, Provincial Court Papers, Md. State Archives. Many of the early manor surveys were woefully inexact, and a number of the original surveys and deeds either were not recorded or have not survived. There was a great deal of litigation about the bounds of manor lands in the 18th century, so much so that a portion of the manor where titles were inextricably jumbled came to be known locally as Bedlam Neck. The court papers sometimes include maps of later resurveys along with depositions about original bounds that aided in plotting the location of many tracts on St. Clement's.

16. *Md. Archives*, LIII, 627–630, 634, 636.

17. For a discussion of social organization, neighborhood associations, and support networks in early Virginia, see James Russell Perry, "The Formation of a Society on Virginia's Eastern Shore, 1615–1655" (Ph.D. diss., The Johns Hopkins University, 1980). In mid-17th-century England, manors varied greatly in strength of organization and influence on the lives of residents. On the most active manors, courts might

Manor court records for 1670–1672 provide our second and last complete profile of St. Clement's inhabitants in the seventeenth century and show a decline in such formal collective identity as had appeared ten years earlier.[18] The composition of the manor's population was changing and the manor itself had ceased to be an effective form of local economic or social organization, insofar as it ever had been.[19] Several circumstances contributed to this decline: diminishing leadership by the lord of the manor, failure of manor courts to assume an essential role in local government, changes in the character of manor residents, decreased religious cohesion, high mortality, and great geographic mobility.

Loss of leadership came first. For reasons that are not entirely clear, Thomas Gerrard ceased to support Lord Baltimore's government. Instead, Gerrard became active in anti-proprietary politics "Aymeing at his owne Greatenes which in unsettled times he might uphould," an opponent later asserted.[20] In 1660 Gerrard was temporarily banished from Maryland and his property confiscated because of his support of the rebel

---

meet as often as every three weeks. On weaker manors, the court usually met but once a year (Joan Thirsk, ed., *The Agrarian History of England and Wales*, vol. V, *1640–1750*, pt. 1 [Cambridge, 1984], 296). St. Clement's followed the second pattern, usually holding one meeting a year.

18. From lists of freeholders and leaseholders kept by the Carroll family, who later owned the manor, one can continue to trace part of the St. Clement's population up to the outbreak of the American Revolution. However, without the manor court records and their lists of all free male residents and female heads of households, one can no longer systematically follow nonlandowners—adult sons at home, free laborers, undertenants, and the like—who continued to form a substantial part of the manor population.

19. The manor court apparently ceased to meet after Thomas Gerrard's eldest son and principal heir, Justinian, died childless in 1688. However, it did not simply fade from memory. Charles Carroll, the richest man in Maryland in the first decades of the 18th century, bought the manor from Gerrard's widow in 1711. In 1729, when Carroll tried to collect manorial rents more assiduously than the Gerrards had ever done, residents asked that the manor court be reconvened to adjudicate titles and sums due. Very probably the court never met again. That manor residents sought to resurrect it after 40 years of inactivity—when it was in their interest to do so—suggests that the earlier abandonment of the court may have been the result of the residents' perception that the court was no longer serving their interests. Joshua Doyne to Charles Carroll, Feb. 7, 1728/1729, Carroll-Maccubbin Papers.

20. *Md. Archives*, III, 354–357. For a discussion of Gerrard's politics, see Edwin W. Beitzel, "Thomas Gerrard and His Sons-in-Law," *Chronicles of St. Mary's*, X (1962), 300–305, 307–311.

governor, Josias Fendall. Although he soon obtained a pardon, Gerrard's political career was ended, as he was barred from holding further office in the colony. Shortly after recovering his property from the proprietor, Gerrard was sued for failing to repay money borrowed in the 1640s. Part of the manor was turned over to his creditor until his debt was repaid out of the profits of manor rents and crops raised on his Mattapany farm. Gerrard moved across the Potomac to Westmoreland County, Virginia, married a propertied local widow (his first wife having died), and turned to developing an estate there. The settlers who remained on St. Clement's Manor had to turn to someone other than the lord of the manor for legal and economic services.

Ample reason existed for Gerrard's apparent disillusionment. While rents constituted an important source of income for most English gentlemen of this period, being a Maryland manor lord simply did not pay very well. There were much easier ways to make a fortune than finding and keeping reliable tenants, hounding recalcitrant freeholders who often failed to pay their almost nominal rents, and collecting traditional manorial dues in capons and corn rather than in currency or in more readily marketed tobacco. By the late 1660s, Gerrard ceased renting manor land to tenants except for the outlying Basford tract, and he turned over large portions of St. Clement's Manor to his eldest son and to three sons-in-law as freehold estates. He also allowed many former leaseholders to purchase their farms outright. Finally, he sold off the remaining undeveloped but marketable waterfront properties to new purchasers (see map 2). In addition, Gerrard had begun purchasing slaves for his Virginia plantation during the 1660s and had acquired others through his second marriage. Slave labor, he may have found, contributed more to a Chesapeake landed empire than did a reluctant and unstable New World peasantry.

Thomas Gerrard died in 1673. His son, Justinian, the new lord of the manor, seems to have lacked his father's commanding personality. Even had the son been more like the father, the outcome might not have been much different. The lord of the manor no longer had a monopoly on political power. Four of the twenty-one St. Clement's freeholders of 1672 also held countywide powers and responsibilities, and three more would be named to such positions within a few years. Moreover, St. Clement's residents had never been a community unto themselves in the sense that they were isolated socially or economically from other county settlers. As common planters developed their own farms and forged their own

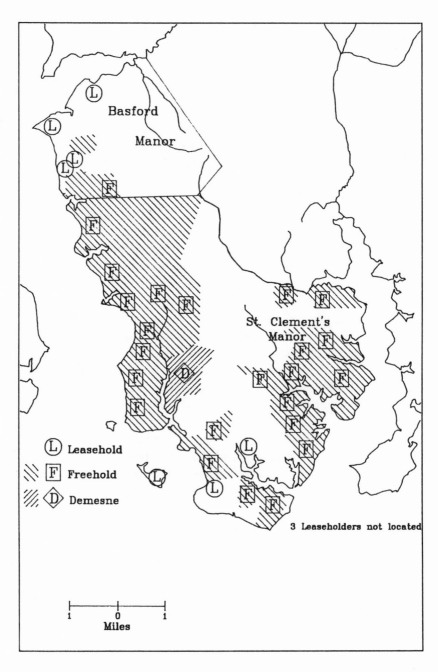

MAP 2. *St. Clement's Manor c. 1671*

ties with English ship captains, economic dependence on local mag-
nates declined proportionately. In addition, St. Clement's residents had
increasingly frequent dealings with nearby planters living outside the
manor and soon turned to more comprehensive agencies than the manor
court to collect debts and to settle most of their disputes. The county
court had concurrent jurisdiction over land boundaries, petty suits, and
breaches of the peace, as well as the right to settle more serious matters.
The manor court met too infrequently and involved too few people to be
either an effective or an essential institution. It soon proved an unnecessary adjunct to justices of the peace and to the county court that was
evolving as an effective agency for settling disputes among neighbors and
for providing the rudimentary administrative machinery needed to keep a
frontier community functioning.[21]

The decade between 1660 and 1670 marked an end to the early close
connection between manor and church. Many of the freeholders who had
arrived during the 1660s were Protestants as were most newly imported
servants and resident ex-servants. Gerrard's own children had been
raised as Protestants, and he himself and his three sons-in-law became
leaders of the anti-proprietary (and hence pro-Protestant) faction. Certainly not all of the manor Catholics shared their lord's political views,
and some must have felt decidedly uncomfortable in the increasingly
anti-Catholic atmosphere that dominated gatherings in the homes of
the likes of Gerrard's son-in-law Nehemiah Blakiston.[22] The remaining
Catholic residents would increasingly seek coreligionists off the manor as
marriage partners, as witnesses to economic agreements and to wills, as
godparents or guardians to their children, and as estate administrators.[23]

21. For the jurisdiction of the county court and its evolution as the predominant
institution of local government in colonial Maryland, see Lois Green Carr, "The
Foundations of Social Order: Local Government in Colonial Maryland," in Bruce C.
Daniels, ed., *Town and County: Essays on the Structure of Local Government in the
American Colonies* (Middletown, Conn., 1978), 72–110, and Carr, "County Govern-
ment in Maryland, 1689–1709" (Ph.D. diss., Harvard University, 1968). Indeed, the
decline of the manor court may have mirrored similar developments in parts of
England. David Grayson Allen has found that in East Anglia manorial responsibilities
were being transferred to parish and county governments at almost the same time. *In
English Ways: The Movement of Societies and the Transferal of English Local Law and
Custom to Massachusetts Bay in the Seventeenth Century* (Chapel Hill, N.C., 1981), 149–
153.

22. *Md. Archives*, XV, 391–392, V, 534–535.

23. See Graham, "Lord Baltimore's Pious Enterprise," chaps. 3, 5, and 7.

At the same time, Thomas Gerrard's policy of converting leaseholds to freeholds soon brought about a marked change in the composition of the free adult male residents on the manor. By 1672 their numbers had increased to eighty-four. However, leaseholders had dwindled to only seven (8 percent of the adult males as compared to 36 percent ten years before), and they were of little importance in the manor hierarchy. Twenty-one freeholders (25 percent, nearly the same as before) now held most of the land, while fifty-six men (67 percent) were *resiants*, a now obsolete term for residents settled by arrangements other than ownership or leasing of land. This decline in the number of tenants, the most feudal of manor residents, removed a relatively responsible but somewhat dependent group of male householders. The manor, like the rest of the tobacco coast in the 1670s, became largely a society of freeholders and landless, often mobile, freedmen (see table 1).

Consequently, by 1670 there was very little to distinguish manor freeholders from other county landowners who did not live on an organized manor. They were a more disparate group than in 1660, reflecting changes during the 1660s and 1670s in immigration and opportunity. Some had resources and connections that outdistanced the Gerrard family's wealth and political power. Others were small planters who had risen to landowning status from tenancy. Only about half of the landowners of 1670–1672 were Roman Catholics, and some of the new Protestant freeholders were something less than loyal to the Catholic proprietary. These families did not benefit from the church and school organized by Catholic residents, and they may have resented the failure of the government to help them establish similar facilities for their children.

Likewise, the nonlandowners were little different from other unmarried men who had not yet established a niche for themselves on Maryland's lower Western Shore. While a few were sons still at home, most were ex-servants who had been transported in the late 1650s and early 1660s and who had worked for freeholders on the manor. Unlike men who had served Gerrard or his family, former servants who had labored on the farms of others had few direct ties to the lord of the manor. Most had not yet married and started families, and most were Protestants who had no organized local church. Thus there was little to tie them to the locality.

Some freedmen would eventually marry women who lived on or near the manor, but clearly these couples found it difficult to set up their own households. Falling tobacco prices made it ever harder for a poor man to

TABLE I. *Status of St. Clement's Manor Residents*

Period	Free-holder No.	Free-holder %	Lease-holder No.	Lease-holder %	Resiant No.	Resiant %	Total No.
1659–1661	9	20.4	16	36.4	19	43.2	44
1670–1672	21	25.0	7	8.3	56	66.7	84

Sources: St. Clement's Manor court records, in William Hand Browne *et al.*, eds., *Archives of Maryland* (Baltimore, 1883–), LIII, 627–637; biographical file of St. Mary's County residents, St. Mary's City Commission, Maryland State Archives, Annapolis.

become established. Like other places on the lower Western Shore, the proportion of such semidependent unmarried boarders rose on St. Clement's Manor in the late 1660s and 1670s. In 1659–1661 there was about one nonhouseholder for every two householders. Ten years later the proportion of boarders had nearly doubled. The presence of so many unattached males worked against a stable local population.

Indeed, the turnover among individuals was even more marked than the change in overall composition. Of the forty-four adult males who lived on St. Clement's Manor in 1659–1661, only eight (18 percent) still lived there ten years later in 1670–1672. Family continuity was as transitory as individual persistence. Only ten of the eighty-four adult male residents of 1672 were sons or sons-in-law of residents of a decade earlier. The others had immigrated within the preceding ten years. High mortality was one reason for so much discontinuity. Of the twenty-five freeholders and leaseholders of 1659–1661, eight (32 percent) had died within these ten years. However, geographic mobility was even more important. Of the surviving seventeen property holders, only five (29 percent of those still alive and 20 percent of the original group) had stayed put. The early nonhouseholders were more footloose still—only two of the original nineteen resiants remained on the manor ten years later. Two had died in the area, one had purchased land nearby, and the rest had simply disappeared.[24]

24. So far as I can determine, there are no comparable studies of persistence and mobility for small geographic subdivisions of 17th-century Chesapeake counties. Since rates of movement into or out of such restricted units are almost certainly greater than movement into or out of a much larger area such as a county, it is

A combination of push and pull was at work. A major push factor was that by 1672, the St. Clement's and Basford Manor complex, for all its 12,500 acres, was filling up. The 1672 density of two to three households per square mile appears thin settlement indeed, but there was in fact not a lot of room for new households. By the early 1670s all the waterfront land well suited to growing tobacco had been granted out. What remained were small, often land-bound, parcels of 50 to 100 acres that promised a barely adequate living for a family. Thus, so long as the earlier-established landowners were unwilling to sell part of their choice holdings, men who aspired to own enough land to endow their children as well as to farm for their own use had to move on (see map 2).

In the 1670s, pull strongly augmented push. Further up the Potomac, undeveloped waterfront land was still available. There, enough recently freed servants and unpropertied immigrants were advancing into the ranks of landowners to encourage those getting nowhere in the slightly older parts of St. Mary's County to head for the new frontier.[25]

Men who already had acquired land faced other imperatives in the early 1670s—and these too encouraged local if not long-distance migration. In families with more than one child, prudent fathers took up additional land off the manor for the majority of the children and designated the manor tract for one child only. Good undeveloped land in St. Mary's County remained a modest investment for anyone with a little spare capital or access to credit, and most landowners took up undeveloped tracts as an inheritance for their male, and sometimes their female, offspring. Since frequently a landowner would bequeath the dwelling

---

impossible to assess whether this degree of local turnover was in any way exceptional. For studies of persistence and migration within entire counties, see Darrett B. and Anita H. Rutman, " 'More True and Perfect Lists': The Reconstruction of Censuses for Middlesex County, Virginia, 1668–1704," *Virginia Magazine of History and Biography*, LXXXVIII (1980), 37–74, and Lorena S. Walsh, "Staying Put or Getting Out: Findings for Charles County, Maryland, 1650–1720," *WMQ*, 3d Ser., XLIV (1987), 89–103. For a discussion of very different (and much higher) rates of migration between individual parishes and within whole counties in England, see Charles Phythian-Adams, "Little Images of the Great Country: English Rural Communities and English Rural Contexts" (paper presented at the conference "The Social World of Britain and America, 1600–1820," Williamsburg, Va., September 1985).

25. Lorena S. Walsh, "Servitude and Opportunity in Charles County, Maryland, 1658–1705," in Aubrey C. Land, Lois Green Carr, and Edward C. Papenfuse, eds., *Law, Society, and Politics in Early Maryland* (Baltimore, 1977), 111–133.

plantation to his widow for her lifetime use, the child who was to eventually inherit the home farm might well marry and take up residence elsewhere before the mother died. Inheritance strategies too, then, tended to disperse family members across the landscape.

The histories of St. Clement's Manor residents of the 1660s and 1670s indicate that a combination of push and pull continued to draw off most free immigrants and ex-servants who did not quickly acquire land in the area. Those who succeeded were indeed much more likely to remain in the county, but not necessarily to stay on the manor. However, the manor population would still continue to increase as long as landowners could readily get new servants to replace those whose time was finished. The freed servants in turn often stayed around for a few years, working as hired laborers before renting or purchasing a small farm or before moving on in search of greener pastures. Thus, although population continued to rise, family continuity on the land remained more problematic as early death, failure to have children, or the lure of better prospects elsewhere removed individuals from the immediate locality. So long as most St. Clement's area residents were immigrants and not native-born, local ties remained weak. Economic success or failure was much more important in determining whether an immigrant would stay or move than often nonexistent or tenuous family connections.[26]

Thus we see that formal, traditional forms of community organization proved short-lived. St. Clement's Manor was for a time a more organized neighborhood than most in the early Chesapeake—economically, politically, and religiously. But Gerrard's departure, competition from the county court, and rapid turnover of population all undid the manor as an institution.

Nevertheless, the decline of the manor court did not mean that informal community ties declined. Rather, these early settlers forged other patterns of association so enduring that to some extent they function even today. To identify these networks we must infer much from our general knowledge of the social and economic order, as well as examine both the social content and the geographic scope of documented relationships. Examples from the manor and surrounding areas illustrate patterns of interaction on the land, but to explore more fully the social content of neighborhood associations, we must search for instances of such encounters throughout the Chesapeake region.

26. Walsh, "Staying Put or Getting Out," *WMQ*, 3d Ser., XLIV (1987).

Many obstacles hindered the creation of community networks. The physical landscape, sheer distance, and available means of transportation restricted the spatial scope of exchanges between families in the St. Clement's area, as they did elsewhere. Scattered, low-density settlement limited the number of other households that one family could physically reach. The numerous rivers and creeks bisecting the region presented barriers of varying degrees of difficulty, while a scarcity of horses before the 1670s and a poorly developed road system tended to confine movement to foot traffic whenever boats could not be procured. Second, social barriers further restricted possible patterns of interaction. Maidservants, for example, could not readily leave the plantation without their masters' or mistresses' consent, nor could they relate as equals to free women. Neither would common farmers ordinarily form close friendships with members of the provincial elite.[27]

The structure of the local economy, too, tended to limit the extent and density of networks. Since most mid-seventeenth-century planters tried to maximize tobacco production, other economic activities were more incidental. The sale of local products and especially of livestock did augment the income of most households. Nonetheless, tobacco was the chief source of farm income, and seasonal routines revolved around its production and annual exchange for manufactured goods. This exchange often occurred directly between the planter and an English merchant, rather than through colonial middlemen. The tobacco trade required almost no local infrastructure. Economic transactions with other planters were too few, and exchanges of local products too irregular, to lead to the development of markets or marketing networks for other commodities.

In years of heavy immigration a number of new households were formed, all requiring corn and livestock to get started. In the absence of towns, however, there were no established local marketplaces where produce could be readily traded. Buyers usually found sellers simply through word of mouth, learning who had a cow or hogs or corn to spare through the neighborhood grapevine. Neither were there stable groups of local producers and consumers; buyers and sellers were seldom the same from one year to the next. New householders soon achieved self-sufficiency and no longer needed to purchase foodstuffs and livestock. Many established planters who could have produced commodities for the local

27. The analysis of geographic networks as part of a community study is discussed in Darrett B. Rutman, "Community Study," *Historical Methods*, XIII (1980), 29–41, and in Rutman, "Social Web," in O'Neill, ed., *Insights and Parallels*.

market seem not to have done so intentionally. Rather they simply sold off accidental surpluses. The limits of the local market are clear in places where we can estimate population. In the area around St. Clement's in the 1660s, 1670s, and 1680s, there were probably no more than half a dozen new families who were buying provisions and livestock in quantity in a given year, and perhaps no more than three or four within the normal reach of most planters.[28]

Still, discernible patterns of association existed, even at this early stage of development. The lands of most St. Clement's householders of the 1650s, 1660s, and 1670s can be located on a tract map and their recorded contacts with other households plotted. Some regularities emerge. All the repeated and ordinary contacts of male residents involved other households lying within an approximate five-mile radius of the home, a journey of an hour or two. As most communications and transactions were oral rather than written, a man's effective communication network seldom exceeded this five-mile area where face-to-face contacts could be conveniently made. Since families living on the periphery of one settler's network regularly gleaned news of those living as much as five miles farther away, the extent of the information network might in effect have been doubled. However, since the first settler was probably unacquainted with many of the individuals known to the second, conversation was likely limited to news about mutual acquaintances living within effective reach of both.[29]

Robert Cole (1628–c. 1663), Richard Foster (c. 1621–c. 1675), John

28. These ideas are expanded and documented in a manuscript in preparation for the Colonial Williamsburg Foundation on plantation management in the Chesapeake, 1609–1820, by the author.

29. Biographies of all 17th-century St. Mary's County residents have been compiled by the St. Mary's City Commission through stripping of relevant record series, and county tract maps for 1642, 1659, 1705, and 1763 were constructed from patents, deeds, surveys, plats, rent rolls, and from later boundary adjudications. These two sources were used to make maps of the networks of all the recorded associations of 15 St. Clement's Manor residents and of 12 individuals living nearby. The discussion of network size and content is based on the results of these maps and on additional analysis of the spatial clustering of residences of appraisers of all extant 17th-century probate inventories for the county and of the decedents whose property they valued. In many cases residence could be located on a specific tract of land and in most others within a small geographic area, e.g., on Basford Manor. Association patterns were then examined both for distance between contacts and for evidence of clustering of associations. All this material is housed at the Maryland State Archives in Annapolis. For discussion of credit networks and additional patterns of individual interaction on

Shanks (c. 1627–1685), and John Hilton (c. 1643–c. 1705), whose association patterns are shown in map 3, were all manor residents: Cole, Foster, and Shanks became middling planters, while Hilton remained a tenant farmer. Cole migrated from England in 1652, along with his wife, four children, and two servants. Foster and his family moved to the manor from Lynnhaven Bay, Virginia, in the same year. Both were able to purchase land at once. Shanks arrived as an indentured servant in 1640, and it took him twelve years to save enough to buy a farm. Hilton also came as a servant, working four years for Robert Cole, and had taken up a leasehold on Basford Manor by 1676. Cole and Foster, the wealthier of the four, had the widest networks, including a few contacts not shown on the map. Cole traded livestock with some Charles County planters living further up the Potomac and attended a meeting of the provincial court in St. Mary's City, while Foster exchanged goods with two Virginians, Francis Yardley of Lynnhaven and William Fitzhugh of Stafford. John

---

the manor, see James Horn, "Adapting to a New World: A Comparative Study of Local Society in England and Maryland, 1650–1700," in this volume.

Any analysis of networks must rest on surviving evidence, and this material is woefully incomplete and inherently biased. Attempting to measure the degree of kinship among 17th-century Maryland settlers, for example, is a formidable task. Until the Anglican church was established in the colony in 1692, neither civil nor church registers of vital events were systematically kept, and many of those that once existed have not survived. Evidence of kin connections among immigrants is even more incomplete than for the native-born, since there are no genealogies showing the English connections of many ordinary settlers. In most cases kinship can be traced only through the male line; connections through the female line were perhaps equally instrumental, but in most cases simply cannot be followed in the absence of marriage records.

Instrumental ties can be effectively traced only through surviving legal documents, occasionally supplemented with highly idiosyncratic evidence of more informal connections recorded in depositions. Appearances as witnesses, securities, guardians, attorneys, appraisers, and legatees thus constitute the bulk of the evidence. For men, such formally recorded associations clearly represent only a tiny proportion of all associations and, in addition, document much better the relationships of the long-lived and of the more prominent and active householders. Female networks cannot be traced, even on this limited basis, since a married woman's legal role (and in the 17th century almost all adult women were married for the better part of their lives) was highly circumscribed. For a discussion of the difficulties in dealing with surviving evidence of association patterns, see Darrett B. Rutman and Anita H. Rutman, *A Place in Time: Middlesex County, Virginia, 1650–1750* (New York, 1984), chap. 5, and *Explicatus* (part 2 of *A Place in Time*), chap. 8.

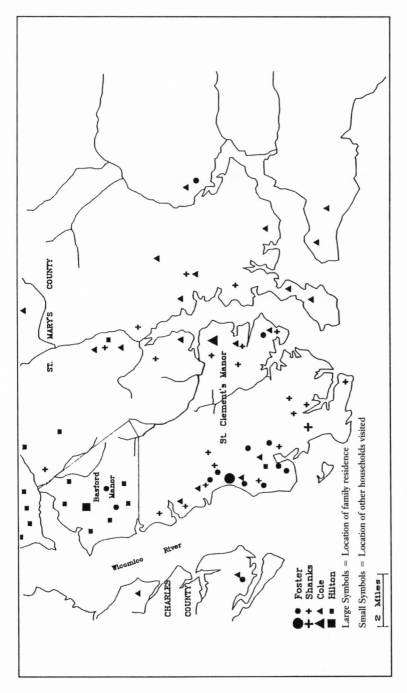

MAP 3 . *Association Patterns for Four Families*

Shanks's most frequent contacts were with other manor residents, including two married children, but government service as an Indian interpreter occasioned at least two longer trips. Hilton, the poorest of the four, had the most circumscribed network.

The most frequent contacts of these four men as well as those of other manor residents involved even shorter distances—within two to three miles of the home.[30] In the early 1660s, this meant that a family's choices were limited indeed. In the St. Clement's area, the typical household of the early 1660s would find only about fifteen other families within a two-and-a-half-mile radius of the home farm and about twenty-five families within five miles (see map 4). With possible contacts so restricted, it follows that most families had a vested interest in maintaining good relations with their neighbors.

By the early 1670s the situation was changing. St. Clement's residents then had about twenty-five households within two and a half miles of their homes and perhaps sixty within five miles (see map 5). Thus it was becoming possible for individuals and their families to choose at least to some extent with whom they would most closely associate. The difficult, dishonest, or ungenerous could be more easily avoided, and neighbors with like views in religion or politics more readily cultivated. This increased luxury of choice may have been one of the factors that contributed to a diminution on St. Clement's Manor of the apparently greater cohesiveness of the earlier years.

30. The Rutmans found an almost identical pattern in Middlesex County. Most associations took place within "relatively tight clusters two to three miles across with only occasional outliers." Circa 1700, 36% of all marriages were between persons living within a half mile of each other, and 95% were between individuals living no more than five miles apart (*A Place in Time*, 120–121). Similarly, Perry found that 80% of all recorded face-to-face contacts between landowners took place within a three-mile radius, and that only 8% of such contacts involved traveling more than six miles ("Formation of a Society," 98). One can find comparative evidence of the similar physical limits to association in other colonies. For example, a North Carolina missionary reported in 1704 that he had to hold a service every ten miles, "for five miles is the furthest they will bring their children, or willingly come themselves" ("Reverend John Blair's Mission to North Carolina, 1704," in Alexander S. Salley, Jr., ed., *Narratives of Early Carolina, 1650–1708* [New York, 1911], 217). Similarly, David Konig found that in 17th-century Essex County, Massachusetts, the optimum distance for smooth-functioning economic relationships did not exceed two miles. Economic transactions were indeed made over greater distances, but these much more often involved litigation than did bargains made closer to home. *Law and Society in Puritan Massachusetts: Essex County, 1629–1692* (Chapel Hill, N.C., 1979), chap. 3.

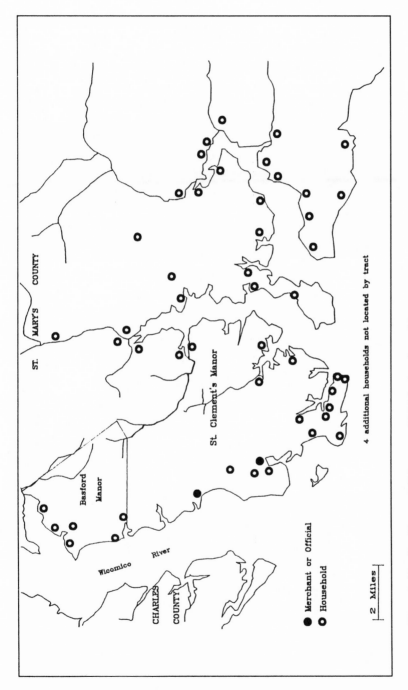

MAP 4. *Households, St. Clement's-Newtown Neighborhood c. 1660*

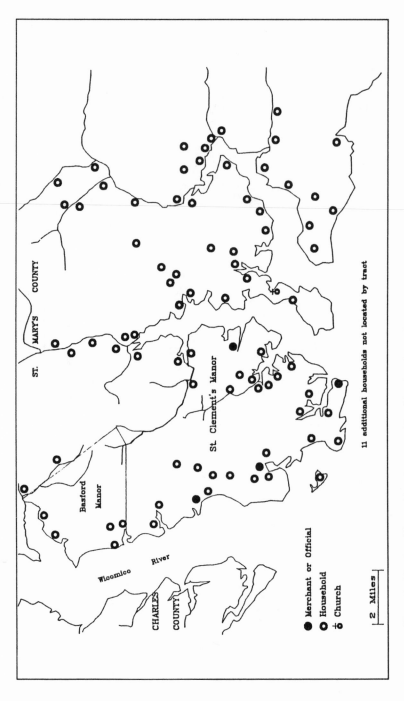

MAP 5 . *Households, St. Clement's–Newtown Neighborhood c. 1670*

In Virginia, fewer settlers encountered the marked religious differences that came to divide some Maryland communities, especially those in St. Mary's and Charles counties, where Roman Catholics remained a substantial minority. However, with continued local population growth, Chesapeake settlers everywhere could become more discriminating in their choice of associates. In Middlesex County, Virginia, for example, although the number of neighbors with whom a householder was friendly did not change much between 1687 and 1724, the character of those associations did. In 1687 only 17 percent of all identifiable friendships between household heads involved a tie by blood or marriage; by 1724, a full 64 percent of friends were also kin. Middlesex residents were coming to select most of their friends from among nearby kin, while families on the lower Western Shore increasingly applied the dual criteria of kinship and shared religion.[31]

For most married women, face-to-face contacts were usually confined to the twenty or so households within two to three miles of home. Since a planter's wife was soon burdened with nursing infants and slightly older toddlers, she could not easily travel very far from her own farm and thus visited most frequently with neighbor women living only a few miles away.[32] Evidence from depositions makes clear that women traveled greater distances also. Such journeys, however, entailed often complicated arrangements for child care and would usually have been undertaken only infrequently. Consequently the planter's wife had to rely on her husband's somewhat wider contacts to glean news of what was going on in the larger neighborhood. Doubtless she learned as much as she could from passersby who stopped at the house on business or to seek refreshment or shelter.[33]

31. See Rutman and Rutman, *A Place in Time*, 103, and *Explicatus*, chap. 8, for Middlesex. Graham, "Lord Baltimore's Pious Enterprise," chaps. 3 and 7, documents the tendency for Roman Catholics to rely on other Catholics, while Allan Kulikoff discusses the importance of both kin and religion in choice of friends in the 18th century in *Tobacco and Slaves: The Development of Southern Cultures in the Chesapeake, 1680–1800* (Chapel Hill, N.C., 1986), chap. 6.

32. Laurel Thatcher Ulrich found that New England women traveled least when pregnant or nursing, but were more apt to stay home for the first 10 months after the birth of a child than during pregnancy (*Good Wives: Image and Reality in the Lives of Women in Northern New England, 1650–1750* [New York, 1982], chap. 7). For women's networks, see also Rutman and Rutman, *A Place in Time*, 103–113.

33. This material is documented and elaborated in Lorena S. Walsh, "Women's Networks in the Colonial Chesapeake" (paper presented at the annual meeting of the Organization of American Historians, Cincinnati, Ohio, 1983).

Although women's visiting networks remained more restricted than men's, by the early eighteenth century there were changes for them as well. The wide availability of horses and greatly expanded and improved road systems facilitated travel. Population growth continued to expand the number of households within convenient distance in many places. However, in areas where slaveholding became most widespread, most of the added households were black. The number of neighboring white households (and thus of potential white women friends) may not have grown significantly beyond late-seventeenth-century concentrations.[34]

For men, the degree of geographic mobility was closely related to their occupation and economic position. Freedmen, who had few livestock and few or no crops to tend and no encumbering families, often moved to seek work. Tailors, coopers, carpenters, and ordinary laborers might live in the households of several employers widely scattered by distance over the course of a year. Conversely, tenant farmers and small landowners were least likely to venture far from home. Heavily reliant upon their own and their wives' labor, they could not leave crops and livestock unattended for long. Middling planters were more likely to have wider connections between five and ten miles of their farms as well as nearer by, and also had more occasion to travel to meetings of the county court or to the provincial capital at St. Mary's City. Such men were likelier to have surplus produce to sell locally and could leave their servants to tend the farm on occasion. Once a planter was appointed to a county office (often a confirmation of his having achieved a leading economic position), his local connections became more dense and his travel within his own county (and to a lesser extent, neighboring counties) more frequent. Civic responsibilities probably also increased a man's access to information. A justice could learn much about local happenings without stirring far from his home. The area constables often needed to consult with him, and dissatisfied servants and litigious neighbors kept him informed about local problems.

Planter-merchants, such as St. Clement's resident Robert Slye or William Fitzhugh in Stafford County across the Potomac, enjoyed the widest communication networks. These men employed sailors and sloop captains to navigate surrounding rivers and creeks and to contact planters not only within the home county but in three or four adjacent counties as

34. Kulikoff describes transportation networks in 18th-century southern Maryland in *Tobacco and Slaves*, chap. 6.

well. Unlike prosperous planters and ordinary county justices, whose connections were usually confined to about a ten-mile radius of their homes, planter-merchants could maintain extensive contacts within a fifteen-mile compass and had some dealings within a twenty-five-mile radius of their home plantations. While these connections were based primarily on trade, they could be turned to political advantage on occasion. Similarly, doctors and ministers also traveled widely and served as links between more localized neighborhoods.[35]

A variety of activities might bring many adult male colonists together whatever their occupation—militia musters and expeditions, hunting forays, trips to the capital or county court, negotiations with ship captains, and in later years, visits to a local store. Such ventures did serve to draw men out of their usual neighborhoods to new areas and sometimes to centers of power. However, for ordinary planters these were infrequent occasions. As late as 1759 the *Maryland Gazette* eulogized Anne Arundel County planter Robert Boone, "an honest and industrious Planter, who Died on the same Plantation where he was Born in 1680, from which he never went 30 Miles in his Life."[36]

Even a planter or a housewife who rarely ventured far afield was part of a neighborhood, a discernible territorial entity that circumscribed his or her most frequent economic and social exchanges. Geography, proximity, greater familiarity, and perhaps mere force of habit led settlers to confine most of their social interactions to households within their neighborhood, and to slight other households, perhaps no further away, whose primary connections were with an adjacent neighborhood cluster. Some external bounds are easily explained—wide rivers, expanses of unsettled land, and large swamps that presented real barriers to travel. In other instances, there were apparently no significant physical barriers, but instead established focal points that channeled the flow of communication in different directions. Collective activities tended to move from the periphery of a neighborhood (within a radius of approximately five miles) inward toward

35. Fitzhugh's activities are documented in Richard Beale Davis, ed., *William Fitzhugh and His Chesapeake World, 1676–1701* (Chapel Hill, N.C., 1963). Generalizations in this and preceding paragraphs are based on the network maps and biographical files discussed in n. 29, above, and on an analysis of bills of particulars found in 17th- and early-18th-century Charles County court records. For similar conclusions about the size of the networks of various occupational groups, see Perry, "Formation of a Society," chap. 4.

36. *Maryland Gazette*, Feb. 15, 1759.

the sites of very early settlement. A study of the interaction patterns of individuals who left inventories between 1658 and 1705 in St. Mary's County showed that settlement clusters established in the 1640s continued to serve as centers for local interaction well into the next century (at St. Mary's City, further south around the Roman Catholic holdings at St. Inigoe's, across the St. Mary's River in St. George's Hundred, and further up the Potomac around Bretton's Bay). In areas that were settled later, clusters that developed in the 1660s served a similar function.

Part of the explanation for this pattern involves population density and topography. Social networks mirrored the original flow of settlement, hugging the edges of rivers and creeks. Where the rivers were not too wide, there was more contact between families living directly across the water than between families living on opposite sides of the same peninsula. This was not necessarily a matter of water transport being quicker or easier, since land travel across gentle Chesapeake divides was not especially difficult. Rather, it appears that functioning networks depended on households being sited at fairly frequent intervals. As long as land without direct water access remained unsettled, neighborhoods did not extend across that divide.

The second part of the explanation is economic and political. A few early settlers who arrived with ready capital usually commandeered the best land and built highly developed and capitalized farms. Subsequently, such choice establishments continued in the possession of influential men—whether through inheritance, purchase, or marriage to the widow of the initial settler. Because the proprietors of such farms almost invariably became county officials and not infrequently planter-merchants, political, economic, and social activities continued to be directed to these early focal points. On St. Clement's Manor in the 1660s, the home of the lord of the manor and the house and store of merchant Robert Slye served as gathering places. In the 1670s the homes of several justices of the peace and of the district naval officer provided the same function. The manor house ceased to operate as a focal point once Thomas Gerrard removed to Virginia. However, even toward the end of the eighteenth century, county justices of the peace and planter-merchants usually lived on the home farms established by Gerrard's son, Justinian, and by his sons-in-law Robert Slye, Nehemiah Blakiston, and Kenelm Cheseldyne, as well as on Luke Gardiner's home farm.

Early court records frequently mention both neighbors and neighborhoods—one's reputation in the neighborhood, the common knowledge of the neighborhood, and the like. When a planter or his wife referred to their neighbors, they generally meant the residents of nearby households living within about two and a half miles. On the other hand, their neighborhood was that territorial unit within which activities were most focused. In Maryland, neighborhoods identified by activity patterns of local residents followed the boundaries of the various hundreds within a county. Settlers themselves provided further corroboration of the self-identifying character of these units. When dealing with other county residents in the seventeenth century, men who wanted to identify themselves by geographic locality most often used a hundred or a watershed, and thus a neighborhood designation (Robert Cole of St. Clement's and William Evans of Bretton's Bay, for example). Map 6 shows the approximate location of these kinds of neighborhoods in seventeenth-century St. Mary's County.[37]

By the second quarter of the eighteenth century, individuals much less often identified themselves with a neighborhood, instead naming themselves as of a particular plantation, of a more specific location (Thomas Spalding Court House as opposed to Thomas Spalding Beaver Dam), or by genealogy (Thomas Spalding of Thomas, Thomas Spalding of William, etc.). But although patterns of self-identification changed—and probably attitudes toward neighborhoods as well—to a surprising degree the early patterns of neighborly interaction have endured. Modern county election districts closely follow the bounds of the seventeenth-century hundreds. And as late as the 1970s, the delivery areas of rural St. Mary's County post offices tended to replicate networks of association traceable from the 1670s.[38]

37. The boundaries shown in map 6 are based on association patterns, which also approximate the boundaries of the hundreds c. 1700 insofar as we know them. Since the county court records have not survived, no full description of hundred bounds is available. Most can be ascertained reasonably well from a 1705 tract map, since the rent roll of 1705 assigned all tracts to a particular hundred. However, precise boundaries for tracts located in the interior could not always be plotted, so interior hundred bounds are also not well defined. Two small hundreds, St. George's and St. Inigoe's, appear not to have functioned as separate neighborhoods and have been included on the map as parts of Poplar Hill and St. Michael's communities respectively.

38. Though most interior tracts remained unpatented and undeveloped in 1705, all had been taken up and most improved by 1790, which resulted in some reorientation of neighborhoods. Regina Combs Hammett, *History of St. Mary's County, Maryland* (Ridge, Md., 1977), chap. 10, demonstrates the continuity between historic neighborhoods and current postal delivery areas. Modern zip code districts are available in ADC, *St. Mary's County, Md., Street Map* (Alexandria, Va., 1983). While post–World War II suburban developments and the construction of the Patuxent Naval Air Station

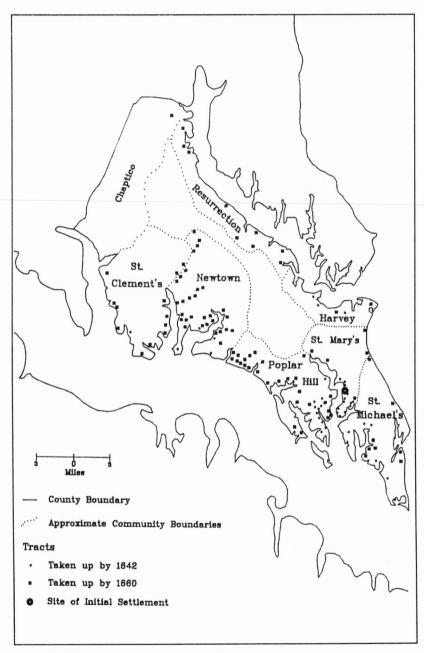

MAP 6. *St. Mary's County Communities c. 1700*

Source: St. Mary's City Tract Maps.

What functions did such neighborhoods perform? What kinds of support might settlers expect from their neighbors and what kinds of obligations did they honor? Surviving records document formalities most fully—which neighbors an individual chose to witness a deed or will, for example, or who appraised an estate or stood security for a litigated debt. But what of the more frequent and much less serious commonplace interactions that were the stuff of normal life? Here formal records tell us little, and in order to address the subject, we must turn to the few eyewitness descriptions of everyday circumstances that survive.[39]

For the seventeenth-century Chesapeake, such testimony is found primarily in depositions. Few in number and preserved either by chance or because they concerned unusual circumstances, surviving contemporary accounts clearly cannot be used to demonstrate anything about the regularity of the informal contacts that they describe. However, they do reveal that, in some places and times in the seventeenth-century Chesapeake, neighborliness involved at least some of the qualitative dimensions that have been ascribed to it in contemporary New England communities. Indeed, the power of neighborly cooperation to help hold together an otherwise disparate, sexually imbalanced, socially unstable, highly mobile, short-lived, and disease-ridden society has often been ignored or at best underestimated.[40]

---

have led to some subdivision and reorientation of 17th-century neighborhoods, present-day communication networks still show remarkable continuity with those of the colonial era.

39. County court records c. 1640 to c. 1680 offer the most examples, for during these years court procedures were extremely informal and supporting depositions often were recorded. See, for example, Susie M. Ames, ed., *County Court Records of Accomack-Northampton, Virginia, 1632–1640* (Washington, D.C., 1954) and Ames, ed., *County Court Records of Accomack-Northampton, Virginia, 1640–1645* (Charlottesville, Va., 1973); selected 17th-century Maryland county records from Charles, Talbot, Kent, and Somerset and period provincial court records published in the *Md. Archives*; later manuscript court and land records for Charles and Somerset counties and depositions concerning land disputes in the Provincial Court Papers (formerly Ejectment Papers), Md. State Archives; Lower Norfolk County, Virginia, Wills and Deeds; Northumberland County, Virginia, Record Books; and Westmoreland County, Virginia, Wills and Deeds (the Virginia records are available on microfilm at the Virginia State Library in Richmond). Such sources are particularly essential since all the colonial St. Mary's County court records were destroyed in a courthouse fire in 1831.

40. Among historians of the American colonies there remains a tendency to consider New England the norm when it comes to considerations of community and neighborliness. There is every reason to suppose that in a society that enjoyed

Early Maryland court records demonstrate that the function of neighborhoods was social in the broadest sense. The touchstones of neighborhood were familiarity and frequent contact. Each family knew well and
was well known by all the others. The economic and social position,
reputation, and everyday affairs of each were familiar to all the rest; few
pretenses were possible. The exchange of news and gossip, the main
means of communication in a predominantly oral culture, continually
supplied fresh information. In addition, informal neighborhood activities—mutual aid, bearing witness, watching and warding, and mediation
of disputes—contributed to the smooth functioning of community affairs.
Land boundaries and economic agreements, for example, were preserved
as much (or more) in the minds of the contracting parties and the memories of the neighbors who bore witness to the transactions as they were by
blazes on trees or words put on paper.[41]

---

extraordinary longevity, social and geographic stability (although the latter has probably been exaggerated), and religious homogeneity, communal and consensual behavior would have been most intense. Yet to suppose that community depends on long-
term relationships, for example, strikes me as an exceedingly myopic perspective.
Even in our own century, only a small proportion of the world's inhabitants have
enjoyed the extraordinary life-spans of 17th-century New Englanders. Among the
works that have dealt with the functions of neighborliness in New England are
Zuckerman, *Peaceable Kingdoms*; Konig, *Law and Society*; Ulrich, *Good Wives*; David
H. Flaherty, *Privacy in Colonial New England* (Charlottesville, Va., 1967); and Lyle
Koehler, *A Search for Power: The "Weaker Sex" in Seventeenth-Century New England*
(Urbana, Ill., 1980).

The quantity of contacts in either region is even more problematic. Only personal
diaries can provide accurate answers, and these are rare enough for New England,
almost nonexistent for the early Chesapeake. It is easy to assume that both the
intensity and the absolute frequency of neighborly interchanges were greater in New
England. Proof, however, is another matter. The evidence about associations in the
two regions is roughly similar and cannot be used to estimate total numbers of
individual contacts. In addition, we need to know much more about settlement
densities, especially the number of households per square mile, in both regions.

41. See Walsh, "Women's Networks in the Colonial Chesapeake"; Walsh, "Charles
County, Maryland, 1658–1705: A Study of Chesapeake Social and Political Structure" (Ph.D. diss., Michigan State University, 1977), chaps. 5 and 7; and Carr,
"County Government in Maryland." Here my discussion emphasizes the similarities
among Chesapeake neighborhoods. There were of course many local variations in
custom within the region—differences in inheritance patterns, for instance, or varying
degrees of zeal or laxity in punishing fornication. In colonies with different demographic, economic, social, and religious histories one would expect to find even
greater differences. Allen, *In English Ways*, discusses some of the many variations in

Social visiting further strengthened relations with neighbors. In 1687 the Huguenot visitor Durand of Dauphiné commented not altogether favorably on the settlers' fondness for these events. He asserted that "the people spend most of their time visiting each other. . . . The land is so rich & so fertile that when a man has fifty acres of ground, two men-servants, a maid & some cattle, neither he nor his wife do anything but visit among their neighbors."[42] Surviving depositions describe a variety of convivial gatherings. Most took place within individual homes, for until well into the 1680s there was almost nowhere else to go for casual conversation, for games, or for large-scale socializing. Chances for social intercourse were sufficiently limited that a neighbor's passing by was reason enough for a pause in the daily rounds, an excuse to exchange news, to "pipe it," and perhaps to have a drink.[43]

On court days, Saturday afternoons, and especially on Sundays, neighbors got together for more organized recreations. This usually meant more smoking and drinking (activities in which, Durand noted, the women were foremost), perhaps singing and dancing, sometimes political discussions, and very often games. Visiting after church was an established practice. Those who lacked either the opportunity or the inclination to attend Sunday services nonetheless met on Sunday for convivial entertainment. Numerous prosecutions for selling cider and "keeping very disorderly doeings" in private houses on the Sabbath attest both to the prevalence of the custom and to the puritan inclinations of some members of the community. Both men and women enjoyed games played with cards or dice, while hustle-cap, stoolball, tenpins, and shooting matches occupied the menfolk alone. A few wealthy planters added the refinement of billiard tables. Gambling usually accompanied most of these games, often for stakes that the participants could ill afford to lose.

A passion for horse racing was also common. By the 1670s there was a "race house" in Charles County somewhere near the courthouse at Port Tobacco where Saturday races were run, attracting a crowd of planters and servants on their afternoon off. References appear to a racecourse on

---

approaches to community life that appeared even within the supposedly homogeneous Massachusetts Bay colony. But variation does not negate some basic underlying similarities.

42. Durand of Dauphiné, *A Huguenot Exile in Virginia; or, Voyages of a Frenchman Exiled for His Religion* . . . , ed. Gilbert Chinard (New York, 1934), 111.

43. Walsh, "Charles County," chap. 5.

St. Clement's Manor about the same time, and there were doubtless other courses in the St. Mary's County area. The races were usually between local horses, but occasional matches with horses from outside the county generated intense excitement. At such matches wagers often ran high. Although only wealthy planters could afford to keep racehorses, as a spectator sport racing brought together large numbers of county residents of all stations.[44]

Rites of passage—marriages and especially the all too prevalent funerals—took on an almost frenetic quality. In 1687 Durand described the wedding of a French freedman that involved more than one hundred guests and enough food for at least twice that number. After the ceremony and the ample late-afternoon meal eaten outside under the trees, the evening and the entire night were spent in drinking beer, cider, and punch, smoking, singing, and dancing. All the beds were put in one room for those women and girls who eventually chose to retire; the men had to make do with the hall floor, which may not have mattered since all were reported thoroughly drunk.[45]

Or a funeral in Charles County in 1662. An unprepossessing planter died, soon followed by his wife and two children. The observance began when the administrator rowed to the nearest store to fetch beer and mourning ribbon for the event. "By reason of the badnes of the weather," the advance party "tarried a day or too thear and drank out one of the three barrells of beear." When the official day finally arrived, "thear wear at the funerall all the neighbour[s] living about," where "thay had intertainment part of too days," shooting off a number of parting volleys and consuming the remaining two barrels of beer plus two bottles of drams. One appalled county justice questioned whether the proceedings were "Christian like," but a local jury ruled that since there were no surviving heirs to be considered, "so long as an Estate sufficient was left . . . [it] only redounded to the Credit and Memory of the Persons deceased."[46]

Some seventeenth-century planting families were doubtless inordinately fond of socializing and prone to turn, upon the flimsiest of excuses, to "thear Carousing Cups," in the words of one scandalized official. However, few could afford to neglect their crops for long, and most attended relatively conscientiously to a staple agriculture that required an

44. *Ibid.*
45. Durand of Dauphiné, *Huguenot Exile in Virginia*, 137–139.
46. *Md. Archives*, LIII, 207–210.

almost unremitting cycle of hard and often lonely toil. Left behind in England were the customary local holidays, market days, or annual fairs that afforded an opportunity for regular, less emotional, social gatherings. For many, only the inevitable rituals of birth, marriage, and death provided a justifiable excuse for a break in the daily work routine. All the talking, feasting, drinking, singing, and dancing that strength permitted had to be packed into a few hours or at most a day or two. With few other outlets available, the resulting celebration or commiseration doubtless served as an essential emotional outlet for hardworking farm families who otherwise had only chance opportunities for gathering together.

Mutual aid and shared labor further strengthened bonds in Chesapeake neighborhoods. The hospitality customarily extended to travelers needs no further comment. Rather less has been said of the extent to which a family used its time and resources to cement good relations with neighbors old and new. A loan of what one could spare when others fell short, for example, was often extended. As one writer put it, "There is no man will ever be denied the loane of Corne for his house-spending, and seed till the Harvest."[47] Near neighbors cooperated in framing buildings, hunting and killing hogs, gathering corn, housing and packing tobacco, mauling rails, carting or rolling produce, threshing grain, cutting wood, and processing yarn. They lent tools and exchanged salt, corn, liquor, meat, and cloth from family stocks when neighbors needed them. Men and women were expected to share of their time when neighbors were ill or shorthanded. The beneficiaries were then under a strong obligation to reciprocate. Aid extended in time of need established a future claim for similar kinds of help, help that could be critical to the family's survival.[48] Indeed, neighborly obligations claimed first precedence, even over more formal duties. For example, the Charles County bench remitted Constable Richard Dod's fine for failing to appear in court when they learned that he was absent, "being out of Charity forst to ride to fetch one to bleed a near neighbour which Lay at the point of Death."[49]

Neighborliness sometimes required that a family concede more than

47. E[dward] W[illiams], *Virginia: More Especially the South Part Thereof, Richly and Truly Valued* . . . (1650), in Peter Force, comp., *Tracts and Other Papers, Relating Principally to the Origin, Settlement, and Progress of the Colonies in North America,* 4 vols. (Washington, D.C., 1836–1846), III, no. 11, 47.

48. Walsh, "Charles County," chap. 5, and Walsh, "Women's Networks in the Colonial Chesapeake."

49. Charles County Court and Land Records, X #1, 340, Md. State Archives.

the mere letter of the law demanded, and indeed even this might not satisfy all. Roving horses, cattle, and hogs presented continual and vexing problems, while difficulties arising over dogs raised issues that even the modern suburbanite can well appreciate. One aggrieved planter in Charles County, for example, when sued for keeping a vicious dog, argued that justice had already been served. The neighbor who prosecuted him "was in the hows and that hee trod upon the bitch and in testimonie of his sorrow for the plantive['s] misfortune in beeing bitt [by] the sayd bitch although it was throughe his owne Carlesnes hee killed his bitch." County courts expected this kind of restitution. The same court released planter William Robinson from a bond restraining him from hunting abroad, but only on the condition that he pay the court costs, "by reason that hee hath partly bin the occasion of this suit or complaint by not killing his doge upon the complaint of his neighbours."[50]

Legal procedures occasionally took into account and formalized some aspects of informal neighborhood cooperation and consensus forming. In cases of unexplained deaths it was usually the neighbors—the persons with the greatest knowledge of the individuals concerned—who sat on the coroner's jury. Disputes about land boundaries were also settled in the locality; a special "jury of the neighborhood" was summoned to consider the evidence of both claimants on the basis of the jurors' knowledge of local geography and of traditionally accepted boundaries. County courts sometimes ordered that the more time-consuming repairs to roads and bridges be made by those living close by. Men of the vicenage (rather than the larger hundreds or parishes that were the usual work units) might be instructed to take full responsibility for making improvements to roads and bridges in the immediate area. When a soldier was pressed for far-ranging expeditions, the local constable was responsible for assigning near neighbors to tend his crops.[51]

There was of course a fine line between friendly neighborly aid, or at least responsible intervention, and downright meddling. Neighbors were likely to proffer admonition and advice without being asked, if they felt that one of their number was violating established community norms, but the overzealous might go much further. Then neighborly intervention heightened rather than relieved tensions. For example, when Cyprian Bishop of Northumberland County, Virginia, informed neighbor Richard

50. *Ibid.*, B #2, 89–90, A #1, 231–232.
51. Walsh, "Charles County," chap. 5.

Flint that a woman had been spreading tales that Flint's mother used to run a bawdy house in England, Flint wanted to ignore the incident. Bishop seems to have taken a certain relish in repeating the story, and Flint "tooke it not as a neighborly curtesy." Doubtless he was even more perturbed when Goodman and Goodwife Bishop proceeded to drag the affair into the county court, apparently hoping to see the offending tale-bearer soundly whipped.[52] Sometimes county justices would refuse to act on this sort of meddling, as in Maryland when the Charles County Court dismissed an action of slander "being by Court lookt one as a frivolous atton and more out of malice than anything else," or another case where they decided that "as it was a dronken busines the Charge shall bee equalie devided."[53]

Passing news along the local grapevine was not necessarily a constructive means of communication. In a predominantly oral culture, gossip was the main way of exchanging all kinds of information from the most trivial to the most grave. Gossip, even in its most modern and pejorative sense, was far from an exclusively feminine preoccupation in the seventeenth-century Chesapeake. With few organized recreational outlets available, speculation about one's neighbors' possible excesses constituted a major source of entertainment for both sexes. Men and women avidly traded news of their neighbors' doings and seem to have taken special delight in discussing marital disputes and supposed sexual irregularities. That sexual tensions should have been high is hardly surprising. With men outnumbering women by two or three to one, few married women were safe from the suggestive comments of unattached males, not to mention their sexual overtures. Unmarried daughters and maidservants were subjected to even greater pressures. At the same time, privacy was difficult to obtain in cramped living quarters that often sheltered boarders and servants as well as family members. Hospitality demanded that the housewife offer a bed to any traveler seeking overnight shelter; if the only one available was her own, some of her neighbors would be unable to resist speculating as to the result.

Lewd conversation seems for many settlers to have been their usual idiom, too common to merit more than an occasional reproach, as when a woman reviling a man was reminded that "civiler language would become

52. Northumberland County, Virginia, Record Book, 1652–1658, fol. 20. Photostat at Va. State Library.
53. Charles County Court and Land Records, G #1, 93; *Md. Archives*, LIII, 418.

her." Gossips were usually formally prosecuted as "disturbers of the neighborhood" or as barrators (a legal term sometimes applied to those who vexatiously raised or incited litigation) when they tried to pass off their more inventive fancies as fact, especially in mixed company where the situation could easily get out of hand. Others, however, used sexual slander less promiscuously, as a powerful and quite calculated weapon. Sometimes the motives were private. A rejected suitor might try to dissuade other men from courting a girl by spreading stories that he had already slept with her. Conversely, one bachelor sued a spinster for slander, contending that her claim to having had sexual relations with him was interfering with his efforts to "attaine a wife." In another case jealousy prompted a spurned woman to fabricate a vivid tale about her lover's alleged liaison with a rival in order to punish both. Attacks on a spouse might wound much more effectually than direct personal insult. More than one man, angered over a soured bargain, managed to provoke a desired free-for-all by calling his erstwhile partner's wife a whore.[54]

But most of all, gossip in the early Chesapeake was a way of challenging authority and of expressing resentment about the social pretensions of the emerging ruling class. Talk about the sexual irregularities or incapacities of county officials or of the alleged promiscuity of their wives served to bring those in power down to the level of the politically powerless. Because many early officials sorely lacked social prestige to bolster their position, they were especially sensitive to such innuendos.[55]

Neighborhood consensus much more than formal statute defined proper standards of behavior, and these were in turn enforced more often by informal sanction than by magisterial intervention. Local residence groups could exert considerable pressures for conformity. The penalties for flagrant and repeated violations of neighborhood norms were so severe that most heads of household were unwilling to risk the consequences of universal condemnation by their neighbors. Informal sanctions, ranging from unfavorable talk to outright refusals of aid, could quickly become formal sanctions if neighbors made complaints to justices or grand juries or refused to stand as sureties. Free men and women who

54. *Md. Archives*, XLI, 550, LIV, 576–577, 534–539; Ames, ed., *County Records of Accomack-Northampton, 1640–1645*, 287, 290–291, 299–300. Mary Beth Norton, "Gender and Defamation in Seventeenth-Century Maryland," *WMQ*, 3d Ser., XLIV (1987), 3–39, analyzes sexual patterns of slanderous talk.
55. For documentation, see Walsh, "Women's Networks in the Colonial Chesapeake." For discussions of the role of gossip in New England, see Ulrich, *Good Wives*, chaps. 3 and 5, and Koehler, *Search for Power*, chaps. 3 and 7.

fell afoul of the law could escape corporal punishment or prison only if their neighbors were willing to act as securities for payment of fines or to post bond for the person's future good behavior. Whatever the merits of the case, county benches were likely to deal more harshly with individuals who did not "live in good fame" among their neighbors, and juries were doubtless influenced by local reputation as well. Even the most law-abiding man needed securities when he wanted to borrow money locally, obtain credit from English merchants, administer an estate, or hold a public office that entailed fiscal responsibility.

A married woman would still have been concerned about maintaining her reputation, although by law she could seldom act directly for herself. She must often have pressured her mate to remain on good terms with at least some of the neighbors, since the family's welfare could all too easily depend on it. Many women must have been aware that there was an excellent chance the husband would die first. A widow would forfeit whatever benefits might arise from administering her husband's estate if male neighbors refused to post bond for her. In addition, if she was left alone with several small children to raise and no one to help with the farming, only the generous assistance of near neighbors would keep the family together.[56]

Neighborly contacts involved a good measure of watching and warding. A community with no organized police had to rely heavily on the sharp eyes of private citizens just to maintain some semblance of order. For example, families who butchered a hog or steer were expected to retain the marked ears of the animal for inspection on demand. Any housewife with pork stewing in her pot was expected to account to her neighbors for its origin. Failure to do so constituted a tacit admission of stealing or at least of being an accessory to poaching, a serious crime.[57] Such an accusation, as one man put it, tended to "strike at the roote of the reputacion of him . . . & tendinge much to the breach of his comfortable liveinge amongst his neighbors."[58] Neighborly watchfulness rendered theft of less perishable possessions difficult indeed. Men and women often knew every article of their nearer neighbors' property, and they would almost certainly notice if a missing pot, coat, or tablecloth appeared in someone else's house. When Mary Clocker stole from her

56. Lois Green Carr and Lorena S. Walsh, "The Planter's Wife: The Experience of White Women in Seventeenth-Century Maryland," *WMQ*, 3d Ser., XXXIV (1977), 542–571.
57. See, for example, *Md. Archives*, LIV, 42–44, 49–51, 88–89, 582–587.
58. Charles County Court and Land Records, E #1, 138.

neighbor and employer, she was reduced to hiding the loot in a hollow tree, not only unable to use the goods, but even to bring them into the house for fear of detection.[59]

Neighborly intervention curbed physical abuse as well, especially of dependent servants and orphans, while the efforts of those living close by to reconcile differences between estranged couples or bickering land-owners sometimes averted other kinds of violent outbreaks. When a fight broke out, those nearest at hand separated the combatants, charging them to "keep the king's peace." The arbitrators listened to both sides of the story and then tried to persuade quarreling husbands and wives or feuding neighbors to reconcile their differences and "be friends" again, living "peacablye as naybours ought to do."[60]

The neighborhood played an especially critical role in supporting otherwise disrupted family life. The great majority of seventeenth-century Maryland colonists lacked nearby kin to give psychological or material support. While we do not yet know much about the ways in which English families involved themselves in the daily affairs of their closer relations, it is clear that many gentry and middle-class families, at least, maintained steady and enduring ties. Both parent-child and sibling relationships may have been close indeed, and in some cases distant members of a nuclear family may have made an effort to be present at family rituals, to visit frequently, and to provide substantial aid to immediate family members in times of illness or economic distress.[61] But in Maryland parents and siblings were usually an ocean away, and few immigrants had relatives anywhere in the colony, much less nearby. So long as age at marriage

59. Examples showing the difficulties thieves encountered appear in *Md. Archives*, LIV, 508–510, XLI, 221–223.

60. For documentation, see Walsh, "Women's Networks in the Colonial Chesapeake"; Walsh, "Charles County," chap. 5; and Walsh, "Child Custody in the Early Colonial Chesapeake: A Case Study" (paper presented at the Fifth Berkshire Conference on the History of Women, Vassar College, June 1981). Examples can be found in Ames, ed., *County Records of Accomack-Northampton, 1640–1645*, 118–119, 271–272, and *Md. Archives*, LIII, 376–383, 628.

61. Alan Macfarlane, *The Family Life of Ralph Josselin, a Seventeenth-Century Clergyman: An Essay in Historical Anthropology* (Cambridge, 1970); William L. Sachse, ed., *The Diary of Roger Lowe of Ashton-in-Makerfield, Lancashire, 1663–1674* (New Haven, Conn., 1938); and Doreen Slatter, ed., *The Diary of Thomas Naish [1685–1728]* (Devizes, Wiltshire, 1965) document the roles of kin in the lives of more privileged folk. Keith Wrightson and David Levine, *Poverty and Piety in an English Village: Terling, 1525–1700* (New York, 1979), chap. 4, and James P. P. Horn, "Social and Economic

remained high and life-spans short, few parents left adult children ready to take over family responsibilities. Instead, neighbors provided witness and companionship during family rituals, attended the planter's wife in childbirth, and nursed the sick. When death struck, the planter's "friends and neighbours" gathered to mourn his passing. They, too, would be the only people to provide assistance to his widow or orphans.[62]

On St. Clement's Manor, then, as elsewhere in the seventeenth-century Chesapeake, informal neighborhood networks helped to bind individuals and disparate households to the larger society, supplementing the more formal institutions of manor, church, and county or provincial government. This was crucial in a region that experienced so much flux due to immigration, out-migration, and high mortality that it remained largely a society of newcomers long after the land itself had been effectively settled. Immigrants continued to draw on many differing traditions—in religious practice, types of agriculture, forms of landholding and estate management, kinds of building construction, customary contributions to community needs, and family arrangements. Only within the collective experience of small local residence groups, the manor or neighborhood, did a common and unique regional culture begin to emerge from a variety of competing forms.

Recent work in Chesapeake political, demographic, and social history has emphasized the extreme disruption seventeenth-century settlers experienced and the numerous tensions that divided them. Where formal institutions failed, as they often did, to resolve problems and prevent conflict, what one observer termed "extraordinary good neighbourhood" proved a crucial countervailing force.[63]

Aspects of Local Society in England and the Chesapeake: A Comparative Study of the Vale of Berkeley, Gloucestershire, and the Lower Western Shore of Maryland, c. 1660–1700" (D.Phil. diss., University of Sussex, 1982), chaps. 5 and 6, discuss the roles of kin, friends, and neighbors in English communities. Poor folk on either side of the Atlantic were usually more mobile than the rich, more often dwelt outside of the effective reach of their families of birth, and thus had to rely more upon friends and neighbors than upon relatives outside of the nuclear family. The peculiar circumstances of early Maryland settlement enhanced the importance of friends and neighbors. However, similarities with many English communities may have been greater than differences.

62. Carr and Walsh, "Planter's Wife," *WMQ*, 3d Ser., XXXIV (1977).

63. John Hammond, *Leah and Rachel, or, the Two Fruitfull Sisters, Virginia and Maryland* (1656), in Clayton Colman Hall, ed., *Narratives of Early Maryland, 1633–1684* (New York, 1910), 297.

Michael   **Meetinghouse and Chapel**

Graham   Religion and Community in

Seventeenth-Century Maryland

ON DECEMBER 4, 1673, Luke Gardiner of
Newtown Manor, St. Mary's County, Maryland, decided that the time
had come to set his affairs in order and so drew up a will. About five years
later and a little further up Chesapeake Bay, William Coale of West River
Hundred, Anne Arundel County, sensed his death approaching and composed a will. In some respects, both documents are unremarkable; they
are what recent scholarship on the early Chesapeake has prepared us to
expect. Both men were planters whose principal gifts to their heirs consisted of the land, tobacco, and servants that were ubiquitous in the
seventeenth-century Chesapeake. Each man bequeathed a few slaves as
well—but only a few, as if to remind us that the transition from servant to
slave labor would not be completed for several decades to come. Coale's
will provides a glimpse of the demographic instability that characterized
the early Chesapeake. His widow was actually his third wife; the first two
died, leaving him one son each. Both men immigrated to Maryland while
young—Gardiner as a minor with his parents, Coale most likely as a
young indentured servant with his brother Thomas. The careers of both
men likewise confirm our understanding of the early Chesapeake as a
reasonably good "poor man's country" for those who survived: Gardiner
left an estate valued at over £600 sterling; Coale's total estate value is
unknown, but he held at least 700 acres of land and thousands of pounds
of tobacco at his death. Finally, neither man was particularly old when the
Chesapeake claimed him. Luke Gardiner died at about the age of fifty-
one; William Coale, a little older, at about fifty-eight.[1]

1. Luke Gardiner's will is in Maryland Colonial Wills (hereafter cited as Wills), I,
631. Unless otherwise noted, all manuscript sources are at the Maryland State
Archives, Annapolis. For additional information on Gardiner, see the Men's Career
File, St. Mary's City Commission, "Career File of Seventeenth-Century Lower
Western Shore Residents," MS, hereafter cited as MCF. See also the entry for Luke
Gardiner in Edward C. Papenfuse *et al.*, eds., *A Biographical Dictionary of the Maryland
Legislature, 1635–1789*, 2 vols. (Baltimore, 1979), hereafter cited as Papenfuse, *Dic-*

But the lives and deaths of these two planters illustrate more than well-known aspects of early Maryland. The colony would remain an immigrant-dominated society, where life was short and kin were uncommon, for several decades after 1673, and yet Luke Gardiner's will indicates that he inhabited a rich social world populated by a large family and many friends who knew one another well. Several months after Coale died, his family and friends gathered for a special tribute to him that suggests that he too was less socially isolated than we might have expected. Gardiner's will called for the disinheritance of disobedient children, a provision we are more accustomed to seeing in patriarchal New England than in the immigrant Chesapeake. Finally, William Coale's will was proven, not by a member of his family, but by his neighbor Thomas Taillor, then a member of the Maryland Governor's Council. Taillor's action did Coale a high honor, and one that we may well wonder at since Coale seems never to have held elective or appointive office of any kind and died leaving hardly a trace in the public records of early Maryland. Clearly, however, Coale commanded major respect.[2]

What do the lives and deaths of Gardiner and Coale teach us about their world? Not only were they fairly typical men of the early Chesapeake—men who immigrated young, grew tobacco, amassed land, bought servants, prospered to some degree, died before they were old, and left orphans behind them—they were also men of deep and evident faith. Luke Gardiner was a Roman Catholic and William Coale was a Quaker, members of two religious groups that had sought out the broad toleration early Maryland guaranteed. An examination of the communities these groups established shows how neighbors in early Chesapeake society became substitutes for kin networks left behind in England. Moreover, these communities grounded in faith provided their members with a strong sense of cohesion and identity that often helped to mitigate the hardships of early Chesapeake life.

The social and economic dimensions of that life are by now well known. Two forces shaped Chesapeake society: tobacco and immigration. Though it was the foundation of the Chesapeake's wealth, the tobacco

---

tionary. William Coale's will is in Wills, IX, 92. For additional information on Coale, see J. Reaney Kelly, *Quakers in the Founding of Anne Arundel County, Maryland* (Baltimore, 1963), 25, 52, 56, 61.

2. In addition to the above, see Testamentary Proceedings (hereafter cited as Test. Procs.), X, 342.

economy was a decidedly mixed blessing. The staple attracted settlers who hoped to improve their fortunes, but it also drove them apart. Tobacco culture and the need for access to shipping combined to disperse Maryland's population along the many creeks, tributaries, and rivers of Chesapeake Bay. But while tobacco was the treasure, labor was the key. The demand for labor to realize Maryland's potential wealth created a market for indentured servants. Usually young and usually male, they made up the bulk of the bound labor force for most of the seventeenth century. If they survived long enough to gain their freedom, these servants became planters, and until late in the seventeenth century immigrant ex-servants predominated in the adult Chesapeake population. That population finally became mainly native-born only in the eighteenth century.[3]

The resulting portrait that many social historians have drawn of early Chesapeake society is hardly an inviting one. They show a rough and often cruel world, where people were fundamentally alone. Frequent sickness, early death, and a shortage of women that curtailed marital opportunities for men warped Chesapeake society, making it a parody of the traditional English world the immigrants had left behind. New England Puritans brought to America the rich texture of English village life with its webs of kinship and acquaintance. Chesapeake immigrants, however, confronted a society in which economic and demographic accidents had obliterated many of the bonds that ordered life in England. Chesa-

3. For the best study of the effects of tobacco culture on Chesapeake society, see Russell Robert Menard, "Economy and Society in Early Colonial Maryland" (Ph.D. diss., University of Iowa, 1975). The most vivid description of the tone of early Chesapeake society is Edmund S. Morgan, *American Slavery, American Freedom: The Ordeal of Colonial Virginia* (New York, 1975). See also several articles in the collection edited by Thad W. Tate and David L. Ammerman, *The Chesapeake in the Seventeenth Century: Essays on Anglo-American Society* (Chapel Hill, N.C., 1979): James Horn, "Servant Emigration to the Chesapeake in the Seventeenth Century" (pp. 51–95); Lois Green Carr and Russell R. Menard, "Immigration and Opportunity: The Freedman in Early Colonial Maryland" (pp. 206–242); and Lorena S. Walsh, " 'Till Death Us Do Part': Marriage and Family in Seventeenth-Century Maryland" (pp. 126–152). See also two essays in the collection edited by Aubrey C. Land, Lois Green Carr, and Edward C. Papenfuse, *Law, Society, and Politics in Early Maryland* (Baltimore, 1977): Lorena S. Walsh, "Servitude and Opportunity in Charles County, Maryland, 1658–1705" (pp. 111–133), and Russell R. Menard, "Immigrants and Their Increase: The Process of Population Growth in Early Colonial Maryland" (pp. 88–110). See also Lorena S. Walsh and Russell R. Menard, "Death in the Chesapeake: Two Life Tables for Men in Early Colonial Maryland," *Maryland Historical Magazine*, LXIX (1974), 211–227.

peake settlers paid a high price for the wealth they came to seek. As one historian has described it, early Maryland was "not only a land of opportunity, but also a place of stark inequality and fragile, oppressive and violent social relations."[4]

Without a doubt, this view of life in the seventeenth-century Chesapeake is overdrawn because it is incomplete. Recent work on both Virginia and Maryland seeks to complement this picture by understanding how Chesapeake society evolved within its own peculiar circumstances. By examining hundreds, neighborhoods, and counties, historians are now revealing the patterns of human interaction and interdependence evident in the seventeenth-century Chesapeake. Through their studies, we are at last discovering the community life that did exist in the harsh world of the early Chesapeake.[5]

Communities in the early Chesapeake were not grounded only in settlement patterns. Religion played a role. The Catholic and Quaker dissenters drawn to early Maryland formed close communities and enjoyed a variety of social, political, and economic benefits through their affiliation. Both groups built places for worship, and these chapels and meetinghouses supplied social centers in an environment where such centers were in short supply. Zealous Catholic priests and Quaker preachers viewed early Maryland as mission territory and were instrumental in maintaining their flocks' faith. The public worship such men initiated gathered congregations together to provide forums for sacred activities and for the rituals that mark the important passages in life: birth, marriage, death. Both priests and preachers sought and gained converts, imparting thereby a sense of dynamism and growth to their separate fellowships. Most important perhaps, each group had a specific religious

4. Paul G. E. Clemens, "The Early Maryland Economy: A Comparative Perspective" (unpublished paper, 1984), 6.

5. See, for example, Lorena S. Walsh, "Community Networks in the Early Chesapeake," in this volume; Lois Green Carr, "Sources of Political Stability and Upheaval in Seventeenth-Century Maryland," *Md. Hist. Mag.*, LXXIX (1984), 44–70; and, especially, Darrett B. and Anita H. Rutman, *A Place in Time: Middlesex County, Virginia, 1650–1750* (New York, 1984). For a brief but perceptive critique of the crisis view of the early Chesapeake, see Clemens, "Early Maryland Economy." The work of Darrett B. Rutman has been important in redefining historical approaches to the study of community. See his "Community Study," *Historical Methods*, XIII (1980), 29–41, and "The Social Web: A Prospectus for the Study of the Early American Community," in William L. O'Neill, ed., *Insights and Parallels: Problems and Issues of American Social History* (Minneapolis, Minn., 1973), 57–89.

self-awareness, one that located the individual believer in a cosmic drama. Maryland Catholics saw themselves as having sprung from the persecuted English remnant of the one true church. Founded in the 1650s, the Quakers had themselves been tested by persecution and had learned to survive by banding together. Paralleling the Catholic church's Counter-Reformation insistence on its own uniqueness, the Quakers believed themselves to be "the true reformed church in Christ Jesus." Consequently, for Catholics and Quakers alike in early Maryland, religion possessed the power to transform rude frontier settlements with their inevitable associations of neighbors into gathered communities with strong identities. The lives of Gardiner and Coale, set against the backgrounds of their communities, reveal the rich texture of Catholic and Quaker life in early Maryland.

I

Maryland's first Catholics arrived aboard the *Ark* and the *Dove* in 1634. The several Jesuit priests on board originally hoped to divide their energies between the English settlers and the native population and quickly developed bases from which to launch both ventures. The Jesuits' English superiors actively recruited priests and brothers for the enterprise, eleven of whom served in Maryland before 1641. The Franciscan order sent several priests of its own in 1672 or 1673, and several more followed during the next decade. Owing to the patronage of native English Catholic authorities, Maryland's Catholics nearly always enjoyed enough clergy to meet their religious needs; for most of the seventeenth century (the disruptions of the 1640s and 1650s excluded), four or five Catholic priests usually labored in the province at any given time.[6]

Suspicion of the Jesuits' work among the Indians in addition to proprietary pressure forced the Jesuits to abandon their mission to the Indians and to confine their ministry to the English colonists after 1648. The reports sent back to England describe the priests' delight in Catholic

6. See David W. Jordan, " 'The Miracle of This Age': Maryland's Experiment in Religious Toleration, 1649–1689," *Historian,* XLVII (1985), 338–359 (esp. p. 343); John Tracy Ellis, *Catholics in Colonial America* (Baltimore, 1965), 315–343; and Gerald P. Fogarty, "The Origin of the Mission," in R. E. Curran, Joseph Thomas Durkin, and Gerald P. Fogarty, *The Maryland Jesuits, 1634–1833* (Baltimore, 1976).

attendance upon the sacraments, their success at reconciling lapsed Catholics, and their zeal for gaining converts. The number of Catholic chapels grew to keep pace with the increasing number of Catholics and their movement northward and eastward from St. Mary's County; nine Catholic chapels had been founded in the province by 1689. Although perhaps 95 percent of Maryland's seventeenth-century Catholic population lived in St. Mary's and Charles counties (and most of the rest in Calvert County), in the eighteenth century Catholics were also well established in Anne Arundel County on the Western Shore and in Talbot and Queen Anne's counties across the Bay. Nevertheless, Maryland's lower Western Shore remained home for the majority of Maryland's Catholics.[7]

There are no reliable figures for seventeenth-century Maryland's Catholic population. Consequently, estimates of their number or their proportion within the overall population are speculative. In attempting to dissuade the Privy Council from levying a church-support tax in 1676, Lord Baltimore claimed that Catholics (along with Anglicans) were "the fewest" in the colony. Records surviving from St. Clement's Manor in St. Mary's County suggest that Catholics constituted at least 10 percent of the manor population in 1661, but the difficulty of identifying Catholics makes this only a rough estimate. The census of 1708 indicates that Catholics then constituted about 7 percent of the total population in the colony, 32 percent in St. Mary's County, 22 percent in Charles, and 7 percent in Prince George's. Perhaps the most that can be said regarding the seventeenth century is that about one in seven of Maryland's population in 1689 was Catholic.[8]

Luke Gardiner was born in 1622, probably in England, and in 1637 he and his parents moved to Maryland from Virginia. Little is known about his family, although his older sister, Elizabeth, married Richard Lust-

7. See Jordan, " 'Miracle of This Age,' " *Historian*, XLVII (1985), 338–359, and Ellis, *Catholics in Colonial America*, 315–343. Distribution of Roman Catholics in the 18th century is based on census figures from 1708 found in William Hand Browne *et al.*, eds., *Archives of Maryland* (Baltimore, 1883–), XXV, 258, hereafter cited as *Md. Archives*. For the 17th century, my analysis depends upon the geographical location of Catholic testators.

8. Lord Baltimore to Privy Council, *Md. Archives*, 133. On St. Clement's Manor, see Walsh, "Community Networks." For the 1708 census for Maryland, see *Md. Archives*, XXV, 258–259. The size of the Roman Catholic population in Maryland in 1689 is estimated in Lois Green Carr and David William Jordan, *Maryland's Revolution of Government, 1689–1692* (Ithaca, N.Y., 1974), 33n.

head, a Maryland planter and burgess who died about 1642. Lusthead
left few traces in the public record; he arrived in Maryland as a servant to
the Jesuits there and was probably a Catholic himself. The year Luke
Gardiner came to Maryland he appears to have been a servant or apprentice to Jesuit mission superior Father Thomas Copley, but Gardiner
subsequently built a career as a planter. He married Elizabeth Hatton, the
daughter of a prominent Protestant but herself a convert to Catholicism.
Through his sister-in-law Elinor Hatton (another Catholic convert, married to Catholic convert Thomas Brooke), Gardiner was connected to
important families throughout the province. He served in a variety of
offices—as a justice of the peace in St. Mary's County, as a county sheriff,
and as a member of the assembly—and held important militia appointments. The modest fortune he acquired before his death in 1674 enabled
him to bequeath tobacco to four Maryland priests. His will instructed his
executors to bury him according to the rites of "the holy Roman Catholiq
Church" and to disinherit any of his children who, before arriving at the
age of twenty-five, "should prove Irreverent and Stubborn and Change
his religion that he be no Roman Catholick."[9]

As an important public figure in St. Mary's County, Gardiner was
associated with many Protestants as well as Catholics. His fellow burgesses from St. Mary's County generally included members of both
groups, and he sat with both on St. Mary's County Court. Catholics and
Protestants owed him tobacco at various times, and he was summoned to
court to testify on behalf of men of both faiths. His largest land transactions were concluded with Dr. Luke Barber, another burgess, who was
almost certainly a Protestant.[10]

Gardiner's Catholic associations quickly multiply and become predominant, however, when we look to the more personal side of his life.
Repeated references identify him as a prominent member of the Catholic
church at Newtown, someone to whom the Jesuits turned for help with
church affairs: Gardiner ensured that testamentary bequests to the
priests were delivered to them; brought a gift from a future Jesuit to
several children of a Catholic friend; and witnessed the conveyance that
put the Newtown church lands firmly in Jesuit hands. While his relationship with his Protestant in-laws was at times less than cordial, he repeat-

9. See the file on Luke Gardiner in the MCF; the entries for Gardiner and
Lusthead in Papenfuse, *Dictionary*; and Wills, I, 631.

10. *Md. Archives*, XLI, 354, 393–394, 476, XLIX, 33–34, 156, 431, 565, LVII,
173, 302, 312, 315, 321.

edly appears in the documents with his Catholic relatives. Both his daughter and his widow married Catholics. He formed his closest friendships with William Evans and William Johnson, fellow members of the Jesuit church at Newtown. The only wills he witnessed were those of Catholics. He served as executor to the estate of one Catholic friend and, with two other Newtown Catholics, as a feoffee in trust for the estate of another.[11] Catholics were a minority not only in the province generally but even in St. Mary's County. Nevertheless, Luke Gardiner lived much of his personal life in Catholic company.[12]

Gardiner lived near Newtown Hundred, where the Jesuits had established an early mission. In 1661 Catholics in the area gave subscriptions for a church and a graveyard, which were to serve the Catholics of Newtown, St. Clement's, and St. George's hundreds. As the focal point of Catholic life, the church provided a social hub in an environment that otherwise lacked one. It drew worshippers together, introduced them to one another, and thereby facilitated other kinds of relationships among them. In addition to Gardiner, twenty-seven men appear to have worshipped at the Newtown church before 1674, the year Gardiner died.[13] These Catholic men interacted on several social levels to a striking degree that illustrates the various layers of this early Chesapeake community.

11. *Md. Archives*, X, 52, 260, 326–327, 387, 418, 450, 465–466, XLI, 143, 489, 531, 579, XLIX, 3, 25–26, 220, 431, 537, LVII, 173, 302, LXV, 212. Also see Test. Procs., V, 381, 472, 506, IC, 16, III, 272; and Wills, I, 129, 517. In 1654, Gardiner was ordered to surrender his sister-in-law Elinor Hatton to her Protestant uncle Thomas Hatton because it was feared that Gardiner was "endeavouring . . . to trayne her up in the Roman Catholick Religion contrary to the mind and will of her said Mother and Uncle." The order did little good as Elinor later converted to Catholicism on her own. See *Md. Archives*, X, 354–356.

12. A provincial court case in which Gardiner testified in 1662 makes the point vividly. The case involved a sale of land that was not completed before the purchaser died, leaving his orphan with a reduced estate. The decedent's executors sued to recover either the land or the tobacco paid out before his death. The case was an almost purely Catholic concern. Of the 21 individuals involved, 18 can be positively identified as Catholics: the executors; the original owner of the land; the buyer; his orphan; the witnesses for the original purchase agreement; most of the witnesses who gave depositions; the clerk who recopied the agreement; and even several of the justices who took the testimony. *Md. Archives*, XLI, 557–566.

13. These men were William Bretton, Nicholas Causine, Robert Clarke, Edward Cotton, Thomas Diniard, William Evans, Thomas Greene, John Greenwell, Walter Hall, Thomas Hebden, John Jarbo, William Johnson, John Jordaine, James Lang-

Members of the church at Newtown publicly supported each other through the signing of one another's documents; that they did so signals the importance of the informal relationships upon which these more formal, legal ones rested. When John Pile sold John Jarbo all his land in Port Tobacco and his land, house, and chattels at Newtown in 1651, James Langworth and William Thompson witnessed the conveyance. On a smaller scale, William Evans witnessed William Bretton's sale of a heifer to Charles Maynard.[14] The approach and consequences of death especially called upon friends to stand by one another through writing, witnessing, and proving wills, calculating inventories of estates and accounts, and administering estates to the benefit of the heirs. Thus, when Thomas Hebden died, his neighbor Nicholas Causine was appointed a feoffee in trust for the estate, along with Luke Gardiner and Barnaby Jackson. Together, the three ensured that a bequest due the Catholic church was paid to Lawrence Starkey, the mission superior. When Starkey received the legacy, William Bretton and Benjamin Gill witnessed his receipt.[15]

Newtown parishioners often married local Catholics or other Catholics living in the southern portion of Western Shore Maryland. Twenty-four of the twenty-seven known members of the Newtown parish married at least once. Nine of these marriages were to widows, seven of whom had been married to men known to be Catholic. Eleven of the wives in the parish contracted new marriages after the deaths of their husbands; at least nine of these women married Catholic men. The marriages and remarriages of Catholic widows and widowers helped weld the community together by creating dense family networks. For example, William Thompson married Mary Bretton, William Bretton's daughter or stepdaughter. Thompson remarried upon her death, and his widow, Ann, later married William Evans. After Ann Thompson Evans's death, Wil-

---

worth, Charles Maynard, Henry Neale, John Pile, George Reynolds, William Rosewell, John Shirtcliffe, Henry Spinke, John Thimbleby, William Thompson, Thomas Turner, John Wheatley, and Richard Willan. Benjamin Gill almost certainly worshipped there as well.

14. *Md. Archives*, X, 20, 110.

15. Likewise, John Pile prepared Edward Cotton's will, and when John Thimbleby died, John Shirtcliffe brought his will to court for recording. Walter Hall wrote John Greenwell's will for him several days before his death, and William Evans signed it. Evans also acted as the guardian of Charles Maynard's orphans after Maynard's death in 1661, and Thomas Turner administered William Johnson's estate. See *Md. Archives*, IX, 207, XLI, 538, 563, LVII, 242; Test. Procs., VII, 55.

liam Evans married Elizabeth, who subsequently married John Jordaine. All were Catholic.[16]

Commercial and business activities further brought the members of the Newtown Catholic community into close contact with one another and with Catholics beyond Newtown. On the average, Catholics interacted more frequently with other Catholics than they did with non-Catholics, and almost twice as often as non-Catholics interacted with Catholics. Analyzing the social relationships of the Newtown parishioners—whom they lived near, conducted land transactions with, contracted debts with, sued in court, retained as attorneys, witnessed documents for, and so on—reveals that 53 percent of the interactions of these Catholic men were with one another or with other known Catholics. In comparison only 29 percent of the social relationships of twenty-six non-Catholic residents of Newtown Hundred involved Catholics. This difference strongly suggests that Catholics actively cooperated with one another socially and economically to their mutual benefit.[17]

The participation of members of the Newtown Catholic community in politics strengthened their other associations, which evolved through residence, religion, marriage, and business. Of course, the very public arena of political life brought Newtown Catholics together regularly with many of their neighbors, both Catholic and Protestant. Yet the political eminence of Catholics in a province whose political life was dominated by a Catholic proprietor, and the strength of Catholic relationships outside of politics, helped further bind these Catholic men together locally and, occasionally, on the provincial level as well. Many of the Newtown parish-

16. Similarly, James Langworth's stepsister married William Johnson, and after Johnson's death, Thomas Turner, and after Turner's death, William Rosewell. See the files for these men in the MCF and in the Genealogy File at the Md. State Archives.

17. For the careers of Newtown non-Catholics, see the MCF. Examples of members of the Newtown church cooperating with one another in social and economic matters could be multiplied almost indefinitely. William Johnson, the agent for a third party, sold servants to James Langworth, his brother-in-law, and to Luke Gardiner as well. Johnson and Gardiner bought land as partners, as did John Jarbo and James Langworth. John Langworth, James's father, transported John Greenwell to Maryland in 1642 as an indentured servant, and John Pile assigned him 200 acres of land. John Shirtcliffe and Henry Spinke speculated in land together. John Jarbo and William Evans joined in a lawsuit against the proprietor for tobacco and corn he owed them. After Benjamin Gill's death, John Thimbleby and William Bretton acted as attorneys for James Neale in Neale's administration of Gill's estate. *Md. Archives*, X, 7, 446, 451, 461, 467, 472, 474, 476, IV, 362, 467, 480, 490, XLI, 166, 210, 265, 372; Rent Rolls, O, 5–6, 27; Patents, AB & H, 166, III, 25; and Wills, I, 9.

ioners held office at one time or another, however minor. What is more impressive, however, is that before 1680 eleven Catholics filled the office of justice of the peace and eight sat as burgesses in the assembly. Robert Clarke and William Evans attained the highest degree of provincial political distinction by sitting on the Governor's Council, which entailed the triple honor of membership on the Council, in the upper house of the assembly, and on the provincial court.[18] Because their advice influenced other appointments, Clarke and Evans no doubt aided the political careers of lesser Newtown Catholic men.

Finally, the cohesiveness of the Newtown Catholic community may be glimpsed by studying the Catholic connections of non-Catholic residents of Newtown Hundred. The relationships of Luke Barber and Walter Peakes, two non-Catholics, are illustrative. Both sat as members of the assembly—Barber in the upper house, Peakes in the lower—and served there at the same time as Robert Clarke, William Evans, and Luke Gardiner. Barber and Peakes were well-to-do planters in St. Mary's County; Peakes was also an innkeeper. As prominent figures, they routinely engaged in a variety of public activities with Catholics, witnessing their documents, requesting their signatures, suing to recover debts from them in court, and so on. Altogether, of Barber's 57 associates, 28 percent were Catholics, and of Peakes's 121 public connections, 22 percent were Catholics; by comparison, among Catholics, Charles Maynard had the fewest interactions with his coreligionists at 37 percent (11/30). The connections Barber and Peakes did have with Catholics came through relatively official forms—in court cases, actions of debt, some official documents, jury duty, or public service of one kind or another. They tended not to interact with Catholics in more personal ways, such as marriage or remarriage, giving gifts to the children of Catholics, or witnessing their wills. This pattern reverses that for Catholics, who reveal

18. Further, Langworth served as justice of the peace in St. Mary's County and, later, in Charles County. Bretton's clerical abilities landed him posts as clerk of the Governor's Council, the secretary's office, the provincial court, and the lower house. He was also St. Mary's County coroner in 1669–1670. Gardiner was the St. Mary's County sheriff from 1672 to 1674, a position for which he relinquished his assembly seat. Gardiner held a number of commissions in the militia as well. Robert Clarke served various clerkships and was either deputy surveyor or surveyor general of the province from 1640 to 1661. William Evans's career included positions as county justice of the peace, sheriff, and militia commander. *Md. Archives*, I, 318, 426, 482, 505, IV, 139, 403, X, 143, 430, XLI, 6. See the entries in Papenfuse, *Dictionary*, for Bretton, Gardiner, Clarke, and Evans.

more associations with other Catholics the more the records rest on informal relationships. For example, while the Newtown Catholics can be linked with other Catholics 53 percent of the time in the public record as a whole, that figure jumps to 65 percent when documents concerning the approach or consequences of death (wills, probate records) are considered.[19]

The social obligations created by and strengthened through family, political, legal, and commercial ties all reflected the common Catholic faith of these men. Their standing together through life and support of one another into death suggest that the strength of their community lent a certain security to their new lives in Maryland. They consequently took their obligations to their church seriously, contributing to its support as they were able. Their church bequests were usually made to individual priests, a practice that underlines both the centrality of the clergy among Maryland's Catholics and the precarious institutional position of the Catholic church there. In his will, Edward Cotton endowed a Jesuit-sponsored free school, gave his chestnut mare to Newtown chaplain Lawrence Starkey, and dedicated his soul "to God my Maker and Redeemer [and] to the fellowship of all the Ho[ly Ang]ells and Saints." Nicholas Causine gave Starkey a steer, "desyring the prayers of the Church." William Johnson left Father Francis Fitzherbert one thousand pounds of tobacco and to Starkey "one hhd of sweet scented tobacco . . . to pray for the Soules of me and my dear wife." Luke Gardiner provided for priests throughout the province, leaving a thousand pounds of tobacco to the Jesuit pastor at Newtown and four hundred pounds each to the Jesuit priest at Port Tobacco and two Franciscans, Mr. Thomas Massey, "living at the Governors," and "Mr. [Henry] Carew, living at the Chancellors." For some—Cotton and Johnson, for example—leaving bequests was singularly appropriate: Jesuits had brought them to Maryland in the first place as indentured servants, and Jesuits bade them farewell when they left Maryland for eternity.[20]

19. See files on Luke Barber and Walter Peakes in Papenfuse, *Dictionary*, and in the MCF.

20. Some Catholics also left legacies for the relief of impoverished Catholics; see the wills of Greenwell, Thimbleby, and Jarbo (*Md. Archives*, XLI, 43; Wills, I, 80, II, 65). In addition to those mentioned in the text, Clarke, Diniard, Evans, Greene, Hall, Hebden, Jordaine, Langworth, Maynard, Rosewell, Shirtcliffe, Turner, Wheatley, and Willan also made bequests to the Catholic church (see Wills, I, 82, 112, 129, 167, 193, 203, 207, 217, 331, 631, VII, 105, IX, 57, 64; *Md. Archives*, IV, 519, X, 90, XLI,

II

The meager details we have of William Coale's life make Luke Gardiner's biography seem rich in comparison. The date of Coale's arrival in Maryland is unknown, though he had immigrated with his brother, Thomas, by 1650. The names of both appear in several routine court documents in the next few years. Thomas Coale was a servant to William Mitchell, an unsavory character charged in 1652 with atheism, blasphemy, and abortion; not surprisingly, Thomas ran away. Whether William Coale was also a servant is not known, but he probably was. Thomas died in 1659, a free man but not a householder. William Coale appears briefly in a court action that same year and then disappears from the provincial records altogether until 1678, when he drew up his will. By that time he had become a respectable planter, outlived two wives, and fathered at least five children.[21]

The slight biography available through civil sources omits, however, the central event of William Coale's life: his conversion or "convincement" as a Quaker. Coale's disappearance from the civil record is accompanied by his rise to prominence in early Maryland Quakerism, and it is through Quaker records that the highlights of Coale's subsequent career can be traced.

A letter from one early Quaker missionary to another in 1657 records that "Will Coale . . . hath . . . made open confession of the truth"; Thomas was convinced about the same time. William Coale subsequently became an important minister in the early Quaker movement. He was instrumental in setting up the first Quaker meetings on the Western Shore of the Bay, at his home, West River Hundred in Anne Arundel County. In 1659, he and several other Friends challenged the provincial court by refusing to swear oaths to administer a Quaker orphan's estate. They lost their challenge, and the court stripped them of the estate to

---

54, 172; Test. Procs., IC, 33, ID, 69, II, 309). Of the 102 bequests to churches left by Maryland testators from 1660 to 1689, 54 were made by Roman Catholics (53%) with the remaining 48 evenly split between Quaker and other testators. Put another way, about 70% (54/78) of identified Roman Catholic testators between 1660 and 1689 left bequests for the support of their churches, compared with 50% of identified Quaker testators (24/48), and less than 2% of all other testators (24/1,110).

21. *Md. Archives*, II, 303, 435, 475, X, 65, 170, 173, 193, 201, 202, 221, 229, 244, 258, 259, 307, XLI, 350–351; Wills, IX, 92.

make an example of them. During the 1660s, William Coale traveled throughout Virginia as an itinerant missionary with several other Friends. He was imprisoned for his efforts, and one of his companions died in jail. Sometime near the end of the 1660s, Coale married Elizabeth Thomas, the daughter of prominent Quaker converts; her father, Philip Thomas, had been one of the councillors appointed by the parliamentary commissioners to govern Maryland in the early 1650s. George Fox himself, during his tour of Quaker settlements in Maryland and elsewhere in 1672 and 1673, made a point of sojourning at Coale's and conducted there "a large and precious Meeting . . . where the Speaker of their Assembly with his wife, and a Justice of the Peace and several other people of Quality were present." After Coale's death, lyrical testimonies to his "sincere love and good behavior" were read into the minutes of the quarterly meeting he had helped to organize; the testimonies of his fellow members were to encourage "all friends both young and old . . . to travaill in the way of truth and Righteousness to the end of their dayes." Considering the significance of Coale in the Quaker movement in Maryland, from his missionary travels to his marriage, it becomes explicable why one of the county's most important men helped Friends settle Coale's estate.[22]

The Quaker awakening in early Maryland—the movement within which William Coale's life gained its meaning—raises an interesting question: Why did the early Quaker missionaries meet such success there? The answer begins with an understanding of the state of Protestantism in the colony when Quaker missionaries first arrived in 1655 or 1656. Protestants found early Maryland troubling in ways that Catholics did not. As dissenters in England, Catholics had developed a variety of strategies to survive in a culture hostile to them, strategies that helped them flourish in the tolerant atmosphere of early Maryland. Catholic Marylanders actively supported their clergy, and Catholic authorities in

22. Kelly, *Quakers in Anne Arundel County*, 16, 25, 52, 56; *Md. Archives*, XLI, 295. For Coale's conversion, see Robert Clarkson to Elizabeth Harris, Nov. 14, 1657; the letter is reproduced in Kenneth L. Carroll, "Elizabeth Harris, the Founder of American Quakerism," *Quaker History*, LVII (1968), 96–111. The testimonies to Coale were given by fellow Quakers Ann Birkhead, Ann Chew, Samuel Galloway, Thomas Hooker, Elizabeth Richardson, George Skipworth, Solomon Sparrow, Edward Talbott, Elizabeth Taylor, Thomas Taylor, Henry Wilcocks, and Coale's wife, Elizabeth, and his son, William Coale, Jr. West River Quarterly Meeting Minutes, 1680–1688, fols. 3–11. All Quaker records referred to are on microfilm at the Md. State Archives.

England responded by providing a steady stream of priests. The Jesuits who founded the Maryland mission proved adept at fending for themselves. They transported many servants and used these servants' headrights to establish plantations that supported Catholic missionary activities. Consequently, the Jesuits had a solid base on which to build Catholic life.[23]

By and large, Protestant clergy, especially Anglican priests, lacked this sort of support. The Church of England had never had to survive on voluntary contributions, nor would it begin to understand the requirements of missionary life until Thomas Bray founded the Society for the Propagation of the Gospel in Foreign Parts in 1702. As a result, few Anglican clergy officiated in Maryland in the seventeenth century. Ministers from Virginia occasionally conducted services in Maryland in the very early years of the colony, but Maryland enjoyed no settled Anglican minister of its own until 1650, when the Reverend William Wilkinson began a career that lasted thirteen years. After another hiatus, three Anglican priests arrived in the early 1670s and were joined by a fourth in 1677. On the eve of Maryland's Glorious Revolution, no more than six, and perhaps only four, Anglican clergy were active in the colony. Petitions to English authorities to provide ministers to people "who have a long while lived as sheepe without a shepherd" were unsuccessful, as were two legislative attempts to settle ministers in 1661 and 1666. When the Privy Council suggested to Lord Baltimore that some sort of a tax be levied to support all Protestant instead of just Anglican clergy, Baltimore parried their request by arguing that Maryland's religious heterogeneity would make enacting such a law "a most difficult task." As the Reverend John Yeo wrote to the archbishop of Canterbury in 1676, the lack of orthodox ministers in Maryland had clearcut consequences. "Not only [do] many Dayly fall away either to Popery, Quakerism or Phanaticisme but alsoe the lords day is prophaned, Religion despised, & all notorious vices committed soe that it is become a Sodom of uncleaness & a Pest house of iniquity."[24]

---

23. For an interesting comment concerning the "depressed" state of the "protestant ministry" in Maryland in the early 17th century, see *Md. Archives*, V, 139.

24. See Jordan, " 'Miracle of This Age,' " *Historian*, XLVII (1985), 345–346 (quotation on p. 344); Nelson Waite Rightmyer, *Maryland's Established Church* (Baltimore, 1956), 1–19; Lawrence C. Wroth, "The First Sixty Years of the Church of England in Maryland, 1632–1692," *Md. Hist. Mag.*, XI (1916), 1–41; John Goodwin Herndon, "The Reverend William Wilkinson of England, Virginia, and Maryland," *Virginia*

One man's "Phanaticisme" is another man's faith, of course, and Yeo's disparagement of the religious life around him reminds us that Catholics and Quakers were not the only dissenters in Maryland. Presbyterians settled in Somerset County on the Eastern Shore in the 1660s and eventually petitioned Scottish church leaders for ministers, three of whom arrived in the 1680s. Nonconformist ministry earlier and on the Western Shore enjoyed less success. Three Presbyterian ministers—all of them former Church of England clergy whose nonconformity caused their ejection from English benefices—preached in Charles County for varying lengths of time between 1659 and 1679, but no minister was available there at all before 1659, between 1665 and 1669, and after 1679. In 1665, Giles Thomkinson of Charles County was able to avoid a conviction of bastardy by claiming that "his marriage was as good as possibly it Coold bee maed by the Protestants hee beeing one becaus that befor that time and ever since thear hath not bin a protestant Minister in the Province." Thomkinson's defense, though overstated, no doubt evoked sympathy from his neighbors who also found themselves without the church services taken for granted in England. Other small groups of dissenters settled in Maryland in the seventeenth century—Labadists in Cecil County on the northern frontier in the 1680s and a scattering of other non-English Protestants chiefly in Baltimore County and northward about the same time. But before 1689, most of Maryland's Protestants were, in effect, unchurched. While Jesuits crisscrossed the countryside administering the sacraments, preaching to Englishmen and Indians, and instructing Catholics and would-be Catholics, Maryland's Protestants had to survive with far too few clergy as best they could.[25]

Like Giles Thomkinson, other Protestants in early Maryland lamented their lack of organized religion. In 1638, when William Lewis, a Catholic, confiscated some of his servants' books because he found their anti-Catholic tone offensive, his "poore bondmen" complained of their ensuing "great discomfort . . . in this heathen country where no godly minister is to teach and instruct ignorant people in the grounds of religion."[26] Four

Magazine of History and Biography, LVII (1949), 316–321; and *Md. Archives*, V, 131, 133.

25. See Louis Dow Scisco, "The First Church in Charles County," *Md. Hist. Mag.*, XXIII (1928), 155–162; J. William McIlvain, *Early Presbyterianism in Maryland* (Baltimore, 1890), 16; and Bartlett B. James, *The Labadist Colony in Maryland* (Baltimore, 1899). For the Giles Thomkinson case, see *Md. Archives*, LIII, 599.

26. *Md. Archives*, IV, 35–36, 37–39.

years later, some Protestants objected that Thomas Gerrard prevented them from holding services by "taking away the Key of the Chapel and carrying away the Books"; Gerrard was fined five hundred pounds of tobacco toward "the maintenance of the first minister as should arrive."[27] The case shows that these Protestants not only lacked a minister, but also their own chapel; the chapel Gerrard locked up was a private Catholic chapel on his own land. Protestant discontent could also have a political edge to it; the disruptions of the early 1650s were exacerbated by Protestant anger over a perceived Catholic dominance not only in religion, but in society and politics as well.[28]

Some Protestants in early Maryland had still other reactions to their lack of a settled religious life. A letter from one early Quaker missionary to another describes well the confused soul-searching of one such man. The text is worth quoting at length.

Richard Beard was in a miraculouse way convinced in the fore pt of the sumer, by a clap of thunder he being at worke in the wood, & one more with him in rany wether, & at that instant it thundered much as is usuall in the summer tyme in soe much that itt wrought a feare in him & put him to thinck of his condition, & it did apeare to him to bee unsafe, hee seeing nothing to hast to, theire being soe many opinions in the world that hee did nott know which to chuse, hee then being in feare not knowing what would become of him in that Condition, desired that the Lord would manifest to him, concerning the way which was knowne amongst us whether it was the true way of god or not, & that it mought bee maide knowne to him by thunder, & at that same instant theire came a clap of thunder which was very greate, in so much that it broake a tree verry near them & shooke him that was with him to the ground, & himselfe could scarse recover from faleing & a powrefull answer came to him at the same Instant, that that which hee had inquired of was the true way of god

27. *Ibid.*, I, 119.

28. See, for example, Daniel R. Randall, *A Puritan Colony in Maryland* (Baltimore, 1886), and Rightmyer, *Maryland's Established Church*, 5–7. Contemporary pamphlets suggest the role of religion in the era of the parliamentary commissioners in the 1650s; see Leonard Strong's 1650 pamphlet, "Babylon's Fall," in Clayton Colman Hall, ed., *Narratives of Early Maryland, 1633–1684* (New York, 1925), 231–246, and "Virginia and Maryland, or the Lord Baltamore's Printed Case Uncased and Answered," *ibid.*, 181–230.

& forthwith hee declayred it abroade & were convinced thereby wherein I hope hee abides.[29]

We cannot know how representative Richard Beard was of other Protestants in early Maryland, yet his case is instructive. Yearning for religion and God-fearing, unsure of his own "condition" but finding it "unsafe," confused by "soe many opinions in the world" and lacking ministers who would instruct him in what "to hast to," he implored heaven for a clear sign. For Beard and perhaps for others, the appearance of the early Quaker missionaries must have come as God's answer to their prayers.

The first Quaker missionaries to Maryland found eager audiences among just these dissenting Protestants who lacked clergy of their own. The missionaries established small groups of Friends in Kent County, where Protestants from Virginia had settled before the arrival of the *Ark* and the *Dove*, and among the Presbyterians of Charles County. They enjoyed their greatest successes, however, in Calvert County and especially among the Puritan settlers along the Severn, West, and South rivers of Anne Arundel County. Driven from Virginia in 1649 and 1650 by increasing pressure to conform to orthodox Anglican practice, four hundred to six hundred Puritans had arrived in Anne Arundel at the invitation of the Calverts. A decade after the missionaries' initial convincements, four Quaker meetings were thriving around West River. Further pressure toward orthodoxy in Virginia forced Quakers out of Accomack and Northampton counties in 1659 and 1660. These Friends quickly spilled up Maryland's Eastern Shore. Soon after their arrival, Eastern Shore Friends had organized four meetings in Talbot County and, by the mid-1670s, another three in Somerset County. By 1679, at least fourteen Quaker congregations were scattered throughout the province. Some of these meetings embraced only a handful of families who worshiped in one another's homes, while others were larger and met in barns until they could build their own meetinghouses. Quaker and civil records alike reveal that these gatherings attracted converts—George Fox rhapsodized over them while the provincial government initially railed against them—and the Quaker population increased steadily. Unfortunately, there are no figures by which to gauge accurately the size of Maryland's seventeenth-

29. Clarkson to Harris, Nov. 14, 1657, in Carroll, "Elizabeth Harris," *Quaker History*, LVII (1968), 103–106. Richard Beard later became the deputy surveyor of Anne Arundel County. *Md. Archives*, XVII, 273–274.

century Quaker population. The suggestion of Lois Carr and David Jordan that Quakers constituted perhaps 13 percent of Maryland's population in 1689 is probably the best estimate possible.[30]

The growth of Quakerism in Maryland is best understood by considering what Friends offered Maryland's disadvantaged Protestants. Quakerism solved the chronic problem of the scarcity of ordained Protestant clergy in the province by emphasizing the priesthood of all believers. Meetings provided a religious environment in which marriages could be solemnized, God worshipped with apostolic purity, and children raised in a vibrant Protestant atmosphere. But the appeal of the Quakers was broader still. Like the Catholics who were bound together by blood ties, emotional bonds, and the shared values and beliefs of their faith, Quakerism added a distinctive religious dimension to some of the neighborhood communities that had already begun to develop among Protestant Marylanders.[31]

Indeed, the enhancement of community stood at the very center of Quakerism. Friends depended on the direct promptings of the spirit—on the "Inward Light"—and they contained the resulting drift toward antinomianism by subordinating the individual to the group. To avoid the distortion of grace through human sinfulness and to check the extravagant claims of enthusiasts, Quaker ceremony and ritual stressed the incorporation of the individual "meeter" into the larger "meeting." All Quaker ritual activities, from counseling backsliders to celebrating weddings to worship itself, served as ways of fostering and extending the intense, personal community of the meeting.

30. A good, quick overview of the rise and progress of Quakerism in 17th-century Maryland is in David W. Jordan's " 'Gods Candle' within Government: Quakers and Politics in Early Maryland," *William and Mary Quarterly*, 3d Ser., XXXIX (1982), 628–654 (esp. pp. 628–632). See also two articles by Kenneth L. Carroll: "Maryland Quakers in the Seventeenth Century," *Md. Hist. Mag.*, XLVII (1952), 297–313, and "Talbot County Quakerism in the Colonial Period," *ibid.*, LIII (1958), 326–370. Useful surveys of specific areas may be found in Phebe R. Jacobsen, *Quaker Records in Maryland* (Annapolis, Md., 1966) and in Kelly, *Quakers in Anne Arundel County*.

31. Because they refused to swear oaths and the proprietor refused to accept their affirmations in this early period, and because they also avoided county courts for matters they could handle within their own meetings, Quakers left comparatively few traces in early Maryland's public record. As a result, this analysis of Quaker life is drawn from their own records, which provide an excellent testimony to the fellowship of Quaker meetings.

Foremost among all Quaker ritual activities were their meetings for worship. Through worship, "the Spirrit of Truth in the Body of Friends" became manifest. If "little of outward busines" presented itself for the community's consideration, Friends found it sufficient "to wayt upon the Lord for his presents to strengthen & refresh us." In 1686, the Yearly Women's Meeting gave a lyrical account of their attendance upon God's mercy. "We being mett together According to our wonted Manner on purpose to wait upon God more and more, to bee renewed with strength in the Inward Man and from A sensible feeling of the same to bee fellow helping of one another, in that inward and spiritual worke which god has made known and requires of goeing forward." The women's testimony gives clear priority to spiritual means over tangible ends, for the true purpose of the meeting was to nourish the inner world of the spirit. If God chose in the process to make known solutions to special problems or to reveal particular courses of action, so much the better. If not, the waiting alone was enough.[32]

Community also supplied the basis for Quaker orthodoxy. By gaining "unity" around issues, Quaker doctrine emerged and a teaching gained authority and prestige as meetings found "true unity with it." Conversely, Friends indicated their displeasure over a teaching or an action by declaring that they had "not unity with it." So strong was the pressure to unity that fractures of it—as when a Friend acted on his own without or against the meeting's advice—were considered grave offenses against the "Body of Friends," and Quaker practice required that the offender present a paper of condemnation to his monthly meeting for its approval before he could be forgiven. Such disciplinary sessions were special, if painful, times in which the meeting emphasized its own unity by defining behaviors that separated a member from Friends' fellowship. When trouble broke out between Friends, the meeting moved quickly to end it, usually appointing overseers or visitors to counsel the disputing parties and settle the matter through arbitration. Disagreements occasionally got out of hand and one or both parties scandalized the community by threatening to lay the case before civil magistrates. The meeting acted swiftly in such

32. Jacobsen, *Quaker Records*, 5–6; Baltimore Yearly Meeting Minutes, 1677–1716, fol. 25; Clifts Monthly Meeting Minutes, 1677–1771, fol. 3 (the minutes of both meetings provide interesting illustrations of Quaker worship). Quotation from the Women's Meeting is in the Half-Yearly and Yearly Women's Meeting Minutes, 1677–1718, fol. 37.

situations, ordering a "full stop to any such proceedings as may be a Dishonour to the Truth."[33]

From time to time, the patient efforts of Friends to break the obstinate spirits of troublesome members proved unsuccessful, however, forcing the meeting to invoke its most extreme sanction, disownment. This excommunication consisted of publishing a paper against a transgressor in which the meeting declared that it had no unity with the spirit that led to the person's action. Disownment was a decision made only reluctantly when the meeting felt it had no other choice, as in the decision of the Third Haven Monthly Meeting to disown John Spooner for defending a group of separatists in June 1681. Despite the attempts of a series of visitors, Spooner "justified himself and [has] been very hard upon friends with many unsavory words inconsistent with the Truth." Consequently, "the meeting can do no less than place true Judgement upon the ungodly and unruly spirit by which he was acted."[34]

Most community actions involved happier occasions. Meetings carefully preserved the unity of their congregations by requesting certificates from traveling Friends and issuing such "traveller's certificates" to local members bound on business elsewhere. The meetings were especially fond of giving these certificates to missionaries. This practice not only eliminated the problem of enthusiasts who took to the road after their home meetings disowned them, but also provided occasions when local meetings gathered to praise the grace evident in the life of one of its members. The certificate that the West River Quarterly Meeting presented to Henry Currier before his departure in 1681 offered a wonderful testimony to his "sober life" and zeal "for the Truth." Calling Currier "a very serviceable instrument in this country," the document concluded with a uniquely Quaker tribute: "we have a great unity with him and the more for that he hath Diligently laboured to heale breaches amongst

33. On the drive toward "unity" of the meetings, see Women's Meeting, fol. 92; Baltimore Yearly, fol. 18; Third Haven Monthly Meeting Minutes, 1676–1717, fol. 45; and Minutes of a Particular and Fourth Monthly Meeting at Richard Harrison's, 1699–1716, fol. 1. For examples of disunity that required disciplinary measures such as a paper of condemnation, see the Third Haven Monthly, fols. 12, 16, 18, 85. The abhorrence Quakers felt for having Friends' affairs land in civil courts may be glimpsed in the Clifts Monthly, fol. 18, and the Third Haven Monthly, fols. 9, 16, 30, 39, 46, 89, 97–98, 119, 124. Quotation is from Baltimore Yearly, fol. 11.

34. Third Haven Monthly, fol. 42.

friends and hath not made any." Ninety-three members of the West River Quarterly Meeting signed this document.[35]

Marriages were additional occasions to recall the underlying unity of the meeting even as the meeting sealed the particular unity of two of its meeters. Prospective candidates for marriages first brought their intentions to their monthly meeting, which appointed overseers to verify the individuals' "clearness" for marriage, the Quaker equivalent of issuing marriage banns. The aspiring bride and groom again presented their desires, and the meeting, if it approved, assigned more Friends to prepare the couple for marriage. For example, in 1679, Elizabeth Morgan and Emmanuel Jenkinson, a non-Quaker, were "cleared" for marriage after the meeting found "the young man to be very loveing to ffriends and willing to be subject to what truth requires."[36] In 1702, Richard Bond and Elizabeth Chew, a widow, were permitted to proceed with their plans to marry after the meeting ascertained that Chew's children would be well provided for and after Bond, recently arrived from Virginia, produced a certificate of unity from his home meeting.[37] Of course, the marriage itself was accompanied by a certificate signed by the meeting members. When Joseph Chew and Mary Smith rose at meeting in 1685 and "took" each other "According to the Example of the holy men of God recorded in the Scriptures of truth," forty-one Friends signed the record of their marriage.[38]

A generation after Elizabeth Harris first preached the Inward Light among the Puritans of Anne Arundel County, Maryland's Quakers embarked upon a course that emphasized their distinctiveness as a community and increasingly isolated them from the surrounding society. A combination of pressures led in this direction. Notable Quaker missionaries such as John Burnyeat, William Edmundson, and George Fox urged

35. West River Quarterly, fol. 16.

36. Women's Meeting, fol. 25. Meetings would withhold permission to marry from members under disciplinary action as well until the individual concerned had satisfied the meeting regarding his transgression. (See Clifts Monthly, fol. 60, for an example.) Likewise, marriage outside the community was a grave matter that required sincere repentance, and if this repentance was not forthcoming, Friends would not hesitate to disown the outmarrier. See Baltimore Yearly, fol. 15; Clifts Monthly, fol. 12; Third Haven Monthly, fols. 1, 8, 71, 114.

37. Clifts Monthly, fol. 28.

38. West River Quarterly, fol. 76.

stricter conformity to Quaker practice upon the Friends in Maryland. But these outside exhortations found a receptive audience. By the 1670s, the era of intense missionary activity had passed and dynamic growth through evangelization had ended. Quakerism in Maryland was coming of age. As a mature religious community, Friends had to ensure the transmission of their faith to their children—who had known no other faith, who had not heard the stirring preaching of the early missionaries, who may not yet have had the galvanizing experience of the Inward Light for themselves. Thus, in the 1680s, Maryland's Quakers undertook a wide-ranging program of internal moral reform to preserve the uniqueness of their witness and to rededicate themselves "to the God of all faith . . . the better to shine before all men."[39]

Friends pursued this effort on a variety of fronts. For example, David Jordan has detailed how their renewed emphasis on maintaining the testimony against taking oaths forced their increasing withdrawal from public office beginning in the mid-1670s. Quakers sought to preserve the integrity of their witness in a variety of other ways as well. Several of these strategies may be glimpsed in their wills. More Quaker testators left bequests to their meetings in the 1680s than testators in earlier decades had; five Quakers (about 30 percent of all Quaker testators) left such gifts in the 1670s, compared with ten, almost 50 percent, in the 1680s. Wills written in the 1680s used Quaker dates more often, whereby simple numbers replaced pagan calendar names as a witness against idolatry (2/17 wills in the 1670s, 17/22 in the 1680s). Quakers increasingly appointed Quaker overseers to manage their estates (1/17 in the 1670s but 11/22 in the 1680s), another practice necessitated by refusing to swear oaths, even those required to prove wills. The number of condemnation papers Quakers gave against themselves also rose in the early 1680s: five from 1676–1680, twenty-six in 1681–1685, fourteen in 1686–1690. Far from suggesting a sudden lapse in Quaker morality, this increase probably reflects a tightening of standards. Quakers increasingly insisted on maintaining the radical witness of self-condemnation in a vain world and on preserving the true unity of the meeting.[40]

For all of this activity, the center of Quaker reform was the family.

39. Quotation from a letter by William Edmundson addressed "To Friends in Maryland and Virginia, and other parts of America," dated Jan. 5, 1676/77. Letter in Herring Creek Quarterly Meeting Minutes, 1682–1716, fol. 60.

40. See Jordan, " 'Gods Candle,' " *WMQ*, 3d Ser., XXXIX (1982), 634–637; Wills, I–XVII.

Friends renewed their insistence that children marry within the community. A slight rise in the percentage of unsanctioned marriages between 1681 and 1685 led to increased counseling of children against the practice, and the rate dropped in the succeeding five years. The meeting also sought to reach those who did marry outside the community and to gain their return. These efforts also met with some success. Seven of the ten Friends known to have married outside the Maryland Quaker community between 1676 and 1685 eventually repented of their marriages, condemned them as "disorderly," and were reconciled to the meeting, presumably with their spouses. Continued incidents of outmarriage did occur, however, leading the Yearly Meeting in 1688 to advise parents to disinherit their offending children and "to let such suffer." Further, the meeting began to lobby actively for the prosecution of "priests or magistrates that doe marry friends children or child without their parents or Guardians consent."[41]

Quaker women took the lead in encouraging the faithful preservation of Quaker customs within the family, and the minutes for the various women's meetings reveal how they sought to raise their children in the gospel's light. They recommended forming special meetings just for young people, and advocated that parents teach their children to strictly observe all Quaker testimonies, "either in Apparell or otherwise, Especially upon Account of Marriage." The women also stressed the role of education in raising proper Quaker children; in 1679, twenty-one of their signatures accompanied this advisement to the Men's Meeting.

The Women's Meeting give a Caution to all ffriends, that he that is the scoole master may be Exhorted to teach ther Children in the practice, both in words, ways of action, which become the Blessed truth & that we Cannot neither will allow them to practice any of the worlds liberty in any maner of practice which the truth allows not & alsoe is desired that ffriends be dilligent to provide ffriends Bookes

41. Baltimore Yearly, fol. 34. The centrality of the family for Quaker life has been perceptively described by J. William Frost in his *The Quaker Family in Colonial America: A Portrait of the Society of Friends* (New York, 1973). It is not clear how well the threat of disownment worked because it is difficult to match up outmarriers with their parents' wills to determine whether outmarrying children were successfully disinherited. Certainly, some were. See, for example, Jane Clothier, daughter of Robert Kemp (Talbot Wills, EM1, fol. 193; Third Haven Monthly, fol. 192), and Mary Young, daughter of Arthur Young (Wills, XIII, 249; Clifts Monthly, fol. 65). These two cases, however, are from the early 18th century.

& if possible to have a ffriend to be Scoole master or mistress, this being presented to our Brethren.[42]

While the women's emphasis on hewing to the hard line of Quaker witness helped accelerate the process by which Maryland's Friends isolated themselves from the outside world, the Friends nonetheless maintained a high degree of social prestige and political leverage throughout the seventeenth century.

III

Thus, by the 1670s, Maryland had become home to communities of Catholics and Quakers. Chapels and meetinghouses provided much-needed focal points for immigrant society, while the aggressive missionary work of priests and preachers helped knit the communities together by reminding them of their sacred identities as people favored by God. These communities based in religion helped replace the familiar social world their members had lost in crossing the Atlantic.

Moreover, the cohesiveness of these communities gave Catholics and Quakers a variety of advantages in the unstable world of early Maryland. For example, historians have generally recognized the significant political role played by Catholics and Quakers in seventeenth-century Maryland. Catholics held important posts at all levels and, in general, were proportionally more numerous the higher the office. Catholics often held the great provincial offices, especially before 1650. They enjoyed disproportionate representation on the Governor's Council, especially before Cecilius Calvert's attempt during the Interregnum to recruit prominent Protestants for the colony. Before 1648 and after 1660, the governor was a Catholic. So, too, was the proprietor. As the careers of several politically successful men indicate—Henry Darnall and Baker Brooke, for example—Catholic faith coupled with marriage into the proprietary family ensured political prominence. Although the early years of the colony were not years of total Catholic control, and although local offices (especially county justices of the peace) rotated among important local planters,

---

42. Quotations are from the Women's Meeting, fols. 22 and 23. Even a casual reading of the Women's Meeting Minutes (esp. fols. 37–78) will impress upon a modern reader the importance of Quaker women in preserving the purity of the Quaker witness.

Catholics were visible in important provincial offices beyond their proportion of the overall population. This was especially true of St. Mary's County, the oldest of Maryland's counties and the seat of the provincial government throughout most of the seventeenth century.[43]

Political power likewise marked Maryland's Quaker community. In an important study of Friends' political activity in early Maryland, David Jordan notes:

> The prosperity, stability, and moral example of Quakers contributed to their political and social importance, for Maryland colonists were still overwhelmingly poor, ill-educated and often illiterate. . . . It is no wonder then, that both the proprietary government and the general populace looked to the Quakers to provide leadership in the young counties of the upper Western Shore and in the rapidly growing Eastern Shore. Lord Baltimore appointed Friends to important local offices such as sheriff and justice of the peace, while freeholders elected numerous Quakers as burgesses in the assembly. Friends also performed a host of other less prominent political duties. . . . It is hardly surprising, then, that Friends were disproportionately represented in positions of political authority.[44]

Jordan proceeds to detail Quaker political appointments, beginning with participation at local levels through the offices of sheriff and justice of the peace and ascending in honor and power through the assembly to the Council itself. Though Quakers would withdraw from public life in the 1680s, until then their disproportionate participation in provincial political life both reflected and enhanced the prestige and importance of early Maryland's community of Friends.[45]

For both Catholics and Quakers in seventeenth-century Maryland, however, political status was the mark of a more fundamental economic and social stability that these groups enjoyed owing to their organization into religious communities. Their economic prosperity is not surprising. Quakers would later be celebrated as industrious, honest, and frugal, and doubtless these virtues characterized them as well in this era, as they

---

43. David W. Jordan, "Political Stability and the Emergence of a Native Elite in Maryland," in Tate and Ammerman, eds., *Chesapeake in the Seventeenth Century*, 243–273. See also the entries for Henry Darnall and Baker Brooke in Papenfuse, *Dictionary*.

44. Jordan, "'Gods Candle,'" *WMQ*, 3d Ser., XXXIX (1982), 633–634.

45. *Ibid.*, 634–636 (esp. nn. 18, 20).

established the foundations for the impressive Quaker fortunes of the eighteenth century. For their part, some Catholics came to early Maryland with an economic advantage. The early gentlemen adventurers of Maryland were virtually all Catholics, and the large majority of the early manors were granted to Catholic gentlemen. As the colony's principal investors, they formed its first upper class and enjoyed the political and economic power that grew from their social status. Further, the strength of the networks in both religious communities suggests that each group might have looked to the economic well-being of its own membership, not only assisting those less fortunate but also trying to advance the prosperity of the group as a whole.[46]

A comparison of the wealth distribution for Catholics and the overall population of St. Mary's County reveals that Catholic decedents tended to have larger, more valuable estates at their deaths than their non-Catholic neighbors (see figure 1).[47] The rough equivalence of St. Mary's County Catholics to the overall county population at the middling levels of wealth (estates worth from £100 to £500) is striking. However, marked contrasts distinguish Catholic and overall wealth at the top and bottom of the scale. Small-estate holders (those with personal estates valued at less than £100) accounted for 59 percent of St. Mary's Catholics but 74

46. Before 1655, Cecilius Calvert, Lord Baltimore, granted 24 patents for manors; at least 18 of the grantees were Catholics. After 1658, Calvert granted another 38 manors, 14 of which went to men who were demonstrably Catholic, most of them members of the proprietary family. While greater Catholic wealth may reflect the, on the whole, wealthier Catholic immigration, other forces may have been at work. If Catholics did indeed begin the transition to a native-born population earlier, this would be reflected in their greater economic prosperity, for the wealth in land and possessions transmitted to offspring would have enabled them to begin their own careers earlier, having no indentures to complete.

47. Comprehensive figures are available only after 1660 because inventory statistics were not kept systematically before then. These figures can be best appreciated when compared to other data on the growth of personal wealth in Maryland. See Russell R. Menard, P.M.G. Harris, and Lois Green Carr, "Opportunity and Inequality: The Distribution of Wealth on the Lower Western Shore of Maryland, 1638–1705," Md. Hist. Mag., LXIX (1974), 169–184; Gloria Lund Main, "Personal Wealth in Colonial America: Explorations in the Use of Probate Records from Maryland and Massachusetts, 1650–1720" (Ph.D. diss., Columbia University, 1972); and P.M.G. Harris, "Integrating Interpretations of Local and Regionwide Change in the Study of Economic Development and Demographic Growth in the Colonial Chesapeake, 1630–1775," Regional Economic History Research Center, Working Papers, I, no. 3 (1978), 35–71.

FIGURE I. *Catholic and Overall Estate Values for St. Mary's County in the Seventeenth Century*

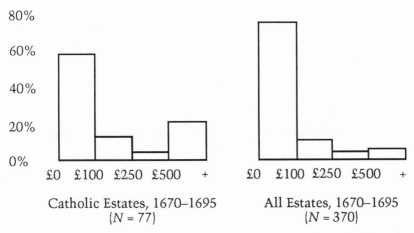

Catholic Estates, 1670–1695
(N = 77)

All Estates, 1670–1695
(N = 370)

Sources: Inventories and Accounts, 1–39, Inventories, 1–7, Accounts, 1–8, Maryland State Archives, Annapolis.

percent of all decedents. Conversely, large personal estates (over £500) were three times more frequent among Catholic decedents than among all decedents in the county. Catholics seem to have been, on the whole, less poor and more prosperous than the population generally.

Within a few years of its establishment, the Quaker community in Maryland also became a center of economic prosperity. Just as movement into the Catholic community provided valuable contacts that aided a planter in building a career, so, too, did entrance into the Quaker community. The distribution of Quaker personal estates, however, differs from that of Catholics' as well as from the overall distribution, and these differences help describe the composition of the Quaker movement in Maryland (see figure 2). While the Catholic and general population differ most at both ends of the scale, Friends' personal estates tend both to cluster in the middle of the range and to be far less represented on the low end of the spectrum. Thus, before 1700, Maryland Quakerism appears to have been predominantly a middle-class movement. Further, the economic leadership of the Quakers, like that of the Catholics, was especially apparent on the Western Shore, a fact of some significance given the political importance of the Western Shore generally throughout Maryland's early colonial period. This evidence supports the traditional notion of Maryland Quakers as "generally solid, prosperous planters and

FIGURE 2. *Quaker Estate Values in Seventeenth-Century Maryland*

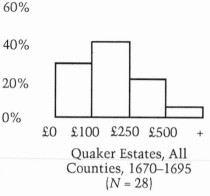

Quaker Estates, All
Counties, 1670–1695
(*N* = 28)

Sources: Inventories and Accounts, 1–39, Inventories, 1–7, Accounts, 1–8, Maryland State Archives, Annapolis.

merchants who enjoyed favorable reputations and provided desirable models for new immigrants."[48]

Catholics and Quakers alike enjoyed social as well as economic advantages. Both communities developed strategies to care for members who suffered from the hardships of Chesapeake life in one way or another. That single men may have been incorporated into the Catholic community by priests and lay Catholics alike is suggested by the often generous bequests that many single Catholic men left to the church, their frequent role as godfathers to Catholic children, and the strength of their associations with other Catholics in general. Three men from the Newtown church are good examples. Thomas Diniard left half of his estate to the Newtown pastor; John Thimbleby gave legacies to the church, to poor Catholics, to two godchildren, and to several Catholic friends; and Edward Cotton endowed a Jesuit school with cattle, bequeathed his horse to his pastor, and left gifts to two godsons. Because much of the social instability of the early Chesapeake has been ascribed to single men, the ability of the Catholic community to incorporate them provided a significant mitigating influence.[49]

48. Jordan, "'Gods Candle,'" *WMQ*, 3d Ser., XXXIX (1982), 633.
49. Wills, I, 80, 82, 203. Men who had never married were the second strongest supporters of the church in their will bequests, exceeded only by men whose spouses had predeceased them and left no children. (See Michael James Graham, "Lord Baltimore's Pious Enterprise: Toleration and Community in Colonial Maryland,

The bequests their husbands left to them suggest that Catholic widows enjoyed special attention within the community as well. Inheritance laws required that widows be left their "dower's portion," one-third of the husband's estate. Catholic widows, however, frequently appear to have received a greater than dower portion of their husbands' estates and may have set the standard for bequests to widows in the county generally. Of fifty-three identifiable Catholic widows in St. Mary's County from 1660 to 1689, thirty-seven (about 70 percent) received a greater than dower bequest from their husbands. This percentage is comparable to Lois Carr's findings for widows in St. Mary's County as a whole in the 1670s (70 percent received a greater than dower bequest) and is greater than that found in non-Catholic areas of the seventeenth-century Chesapeake. The enhanced position of the widow within the Roman Catholic community may reflect an adaptation made within the English Catholic community in the Elizabethan period. At that time, the status of Catholic women rose because the survival of Catholicism depended upon them. While Catholic men had to demonstrate occasional conformity to the Anglican church to avoid the penal laws, women maintained the rhythm of Catholic life in their households by enforcing the complex schedule of feast and fast days and by raising their children as Catholics.[50] The improved status of Catholic women did not vanish in Maryland where the penal

---

1634–1724" [Ph.D. diss., University of Michigan, 1983], 105.) The contributions of men who left no heirs suggest that the Catholic clergy may have targeted them as good potential benefactors, since inheritance laws required the reversion of the estate to the proprietary government in the event that a man left no designated heirs. While this accounts somewhat for the bequests of single men, it is also possible that the greater attention the Jesuits directed to such individuals would have more completely incorporated them into the Roman Catholic community. On single men as the preeminent source of the early Chesapeake's instability, see Morgan, *American Slavery, American Freedom*, especially Book III.

50. Wills, I–XVII, and MCF. Also see Graham, "Lord Baltimore's Pious Enterprise," table 3B, 106, and John Bossy, *The English Catholic Community, 1570–1850* (New York, 1976), 158–162, 170–172. Bossy refers to the late Elizabethan era as the "matriarchal period of English Catholicism" (p. 170). This picture of Catholic support of widows comports with general patterns of inheritance for areas of the colony in which there was a sizable proportion of Catholic settlers, patterns that endured far into the 18th century. For a study of these patterns, and a discussion of their implications, see Lois Green Carr, "Inheritance in the Colonial Chesapeake," in Ronald Hoffman and Peter J. Albert, eds., *Women in the Era of the American Revolution* (Charlottesville, Va., forthcoming).

laws did not extend (except in 1654–1658) but instead continued and found new forms. There, the economic advantages a Catholic widow enjoyed not only ensured her independence after her husband's death but also gave her greater bargaining power in contracting a future marriage.

Similarly, it is impossible to read the Quaker meeting minutes and not be impressed by the degree to which Quakers took care of their own. Orphans were assigned overseers to guard their inheritances and raise them in the "Fear of God."[51] Friends took subscriptions for livestock to care for their poor, as when, in 1683, John Keelid and his children received a cow and 650 pounds of tobacco from the Third Haven Monthly Meeting to ease their need.[52] Friends' refusal to swear oaths produced problems in proving wills, but the meetings usually appointed Quaker overseers to manage Friends' estates, thus ensuring Quaker management of Quaker property.[53] Elderly Quakers merited special concern from their coreligionists. When William Fisk and his wife alerted their monthly meeting that they were too old and infirm to travel to their weekly meeting for worship, the weekly meeting was moved to the Fisks' home.[54] Widows and widowers also received the solicitous care of the community, as when William Berry informed the Widow Wilcox on behalf of the meeting that Friends would take care of her "if she freely Resigns her self and her children to friends" and if she would appear at "our next monthly meeting."[55] Together, the Quakers' tender regard for those peo-

51. Quaker orphans were without a doubt among the best protected and cared for in the province. See minutes from the following meetings: West River Quarterly, fols. 22, 25, 26, 28, 83, 86; Baltimore Yearly, fols. 4, 6, 11, 12, 19, 25, 54, 60; Herring Creek Quarterly, fols. 23, 56; Women's Meeting, fol. 55; Third Haven Monthly, fols. 10, 16, 20, 31, 34.

52. Third Haven Monthly, fol. 55. See also Baltimore Yearly, fols. 3, 4; Herring Creek Quarterly, fols. 2, 11; Women's Meeting, fols. 23, 24, 30, 33, 38, 120; West River Quarterly, fols. 32, 60; Clifts Monthly, fols. 8, 13, 19; Third Haven Monthly, fols. 1, 2, 5, 7, 21, 30, 49, 54, 63, 116, 313.

53. Baltimore Yearly, fols. 29, 32, 37, 49, 51, 60; West River Quarterly, fols. 2, 57, 82–84; Clifts Monthly, fols. 5, 6, 14, 16, 22, 79, 86, 91. In 1688, Lord Baltimore finally allowed a declaration instead of an oath in the prerogative court and Quakers then stopped bypassing it. The meeting decided who was to administer the decedent's estate and then sent that person to the prerogative court to apply for administration. Thus, though provincial policy eventually took Friends' refusal to swear oaths into consideration, the Quaker meetings nonetheless continued to oversee Quaker estates. (I am indebted to Lois Carr for pointing this out to me.)

54. Third Haven Monthly, fol. 72.

55. *Ibid.*, fol. 28. See also Baltimore Yearly, fols. 7, 10, 28, 40; Herring Creek Quarterly, fols. 6, 7, 9, 48, 56–57; Women's Meeting, fols. 46, 61; Clifts Monthly, fols.

ple in early Maryland who would have suffered the greatest hardships—orphans, the elderly, and widows—emphasized the stability of the Quaker community and aided Friends in winning both converts and political power.

All of the advantages—religious, social, economic, and political—that Catholics and Quakers together enjoyed in early Maryland are reflected in one other detail of Catholic and Quaker social life: they tended more often to be married than their non-Catholic and non-Quaker counterparts. Between 1650 and 1670, just over three-fourths of Catholic testators (31 out of 41, or 76 percent) had married, as compared with just under two-thirds (219 out of 335, or 65 percent) of all testators. For Quakers, the figures are greater: 40 out of 45 identifiable Quaker testators before 1690 had been married (nearly 90 percent).[56]

How do we explain the greater frequency of marriage for Catholics and Quakers than for the population as a whole? In a society where men predominated, women could be selective in choosing future husbands. Membership in the Catholic and Quaker communities conferred exactly those advantages—the multiple comforts of extensive social relations, greater political influence, economic security, and a religious community in which the marriage itself could be celebrated and legitimated—that would have attracted a wife in early Maryland. Further, women held prominent places in Catholic and Quaker society. The status of Catholic women has already been indicated. Quaker women served as important missionaries and became moral conservators within the movement. So central was their role that they held their own meetings to consider issues important to them and to the Quaker movement generally on which they regularly advised the men's meetings. Signatures on several certificates in the early 1680s suggest that women made up fully 40 percent of the adult membership of the West River Quarterly Meeting, the oldest and most important of the general meetings on the Western Shore.[57] The advan-

---

50, 70–71, 78; and Third Haven Monthly, fols. 18, 20, 25, 26, 30, 31, 34, 111, 116, 117.

56. Wills, I, 2, 8.

57. These certificates are in the West River Quarterly Minutes, fols. 16, 38, 76. Of the 93 signatures attesting to Henry Currier's unity, 37 were women's (40%); 14 of the 41 signatures condemning Stephen Kaddy were women's (34%); and 18 of the 42 witnesses to the marriage of Joseph Chew and Mary Smith were women (43%). Thus, of the 176 signatures on these various documents, 69 (39%) were those of women. For an illuminating study of the importance of women in colonial American Quaker communities, see Jean R. Soderlund, "Female Authority in Colonial Pennsyl-

tage Catholics and Quakers enjoyed in settling households raises a provocative possibility and defines the ultimate meaning of stability for these communities. If Quakers and Catholics were more likely to be married than their Protestant contemporaries, they were also more likely to have children. Thus both groups may have begun the transition from immigrant to native sooner than the population as a whole. This is an important possibility since it is generally agreed that only the growth of a native population eliminated early Maryland's multiple demographic problems.[58]

Seventeenth-century Maryland was thus in some ways what the first Lords Baltimore had hoped it would be, though for reasons larger than they could have imagined. The colony fulfilled their dream of a sanctuary for religious dissenters, especially Roman Catholics. With sharp memories of persecution little more than a generation away, and still mistrusted and excluded from important roles in English society, Catholics experienced a freedom in Maryland unavailable to them in England. So, too, with Quakers, whose insistence on the direct promptings of the spirit made them antinomian heretics in England and a threat to Puritans and Anglicans alike. In Maryland, however, the Baltimores' program of religious toleration liberated Catholics and Quakers, and both groups capitalized on the fresh opportunities Maryland offered. But the lessons they had learned as dissenters in England also served them well. Their banding together as religious communities both ensured the vitality of their faiths and provided them with powerful advantages in a fledgling province where immigration patterns, disease, and death conspired against social development. While seventeenth-century Maryland was a harsh world indeed, for Catholics and Quakers alike it provided not only a sanctuary, but also a home.

---

vania and New Jersey Friends Meetings, 1680–1760" (paper presented at the Philadelphia Center for Early American Studies Seminar, 1985).

58. This is the overwhelming consensus of the modern historians of the 17th-century Chesapeake. See, for example, Menard, "Immigrants and Their Increase," in Land, Carr, and Papenfuse, eds., *Law, Society, and Politics*, 88–110; Carr, "Sources of Political Stability and Upheaval," *Md. Hist. Mag.*, LXXIX (1984), 44–70; Harris, "Integrating Interpretations," Regional Econ. Hist. Research Center, *Working Papers*, I, no. 3 (1978), 35–71; and Jordan, "Political Stability," in Tate and Ammerman, eds., *Chesapeake in the Seventeenth Century*, 243–273.

Douglas Deal

A Constricted World

Free Blacks on Virginia's Eastern Shore, 1680–1750

LATE IN the summer of 1738, Azaricum Drighouse of Northampton County on Virginia's Eastern Shore died. The name Azaricum may have come from the Old Testament Azrikam (1 and 2 Chronicles); Drighouse was an anglicized form of the Iberian Rodriggus. Though the name was unusual, Drighouse's family had been in Virginia for nearly a century. He was a slave owner whose estate included sizable herds of livestock, a boat and a canoe, various craft tools and raw materials, a gun with powder and shot, a Bible and some other books, and assorted personal effects. When appraised these possessions came to more than £100 in the current money of Virginia.[1] Neither poor nor rich, this man of middling wealth stood out in only one respect: he was a mulatto.

Drighouse was certainly not typical of his free black contemporaries on the Eastern Shore. He was wealthier than most, and none of the others appear to have owned slaves. But he was not unique either. During the 1730s, at least two and probably three free black families in Accomack County, Northampton's larger neighbor up the Shore, owned land—between 100 and 200 acres each. These farm families were also the descendants of generations of free black men and women who had lived in the area since the middle of the seventeenth century.[2]

The research upon which this essay is based was supported by a National Science Foundation doctoral dissertation grant. I would like to thank Richard Dunn, Allan Kulikoff, and Philip Schwarz for their comments on an earlier draft. Jean Russo, Lois Green Carr, and, in particular, Philip Morgan have improved the final version by offering first-rate editorial advice.

1. Northampton County Wills & Inventories, 1733–1740, 279–280. All Northampton County court records referred to are in the county clerk's office in Eastville, Va., and are available on microfilm at the Virginia State Library in Richmond.

2. They were the Harman, Longo, and Johnson families. For details, see Joseph Douglas Deal III, "Race and Class in Colonial Virginia: Indians, Englishmen, and Africans on the Eastern Shore during the Seventeenth Century" (Ph.D. diss., University of Rochester, 1981), pt. 2.

What are we to make of them? Most historians, after all, would agree that the free black residents of Virginia suffered a serious decline in status and opportunities between the late seventeenth century and the middle of the eighteenth.[3] A plantation society based upon the exploitation of black slaves was emerging in Virginia, and along with it came increasingly racist attitudes and practices among whites that denied to free blacks the social "space" that they, or at least their ancestors, had enjoyed in earlier decades. They could no longer mingle easily with whites and were lumped indiscriminately with slaves and Indians as objects of the ever more repressive legislation of the colony. Socially and economically marginal, many free blacks tottered quite literally on the brink of de facto enslavement. Theirs was a constricted world.

These generalizations, while accurate enough at one level, tend to obscure the variety and idiosyncrasy in the lives of even the most typical free blacks and mulattoes, let alone the exceptions like Azaricum Drighouse and his propertied counterparts. To illustrate that individual variety, as well as the general patterns, I offer here some portraits of free black life on Virginia's Eastern Shore from the late seventeenth century to about 1750, with a few glimpses beyond. The periods before 1700 and after 1775 are much better known,[4] so the general statements presented here should be taken as provisional at best. Further, the detailed portraits may not be representative of free black life in other regions of colonial Virginia or Maryland.

As Michael Nicholls has observed, the legal codes that evolved in Virginia between the 1660s and the 1720s to handle questions of slavery and race set certain limits on the development of the free black caste.[5] Step by step, various liberties that had been permitted to the small free black community of early Virginia were abridged or eliminated, and their

3. For two recent arguments along these lines, see Ira Berlin, "Time, Space, and the Evolution of Afro-American Society on British Mainland North America," *American Historical Review*, LXXXV (1980), 44–78, and T. H. Breen and Stephen Innes, *"Myne Owne Ground": Race and Freedom on Virginia's Eastern Shore, 1640–1676* (New York, 1980), especially chaps. 4 and 5.

4. See Deal, "Race and Class"; Breen and Innes, *"Myne Owne Ground"*; and Richard S. Dunn, "Black Society in the Chesapeake, 1776–1810," in Ira Berlin and Ronald Hoffman, eds., *Slavery and Freedom in the Age of the American Revolution* (Charlottesville, Va., 1983), 49–82.

5. Michael L. Nicholls, "Passing Through This Troublesome World: Free Blacks in the Early Southside," *Virginia Magazine of History and Biography*, XCII (1984), 51–53.

freedom to interact with white neighbors severely curtailed. The growth of the free black caste was itself hampered by legislation making manumission much more difficult than it had been during much of the seventeenth century. Most of the pertinent laws were passed or revised between 1691 and 1723, the years that also marked a decisive transition in Virginia to black slavery as the mainstay of the economy.[6]

The very creation of a free black caste, mostly via manumissions, had been an important feature of slavery in seventeenth-century Virginia. As I argue elsewhere, the small but significant free black population—on the Eastern Shore at least—acted to subvert the logic of black slavery and retard the development of racism among whites.[7] Manumissions of slaves demonstrated that slavery could be undone, and the behavior of ex-slaves among their predominantly white neighbors seriously weakened (but did not obliterate) the proposition that the races neither should nor could get along reasonably well together. But, as slaves grew in number, their owners and the officials of the colony deemed it important to define and secure the institution of slavery with laws. The escape hatch of manumission was all but closed in 1691, not simply to limit the increase of the free black population, but also to demonstrate that, for all practical purposes, slavery could *not* be undone, even if apostate slave owners willed it.[8] Forcing whites to close ranks and crushing the hopes of enslaved blacks went hand in hand.

At the same time, the colony's legislators moved to limit the reproduction of the existing free black population by erecting a racial barrier around it. Until 1691, white women and free black men could, and did, marry with impunity. In that year, intermarriage between the white and the non-white peoples of Virginia became a crime punishable by banishment from the colony (the penalty was later changed to six months in prison and a £10 fine).[9] Again, the symbolic effects of the legislation probably weighed as heavily as the practical results.

Since interracial reproduction could occur outside of marriage as well

6. This period of transition is specified and explained in Russell Menard, "From Servants to Slaves: The Transformation of the Chesapeake Labor System," *Southern Studies*, XVI (1977), 355–390.

7. Deal, "Race and Class," chap. 3 and pt. 2.

8. William Waller Hening, ed., *The Statutes at Large: Being a Collection of All the Laws of Virginia, from the First Session of the Legislature in the Year 1619* (Richmond, New York, and Philadelphia, 1809–1823), III, 86–88.

9. *Ibid.*, 87, 453–454.

as within it, laws were also needed to stiffen the penalties for bearing illegitimate mulatto offspring, which were already (i.e., before 1691) worse than those for intraracial bastardy.[10] Now a white woman who bore a mulatto bastard would be fined £15 or be sold for a five-year term of service, and her child bound over to a master for thirty years of servitude (increased in 1705 to thirty-one years).[11] The cycle was repeated for those mulatto children. If young mulatto women still in service bore illegitimate children, the children were to be bound out as servants to the same masters for terms equivalent to those of their mothers. So decreed the legislature of the colony in 1723, when that second mulatto generation was emerging.[12]

A society devoted to forced labor for blacks thus found an obvious sanction to support its regime of racial separation and oppression: more forced labor. This quasi slavery was the nemesis of many free black families in eighteenth-century Virginia. They struggled constantly to hold on to the residual years of freedom, to move away from the abyss of lifelong, hereditary slavery.

For those who weathered these storms or steered clear of the "racial" infractions just described, what did freedom mean? Between 1670 and 1723 it came to mean less and less. At the beginning of this period, free blacks lost the right to employ white indentured servants, the only source of extra labor (except for slaves, who were still scarce and expensive) for families attempting to rise above the level of subsistence production.[13] In 1705, they lost the right to hold offices of any kind and, in a ruling of more practical concern, were deemed criminals if they struck any white person, even in self-defense. No longer could free blacks testify as witnesses in the courts of the colony.[14]

By 1723, the disabilities and burdens of color had grown even greater. Though still nominally free, blacks (and Indians, the legislators always added) could not serve with arms in the local militias (they could be trumpeters and drummers, and in an emergency serve as menial laborers). Free blacks could testify in trials of slaves accused of capital crimes, but not under the oath used for white Christian witnesses (a different oath and a terrible corporal punishment for perjury were prescribed).

10. *Ibid.*, II, 170.
11. *Ibid.*, III, 87, 453–454.
12. *Ibid.*, IV, 133.
13. *Ibid.*, II, 280–281.
14. *Ibid.*, III, 251, 459, 298.

They could not vote in any election. Yet they paid more in taxes than comparable white families, for free black women above the age of sixteen were—unlike their white counterparts—declared to be tithable.[15]

In practice, of course, many of these issues were confronted in local courts long before the colonial legislators handed down their decrees.[16] Without clear-cut laws to follow, county justices of the peace had to fashion their own rules and decisions. Free black residents of the Eastern Shore, at least, were active participants in this legal process. With some success, they battled efforts to twist already skewed statutes to their disadvantage or to obliterate their last vestiges of freedom.

By the eighteenth century, however, free men and women of color had precious few white allies. Indeed, the leading whites of Northampton County twice complained to the colonial legislature about free blacks. In 1723, they bemoaned the "great Numbers of free Negros of which the women pay no Taxes" and persuaded the assemblymen to do something about the latter; in 1758, white residents tried but failed to convince the same body to send "all free Negroes out of the Colony."[17] The "great Numbers of free Negros" in the 1720s were, according to the tithable lists, about 4 percent of the total population of Northampton County: there were ten to fifteen free black men on the lists in 1723, and just under twenty free black women were listed the following year, once the tithables law changed.[18] It seems clear that the discriminatory measures concocted by the county's elite had little to do with the size of the free black population.

The attitudes of ordinary whites are harder to identify, though animosity and a determination to take advantage of free blacks seem to have been common. One sign of growing hostility appears in episodes of slander. By the middle decades of the eighteenth century, it became increasingly common for whites to taunt each other with racially tinged epithets. "You are a Negro whore and Negros strumpet and you would have Jumpt over

15. *Ibid.*, IV, 119, 127, 133–134.

16. See the instances described below.

17. For 1723, Northampton County Orders, 1719–1722, 192; quotation from H. R. McIlwaine, ed., *Journals of the House of Burgesses of Virginia* (Richmond, Va., 1905–1915), *1712–1714, 1715, 1718, 1720–1722, 1723–1726*, 369. For 1758, see *ibid.*, *1758–1761*, 73.

18. Calculated from the lists of tithables in the loose papers for Northampton County in the county clerk's office in Eastville, Va., hereafter cited as NCo L.P. The figures are approximate because in a few cases it was not possible to determine whether the blacks listed were free or slave.

nine hedges to have had a Negroe," one white woman accused another in 1729.[19] In 1750, one white man was called by another "a Negro frigging son of a bitch."[20] Three years later, in a more unusual case, a young fellow allegedly went to "bugger a Negro man called Frank" and had to be driven "two or three times out of the kitchin from the Negro Wenches for they could have no rest for [from?] him."[21] All of the accused denied the charges against them; two sued successfully for slander.

Even in the absence of the predictable sexual tensions of a stratified multiracial community, racial slander could sting. In October of 1748, an outraged John Cobb complained in Northampton County Court that Henry Stott damaged his reputation by calling him a mulatto in public. According to Cobb, Stott was plotting to destroy his ability to prove debts or give evidence in court by declaring, "you are a mulatto and I will prove it." As this case suggests, physical appearance was of little relevance, for even a man who was the great-grandchild of a Negro (i.e., who had at least one-sixteenth part Negro blood) was legally a mulatto in the colony of Virginia. Cobb countered this accusation by arguing that he had collected plenty of debts, often gave evidence in controversies "between other white persons and free subjects," and possessed the goodwill and esteem of his neighbors and others.[22] By implication, a mulatto could claim none of these things in Northampton County in 1748.

What, then, did free black men and women make of their half freedom, their constricted world? The evidence is displayed in some biographical portraits compiled from the court records of Northampton and Accomack. It seems reasonable to begin with the family of Azaricum Drighouse, the mulatto slave owner of Northampton County. As figure 1 illustrates, his great-grandfather was Emanuel Driggus, who had arrived in Northampton as a slave by 1645. Though Driggus won his own freedom by 1660 or so, several of his children remained slaves. One who did was Thomas Driggus, the grandfather of Azaricum. He married a free

19. *Anne Batson v. John Fitchet and wife Mary* (NCo L.P., 1731). Batson, the plaintiff, won the case.

20. *Solomon Bunting v. Peter Kellum* (NCo L.P., 1751). Bunting was awarded £2 in damages. Northampton County Orders, 1748–1751, 397.

21. *Michael Rickards Tathom v. Hannah Grafton* (NCo L.P., 1752–1753). This case was dropped by agreement of both parties. Northampton County Orders, 1751–1753, 261.

22. *John Cobb v. Henry Stott* (NCo L.P., 1748). Early in 1749 Cobb and Stott agreed to drop the case (Northampton Orders, 1748–1751, 37). The definition of a mulatto was given in 1705. Hening, ed., *Statutes at Large*, III, 252.

black, Sarah King, and thanks to her status, the couple's children were also free. But a marriage that crossed the chasm between slavery and freedom was destined to be difficult; Sarah Driggus lived with her enslaved husband for a few years, but established her own household in 1674. She neither remarried nor dropped the surname Driggus. Perhaps she was simply determined to rear her children in a free household instead of the slave plantation where her husband remained.[23]

Sarah and her children lived at the southern tip of Northampton County, near Magotha Bay. In an unusual episode that began early in 1688, when the children were adolescents and their mother nearly forty years of age, they fled in the company of several other free blacks all the way to Somerset County in Maryland. A few years later, having returned home to Northampton County, Sarah Driggus was to explain, at least in part, what had prompted their sudden flight. Though limited in scope, the circumstances surrounding this episode indicate clearly how precarious, not to say dangerous, some free blacks considered their situation to be, when Virginians were importing African slaves in ever-increasing numbers and experiencing both expected and novel forms of social unrest.[24]

In these uncertain times, Robert Candlin, a tenant farmer of modest means and devious intent, concocted a scheme to defraud some of his free black neighbors of their property. He told Peter George, who had been manumitted just six years earlier, that "there was a law made that all free Negroes should bee slaves againe."[25] George passed the rumor on to Sarah Driggus, though Candlin, for obvious reasons, had urged him not to breathe a word of it. Sarah went to Candlin's house and confronted him with the story. He recanted nothing, adding that he had already advised Peter George to leave the colony as quickly as possible lest he be trapped and reenslaved. On hearing this, she made for George's house, where she saw Candlin's cart already loaded with George's goods. Candlin, his wife, and William Howard, another white neighbor, had promised

---

23. This summarizes Deal, "Race and Class," 326–349.

24. The context is sketched briefly in Allan Kulikoff, "The Origins of Afro-American Slavery in Tidewater Maryland and Virginia, 1700 to 1790," *William and Mary Quarterly*, 3d Ser., XXXV (1978), 230, and more thoroughly in Edmund S. Morgan, *American Slavery, American Freedom: The Ordeal of Colonial Virginia* (New York, 1975), chap. 15.

25. Northampton County Orders & Wills, 1689–1698, 116. For more on George and his family, see Deal, "Race and Class," 443–449.

FIGURE 1. *A Partial Genealogy of the Driggus (Drighouse) Family*

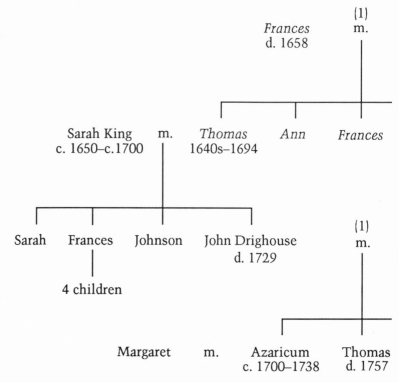

Note: Italics indicate slave status; all other individuals are free blacks unless otherwise noted.

Peter George that they would preserve his estate for him while he fled. They told him to send for it later in his own hand and to be sure to have another black man deliver the message. The goods would be his again, and he would be safe. With these words, they parted company. The whites, with nearly all of Peter George's worldly possessions, including three head of cattle and some hogs, made for the Candlin farm. The blacks, including Sarah Driggus, sped northward up the Shore carrying as little with them as possible.[26]

When they discovered the ruse or what they did once they reached Maryland is not clear. Only a few pieces of evidence remain to confirm their presence there. On August 14, 1688, the court of Somerset County heard

26. Northampton Orders & Wills, 1689–1698, 106, 115–116.

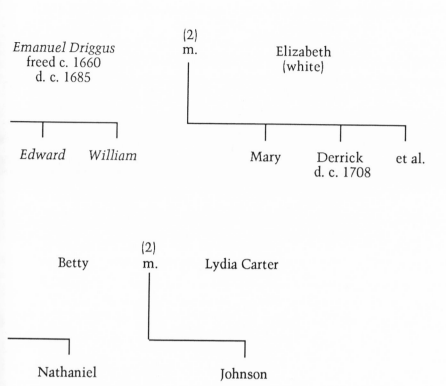

the peticon of Sarah Driggers and the rest all Negroes desiring that they might be putt out of the list of Tythables from paying any Taxes as being free borne Negroes whereupon it was the same day Ordered that the four women be exempted and that the mn [men pay?] taxes for this yeare and that they bring a Certificate under the Ministers hands where they formerly did live or were borne that they are free Negroes and baptized.[27]

The other Negroes referred to in this document were probably Driggus and George family members. Derrick Driggus, one of Emanuel Driggus's free mulatto children, was in their company. In November 1689, he subscribed, along with a hundred or so "Inhabitants of the County of

27. Somerset Court, Liber AW, 1690–1691, p. 58, cited in Clayton Torrence, *Old Somerset on the Eastern Shore of Maryland: A Study in Foundations and Founders* (Richmond, Va., 1935), 492.

Somersett," to a profession of loyalty to the Protestant cause and the king and queen of England.[28]

Derrick Driggus and perhaps one or two others decided to stay in Maryland.[29] Sarah Driggus and Peter George stayed for three years, but in the spring of 1691, they returned to Northampton County. At that very moment, the Virginia Assembly was engaged in drafting and passing its harshest act yet concerning slaves and free blacks. This expressly forbade future manumissions of blacks, except in cases where the former owners were prepared to arrange for the transportation of the freedmen out of the colony.[30]

Once back in Virginia, Peter George successfully brought suit to recover his cattle and hogs from the widow Elizabeth Candlin. Sarah Driggus had even more important business to look after; she, however, failed in a last-ditch attempt to prevent her eldest daughter, Sarah, from being taken out of the colony by a white family. The younger Sarah, by then about twenty-three years old, had lived nearly all her life with a free black couple, John and Christian Francisco.[31] In midsummer 1691, her mother learned that Sarah had apparently been bound over to a white family, the Kennys, and was "to goe to the Southward" with them. The details are sketchy and confusing, but it is clear that the elder Sarah Driggus thought the arrangement unlawful and tried to persuade the Northampton County Court to invalidate it. The court ruled against her, and she thereby lost contact with a daughter she had hardly even known, a young woman who at age twenty-one in 1689 was to have been set "free for ever from the claim of any person to make [her] a slave."[32]

After these years of flight, confusion, and separation, Sarah Driggus settled once again in Northampton County. As other poor families, white and black, were doing in this period, she bound out her younger daugh-

28. Torrence, *Old Somerset*, 349.

29. According to information supplied by Lois Green Carr from the land records of Maryland and the court records of Somerset County, Derrick (or Devorix) Driggus may have arrived in Maryland as early as 1677; he remained until his death in 1708 or 1709. Other Drigguses appeared on the county's tax lists until the 1740s.

30. Hening, ed., *Statutes at Large*, III, 86–88.

31. Northampton Orders & Wills, 1689–1698, 106. For details, see Deal, "Race and Class," 370 n. 97.

32. Northampton Orders & Wills, 1689–1698, 121, 125; Deal, "Race and Class," 339–340.

ter, Frances, as a servant to John Brewer, a local blacksmith.[33] Sarah's husband, Thomas Driggus, at the age of fifty or thereabouts, died early in 1694.[34] Their daughter Frances and their sons were reaching maturity, and so beginning to experience for themselves the frustrations of constricting horizons and the racist pressures their white neighbors and superiors brought to bear on nominally free men and women of another color.

In May of 1694, Frances was hauled before the grand jury by John Brewer, her master, and presented for the sin of fornication. No partner was named. She was ordered to receive thirty lashes of the whip on her bare shoulders and to serve her master an additional two years.[35] Exactly one year later, she found herself in court again: this time her sin, as the jurymen and justices saw it, had led to conception, and Frances had given birth to an illegitimate child. Not about to suffer in silence, she threw the court into an uproar by identifying her master as the father of the infant. This Brewer heatedly denied, declaiming under oath that he had been one hundred miles from home when her bastard was conceived. Furthermore, "hee never knew her or was concerned with her in any such way." The justices were clearly unsettled by the charge and worried about "what evil consequence such presidents [precedents] may futurely be if unduely grounded." They were not prepar.:d to accept the oath of a black woman in "soe tender a case" and thus decided to pass the matter on to the governor and Council for their opinion and advice. Meanwhile, the justices ordered Frances Driggus to pay her fine or suffer corporal punishment—thirty lashes again.[36]

Shortly thereafter, Brewer decided he had had enough and sold her

33. Accomack County Orders, 1690–1697, 158a. All Accomack County court records referred to are in the county clerk's office in Accomac, Va., and are available on microfilm at the Virginia State Library. Frances was then about 14 years old. Brewer lived just north of King's Creek, not far from the land Emanuel Driggus once rented from William Kendall (see n. 37, below). On the general practice of apprenticing poor children, see Richard B. Morris, *Government and Labor in Early America* (New York, 1946), 384–386. For other Eastern Shore examples in the same period, see Accomack County Wills Etc., 1692–1715, 328, 424–425.

34. Driggus seems to have had some livestock to pass on to his survivors, for in March 1694 Sarah had a cattle mark put on record for the first time. Northampton County Deeds, Wills, Etc., 1651–1654, 28 (at the end of the volume).

35. Northampton Orders & Wills, 1689–1698, 274, 279.

36. *Ibid.*, 322.

to one Thomas Mills, the brother of his son-in-law Edward Mills, in Accomack County. Frances was at their mercy and grudgingly made the trip of over forty miles to the farm of her new master. But soon she caught wind of what she considered to be a plot by Brewer and Mills to "transport her to some parts of the world where her free condition could not be made app[arent] and thereby indangered to be made a slave." The spirited eighteen-year-old took her case to the Accomack County Court, where she petitioned in September 1695 to be discharged from servitude once and for all. Brewer enlisted the legal services of the eminent John Custis, who was instructed by the court to give evidence at the next session proving his client's right to the service of Frances Driggus. In November, Custis presented the court with a letter from Sarah Driggus binding her daughter out to Brewer. The justices ruled the letter, which was not a formal indenture, invalid in law and declared Frances a free woman.[37]

Frances Driggus probably went to live with her mother again. By then a widow, Sarah Driggus was also joined by her sister-in-law Jane Driggus's mulatto daughter, Sarah Landum.[38] The earliest (and only) reference to this domestic arrangement came in February 1698, when Landum and Sarah Driggus were accused by another free black woman, Black Nanny, of stealing some linen yarn and dressed flax out of her house.[39] Black Nanny took her complaint to John Custis, the nearest justice of the peace, and obtained a warrant authorizing the local constable to search the Driggus house for the stolen goods, some of which were found there. The constable took these and the two accused women back to Custis, who had them jailed until they entered into bond with good security to appear for trial at the next court. Black Nanny was bound by recognizance to prosecute them. At the trial, there was apparently some initial uncertainty as to whether she would be allowed to testify under oath.[40] But the justices finally found her "capable of an oath" and let her speak. It is clear

37. Accomack Orders, 1690–1697, 158a, 169a–170. The information on Brewer and Mills comes from Ralph T. Whitelaw, *Virginia's Eastern Shore: A History of Northampton and Accomack Counties*, 2 vols. (Richmond, Va., 1951), 166–167, 1118. Brewer appealed the court's ruling, apparently to no avail.

38. Sarah Landum, born in 1663, was the illegitimate child of Jane Driggus and an Irish freedman, Dennam Olandum. See Deal, "Race and Class," 334.

39. For more on the life of Black Nanny, see *ibid.*, 457–459.

40. Here we see local justices confronting an issue before the Virginia Assembly ruled on it in 1705 (see above). Even the new law did not put an end to the uncertainty; see the material on Jane Webb in the text below.

that she took the oath as seriously as they did, for she readily identified the yarn found in the possession of Landum and Driggus as her own, but would not go so far with the dressed flax, which "shee believed to be hers by colour, length, and the manner of its dress and twist, but said she would rather loose it then sweare for it." If the accused offered any defense it was not recorded. Each was sentenced to twenty-five lashes on the bare back and ordered to pay all the costs in the suit.[41]

Within two years of this humiliating experience, Sarah Driggus was dead. Like her husband before her, she did not live past the age of fifty. Born in Virginia of free black parents, she had as much opportunity to conform or assimilate to the ways of white society as anyone of her color and sex had. Yet she married a slave, and though she lived apart from him for twenty years, she bore his surname to her death. In fact she seemed to keep her dealings with whites to a minimum. Apart from one brief reference near the end of her life to a cure she performed on a white man's arm,[42] there is little evidence that she ever hired herself out or provided services to anyone. Her life was bounded by relationships with her own family and a few black neighbors.

As her mother was dying Frances Driggus was reduced to stealing food and other supplies from the houses of white farmers. In January 1700, she was caught and given thirty lashes for thefts from the house of Arthur Roberts. A month later, she was briefly imprisoned on the charge of stealing some meat from Charles Trelfo, but Trelfo decided not to prosecute and she was discharged.[43] That October, after her mother died, she entered into a contract to serve Isaac and Bridget Foxcroft, a wealthy couple, for the term of ten years. Half a century earlier, Bridget's father, Stephen Charlton, had briefly owned Emanuel and Frances Driggus, the grandparents of young Frances Driggus, or Drighouse, as the name was spelled by 1700.[44]

Though she was not a slave, Frances Drighouse was in a desperate situation. Three weeks before signing the agreement with the Foxcrofts, she had given birth to another illegitimate child. Unable even to pay the family who had seen her through the delivery, she was forced to indenture not only herself but also her infant and any other children she might bear during the next ten years. Each child was to serve until he or she reached

41. Northampton Orders & Wills, 1689–1698, 463.

42. *Ibid.*, 521.

43. Northampton County Orders, Wills, Etc., 1698–1710, 35, 36.

44. Northampton County Deeds & Wills, 1692–1707, 348–349.

the age of twenty-five. In return, Drighouse and her children were to be adequately maintained, but they would receive neither wages nor "freedom dues."[45] Here, in local practice, was an example of the sort of arrangement for mulatto children that would be inscribed in law in 1723.

Late in 1702, Drighouse gave birth to a third illegitimate child. No father was named but he may have been a slave, since she was ordered by the court to post bond herself to "save the parish harmless."[46] Her spirits were lifted temporarily a few months later, when Isaac Foxcroft, on his deathbed, promised to set her free. But the promise was broken by Foxcroft's widow when, several months after her husband's death, she assigned Frances Drighouse to one Thomas Ward. Drighouse protested this breach of faith in Northampton County Court in November 1703, to no avail. Declaring that the matter was not adjudicable, the judges advised "the said Drighouse to go home to the said Thomas Ward, and serve him faithfully."[47]

About the time her mistress Foxcroft assigned her to Ward, Frances Drighouse became pregnant with a fourth illegitimate child. Ten months later, in May 1704, she was presented in court by the grand jury for bastardy.[48] The next year her master moved up to Accomack County. Whether Frances went with him is unknown, but she probably did. A Comfort Driggus—perhaps one of her children—was presented for bastardy in the Accomack County Court in May 1715. The mulatto Francis Johnson agreed to pay her fine and to see that the child was maintained.[49] Apart from this one piece of evidence, we know nothing about the fate of Frances Drighouse and her children.

Her brothers, John and Johnson Drighouse, remained in Northampton County. Along with another free black, Samuel George, they were prosecuted in 1702 for stealing a hog and then abusing and threatening several whites "in an insolent manner." The court ordered them to pay a fine of 2,000 pounds of tobacco for the theft and to receive whippings—thirty-nine lashes each—for the abuses and threats.[50] Johnson Drighouse seems to have left the county sometime after this incident and moved to North Carolina. Three different "Driggers" appear in the published

45. *Ibid.*
46. Northampton Orders, Wills, Etc., 1698–1710, 122–123, 129.
47. *Ibid.*, 178; Northampton Deeds & Wills, 1692–1707, 351.
48. Northampton Orders, Wills, Etc., 1698–1710, 193.
49. Accomack County Orders, 1714–1717, 7a, 9; Whitelaw, *Virginia's Eastern Shore*, 616.
50. Northampton Orders, Wills, Etc., 1698–1710, 102, 106.

military records for that colony after 1700. And, in 1790, a Johnston Driggers headed a free black household in Craven County.[51]

John Drighouse spent the rest of his life in Northampton County. He never acquired any land and was quite poor when he died in 1729. His estate was worth a little more than £10 in the current money of Virginia, and most of that sum had to be paid to a creditor, Gertrude Harmanson. Drighouse's young widow, Lydia, had to bind out her nine-year-old stepson, Nathaniel, and her two-year-old son, Johnson, to a planter early in 1730. She tried to recover a small part of her husband's estate for his funeral expenses. The justices agreed to allow her 150 pounds of tobacco if that much was left after the debt to Harmanson was liquidated.[52]

This grim picture is at least partly misleading. John Drighouse had been living with his wife, Lydia, for only a couple of years before he died. Before his marriage to Lydia Carter, Drighouse had had a wife named Betty. She, or perhaps an earlier wife, appears to have borne him two sons, Azaricum and Thomas, between about 1700 and 1710.[53] The material success of these sons stands in stark and surprising contrast to the poverty of their father at the end of his life.

Azaricum (or Rica) Drighouse was apprenticed to Richard Carver between 1715 and 1717. The most unusual provision of the agreement between them was the stipulation that Carver was to provide Drighouse with two months of schooling each fall.[54] After 1717, Drighouse went to work in the households of two other small planters, Francis and Jonah Batson. By 1722, Azaricum and his wife, Margaret, had established their own household, probably on land leased from a white neighbor.[55]

In later records, Drighouse is identified as a carpenter. This artisanal skill and the brief education he had received as a youth may have helped him to acquire more property than any of his black, and a good many of

51. See William L. Saunders *et al.*, eds., *The Colonial Records of North Carolina* (Raleigh, N.C., 1886–1909), IV, 803, 897, 965, IX, 725, 771, and U.S. Bureau of the Census, *Heads of Families at the First Census of the United States Taken in the Year 1790, North Carolina* (Washington, D.C., 1908), 134.

52. Northampton County Wills, Deeds, Etc., 1725–1733, 216; Northampton County Orders, 1722–1729, 394; *ibid.*, 1729–1732, 4, 37, 44.

53. See the Northampton County lists of tithables for 1724–1726, NCo L.P. Azaricum and Thomas may have been two of the illegitimate children borne by Drighouse's sister Frances just before and after 1700 (see the text above). Unfortunately, none of the court records provide evidence about who their parents were. That John Drighouse was their father is simply my best guess.

54. Northampton County Orders, Wills, Deeds, Etc., 1711–1718, 83.

55. See the lists of tithables for 1720–1728, NCo L.P.

his white, contemporaries. He even became a slaveholder: in 1736, he purchased a girl, Bridget, who was judged in court to be nine years old; the next year, he bought a twelve-year-old boy named Harry.[56] The two slaves probably accounted for more than one-third of the total value of Drighouse's estate when he died in the summer of 1738. Although the boy died or was sold sometime between the writing of Drighouse's will and the appraisal of his estate three months later, his property was still valued at more than £100 in the current money of Virginia.[57] The estate included livestock of all kinds, carpentry and shoemaking tools, farm implements, wool-processing equipment, two boats, crops of corn, wheat, and flax, lumber, cloth, leather, and personal effects, among them a Bible, five other books (no titles were given), and a gun. Using figures on wealth distribution compiled by Lois Green Carr for nearby Somerset County, Maryland, we can estimate that Azaricum Drighouse was wealthier at his death than nearly two-thirds of all white decedents on the lower Eastern Shore in this period.[58]

The acquisition of slaves and significant amounts of property by men like Drighouse betokened nascent class divisions within the free black caste. But these divisions dissolved rapidly with the dispersal of the estates of the few property-holding free blacks on the Eastern Shore by midcentury. The properties of Azaricum Drighouse were divided into three parts after his death.[59] His widow, Margaret, married a free mulatto, Mark Becket, but neither Becket nor Drighouse's children came close to matching his material accomplishments.[60] Only his brother, Thomas Drighouse, did that; and his estate, valued at just over £80 after his death in 1757, was divided among four heirs.[61]

56. Northampton County Orders, 1732–1742, 22, 275. The name that Drighouse gave the slave girl may hold some meaning: Bridget Foxcroft was the unsympathetic mistress of Frances Drighouse, who was either the aunt or the mother of Azaricum.

57. See the will and inventory in Northampton Wills & Inventories, 1733–1740, 279–280.

58. In a letter to the author, May 6, 1987, Carr generously shared information on recently devised currency deflators and a table on inventoried wealth distribution in three Chesapeake counties (including Somerset) that will appear in her essay "Inheritance in the Colonial Chesapeake," in Ronald Hoffman and Peter J. Albert, eds., *Women in the Era of the American Revolution* (Charlottesville, Va., forthcoming).

59. For the provisions of his 1738 will, see Northampton Wills & Inventories, 1733–1740, 279.

60. See Northampton County Orders, 1742–1748, 33, 56, 69, 97, 101, 107–108.

61. Northampton County Wills & Inventories, 1754–1763, 281, 284–285.

Changing economic conditions in the Chesapeake may have closed off the few opportunities available to free blacks like Azaricum and Thomas Drighouse. As the use of slave labor increased, slaves began to take over the basic artisanal functions that had previously been commanded by independent white, and occasionally free black, craftsmen.[62] Without land of their own, most free black men and women had little recourse after 1750 except to work as tenant farmers and hired laborers, adjusting to the new seasonal demands of the diversified grain economy on the Eastern Shore.

In his apparent literacy, his material possessions, and his status as a slave owner, Azaricum Drighouse was atypical of free blacks on the Eastern Shore during the first half of the eighteenth century. Far more common were the poverty, servitude, bastardy convictions, and brushes with de facto enslavement experienced by some of his ancestors and contemporaries. The following portrait of another family further illustrates these prevailing hardships.

The Carter genealogy can be traced back to Paul and Hannah, two slaves imported by the Littletons of Northampton County in 1640. The Carters had six children (Elizabeth, Edward, Mary, Thomas, James, and Paul) between 1640 and about 1655. By 1665, Paul Carter had died and the other members of his family had become the property of Francis Pigot, who had just married the widow of one of the Littleton heirs. In May of that year, Pigot manumitted Hannah Carter, and some of her free black neighbors (including Emanuel Driggus) saw to her support over the next decade or so.[63]

Though she survived her husband by more than twelve years, Hannah Carter may not have lived long enough to see any of her children attain freedom. In 1684, having been a sheriff and a justice of the peace in Northampton County and having outlived two wives, Francis Pigot wrote his last will and testament.[64] It is a lengthy document that contains elaborate provisions for the disposition of his estate and maintenance of his children, most of whom were still in their minority. Among other bequests to his children, Pigot left nine slaves, three of whom were sons

---

62. See Berlin, "Time, Space, and Evolution," *AHR*, LXXXV (1980), 73–74, and David W. Galenson, "White Servitude and the Growth of Black Slavery in Colonial America," *Journal of Economic History*, XLI (1981), 39–47.

63. See Deal, "Race and Class," 431–434, for more details.

64. Whitelaw, *Virginia's Eastern Shore*, 138, 181, 414; Susie M. Ames, *Studies of the Virginia Eastern Shore in the Seventeenth Century* (Richmond, Va., 1940), 154.

FIGURE 2. *A Partial Genealogy of the Carter Family*

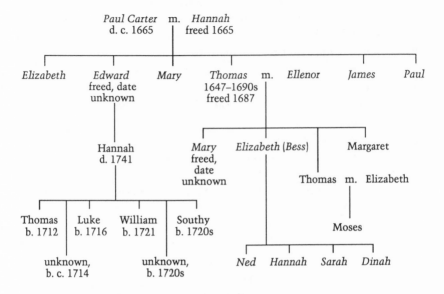

Note: Italics indicate slave status; all other individuals are free blacks.

of Paul and Hannah Carter: Edward, James, and Paul. The provisions in the will regarding their brother Thomas, whom Pigot called "my Negro servant Thomas Carter," and his family were quite different.[65]

Thomas Carter, who in 1684 was thirty-seven years old, had married another slave named Ellenor.[66] She had borne him two children and was expecting another. For reasons that are unspecified in the will, Francis Pigot laid out in detail a procedure by which Thomas and Ellenor Carter might become free. First, they had to agree that their daughters, Mary and Elizabeth, would serve two of Pigot's sons; their unborn child was to serve Pigot's daughter. Each of the Carter children would be free from service when she or he reached the age of twenty-four. Next, Thomas and Ellenor Carter themselves had to serve Pigot's heirs for two years

65. Northampton County Orders & Wills, 1683–1689, 119–123.
66. In a 1663 document Carter is identified as age 16. Northampton County Deeds, Wills, Etc., 1657–1666, 168.

after his death. They would then be required to begin paying his heirs the sum of 10,000 pounds of tobacco in ten annual installments. During those ten years they would be permitted to live rent free on the land of one of Pigot's sons. Finally, the Carters had to agree that they would leave the county for good, once all the payments had been made. Only if these conditions were met would freedom be theirs.[67]

Pigot's plan for the manumission of the Carters seems to have been finely calculated to capture the fruits of their labor until they were too old and worn out to produce more than enough to maintain themselves, at which point they would be cast off.[68] Pigot knew that the incentive of attaining freedom for their children as well as themselves would be sufficient to induce the Carters to comply with his conditions. By promising to deposit 1,000 pounds of tobacco per year into the hands of Pigot's heirs, the Carters would in effect be assuming the risks normally borne by their owners. In periods of chronically low tobacco prices like the 1680s and 1690s, with essentially fixed costs of subsistence, masters could not always extract a profit out of the labor of their slaves.[69] To be guaranteed a handsome annual return, if only for ten years, and to be relieved of the burden of maintaining two elderly slaves in the bargain was almost a godsend. If the Carters failed to satisfy the conditions set by Pigot, they and their children would remain slaves. If they succeeded, the only substantial cost to Pigot's children would be the foregone profits that would have accrued from owning the Carter daughters from the age of twenty-four until their deaths.

As it turned out, Pigot's own heirs foiled this elaborate scheme after his

67. Northampton Orders & Wills, 1683–1689, 119–123.

68. Even if Pigot had died immediately after writing his will (he actually died about a year later), Carter would have been 49 years old at the end of the 12-year manumission process outlined in the will. This is close to the average age of death for native-born whites and blacks in the Chesapeake at the close of the century. In fact, Carter died at the age of 51 or 52. See the text below; Russell R. Menard, "The Maryland Slave Population, 1658 to 1730: A Demographic Profile of Blacks in Four Counties," *WMQ*, 3d Ser., XXXII (1975), 32, 43, 45, 48; and Lorena S. Walsh and Russell R. Menard, "Death in the Chesapeake: Two Life Tables for Men in Early Colonial Maryland," *Maryland Historical Magazine*, LXIX (1974), 218–219.

69. The slump of those decades was interrupted only by a brief boom in the mid-1680s. See Russell R. Menard, "The Tobacco Industry in the Chesapeake Colonies, 1617–1730: An Interpretation," *Research in Economic History*, V (1980), 137–140.

death in 1685. Two years later, Ralph and Thomas Pigot decided to release Thomas Carter from "certaine payments, articles, clauses, services and provisions" upon which, according to the terms of their father's will, Carter's manumission depended.[70]

Thus, Carter and his wife Ellenor were set free. Whether they remained tenants on land belonging to the Pigots is unknown. They do appear to have lived in the same general area, between Old Plantation Creek and Magotha Bay. Court records of the early 1690s document their ties with local farmers and free blacks.[71] In 1690, Thomas Carter promised to pay the fine for fornication levied by the Northampton County Court against Frances Harman, a young free black woman. During the Carters' first few years as free blacks, Harman had been employed as a domestic servant on the nearby estate of John Custis. A few years later, she would marry one of the Pigot family's slaves, Anthony George.[72]

In 1693 Thomas Carter signed a deed that reflects his precarious economic condition and his concern for the future of his children. In it he agreed to apprentice his son Thomas and daughters Elizabeth and Margaret to his "loving friend" William Gelding, a yeoman farmer who lived on a 200-acre tract at Magotha Bay. The children were to serve Gelding from the time of their father's death until each reached the age of nineteen. Gelding promised to teach them to read and provide them with freedom dues similar to those received by white indentured servants: three barrels of corn and some suits of clothing.[73]

Carter died sometime during the next six years. In May 1699, Ellenor Carter is identified in the records as a widow.[74] Thomas Carter had enjoyed a decade or so of freedom—not much, but more, apparently, than some of his own children. According to Francis Pigot's will of 1684, three of those children, who had been born while their parents were still slaves, were to continue serving members of the Pigot family until the age of twenty-four.

The first, Mary Carter, assigned to Thomas Pigot, was a free woman by 1699, perhaps because Pigot had died without heirs some years ear-

70. Northampton County Deeds, Wills, Etc., 1680–1692, 159–160.

71. Northampton Orders & Wills, 1689–1698, 46, 48–49, 194, 250; Whitelaw, *Virginia's Eastern Shore*, 132, 142.

72. Northampton Orders & Wills, 1689–1698, 58. See the sketch of the Harman family in Deal, "Race and Class," 398–412.

73. Northampton Orders & Wills, 1689–1698, 250; Whitelaw, *Virginia's Eastern Shore*, 132.

74. Northampton Orders, Wills, Etc., 1698–1710, 8.

lier.[75] She seems to have returned to live with her mother and father. After her father died, she bore an illegitimate child whose father she identified in court as Daniel, a slave belonging to Daniel Benthall, a nearby landowner.[76] Just four years later, in 1703, Mary Carter was again presented in the county court for bastardy. This time, she was designated as a widow, though the identity of her deceased husband is not known. Two local farmers agreed to pay her fine and find a home for her youngest child.[77] She does not appear in the court records again.[78]

The second daughter of Thomas and Ellenor Carter, Elizabeth, was to serve Ralph Pigot. Well after she should have been set free, she was listed, as Bess Carter (age twenty-seven), in a 1705 inventory of Ralph Pigot's slaves. So, too, were four children of hers: Ned (age ten), Hannah (seven), Sarah (four), and Dinah (two). Bess Carter's uncles, James and Paul Carter, lived on the same plantation.[79] Fifteen years later, Bess Carter was working for yet another Ralph Pigot, grandson of her first master, Francis Pigot. She and her children all labored as slaves for various members of the Pigot family through the 1720s.[80]

The fate of the child that Ellenor Carter was pregnant with in 1684, when Francis Pigot wrote his will, is unknown. That child, if it lived, was to serve Pigot's daughter, Elizabeth, who married Matthew Moore. Listed among their slaves in the early decades of the eighteenth century were two who bore the names Paul and Hannah, the same as those of the progenitors of the Carter family.[81] Whether these slaves descended from one of the Carters remains an open question.

Some of the children of Thomas and Ellenor Carter had the good fortune to be born free, though that freedom was often tenuous. Their

75. On Mary Carter, see Francis Pigot's will (Northampton Orders & Wills, 1683–1689, 119–123). Thomas Pigot appears to have died by 1692. Whitelaw, *Virginia's Eastern Shore*, 181.

76. Northampton Orders, Wills, Etc., 1698–1710, 8, 18. Since Mary is here identified as the "daughter of Ellenor Carter widow," I assume she was living at home. On Benthall, see Whitelaw, *Virginia's Eastern Shore*, 124.

77. Northampton Orders, Wills, Etc., 1698–1710, 162, 165.

78. A "Mary Carter alias Hiram" was presented in court for bastardy in 1717. She may have been the first child (b. 1699) of the Mary Carter discussed here, though there is no direct evidence to establish the connection. See Northampton County Orders, 1716–1718, 34.

79. Northampton Deeds & Wills, 1692–1707, 417.

80. See the lists of tithables for 1720–1729, NCo L.P.

81. The genealogy of these slaves can be reconstructed from a dispute in Northampton County's chancery court in 1749 and 1750. See, in particular, the bill of

son Thomas may have stayed, as his father had arranged, with William Gelding for a few years at the turn of the century. But Gelding left the county in 1702.[82] Carter does not appear in the court records again until 1716, and in 1720 he was listed as a tithable in the household of Daniel Jacob, another free black, whose father had been freed in the 1690s by John Custis.[83] With his wife, Elizabeth, and young son, Moses, Thomas Carter eventually established his own household in Northampton County.[84]

Little evidence about Carter's relations with his neighbors has survived. In 1724, though, he was implicated in a case of larceny that involved an informal network of whites, slaves, and free blacks. Carter harbored a runaway slave who had stolen some linen from a local planter. The slave wanted Carter's wife, Elizabeth, to make a shirt out of the cloth, which she and her husband testified they did not do. Thomas Carter did confess to giving the slave shelter and food on a few occasions, even though they knew he was outlawed. Elizabeth Carter denied that "she ever gave the said Negro any victuals or that he ever eat any or drank in her house to her knowledge."[85] The slave was caught and sentenced to hang. Thomas Carter and a poor white widow were both found guilty of a "great misdemeanor in harbouring and entertaining the said Negro." The widow received twenty-five lashes and a month in jail; Carter was given twenty-nine lashes and an hour in the pillory, and was put in jail until he could pay the court fees.[86]

During the 1710s and 1720s, another group of free blacks with the surname Carter appears in the Northampton court records. They seem to have been the descendants, not of Thomas and Ellenor Carter, but of Thomas's brother Edward. In 1684, Francis Pigot had bequeathed Ed-

---

complaint entered on Dec. 12, 1749, by John Moore and Leah Evans, NCo L.P., 1751.

82. At least, Gelding sold his land in 1702 and was not mentioned on the rent roll of 1704. See Whitelaw, *Virginia's Eastern Shore*, 132, and Thomas J. Wertenbaker, *The Planters of Colonial Virginia* (Princeton, N.J., 1922), 245.

83. In 1716, Carter was sued by Jacob for a debt of 1,100 pounds of tobacco (Northampton County Orders, 1711–1716, 255, 256–257). For the 1720 list of tithables, see NCo L.P., 1720. On Jacob's father, Gabriel, see the 1696 will of John Custis (Northampton Orders & Wills, 1689–1698, 357). In this instance, the 1691 law regarding manumissions seems to have been ignored.

84. See the lists of tithables from 1722 onward, NCo L.P.

85. See *ibid.*, 1724.

86. Northampton Orders, 1722–1729, 146.

ward Carter to his son Thomas, who owned him for at least a few years.[87] In 1687, just after Thomas Carter had been manumitted by Ralph and Thomas Pigot, Edward Carter was brought into court for assaulting a white woman. William Sterlinge and his wife, Elizabeth, testified that Carter "insolently abused her strikeinge her severall blowes and tore her hood to peeces of[f] her head." No reason for the alleged attack was given, but Carter was summarily sentenced to be whipped (thirty lashes) for the crime.[88]

Within five years, Thomas Pigot would be dead.[89] No will or deed of manumission has survived to establish when or how Edward Carter won his freedom. By 1714, however, he and a mulatto daughter named Hannah are mentioned in the court records as free persons. His daughter had just given birth to an illegitimate child. Carter and a white neighbor—one who also had come to the assistance of Hannah's cousin Mary Carter in a similar predicament in 1703—posted bond together to arrange for maintenance of the child and to pay Hannah's fine and the court fees.[90]

This was not Hannah Carter's first child. A son, Thomas, had been born in 1712. She apprenticed him, when he was four, to a local farmer since she could no longer afford to take care of him herself. In 1716, she bound over another illegitimate child, a son named Luke, to a white farmer, Absalom Satchell, who paid her fine in court. In 1721, it was a free black, William Harman, who came to her assistance, although there was some suspicion, never substantiated in court, that William Brumfeild, a white man, was the father. Hannah Carter called this child William. She bore two more illegitimate children in the 1720s, one a son named Southy. In both cases, her fines were paid and maintenance of the children arranged by prominent planters in the neighborhood, Ralph Pigot and John Robins.[91]

Although William and Southy were reared in the households of white neighbors, Hannah Carter never formally bound over these two sons. This lapse brought complaints from their white custodians when the boys reached working age. As the case of William Carter makes clear, Hannah

87. See Pigot's will, Northampton Orders & Wills, 1683–1689, 119–123.

88. *Ibid.*, 299, 309.

89. Whitelaw, *Virginia's Eastern Shore*, 181.

90. Northampton Orders, 1711–1716, 149.

91. See Northampton Orders, 1711–1716, 244, 252, 1716–1718, 34, 136, 1719–1722, 144, 146, 150, 1722–1729, 181, 190, 382, 384, 387; NCo L.P., 1741, 1740. The fathers were not identified in these cases.

Carter's motive was to avoid losing all rights to her children, even though she lacked the resources to rear them herself while they were young. William Carter's former master, John Wilson, complained in 1740 that the boy's mother had promised "at sundry times to bind the said child to your petitioner according to law but instead of complying with her promise, she induced the said child to leave your petitioner and hath kept him from your petitioner about 16 months." The court granted Wilson's petition that William Carter be bound to him legally.[92]

Perhaps Hannah Carter was reluctant to formally apprentice her son William because she had had difficulty enforcing the contract that bound her eldest son, Thomas Carter, to Thomas Costin. In 1728, she petitioned the county court that Costin "hath never endeavoured to learn her said son any trade or to give him schooling as the law directs." She had also discovered that Costin was planning to leave the colony and either take Thomas Carter with him or sell him to another master for a much longer term of service—"both which will be illegal," Hannah Carter said. She asked the justices to order Costin not to remove him from the colony or sell him to anyone else without the court's approval.[93] Costin did not abscond with Carter, but neither did he make any effort to give the boy an education. Five years later, Hannah Carter again petitioned the court to order Costin to fulfill his contractual obligations. Instead of contesting the petition in court, Costin sold Thomas Carter to another planter, William Satchell. In the fall of 1733, the justices duly ordered Satchell to provide Carter with some education.[94] But the question had become moot. Early in 1734, after he turned twenty-one, Carter himself successfully petitioned the court for his freedom and freedom dues.[95]

Hannah Carter died in 1741.[96] A few of her descendants and relatives remained in Northampton County through the eighteenth century. Others migrated up the Eastern Shore into Maryland and Delaware, or southward to the Carolinas. So did many members of the Johnson, Harman, and Longo families, who were the last free black landowners in

92. See NCo L.P., 1740–1741, and Northampton Orders, 1732–1742, 395. For some reason, William Carter did not return to Wilson's household. On the tithable lists from 1740 to 1744 he appears in the households of Muns Bishop, Richard Respess, and John Warren. See NCo L.P.

93. NCo L.P., 1728.

94. Northampton Orders, 1732–1742, 39, 65, 68, 76.

95. NCo L.P., 1733; Northampton Orders, 1732–1742, 95, 96.

96. NCo L.P., 1741; Northampton Orders, 1732–1742, 461, 467.

Accomack County before the Revolution. These families generally migrated in groups—which makes them easier to trace in the records of other colonies and suggests that the decision to move was often a collective one.[97]

As the work of Thomas Davidson demonstrates, those who stayed in Maryland found no panacea, but they probably did enjoy somewhat greater economic opportunities than their contemporaries who remained in the more congested, southernmost counties of the Eastern Shore.[98] At least some of the migrants intermarried with whites and Indians and founded triracial communities in southern and northern Delaware, known subsequently as the Nanticokes and Moors.[99] The same mixing with local Indians occurred in Northampton County during the eighteenth century, but the descendants of the Delaware groups have been far more adamant in denying the black component of their ancestry and claiming an exclusively Indian cultural heritage.

Among Virginia blacks, free and slave, a reasonably cohesive racial and cultural identity probably began to take shape by the middle decades of the eighteenth century. Only rarely does direct evidence of such a process appear, but there are a few interesting signs in the story of one free black family of Northampton County, the Webbs.

Born free in the early 1680s, Jane Webb spent most of her childhood in the household of Henry Warren, a Northampton County planter, and later lived with his widow, Susanna Warren. Jane and her younger sister, Anne, were both the mulatto children of an unidentified white woman and a black or mulatto man, and both children used the surname Williams. Anne Williams was bound as a servant until her eighteenth birthday to Hamon Firkettle, the second husband of Susanna Warren. If Jane's term of service was more or less the same, she would have been a free woman by about 1700.[100]

97. For details, see Deal, "Race and Class," pt. 2.

98. See Thomas E. Davidson, "Free Blacks on the Lower Eastern Shore of Maryland," pt. 1, "The Colonial Period: 1662–1775" (unpublished paper, 1983), chaps. 2 and 3.

99. See the account of Aminadab Hanser and the Johnson family in Deal, "Race and Class," 274–275. On the Harmans, some of whom probably joined the same communities, see *ibid.*, 411–412.

100. The information in this paragraph is based on Henry Warren's will (Northampton Orders & Wills, 1689–1698, 261–262), the indenture of Anne Williams (Northampton Orders, Wills, Etc., 1698–1710, 30), and a later petition by Jane Webb, Aug. 16, 1722 (NCo L.P., 1722). See also Whitelaw, *Virginia's Eastern Shore*, 274.

In 1703 Jane decided that she wanted to marry Left, a slave on the nearby plantation of Thomas Savage. Savage agreed to their marriage on the following conditions: first, Jane Webb (as she then called herself) had to indenture herself to him for a term of seven years; second, any children that she had during her term of service were to be bound over to Savage until each reached the age of eighteen. Jane Webb later claimed that Savage had also promised to discharge her husband, Left, "from any slavery or servitude what ever" and had disclaimed any interest in children born after her seven-year term had expired.[101] If Savage did make such promises, he was to break all of them.

Jane Webb and Left had three children during their first five years together: Dinah (born in 1704), Daniel (1706), and Frances (1708). When Jane's term of service ended in 1711, Savage had the court formally bind over her three young children to him "according to the law."[102] Left remained a slave, and Jane decided to stay with him and their children in Savage's household. The couple had two more children, Ann and Elizabeth, by 1716. Thomas Savage had the court bind these children to him as well.[103]

In 1722, when Dinah Webb turned eighteen, her mother began petitioning the court for her freedom. The justices dismissed these petitions as "frivolous."[104] When Dinah was twenty-one, Jane Webb again attempted to secure her daughter's release from Savage, to no avail.[105] Ultimately Dinah Webb presented the petition herself, along with a note from the parish certifying her date of birth, and the court relented.[106]

In this instance, the justices appear to have adhered to the letter of the law, which required children bound out as the Webbs had been in 1711 to serve until the age of twenty-one. Jane Webb had assumed, incorrectly, that the terms of service specified in her original agreement with Savage

101. Whitelaw, *Virginia's Eastern Shore*, 221; bill in chancery, *Jane Webb v. Thomas Savage*, Mar. 11, 1726, NCo L.P., 1727.

102. Northampton Orders, 1711–1716, 10; note from Peter Roscoe, clerk of Hungars Parish, NCo L.P., 1725; petition of Jane Webb, Aug. 16, 1722, NCo L.P., 1722.

103. Northampton Orders, 1711–1716, 255.

104. Petition of Jane Webb, Aug. 16, 1722, NCo L.P., 1722; Northampton Orders, 1722–1729, 46.

105. Petition of Jane Webb, Feb. 9, 1725, NCo L.P., 1724; Northampton Orders, 1722–1729, 163.

106. Northampton Orders, 1722–1729, 173, 179; petition of Dinah Webb, Mar. 9, 1725, NCo L.P., 1725.

were still legally valid. By having the court apprentice the children to him formally in 1711, Savage had cleverly added three years to the term of each one.[107]

Dinah Webb proceeded to marry a free mulatto, Gabriel Manly, who worked for another planter, John Wilkins. Manly—like Dinah's mother, the illegitimate child of a black man and white maidservant—by law had to serve his master until he reached the age of thirty (in his case, 1733).[108] Dinah chose not to live in the Wilkins household.[109] Perhaps she was afraid of losing her own freedom again, or worried about the status of any children she might have. Her father, brothers, and sisters were, after all, still held in service by Thomas Savage.

A year after losing the services of Dinah Webb, Savage legally secured those of her youngest sister and brother, Lisha and Abimilech. He complained to the court that Jane Webb had recently "decoyd [Lisha] away" and detained her. Savage argued that he had "the best right to the said children" because "the said Jane hath no visible means to support the said children as the law requires and they may be induced to take ill courses."[110] In response, Jane Webb entered a bill of complaint against Savage in the court of chancery, in which she charged that he had violated several of the terms of their original agreement, especially those that related to her husband and to their children born after 1711. She also accused Savage of concealing the original indenture itself.[111]

To the charges that Webb made in chancery, Savage replied in court that he had never agreed to free her husband. He disingenuously pleaded that he could not remember how long her children were to serve.[112] Savage brought two of his neighbors to testify about the contents of his agreement with Webb, but he never produced the document in court. Without any document to support her case, Jane Webb was forced to rely upon the oral testimony of friends. The justices' decision was to bind over

107. The court seems to have bound the Webb children to Savage as if they were orphans. See Hening, ed., *Statutes at Large*, III, 375.

108. On Manly, see Northampton Deeds & Wills, 1692–1707, 362–363; Northampton Orders, Wills, Etc., 1698–1710, 183, 234; and the lists of tithables for 1720–1729, NCo L.P.

109. See the lists of tithables for 1726–1728, NCo L.P. She was listed as a single tithable, Dinah Manly, in 1726, not listed in 1727 (her own oversight), and listed in her mother's household in 1728.

110. Petition of Capt. Thomas Savage, Feb. 10, 1726, NCo L.P., 1725.

111. Bill in chancery, *Jane Webb v. Thomas Savage*, Mar. 11, 1726, NCo L.P., 1727.

112. Northampton Orders, 1722–1729, 260.

Lisha and Abimilech Webb to Savage formally. Bristling at this verdict, Webb blurted out that "if all Virginia Negros had as good a heart as she had they would all be free." For these "dangerous words tending to the breach of the peace," she received ten lashes at the courthouse whipping post the next day.[113]

Later in 1726, when she brought another free black to testify in her behalf, the justices could not agree on whether to allow this "Negro evidence." Four months passed before they finally decided "none such ought to be allowed." With so little evidence left to buttress her appeals, Webb gave up. She failed to appear in court the next time the case came up, and her bill was accordingly dismissed.[114]

When Savage died in 1728, he still possessed three of Jane Webb's children, Nanny (Anne), Lisha, and Abimilech, as well as her husband, Left, and seven other slaves. The children had four, nine, and thirteen years left to serve, respectively.[115] Nanny Webb herself had two children, Daniel and Abraham, whom one of Savage's daughters tried to "detain in servitude." Webb filed a petition against her in 1732, and the court ruled that the children should not be so detained.[116]

Having snubbed most of Jane Webb's earlier petitions, the justices of the Northampton County Court finally took pity on her when she was an old woman. In 1740, nearly sixty years old, she wrote to them, "Whereas your petitioner is very old and likewise decriped and am not able to git tobbco to pay my leavy therefore I crave your worships order to be sot tax free."[117] This time they granted her request.

Jane Webb came to court no more, but she evidently passed some of her spirit and determination on to her children. They sought the same goal—freedom—but changes in Chesapeake society had begun by the middle of the eighteenth century to effect a shift in the political perspective of Afro-Americans, both free and slave.

An incident in 1750 illuminates these changes. One midsummer day

113. *Ibid.*, 247–248.

114. *Ibid.*, 265, 278, 287. As this case shows, the question of testimony by blacks—supposedly forbidden by the assembly in 1705 (with a small revision in 1723)—was still being debated in the county courts in the 1720s.

115. Northampton Wills, Deeds, Etc., 1725–1733, 229.

116. Petition of Nanny Webb, May 9, 1732, NCo L.P., 1732.

117. Petition of Jane Webb, Aug. 1740, NCo L.P., 1740. On the tithable list for the previous year, she appeared in the household of one Henry Warren, perhaps the grandson of her original master. NCo L.P., 1739.

that year, Abimilech Webb—then in his late twenties—was husking corn with another hired laborer of about the same age. Webb quizzed his companion, a white woman named Barbary White, about the comings and goings of Littleton Eyre, a prominent local planter and one of Northampton County's representatives in the assembly. According to Webb, Eyre "had had orders to sett the Negroes free . . . but he would not do it." Whatever happened, Webb went on, "they would be free." White asked him "how they would go about it," and Webb replied, "with their one indeavour [an]d godalmightys assistance or blessing, for what would it be for the Negroes to go through this County in one nights time[?]"[118]

On the strength of this evidence and the suspicious behavior of some slaves in the vicinity, the county court found Webb guilty of "combining with sundry Negros in a conspiracy against the white people of this county." He was given thirty-nine lashes at the whipping post and jailed until he could post bond of £100 for his good behavior.[119] The conspiracy evidently was never put into effect. Still, the consciousness of racial identity and of the potential for collective action is noteworthy. Abimilech Webb was, like his mother before him, too sanguine about the slaves' prospects for freedom, but there was a kernel of realism in his wishful thinking. Twenty-five years later, some Eastern Shore slaves would, in fact, steal away "in one nights time" to the British fleet of Lord Dunmore.[120]

Until the changes of the Revolutionary era, however, the small free black community was driven by the emerging slave system and its racist ideology into an increasingly marginal existence. Timothy Breen and Stephen Innes, in their discussion of this community, overemphasize access to property as the determining variable in how much liberty free blacks could enjoy in the colony. As the cases of Azaricum Drighouse and others demonstrate, it is not strictly true that "they lost the possibility to acquire property" in the eighteenth century.[121] The continuing struggles

118. Deposition of Barbary White, Sept. 1, 1750, NCo L.P., 1750.

119. Northampton Orders, 1748–1751, 272; court order against a slave belonging to Mrs. Katherine Robins, Oct. 9, 1750, NCo L.P., 1750–1751.

120. See Gerald W. Mullin, *Flight and Rebellion: Slave Resistance in Eighteenth-Century Virginia* (New York, 1972), 131–136, and Sylvia R. Frey, "Between Slavery and Freedom: Virginia Blacks in the American Revolution," *Journal of Southern History*, XLIX (1983), 375–398.

121. Breen and Innes, *"Myne Owne Ground,"* chap. 5; the quotation is drawn from the concluding sentence of the book (p. 114).

of free black property owners in the South after 1800 only confirm the point.[122] What had changed was not access to property per se, but the contours of the larger society within which the free blacks were living. A society increasingly dependent upon the labor of black slaves could no longer accord dignity or respect to the few blacks who were free, whether they owned some property or not.

Choices for marriage, family, and work all narrowed considerably. Many free blacks were forced by circumstances or law to spend much of their lives, as children and adults, in the households of white masters and employers. Some married slaves; some married Indians (if anything, an even more marginal group, barely hanging on to survival); some bore large numbers of children outside of formal marriage. Unfortunately, the only available sources—court records, with their biases and omissions— make it nearly impossible to ascertain what sorts of concrete family arrangements and affective relationships lay behind the sparse evidence of tithable lists, grand jury presentments, and civil suits. The records clearly reflect censure, for example, as justices convicted and sentenced free black women for those "illegitimate" births. What the mothers them- selves felt is mostly hidden from view.

This was a fettered freedom. Those fetters spurred some into legal activism. As free black liberties were curtailed and laws were designed to extract greater quantities of forced labor and taxes from them, many individuals used the county courts as an arena of struggle and self- defense.[123] Others no doubt crumpled under the burdens, left the region, or adopted the extralegal tactics of survival and struggle. A few, like Abimilech Webb, contemplated bringing an end to slavery itself in Vir- ginia, thus confirming the inevitable fears of slaveholding whites that free blacks were not only an anomaly but also a threat to the social order. Such fears were never to dissipate entirely.

Some broad patterns can be seen in the collective fortunes of colonial Virginia's free blacks in the seventeenth and eighteenth centuries. Three long swings, or overlapping periods, stand out (though only the first two figure in this essay): first, a period of relative opportunity and relative fluidity in race relations, extending from the early decades of settlement to 1700 or so; second, a period characterized by constriction of opportu-

122. See Ira Berlin, *Slaves without Masters: The Free Negro in the Antebellum South* (New York, 1974).

123. Cf. Nicholls, "Passing Through This Troublesome World," *VMHB*, XCII (1984), 58–59.

nity, decline in status, and a hardening of racism—coinciding with the consolidation of a slave-based economy—from the 1670s to the Revolution; and third, a period of "awakening," new openings, and potentially radical (but ultimately quite limited) change from the 1770s to 1800.

This pattern probably holds best for the older, coastal regions of Virginia. Areas settled later (for example, the piedmont) might have gone through similar phases but at a different pace. Regionally uneven development itself constituted a motor of change—for example, through the migration of people from an area of declining opportunity into a county or town with better prospects. From the 1660s on, free blacks left Virginia's Eastern Shore for Maryland, Delaware, North Carolina, and towns such as Norfolk.[124]

Though many were driven to leave their homes for good, some stayed behind and endured the succession of repressive and purgative efforts launched by local whites during the eighteenth and nineteenth centuries. The survival of these free black families on the Eastern Shore through some very difficult times was a potent reminder that, since the 1630s, a minority of slaves had managed to find routes out of bondage, sometimes with the assistance of their masters or other whites, but at other times despite heavily unfavorable odds. This rivulet of freedom, the treasured heritage of a few, nourished many others with the hope that their day, too, would come.

124. Cf. *ibid.*, 69.

Jean Butenhoff Lee

Land and Labor

Parental Bequest Practices in Charles County, Maryland, 1732–1783

"PROPERTY RELATIONSHIPS," Rhys Isaac has emphasized, constitute a "basic code" for interpreting social systems, for understanding "the domestic arrangements of the past."[1] Scholars of early American history have frequently examined such relationships in terms of inheritance, no doubt because testamentary records are the most accessible and plentiful source illuminating the distribution of property among large numbers of people. From this work has emerged a largely androcentric interpretation of bequests to children, which, in oversimplified imagery, could be phrased as follows: when men settled their temporal affairs, sons inherited land and daughters feather beds.[2] Providing sufficient land for new generations of sons amid shrinking supplies is a central theme of many recent studies of the eighteenth-century New England town. Land scarcity has been seen as contributory to everything from intergenerational conflict to the constitutional crisis with Great Britain.[3] By implication or otherwise, the association of fathers, sons, and

Merrill D. Peterson, Stephen Innes, William W. Abbot, Mary Beth Norton, and Christopher F. Lee read earlier versions of this essay and offered many valuable suggestions. Financial support came from the Danforth Foundation, the Thomas Jefferson Memorial Foundation, the American Association of University Women, the Carter G. Woodson Institute for Afro-American and African Studies at the University of Virginia, the Society of the Cincinnati in the State of Virginia, the Institute of Early American History and Culture, and the National Endowment for the Humanities.

1. Rhys Isaac, review of *Inside the Great House: Planter Family Life in Eighteenth-Century Chesapeake Society*, by Daniel Blake Smith (Ithaca, N.Y., 1980), in *William and Mary Quarterly*, 3d Ser., XXXIX (1982), 230.

2. See, for example, Mary P. Ryan's widely used textbook, *Womanhood in America: From Colonial Times to the Present*, 2d ed. (New York, 1979), 7.

3. Charles S. Grant, *Democracy in the Connecticut Frontier Town of Kent* (New York, 1961); Richard L. Bushman, *From Puritan to Yankee: Character and the Social Order in Connecticut, 1690–1765* (Cambridge, Mass., 1967); John Demos, *A Little Commonwealth: Family Life in Plymouth Colony* (New York, 1970); Philip J. Greven, Jr., *Four*

wealth in land reinforces the idea that daughters customarily were left out and, indeed, that they were less important than their brothers. In his work on eighteenth-century Guilford, Connecticut, for example, John J. Waters finds a belief "that land belonged to the male line," from which he draws "the obvious implication of the greater worth of males over females."[4] In cases where daughters did come into substantial inheritances, it is often assumed that the decedent lacked a male heir or that females received lesser estates, meaning possession of property only until marriage or during their own lifetimes.[5]

An androcentric interpretation overemphasizes both males and land. Men almost always appear as the only transmitters of major assets, so that a dearth of knowledge exists with respect to the kinds and amounts of property women passed on to their offspring.[6] Among recipients of bequests, sons have attracted the greatest attention. Some scholars, however, have recently undertaken systematic investigations of what husbands left their wives and then have probed the ramifications of those bequests for widows' status within their families and communities. Focusing on wealth placed in widows' hands, it should be noted, reveals property they took away from their marriages, not what they may have contributed to those marriages. To date, few scholars have analyzed daughters' inheritances.[7]

Generations: Population, Land, and Family in Colonial Andover, Massachusetts (Ithaca, N.Y., 1970); Kenneth A. Lockridge, *A New England Town, the First Hundred Years: Dedham, Massachusetts, 1636–1736*, 2d ed. (New York, 1985); Lockridge, "Social Change and the Meaning of the American Revolution," *Journal of Social History*, VI (1973), 403–439; Robert A. Gross, *The Minutemen and Their World* (New York, 1976); Linda Auwers, "Fathers, Sons, and Wealth in Colonial Windsor, Connecticut," *Journal of Family History*, III (1978), 136–149.

4. John J. Waters, Jr., "Patrimony, Succession, and Social Stability: Guilford, Connecticut, in the Eighteenth Century," *Perspectives in American History*, X (1976), 139–140.

5. Lawrence M. Friedman, *A History of American Law*, 2d ed. (New York, 1985), 251; Smith, *Inside the Great House*, 246. In his classic study of women's legal rights in early America, Richard B. Morris speaks of "a mere life estate." *Studies in the History of American Law*, 2d ed. (Philadelphia, 1959), 161.

6. Suzanne Lebsock's *The Free Women of Petersburg: Status and Culture in a Southern Town, 1784–1860* (New York, 1984), 130–145, attests to the value of examining women's bequest practices.

7. Recent work on colonial widows includes the following: Alexander Keyssar, "Widowhood in Eighteenth-Century Massachusetts: A Problem in the History of the

The tendency to concentrate on the descent of land, to the exclusion of other forms of wealth, may be justifiable for the agricultural communities of New England and the Middle Atlantic region. It is patently untenable for the South because of indentured servitude and, to a much greater degree by the eighteenth century, slavery. In plantation economies, bound laborers often were more valuable than the land they tilled. As Gov. Horatio Sharpe of Maryland observed in 1757 in explaining why labor, not land, was taxed in the province, "our Estates consist for the most part in Servants & Negroes [so that] those who have most property pay the greatest Share of the Tax."[8] Slave property was particularly important to daughters because human chattel was almost always classified as personal property, and a strong tradition to divide personalty equally among children, without regard to gender, existed in the Anglo-Ameri-

---

Family," *Perspectives Am. Hist.*, VIII (1974), 83–119; Christine H. Tompsett, "A Note on the Economic Status of Widows in Colonial New York," *New York History*, LV (1974), 319–332; Lois Green Carr and Lorena S. Walsh, "The Planter's Wife: The Experience of White Women in Seventeenth-Century Maryland," *WMQ*, 3d Ser., XXXIV (1977), 542–571; Kim Lacy Rogers, "Relicts of the New World: Conditions of Widowhood in Seventeenth-Century New England," in *Woman's Being, Woman's Place: Female Identity and Vocation in American History*, ed. Mary Kelley (Boston, 1979), 26–52; Marylynn Salmon, *Women and the Law of Property in Early America* (Chapel Hill, N.C., 1986), 141–184; Smith, *Inside the Great House*, chap. 6; David Evan Narrett, "Patterns of Inheritance in Colonial New York City, 1664–1775: A Study in the History of the Family" (Ph.D. diss., Cornell University, 1981); Narrett, "Preparation for Death and Provision for the Living: Notes on New York Wills (1665–1760)," *N.Y. Hist.*, LVII (1976), 417–437; Linda E. Speth, "More Than Her 'Thirds': Wives and Widows in Colonial Virginia," in Linda E. Speth and Alison Duncan Hirsch, *Women, Family, and Community in Colonial America: Two Perspectives* (New York, 1983), 5–41; Gail S. Terry, "Wives and Widows, Sons and Daughters: Testation Patterns in Baltimore County, Maryland, 1660–1759" (M.A. thesis, University of Maryland, 1983). Narrett and Terry discuss both wives' and daughters' inheritances. See also Lois Green Carr and Lorena S. Walsh, "Woman's Role in the Eighteenth-Century Chesapeake" (paper presented at the conference "Women in Early America," Williamsburg, Va., November 1981), 36–37. Mary Beth Norton synthesizes much of the recent research in "The Evolution of White Women's Experience in Early America," *American Historical Review*, LXXXIX (1984), 602–603. For the Chesapeake, see Lois Green Carr, "Inheritance in the Colonial Chesapeake" (paper presented at the U.S. Capitol Historical Society conference "Women in the Age of the American Revolution," Washington, D.C., 1985).

8. Horatio Sharpe to Cecilius Calvert, Nov. 9, 1757, *Archives of Maryland*, ed. William H. Browne *et al.* (Baltimore, 1883–), IX, 100–101, hereafter cited as *Md. Archives*.

can world.[9] Slaves, moreover, multiplied and were readily parceled out among legatees, whereas there were limits on the extent to which land could be subdivided and still comprise viable economic units.[10]

Still another problem with much of the literature on early American inheritance practices involves the impression that women alone received "lesser estates." Both daughters and wives who inherited land for use until marriage or death certainly had limited rights to the property, for they could neither mortgage nor transfer it to other persons through deed or will. But the male recipient of entailed land also held what in effect was a life estate, which theoretically he could not alienate.[11] A so-called lesser estate, moreover, might actually be more valuable to the legatee than fee-simple ownership. Nowhere was this more true than in the case of married women (*femes covert*). Suppose a parent willed his or her daughter

9. From the days of the Norman Conquest, in England land and personalty were treated as two distinct categories of property. Land was devised in wills, which were administered in common law courts, while personalty was bequeathed in testaments, over which ecclesiastical courts had jurisdiction. Whereas, in the absence of a will, land devolved upon the eldest male heir, personalty was equitably distributed among all the decedent's children. The differing treatment, under the law, of the two kinds of property remained in force even after the will and testament became one document. In the British American colonies, a 1705 Virginia statute modified the definition of real estate by declaring that slaves were real property for inheritance purposes, thus subjecting them to the rule of primogeniture in intestate cases. Virginia was the only colony to adopt this practice. Alison Reppy and Leslie J. Tompkins, *Historical and Statutory Background of the Law of Wills, Descent and Distribution, Probate and Administration* (Chicago, 1928), 4–5; Friedman, *History of American Law*, 86; Joan R. Gundersen and Gwen Victor Gampel, "Married Women's Legal Status in Eighteenth-Century New York and Virginia," *WMQ*, 3d Ser., XXXIX (1982), 121.

10. On the importance of slave legacies for daughters, see John E. Crowley, "Family Relations and Inheritance in Early South Carolina," *Histoire Sociale—Social History*, XVII (1984), 51–57; Terry, "Wives and Widows," 78; Carr, "Inheritance in the Colonial Chesapeake," 6 and table 1.

11. General and special fee tail are described in William Blackstone's *Commentaries on the Laws of England* (1765–1769), facsimile reprint (Chicago, 1979), II, 113–115. Breaking or docking the tail on land was possible in colonial America, but uncommon because of the expense involved. Not until the War of Independence did any of the 13 former colonies abolish the practice. C. Ray Keim, "Primogeniture and Entail in Colonial Virginia," *WMQ*, 3d Ser., XXV (1968), 547; Maryland General Assembly, *Laws of Maryland, Made and Passed at a Session of Assembly [November Session, 1782]* (Annapolis, Md., n.d.), chap. 23, hereafter cited as *Laws of Maryland*; Stanley N. Katz, "Republicanism and the Law of Inheritance in the American Revolutionary Era," *Michigan Law Review*, LXXVI (1977), 11–13.

land in fee simple. Under the English common law, her husband could not of his own volition alienate the property, but he might convince his wife to agree to a sale. That accomplished, he acquired unrestrained control over the proceeds. So, too, with all personalty, including slaves: the husband could mortgage or sell it at any time, or his creditors could seize it. If, on the other hand, the parent restricted the bequest by giving the daughter a life estate in the property and naming an ultimate owner, neither the husband nor his creditors had such recourse. True, the husband's common law rights accorded him management of the property, but he could not dispose of it. If he predeceased his wife, the life estate reverted to her control. For the *feme covert*, therefore, a lesser estate might prove the greater estate.[12]

In any study of inheritance practices, then, it is essential to know not only who received what property, but also when children took possession and whether parents restricted legatees' power to utilize, fully profit from, or dispose of their legacies. In sum, one needs to examine the terms as well as the incidence of inheritance. Even though testators usually were mute as to their motives, it is also useful to probe the rationale for the patterns that emerge, as well as the possible consequences of parental decisions. Only then can the social context of the tedious devising of property in will after will come into sharper focus.

This essay analyzes the testamentary provisions that fathers and mothers made for their children, with specific reference to land and slaves, in one area of the Chesapeake during the eighteenth century. Charles County, Maryland, was located in the heart of the tobacco coast, the labyrinth of land and water, rivers and bays, that made the Chesapeake renowned for unsurpassed navigable waters and "the best laid out for trade of any [country] in the world." At waterside landings and in the towns of Port Tobacco, Benedict, and Newport, Charles County residents exchanged tobacco and grain for the wares of local artisans and for African slaves, West Indian sugar, and European manufactured goods. Among white inhabitants, nearly nine out of ten were of English stock.[13]

12. A good general discussion of women's legal status in early America is in Norma Basch, *In the Eyes of the Law: Women, Marriage, and Property in Nineteenth-Century New York* (Ithaca, N.Y., 1982), chaps. 1 and 2. See also Salmon, *Women and the Law of Property*.

13. E. I. Devitt, ed., "Letters of Father Joseph Mosley, 1757–1786," *Woodstock Letters*, XXXV (1906), 40; U.S. Bureau of the Census, *A Century of Population Growth: From the First Census of the United States to the Twelfth, 1790–1900* (Washing-

The wealth of the county lay in land and labor. As of 1782, real property constituted one-half of the assessed wealth, slaves another third.[14]

A detailed analysis of all parents' wills filed for probate over almost half of the eighteenth century reveals a rich, complex tapestry of property relationships, relationships woven of both Anglo-American legal tradition and individual family circumstances. In the aggregate, parents favored daughters when devising slaves, and sons when devising land. Yet, when one considers use provisions as well as outright ownership, bequests of land to female children were surprisingly frequent, probably because of the availability of slaves to work the land. In addition, many testators established priorities requiring the successive sharing of finite resources among widows, sons, and daughters. Sons often had to wait to possess plantation lands until female family members no longer occupied them. Daughters, moreover, were doing particularly well in inheriting land and slaves at the time of the War of Independence. Overall, the evidence from Charles County yields a complicated picture, one in which both sons' and daughters' legacies contributed importantly to the family economies of a plantation society.

The data base is comprised of all parents' wills ($N = 594$) written between 1732 and 1783 and probated between 1740 and 1784.[15] Be-

---

ton, D.C., 1909), 272; Jean Butenhoff Lee, "The Social Order of a Revolutionary People: Charles County, Maryland, 1733–86" (Ph.D. diss., University of Virginia, 1984).

14. Of the 14 hundreds into which the county was divided in 1782, tax lists have survived for 10, in which two-thirds, or 11,868 of the inhabitants lived. Slaves comprised 44.7% of the total population of 17,724. All property was appraised except ready money, clothing, plantation and artisans' tools, and the provisions, livestock excepted, that would feed the property holder and his or her household for the year. The average assessed value of real estate in the county was £1 11s. 2d. current money per acre, whereas the assessed rate for a male slave between 14 and 45 years of age was £70. Charles County assessment lists, 1782, Maryland State Papers, Ser. Z— Scharf Collection, box 96, items 7–10, 12–17, Maryland State Archives, Annapolis; "Population of Maryland—1782," *The American Museum, or, Universal Magazine,* VII (1790), 159; *Laws of Maryland [November Session, 1781],* chap. 4; *An Account of the Gross and Average Value of the Land in the Several Counties of This State . . . [1781, 1782, 1783],* broadside in the Maryland Diocesan Archives, on deposit at the Maryland Historical Society, Baltimore.

15. Two sets of the wills filed for probate before May 1777 were recorded for Charles County, and both are at the Md. State Archives. The first set is among the papers of the colonial prerogative court at Annapolis, which was the centralized probate court headed by a commissary general. These wills are described in Elisabeth

cause the common law, which was observed in Maryland, barred *femes covert* from leaving wills, four out of five testators ($N = 471$) were fathers. With one exception, all of the female testators were widows. Together the 594 wills and associated probate entries identify more than 2,700 children, of whom approximately 1,495 were sons and 1,260 daughters.[16] About 54 percent of all persons whose estates were entered into probate were testators. As a group they undoubtedly reflect the wealth bias of wills, for 70.4 percent ($N = 418$) were landowners, 53.5 percent ($N = 318$) slave owners, which is in excess of comparable figures for the living population.[17]

Hartsook and Gust Skordas, *Land Office and Prerogative Court Records of Colonial Maryland* (Annapolis, Md., 1946), 100–104, and indexed in James M. Magruder, Jr., comp., *Index of Maryland Colonial Wills, 1634–1777, in the Hall of Records, Annapolis, Md. Reprinted with Additions and a New Introduction by Louise E. Magruder* (Baltimore, 1967). In February 1777 the General Assembly abolished the colonial prerogative court, placed testamentary proceedings under the jurisdiction of county orphans' courts, and ordered each county to acquire a transcript of all relevant prerogative court documents. The Charles County transcript terminates as of April 21, 1777, and thereafter the wills in the orphans' court set are the original recordings. My study relies on this series (hereafter cited as Wills), supplemented with 11 additional wills found in the prerogative court set (*Laws of Maryland [February Session, 1777]*, chap. 8; Wills, AE6, 315, AF7, 2A). Computer-based analysis of the quantifiable data was carried out at the Academic Computing Center at the University of Virginia, using the Statistical Package for the Social Sciences (SPSS). See Norman Nie *et al.*, *SPSS: Statistical Package for the Social Sciences*, 2d ed. (New York, 1975).

16. The exact number of children cannot be ascertained. Thirteen testators mentioned having sons and thirteen mentioned having daughters without naming them or indicating their numbers. In calculations incorporating these cases, the number of children of each gender was arbitrarily placed at one, which assuredly underestimates the true number. On the other hand, because the data base includes wills of men whose wives also later left a will, some children were counted twice. The author is unable to demonstrate why sons mentioned in the wills outnumbered daughters. Perhaps any other surviving female children had already received dowries. Or perhaps they did not share in parental wealth.

17. Some idea of the wealth bias of the wills, compared to the living population, may be gained from county tax lists for 1758 and 1782. Of 642 taxpayers living in six taxing districts in 1758, which were scattered across the county, 40.5% owned slaves. By comparison, during the years 1753 through 1763, 56.9% of 137 parent-testators owned slaves. Among 1,667 property holders whose wealth was assessed in 1782, 41.1% owned plantation land and 46.5% owned slaves. Charles County tax lists, 1758, Papers of the Secretary in Maryland, 1637–1776, items 8–13, Md. State Archives; Charles County assessment lists, 1782, Scharf Collection, box 96, items 7–10, 12–17; Wills.

Two caveats are in order. First, wills may not dispose of all of the property that the decedent owned at the time of his or her death. Such was the case with Randolph Morris Hawkins and the Reverend Theophilus Swift. So preoccupied was Hawkins with his debts that his entire 1769 will and codicil are concerned with selling some acreage to satisfy his creditors. Swift, on the other hand, devoted his last testament to disposition of personalty, never hinting that he was also a substantial landowner.[18] Most Charles County testators, many of whom followed their specific devises with a general bequest of any residue estate, fortunately were more thorough than Hawkins or Swift.

More important, if one is concerned with comparing the amounts of property passed on to sons and daughters, as well as the social meaning of such descent, then Jack Goody's warning bears repeating: transfer of wealth "should be seen as a whole over time; whether a son or daughter receives a 'portion' by dowry or by inheritance is, from the standpoint of equity, of little importance; the fact is that the child of either sex shares in the parental wealth."[19] During their lifetimes, Charles County parents

----

On the biases of probate records, see Russell R. Menard, P.M.G. Harris, and Lois Green Carr, "Opportunity and Inequality: The Distribution of Wealth on the Lower Western Shore of Maryland, 1638–1705," *Maryland Historical Magazine*, LXIX (1974), 169–184; Gloria L. Main, "The Correction of Biases in Colonial American Probate Records," *Historical Methods Newsletter*, VIII (1974), 10–28; Main, "Probate Records as a Source for Early American History," *WMQ*, 3d Ser., XXXII (1975), 95–99; Daniel Scott Smith, "Underregistration and Bias in Probate Records: An Analysis of Data from Eighteenth-Century Hingham, Massachusetts," *ibid.*, 100–110; Lois Green Carr and Lorena S. Walsh, "Inventories and the Analysis of Wealth and Consumption Patterns in St. Mary's County, Maryland, 1658–1777," *Historical Methods*, XIII (1980), 81–104.

18. Wills, AE6, 65–66, AD5, 236–237, respectively. The 1753 Charles County Debt Book, fol. 38, credited Swift with 10 tracts of land amounting to 1,370 acres. In 1774 his widow retained 457 of those acres, undoubtedly her dower right. Charles County Debt Book for 1774, fol. 16. This series of land records is at the Md. State Archives.

19. Introduction to Jack Goody, Joan Thirsk, and E. P. Thompson, eds., *Family and Inheritance: Rural Society in Western Europe, 1200–1800* (Cambridge, 1976), 2. See also Goody, "Inheritance, Property, and Women: Some Comparative Considerations," *ibid.*, 23, 26, 29. For colonial New England, Christopher M. Jedrey's research on Chebacco Parish, Ipswich, Massachusetts, and Daniel Scott Smith's investigation of Hingham, Massachusetts, testify to the applicability of Goody's remark. For the Chesapeake, no study of premortem and postmortem distribution of parental wealth has yet appeared. Jedrey, *The World of John Cleaveland: Family and Community in*

formally and informally conveyed property to their children. Thus, on the day of her marriage in 1782, Rebeckah King went before a justice of the local court and deeded to a daughter by an earlier marriage the following items, which were typical components of young women's dowries: a slave girl, a riding horse and saddle, a bed and furniture, and two cows with calves.[20] Deeds of gift from parent to child are commonplace among the local records.

Wills, too, indicate or intimate premortem distribution. John Matthews articulated what other testators only implied: the property he had already given several of his children was to be "Counted with what they are to receive so as every one may have an equal part from the beginning." A few parents explained the meagerness of certain legacies by stating that they previously had given the child "Suitable to my Circumstances," or "what provision I cou'd prudently afford from my Fortune," or "what negroes and other thing[s] I could prudently spare."[21] Some children—including married daughters who presumably had earlier received bridal portions— were bequeathed only token bequests, such as an English shilling. For other children, usually sons, the will transferred ownership of land they already possessed.[22]

Descent of Land to Children: General Patterns

Land that had belonged to intestate parents, or to those who did not devise it in their wills, was distributed by law according

---

Eighteenth-Century New England (New York, 1979), 69–70; Smith, "A Perspective on Demographic Methods and Effects in Social History," *WMQ*, 3d Ser., XXXIX (1982), 463.

20. Charles County Court Records, Z3, 10, Md. State Archives.

21. In order quoted: Wills, AD5, 308, AE6, 153; Prerogative Court Wills, Lib. 32, fol. 163; Wills, AD5, 286.

22. In families with at least two known daughters ($N = 362$), 150 testators (41.5%) did not leave legacies to their female children equally. Of those 150 testators, 64 demonstrated a decided or apparent preference for daughters known to be minors or unmarried or both. For sons settled on plantations prior to receiving ownership through a parent's will, see Wills, AC4, 154–156, AD5, 115–116, 126–128, 201–202, 215–216, 273–275, 300–302, 314–315, AE6, 19–22, 27–28, 51–52, 82–83, 102–104, 110–111, 141–143, 309–311, AF7, 96–97, 226, 409–411, 565–568, 692–693, B1, 68–69. For daughters in this situation, see AC4, 178–179, AD5, 46–47, 257–259, AE6, 4–5, AF7, 2A–3, 14–16.

to primogeniture and lineal descent that favored male children. Inheritance was from parent to eldest son and his heirs, but in the absence of such heirs the land devolved successively upon each younger male child and his heirs. Should the deceased leave neither a son nor a descendant of any son, then the land was to be equally divided among the daughters of the deceased. Under the law, primogeniture applied only to sons.[23]

Charles County parents displayed much more numerous and varied bequest practices. A few people were more rigid than the law of descent prescribed, but most were more lenient. Certainly individual family circumstances and the greater availability of land in the Chesapeake, compared to the mother country from whence the law of primogeniture was derived, affected parental decisions. John Scrogin and Sarah Woodman represent opposite poles of a broad spectrum. Scrogin's 1743 will is even more restrictive than the law of descent. He stipulated that his land should descend only to male issue of his sons. If Scrogin died without any surviving male descendant, however, his land was to devolve successively upon any female heir of each of his deceased sons, in birth order. Failing that, his own daughters would receive the property according to primogeniture, not partible inheritance as prescribed in law. At the opposite end of the spectrum from Scrogin stood Sarah Woodman, whose 1758 will ignored legal tradition. To each of two sons she bequeathed a cow, and to her widowed daughter a tract of land on the Potomac River. Nor was Sarah Woodman's grant of land to a daughter an anomaly. James Gates in 1749 left his dwelling plantation first to his wife, then to two daughters in succession, and only then to his eldest surviving son. Walter Pye formulated an even more complicated line of descent in 1772 when he devised 500-acre tracts to each of three daughters. If any died without issue, her share was to be divided among the surviving daughters, and only if all three women died without issue was the land to descend to Pye's two sons. Finally, Peter Montgomery, a Frenchman who was a naturalized citizen of Maryland, reversed the classic stereotype in 1752 by giving land to his married daughter Mary and a feather bed and a cow with calf to his son Richard.[24]

23. Elie Vallette, *The Deputy Commissary's Guide within the Province of Maryland, Together with Plain and Sufficient Directions for Testators to Form, and Executors to Perform Their Wills and Testaments* . . . (Annapolis, Md., 1774), 96–100.

24. In order: Wills, AC4, 173–174, AD5, 103–104, AC4, 305–307, AE6, 139–141, AD5, 31–33; Jeffrey A. Wyand and Florence L. Wyand, *Colonial Maryland Naturalizations* (Baltimore, 1975), 13.

Most landowning parents whose wills were probated in the county between 1740 and 1784 stood somewhere between these poles. Bequeathing real estate was predominantly a paternal function, for only 6.5 percent ($N = 27$) of the landed testators were mothers, all of them widows.[25] As would be expected, parents in the aggregate preferred to give ownership of their land to male children and bequeathed acreage to nearly three-fifths of them. Yet more than one-fifth of all daughters—including those in families with both male and female children—also received use *or* ownership of land, sometimes to the exclusion of their brothers.[26] In addition, many testators barred their sons from exercising full sovereignty over the use and disposition of their legacies. Often such restrictions had the effect of placing female family members, both wives and daughters, ahead of sons in regard to actual occupancy and benefit from the land.

Sons and Land

Of the 395 landowning parents who identified male issue in their wills, 86 percent left realty to at least one son. Yet many sons did not inherit land, a situation that is probably most attributable to the following circumstances: premortem distribution, fathers' granting all of their realty to their wives, or testators' determination not to divide plantations into units too small to be economically viable. Out of all potential male legatees ($N = 1,196$), 57.5 percent ($N = 688$) actually inherited parental land. Even when testators identified only one son, descent of realty was not assured; 73.8 percent devised land to that son (see table 1). The greater the number of male children, the less likely each was to inherit real property. Among parents with more than one son,

25. If a woman owned land upon marriage and was not protected by a prenuptial agreement, she lost control of the realty when she said her wedding vows. As long as she remained *feme covert* she had no legal right to dispose of the property by will or in any other manner, and her husband could use it as he wished. If she predeceased him, the husband by the common law right of curtesy held a life estate in all of her fee-simple and entailed land, provided the marriage had produced at least one live birth, even if the child did not survive. If he predeceased her, she resumed control of the land. Henry Campbell Black *et al.*, *Black's Law Dictionary*, 5th ed. (St. Paul, Minn., 1979), 346.

26. For testators who named both male and female children, 55.4% of the sons and 21.3% of the daughters received land under their parents' wills. See table 4.

TABLE I. *Testators' Land Bequests to Sons, 1732–1783*

No. of Sons per Testator[a]	Total Testators	Testators Bequeathing Land to Each Son		Testators Not Bequeathing Land to Each Son	
		No.	%	No.	%
1	84	62	73.8	22	26.2
2	90	47	52.2	43	47.8
3	79	28	35.4	51	64.6
4	62	10	16.1	52	83.9
5	46	6	13.0	40	87.0
6	13	2	15.4	11	84.6
7	11	1	9.1	10	90.9
8	5	2	40.0	3	60.0
9	1	0		1	100.0
10	1	0		1	100.0
Total	392[b]	158	40.3	234	59.7
Total testators with more than 1 son:	308	96	31.2	212	68.8

Source: Charles County Wills, Maryland State Archives, Annapolis.

[a] Sons who *first* inherited land at age of majority, testator's death, or remarriage or death of testator's widow. Sons who were no more than contingent heirs (for example, if a brother died and left no heirs) were not classified as recipients of land under the testator's will.

[b] Among all 395 landowning testators, the number of sons is unknown in three cases.

68.8 percent did not bequeath acreage to all. Only in families with two sons did a majority of testators leave land to each. This pattern held constant throughout the period 1732–1783.[27]

27. The extent of primogeniture is uncertain because not many parents identified sons according to birth order. Based on all wills in which the testator had at least two sons ($N = 311$), no more than 27% of the fathers and 39% of the mothers observed the ancient custom. The latter may have been more likely to single out one son because women, on balance, had fewer acres to dispose of. Primogeniture was not widespread in colonial America. Cf. Keim, "Primogeniture and Entail in Colonial

In addition to whether a child inherited real property, when he did so could assume crucial importance in his life. Timing could influence such factors as the amount of wealth he accumulated over a lifetime, whether he qualified as a voter or officeholder, when he married, whether he worked as someone else's tenant or day laborer until he came into possession of the land bequeathed him, and whether he migrated to the frontier. From the son's point of view, the most advantageous arrangement was to assume ownership of the land as soon as his parent died or upon reaching the age of majority for males, twenty-one.

Testators without spouses, both widowers and widows, uniformly adopted this practice in Charles County. Married fathers could not always do so because they first had to provide land, dower or more, for their widows. In the cases where the wives survived their husbands, one of every three sons who inherited paternal land under the wills did not obtain ownership of a single acre until his father's widow remarried or died (see table 2).[28] During the American Revolution, the proportion of fathers who gave their sons land at the most favorable time, the testator's death or when the child came of age, reached a low of 54.1 percent (see table 3). Simultaneously, more fathers required their sons to wait until the widow's remarriage. That could work to the sons' advantage if widows wed quickly, but by the Revolution many propertied widows in the county were choosing to remain *feme sole* (single).[29] Waiting carried risks for sons because the widow or her subsequent husband might abuse the land by cutting too much timber, exhausting the soil, or allowing buildings, fencing, and orchards to deteriorate.[30]

Virginia," *WMQ*, 3d Ser., XXV (1968), 551–552; James W. Deen, Jr., "Patterns of Testation: Four Tidewater Counties in Colonial Virginia," *American Journal of Legal History*, XVI (1972), 158, 162, 173; Narrett, "Preparation for Death," *N.Y. Hist.*, LVII (1976), 419–420; Katz, "Republicanism and the Law of Inheritance," *Mich. Law Rev.*, LXXVI (1977), 13, 26; Smith, *Inside the Great House*, 244–245; Speth, "More Than Her 'Thirds,' " in Speth and Hirsch, *Women, Family, and Community*, 15.

28. The proportion probably was somewhat higher because 14.6% of the widows whose husbands' wills were probated between 1740 and 1784 renounced them and instead claimed dower in land, which secured a widow a life estate in one-third of her husband's realty. Such realty could not descend to sons, even if their fathers had bequeathed it to them outright, until the widows died.

29. Lee, "Social Order of a Revolutionary People," 91–94, and research in progress.

30. Legal remedy in such cases was through complaint or suit, brought in the local court, alleging that the son's estate was being wasted. *Md. Archives*, XXX, 345; Vallette, *Deputy Commissary's Guide*, 147–148.

TABLE 2. *Time Sons First Acquired Land under Wills Written between 1732 and 1783*

Marital Status of Testator	Total Sons	At Testator's Death or at Age of Majority		At Re-marriage of Testator's Widow		At Death of Testator's Widow	
		No.	%	No.	%	No.	%
Married fathers	521	349	67.0	42	8.0	130	25.0
Widowers	138	138	100.0	0		0	
Widows	29	29	100.0	0		0	
Total	688	516	75.0	42	6.1	130	18.9

Source: Charles County Wills, Maryland State Archives, Annapolis.

Note: If a husband left land to his wife until her remarriage or death, whichever came first, the case was classified under remarriage of the widow.

Bequeathing a son possession of land upon the remarriage or death of his father's widow was but one form of delayed inheritance found in the county. A second involved giving use but not ownership of real property to someone else ahead of the son. Usually that person was the testator's daughter, who received the real estate either during her single life or until death (see table 6). The practice was not as common as setting aside land for widows, since, among other things, daughters had no claim on their fathers to dower rights. Furthermore, before the War of Independence, parents who had children of both genders rarely gave daughters use of land for their single lives. During the forty-two years preceding 1774, only nine testators did so. Then, in the decade between 1774 and 1783, twenty-five parents adopted the practice. Unlike reserving acreage for widows, which only married men did, widowers and mothers also reserved use of land for daughters. Unfortunately, not one testator articulated his or her motives.

Delayed inheritance introduced an element of uncertainty into sons' lives because the date they would possess their legacies was indeterminate. Some waited a long time for their property. Samuel Cooksey was forty-five years old and his brother John was forty when their father's will was probated in 1778. Neither owned land in Charles County according to the 1774 Debt Book, the last accounting of the proprietary period. Nor

TABLE 3. *Time Sons First Acquired Land under Married Fathers' Wills Written between 1732 and 1783*

Date of Will[a]	Total[b]	At Father's Death or at Age of Majority		At Re-marriage of Father's Widow[c]		At Death of Father's Widow	
		No.	%	No.	%	No.	%
1732–1747	48	31	64.6	2	4.2	15	31.2
1748–1763	108	68	63.0	7	6.4	33	30.6
1764–1773	54	37	68.5	3	5.6	14	25.9
1774–1783	74	40	54.1	15	20.2	19	25.7
Total	284	176	62.0	27	9.5	81	28.5

Source: Charles County Wills, Maryland State Archives, Annapolis.

[a] The periods used in this table and those following delimit significant economic and political eras in Maryland history, which may have influenced testation practices. The years 1732–1747 fall before the establishment of a public tobacco inspection system in the colony and were characterized by frequent depressions in the tobacco trade. The second period, 1748–1763, begins with the implementation of the Tobacco Inspection Act of 1747 and ends with the close of the Seven Years' War. Between 1764 and 1773, the population grew rapidly and Marylanders enjoyed the greatest era of prosperity of the entire colonial period, until the onset of a severe depression in late 1772. Revolution and war dominated the final period.

[b] Some fathers are counted twice because their sons received land under different terms. The actual number of fathers is 265.

[c] If a husband left land to his wife until her remarriage or death, whichever came first, the case was classified under remarriage of the widow.

did they receive any in 1778, because their father willed his widow a life estate in all of his real property, "the better to maintain" herself and the couple's unmarried daughters. Only at the widow's death would the two sons become landowners.[31] John Biggs's fortune hinged upon the fate of not one but six women, for in 1758 Biggs's father bequeathed his wife a

31. Wills, AF7, 106–107; Trinity Parish Register, in "Abstracts of Early Protestant Episcopal Church Records of Charles County, Maryland" (typescript on deposit at the Martha Washington Chapter, Daughters of the American Revolution, Washington, D.C.), 44. The elder Cooksey owned 147 acres according to the Charles County Debt Book for 1774, fol. 54.

life estate in his plantation, "and after her Decease to my five Daughters Mary Sarah Elizabeth Charity and Ruth to live on it till they marry[;] as they marry they must go off and afterword to my son John." Each of Joseph Jameson's three sons also had six women to wait for. Not until his widow died and all five daughters married or died would the sons receive his dwelling plantation. In the meantime, Jameson admonished them "not [to] disturb there Mother . . . nor there Sisters." Alexander McPherson, too, gave his daughters obviously unrestricted access to land that would actually belong to their brother. A month after the battles of Lexington and Concord, McPherson signed his will devising 175 acres to his son Samuel but stipulating that he was not to "enjoy any part of the said Land till my two Daughters Chloe and Anna Shall Marry or Die that they . . . shall have my Dwelling house and all my Land as long as they live Single."[32]

The impact that delayed inheritance might have upon a son's life is amply illustrated in the case of James Farnandis, whose father died possessed of 200 acres in 1775. The elder Farnandis bequeathed to his wife, during her lifetime, and his four daughters, while they remained single, joint use of all his real and personal estate. His son James had to content himself with the gift of a feather bed and the knowledge that 100 acres would descend to him after the widow died and all four daughters married. He did not own any realty in the county at the time of his father's death. Faced with an extended wait for his legacy, Farnandis entered the army as an ensign in early 1776, was captured and imprisoned on Long Island a few months later, exchanged in 1777, and then endured the winter of 1777–1778 at Valley Forge. Weakened by the rigors of military life, he was back in Charles County by the spring of 1779 as a recruiting officer for the army. That summer he resigned his commission as captain-lieutenant and returned to civilian life. Still without his landed legacy, he finished out the war as commissary of purchases in the county, buying country produce and forwarding it to the army. Farnandis died landless, leaving a widow and four young children, in 1790.[33]

32. Wills, AD5, 115–116, AF7, 627, AE6, 272–273, respectively. See also AC4, 189–190, AD5, 81–82, 271–272, AE6, 72–73, AF7, 14–16, 28–30, 45, 699–700, B1, 274–275.

33. *Ibid.*, AE6, 253–256; Charles County Debt Book for 1774, fol. 19; Compiled Service Records of Soldiers Who Served in the American Army during the Revolutionary War (M881), reel 397, Record Group 93, National Archives and Records Service, Washington, D.C.; Rieman Steuart, *A History of the Maryland Line in the*

Other parents did not postpone sons' actual possession of land, yet still encumbered their bequests. Some testators, while they did not specifically set aside land for daughters' use, nevertheless instructed their sons "not to let their unmarried Sisters . . . while they are Single be Destitute of a home" or to give "two Rooms in my dwelling house one with a fire place . . . to my four youngest Daughters During their single Lives for a place of Residence." Concerned lest his two unmarried daughters not be properly supported after his death, James Key not only encumbered his son's landed estate, but he also asked the justices of the local orphans' court to determine the appropriate level of sustenance. If the son refused to comply, he would lose his right to the land. Key's wife was pregnant when he wrote the will shortly before his death; if she delivered a daughter who survived, the son could have anticipated his inheritance being encumbered for at least sixteen years. Priscilla Smallwood, a wealthy widow, adopted a different approach. She wanted her daughter, also named Priscilla, to remain in Charles County, "adjacent to her friends and connections." Therefore, when Mrs. Smallwood bequeathed 800 acres in Virginia to her son William, the Revolutionary War general, she attached a condition. He had to furnish his sister, so long as she remained single, with two local plantations. He posted a performance bond for one hundred thousand pounds of tobacco to confirm the arrangement. During Smallwood's lifetime, his sister never married.[34]

Many parents barred sons not from using their land but from disposing of it. Depending on how the terms of succession contained in the wills are interpreted, as many as two-thirds of the landowning testators may have prevented sons from mortgaging, selling, or bequeathing inherited realty. The uncertainty arises because it is not clear exactly what legal language created a general fee tail in Maryland. But half of the testators ($N = 202$) used phrases such as "to him and his heirs forever," or "to him and the heirs of his body." Only a study of the subsequent disposition of the land will answer the question whether such language did create fee tails, or

---

Revolutionary War, 1775–1783 (n.p., 1969), 79–80; Maryland State Papers, Ser. A—Executive Papers, box 16, items 126–128, box 42, folder 18, box 46, item 57; Charles County assessment lists (5th District), 1783, microfilm at the Md. Hist. Soc., Baltimore; Wills, AI10, 386–387.

34. In order, Wills, AE6, 247, AF7, 459, 366–369, B1, 409–411; see also AD5, 328, AE6, 151–152. Unlike New England custom, formal setting aside of rooms in the testator's house for use of female family members was not common in Charles County.

whether testators thereby invoked less severe forms of restriction.[35] The prohibitions of other testators are not ambiguous. A few invoked the special fee tail that barred female lineal descendants from inheriting the land, or the life estate, in which the testator specified both the original legatee and his successor. Others placed daughters ahead of sons as successor legatees; barred a son's descendants from inheriting, in favor of other children of the testator; or, as did Edmund Burch in 1763, ordered that a son who wanted to sell his legacy had to "sell to his brother or not at all." Catholics comprised a sizable religious minority in the county, and a few Catholic parents bequeathed realty on condition that male children not become priests. The purpose was not to deter them from religious vocations but—like all testators who prevented children from alienating or bequeathing property—to ensure that it remained within the family.[36]

Daughters and Land

Whether, when, and upon what conditions women inherited parental lands did not follow the same patterns found among their brothers. Women married, and thereby lost control of their estates unless they were protected by a trust or a prenuptial agreement. So far as the official records reveal, such agreements were rare in the county, so that most husbands were legally free under the common law to conserve or waste their wives' realty. Not surprisingly, therefore, daughters received legacies to land at a rate less than half that of sons. Whereas 57.5 percent of the male children of landowning parents were bequeathed tracts, only 23.2 percent of daughters were similarly endowed (see table 4). The frequency with which testators willed land to female children varied according to whether the family also included sons, with the rate

35. Blackstone's discussion of the terminology of entail demonstrates why the uncertainty exists (*Commentaries*, II, 113–115). For a local example of land tenure cast in doubt by the terminology of a will, see Wills, AC4, 307–308; Charles County Court Records, Z3, 82–83. See also the cases cited in Thomas Harris, Jr., and John McHenry, comps., *Maryland Reports, Being a Series of the Most Important Law Cases, Argued and Determined in the Provincial Court and Court of Appeals of the Then Province of Maryland, from the Year 1700 down to the American Revolution* (New York, 1809), 582, 588. The Maryland legislature abolished entail in 1782. *Laws of Maryland [November Session, 1782]*, chap. 23.

36. Wills, AC4, 218–221, 240–242, 243–248, 333–334, AD5, 118–119, 222, 224, 336–338, 361 (Burch's will), AE6, 48–49, 53–54, 88–90, 170, AF7, 506, 508–511.

two and one-half times higher in estates where daughters alone were named. For daughters in either category, the proportion of those who received realty was appreciably lower than the companion figure for sons.[37]

Association of males with land and females with personalty was strong in some families, so strong that a few fathers willed their lands to their sons-in-law or, before admitting their own daughters, to all conceivable male descendants.[38] Others ordered tracts sold and the proceeds distributed among female children. Henry Brent did so in 1769 because his property lay in Virginia, and he obviously had no intention of uprooting his three daughters. But Peter Harout a decade earlier had directed that his lot at Port Tobacco, the county seat, be sold for the benefit of his daughters, while at the same time he devised his plantation to a grandson. Joseph Jameson's realty was encumbered with debt when he wrote his will in 1774. If his three sons satisfied the creditors, they were to divide the property; if not, it was to be sold and the profit divided among his daughters and sons.[39]

The exclusive association of males with land that was characteristic of many families, however, should not mask different arrangements found in others. Of 961 landowners' daughters identified in the wills, 223 received some form of landed estate. Three-fourths of the parents who had daughters only ($N = 23$) willed realty to at least one of them. And among testators with children of both sexes ($N = 327$), more than one-quarter ($N = 92$) willed use *or* ownership of land to daughters. Furthermore, twenty-two of those ninety-two parents did not bequeath *any* acreage to sons.[40] Among all landowning testators who had daughters, nearly one-

37. The figures for daughters do not include the uncommon instances where testators permitted them to occupy a portion or all of the dwelling house but did not specifically allow them use of land. For example, Samuel Turner, Sr., in 1746 gave his widow a life estate in his plantation. He clearly intended his daughters to live there and have "a place of byding . . . till they alter their Condition," yet did not give them the right to work the soil. Wills, AC4, 225–227; see also AC4, 203–206, AE6, 149–150, 258.

38. *Ibid.*, AC4, 333–334, AD5, 222, 224, 257–259, AE6, 85–87, 115–116, AF7, 28–30. Cf. AC4, 225–227, AE6, 70–71, 176–178.

39. In order: *ibid.*, AE6, 53, AD5, 142–143, AF7, 626–628.

40. The parents, 18 men and 4 women, collectively accounted for 90 daughters, 50 of whom received land, and 72 sons. Only one of these wills was written between 1732 and 1747; the remaining 21 were evenly distributed across the periods 1748–1763, 1764–1773, and 1774–1783.

TABLE 4. *Number of Daughters and Sons Bequeathed Land in Wills,*
1732–1783

	Total Sons	Sons Bequeathed Land		Total Daughters	Daughters Bequeathed Land	
		No.	%		No.	%
Testators naming sons only (*N*=68)	165	117	70.9			
Testators naming daughters only (*N*=23)				54	30	55.6
Testators naming both sons and daughters (*N*=327)	1,031	571	55.4	907	193	21.3
Total	1,196	688	57.5	961	223	23.2

Source: Charles County Wills, Maryland State Archives, Annapolis.

third of the fathers and almost half of the mothers vested one or more of their daughters with land. This practice was especially common during the years of the American Revolution (see table 5). The higher incidence among mothers may have occurred because their deceased husbands already had furnished sons with realty, which left the women free to discriminate among their children.[41]

Restrictions placed on daughters' estates also differed, in the aggregate, from those set down for sons. Testators encumbered daughters' use of their legacies less than sons'. For example, while some men had to support their sisters out of the profits of their inherited plantations, the reverse never happened. As to the power to dispose of their property, a higher proportion of daughters could neither sell nor devise in a will (see table 6). Again, exact proportions are not certain because of the unresolved questions regarding entail, but if two of three testators barred sons from disposing of their lands, comparable figures are four out of five for

41. Cf. Lebsock, *Free Women of Petersburg*, 135.

TABLE 5. *Parental Bequests of Use or Ownership of Land to Daughters,*
1732–1783

Date of Will[a]	Total Fathers	Fathers Bequeathing Land to Daughters		Total Mothers	Mothers Bequeathing Land to Daughters	
		No.	%		No.	%
1732–1747	44	13	29.5	2	1	50.0
1748–1763	104	23	22.1	9	4	44.4
1764–1773	84	24	28.6	8	1	12.5
1774–1783	91	37	40.7	8	6	75.0
Total	323[b]	97	30.0	27[c]	12	44.4

Source: Charles County Wills, Maryland State Archives, Annapolis.

[a] See table 3 for explanation of the periods used.

[b] Fathers willed use or ownership of land to 196 (22.1%) of 887 daughters.

[c] Mothers willed use or ownership of land to 27 (36.5%) of 74 daughters.

daughters' estates. Daughters alone received use of land until marriage, and the practice was found only in families with both male and female children. With one exception, invoking life estates also was limited to such families.[42]

The forms of bequest could affect daughters' lives appreciably. The woman given use of a plantation until her wedding day had a secure place to live and could support herself either by working slaves on the land or by renting it out. If she married, any accumulated profits from her exploitation of the property accrued to her husband's financial well-being. If she never took a husband, use until marriage in practice became a life estate. On the other hand, the daughter bequeathed fee-simple title to real

42. Except for the marked increase from 1774 to 1783 in the number of testators who willed land to female children for use during their single lives (see p. 319), the incidence of the various forms of bequest did not change significantly over time. Nor did fathers and mothers will tracts in appreciably different ways, with the exception of estates given to daughters so long as they remained single, which fathers used almost exclusively; 94.1% of the testators employing this form were men.

TABLE 6. *Restrictions on Daughters' Disposal of Land, 1732–1783*

	No. of Testators	Unrestricted (i.e., fee simple)	Use during Daughters' Single Lives	Life Estate	Presumed Entail upon Legatee and Her Heirs	Other
Testators with daughters only	17	7	0	1	8	1
Testators with daughters and sons	92	18	34	13	28	5
Total	109	25	34	14	36	6

Source: Charles County Wills, Maryland State Archives, Annapolis.

Note: The number of bequest provisions exceeds 109 because several testators employed more than one kind of devise.

property could sell, exchange, mortgage, or will it away so long as she was a *feme sole*, whether spinster or widow. Unless protected by a prenuptial or trust agreement, however, she lost control of the property upon marriage. If she agreed to sell the land, her husband was free to spend the proceeds as he pleased, with or without her approval.

Entailing land upon a daughter therefore had its advantages if she was or subsequently became *feme covert*. Even though the legal liabilities of the married state prevented her from controlling or willing the property, she could rest assured that it ultimately would descend to her children and grandchildren. The disadvantage of land held in fee tail, from the daughter's point of view, was that she could not alienate it if she was *feme sole*. A life estate, under which the testator usually designated the person who would succeed to the property upon the daughter's death, similarly prevented her and her husband from selling it; but such a devise was less restrictive than fee tail because the land could pass in fee simple to the successor legatee. Other things being equal, the woman with a life or an entailed estate would be a more attractive marriage partner than one given use of land until her wedding day. Although the husband could not dispose of the legacy, common law accorded him full access to it.

That at least some testators understood the consequences of the forms of bequest they adopted is evident from the language in a number of wills. Charles Alasan Ford in 1783 stated as forcefully as he could that a recently purchased tract was to benefit his daughter and her children, not her husband: "I hereby declare the said purchase to have been made Solely and only, for my Daughter Sarah Maddox and the Heirs of her body." Robert Hanson demonstrated his awareness of the relative advantages of fee simple and entailed estates when he left his unmarried daughter the former and his married daughters the latter. For his part, John Woodward in 1766 took steps that would defeat any attempt his daughter and son-in-law might make to dock the tail on a tract where they lived, which Woodward devised to her "and the heirs of her body lawfully begotten forever." "The day she . . . shall offer to sell the said Land," Woodward wrote, "it shall become the inheritance of my Daughter Violetta."[43]

For the 109 parents who left use or ownership of land to daughters, the exact amounts bequeathed are known in thirty cases and ranged from one to 1,500 acres, with a mean of 238 acres.[44] In another twenty-four cases, daughters received whole dwelling plantations, and in three more they acquired plantations plus additional acreage (see table 7). Therefore, when Ann Price in 1778 set aside a single acre, enough to furnish two daughters with a place to live, water, firewood, and a garden plot, she was an exception. So far as the data reveal, only four parents bequeathed tracts of less than 50 acres; the rest provided sufficient realty to enable their daughters to operate viable plantations.[45]

Not only that, parents often bequeathed the personalty necessary to exploit the land. Particularly revealing in this respect is Godshall Barnes's

43. In order: Wills, B1, 284–286, AC4, 252–255, AE6, 4–5.

44. As of 1782, 29.6% of the tracts in the county were 100 acres or less, 44.5% ranged between 101 and 300 acres, 23.0% between 301 and 1,000 acres, and 2.9% were more than 1,000 acres. Charles County assessment lists, 1782, Scharf Collection, box 96, items 7–10, 12–17.

45. Wills, AF7, 244–246. Historians of colonial Maryland generally regard 50 acres as the minimum necessary for a viable plantation. Paul G. E. Clemens, "Economy and Society on Maryland's Eastern Shore, 1689–1733," in Aubrey C. Land, Lois Green Carr, and Edward C. Papenfuse, eds., *Law, Society, and Politics in Early Maryland* (Baltimore, 1977), 158; Gloria L. Main, *Tobacco Colony: Life in Early Maryland, 1650–1720* (Princeton, N.J., 1982), 41.

TABLE 7. *Land Bequests to Daughters, 1732–1783*

Bequests	Testators with Daughters Only	Testators with Daughters and Sons
1–49 acres	0	4
50–100 acres	1	8
101–300 acres	1	10
301–1,000 acres	2	2
1,000–1,500 acres	0	2
Dwelling plantation (acreage unknown)	3	21
Dwelling plantation plus additional acreage	0	3
Acreage unknown	10	42
Total	17	92

Source: Charles County Wills, Maryland State Archives, Annapolis.

1766 will, in which he left two unmarried daughters a life estate of 170 acres "without any Disturbance." He also gave them 2 male slaves, 18 head of cattle, sheep, and pigs, all of his poultry, a horse, 1,000 pounds of crop tobacco, 10 bushels of wheat and 10 barrels of corn, hoes and axes, and 1,000 nails. Perhaps the best-endowed daughter in Charles County was Priscilla Smallwood, who acquired (in addition to the plantations her brother William had to furnish her) 110 head of cattle, 100 sheep, 9 horses, 48 hogs, 15 lambs, and 21 slaves under her mother's will. Parents were especially explicit when giving daughters slave labor to till their land. References abound to daughters being told to work their "people," "Negroes," and "slaves" on their estates. Indeed, the possession of slave labor probably accounted for parents' willingness to bequeath acreage to female children, even those with brothers. Such daughters had the means to support themselves.[46]

46. Wills, AE6, 19–22, B1, 409–411. For references to slaves, see AD5, 284–285, AE6, 23, 104–105, 146–149, AF7, 48–49, 683–684, B1, 409–411; Prerogative Court Wills, Lib. 40, fols. 290–292.

Personalty

Under Maryland intestacy law, children of both sexes inherited personal property in equal shares. If the decedent also left a widow, she received one-third and the children divided the residue. If, on the other hand, the decedent was either a widow or a widower, the offspring received the entire personal estate. Children of deceased heirs succeeded to their parent's share as his or her legal representatives. Thus the personalty of a man who died intestate leaving a widow, three living children, and four grandchildren whose parent was dead was distributed as follows: the widow received one-third, each living child one-sixth, and each of the orphaned grandchildren one twenty-fourth.[47]

The law calculated premortem distribution of personalty, however, in ways that potentially favored sons over daughters and could effectively negate the equitable division of an intestate's inventoried estate. Children deemed to have received "advancements" during their father's life were entitled not to an equal share but only to the amount beyond what they already had been advanced. As defined in Elie Vallette's *Deputy Commissary's Guide within the Province of Maryland . . . ,* an advancement made the recipient independent of the father and therefore included daughters' dowries. Excluded from the term, however, were broadly defined educational expenses that most often benefited sons: "maintenance money, or allowance made by the father to his son at the university; or in travelling; putting a child apprentice; keeping him at school; and such like expences, having for object the child's improvement and education only."[48]

Parents, of course, were free to bequeath their personal wealth as they pleased. Among the 594 Charles County testators, some simply gave each child a percentage or child's share of the personalty, thereby leaving the actual distribution to the executor. Far more often, parents were specific in at least some of their bequests, so that it is possible to identify children

47. Vallette, *Deputy Commissary's Guide,* 13, 107; *Md. Archives,* XXX, 332. Included in personalty were goods, chattel, money and debts, and crops already in the ground when the deceased expired. Land, buildings, and surviving widows' apparel alone were excluded.

48. Vallette applied the advancement restriction only to fathers' estates on the grounds that the relevant English statute that served as precedent in Maryland covered persons "capable of having a wife . . . which must be husbands only." Vallette, *Deputy Commissary's Guide,* 90, 107, 114–118; *Md. Archives,* XXX, 332–333.

TABLE 8. *Time Children Received Personalty, 1732–1783*

Acquisition of Major Share of Personalty	Testators with Sons		Testators with Daughters	
	No.	%	No.	%
At testator's death or at age of majority	407	75.4	419	84.3
At remarriage of testator's widow	24	4.4	16	3.2
At death of testator's widow	47	8.7	36	7.2
Other	24	4.4	9	1.8
No bequest	38	7.0	17	3.4
Total	540	99.9	497	99.9

Source: Charles County Wills, Maryland State Archives, Annapolis.

who inherited household goods or valuable capital assets such as slaves, livestock, money, or tobacco.[49] On the whole, personal wealth descended to children much sooner than did land, and in this respect daughters were somewhat favored over sons. Seventy-five percent of the testators with sons stipulated that the son would inherit his personal estate at the parent's death or at the age of majority. Of the testators with daughters, nearly 85 percent similarly ensured early access to legacies (see table 8).

No capital asset figured more prominently in the distribution of personal wealth than slaves because of their productive worth and reproductive potential. Maryland law protected young children's slave inheritances,[50] and parents, too, testified to the importance of the labor in their

49. Of all parent-testators, 74.9% willed property under at least one of these categories.

50. First, unless no other form of personal property remained in the estate, slaves could not be sold to satisfy claims against it. Second, guardians could appropriate the profits of slave labor, beyond what it cost to maintain the orphan, but could not sell their ward's chattel or the slaves' offspring. When a child attained the legal age of majority (21 for males, 16 for females), he or she was entitled to "the like number of slaves, of like ability of body" as was his or her due at the parent's death. If the slaves

estates by specifically willing slave property more often than any other kind of personalty. Of the 594 parents whose wills were probated between 1740 and 1784, 53.5 percent ($N = 318$) bequeathed slaves to members of their immediate family. Collectively they mentioned 866 sons and 740 daughters, among whom they distributed more than 1,600 slaves. Only 3.5 percent ($N = 11$) of the slave owners did not leave chattel to any of their offspring.[51]

By tabulating the number of slaves whom each testator willed to his or her children, one can ascertain whether equal distribution between the sexes was the rule in practice as it was under the law of intestacy. By tabulating the gender distribution of the bondmen and bondwomen, one can also gain an idea of the composition of the labor force that descended from one generation to the next. Moreover, it is possible to ascertain whether fathers' and mothers' bequest practices varied significantly. The wills of 228 parents known to have had both male and female children, and who willed slaves by name or number, provide the data to answer these questions. Persons with sons alone or daughters alone were excluded because they did not face the same distributive choices as did parents who had children of both sexes.[52]

The first consideration is whether slave property was equitably apportioned between sons and daughters. Distribution within families obviously varied according to individual circumstances, and no attempt has been made to judge the extent to which each child in each slave-owning family did or did not receive an equitable share. What the body of data does show, when analyzed in terms of gender, is that daughters received proportionally more slaves than did sons (see tables 9 and 10). Over the entire period 1732 through 1783 the mean number of slaves willed to

---

had grown old, lame, or "otherwise impotent" in the interim, so that they and their increase were less valuable than the child's original devise, then the guardian had to pay the difference. *Md. Archives*, XXX, 333–336; Vallette, *Deputy Commissary's Guide*, 135, 149.

51. The exact number of slaves is unknown because, of the 307 testators who left slaves to their children, 29 bequeathed percentages rather than specific numbers of slaves. The count of those known to have been bequeathed is 1,637. Men constituted 79.3% of parent-testators and 79.2% of slave owners. Women accounted for 20.5% and 20.8%, respectively. The gender of one testator is unknown.

52. Since the 228 parents constituted 92.7% of those with both sons and daughters—the remaining 7.3% ($N = 18$) being those who willed a percentage or an unknown number of human chattel—one can feel quite confident of the results.

TABLE 9. *Per Capita Distribution of Slaves to Sons, 1732–1783*

Date of Will	No. of Testators	No. of Sons	No. of Slaves	Per Capita Distribution
1732–1747	21	71	84	1.18
1748–1763	78	250	205	.82
1764–1773	61	187	187	1.00
1774–1783	68	187	230	1.23
Total	228	695	706	1.02

Source: Charles County Wills, Maryland State Archives, Annapolis.

Note: Testators limited to those with children of both sexes.

daughters was 1.19 and to sons, 1.02. Except for the years 1764 through 1773, when the per capita distribution was nearly identical, female children consistently inherited more slaves, with the greatest disparity between the sexes occurring during the years of the Revolution. At that time seven of every twelve slaves willed to children went to daughters. These are the same years, moreover, when the proportion of landowning testators who gave female children use or ownership of plantations also increased appreciably. Furthermore, although there were fewer daughters than sons, the former received more slaves: 620 daughters acquired 740 slaves, while 695 sons inherited 706. That is a surprising finding, especially when one remembers that many married daughters probably had already received slaves as part of their dowries.

Analysis of the Charles County data therefore yields an unexpected result: strictly in terms of the number of slaves willed to children, parents favored daughters over sons. Just as testators did not adhere rigidly to common and statutory law concerning descent of land, neither did they follow legal prescriptions about the most valuable personal property in their estates. In the aggregate, they preferred sons when devising land, but favored daughters when dividing slaves.

Taking the same 228 parents, one can also trace the gender distribution of the unfree labor force willed to the rising generation. Over a fifty-year period, the distribution rate for female slaves changed little, hovering around 40 percent for sons and 60 percent for daughters (see table 11). Division of male slaves showed a different pattern. Through 1773, ap-

TABLE 10. *Per Capita Distribution of Slaves to Daughters, 1732–1783*

Date of Will	No. of Testators	No. of Daughters	No. of Slaves	Per Capita Distribution
1732–1747	21	56	78	1.39
1748–1763	78	235	212	.90
1764–1773	61	156	154	.99
1774–1783	68	173	296	1.71
Total	228	620	740	1.19

Source: Charles County Wills, Maryland State Archives, Annapolis.

Note: Testators limited to those with children of both sexes.

proximately three-fifths of the males descended to sons. Then, once again, the traditional practice was interrupted during the Revolution, for suddenly the male labor force was bequeathed to sons and daughters in nearly equal shares. Thus, the distribution of land, the total proportion of slaves, and the percentage of male slaves willed to daughters all increased during the war years.

Considering that the inventoried value of bondmen was higher than that of bondwomen of comparable age and physical vigor, it could be argued that—until the pattern changed during the Revolution—daughters really were not at an advantage over sons in inheriting slaves. True, their per capita share was greater, but as a group they received fewer male field hands and a larger percentage of the less valuable bondwomen. Such an interpretation, however, would focus on only one point in time, the day the estate assessors put a price on the head of the deceased's bond laborers; it would not account for the progeny of female slaves. Every time a slave woman gave birth and the child survived, she increased her master's personal wealth. The children produced by any one woman during her lifetime, in addition to her own assessed worth as a field or domestic laborer, could far outstrip the valuation of any prime field hand or slave artisan.[53]

53. Thomas Jefferson made the point succinctly toward the end of his life. On Jan. 17, 1819, he wrote to Joel Yancey, "I consider the labor of a breeding woman as no object, and that a child raised every 2. years is of more profit than the crop of the best laboring man." And on June 30, 1820, he told John Eppes, "I consider a woman who

TABLE 11. *Distribution of Slaves, by Sex, to Sons and Daughters, 1732–1783*

| | Male Slaves (N = 724) | | | | Female Slaves (N = 722) | | | |
| | Willed to Sons | | Willed to Daughters | | Willed to Sons | | Willed to Daughters | |
Date of Will	No.	%	No.	%	No.	%	No.	%
1732–1747	53	60.2	35	39.8	31	41.9	43	58.1
1748–1763	126	58.9	88	41.1	79	38.9	124	61.1
1764–1773	113	65.3	60	34.7	74	44.1	94	55.9
1774–1783	126	50.6	123	49.4	104	37.5	173	62.5
Total	418	57.7	306	42.3	288	39.9	434	60.1

Source: Charles County Wills, Maryland State Archives, Annapolis.

Note: Testators limited to those with children of both sexes (N = 228).

Where slave property was involved, testation practices of mothers and fathers varied. Both willed daughters, on the average, more slaves than sons received (see table 12). Fathers, however, apportioned slaves among daughters and sons in nearly equal lots. Mothers, on the other hand, set aside only 44.3 percent of the slaves they bequeathed to their children for their sons, and 55.7 percent for their daughters (see tables 13 and 14). In parceling out their bound labor by gender, fathers treated sons and daughters almost exactly the opposite: three-fifths of the bondmen went to sons and three-fifths of the bondwomen to daughters. But mothers as a group divided bondmen almost evenly between sons and daughters, while granting the latter somewhat more than three-fifths of the bondwomen.

Children gained unencumbered access to their slave legacies more frequently than they did to their landed estates. About two-thirds of the testators granted sons fee-simple possession; 56.5 percent treated

---

brings a child every two years as more profitable than the best man of the farm. what she produces is an addition to the capital, while his labors disappear in mere consumption." Edward Morris Betts, ed., *Thomas Jefferson's Farm Book: With Commentary and Relevant Extracts from Other Writings* (Princeton, N.J., 1953), pt. 2, 43, 46.

TABLE 12. *Parental Distribution of Slaves to Sons and Daughters,*
1732–1783

Date of Will	Distribution of Slaves to Sons (per capita)		Distribution of Slaves to Daughters (per capita)	
	Fathers	Mothers	Fathers	Mothers
1732–1747	1.14	1.80	1.51	.20
1748–1763	.87	.63	.86	1.09
1764–1773	1.02	.92	1.08	.66
1774–1783	1.26	1.09	1.72	1.69
Overall	1.04	.89	1.21	1.12

Source: Charles County Wills, Maryland State Archives, Annapolis.

Note: Testators limited to those with children of both sexes. Fathers ($N = 178$) willed 597 slaves to 572 sons and 603 slaves to 498 daughters. Mothers ($N = 50$) willed 109 slaves to 123 sons and 137 slaves to 122 daughters.

daughters in similar fashion. Parents who restricted children's ability to dispose of slaves employed a variety of techniques, including entail and, less frequently, life estates and trusts.[54] They invoked a wider array of devises, and were more articulate in describing their motives, when bequeathing to daughters. As with land, the underlying intention was to preserve the property for them despite husbands' common law rights to ownership of their wives' personalty. Thus did Benjamin Dent in 1778 will slaves to each married daughter "during her natural life and [then to] the Heirs of her Body," while his unmarried daughter gained her legacy in fee simple. Husbands' legal rights notwithstanding, parents gave slaves to daughters "in full and perfect property," "to her and her Children forever," and "for the use of her & the heirs of her body & no other person."[55]

54. The language of one-fourth of slave owners' wills suggests entail. Under Maryland law chattel could not be entailed, although the probate court recognized such bequests in a restricted manner. Vallette, *Deputy Commissary's Guide*, 91.

55. In order quoted: Wills, AF7, 207–209, B1, 357, AD5, 348, AE6, 307–308. See also AC4, 145–147, 359–361, AD5, 37–39, 55–57, 130–134, 265–266, 300–302, AE6, 14–15, B1, 284–286.

TABLE 13. *Distribution of Fathers' Slave Bequests, by Sex, to Sons and Daughters, 1732–1783*

Slaves	Total Slaves	Willed to Sons		Willed to Daughters	
		No.	%	No.	%
Male	596	352	59.1	244	40.9
Female	604	245	40.6	359	59.4
Total	1,200	597	49.8	603	50.2

Source: Charles County Wills, Maryland State Archives, Annapolis.

Note: Testators limited to fathers with children of both sexes (*N* = 178).

Notably adamant in this regard was Prudence Green, who had ample reason to be wary of her son-in-law James Livers. Described as unable to look any man in the face and possessed of "a low womanish Voice," Livers had broken out of debtor's prison in 1748 and apparently had not mended his ways by the time the widow Green wrote her will a decade later. Therefore, in bequeathing her daughter Mary Livers a life estate in five slaves and other personalty, Mrs. Green stipulated that they were to go to Mary "Exclusive of her husband James Livers who shall have no power to give Dispose of or intermeddle with the same or any part Thereof." Nor was the property to be liable for Livers's debts.[56]

Samuel Love, Sr., sought to shield his child Nancy's inheritance, two female slaves and their future increase, in yet another fashion. He willed them in trust to his son Samuel, Jr., and ordered that each year Nancy was to receive "the full hire or annual Value of the Clear profits that may arise" from the slaves' labor, to be used solely for her benefit and that of her children.[57] If the husband acceded to the terms of such a trust, no problem could arise. He simply waived his common law right to the income due his wife. Or, if he demanded the money and she acceded, again no problem arose. But an impasse developed if the husband was determined not to relinquish his prerogative and met resistance from his wife or the trustees of her estate.

That very situation came before the Charles County probate court in

56. *Ibid.*, AD5, 87–89; *Maryland Gazette* (Annapolis), Oct. 26, 1748.
57. Wills, AE6, 154–155.

TABLE 14. *Distribution of Mothers' Slave Bequests, by Sex, to Sons and Daughters, 1732–1783*

Slaves	Total Slaves	Willed to Sons		Willed to Daughters	
		No.	%	No.	%
Male	128	66	51.6	62	48.4
Female	118	43	36.4	75	63.6
Total	246	109	44.3	137	55.7

Source: Charles County Wills, Maryland State Archives, Annapolis.

Note: Testators limited to mothers with children of both sexes (*N* = 50).

1780 in the case of *Henry Britt v. William Godfrey Adams and Mary Adams.* The defendants were executors of the estate of Benjamin Gray, the father of Mary Adams and Tabitha Britt, Henry's wife. In Gray's will, filed for probate two years earlier, he had provided "that my Negro fellow named George ... be hired out by my said Ex[ecuto]r" and that his daughter Tabitha was "to receive the Wages of the said Negro for and during her Life." At issue in the dispute was whether George's wages should be paid to Tabitha or to her husband, as he maintained. Having heard witnesses for both sides and having considered Gray's will and "intentions," the court decided against Henry Britt. His wife was to receive the slave's wages. When the question arose, therefore, the local justices decided that a parent's final wishes took precedence over legal prescription.[58]

Reflections

Recent discussions of inheritance practices underscore the diversity characteristic of seventeenth- and eighteenth-century America. When John E. Crowley, in an article published in 1984, contrasted practices found in northern agricultural areas with those in commercial areas, he may have identified opposite poles on a broad continuum. In the agricultural regions, typified by rural New England,

58. *Ibid.,* AF7, 145, 476.

patriarchy predominated. Land was the principal form of family wealth, and since men worked the land, it customarily descended to sons. Conversely, in at least some northern and southern commercial centers, more equitable distribution between sons and daughters prevailed because land was but one among several kinds of major assets. In his own investigation of testation in Charleston and the surrounding South Carolina low country, Crowley argues that "a feminine orientation, with relative disregard to lineage, impartiality to children, and minimal sexual stereotyping of property" developed during the eighteenth century.[59]

In both locality and testation practices, Charles County, Maryland, lay between rural New England and commercial Charleston. Along the tobacco coast, agriculture was highly commercialized. Both land and slaves figured prominently in family resources, and inheritance patterns were neither entirely patriarchal nor entirely equitable. Regarding land, the most common situation was descent of ownership from father to son, for it was white men who usually tilled the soil and supervised the enslaved labor force. That fewer daughters inherited outright ownership of realty is not surprising in view of both the practicalities of plantation management and women's common law liabilities. Yet family resources were finite, so many sons had to wait to possess or fully exploit their legacies. Ahead of them were their fathers' widows, with dower claims to one-third of their husbands' lands, and daughters allowed to occupy and exploit plantations until they married. Parents who provided for daughters' use of land while single obviously did not envision them as permanent, independent agricultural entrepreneurs. Rather, such bequests reflect the limited options open to women in the eighteenth-century Chesapeake. Whether a daughter's tenure was temporary or lifelong, collateral bequest of slaves made that tenure economically viable. Most *femes sole* in Charles County who lived comfortably by eighteenth-century standards had access to land, slave labor, or both.[60]

At any one time, however, the majority of adult women were *femes covert*, not *femes sole*. To the family economies they established with their husbands, women contributed their labor, dowries, and inheritances. Given their legal status, wives' property did not secure their autonomy

---

59. Crowley, "Family Relations and Inheritance," *Histoire Sociale—Social History*, XVII (1984), 53–57.

60. This statement is based on examination of Charles County Inventories, 1735–1784, at the Md. State Archives, and the Charles County assessment lists, 1782, Scharf Collection, box 96, items 7–10, 12–17.

but rather their material well-being. Since most women presumably moved onto their husbands' land, it seems reasonable that daughters would bring movables, including slaves, to their marriages. Their slaves, added to husbands' land and laborers, formed the productive units of the county's agricultural economy.[61] Examining daughters' contributions to the family economies of the Chesapeake should produce a heightened appreciation of how marriages (and not just those of the great planters) created the wealth networks that were vital to the region's social order.

Nor was daughters' property a static matter. The Charles County women who brought to their marriages more slaves per capita than did their husbands may well have been responsible for the larger share of the family's personal property. In addition, by contributing proportionally more female slaves, wives' inheritances may have been the source of the greatest increase in their husbands' personal wealth, in the form of an increasing slave population. And, if one hypothesizes about the life cycles of such women who subsequently became widows, one can suggest that parental decisions and common law protections blended to produce a greater measure of equity for them, as to property, than has so far been appreciated. Although they may have contributed more than half of their families' inherited slaves and yet had dower rights to only a third of them, these women also had common law rights to one-third of the family land, which in most cases the husbands had brought to their marriages.

It would be valuable to learn whether parents elsewhere in the Chesapeake duplicated salient bequest features encountered in Charles County, especially the web of limitations that parents spun around sons' legacies, the surprising number of bequests of land to female children, and the advantage sisters collectively enjoyed over their brothers in inheriting slaves. In addition, it should be instructive to compare the *value* of the assets devised to sons and daughters. Comparisons admittedly would be difficult for the colonial Chesapeake because estate inventories and tax lists usually did not include real estate. Still, an occasional estate assessor did appraise land or leaseholds, and other records—estate sales, deeds of conveyance, orphans' court valuations, and the Maryland rent rolls and debt books, for example—make educated guesses feasible. Beginning with the 1780s, greater assurance is possible because tax lists in Virginia

61. Lois Green Carr and Lorena S. Walsh called attention to this process in "Woman's Role in the Eighteenth-Century Chesapeake," 37.

and Maryland enumerated both land and personalty.[62] These sources, if used in conjunction with the probate records of persons who died about the same time, would permit scholars to speak with much greater confidence about the accumulation and transfer of wealth within families, both the female and male lines.

Finally, the Revolutionary crisis appears to have had a demonstrable impact on testation practices in Charles County. For it seems unlikely that, at the time of the war, mere coincidence explains why parents suddenly increased their bequests of land and slaves to daughters, or why fathers concurrently required a higher proportion of sons to stand in line—behind widows and unmarried sisters—for land. Probate materials are notoriously devoid of explicit statements of motivation, which leaves the historian in the uncomfortable position of conjecturing possible motives behind observed behavior. Some parents may have responded to the egalitarian rhetoric of the Revolution by permitting their unmarried daughters greater control over their lives than had been the case in the colonial period. More plausibly, the unsettled war years prompted testators to expect that sons away on military duty would leave unprotected the unmarried women of the family, or that wartime casualties would reduce the number of potential husbands. If testation changes reflected the insecurities attendant upon the war, lower incidences of granting land and slaves to women may have reemerged with the peace. Or, as so often happens as a result of wars, altered habits may have persisted. Certainly the trend in inheritance in post-Revolutionary America was toward partibility.

62. The 1782 and 1783 Maryland tax lists are in the Scharf Collection. Comparable lists for Virginia are at the Virginia State Library, Richmond.

Lois
Green
Carr

Diversification in the Colonial Chesapeake

Somerset County, Maryland, in

Comparative Perspective

OVER THE eighteenth century, major changes occurred in the economy of the tidewater Chesapeake. Everywhere in the seventeenth century, tobacco was the cash crop; by the time of the American Revolution, wheat or corn or both were at least supplementary exports from most areas. Over most of the seventeenth century, all manufactures were imported in return for tobacco; by 1776 there was an extensive network of local industry that supplemented imports. This essay will look at that process of change and consider its implications. What was the relationship between soil resources, new crops, and the development of local crafts and home industries? Did these developments bring self-sufficiency to planters or instead encourage local exchange? Did diversification affect the amount and distribution of wealth created? And what quality of life could the resulting economy support?[1]

In discussing these questions, the essay will focus on Somerset County on the lower Eastern Shore of Maryland, which diversified early and intensively. Using primary evidence from estate inventories,[2] the essay

I wish to thank Stanley Engerman, Russell R. Menard, Philip D. Morgan, Jean B. Russo, and Lorena S. Walsh for helpful comments on earlier versions of this essay. I alone am responsible for its deficiencies.

1. This work is part of a larger study of social and economic developments in the colonial Chesapeake tidewater, which has been funded by grants to the St. Mary's City Commission from the National Science Foundation (GS32272) and the National Endowment for the Humanities (RO6228-72-468; RO10585-74-267; RS23687-76-431; and RS20199-81-1955, jointly with Historic Annapolis, Inc.). My colleagues in the grants are P. M. G. Harris, Russell R. Menard, Lorena S. Walsh, Billy G. Smith, Nancy Baker, and Jean B. Russo. Grateful thanks are due to the valiant research assistants who, over the years, have done the coding and collected the prices: Christopher Allan, Victoria Allan, Elizabeth Blistein, Mary Anne Braun, Dreama Greaves, Emily Kutler, Jean E. Russo, and Janice Watson.

2. A discussion of bias in inventories and the ways we have dealt with it is presented in the appendix to Lois Green Carr and Lorena S. Walsh, "Inventories and the

will attempt to show the progress of diversification in Somerset from both internal and external perspectives, the emergence within the county of differing economic areas, and the ways in which the area as a whole resembled or differed from other parts of the tidewater Chesapeake. Included for comparison are three counties on Maryland's lower Western Shore, St. Mary's, Prince George's, and Anne Arundel, which grew oronoco tobacco of varying quality, but much of it better than Somerset could produce; Talbot on the upper Eastern Shore, where planters grew oronoco but by mid-eighteenth century had added wheat to their crop base; and York County, Virginia, the earliest-settled county in the study, where soils produced sweet-scented tobacco, especially valued in the London market.

Colonial Somerset included present Wicomico County, and until 1742, present Worcester County as well. The first settlers came from the lower

---

Analysis of Wealth and Consumption Patterns in St. Mary's County, Maryland, 1658–1777," *Historical Methods*, XIII (1980), 96–100 (on p. 100 the denominator in II, 1700–1776, should be 5, not 2). Other discussions of inventory bias are Alice Hanson Jones, "Wealth Estimates for the American Middle Colonies, 1774," *Economic Development and Cultural Change*, XVIII, no. 4, pt. 2 (1970), 109–121, and Gloria L. Main, "The Correction of Biases in Colonial American Probate Records," *Historical Methods Newsletter*, VIII (1974), 10–28. Age biases appear before about 1710 in York and Anne Arundel counties, 1720 in St. Mary's County, and 1740 in Somerset. With adjustments made for age, mean inventoried wealth was almost always higher but the trends were the same. The problem did not seem severe enough to make adjustments for the purposes of this paper. There was no bias in Talbot from 1720. On biases from reporting rates, see appendix 1, below.

The deflator used in this paper to create constant values in inventories is based on a Chesapeake-wide commodity price index, which uses prices from all the counties represented in this study. Separate indexes were constructed for five areas: the lower Western Shore, Talbot County, and Somerset County in Maryland, and Lower Norfolk and York counties in Virginia. These indexes differ from that described in Carr and Walsh, "Inventories and the Analysis of Wealth," *Hist. Methods*, XIII (1980), 96–100, in that bound labor is omitted and the remaining two parts of the index are given equal weight. All the indexes are reduced to sterling, using Maryland and Virginia sterling exchange rates listed in John J. McCusker, *Money and Exchange in Europe and America, 1600–1775: A Handbook* (Chapel Hill, N.C., 1978), 189–214. The Maryland sterling indexes are then averaged, as are those of Virginia, and then Virginia and Maryland are averaged to create a Chesapeake sterling index. Finally, separate Virginia and Maryland deflators are created from the Chesapeake-wide sterling index by using the exchange rates to return the index to local money values. P. M. G. Harris, who devised this overall Chesapeake deflator, plans a publication soon to explain it in greater detail.

Eastern Shore of Virginia. These included Quakers who came to Anna-messex in 1662 to take advantage of Lord Baltimore's policy of toleration, which, combined with a liberal land policy, made the Somerset frontier attractive. Others, less influenced by religion, settled at Manokin at the same time, and settlers soon began to emigrate directly from the British Isles, many from Scotland or northern Ireland (see map 1).[3]

As in other parts of the early Chesapeake, tobacco was the cash crop, but there was much less prime tobacco soil and more tidal marsh and beach in Somerset than in most parts of the Chesapeake tidewater. Table 1 shows that only a fifth of present Somerset soil could ever have pro-duced high yields of tobacco and that the quality was generally low. By contrast, in Talbot on the upper Eastern Shore and in the Western Shore counties of Maryland more than half the land produced high yields and a much higher proportion of the tobacco land produced high-quality leaf. In Maryland, all tobacco was of the oronoco variety, but in Virginia between the James and Rappahannock rivers, many planters raised sweet-scented tobacco as well.[4] All these areas were more productive for tobacco than was Somerset. Only on the south side of the lower James were conditions as unfavorable; in Lower Norfolk County tobacco pro-duction essentially stopped as early as the 1680s.[5]

Eventually, as we shall see, in most areas corn or wheat began to compete with tobacco as an export crop. But Somerset was slow even in this development, although its productivity in grains was not as dismal as in tobacco. Today less than a fifth of its land produces high yields of corn, but another half produces medium yields, making its overall productivity higher than that of several other areas.

In the past, parts of Somerset were more productive. The area between the lower Nanticoke River and the Pocomoke River lies very low and flat, especially the parts between the Wicomico River and the Pocomoke Sound (see map 1). Here, in the present limits of Somerset County, 26 percent of the land is tidal marsh, and 30 percent is Othello silt loam, land that drains poorly and is very unsuited to tobacco. Of the Othello silt loam about 6 percent is flooded by brackish water during extremely high

3. Clayton Torrence, *Old Somerset on the Eastern Shore of Maryland: A Study in Foundations and Founders* (Richmond, Va., 1935).
4. Arthur Pierce Middleton, *Tobacco Coast: A Maritime History of Chesapeake Bay in the Colonial Era* (Newport News, Va., 1953), 97–98.
5. St. Mary's City Commission inventory file for Lower Norfolk County.

tides. But in the seventeenth and eighteenth centuries, much of this land had a different character. The subsidence of the East Coast plus melting of the polar icecaps has raised the seawater level about twelve inches over the last hundred years and possibly twenty inches or more since the seventeenth century. In the Somerset area this process has wiped out many islands and much shoreline and has pushed the tidal marshes inland. Much of what is now tidal marsh was probably once the Othello silt loam, and areas of what is now Othello silt loam might have been a better-drained soil that could produce a medium-yield, low-quality tobacco. How much, of course, is the question. Should we say one-half of the Othello in the especially low-lying areas, then 33 percent of colonial Somerset-Worcester would have had soils suitable for tobacco, although of low quality; if all this Othello was once much better drained land, 38 percent of the soils could have grown tobacco. Nevertheless, even this is still well below the proportion of tobacco land available in other tidewater localities, the Norfolk area excepted.[6]

Somerset, then, was a poor area for tobacco and probably one of the poorest places in the tidewater. Probate inventories bear out this conclusion. Figure 1 shows that mean inventoried wealth in Somerset was lower than in the other five counties studied, with a brief exception; St. Mary's and Talbot fell below Somerset over three decades in the middle eighteenth century. However, differences in inventory reporting rates account for this seeming discrepancy. In reality, Somerset planters on the average died poorer than planters studied elsewhere over the whole colonial period.[7]

Although mean property accumulation was less, the development of

6. U.S. Department of Agriculture, Soil Conservation Service, *Soil Survey, Somerset County, Maryland* (Washington, D.C., 1966), 9, 34–35; Roy G. Metzgar, *Wetlands in Maryland*, Maryland Department of State Planning, Publication no. 157 (Baltimore, 1963), XII, 1–2, XIII, 1–2, 8–9; personal communication from James Brewer, Soil Conservation Service, Dorchester County, Md. I am grateful for the assistance of Dr. Richard Weismiller and Dr. Thomas Simpson of the Departments of Agronomy at the University of Maryland and Virginia Polytechnic Institute, respectively, and especially for that of James Brewer, in obtaining and interpreting the information in table 1. I am responsible for any errors.

7. In St. Mary's and Talbot—as opposed to Somerset—a larger proportion of people, and hence a large proportion of poor people, went through probate at death, bringing down the level of mean wealth as revealed in figure 1, whereas a low reporting rate for Somerset raised the mean wealth shown. See appendix 1.

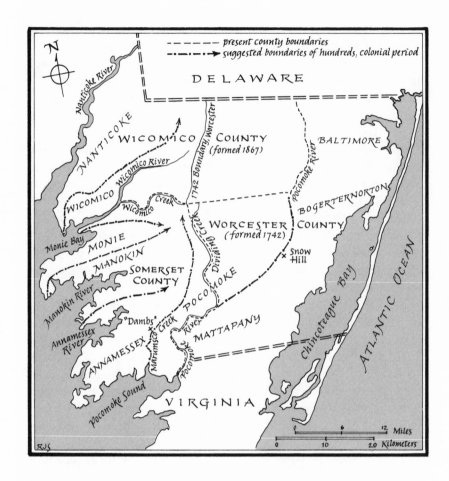

MAP 1. *Somerset County and Its Later Divisions*

Drawn by Richard Stinely

Sources: Harry L. Benson Tract Maps of Somerset and Worcester Counties, Maryland, by Election District, MSS, Maryland State Archives, Annapolis; Ruth T. Dryden, *Land Records of Somerset County, Maryland* (n.p., n.d., privately printed); Somerset County Lists of Taxables, 1757, MSS, Md. State Archives.

Note: Hundred boundaries as laid out in 1666 ran along the dividing lines of the watersheds of rivers, with two exceptions. The Pocomoke River was the eastern boundary of Pocomoke Hundred, and Marumsco Creek was the western boundary as far as the "Dambs," near present-day Hudson's Corner. Tract maps for Somerset and part of Worcester, prepared by Harry L. Benson, and title histories prepared by Ruth T. Dryden, combined with various Somerset County tax lists taken by hundred indicate that these boundaries were retained over the colonial period, although much more work is needed to determine where they were precisely. These materials also indicate that above the head of Marumsco Creek the boundary between Pocomoke and other hundreds within the limits of present-day Somerset ran between the headwaters of creeks that fell into the Chesapeake Bay and those that ran into Dividing Creek, creating the narrow strip of Pocomoke Hundred that remained in Somerset after the creation of Worcester in 1742. Boundaries of hundreds between the Pocomoke River and the ocean, created later in the seventeenth century, are unknown.

TABLE I. *Modern Chesapeake Tidewater Soils, by Region (in Percents)*

	Tobacco				Corn			Wheat or Barley			Tidal Marsh, Swamp, Muck, Sand
	Total Land Suitable	High Yield	High Quality	High Yield & Quality	Total Land Suitable	High Yield	Medium Yield	Total Land Suitable	High Yield	Medium Yield	
MARYLAND											
Upper Eastern Shore:											
Talbot	55.0	46.6	29.2	28.9	91.1	35.4	55.7	91.1[a]	48.5[a]	42.3[a]	7.5
Lower Eastern Shore:											
Somerset[b]	29.1	21.7	11.9	7.8	82.6	18.0	51.4	74.6[a]	34.8[a]	39.9[a]	17.4
Lower Western Shore:											
Anne Arundel	55.6	36.2	43.6	25.4	67.3	30.1	37.1	67.3	22.6	19.0	1.6
Prince George's	59.4	49.6	34.0	26.4	68.3	7.1	43.0	66.4	0.0	32.9	2.3
St. Mary's	59.7	50.8	18.4	12.6	78.3	31.8	41.9	59.7	16.8	40.3	4.4

VIRGINIA

	Good Crops	Moderate Crops								
Lower Potomac River:										
Westmoreland	45.7	30.8	14.9	63.3	37.3	25.4	63.3	20.7	22.7	4.5
Northumberland	44.8	32.1	12.7	40.5	0	40.5	63.1	57.2	5.8	22.7
Rappahannock River:										
Lancaster	55.0	41.1	13.9	28.1	0	28.1	65.3	62.0	3.3	20.6
York River:										
York[c]	37.5	8.8	28.7	56.2	26.7	9.9	56.2	11.5	23.2	6.8
Gloucester				50.9	36.8	12.3	49.1	46.5	1.4	0
Lower James River:										
Virginia Beach	14.3	4.5	9.8	66.2	56.6	9.6	66.2	57.2	9.0	17.2
Suffolk City	45.8	9.2	21.4	73.1	35.1	30.9	73.1	52.8	18.7	19.4

Sources: U.S. Department of Agriculture, Soil Conservation Service, *Soil Survey, Anne Arundel County, Maryland* (Washington, D.C., 1973), *Soil Survey, Prince George's County, Maryland* (Washington, D.C., 1967), *Soil Survey, St. Mary's County, Maryland* (Washington, D.C., 1978), *Soil Survey, Somerset County, Maryland* (Washington, D.C., 1966), *Soil Survey, Wicomico County, Maryland* (Washington, D.C., 1970), *Soil Survey, Worcester County, Maryland* (Washington, D.C., 1973), *Soil Survey, Talbot County, Maryland* (Washington, D.C., 1970), *Soil Survey, James City and York Counties and the City of Williamsburg, Virginia* (Washington, D.C., 1985), *Soil Survey, Westmoreland County, Virginia* (Washington, D.C., 1980), *Soil Survey, Northumberland and Lancaster Counties, Virginia* (Washington, D.C., 1963), *Soil Survey, Virginia Beach, Virginia* (Washington, D.C., 1985), *Soil Survey, City of Suffolk, Virginia* (Washington, D.C., 1981).

Note: Lands with more than 10 to 15 percent slopes and not now cultivated have been omitted. Such lands are now heavily eroded and some surely have been cultivated, but not necessarily in the colonial period. Urban land, made land, gravel pits, cut and fill land, and mixed alluvial soils have also been omitted, since their earlier use is uncertain or their soil types not sufficiently identified. No information on crop is available for any of these omitted soils.

[a] Where wheat is no longer a crop, data for barley are used instead. Yields per acre of soil varieties are similar.

[b] Includes present Wicomico and Worcester counties.

[c] City of Williamsburg omitted.

FIGURE I. *Mean Total Estate Value, Six Counties, 1636–1777*

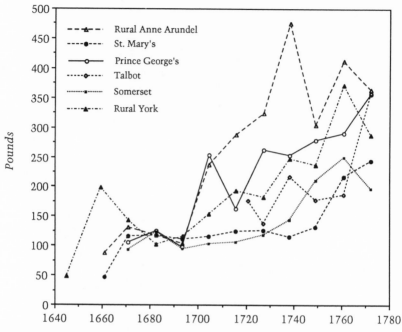

Source: St. Mary's City Commission inventory files.

Note: Points are placed at the midpoints of year groups. Data for Anne Arundel and St. Mary's counties begin in 1658 instead of 1655, hence the midpoint of the first year group is at 1661 instead of at 1659 and a half. Similarly, Talbot County data begin in 1720 instead of 1710, hence the midpoint of its first year group is 1721. Prince George's County data end in 1769, instead of 1777, hence the midpoint of its last year group is 1768 and a half.

The high for the year group 1733–1744 in Anne Arundel County is produced by 3 exceptionally large estates, 2 worth more than £7,000 and 1 more than £5,000, out of a total of 215 rural estates. The high in the same county for the year group 1755–1767 is produced by 1 estate valued at more than £12,000.

early Somerset paralleled that of other counties. Settlers invested their time in clearing land, building houses and barns, fencing fields and orchards against the predation of deer and livestock, and raising tobacco and corn. Corn was the basic food crop; tobacco was the crop sold on a European market in return for European manufactures. Until the late seventeenth century it was more cost effective to raise tobacco to pay for manufactures than to support local craftsmen or industries such as yarn spinning, weaving, or leather manufacture. Such craftsmen as there were,

were mostly carpenters and coopers needed to create shelter for people and containers for shipping the crop. Most, furthermore, were not specialists; they combined their skills with planting.[8]

It was also true everywhere, as Aubrey Land long ago showed, that major fortunes were not made just by planting and selling tobacco.[9] The men who achieved great wealth were merchants as well as planters. They bought up the crops of their neighbors and imported the manufactures their neighbors purchased. Almost any planter whose estate came to more than, say, £1,000, was a "dealer," in the words of one early Maryland governor.[10] Probate inventories of every county show huge gaps between the estates of successful merchants and those of the next richest planters. But in seventeenth- and early-eighteenth-century Somerset, the gaps were larger and the number of successful inventoried merchants proportionally smaller than in other Maryland counties.[11]

Early in the eighteenth century the economic characteristics of the tidewater Chesapeake began to change. A much greater variety of craft activities began to appear, and value in tools and materials began to

8. Gloria L. Main, *Tobacco Colony: Life in Early Maryland, 1650–1720* (Princeton, N.J., 1982), 77–78 and table II.12.

9. "Economic Base and Social Structure: The Northern Chesapeake in the Eighteenth Century," *Journal of Economic History*, XXV (1965), 639–654. See also Main, *Tobacco Colony*, 87–91.

10. Gov. John Seymour to the Board of Trade, Mar. 10, 1708/1709, William Hand Browne *et al.*, eds., *Archives of Maryland* (Baltimore, 1883–), XXV, 269, hereafter cited as *Md. Archives.*

11. Main sees rich Somerset planters as more committed to mercantile and shipping activities than those of Charles, Calvert, Anne Arundel, Baltimore, or Kent counties (*Tobacco Colony*, 89 and table II.17). But of the 96 estates in her six-county inventory file, 1658–1719, with £600 or more in capital assets, only 5 were in Somerset. The following table, made from the St. Mary's City Commission inventory files, shows the disparity in percentages of total inventoried decedents between the very rich and those who were poorer in the five counties, 1658–1722, studied here.

	Less than £226		£226–£999		£1,000+	
	No.	%	No.	%	No.	%
Somerset	715	91.2	58	7.4	10	1.3
Anne Arundel	627	79.7	129	16.4	31	3.9
Prince George's	364	86.3	42	10.0	17	4.0
St. Mary's	933	88.1	110	10.4	16	1.5
York	350	81.7	72	16.8	7	1.6

FIGURE 2. *Mean Diversification Scores for Craft, Six Counties, 1655–1777*

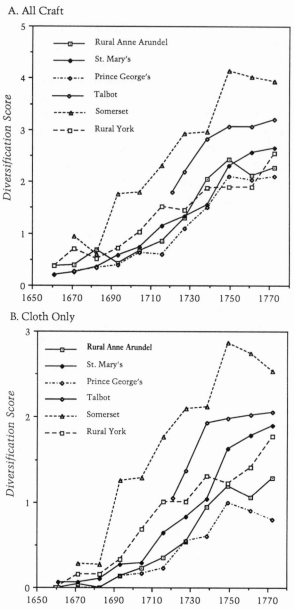

A. All Craft

B. Cloth Only

Source: St. Mary's City Commission inventory files.

Note: This index shows the increase over time in the kinds of tools and materials per inventoried estate that indicate craft activity. For each time period, the total number of kinds of increase (see table 2, below, and figure 2).[12] Four kinds of underlying changes were at work. First was a thirty-year stagnation in the tobacco industry that began in the 1680s. Until that time it had been a new and expanding industry, characterized by falling prices but rising production such as has occurred today in the calculator industry. Tobacco in the 1620s, or a hand calculator in the early 1970s, was a high-priced luxury product with a small market. Increased production in response to high profits drove prices down, but markets expanded as prices fell. Expanding markets encouraged finding ways to increase efficiency to make profits possible at lower prices. Such a process eventually ends when increased efficiencies no longer are possible. In the Chesapeake by the 1680s the major efficiencies had been achieved. They occurred largely in increases in crop production per hand that lowered labor costs and in decreases in freight rates for shipping through improved packing into hogsheads. Prices, therefore, could fall no further. Prices, production, and markets then stabilized and the industry ceased to grow.[13] Tobacco prices fell low enough to finally make it effective to put labor into activities that supplemented imports: spinning yarn, weaving cloth, and making leather and metal products.

Second, even without the pressure from low tobacco prices, crafts and also new crops began to appear because planters and their families had more available time. As land was cleared and housing and fencing were put in place, planters took time to remove stumps from their fields, making plowing a practical possibility. With the ability to plow, planters also took time to plant grain crops, especially wheat, that added more

---

tools in all estates is divided by the number of estates, giving a mean number of tool categories per estate. Twelve categories are included: carpenter tools, cooper tools, tailoring equipment, shoemaker tools, smith tools, wool or cotton cards, spinning wheels, looms, flax hackles or breaks, candlemolds, spoonmolds, and soapmaking equipment or soap. The clothmaking index contains the cards, wheels, looms, and hackles or breaks. For further discussion, see appendix 2.

12. Main also documents this change through 1719 (*Tobacco Colony*, table II.12). See appendix 2, below, for a discussion of table 2 and the diversification index in figure 2. Carville V. Earle, *The Evolution of a Tidewater Settlement System: All Hallow's Parish, Maryland, 1650–1783* (Chicago, 1975), 103–113, pioneered in the use of a diversification index, but used a much more complex system than the one developed here. See also comments on Earle's work in n. 44, below.

13. Russell R. Menard, "The Tobacco Industry in the Chesapeake Colonies, 1617–1730: An Interpretation," *Research in Economic History*, V (1980), 109–177, esp. 142–155.

variety to their diet. These crops not only encouraged plowing and harrowing but also required carts for moving the grain from the field to the barn. Plows and carts required traces, cart bodies, and wheels and meant work for blacksmiths and woodworkers.[14] Tobacco, by contrast, required only hoes and provided less encouragement for crafts.

Third, as the population became predominantly native-born and sex ratios evened out, women were no longer in short supply.[15] Until this occurred the shortage of women had discouraged much development of home industry. Now, women spun yarn and knitted it, made butter and cheese, salted down meat, and helped make cider and beer.[16] Women not only could make things that otherwise would be paid for with tobacco but also could produce salable surpluses of products that generally improved the standard of living.

Finally, a native-born population produced both more and larger families than had the immigrant predecessors.[17] Parents wanted to provide for children's welfare with greater variety of food and with clothing and shoes made at home or nearby if tobacco to buy such goods from abroad was insufficient. Equally or more important, from age eight the labor of a child could be sufficient to support him or her and made a further contribution to time for diversified activity.[18] On plantations where slaves began to produce families, the number of slave children was significant.[19]

14. Main also documents these changes (*Tobacco Colony*, 76–78 and tables II.11, II.12, II.13). Carville Earle and Ronald Hoffman first suggested the connection between crop bases and craft activities in "Staple Crops and Urban Development in the Eighteenth-Century South," *Perspectives in American History*, X (1976), 5–78.

15. Russell R. Menard, "Immigrants and Their Increase: The Process of Population Growth in Early Colonial Maryland," in Aubrey C. Land, Lois Green Carr, and Edward C. Papenfuse, eds., *Law, Society, and Politics in Early Maryland* (Baltimore, 1977), 98–99.

16. Any of the 16th- or 17th-century handbooks of housewifery make this clear. See, for example, Gervaise Markham, *Country Contentments . . . The English Housewife: Containing the Inward and Outward Vertues Which Ought to Be in a Compleate Woman: as Her Phisicke, Cookery, Banqueting-Stuffe, Distillation, Perfumes, Wooll, Hemp, Flaxe, Dairies, Brewing, Baking, and All Other Things Belonging to an Household* (London, 1615; reprinted New York, 1973).

17. Menard, "Immigrants and Their Increase," in Land, Carr, and Papenfuse, eds., *Law, Society, and Politics*, 88–110.

18. This estimate is based on Fogel and Engerman's finding that net earnings of male slaves in the Old South about 1850 were positive beginning at age eight. Robert William Fogel and Stanley L. Engerman, *Time on the Cross: The Economics of American Negro Slavery*, 2 vols. (Boston, 1974), I, 74.

19. See Russell R. Menard, "The Maryland Slave Population, 1658 to 1730: A

Slave children, once grown, would not leave the household unless sold or given away, and thus constituted a permanent labor force. In households wealthy enough to have slaves, more diversification was possible.

More time, more women, and larger families, both free and slave, probably affected the use of labor time sooner in some places than in others, depending on when settlement had begun. However, the depression in tobacco prices created pressure for import supplement and new sources of income throughout the economy. By 1720 inventories in every area showed increases in value of craft tools and materials.

Import supplement appeared earlier in Somerset County than elsewhere. Here Scottish and Scotch-Irish settlers had brought skills as weavers, with results that were evident by the 1680s. In 1688, when Maryland tobacco prices were the lowest ever over the colonial period, the Maryland Assembly sought to encourage economic diversification with acts authorizing the payment of bounties for the production of various manufactures, among them cloth. The county courts were to levy local taxes to pay these bounties.[20] The response of the Somerset court was to seek permission from the Council to declare the act null and void in the county, where families were already producing enough cloth to make such bounties a heavy burden.[21] This is probably the earliest act of nullification of a law in American history.

Diversification into craft and other manufacturing activity was clearly of great economic importance throughout the Chesapeake over the long period of hard times in the tobacco industry. The population and the number of working hands continued to grow but not the production of tobacco.[22] Labor was put to additional uses, and these new activities supplied sufficient income to prevent a drop in property accumulation.

Demographic Profile of Blacks in Four Counties," *William and Mary Quarterly*, 3d Ser., XXXII (1975), 29–54.

20. *Md. Archives*, XIII, 220–222. For sterling tobacco prices at the farm through 1730, see Menard, "Tobacco Industry," *Research Econ. Hist.*, V (1980), 157–161. We believe that the series published for 1711–1755 in U.S. Bureau of the Census, *Historical Statistics of the United States: Colonial Times to 1970*, 2 vols. (Washington, D.C., 1975), I, 1198, undervalues tobacco to about 1750.

21. Lois Green Carr, "County Government in Maryland, 1689–1709" (Ph.D. diss., Harvard University, 1968), text p. 465; Somerset County Judicial Record, 1687–1689, fol. 103. All manuscript materials cited are at the Maryland State Archives, Annapolis, unless otherwise noted.

22. The figures are compiled in Menard, "Tobacco Industry," *Research Econ. Hist.*, V (1980), 157–161. See also Gloria Main, "Maryland and the Chesapeake Economy, 1670–1720," in Land, Carr, and Papenfuse, eds., *Law, Society, and Politics*, 134–135.

Somerset experienced a slight decline, but otherwise the average value of estates leveled out or even rose (see figure 1).

The tobacco industry began to expand once more with rising prices in the second decade of the eighteenth century.[23] Demand for tobacco in Europe increased, helped along by two developments. First, the French government licensed a monopoly that bought up and then sold a very large part of the Chesapeake tobacco crop and provided an efficient marketing system in Europe.[24] Second, a growing taste for snuff created new demand.[25] Consequently the price of tobacco in the Chesapeake began a rise that continued—with fluctuations common to any staple crop—across the whole colonial period.[26]

Every part of Maryland responded to rising tobacco prices with an increase in the production of tobacco and in the proportion of planters who raised it (see tables 2 and 3).[27] Nevertheless, differences among localities emerged that were clearly based on differing soil resources and perhaps distances from markets. Some areas studied stayed tightly tied to tobacco, whereas others began to diversify into supplementary crops for export. St. Mary's County on the lower Western Shore relied more heavily than any other place on exports of tobacco alone.[28] By contrast,

23. Menard, "Tobacco Industry," *Research Econ. Hist.*, V (1980), 154–155.

24. Jacob M. Price, *France and the Chesapeake: A History of the French Tobacco Monopoly, 1674–1791, and of Its Relationship to the British and American Tobacco Trades*, 2 vols. (Ann Arbor, Mich., 1973), I, *passim*.

25. *Ibid.*, 266.

26. On tobacco prices at the farm, see figure 3.

27. York County, Virginia, does not show this pattern. In rural York the mean value of inventoried tobacco dropped steadily from the 1720s and across every wealth group. Yet the number and value of slaves rose and the price of land increased at least somewhat (unpublished research from St. Mary's City Commission inventory files and the Colonial Williamsburg York County Project). Clearly, tobacco crop was not as systematically inventoried in York as it was in the Maryland counties, and the same may be true for corn. Lorena S. Walsh has recently established from plantation account books figures for production per hand of tobacco that indicate much higher levels of production in York than the inventories indicate. Tables 2 and 3 do show increases in mean value of, and participation in, growing corn, which fit with Walsh's findings.

28. Table 3 shows a decline in the proportion of St. Mary's County planters who had an inventoried tobacco crop after 1744. This is undoubtedly the result of a drastic decline in the proportion of accounted estates in St. Mary's that began in the 1740s. Tobacco crop usually appeared in the administration accounts of estates on the lower

Talbot on the upper Eastern Shore began to move into corn and especially wheat. Somerset County on the lower Eastern Shore and Anne Arundel and Prince George's counties on the lower Western Shore did not grow much wheat but began to produce large quantities of corn (see table 2). The changes took place in response to new opportunities. Markets for wheat expanded vigorously at midcentury with crop failures in southern Europe and relaxation of British regulations that otherwise would have prevented direct shipment to these markets. And there was an increasing need for corn in the British West Indies, which imported much of their food in order to concentrate on raising sugar.[29]

The shift to new crops had significant differential effects on planters' investments and by-employments. While diversification into crafts began well before changes in crop bases had achieved importance, increases in value of inventoried craft tools and materials continued longer and attained higher levels where grain and corn became important export crops (see tables 2 and 3). Like wheat, when grown for market corn encouraged crafts, since it too required carts and wagons for transport, although plows would not be required for preparing the ground. In St. Mary's and York counties, where crop diversification was smallest, value in crafts grew much more slowly than elsewhere and attained much lower levels per estate. In Talbot, where wheat and corn crops were large, craft value was very high. However, the crop base cannot have been the only element affecting crafts. Planters of Prince George's County, a corn-producing area, resembled those of St. Mary's in level of overall value of craft-related assets and showed the lowest participation in craft activity found

---

Western Shore. Before 1740, 80 to 90% of St. Mary's County estates were accounted. By the 1770s, only half were. This fact also lowers the mean value of crop shown in table 2, since all estates, whether or not they have crop, are included. In coding tobacco crop on the lower Western Shore, every effort was made to exclude tobacco that was not crop. This procedure proved impossible on the Eastern Shore, hence Talbot and Somerset crops are probably somewhat exaggerated. On York County, see n. 27, above.

29. Paul G. E. Clemens, *The Atlantic Economy and Colonial Maryland's Eastern Shore: From Tobacco to Grain* (Ithaca, N.Y., 1980), 174–179; David C. Klingaman, "The Significance of Grain in the Development of the Tobacco Colonies," *Jour. Econ. Hist.*, XXIX (1969), 268–278. Raw prices of corn and wheat rose abruptly in the mid-1730s. These price changes undoubtedly affected planter decisions, but do not account for the increased mean value of these crops as seen in the tables. Values in the tables are deflated into constant pounds.

TABLE 2. *Mean Value of Inventoried Export Crops and Craft Tools and Materials, Six Counties, 1658–1777*

	Tobacco						Corn					
	Somer-set	Rural Anne Arundel	Tal-bot	St. Mary's	Prince George's	Rural York	Somer-set	Rural Anne Arundel	Tal-bot	St. Mary's	Prince George's	Rural York
1658–1664		.44		.27		7.83		.21		NC	NC	.34
1665–1677	3.09	3.71		4.24	4.00	4.47	1.13	1.22		NC	NC	.16
1678–1687	2.33	6.70		1.32	7.17	6.19	.58	1.15		NC	NC	.34
1688–1699	1.90	10.56		2.63	5.07	6.68	.25	1.31		NC	NC	.10
1700–1709	3.03	13.62	10.72[b]	4.36	11.34	5.52	.90	3.47	6.63[b]	.35[a]	NC	1.16
1710–1722	2.56	12.46	9.15	4.51	8.66	2.42	.88	4.85	5.05	1.65	2.38	1.59
1723–1732	2.44	12.83	16.70	7.73	10.35	2.40	1.74	5.27	6.09	2.05	6.61	1.24
1733–1744	3.09	20.61	13.38	7.44	13.29	3.00	2.45	10.95	5.14	1.78	7.98	1.55
1745–1754	3.67	13.17	7.01	6.08	13.01	2.25	4.71	6.48	6.52	1.53	7.75	2.24
1755–1767	3.85	10.47	11.24	9.71	16.57	.81	5.94	8.56	7.90	3.28	9.13	3.64
1768–1777	4.36	10.44		8.87	25.13[c]		5.88	7.91		3.53	10.80[c]	4.27

	Wheat						Craft					
1658–1664		.00		NC	NC	.00		.25		.26		.45
1665–1677	.25	.31		NC	NC	.19	1.21	.71		.34	.84	1.48
1678–1687	1.04	.28		NC	NC	.05	1.08	1.19		.28	1.40	.40
1688–1699	.12	.28		NC	NC	.02	1.60	.68		1.04	.58	.40
1700–1709	.21	.43		.01[a]	NC	.09	1.63	1.30		1.47	1.50	1.29
1710–1722	.18	.58	1.39[b]	.25	.21	.17	2.04	1.64	1.85[b]	1.49	.82	1.74
1723–1732	.16	.75	.80	.27	.53[d]	.16	2.74	2.36	2.67	1.39	1.82[d]	1.45
1733–1744	.24	1.12	1.56	.19	*	.26	3.10	3.35	2.89	.59	NC	2.20
1745–1754	.44	.84	1.58	.24	*	.10	4.41	2.44	3.19	1.72	1.30	2.23
1755–1767	.48	1.46	6.16	.42	*	.27	3.90	2.89	3.05	1.93	1.28	2.15
1768–1777	.62	1.78	8.94	1.31	*[c]	.84	2.93	3.15	4.09	1.92	2.07[c]	2.58

Source: St. Mary's City Commission inventory files.

Note: From 1745 through 1777 in Prince George's County only craft tools were coded. Craft materials and products, which were included in the coding of the other counties, were excluded, and consequently the values are a lower bound. However, table 5 shows that participation was low compared to other areas, so mean value was probably lower also.

NC = not coded.

* Included in corn.

[a]1706–1709.

[b]1720–1722.

[c]1768–1769.

[d]1723–1729.

TABLE 3 . *Proportion of Estates with Export Crops and Craft Tools and Materials, Six Counties, 1658–1777*

	Somerset					Rural Anne Arundel					Talbot				
	No.	To-bacco %	Corn %	Wheat %	Craft %	No.	To-bacco %	Corn %	Wheat %	Craft %	No.	To-bacco %	Corn %	Wheat %	Craft %
1658–1664						8	12.5	12.5	0	37.5					
1665–1677	18	27.8	33.3	16.7	77.8	103	31.1	31.1	11.7	68.9					
1678–1687	48	18.8	12.5	14.6	64.6	100	40.0	36.0	18.0	73.0					
1688–1699	139	11.5	10.1	7.9	77.7	157	45.9	28.0	8.9	58.6					
1700–1709	208	25.0	18.3	8.9	74.5	163	52.8	41.1	14.7	63.8					
1710–1722	386	38.3	25.1	8.5	81.9	199	53.8	45.7	20.6	59.3	76[a]	72.4[a]	59.2[a]	32.9[a]	72.4[a]
1723–1732	237	40.9	37.1	12.2	85.2	115	64.3	58.3	26.1	75.7	194	70.1	68.0	44.8	84.5
1733–1744	329	52.0	48.0	21.3	84.8	215	66.0	67.9	34.9	81.4	251	80.1	78.1	53.0	92.0
1745–1754	195	46.2	70.8	36.9	95.4	167	55.7	64.7	39.5	88.6	172	82.0	73.8	58.1	94.2
1755–1767	261	40.6	68.6	33.0	94.6	251	46.2	56.6	34.7	86.5	124	54.5	71.0	67.7	90.3
1768–1777	261	41.1	71.3	42.5	93.5	181	44.8	68.0	37.6	82.3	88	58.0	63.6	59.1	89.1

	St. Mary's					Prince George's					Rural York				
1658–1664	35	8.6	22.9	0	48.6						19	31.6	36.8	0	31.6
1665–1677	183	29.0	30.6	6.0	42.5	18	27.8	27.8	0	55.6	38	27.5	10.5	10.5	57.9
1678–1687	143	59.4	22.4	8.4	51.0	29	37.9	31.0	3.4	62.1	51	26.7	11.8	3.9	56.9
1688–1699	179	20.1	16.8	6.1	52.5	77	37.7	23.4	22.4	53.2	60	15.1	6.7	3.3	55.0
1700–1709	160	27.6	10.3	1.5	59.4	76	43.4	34.2	22.4	57.9	73	24.4	20.5	2.7	61.6
1710–1722	359	39.0	20.8	7.2	65.5	222	45.9	38.2	15.3	55.8	164	19.3	17.7	8.5	72.6
1723–1732	241	53.9	23.0	12.0	73.0	174	46.0	57.0	21.7	68.8[b]	88	17.1	17.0	11.4	67.0
1733–1744	361	62.0	18.0	7.0	75.9	282	53.5	49.0	36.6	NC[c]	123	17.5	20.3	10.6	77.2
1745–1754	301	47.5	27.0	14.0	85.4	181	57.5	49.2	29.3	60.8	120	14.4	25.0	12.5	74.2
1755–1767	367	43.1	33.0	16.0	83.7	216	47.7	50.0	30.6	59.3	124	6.0	37.1	17.7	76.6
1768–1777	255	39.5	36.0	22.0	86.7	39[d]	53.8[d]	61.5[d]	38.5[d]	66.7[d]	84		44.0	25.0	88.1

Source: St. Mary's City Commission inventory files.

NC = not coded.

[a] 1720–1722.

[b] 1723–1729.

[c] 1730–1744.

[d] 1768–1769.

in any county studied. By contrast, planters of Anne Arundel and parts of Somerset, also heavily dependent on corn as a secondary crop, showed much larger value per estate in craft and higher overall participation.[30]

The reason for the difference probably lies in varying corn cultivation practices. Evidently Prince George's County planters hoed rather than plowed their corn land and depended less than other planters on carts.[31] The proportion of estates in this county containing such equipment, especially plows, was lower than in the other Maryland counties, although not as low as in York.[32] Unfortunately, in the absence of breakdowns of value by craft the proposition cannot be fully tested. Fewer carts and plows should accompany lower mean value in carpenter and blacksmith tools, but whether this was the effect remains to be seen. For the moment it can be said only that where corn was the main secondary crop it could, but did not necessarily, encourage crafts.

Tobacco, wheat, and corn were the chief products grown for export, but other agricultural products began to appear that must have provided a network of local exchange and improved the standard of living. Over the eighteenth century, beans, peas, oats, buckwheat, barley, and rye appeared in inventories everywhere, although in small amounts. When they were traded it must have been in a local market.[33] Beans and peas were especially important, since when added to a diet of corn they provided a balanced nutrition. Lumber products—plank, staves, shingles—and preserved meat also began to be inventoried.[34] At first these, too, were

---

30. Prince George's developed comparatively high participation in some crafts, particularly carpentry and shoemaking, but from the 1740s the proportion of estates with no craft investment was the largest of any county, as indicated in table 3. Tables to show participation by craft in each county can be obtained from the author.

31. I am indebted to Lorena S. Walsh for suggesting this point.

32. In the 1720s, for example, estates in rural Anne Arundel County were nearly four times as likely to have a plow and twice as likely to have a cart as those of Prince George's. Over time this difference diminished, especially with respect to carts. After 1755, Anne Arundel rural estates were only 18% more likely than those of Prince George's to have plows and 9% more likely to have carts. Increase in value of craft in Prince George's did not accompany the increase in percentage of estates with plows and carts until 1768–1769, when mean value of craft-related assets rose 63% over what it had been since 1745 (see tables 2 and 3). These two years may not represent a long-run change.

33. By the 1770s, mean value of these small grains ranged from £.22 in St. Mary's to £1.47 in rural Anne Arundel. Appearance in inventories had risen from under 10% in the 1670s to 40–55%. St. Mary's City Commission inventory files.

34. By the 1770s, mean value of preserved meat ranged from £1.14 in rural York to £4.97 in Talbot; lumber ranged from £.04 in rural York to £1.40 in Talbot. For meat

probably mostly for home use, but the gradual increase of their appearance in inventories suggests an increase in local exchange. When lumber was cut and animals were butchered only as needed, the chances of either appearing in an inventory were much less than when quantities were being prepared for sale.

Cider was another product that may have contributed to local exchange.[35] Orchards were planted on most estates early on—the terms of any lease required this—but trees started from seeds required care for survival and making cider took time. In seventeenth-century Somerset twenty years elapsed after settlement before planters' estates began to show much evidence of cider production for more than immediate use, usually in the form of casks for storage rather than cider itself. Before 1700 value in cider was everywhere small and appeared in less than 10 percent of estates. However, as with meat and lumber, the value of cider-related assets per estate began to rise in the early eighteenth century and the percentage of estates participating increased. Wills as well as inventories suggest that some eighteenth-century planters of Somerset County were particularly conscious of the value of their fruit. They devised interests in their orchards and stills, and their inventories often included fruit brandy.[36]

A closer look at Somerset County provides an illustration of the importance of soils and location in guiding planter choices. During the stagnation of the tobacco industry, Somerset tobacco prices fell much lower than elsewhere and did not achieve parity with those of other areas until the 1730s (see figure 3). The consequence might have been a county-wide withdrawal from tobacco, followed by a return to production when prices had sufficiently improved. Instead, economic patterns tied to variations in resources divided Somerset into at least two, and probably three, major areas, each with its own behavior. These areas on the whole fol-

---

products, participation rose from 0–11% in the 1670s to 40–65%, except in rural York, which reached only 21%. For lumber products participation increased only slightly, from 4–8% in the 1680s to 11–16%, except again in rural York, where it never exceeded 3.3%. Values for these products were coded only if there was at least £1 worth in an inventory. Values were not coded in St. Mary's and Prince George's. Tables showing these data can be obtained from the author.

35. By the 1770s, mean value of cider-related assets ranged from £.24 in rural York to £1.66 in rural Anne Arundel. Participation rose from 6% or less in the 1670s to 22–40%, except in York, where it never exceeded 16%. Values were coded only if an inventory had at least £1 worth. Values were not coded in St. Mary's and Prince George's. Tables showing these data can be obtained from the author.

36. See n. 43, below.

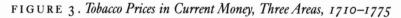

FIGURE 3. *Tobacco Prices in Current Money, Three Areas, 1710–1775*

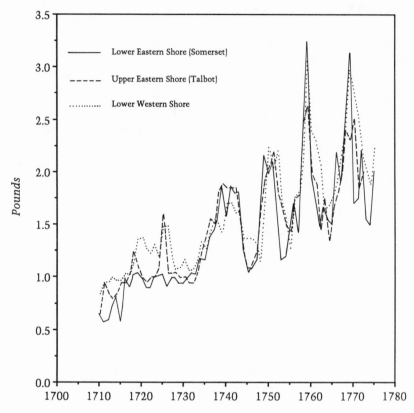

low the boundaries of the present Somerset, Wicomico, and Worcester counties.[37]

Most of present Somerset County—Annamessex, Manokin, and Monie hundreds, which run along Chesapeake Bay—continued production of tobacco throughout the period of low prices. In the 1740s the value of tobacco per estate increased following a region-wide improvement in prices. By the 1760s and 1770s the mean value of the tobacco crop here was as great as in most other tobacco-producing regions, and by then corn was a cash crop of almost equal value. From the mid-1740s,

37. A fourth area, called Pocomoke Hundred, is not discussed here. This was a small area along Pocomoke Bay and the west side of the Pocomoke River. Half fell into Worcester County at its creation in 1742. The investment patterns of the area resemble those of Wicomico in some respects but Somerset in others. I finally decided not to unite the Pocomoke decedents with those of any of the other three

FIGURE 4. *Mean Total Estate Value, Three Areas of Somerset County,*
1665–1777

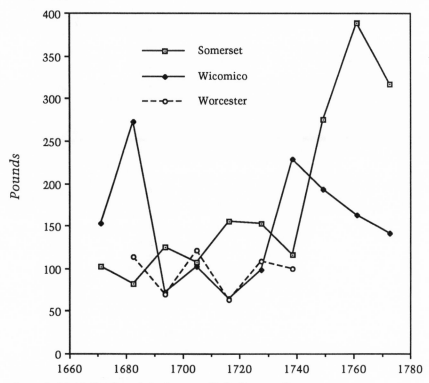

Source: St. Mary's City Commission inventory file for Somerset County.

Note: Points are at midpoints of year groups (see figure 1).

furthermore, the Somerset area had much the largest stocks of craft-related assets in the county, a fact probably connected at least in part to the increase in corn production.[38] Dating from this same time, the area was the richest part of the county (see table 4 and figures 3 and 4).

---

areas. Discussion of the area as a separate unit is omitted because of its small population of inventoried decedents and its mixed character.

38. In the absence of breakdowns by type of craft for the value of craft tools and materials this proposition cannot yet be fully tested. However, the Somerset area had more estates, proportionately, with plows and carts than did the other lower Eastern Shore areas and more with blacksmith and carpenter tools. At the same time, estates with spinning and weaving equipment were not proportionately more numerous. This suggests that the greater mean value of craft in the Somerset area was in carpenter and blacksmith tools and materials that carts and plows would encourage. Tables showing these data can be obtained from the author.

TABLE 4. *Diversification in Three Regions of Somerset County, 1665–1777*

A. Mean Value of Exported Crops and Craft Tools and Materials

	Tobacco			Corn			Craft		
	Somerset[a]	Wicomico[b]	Worcester[c]	Somerset	Wicomico	Worcester	Somerset	Wicomico	Worcester
1665–1677	.60	17.96	1.95	.57	3.61	.29	1.14	1.46	0.00
1678–1687	3.24	5.43	0.00	1.42	0.00	.32	2.18	.54	.72
1688–1699	5.76	.65	.54	.69	.20	.07	1.68	1.09	2.12
1700–1709	4.56	1.86	4.02	1.26	1.86	.48	1.47	1.55	2.22
1710–1722	3.52	1.89	1.98	1.22	1.31	.48	2.65	1.64	1.78
1723–1732	3.84	1.91	1.90	1.30	2.47	1.01	3.22	2.69	1.94
1733–1744	4.09	3.01	1.65	2.61	3.43	1.17	2.71	3.72	2.61
1745–1754	7.97	1.36		6.90	3.89		5.83	3.76	
1755–1767	7.73	1.88		7.54	5.25		8.94	3.45	
1768–1777	9.55	1.98		8.55	4.60		3.69	2.35	

B. Proportion of Estates Showing Export Crops and Craft Tools and Materials

	Somerset				Wicomico				Worcester			
	No.	Tobacco %	Corn %	Craft %	No.	Tobacco %	Corn %	Craft %	No.	Tobacco %	Corn %	Craft %
1665–1677	11	10.1	10.1	81.8	2	50.0	50.0	100.0	1	100.0	100.0	0
1678–1687	16	37.5	18.7	87.5	11	27.3	0	36.6	15	0	13.3	66.7
1688–1699	39	17.9	12.8	74.3	18	16.7	11.1	83.3	53	11.3	11.3	84.9
1700–1709	48	22.9	16.7	75.0	45	26.7	24.4	77.7	69	23.3	17.4	78.3
1710–1722	110	45.4	18.2	78.2	80	37.5	32.5	83.7	134	35.1	26.9	82.8
1723–1732	61	41.0	34.4	90.2	84	35.7	44.0	90.5	62	43.5	25.8	71.0
1733–1744	98	57.1	54.1	84.7	99	52.5	53.5	92.9	82	42.7	25.6	76.8
1745–1754	65	69.2	69.2	98.5	109	32.1	73.4	95.4				
1755–1767	78	52.6	69.2	92.3	142	30.3	68.3	94.4				
1768–1777	78	53.8	66.7	92.3	149	32.9	69.1	92.6				

Source: St. Mary's City Commission inventory file for Somerset County.

Note: Figures for the Pocomoke area are omitted from this table. In value of tobacco production per estate Pocomoke exceeded the Wicomico area, but did not share in Somerset's great rise after 1750. In value of corn production and stocks of craft equipment per estate Pocomoke most resembled the Wicomico area. See n. 37, above.

[a]The Somerset area as defined in this table excludes the portions of the Pocomoke area that fall into the present Somerset County at its southeastern end.

[b]The Wicomico area as defined in this table includes all of the present Wicomico County, which was established out of Somerset and Worcester counties in 1867. However, in 1742 nearly half of the Wicomico area became part of the newly created Worcester County. Most of the good tobacco land remained on the Somerset County side. Otherwise soils were similar with respect to productivity in the two parts of the Wicomico area (see table 5). Note that an increase in the proportion of good tobacco land in the Wicomico area after 1742 did not result in an increase in the proportion of tobacco producers or in the mean value of tobacco per estate.

[c]The Worcester area as defined in this table excludes the portions of the Pocomoke area and the Wicomico area that fell into Worcester County at its creation.

TABLE 5. *Soils of Colonial Somerset County*

	Total Land Suitable %	High Yield %	Medium Yield %	Low Yield %	High Quality %	High Yield, High Quality %
			Tobacco			
Present Somerset[a]	16.8	15.5	1.3	0.0	4.5	4.3
Present Somerset, colonial period	39.6	15.5	24.1	0.0	4.5	4.3
Present Wicomico[b]	37.8	19.7	18.1	0.0	14.8	2.5
Present Wicomico, colonial period	19.7	19.7	0.0	0.0	2.7	2.7
Present Worcester[a]	32.8	30.0	2.8	0.0	16.5	16.5
			Corn			
Present Somerset[a]	62.8	10.9	51.8	0.1		
Present Somerset, colonial period[b]	88.8	33.7	29.0	26.1		
Present Wicomico[b]	90.1	0.0	35.0	55.1		
Present Wicomico, colonial period	90.1	0.0	53.0	37.1		
Present Worcester[a]	90.6	43.2	40.9	6.5		
			Barley			
Present Somerset[a]	64.9	17.7	47.2	0.0		
Present Wicomico[b]	78.0	47.3	30.7	0.0		
Present Worcester[a]	81.1	39.3	41.8	0.0		
		Land in Tidal Marsh, Swamp, Beach, or Muck				
Present Somerset[a]	28.4					
Present Wicomico[b]	8.1					
Present Worcester[a]	12.4					

Sources: See source note for table 1.

Note: See table 1 for explanation of omitted soils. In present Somerset County, 26.0% of the land is tidal marsh. In the colonial period, much of this land may have been Othello silt loam

This wealth at first comes as a surprise. Table 5 shows that today the area's soil resources are far and away the poorest of the three subregions. This poverty must be the result of the rising water table, which over time has increased the poor drainage.[39] Most of present Somerset is now covered in loblolly pine; in the colonial period, perhaps with the help of ditches, planters created productive fields of tobacco and corn. In addition, woodlands of hard timber as well as pine may have provided a less dreary landscape than we see today.

In present Wicomico County—Wicomico and Nanticoke hundreds—which runs well into the interior along the Wicomico and Nanticoke rivers, about 20 percent of the soils are droughty and today require irrigation for good yields. Another 11 percent are somewhat droughty. Here, after the 1680s value of tobacco per estate never reached more than one-half of that in the Somerset area and participation of planters in growing the weed was seldom as high. Value in tobacco dropped steeply in the late 1680s and 1690s, although it did not disappear, and then rose with improvement in prices, but this process ended in the 1730s. Corn by

---

usable for corn, but probably with low yields. In present Somerset 22.8% is usable Othello silt loam, but earlier this now very low area may have been higher, much better drained, and perhaps with shallow ditching, capable of high yields of corn and medium yields of tobacco, although the tobacco would have been of low quality (see text and n. 6, above). The data for colonial Somerset assume Othello silt loam for the tidal marsh and relatively well drained Othello where poorly drained Othello now prevails. The resulting productivity estimates are of course an upper bound. The data for colonial Wicomico tobacco yields exclude soils capable today of producing medium yields—Evesboro, Galestown, and Klej—but that require irrigation, which was not practiced in the colonial period. For the corn data, these soils have been moved from medium to low production. Present-day Somerset and Worcester counties include the Pocomoke area excluded from table 4. We do not know the exact boundaries of Pocomoke. In Somerset it ran along Pocomoke Sound, beginning near Marumsco Creek, up the Pocomoke River to Dividing Creek, and then some unknown distance up Dividing Creek. It probably constituted about one-sixth of present Somerset County. This land was mostly tidal marsh or muck and Othello silt loam, very like the county overall. In Worcester the Pocomoke part was probably the land between Dividing Creek and the Pocomoke River about up to the present Wicomico County boundary. This constitutes about one-fifth of present Worcester County. The land is somewhat wetter overall than is the rest of Worcester County. For the productivity of the Pocomoke area in the colonial period, see the note to table 4. No tobacco is now grown in the three-county area. Estimates of productivity are made from those supplied for lower Western Shore soils of the same classification.

[a]Includes land in colonial Pocomoke area.

[b]Includes land that became part of Worcester County in 1742.

39. See text and n. 6, above.

that time was a cash crop and began to surpass tobacco in value.[40] However, after the late 1740s Wicomico did not produce as much corn per estate as did the Somerset area. Nor was craft per estate as large, or mean inventoried wealth as high (see table 4 and figure 4).

The area that became most of Worcester County, between the swamps of the Pocomoke River and the beaches of the Atlantic Ocean, can be followed only until 1742, but at that time it was developing differently from both the other sections. From the 1690s the value of tobacco per estate followed the Wicomico pattern, leaving production for the region primarily to Somerset area planters, but corn did not become an export crop. Neither the mean value of corn, nor the proportion of planters who raised it, came close to the figures for Wicomico. At the same time, there is little indication that Worcester planters were putting other resources to work more intensively than were their neighbors. Much of Worcester County has good land for pasture, but value of livestock per estate was not higher here than in the other two areas and there was less evidence of meat production. Nor did Worcester area planters show more signs of lumber or fruit production, and mean value in craft was not superior.[41] In 1742, the Worcester area was chiefly distinguished from the rest of Somerset by its failure to develop a substantial export crop, but this difference had a major consequence. Without a crop that paid for im-

40. Droughty soils are Evesboro (9.3%), Galestown (2.8%), and Klej (5.9%); somewhat droughty is Matawan (10.7%). Soils of more than 15% slope are omitted. For determination of what was a cash crop, see appendix 2.

41. In the Worcester area, mean value in livestock fluctuated between £25 and £39; in Somerset before 1745, between £25 and £38; in Wicomico before 1745 between £23 and £42. In all three areas most estates had animals. Mean values of meat in Worcester ranged from £.85 to £2.04, but the proportion of estates that showed it (value of meat worth less than £1 was not coded) never exceeded 15%. In the Somerset area before 1745, mean values of meat ranged from £.78 to £2.75, and in Wicomico from £.39 to £2.73, except that a single estate with £77 worth of meat out of 11 inventoried between 1678 and 1687 pushed the mean for that period to £7.12. Participation of estates in both areas much exceeded that of the Worcester side of the county, reaching a third or more in the period 1733–1744. After 1744, Somerset area planters began to exploit meat resources more fully, but Wicomico area planters did not follow suit. In none of the three areas were mean values of stocks of lumber or cider-related equipment exceptional, but there was somewhat more in the Somerset area than elsewhere. Diversification scores, which show the variety of activity, did not vary much among the three areas. Tables showing the data can be obtained from the author. On land resources for pasture in the three-county area, see the soil surveys noted in the sources for table 1.

ports, the area must have been more heavily dependent than other parts of the county on local crafts and home industries to supply planters' needs (see table 4).

Were Worcester area inhabitants poorer than their neighbors? Somerset area planters were certainly richer, but from the 1690s, mean total estate value of Wicomico and Worcester planters was similar until the very last period of Worcester history as part of the county (see figure 4). Perhaps Wicomico planters did not begin to benefit from their turn to corn until its production reached the level obtained by the 1730s. Or perhaps until then, crafts and home industry in the Worcester area maintained income and hence accumulation of wealth at the level established in Wicomico. In the absence of information about the later history of Worcester, it can be said only that the movement of Wicomico area planters into corn brought them benefits.

Location rather than soil resources seems to have directed the economy of the Worcester area. In present-day Worcester County 43 percent of tillable land can produce high yields of corn, as opposed to 36 percent in Somerset (assuming that all the present-day Othello silt loam was then well enough drained to produce high yields) and none in Wicomico, where many soils are droughty. In addition, 30 percent of Worcester's land is of a type that can grow high yields of tobacco, half again as much as in Wicomico and twice as much as in Somerset (see table 5). Why, then, was Worcester area production of tobacco and corn no greater? The reason probably lies in Worcester's relative distance from markets. Because of marshes, Snow Hill, well up the Pocomoke River, was the only landing easily accessible to shipping on the west side of the Worcester area. On the ocean side there was no anchorage for ships unless they could make their way inside the barrier islands. Some preliminary investigation of Worcester County inventories, 1752–1761, indicates that while tobacco continued to play a minor role, by the 1750s corn was taking on greater importance than earlier. Shallop men from New Castle and Philadelphia, who collected corn and wheat from planters further up the Delmarva Peninsula, probably by then were coming this far south.[42]

42. On the shallop men, see David E. Dauer, "Colonial Philadelphia's Intraregional Transportation System: An Overview," Regional Economic History Research Center, *Working Papers*, II, no. 3 (1979), 1–16. Some estimates of value of corn per estate in Worcester County for these years, made in connection with another study, show a greater than fourfold increase over the value from 1733 through 1742, which

Regardless of variations in resources, men in all areas of Somerset County had to make the most of everything they had in order to gain a living. Wills as well as inventories reveal this. Systematic studies of wills in a number of Maryland and Virginia counties reveal that very few testators made the complex arrangements for use of marshland, pasture, orchards, and equipment that often appear in Somerset wills. For example, William McClemmey of Manokin at his death in 1750 left his oldest son, Whitty, the dwelling plantation, including the marsh and the orchard. Whitty also received the still and worm. But his younger brother William, who got the rest of the land, also inherited the right to use the still to make sixty gallons of brandy each year, provided he did not remove the still without Whitty's permission. In 1759 Stephen Horsey of Manokin left land to his son Revell, but required him to allow his brother Stephen the privilege of pasturing twelve head of cattle in the marsh. Henry Newman of Monie gave land to two sons while bequeathing privileges to cut timber on these lands to a third. His widow and two of the sons were to share the still. Even a man as wealthy as Isaac Handy of Pemberton in Wicomico made a point of giving his marsh, valuable for its pasture, to all his sons jointly. A man's orchard was usually part of his dwelling plantation, but planters sometimes ruled in their wills that several children should share in the produce.[43] While values in cider, cider casks, and stills were not higher in Somerset than elsewhere, wills suggest that income from fruit may have been more important here than in other counties studied.

Historians have argued that diversification of agricultural products and crafts represented increased self-sufficiency for individual plantations,

---

brings the figure to the level found in the Wicomico area of Somerset, 1755–1767. Worcester incorporated part of Wicomico and Pocomoke hundreds. However, the number of families that were shifted into Worcester County was too small to have been the sole cause of the increase.

43. Wills, XXVII, 513, XXXI, 405, 942, XXXIX, 847. Between 1760 and 1769, of 109 fathers who left wills, 20, or 22%, provided for shared use of pasture, woodlots, or equipment. An additional 42, or 38% more, showed special recognition of land use, noting orchards, marshes, and timber, or made elaborate arrangements for division of equipment. I have not found these concerns dominating the wills of St. Mary's and York counties, where I have made detailed studies. In St. Mary's County in the 1730s, for example, only 1 out of 77 fathers' wills ordered shared use of anything, and none mentioned an orchard or a marsh. Jean B. Russo, Allan Kulikoff, Nancy Baker, and Gail Terry have studied the wills of Talbot, Prince George's, Anne Arundel, and Baltimore counties, respectively, and have informed me that they do not find a noticeable proportion of wills showing these concerns.

but more important was the local exchange created.[44] In every county studied, few planters had all the craft tools necessary for self-sufficiency. Of particular craft tools, only those related to spinning yarn and thread appeared in a majority of inventoried estates, except that in Talbot and Prince George's, by the 1770s, 56 and 64 percent, respectively, had tools for carpentry. Clearly, most families had to turn to others in their communities for a variety of locally offered goods and services. Spinning, indeed, required exchanges with neighbors, since weaving was far less prevalent.[45] Spinners of woolen yarn may have knitted some or all of their product, but linen and cotton thread necessarily went to the weaver. Perhaps the weaver paid the spinner in cloth, but he or she also had a surplus of cloth to sell.[46]

This local exchange brought increased stability to an economy tied to staple export crops, especially tobacco. Bad weather and the violent price fluctuations that characterized tobacco were less devastating to eighteenth-century Chesapeake inhabitants than such hazards had been in the seventeenth century. Planters could make clothing or shoes or obtain income from selling such items to neighbors, who could pay with other services. The complaints of the naked condition of planters heard during the depressions of the seventeenth or early eighteenth century are not

44. Carville Earle, especially, ties increases in diversification to a desire for plantation self-sufficiency (*Tidewater Settlement System*, 103–113). See also John J. McCusker and Russell R. Menard, *The Economy of British America, 1607–1789* (Chapel Hill, N.C., 1985), 126–127, and Allan Kulikoff, *Tobacco and Slaves: The Development of Southern Cultures in the Chesapeake, 1680–1800* (Chapel Hill, N.C., 1986), 101–104.

45. By the 1750s, the percentage of inventories with spinning wheels was fluctuating around 50% in York, Anne Arundel, and Prince George's counties, around 70% in St. Mary's and Talbot, and 80 to 90% in Somerset. But everywhere, except in Somerset, looms appeared in less than 20% of inventoried households. In Somerset this figure was 50%. For a detailed analysis of the self-sufficiency versus local exchange argument and a demonstration of local exchange networks, see Jean B. Russo, "Self-sufficiency and Local Exchange: Free Craftsmen in the Rural Chesapeake Economy," in this volume. Bettye Hobbs Pruitt, "Self-sufficiency and the Agricultural Economy of Eighteenth-Century Massachusetts," *WMQ*, 3d Ser., XLI (1984), 333–364, demonstrates local exchange networks for Massachusetts.

46. For a good example, see Somerset Judicial Record, 1692–1693, fol. 205. In March 1692, John Rowell, cordwainer, sued Hope Taylor, weaver, for 12 yards of cloth. Rowell's wife had supplied Taylor with the yarn and promised to pay for the weaving with one pair of shoes or one bushel of salt. Rowell had taken the shoes to Taylor and found that Taylor had made the cloth and sold it. I am indebted to Jean B. Russo for this reference.

repeated in the 1730s or after. The more complex the network of exchanges became, the less dependent a planter was on tobacco or grain as his only source of income and the better able he was to maintain or improve his standard of living.

What kinds of planters were diversifying? Did poor men stretch meager incomes from tobacco with income earned from other activities? Or was it the rich, with the means to invest in equipment and more time to spare, who led the way? The answer is that it was the rich who diversified soonest and achieved the highest levels. Everywhere poor men—those with less than £50 of movable wealth at death—diversified least and most slowly (see figure 5). Such men often did not own land, although among those inventoried in Somerset, landowners were well represented.[47] Planters at this level had the least surpluses of farm products and were the most dependent on tobacco for purchase of necessities, even in Somerset County. Diversification came soonest and was most visible in estates worth £226 or more. Planters at this wealth level owned both land and slaves. They moved soonest and most heavily both into new crops and into crafts, especially those like blacksmithing or tanning, which might serve a large neighborhood.[48]

A comparison of two inventories, one from the early eighteenth century and one from the 1760s, will show how these changes progressed in Somerset County. George Gale, an immigrant from a merchant family of Whitehaven in Cumberland County, near the Scottish border, died in 1712 with an estate of more than £3,300.[49] Most of this was in debts receivable, cash money—an astounding £850—and several ship cargoes. He owned a sloop, a half share in another, a shallop, and a share of the *Cumberland*, a ship of two hundred tons in the Whitehaven trade. George Gale's mercantile business was the largest inventoried on the lower Eastern Shore before mid-eighteenth century. As a planter he was somewhat diversified. He had a plow and harrow and a cart, indications that tobacco

47. In Somerset County, especially, very few tenant farmers went through probate.

48. The proportion of estates with blacksmith or tanning equipment was small in all areas and in all wealth groups. Over the 18th century, in estates worth less than £50, the maximum proportion showing signs of these activities was 6%; in estates worth more than £226, the maximum was 26%, but 10 to 20% was more usual. Although figure 5 shows diversification by wealth only for Somerset County, the pattern was the same everywhere.

49. Inventories and Accounts, XXXIV, 131; records for the port of Carlisle, Whitehaven Creek, tobacco imports, December 1711–December 1712, E190/1450/17, Searcher, Public Record Office.

FIGURE 5. *Mean Total Diversification Scores by Wealth, Somerset County, 1665–1777*

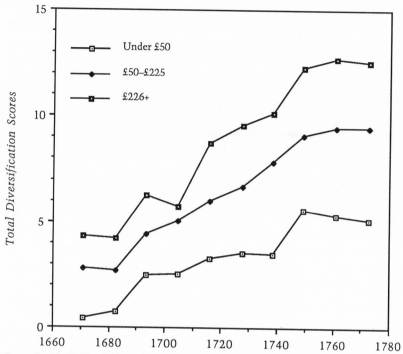

Source: St. Mary's City Commission inventory file for Somerset County.

Note: This index shows the increase over time in all indicators used for evidence of diversification in agricultural and craft activity. For each time period, the total number of indicators in all estates is divided by the number of estates, giving a mean number of indicators. The indicators are listed in appendix 2.

Points are at midpoints of year groups (see figure 1).

and corn were probably not his only field crops, although only corn appears in the inventory. He raised sheep for wool. He had cider casks and a small still. He had lots of wood plank and two pairs of wooden screws, which suggest a construction operation of some kind, perhaps shipbuilding. His wife spun yarn, and Gale's inventory includes two pounds of linen.

In 1762 Isaac Handy, also a merchant, left us signs of a much more diversified agriculture and craft operation, although he was a far less wealthy man.[50] The family ship, called the *George*, was owned by his son

50. Inventories, LXXXI, 303; Wills, XXXI, 942.

George, who was its captain and traded to Bermuda and the West Indies. Handy had three yokes of oxen and one hundred pounds of plow and harrow iron—probably at least twice what Gale had had. Since the inventory was made in July, no surplus of corn appears, but ten bushels of oats are listed. He had twice as many sheep as Gale and evidently grew flax and cotton for their fibers. Overall his investment in home industry was much greater than Gale's. He had a wheel for spinning wool and two wheels for spinning linen, hackles for preparing flax, forty-three pounds of washed wool ready for carding, thirty pounds of hackled flax ready for spinning, thirty pounds of tow, and ten pounds of cotton. There was, furthermore, a loom and tackle for weaving the yarn. In addition, shoe-maker's tools and quantities of leather indicate a shoemaking operation. Finally, a large still—worth £10 as opposed to Gale's £2 still—and one hundred gallons of cider indicate that in Handy's household considerable time went into orchard products, some of which were probably sold. Gale's inventory shows the beginnings of plantation diversification; Handy's shows its great advance.

While the rich diversified first and most intensively, poorer planters eventually did so too, and especially in Somerset. For example, by the 1740s inventoried estates of Somerset householders worth less than £50 usually contained spinning equipment. However, even in Somerset, weaving at this wealth level was not as common an activity.[51] As elsewhere, poor men—or rather their wives and daughters—spun yarn for richer households to weave. Poor men's shoes were also often made on richer men's plantations, doubtless in exchange for cattle hides; plows and carts, when small planters had them, were kept in repair in the same way. Nevertheless, over time more poor and middling planters acquired the tools necessary to enter into activities that might contribute income beyond the sale of crops. The more time the poor had for activities beyond the production of tobacco, the denser became the network of local exchange and the broader the opportunities for improving one's economic condition.

Did the extent of diversification determine differences in mean inventoried wealth from area to area in the Chesapeake region? The answer

51. From the 1740s, 60 to 80% of Somerset County estates worth less than £50 had spinning wheels, depending upon the time period, but only 30 to 40% had looms worth at least £1. In the other five counties in estates at this wealth level 30 to 60% had spinning wheels, but none of the five showed more than 17% of estates with looms worth £1 or more in any time period.

so far is, not in any simple way. Where soil resources, as in Talbot, encouraged the development of new export crops that provided hedges against lows in the tobacco industry, agricultural diversification may have brought greater wealth than appeared in areas like St. Mary's that stayed tied more exclusively to tobacco (see figure 1).[52] On the other hand, strong diversification into nonagricultural activities in Somerset did not enable it to outstrip the other areas. Nevertheless, the experience of Somerset illustrates the importance of diversification in improving on available resources. Had planters there relied primarily on tobacco exports, they would have accumulated less property and suffered a lower standard of living.

What quality of life did the resulting economy support? Over the eighteenth century it allowed most free Chesapeake inhabitants to participate in changes taking place throughout the north Atlantic world, changes that were making life more comfortable and, for some, more luxurious than in earlier times. Those changes came first and most dramatically among the very rich. Recent research demonstrates that in seventeenth-century Chesapeake households wealthy people had more material comforts than their poorer neighbors had, but the life-style of the wealthy was not otherwise much different.[53] A poor man might do without chairs and sit on stools, chests, or overturned casks. A rich man might have many chairs, but his chairs would not be elegant works of craftsmanship made from rare mahogany. A poor man might pass a mug or pewter tankard from hand to hand; a rich man's tankard might be fashioned from silver, but he would not necessarily see the need for

52. Unfortunately, the evidence before us is ambiguous. Only if the reporting rates of Talbot and St. Mary's are similar after 1750 did Talbot clearly outstrip St. Mary's in mean wealth by the 1770s. See appendix 2.

53. Barbara Carson and Cary Carson, "Styles and Standards of Living in Southern Maryland, 1670–1752" (paper presented at the annual meeting of the Southern Historical Association, Atlanta, Ga., 1976); Lois Green Carr and Lorena S. Walsh, "Changing Life Styles in Colonial St. Mary's County," Regional Econ. Hist. Research Center, *Working Papers*, I, no. 3 (1978), 72–118; Carr and Walsh, "Inventories and the Analysis of Wealth," *Hist. Methods*, XIII (1980), 83-96; Lorena S. Walsh, "Urban Amenities and Rural Sufficiency: Living Standards and Consumer Behavior in the Colonial Chesapeake, 1643–1777," *Jour. Econ. Hist.*, XLIII (1983), 109–117; Cary Carson and Lorena S. Walsh, "The Material Life of the Early American Housewife," *Winterthur Portfolio* (forthcoming); Lois Green Carr and Lorena S. Walsh, "Changing Life Styles and Consumer Behavior in the Colonial Chesapeake," in Cary Carson, Ronald Hoffman, and Peter J. Albert, eds., *Of Consuming Interests: The Style of Life in the Eighteenth Century* (Charlottesville, Va., forthcoming).

individual drinking vessels. Elegance and ceremony did not begin to appear until the eighteenth century, and as these became characteristic of life at the top they marked a different way of living and using objects that set apart those who participated from those who did not.

Again, the households of George Gale in 1713 and Isaac Handy in 1762 illustrate the change. Gale's more than £3,300 put him in the top .3 percent of inventoried Somerset wealth holders both in the early eighteenth century and over the whole colonial period. Isaac Handy, with a fifth as much inventoried property, still ranked in the top 6 percent of inventoried wealth holders who died in Somerset in the third quarter of the eighteenth century and in the top 3 percent of those who died inventoried in the Wicomico area.[54] Among the living population his position must have been even more exceptional.

Gale owned a comfortably furnished house with plenty of beds and chairs, pictures and maps for decoration, and £28 worth of silver plate to show his wealth and gentility. But there was little sign of elegance, except for drinking glasses and six knives and forks, both unusual items. Individual forks for eating were a very recent development even in England, and only a handful of estates in all of Maryland had them in the early eighteenth century. By contrast, Handy's style of living indicates much more elegance and attention to ceremony, especially the ceremony of drinking tea. He owned a tea table and a teakettle, along with silver teaspoons, silver sugar tongs, and a silver tea strainer. He could also offer coffee. Fine china in a china closet undoubtedly included a teapot and cups. The china closet itself offered an opportunity for elegant display of the china and glassware within. Anyone invited to Handy's house would know that here there was leisure for ceremony and training in the manners to practice it, as well as the wealth to provide the equipment.

These differences were not tied to great differences in investment in consumption. The value of Isaac Handy's accumulation of consumption as opposed to capital goods was about one-third less than that of Gale's. It is the evident uses of consumption for display and the message carried to others of what gentility required that make Handy's inventory an indication of social change. These changes were occurring in England as well as in the Chesapeake, but they occurred later in the colonies. An early-eighteenth-century woman like Madam Betty Gale, who had high social and economic status in the Chesapeake, was too occupied with keeping

54. These values are in constant pounds. Undeflated the value of Gale's estate was £3,387 and Handy's, £963.

the family plantation running to begin developing the habits that her English counterparts had already established. Although her husband owned six adult slaves, only two were women, and they were valued as full working hands. At least one, if not both, probably did field work. All the Gale children, furthermore, were young. On Mrs. Handy's plantation there were eight adult hands, of whom half were women, two of them old. By this time the slave population was becoming native-born with more-even sex ratios and broader ranges in age distribution. Older slaves could be spared from field work for household tasks, and the two older women may have helped in the house. In addition, Mrs. Handy had an unmarried daughter of age to be of assistance. Consequently there was time for ceremony as well as social pressure to encourage it.

Such changes were not confined to the wealthy. In eighteenth-century Chesapeake society what we might call amenities, as opposed to expensive and leisure-consuming luxuries, began to appear at all wealth levels, although, of course, sooner and more visibly among the rich than among the poor. Somerset County participated fully in these developments. Figure 6 uses a twelve-item index to show the progress of three wealth groups in acquiring amenities. The index consists of coarse earthenware and bed or table linen for convenience and sanitation; table knives, forks, and fine earthenware for refinements in convenience and for increasing elegance at the table; spices for variety in diet (using signs of spice, such as pepperboxes, as well as stocks of spices themselves); religious and secular books for education and some use of leisure time; and wigs, watches or clocks, pictures, and silver plate for signs of luxury and display. Even the poorest group shows a major increase in mean scores beginning about 1710. Over the eighteenth century to the Revolution, these households were acquiring coarse earthenware, linens, table knives and forks, and religious books as they approached a score of four. The middle group added good ceramics and spices as these planters reached and exceeded a mean score of five. At this stage refinements in dining were of growing importance. Only the rich went in much for luxuries, although silver plate began to penetrate the households of middling planters. But tea and tea ware—not included in the index—had reached every group by the 1770s. A third of the poor and more than half of the middle were indulging in this form of inessential expenditure.[55]

On the whole, Somerset mirrored the consumer behavior found in

---

55. See Carr and Walsh, "Changing Life Styles," in Carson, Hoffman, and Albert, eds., *Of Consuming Interests*.

FIGURE 6. *Mean Amenities Scores, Somerset County, Overall and by Wealth, 1665–1777*

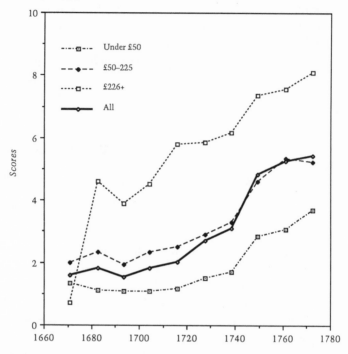

Source: St. Mary's City Commission inventory file for Somerset County.

Note: Points are at midpoints of year groups (see figure 1).

other Chesapeake counties examined. Nevertheless, there were some differences that appear tied to special characteristics of the area. Somerset planters had a penchant for books that was probably the result of the sizable Quaker and Presbyterian elements in the population. Both these religions encouraged reading the Bible. Less surprising was the appearance of bed and table linens both sooner than in the other counties and in a larger proportion of poor and middling estates. The comparatively early and permanent advance over other regions in clothmaking seems a likely explanation.[56]

56. For comparative information on books and linens, see *ibid*. On religious groups in Somerset, see Torrence, *Old Somerset, passim*. Just what proportion of the population was Quaker or Presbyterian is unknown, but there is no doubt that Somerset County (and Worcester County after its establishment) was the main location of Presbyterians in Maryland, although there was also an early congregation in Charles

Certainly in Somerset and undoubtedly throughout the Chesapeake, economic diversification contributed to the rising standard of amenities. Diversification strengthened the economy, making it less dependent on fluctuations of the tobacco industry. And even small amounts of additional income from local exchange—home industries carried on by women, for example—could encourage expenditures on amenities. In addition, some goods, such as linens, could be used at home as well as sold in a local market. Clearly the eighteenth-century economy of the Chesapeake region, even in poorly endowed localities, supported an improving quality of life for almost all of the white population.

The eighteenth century, then, saw region-wide changes in the tidewater Chesapeake as virgin forest gave way to farms and as a predominantly native-born population brought more-equal sex ratios, more families, and larger numbers of children per family, including slave families. In early stages of development more people per family meant more people to cooperate in making the most of available resources. Stagnation in the tobacco industry late in the seventeenth century gave a major push to import supplement, which these demographic changes further encouraged, and new export crops, where they appeared, tended to support a variety of craftsmen. By the 1770s even places like St. Mary's County, which remained closely tied to tobacco exports, had greatly expanded networks of local exchange.

Somerset County, Maryland, is an especially interesting place to look closely at these developments because planters had to work with inferior agricultural soils. Here, diversified activities that extracted the most possible from the resources available were essential to maintaining a standard of living similar to that attainable in places where more land was

---

County and a later one in Prince George's County. See Lois Green Carr and David William Jordan, *Maryland's Revolution of Government, 1689–1692* (Ithaca, N.Y., 1974), 34. The Philadelphia synod established a presbytery at Snow Hill (Worcester County area) in 1716; this later was absorbed into various Pennsylvania (now Delaware) presbyteries. There are references to at least four Somerset County congregations that probably maintained a continuous existence over the colonial period. At least two, one at Snow Hill and one in Manokin, are still in existence. Single congregations appeared in Dorchester, Kent, and Queen Anne's counties in the 1750s. *Records of the Presbyterian Church in the United States of America, 1706–1788* (Philadelphia, 1841), 23–25, 45–46, 172, 184, 288, 310, and appendix VI, table 4; Harry Pringle Ford, *History of the Manokin Presbyterian Church, Princess Anne, Maryland* (Philadelphia, 1910), 1–19, 34–35; J. William McIlvain, *Early Presbyterianism in Maryland* (Baltimore, 1890), 7–13. For clothmaking, see n. 45, above.

suitable for export crops. Diversification enabled Somerset inhabitants to share the improving standard of comfort and the development of a genteel life-style that characterized the eighteenth century. Such adaptations resulted in a distinctive mix of economic activities while allowing Somerset to participate in the broad changes that occurred in the Chesapeake region, and indeed, throughout the north Atlantic world.

APPENDIX 1. *Reporting Rates*

Tests for discovering when and how decedent inventory reporting rates changed within a county are essential to inventory analysis. If reporting rates did not change, shifts that inventories show in the distribution of wealth and its components indicate such shifts in the wealth of the living population, although one still will not know the actual size of economic groups among the living. If changes in reporting occurred, one must determine which kinds of estates were dropping in or out before trying to interpret what inventories reveal. Two tests have proved useful. Comparison of numbers of inventories with numbers of taxables, making allowances for slaves, generally shows a similar pattern over time in the counties examined for this project, although short-term variations can be severe. In addition, P. M. G. Harris has found that in Anne Arundel, St. Mary's, Charles, Prince George's, and Somerset counties and in parts of these counties, servants appeared in inventories and free immigrants and native-born appeared among decedents in patterns that fit predicted growth curves.[1] Together these findings suggest that in these places reporting rates over the long run varied little. Large changes, at least, in the distribution of wealth can be trusted. However, in Somerset there is some evidence that reporting rates dropped in the Worcester area in the 1720s and in Manokin Hundred of the Somerset area in the early 1750s. Luckily a set of tax lists for many of the years over 1723–1759 has permitted testing economic groups in the inventories against economic groups in the living population. The results show that the drop in reporting was across all wealth groups, not at the expense of just the poor. Adjustments for the change in reporting need not be made.

Information on population growth and composition needed for this kind of analysis is still insufficient for York and Talbot. But since the evidence from other counties indicates that on the whole the propensity of various kinds of people to be inventoried does not vary so much over time that gross changes shown in wealth cannot be accepted, I and my colleagues believe that information from inventories in these counties can also be trusted.

Knowledge of changes in reporting rates is sufficient for interpreting changes in the distribution or composition of wealth within a county, but comparison of wealth levels from county to county requires more: some knowledge of the *level* of reporting in each place. Are the decedents of one county richer than those of another, given differences in their mean total estate values, or does a difference in the level of reporting make the difference spurious? Table A1 shows information on levels of reporting at various dates for St. Mary's, Anne Arundel, Somerset, and York.

The procedures for establishing the reporting rates shown for Somerset, Anne Arundel, and St. Mary's apply age-specific mortality rates—taken from the Coale and Demeny population tables[2]—to estimated age structures of white male taxables in

1. "The Nativity, Migration, and Landowning of Anne Arundel Decedents in Comparative Perspective" (unpublished MS).

2. Ansley J. Coale and Paul Demeny, *Regional Model Life Tables and Stable Populations* (Princeton, N.J., 1966).

TABLE AI. *Inventory Reporting Rates for Four Chesapeake Counties by Selected Time Periods: Male Decedents*

A.
Somerset County

	Estimated Deaths per Year	Inventories Dates	No.	Decedents Inventoried per Year	% Decedents Inventoried
1671	3.5	1671–1674	2	.50	14.3
1675	8.7	1675–1677	8	2.67	30.7
1704	27.2	1703–1706	83	20.75	76.3
1710–1712	33.6	1710–1712	48	16.00	47.6
1733	44.7	1733–1735	116	38.67	86.5
1739	61.7	1739–1741	79	26.33	42.7
1754	38.9	1752–1754	38	12.67	32.6
1757	42.2	1755–1757	50	16.67	39.5
1759	43.3	1752–1760	127	14.11	34.0
1766	53.3	1765–1767	63	21.00	39.4

B.
York County

	Decedents in Probate	Reporting Rate of Probates	Total Decedents	No. of Inventories	% Decedents Inventoried
1670–1679	153	.47	325	42	12.9
1699–1703	76	.305	250	25	10.0
1730–1739	119	(.45)	264	97	45.3
1750–1759	135	.45	300	112	37.3
1770–1776	90	(.45)	218	70	32.1

TABLE AI. *(continued)*

C.
Anne Arundel County

	Estimated Deaths per Year	Inventories Dates	No.	Decedents Inventoried per Year	% Decedents Inventoried
1667	8.97	1665–1668	13	3.25	36
1671–1675	11.97	1669–1675	58	8.29	69
1694–1696	20.63	1693–1696	35	8.75	42
1700–1704	22.81	1700–1704	96	19.20	84
1710–1712	23.95	1710–1712	33	11.00	46
1733	27.54	1733–1735	83	27.70	100
1755	31.72	1755–1757	56	18.70	59
1782	32.10	1781–1783	51	17.00	53

D.
Four Counties Compared

St. Mary's Dates	% Inv.	Anne Arundel Dates	% Inv.	Somerset Dates	% Inv.	York Dates	% Inv.
1670–1679	80	1669–1675	69	1671–1674	14	1670–1679	13
				1675–1677	31		
1700–1712	80	1700–1704	84	1703–1706	77	1699–1703	10
		1710–1712	46	1710–1712	34		
1730–1739	80	1733–1735	100	1733–1735	86	1730–1739	45
1750–1759	65	1755–1757	59	1752–1760	34	1750–1759	37
1770–1776	65	1781–1783	53	1765–1767	39	1770–1776	32

order to produce estimated white male deaths at the times for which information on white taxables is available. (White taxables were white men aged sixteen and above.) The number of estimated deaths can then be compared with the number of inventories. In St. Mary's County, Russell R. Menard found that estimated deaths and the number of inventories suggested 100 percent reporting until a drop of about 15 percent appeared in the 1740s.[3] Since the reporting rate was surely not 100 percent, I have lowered the rate to 80 percent, with a drop to 65 percent. In evaluating the results for Somerset and Anne Arundel, one needs to be aware that death crises in the early eighteenth century and in 1733 produced exceptionally high numbers of inventories but that the procedures for estimating deaths could not take these crises into account. High reporting rates for these dates are the consequence and should be ignored. The results then suggest that the eighteenth-century level of reporting in Anne Arundel County ranged from 40 to 60 percent of male adult decedents and in Somerset from 30 to 40 percent.

The York County estimates are based on information supplied by Kevin Kelly of the Colonial Williamsburg Foundation. Parish burial records supply male deaths for selected periods, which can be compared to all references to decedents in probate over the same years. This produces a reporting rate for male probates from which estimates of the total number of male decedents for a decade or so can be made. Unfortunately, in Virginia entering probate did not always produce an inventory, as it did in Maryland, so that the reporting rate for inventories is lower than that for probates. Since information from burials for the eighteenth century is confined to dates at the beginning and in the middle, I have applied the midcentury reporting rate for all probates to the 1730s and the 1770s. The results suggest a possible drop in the reporting rate for inventories, but the method is too crude to justify such a conclusion. If in the 1730s the rate for 1700 is applied instead of that for 1750, the inventory reporting rate is 25 percent instead of 45 percent. The chief results obtained from this exercise are twofold: the inventory reporting rate for the seventeenth century is so low that great care must be used in interpreting information from these inventories; the reporting level for the eighteenth century probably was close to that for Somerset.

Jean B. Russo has estimated that in Talbot County the level of reporting was close to 60 percent over the years to 1760. Her method was to count every reference or inference for an adult male death that she found in any record and compare these to the number of inventoried males.[4] The result probably exaggerates the reporting rate, but the rate was probably considerably higher than in Somerset and York, perhaps about 50 percent.

No reliable estimates have yet been developed for Prince George's County. However, a comparison I once attempted for reporting rates for all Maryland counties in the 1750s put the Prince George's County rate somewhat below that of Somerset County.

3. "The Comprehensiveness of Probate Inventories in St. Mary's County, Maryland, 1658 to 1777: A Preliminary Report," MS, St. Mary's City Commission, Annapolis, Md., 1976.

4. Personal communication.

APPENDIX 2. *Problems in Interpretation of the Data*

The data for this paper come from the St. Mary's City Commission computer inventory files. For the Talbot file, SMCC had the use of Paul G. E. Clemens's card file on inventories, which saved us time in coding. For Prince George's from 1730, Allan Kulikoff generously made his own computer inventory file available. We are grateful to both scholars for this assistance. In general Kulikoff followed SMCC procedure, but there are occasional differences.

Several problems arise in interpreting the tables that show the appearance or values of agricultural products. First, the month of the year in which the inventory was taken affected the amount and therefore the values of inventoried agricultural products. Should certain crops tend to appear only in inventories taken in a few specific months, and should the distribution of appraisals by month of the year change markedly over time or vary widely from one area to another, one could not draw reliable comparative information on changes in crop mixes from the inventories (at least not without some elaborate weighting procedure to control for differing seasonal distributions). Since I and my colleagues became aware of this potential problem only recently, we have not coded for month of the year everywhere, but we do have such coding for Anne Arundel and York counties and for Somerset in selected periods. Jean Russo supplied month of the year for Talbot and Gloria Main lent us her monthly counts to 1720 from her six counties added together (Charles, Calvert, Anne Arundel, Baltimore, Kent, and Somerset). Month of appraisal did not average out over time as we hoped, but the seasonal pattern was generally the same in every area beginning about 1700. Since in these four different areas and in Main's counts patterns were similar, we see no reason to suppose that there were drastic variations in the areas not coded for month. We also believe that gross changes inferred from differing crop mixes found in inventories across time and between regions are not grossly distorted by seasonality in inventories.

Another problem arises in considering the meaning of Indian corn found in inventories. Since corn was a basic part of the Chesapeake diet, it surely was always on hand in a household, but clearly it was not always inventoried. Did appraisers set aside some for the use of the family, and if so, was the practice consistent or did it vary from place to place? Table 3 shows that the proportion of estates containing corn was under 40 percent everywhere in the seventeenth century and increased everywhere across the eighteenth century, reaching two-thirds or more of estates in Talbot and Somerset, but remaining little more than one-third in St. Mary's. Given this pattern and the absence of information about appraisal practices, I have adopted the following rule: any area that is showing more value per estate in corn than St. Mary's is producing a corn surplus. The comments on corn as a paying crop in this paper are based upon this rule. St. Mary's County probably did in fact produce some corn for export, at least by the 1750s. I have accounts for a store on the St. Mary's town lands in the late 1750s that were kept in corn and wheat as well as tobacco. But neither corn nor wheat—and especially not wheat—had the importance in St. Mary's that they developed elsewhere.

The diversification scores shown in figures 2 and 5 and described in the notes to these figures deserve further explication. The total index contains 27 indicators for nonagricultural and agricultural diversification. They are arranged as follows:

Agriculture: Total 15

tools	*crops*	*livestock*	*other*
plows	corn	sheep	seines
sickles or scythes	winter grains	poultry	cider casks
carts	spring grains	bees	stills
wheat fans	legumes		
	flax or hemp		
Total: 4	Total: 5	Total: 3	Total: 3

Craft: Total 12

clothmaking	*tools*	*other household industry*
cards	carpenter	candle molds
spinning wheels	cooper	spoon molds
looms	blacksmith	soapmaking utensils
hackles or breaks	tailor	
	shoemaker	
Total: 4	Total: 5	Total: 3

There are a few discrepancies. In seventeenth-century St. Mary's and Prince George's counties seines and wheat fans and the category *other household industry* were not coded, but also did not appear to speak of in dead men's estates. The difference creates no distortion. A somewhat greater problem arises in Prince George's County, 1730–1769. Here there are only 9 agricultural and 8 nonagricultural indicators for a total of 17. However, some of the missing items contribute very little to the indexes of the other counties. Within the craft index, the only index presented here for all the counties, these are the items in the *other household industry* category. In other lower Western Shore counties, furthermore, hackles and breaks were very rare and their absence in the Prince George's County craft index probably counts for little. The craft index as shown for Prince George's is not much affected.

The diversification index offers many opportunities for analysis not attempted here and raises many questions not asked or answered. Much of it is not presented. Many problems must be faced. The index needs careful coordination with the evidence from the value of craft investment, which unfortunately was not coded by craft. For example, low scores for the presence of craft tools may indicate specialization, not small craft investment. Nevertheless, I believe that the index offers a measure of the density of local exchange and gives additional clues to differences in the economies of various areas.

<table>
<tr><td>Jean B.
Russo</td><td>

Self-sufficiency
and Local Exchange

Free Craftsmen in the Rural

Chesapeake Economy
</td></tr>
</table>

THE STUDY of free craftsmen does not occupy a prominent place in the historiography of southern plantation economies. When colonial Chesapeake historians take note of independent artisans, it is usually to observe how unsuitable the society was to their prospects for success. From Eugene McCormac in 1904 to Gloria Main in 1982, historians have seen the plantation system as inimical to the interests of free craftsmen. Scholars identify two related factors as primarily responsible for the limited opportunities afforded independent craft workers: efforts by individual planters to achieve a measure of self-sufficiency in their operations, and their concomitant reliance upon skilled bound labor to meet that goal.[1] This scholarship asserts that planters strove to create autarkic plantations that would offer some protection against the vagaries of the tobacco market.[2] When tobacco prices fell, the planter who could supply his own shoes or cloth or clothing needed to spend less of his reduced income on purchased goods and

1. Eugene Irving McCormac, *White Servitude in Maryland, 1634–1820* (Baltimore, 1904), 7–112; Margaret Shove Morriss, *Colonial Trade of Maryland, 1689–1715* (Baltimore, 1914); Victor S. Clark, *History of Manufactures in the United States*, vol. I, *1607–1860*, rev. ed. (Washington, D.C., 1929); U.S. Bureau of Labor Statistics, *History of Wages in the United States from Colonial Times to 1928* (Washington, D.C., 1929); Marcus Wilson Jernegan, *Laboring and Dependent Classes in Colonial America, 1607–1783* (Chicago, 1931); Richard B. Morris, *Government and Labor in Early America* (New York, 1946); Carl Bridenbaugh, *The Colonial Craftsman* (New York, 1950); Edmund S. Morgan, *Virginians at Home: Family Life in the Eighteenth Century* (Williamsburg, Va., 1952); Gerald W. Mullin, *Flight and Rebellion: Slave Resistance in Eighteenth-Century Virginia* (New York, 1972); Carville V. Earle, *The Evolution of a Tidewater Settlement System: All Hallow's Parish, Maryland, 1650–1783* (Chicago, 1975); Gloria L. Main, *Tobacco Colony: Life in Early Maryland, 1650–1720* (Princeton, N.J., 1982).

2. Earle, *Tidewater Settlement System*, 101–131; Mullin, *Flight and Rebellion*, 19, 32–33; Main, *Tobacco Colony*, 164.

services than did the planter who had to rely upon others for such items. By their attempts to "live in a kind of Independence on every one but Providence," these planters created the plantations described as "a complete society in miniature, containing within [themselves] almost all the trades and professions necessary for a civilized life."[3]

On closer inspection, two different lines of argument relate the search for self-sufficiency to the declining fortunes of free artisans. Some historians have reasoned that the movement toward self-sufficiency severely restricted the supply of free craftsmen. As planters voluntarily developed self-sufficient plantations, reliance upon the skills of free workers declined, with plantation workers taking over their functions. Lewis C. Gray, for example, argued that "gradually . . . slaves acquired the necessary skill to displace both indentured servants and white artisans." At the same time, it is argued, the association of skilled labor with black slaves accelerated a natural movement away from manufacturing to planting. Artisans either abandoned their callings in favor of agriculture or moved elsewhere in search of a more suitable environment in which to continue as craftsmen.[4]

Other historians see the process in reverse, with plantation owners forced (rather than choosing) to become self-sufficient in order to compensate for a scarcity of free skilled labor. Artisans abandoned their trades for planting not because of competition from slaves but because of the lack of concentrated demand, the failure of the region to provide central markets, and the inevitable lure of readily available land. Carl Bridenbaugh found that "in Virginia and Maryland, prospects of a quick cash crop and easily acquired land lured free workers into tobacco culture. Nearly every artisan . . . at the end of his service, also set up as a farmer." Planters, as a result, necessarily had to depend upon bound workers, purchased or trained as skilled artisans, to satisfy the plantation's requirements for the services of carpenters, coopers, blacksmiths, and the like. In sum, as Richard B. Morris argued, "failing to maintain an adequate number of white artisans, the Southern colonies then trained Negro slaves for the skilled trades."[5]

3. Mullin, *Flight and Rebellion*, vii, 10–12; Morgan, *Virginians at Home*, 52.

4. Lewis C. Gray, *History of Agriculture in the Southern United States to 1860* (Washington, D.C., 1933), I, 500. Bridenbaugh also argues for "the gradual but relentless replacement of white by Negro labor." Bridenbaugh, *Colonial Craftsman*, 15.

5. See, for example, Jernegan, *Laboring and Dependent Classes*, 7–10, and David W. Galenson, "White Servitude and the Growth of Black Slavery in Colonial America,"

Taking different courses, both groups of historians arrive at the same conclusions. Within the plantation a skilled labor force produced the necessary craft products and services while at the same time the number of free craftsmen in the population was sharply curtailed. They both see the Chesapeake region developing an economic system based upon self-sufficient plantations, with skilled workers supplying the craft services that independent artisans provided in a nonplantation economy. According to Marcus Jernegan, "it is hard to see how the eighteenth-century plantation could have survived if the negro slave had not made his important contributions as an artisan, in the building and other trades." For Gerald Mullin, ordinary planters "often required services . . . that were provided by either the large planters' slave-artisans or an occasional itinerant white craftsman." Carville Earle and Ronald Hoffman describe a society in which small planters performed their own routine craft and repair work, relying for specialized aid again upon itinerants or upon their "roughly-skilled" neighbors. The few dissenting views place the source of craft work not in skilled slaves or itinerants but in continued use of indentured servants. None of the portrayals grants a major role to local craftsmen firmly tied to their rural communities.[6]

This essay tests the validity of such a depiction of the rural Chesapeake by studying the free craftsmen working during a seventy-year period in one Chesapeake county. Talbot County, located midway along the Chesapeake Bay on Maryland's Eastern Shore, was part of a tobacco- and wheat-producing region during the colonial period. An area of approximately 200,000 acres, Talbot is almost entirely surrounded by water; a seven-and-a-half-mile land border joins the county to the mainland, while its shoreline extends for nearly five hundred miles. Four river

---

Journal of Economic History, XLI (1981), 40–41. Quotations from Bridenbaugh, *Colonial Craftsman*, 5, and Morris, *Government and Labor*, 31.

6. Jernegan, *Laboring and Dependent Classes*, 23; Mullin, *Flight and Rebellion*, 8–9; Carville Earle and Ronald Hoffman, "Staple Crops and Urban Development in the Eighteenth-Century South," *Perspectives in American History*, X (1976), 24–26. Herbert Klein, contrasting the Chesapeake with the Caribbean, argues that skilled labor was performed largely by indentured white artisans "who continued to dominate the skilled trades right through the colonial period" ("Slave Economies of Cuba and Virginia," in Allen Weinstein *et al.*, eds., *American Negro Slavery: A Reader* [New York, 1979], 123). Eugene McCormac states that "for many years the only skilled laborers in [Maryland] came as servants from England and Ireland. Manufacturing was not carried on to any great extent in Maryland till after the Revolution, but what few manufacturers there were, were servants." McCormac, *White Servitude*, 35.

systems divide the county into a series of large necks reaching out into the Bay; these necks provided plantations with the waterfront landings needed for participation in the Atlantic staple economy. Settlement in Talbot originated in the 1650s when tobacco planters moved across the Bay and began to cultivate the weed on the Eastern Shore. During the eighteenth century, wheat became an increasingly important crop for Talbot planters, as the Philadelphia milling industry reached farther and farther down the Bay for supplies of grain.[7] Although Talbot never ranked among the tidewater counties most dependent upon slave labor, slaves made up 15 percent of the population in 1704 and 29 percent by 1755.[8] To encompass the effects of both the increasing reliance upon slave labor and the increasing emphasis upon wheat as a staple crop, this study starts in 1690, at the beginning of the shift from indentured servitude to slavery as the predominant form of bound labor. The study ends by 1760, well after the addition of a staple with very different processing requirements from those of tobacco.

The analysis of Talbot's craft sector begins with an examination of the trades actually represented in the county and of the factors responsible for their presence. It then considers changes that occurred over time within the persistent craft groups, in order to explore the self-sufficiency argument directly. Use of skilled labor and ownership of craft tools reveal the potential for self-sufficiency; persistence rates for selected crafts and training provided for needy children demonstrate the areas in which self-sufficiency most affected opportunities for free craftsmen. Finally, the county is compared to other rural Anglo-American communities to determine the extent to which a plantation economy distorted the supply of free craftsmen who offered their services to its residents. This analysis indicates that the historiographical arguments outlined above, while accurate in some respects, fail to describe fully either the composition of the rural Chesapeake's craft networks or the role that indigenous craftsmen played in the local economy. Rather than following a model of self-

7. Ronald Hoffman, *A Spirit of Dissension: Economics, Politics, and the Revolution in Maryland* (Baltimore, 1973), 6, 62; Paul G. E. Clemens, *The Atlantic Economy and Colonial Maryland's Eastern Shore: From Tobacco to Grain* (Ithaca, N.Y., 1980), chap. 6.

8. Russell R. Menard, "Five Maryland Censuses, 1700 to 1712: A Note on the Quality of the Quantities," *William and Mary Quarterly*, 3d Ser., XXXVII (1980), 620; "The Population of Maryland, 1755," *Gentleman's Magazine*, XXXIV (1764), in Edward C. Papenfuse and Joseph M. Coale III, *The Hammond-Harwood House Atlas of Historical Maps of Maryland, 1608–1908* (Baltimore, 1982), 37.

sufficiency, the economy was characterized by a system of local exchange of goods and services in which craft specialists firmly rooted in the rural community played a necessary part.

DURING THE seventy years between 1690 and 1760, over eight hundred craftsmen lived in Talbot County,[9] but they found employment in only a few basic crafts (see tables 1 and 2). Carpenters alone constituted about 25 percent of all artisans. With the addition of other wood-processing craftsmen (primarily coopers and sawyers), workers in wood accounted for 50 percent of the county's total. Weavers and tailors, who

9. The analysis of Talbot's artisan population draws upon biographical data collected for all craftsmen known to have worked in the county between 1690 and 1759. Individuals selected for inclusion in the file were those identified (primarily in the Judgments and Land Records libers) by an "addition" (an appendage to the name used to indicate status or occupation) that associated them with a craft skill. A smaller group merited inclusion because disputed accounts or contracts clearly indicated their employment as craftsmen. A very few men were added on the basis of a significant collection of tools and raw materials (and no bound labor) among their assets.

The artisan population consists solely of adult free males. Bound laborers and children are excluded because I am interested in examining the ways in which free craftsmen found employment within a plantation economy, although the other groups are necessarily involved when examining the framework within which free artisans worked. I have not similarly excluded women, but the society in which they lived did. No Talbot woman defined herself or was defined as an artisan; all free women were categorized as spinsters or widows or were subsumed under their husband's identity. Women did work for wages, but that work tended to be domestic—housekeeping, washing, nursing—or field work. The women so employed were never publicly defined by that work. Furthermore, the county court specified craft training for many of the boys who came under its supervision, but it never required that girls be taught more than traditional domestic skills, that is "to sew, Spin, knitt and other House-wifery work." See Jean Burrell Russo, "Free Workers in a Plantation Economy: Talbot County, Maryland, 1690–1759" (Ph.D. diss., The Johns Hopkins University, 1983), chap. 2, for a fuller discussion of hired labor, child employment, and women's work experience.

I have included as artisans those men who were not full-time planters or professional men or merchants or tradesmen, but instead practiced a handicraft skill, in which they fabricated by hand a product—whether a building, a pair of shoes, a hat, a wig, a piece of ironware, a ginger cake, a boat, a barrel, a piece of cloth, or a suit of clothes—that they sold or bartered to a customer. Very few of the men counted as artisans, however, earned a living exclusively from craft work; at least 90% of the householders among them also planted crops and raised livestock. Finally, I have used the terms *artisan* and *craftsman* interchangeably.

supplied cloth and clothing, made up an additional 16 percent of the artisans, while leatherworkers—mostly shoemakers and tanners—added another 12 percent. Metalworkers, almost all blacksmiths, formed the only other sizable group, encompassing about 7 percent of the craftsmen. A variety of trades, from ship carpenters to glaziers, claimed a few each of the remaining 15 percent.

The presence and absence of particular trades formed a changing pattern woven of several different strands. A nucleus of trades, those best adapted to the local economy, persisted throughout. A few reflected the occupations of early immigrants and vanished as those individuals died or left the county. Some required a level of population or income that would not be satisfied until midcentury or later. Still others—most of the potential skills—never found a place in the county's economy. As specialized crafts they were unlikely prospects, needing the support of a large and wealthy urban population or a substantial external market. The rural Chesapeake economy provided neither.[10] This attenuated craft structure can be explained in three major ways.

First, some trades failed to find a secure place in the local economy because of insufficient local demand. Food-processing trades, seemingly essential to any society, are conspicuous by their absence. Only butchers and bakers, in the persons of just four men, enjoyed any presence in Talbot County. In an area with a relatively abundant supply of land, most householders owned or rented enough ground to provide their own food. The few town dwellers might have needed to purchase meat and bread, but many of them also held land outside the town. Thus, we know butcher John Williams only for his appearance as a defendant in three court cases in 1707 and 1708, while the second butcher, Abraham Pearcell, made an even more fleeting appearance in 1727, also as the defendant in a suit. Of the county's two bakers, John Price can be identified with assurance simply as the defendant in three suits in 1697 and 1700, although one case placed him in the county as early as 1694.[11]

---

10. For example, in 1747 Richard Campbell described the education, training, materials used, and skills needed for approximately 170 trades. Talbot County trades accounted for only about 15% of those pursued by London craftsmen during the same period. R[ichard] Campbell, *The London Tradesman* (Newton Abbot, Devon, 1969 [orig. publ. London, 1747]).

11. For Williams, Judgments, RF 11, 3/07 and 6/08 courts; for Pearcell, Judgments, #9101, 3/27 court; and for Price, Judgments, AB 8, 9/97 court, #9093, 8/00 court. All manuscript sources are located in the Maryland State Archives, Annapolis.

TABLE I. *Talbot County Artisans, 1690–1759*

Craft Group	No.	%	Craft Group	No.	%
Woodworkers			Metalworkers		
Carpenters	228	28	Blacksmiths	53	7
Coopers	59	7	Silversmiths	3	*
Sawyers	53	7	Braziers	1	*
Joiners	40	5			
Wheelwrights	19	2		57	7
Cabinetmakers	7	1			
Millwrights	6	1	Shipbuilders		
Turners	3	*	Ship carpenters	42	5
House carpenters	3	*	Caulkers	4	*
Chairmakers	1	*	Sailmakers	2	*
			Blockmakers	2	*
	419	52			
				50	6
Clothworkers					
Tailors	74	9	Builders		
Weavers	57	7	Bricklayers	25	3
Hatters	1	*	Plasterers	13	2
Fullers	1	*	Brickmakers	4	*
			Glaziers	2	*
	133	16			
				44	5
Leatherworkers					
Shoemakers	72	9	Miscellaneous		
Tanners	16	2	Barbers	4	*
Saddlers	7	1	Butchers	2	*
Glovers	4	*	Bakers	2	*
	99	12		8	1
Grand Total	810				

Source: Artisan file for Talbot County compiled from county and provincial records, Maryland State Archives, Annapolis.

*Figures less than .5.

TABLE 2. *Talbot County Artisans, by Period*

Craft Group	1690–1719 No.	%	1720–1739 No.	%	1740–1759 No.	%
Woodworkers						
Carpenters	127	32	74	28	82	26
Coopers	39	10	24	9	12	4
Sawyers	25	6	16	6	15	5
Joiners	8	2	18	7	25	8
Wheelwrights	10	3	6	2	8	3
Cabinetmakers	0	0	0	0	7	2
Millwrights	3	1	2	1	3	1
Turners	1	*	2	1	0	0
House carpenters	0	0	0	0	3	1
Chairmakers	0	0	0	0	1	*
	213	54	142	54	156	49
Clothworkers						
Tailors	34	9	17	6	26	8
Weavers	27	7	18	7	26	8
Hatters	1	*	0	0	0	0
Fullers	0	0	0	0	1	*
	62	16	35	13	53	17
Leatherworkers						
Shoemakers	33	8	29	11	26	8
Tanners	10	3	6	2	6	2
Saddlers	3	1	1	*	4	1
Glovers	4	1	0	0	0	0
	50	13	36	14	36	11
Metalworkers						
Blacksmiths	18	5	22	8	27	9
Silversmiths	0	0	2	1	2	1
Braziers	1	*	0	0	0	0
	19	5	24	9	29	9

TABLE 2. *(continued)*

Craft Group	1690–1719 No.	%	1720–1739 No.	%	1740–1759 No.	%
Shipbuilders						
Ship carpenters	22	6	12	5	19	6
Caulkers	4	1	0	0	0	0
Sailmakers	0	0	1	*	1	*
Blockmakers	1	*	0	0	1	*
	27	7	13	5	21	7
Builders						
Bricklayers	9	2	9	3	14	5
Plasterers	4	1	2	1	7	2
Brickmakers	2	1	1	*	1	*
Glaziers	2	1	0	0	0	0
	17	4	12	5	22	7
Miscellaneous						
Barbers	4	1	0	0	0	0
Butchers	1	*	1	*	0	0
Bakers	2	*	0	0	0	0
	7	2	1	0	0	0
Grand Total	395	100	263	100	317	100

Source: Artisan file for Talbot County compiled from county and provincial records, Maryland State Archives, Annapolis.

Note: Because individual careers spanned more than one time period, the sum of the number of artisans present in each of the three periods is greater than the 810 present during the seventy-year period shown in table 1. Percentages have been rounded off.

* Figures less than .5.

Only the second baker, a man with the unlikely name of Belshazzar Frederick, can be located in a specific working context for a period of years. In June 1708, Frederick signed a renewable lease with Robert Grundy for rental of a house in Oxford, which he occupied until June 1713. When Grundy took him to court in 1715, the rent was £30 in arrears, indicating that Frederick had paid for only one of the five years that he lived in the house. He was still in Talbot in 1716, when he sued to collect an account that ran from 1709 to 1712. During that period, Frederick had sold Cornelius Collins £3 6s. 11d. worth of bread and ginger cakes, usually in twenty-five-pound lots of bread at 5s. each, and individual cakes costing 6d. apiece. The picture of the residents of Oxford strolling along the town's main street, munching one of Frederick's ginger cakes, is an engaging one, but clearly there were never enough customers to pay Frederick's rent.[12]

A second group of crafts was absent for much of the eighteenth century because they provided "luxury" items or specialized services for which too few customers existed until well into the century. As the economy expanded, goldsmiths, fullers, and cabinetmakers made their appearance in Talbot no earlier than the second quarter of the century. Absalom Friston, the one fuller, did not arrive until the 1740s. All of the cabinetmakers (mostly native-born men who were often relatives of other Talbot woodworkers) began practicing in the 1750s. This elaboration of the craft structure continued as the economy expanded. Coachmakers and watchmakers, for example, took up residence in the last quarter of the century, part of a continuing response to the growth of population, the increase in household wealth, and the rise in the standard of living that gained momentum in the second half of the century.[13]

Finally, competition from imports served as the most important restraint on local crafts, an effect most vividly illustrated by the complete absence of potters. No craftsman working in Talbot ever identified himself or was identified as a potter, despite the availability of raw materials for making pottery and evidence of a strong market for earthenware.[14] Studies of rural crafts uniformly cite potteries as one of the basic rural

12. Judgments, FT 1:33, 6/15 court (Grundy suit) and FT 1:109, 3/16 court (Collins suit).

13. Mean total estate value rose from a low in the early 1700s of £126 to £182 in the 1750s. The percentage of inventoried households with supplies of meat rose from 13 in the 1690s to 67 in the 1750s. Over the same time period, households possessing pottery increased from 48% to 92%, those with books from 46% to 70%, and those with equipment for participating in the rituals of tea and coffee drinking from 2% to 43%. The largest rise in these percentages occurred after 1725. See Russo, "Free Workers," appendix I, for a description of the Talbot County inventory file. All inventory values have been deflated according to a price series developed for the St. Mary's City Commission (National Endowment for the Humanities Grant RS23687-76-431). I am grateful to Lois Green Carr for allowing me to use it.

14. As early as 1700, more than one-half of all households owned some type of earthenware.

industries. Warren Roberts, for example, claims, "Wherever suitable clays could be found, potters supplied local needs; the countryside used to be dotted with small potteries operated often by a single family," and Scott Williamson asserts, "With carpentry and cabinetmaking, pottery-making was among the first crafts practiced on a wide scale in America." Some writers have noticed the discrepancy between their abstract descriptions and the reality of colonial life. Williamson goes on to observe that although "every community of importance must have had its pottery, . . . the records of these enterprises are surprisingly meagre," while Sigmund Lavine offers this explanation: "Evidently, the establishment of a pottery was so commonplace that . . . it was rarely entered in the official records of a settlement."[15]

D. E. C. Eversley, however, provides a far more plausible explanation for the absence of potters in Talbot and, by implication, for the absence of a number of other craftsmen as well. Writing of the growing domestic market in England, Eversley observes that the expanded home market furnished the basis as well for an expanded export trade by providing a "foundation for mass production, so that the cost per unit could be reduced to levels which made it feasible to export articles with a relatively unfavourable weight/value ratio, like pottery."[16] As Joan Thirsk persuasively argues, what was true for a bulky, fragile article such as pottery also applied to a variety of other goods. Mass production in England for a growing domestic market underlay successful exportation of a wide range of consumer goods, including staples such as agricultural tools, cloth, pins and needles, nails, and stockings,[17] all articles that traditionally had been made within the household or by *local* craftsmen.

Competition from relatively cheap imported goods was particularly effective in the Chesapeake region for several reasons. Low population density limited the size of the local market. Because of the labor-intensive nature of the region's agriculture, the area did not possess the substantial group of underemployed agricultural workers who produced consumer

15. Warren E. Roberts, "Folk Crafts," in Richard M. Dorson, ed., *Folklore and Folklife: An Introduction* (Chicago, 1972), 245, 329; Scott Graham Williamson, *The American Craftsman* (New York, 1940), 48; Sigmund A. Lavine, *Handmade in America: The Heritage of Colonial Craftsmen* (New York, 1966), 81.

16. D.E.C. Eversley, "The Home Market and Economic Growth in England, 1750–80," in E. L. Jones and G. E. Mingay, eds., *Land, Labour, and Population in the Industrial Revolution* (London, 1967), 234.

17. For production in England, see Joan Thirsk, *Economic Policy and Projects: The Development of a Consumer Society in Early Modern England* (Oxford, 1978).

articles during seasonal slack periods in England's pastoral regions.[18] Moreover, the bulky nature of the region's export crop ensured an abundance of shipping to carry goods back from England to the colonists. In the face of such competition, rural Chesapeake artisans tended to be confined to those trades whose products could not be imported, such as houses, barns, and bridges, or whose raw materials were readily available, such as wool, flax, and hides.

Store inventories clearly reveal the range and volume of goods exported to the colony. William Troth in 1710 offered his customers stocks that included about 100 pairs of shoes, saddles, bridles, hats, buttons, yards and yards of cloth, thread, stockings, gloves, wooden trenchers, and woodworking tools. The largest of Edward Lloyd's three stores in 1719 contained hundreds of bolts of imported cloth, with a total value of over £400. Customers could also choose among more than 450 pairs of shoes, over 130 hats, more than 200 pairs of gloves, about 175 pairs of stockings, and somewhat more than 1,100 dozen buttons, as well as ironware, tinware, and earthenware. Goods "in the store" covered eleven pages of George Robins's 1744 inventory. Contents included numerous tools; 15 dozen pairs of gloves; 28,000 nails, 15,000 saddler's tacks, and 6 dozen saddle nails; 27 dozen pins and 65 brass thimbles; hats; saddles, bridles, girths, and stirrups; earthenware jugs, tea sets, coffee cups, bowls, and plates; and a miscellany of other items from chamber pots to window lead and solder. The Oxford store managed by Robert Morris for the Liverpool firm of Foster Cunliffe & Sons (one of several stores in town by the middle of the century) among its wares offered hats (nearly 85 dozen), shoes, caps, gloves, stockings, handkerchiefs, cloth, china, and saddles.[19]

Purchases by individual settlers frequently encompassed a wide range of goods. Planter Edward Harding's account at Henry Mercer's store in 1740 exemplifies the broad selection. Harding bought two saddles and bridles, two pairs of gloves, a handkerchief, shoes, buckles, scissors, thread, awl blades, a weeding hoe, nails, pins, buttons, a frying pan, and cloth, as well as spices, sugar, cheese, and some odd items like a quire of

18. For Chesapeake agriculture, see Darrett B. and Anita H. Rutman, *A Place in Time: Middlesex County, Virginia, 1650–1750* (New York, 1984), 42–43, and David O. Percy, "Agricultural Labor on an Eighteenth-Century Chesapeake Plantation" (paper presented at the Forty-Fifth Conference on Early American History, Baltimore, Md., September 1984). For English by-employment, see Thirsk, *Economic Policy*, 167.

19. Talbot Inventories, IB 3:43; Provincial Inventories, 3:1; Talbot Inventories, IB & IG 4:33, 5:348.

history books and a pack of cards. Another planter, John Auld, in 1747 purchased not only buttons, gartering, a whip and bridle, and pins but also a remarkable stock of pottery: 10 dozen porringers, 5 tea sets, 2 large butter pots, 1 dozen small yellow cups, 1 dozen yellow jugs, 1 dozen butter dishes, 6 small butter cups, 6 yellow posset cups, 3 small stew pots, and 2½ dozen half-pint, pint, and quart pots.[20]

The Chesapeake region was not alone among the colonies in relying upon English manufactures for much of its consumer goods. In Ireland, as Aidan Clarke points out, "demand for better-quality products and inessential consumer goods was met by importation, rather than by manufacture." He identifies as entering Irish ports a "constant stream of small quantities of such articles as looking glasses and urinals, wooden tableware and household pottery, hats and gloves, spurs and stirrups, tennis rackets and playing cards." Irish dependence upon English manufactures was probably as great as that of the Chesapeake.[21]

Competition from the abundant imports pouring into the colony explains not only the complete absence of such crafts as pottery or stocking manufacture, but also the short-lived presence of other artisans such as hatters and glovers. Glovemaking in Talbot, for example, depended solely upon the presence of William Dixon, a Quaker who arrived in the colony by the 1680s. Dixon prospered in Maryland, acquiring over 400 acres of land and a lot in Oxford, six slaves, and more than 125 head of cattle. By the time of his death in 1709, his estate amounted to £437, placing him in the top 10 percent of decedents whose estates were inventoried during that decade. Dixon's career is easily followed because the records almost always refer to him as "William Dixon, glover." He continued to follow his calling until his death, by which time he had trained at least three apprentices. In his estate Dixon left glover's tools, skins, cut leather, and finished gloves. None of Dixon's apprentices, however, continued to work as a glover and no immigrant arrived to take his place in the trade. Instead, merchants and ship captains satisfied local demand for gloves, offering an abundant supply in a range of quality and price.[22]

20. Judgments, JL 3:204 11/40 court; Civil Judgments, 1748–1750, 3/49 court.

21. Aidan Clarke, "Irish Economy, 1600–1660," in T. W. Moody, F. X. Martin, and F. J. Byrne, eds., *A New History of Ireland*, vol. III, *Early Modern Ireland, 1534–1691* (Oxford, 1976), 183.

22. Rent Roll, Talbot County, 1707; Land Records, RF 11:55; Talbot Inventories, JB 1:461, IB 3:193; AdminAccts, RF 6:42; Land Records, LL 7:107, 220, and RF 9:327 (apprenticeships).

Similarly Thomas Ball, also a Quaker, functioned as Talbot's only hatter until his death in 1722. Born in Ireland, Ball emigrated to Maryland in 1686, with his parents, brother, and sister. It is unclear how extensively Ball practiced his trade, but he did refer to himself as a "felt maker" in legal documents such as the will he wrote in 1720. Hatter's tools are listed among his assets. No other hatter, however, attempted to establish a trade in the county for a half-century after Ball's death. Local manufacturers of small accessory items such as gloves and hats could not compete with the mass-produced wares of English by-industries.[23]

The pattern of Talbot's temporal distribution of artisans, then, consisted of a nucleus of men working in trades that were always present. This group included carpenters, coopers, wheelwrights, sawyers, and joiners; shoemakers, tanners, and saddlers; tailors and weavers; and blacksmiths, bricklayers, and shipbuilders. They were joined initially by some English-born specialists whose trades could not flourish in the rural Chesapeake economy (glovers, hatters, bakers, butchers) and later by those whose products and services required a more fully developed economy. The fundamental outlines of the craft sector were thus determined by the county's relationship to the international market and by the level of local economic development, rather than by the efforts of individual planters to develop self-sufficient plantations.

The broad pattern outlined above was not a static one, however. Changes within the persistent craft groups did take place over the course of seventy years, some of which, it will be seen, were related to efforts by county residents to achieve a measure of self-sufficiency. The most marked change to occur was the decline in numbers of independent craftsmen, both collectively and within most individual crafts, relative to total population (see figure 1 and table 2). While the county's population doubled between the 1690s and midcentury, the number of craftsmen working in the county shrank. Figure 1, based upon consideration of the living population, is corroborated by evidence drawn from the decedent population. Artisans constituted one-fifth of all male decedents through the 1730s but only one-seventh in the 1740s, and one-tenth by the 1750s.

The different craft groups did not share a uniform decrease in size nor did all undergo an uninterrupted decline. Every category of artisan exhib-

23. Francis B. Culver, "Ball of Bayside, Talbot County, Maryland," *Maryland Historical Magazine*, XL (1945), 155; Provincial Wills, 18:29; Provincial Inventories, 13:18.

FIGURE I. *Talbot County Artisans in Major Craft Groups*

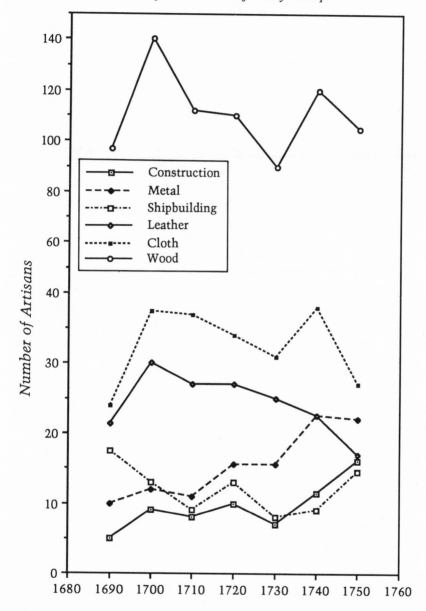

its a peak in numbers around the beginning of the eighteenth century, followed by a period of decline. The shape of the peak varied from craft to craft, however, as did the duration of the decrease. Only blacksmiths and construction workers (primarily bricklayers and plasterers) experienced a small drop and then rapid recovery. The actual number of practicing free blacksmiths most likely remained constant. A smith's shop represented a sizable capital investment; it was unlikely to remain idle for long upon the death of an owner or occupant. On the other hand, because entry into the field required a higher level of investment than did most of the county's crafts, wholly new establishments would be infrequent. Increased employment of bricklayers and plasterers (as well as the appearance by the 1750s of house carpenters as a separately identified group of woodworkers) reflected the expanded building activity that occurred throughout the county as a result of economic improvement.[24]

A long period of stagnation in the tobacco industry, from the 1680s to the 1710s, has been credited by both contemporaries and historians with encouraging diversification within the economy, especially a new emphasis upon manufactures.[25] This movement received additional encouragement from the disruptions suffered by Atlantic trade during King William's and Queen Anne's wars, when Maryland settlements experienced severe shortages of imports.[26] Certainly, the peaks revealed by figure 1 support the contention that local crafts proliferated when the tobacco economy suffered a prolonged depression. Nevertheless, as table 1 demonstrates, any growth of domestic manufactures in the late seventeenth and early eighteenth centuries occurred only within long-established channels of local craftsmanship. Adverse economic conditions in the tobacco trade did not encourage the activities of potters or stocking

24. Inventories taken in the years after 1720 record more rooms per house; orphans' estates appraised after 1720 contained an average of six buildings, double the number for the few appraisals recorded in the earlier decades. Paul G. E. Clemens, "Economy and Society on Maryland's Eastern Shore, 1689–1733," in Aubrey C. Land, Lois Green Carr, and Edward C. Papenfuse, eds., *Law, Society, and Politics in Early Maryland* (Baltimore, 1977), 153–154; Russell R. Menard, "The Tobacco Industry in the Chesapeake Colonies, 1617–1730: An Interpretation," *Research in Economic History*, V (1980), 113.

25. Menard, "Tobacco Industry," *Research Econ. Hist.*, V (1980), 141.

26. Morriss, *Colonial Trade*, 89n; Menard, "Tobacco Industry," *Research Econ. Hist.*, V (1980), 126; Arthur Pierce Middleton, *Tobacco Coast: A Maritime History of Chesapeake Bay in the Colonial Era* (Newport News, Va., 1953), 159, 294–295.

manufacturers or glovers, but rather those of tailors, weavers, shoemakers, and carpenters—men working in trades that offered viable options within the Chesapeake economy.

During the years of stagnation, the colonial population still contained a large proportion of immigrants. Lack of opportunity within the agricultural sector may have served to keep immigrant craftsmen at the practice of their trades, forestalling for longer than usual an inevitable sorting-out process in which both the less skillful and the more ambitious sought new opportunities. Consider, for example, Richard Feddeman, a tailor who arrived in Maryland during the 1680s. Although he had acquired land by 1691, Feddeman continued to identify himself as a tailor until the early 1700s; only then did he begin to shift his identity, and presumably the direction of his economic activity, to that of "planter," a shift that might well have occurred earlier in a more favorable economic climate. At the same time, while the immigrants who swelled the initial ranks of craftsmen were being replaced by native-born artisans, they may not have been replaced on a one-to-one basis. Ownership of land, through either inheritance or out-migration to a frontier area, may have been a more likely prospect for the son of a colonist than for a comparable English youth. The result may have been that fewer native-born sons prepared for an alternative career.[27]

The downward trend in artisan population for most crafts coincided with the period of renewed prosperity for the tobacco economy. Improvement in the tobacco market allowed planters to increase their reliance upon bound labor; more planters owned servants and slaves, while the size of individual holdings of workers increased. Nevertheless, the secular improvement in tobacco prices overlay a cyclical pattern of boom and bust that stimulated efforts to buffer "the extremes of depression by expanding the variety of plantation activities." Thus, these were the years when the twin pressures of the drive for self-sufficiency and competition from slave labor should have been strongest. To test whether these forces were the primary influences upon the fortunes of free craft workers, we must first look within individual plantations for the presence of the two

27. While Richard Feddeman and other immigrants did succeed in acquiring land early in the century, both immigrants and the native-born found their opportunity to become landowners more restricted as the century progressed. But would not the expectation, at least in the earlier part of the century, have been greater for the native-born colonist than for his counterpart in rural England?

components upon which the self-sufficiency model is based: skilled bound workers and the necessary tools and equipment. To what extent did Talbot planters include these two elements within their plantations?[28]

Servants, either those who left England with indentures or those who arrived without indentures and served by "custom of the country," constituted the earliest source of unfree labor. Indeed, indentured servants and landownership arrived in Talbot together, because the initial large land grants represented headrights given to men who imported servants into the colony. Indentured servants remained the primary source of servile labor until the end of the seventeenth century. Improved economic conditions in England that led to a decline in the number of emigrating servants, establishment of colonies that proved more attractive destinations than the Chesapeake, and better access to supplies of slaves resulted in the servant/slave ratio for the colony's labor force shifting by the early eighteenth century to one in which slaves predominated.[29] Although servants remained a part of the labor force, the percentage of men owning servants showed a slight decline during the eighteenth century, while slave ownership and all ownership of labor rose over time (see figure 2).

Given the short terms of service (generally within a range of four to seven years),[30] large holdings of servants meant a substantial investment of capital within a brief period of time; a planter with those resources more likely bought slaves. Although he acquired fewer workers (because of the higher cost of slaves), he could hope to have the benefit of their labor over a longer period of time.[31] It is not surprising, therefore, that

28. Aubrey C. Land, *Colonial Maryland: A History* (Millwood, N.Y., 1981), 166; Clemens, *Atlantic Economy*, 165–166; Lorena S. Walsh, "Anne Arundel County Population," in "Annapolis and Anne Arundel County, Maryland: A Study of Urban Development in a Tobacco Economy, 1649–1776" (National Endowment for the Humanities Grant RS20199-81-1955), 4; Russo, "Free Workers," appendix V, 454–459; Earle, *Tidewater Settlement System*, 102.

29. Menard, "Tobacco Industry," *Research Econ. Hist.*, V (1980), 114; Clemens, "Economy and Society," in Land, Carr, and Papenfuse, eds., *Law, Society, and Politics*, 154; Lois Green Carr and David William Jordan, *Maryland's Revolution of Government, 1689–1692* (Ithaca, N.Y., 1974), 234.

30. Transported convicts served longer terms (7 or 14 years depending upon their crime), but few Talbot servants were identified as convicts and few of those included in inventories had unexpired terms long enough to indicate that they had arrived as convicts.

31. Although illustrating the inherent risks of investing in slave labor, the Rutmans nevertheless acknowledge that for 18th-century planters, "an investment in slaves seemed the only way to secure or improve a position," with the result that "men

FIGURE 2. *Talbot County Ownership of Servants and Slaves*

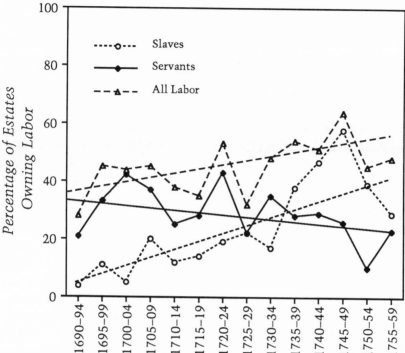

planters rarely owned more than a few servants. At the beginning of the eighteenth century, the average owner held only three servants; the mean declined to just over one servant by midcentury.[32] For the planter, it was

without slave labor sought to buy or inherit it" (Rutmans, *A Place in Time,* 184). The rate of success or failure for those in Talbot County who took "the negro road" (to use the Rutmans' metaphor) can be estimated only for individuals appearing on the 1733 tax list whose estates subsequently went through probate. Of 230 such men, 84 (37%) improved their position (that is, at the time of death their slaveholdings had increased in size); 12 (5%) had lost ground; and the remaining 58% either did not own slaves or showed no appreciable change in their holdings. Of course, men who were not owners or who held static numbers of slaves also must be counted among those who lost. Few men accumulated wealth in the Chesapeake who did not own slaves; slave owners certainly expected that their holdings would increase in size and value. "A List of Taxables in Talbot County Anno Dom. 1733," *Maryland State Papers,* #19999-118/47.

32. Only seven decedents in 70 years (2% of all owners) employed more than five servants: three men (1700–1705) who each owned six, two (1720–1725) with seven

ownership of labor in general that was significant; for the purposes of a study of craft skills, however, possession of adult males constitutes the significant variable.[33] Although adult males formed the largest group within the servant population during the period studied, the small number of servants owned in general translated this predominance into an average ownership of just one male servant.

A planter owning only one male servant was highly unlikely to have chosen a skilled worker, for whom he would have had to pay a higher price or accept a shorter term of indenture.[34] To utilize fully the craft skill of the servant, the small planter would deprive himself of that servant's agricultural labor. Yet because his own scale of operations would be too small to make efficient use of his worker's skill, he would need to find other planters willing to rent the services of his skilled servant, while still requiring assistance with his crops. As will be seen shortly, only those planters whose ownership of labor exceeded the average possessed skilled workers as part of their labor force. For the vast majority of servant owners, possession of bound labor meant the opportunity to produce larger crops of tobacco, not shoes or clothing or cloth.

Until 1720, less than 20 percent of decedents owned slave labor at the time of death, but after that date the percentage of owners began a steady rise, reaching 50 percent by midcentury (see figure 2). The average number of slaves per master was both higher than that for servants and was increasing, rather than decreasing, over time, from between two and three slaves per owner at the beginning of the century to approximately six by midcentury. Among servant owners, only 2 percent held six or more workers, and the presence of such owners declined over time. For slave owners, however, 30 percent possessed six or more slaves; three-quarters of those owners were clustered in the years from 1735 to 1759. No one owned more than ten servants, but 14 percent of slave owners held at least that many slaves, and two-thirds of those masters also were active between 1735 and 1759.[35]

---

each, one (1740–1745) who had purchased eight workers, and one (1720–1725) with ten men and three boys. On the 1733 list of taxables, of the 327 households that included servants, eight had four workers, five had five men, one had seven servants, and one had nine. In that year, the average number was 1.6 workers.

33. See n. 9, above, for an explanation of the concentration upon male workers.

34. David W. Galenson, *White Servitude in Colonial America: An Economic Analysis* (Cambridge, 1981), 107.

35. A comparison of slaveholding among the living population with ownership among the decedent population can be made only for the 1730s, using the surviving

As with servants, the males are of particular interest among the slaves, for they would have been purchased for their skill or trained to be craftsmen. Adult male slaves, unlike adult male servants, did not predominate, constituting only 32 percent of all slaves throughout the seventy years. Thus, although planters owned slaves in greater numbers than they did servants, the average owner held only two adult male slaves. The same arguments against widespread ownership of skilled servants thus apply to slave labor as well. Few planters owned enough adult males to make possession of a skilled slave very likely, although the likelihood would increase with time as slaveholdings grew in size and as larger holdings became more widely diffused among the planter population.[36]

The presence of skilled workers and the range of their skills can be approached more directly, however. In addition to providing information about aggregate holdings of servants and slaves, inventories also describe individual laborers, noting attributes such as name, age, sex, length of service, and skill. That the inventories rarely mention skill serves as additional confirmation that ownership of skilled labor was not widespread. Only 5 percent of plantations with bound labor included workers characterized as having a skill. To those workers a second group may be added on the basis of unusual stocks of raw materials and craft tools or above-average slave values found in the estate. Table 3 summarizes the skilled bound workers identified in inventories, accounts, and suits, as well as those whose presence is suggested by unusually high valuations of workers or above-average holdings of craft equipment.

The concentration of skilled labor in just a few areas is pronounced: tailors, shoemakers, woodworkers (mostly carpenters), blacksmiths, and weavers account for all of the craftsmen. Woodworkers represent two-fifths, with tailors and shoemakers each supplying one-fifth, and smiths and weavers almost equally making up the balance. The emphasis, then,

---

tax list for 1733. In that year, slave owners accounted for 24% of heads of households, the same figure as that obtained from inventories for the period 1730–1734. Average ownership of all slaves (six) and of all adult males (two) proved to be slightly higher, by one slave for each group, than the inventory data indicated. Of both groups 17% owned more than five slaves; 7% of the living slaveholders held at least ten slaves, but no decedents had acquired more than nine.

36. Russell Menard, in considering skills among 17th-century Western Shore slaves, argues that few plantations were large enough to require the services of full-time craftsmen. His arguments apply as well to most masters and their holdings in early 18th-century Talbot. Russell R. Menard, "The Maryland Slave Population, 1658 to 1730: A Demographic Profile of Blacks in Four Counties," *WMQ*, 3d Ser., XXXII (1975), 36–37.

TABLE 3. *Talbot County Skilled Bound Artisans, 1690–1759*

Decade	Wood-workers	Shoe-makers	Tailors	Weavers	Black-smiths	Total
1690–1699	2	3	1	0	1	7
1700–1709	13	0	7	0	1	21
1710–1719	5	1	2	2	3	13
1720–1729	6	3	4	1	1	15
1730–1739	2	3	2	3	0	10
1740–1749	6	10	4	4	3	27
1750–1759	8	2	1	2	0	13
	42	22	21	12	9	106
	(40%)	(21%)	(20%)	(11%)	(8%)	

Source: Artisan file for Talbot County compiled from county and provincial records, Maryland State Archives, Annapolis.

is again upon those crafts whose products were in great demand—clothing, shoes, and cloth—and those skills that could not be replaced through imports—sawing, construction, barrelmaking, tool repair, and horseshoeing.

The mixture of skills did not undergo any significant change during the years from 1690 to 1759, nor did the characteristics of men owning skilled workers. As a group, the owners possessed estates of above-average value—from Philemon Lloyd to George Robins to Richard Bennett they were often the wealthiest men in the area—and their holdings of all servants and slaves exceeded the average. They tended, often, to be not merely planters but also merchants (or those with mercantile connections) or innkeepers. Members of both groups operated businesses that provided a steady flow of customers. A supply of shoes or cloth would find a ready purchaser, a tailor would have many clients, and a planter needing a piece of ironware repaired or a horse shod could shop or have a drink and visit with his neighbors while he waited.

To estimate the extent to which skilled servants and slaves competed with or eliminated the need for free craftsmen is not an easy task. The evidence with which to make such a judgment is fragmentary, but it may be precisely its fragmentary nature that offers a basis for interpretation. Few appraisers attributed a skill to the workers whom they enumerated. Court cases involving suits seeking payment for work done by bound craftsmen are far smaller in number than those involving free craftsmen. The lacunae in the records do not reflect any systematic biases. If the records speak only fleetingly of skilled servants and slaves, it may well be that relatively few such workers existed.

What of the tools utilized by the various crafts? Does the pattern of ownership reveal any increase within plantations of the equipment needed to pursue an artisanal skill? The only major expansion occurred within the woodworking fields (see table 4). In the 1690s, 38 percent of the population owned axes, wedges, and saws; by the 1750s, 75 percent owned such equipment and nearly 50 percent held an assortment of carpenter's and cooper's implements. Possession of these tools generally extended across all occupational groupings. In the 1750s, owners of woodworking tools included over half of the men with no clear status (most were probably planters, either landholders or tenants, or the sons of such men) and all members of other occupational groups, except for one of the two merchants. No more than 10 percent of the population, however, owned any other type of tool until the 1730s. Even after that date only shoemaking equipment could be found in more than 20 percent of households. Ownership of any tools other than those used in woodworking thus remained quite limited.

Examining in detail the status of owners of particular types of craft tools further illuminates this point. For example, only thirty-one decedents in all owned smith's tools. Nineteen of them were blacksmiths and another three were relatives of smiths. Free artisans therefore made up 75 percent of those who possessed any of the tools used by blacksmiths. With but one exception, wealthy planters—those whose estates both included bound labor and placed them in the top 10 percent by wealth of all decedents—accounted for the balance of the owners. The presence of only eight such men over a seventy-year period hardly argues for significant practice of that skill by members of the plantation labor force.

Tailors, unlike smiths, needed only a minimal investment in equipment—a pair of shears, a tailor's goose, and some needles and pins—to practice their craft. Any planter who so desired could supply himself with the necessary articles by investing just a few shillings.[37] Yet not until the 1740s did as many as 10 percent of decedents own even a pair of shears,

37. The shears, thimbles, and goose belonging to William Curtis were valued at 3s. 6d.; William Hadden owned only three pairs of shears, worth 3s.; and Marmaduke Harrison's more extensive collection of shears, hone, scissors, and needles still represented only 4s. in his estate. Talbot Inventories, JB 1:510 (Curtis), JB 1:464 (Hadden), and IB 3:29 (Harrison).

TABLE 4. *Ownership of Craft Tools by Male Decedents, 1690–1759*

Male Decedents

	1690–99 (N=65)		1700–09 (N=192)		1710–19 (N=152)		1720–29 (N=78)		1730–39 (N=148)		1740–49 (N=221)		1750–59 (N=173)		1690–1759 (N=1,029)	
	No.	%	No.	%	No.	%	No.	%	No.	%	No.	%	No.	%	No.	%
Carpenter	5	8	27	14	21	14	18	23	24	16	63	29	45	26	203	20
Cooper	6	9	26	14	11	7	11	14	18	12	31	14	19	11	122	12
Carpenter or cooper	6	9	21	11	16	11	13	17	16	11	37	17	21	12	130	13
Sawyer	0	0	5	3	9	6	7	9	18	12	27	12	24	14	90	9
Plasterer and bricklayer	1	2	2	1	1	1	0	0	5	4	10	4	7	4	26	2
Blacksmith	0	0	4	3	8	5	1	1	9	6	4	2	5	3	31	3
Shoemaker	4	6	8	4	9	6	4	5	31	21	64	29	50	29	170	17
Tanner and currier	2	3	2	1	1	1	2	3	4	3	7	3	12	7	30	3
Tailor	2	3	6	3	8	5	5	6	13	9	21	10	9	5	64	6
Weaver	2	3	3	2	8	5	4	8	17	11	23	10	27	16	84	8
Axes, saws, and wedges	25	38	82	43	78	51	52	65	110	74	189	86	130	75	666	65
General woodworking	19	29	76	40	44	29	29	37	57	39	77	35	63	36	365	35

while in all decades the estates of the wealthiest planters, those most capable of pursuing self-sufficiency and most likely to own trained slaves, rarely included tailoring equipment. Only six men of the fifty-eight with ten or more slaves, for example, owned shears or tools identified as "tailor's," while just 13 percent of men owning more than £225 of property included tailoring equipment among their assets.

Thus, at both the high and low ends of investment, the capability for plantation self-sufficiency or for development of a skilled force of bound workers appears to have been limited. Only a very few plantations fit the portrait of the self-contained world described by Mullin and others. James Lloyd (1680–1723), a justice of the peace, General Assembly delegate, millowner, merchant, and owner of thirty-seven slaves and two servants (identified as a weaver and a shoemaker), was one such planter. His plantation equipment included a set of smith's tools, shoemaker's tools as well as leather valued at £20, and an assortment of carpenter's and cooper's tools, plus a whipsaw for sawing timber. George Robins (1697–1742), also a justice, delegate, millowner, merchant, and planter (and husband of Lloyd's niece), was another. He lived on an estate on Peachblossom Creek, part of the 5,500 acres that he owned. Robins's work force of fifty-six slaves included a joiner, a cooper, and a tanner, and of his three servants, one was a tailor and one was a shoemaker. Robins possessed a smith's shop containing £9 worth of equipment, an extensive supply of woodworking tools, and a shoemaker's shop.[38]

On plantations like Lloyd's and Robins's—those with extensive holdings of land and labor—economies of scale encouraged investment in skilled workers. There were enough trees to be felled, buildings to be constructed to hold people, livestock, and crops, and household members to be clothed and shod to warrant ownership of craftsmen. However, these conditions existed on only a small percentage of plantations. Whether landowner or tenant, the ordinary planter (the vast majority of the county's householders) worked his land with the help of his family and perhaps a slave or servant, owning only those tools needed for cultivation, for clearing land, and for simple woodworking chores. If such men owned a skilled worker, the likelihood was that he was employed in the fields during the growing season and at his craft during slack periods, rather than as a full-time craftsman serving a network of customers.

Examination of the components of self-sufficiency thus suggests a picture different from the one outlined by the self-sufficiency model.

38. *Ibid.*, IB & IG 4:426, 428 (Lloyd), and IB & IG 4:33 (Robins).

Skilled bound laborers did impinge on the opportunities of free artisans in two ways: the occasional large planter, who could afford to have specialists among his workers, might rent the services or sell the products of his skilled slaves or servants to neighbors as well as rely upon them himself; small planters might own occasional part-time craft workers who primarily supplied the needs of their owners.[39] However, such workers were too few in number to have more than a limited impact. A more substantial influence on the prospects of free artisans was the growing skills of planters themselves, as shown in their ownership of craft tools. The widespread presence of woodworking tools and the relatively small percentage of coopers and carpenters among skilled bound workers suggest that ordinary planters possessed woodworking skills adequate for much of the carpentry and cooperage needs of a small plantation. By the 1740s and 1750s a similar pattern existed for shoemaking equipment as well.

We can pursue further the effect of this form of self-sufficiency by studying changes over time in persistence rates for different crafts (see table 5). Over the entire seventy-year period, craftsmen with more than a temporary presence in Talbot (two-thirds of the total) remained for an average of fifteen years. However, the average for the whole period masks significant variations across time. Mean years of persistence reached eighteen for those who began their careers between 1690 and 1709, declined to thirteen and one-half for men entering between 1710 and 1729, and dropped further to just below twelve years for those who started after 1730.

Coopers experienced an especially marked decline. The number of persistent coopers dropped by one-half in each time period, while the percentage who were long-term residents declined as well, from 75 percent of all coopers in the earliest period to 55 percent in the latest. The twenty-one men who made barrels and hogsheads between 1690 and 1710 remained at their trade for an average of sixteen years, but the six working as independent artisans in the last thirty years stayed an average of less than ten years. The decline in coopers did not stem from a decline in demand for their wares; on the contrary, the need for contain-

39. All specific examples of the hiring of skilled bound workers are represented in table 3. Administration accounts most frequently document the hiring of agricultural labor, not skilled workers. Where the services of artisans are mentioned, generally to make coffins and to provide clothing for the family, the men involved were always free craftsmen.

ers increased with the expanding volume of tobacco exports and growing markets for flour, meat, and the raw materials of wooden containers themselves. Rather than diminishing in scope, cooperage moved from the workshop of the free artisan onto the plantation, to be performed as part-time work by small planters supplying their own needs or by bound laborers on large plantations. Neither ownership of land nor the advantage of local birth stemmed the decline of coopers as a craft group: after 1730 only 40 percent of the coopers who held real property or were Talbot natives left visible evidence of having tried their chances for more than three years. The demand for their wares was large enough, the necessary equipment inexpensive enough, and the skill involved readily enough acquired to induce planters to incorporate cooperage into their households as part of the effort to achieve self-sufficiency.

Long-term prospects for independent woodworkers and shoemakers are revealed also in the placement patterns for children in need of care. Orphans, bastards, children abandoned by runaway parents, and those whose parents were too poor to support them all came before the county court to be placed in households where they could be both nurtured and trained to support themselves as adults.[40] In making their decisions about placement of children, the justices were guided by legislation that stipulated, "If the Estate be soe meane & in Considerable tht itt will not extend to a Free Educacon That itt is Enacted tht such Orphans shalbe bound Apprentices to some Handicraft Trade or other pson att the discretion of the Cort untill one & Twenty yeares of Age."[41]

Particularly for older children, the justices undoubtedly received further guidance in their decision making from men who came to court seeking workers. Finally, and especially for younger children, whose age likely made them less attractive to men wishing immediately to increase their labor supply, the justices sought to ensure that the children would not become charges upon the county. The specific assignments for training thus demonstrate both the practical nature of the justices' efforts to

40. The following section is based upon an analysis of all children supervised by the county court. Entries regarding the status of orphaned children and others under the care of the court were recorded as part of the miscellaneous matters covered during each session. The records are for the most part complete for the years 1690 to 1759. The principal gaps appear from 1709 to 1714 and from 1734 to 1738, when the libers are either missing or too fragile to use. Judgments, 1690–1759.

41. William Hand Browne *et al.*, eds., *Archives of Maryland* (Baltimore, 1883–), I, 494.

TABLE 5. *Persistence Rates for Selected Talbot County Artisans, 1690–1759*

Artisans	Long Term						Short Term				
	No.	%	Mean Years	Native-born (%)	Land-owners (%)	Talbot deaths (%)	No.	%	Native-born (%)	Land-owners (%)	Talbot deaths (%)
1690–1709											
Blacksmiths (N=14)	9	64	25.4	0	100	100	5	36	0	0	0
Tailors (N=26)	21	81	18.1	0	67	76	5	19	0	0	0
Coopers (N=28)	21	75	16.1	29	67	67	7	25	0	14	14
Leatherworkers (N=37)	27	73	18.4	26	74	56	10	27	10	40	20
Joiners (N=4)	4	100	13.2	0	75	75	0	0	0	0	0
Ship carpenters (N=22)	11	50	16.7	27	73	45	11	50	0	9	18
Total	93	71	18.1	17	73	67	38	29	3	16	13
1710–1729											
Blacksmiths (N=11)	9	82	15.0	78	67	78	2	18	0	50	50
Tailors (N=19)	12	63	9.4	25	33	25	7	37	0	0	29
Coopers (N=17)	11	65	13.6	82	91	82	6	35	50	33	17
Leatherworkers (N=24)	20	83	14.7	55	75	50	4	17	0	25	0

Joiners (N=12)	8	67	11.7	38	50	50	4	33	50	50	75
Ship carpenters (N=5)	5	100	24.6	40	80	60	0	0	0	0	0
Total	65	74	13.4	51	66	55	23	26	22	26	30

1730–1759

Blacksmiths (N=32)	20	63	13.0	65	60	25	12	37	42	25	33
Tailors (N=29)	16	55	12.5	38	19	50	13	45	8	0	15
Coopers (N=11)	6	55	9.7	33	33	0	5	45	60	60	0
Leatherworkers (N=37)	20	54	13.2	55	55	35	17	46	53	29	6
Joiners (N=32)	26	81	10.8	54	42	15	6	19	67	33	83
Ship carpenters (N=17)	11	65	10.2	73	55	9	6	35	33	50	0
Total	99	63	11.8	56	45	25	59	37	41	27	20

Source: Artisan file for Talbot County compiled from county and provincial records, Maryland State Archives, Annapolis.

Note: Persistence rates were calculated by first dividing all artisans into two groups: those whose presence could be verified only for a period of three years or less and those who remained in the county for four or more years. The craftsmen in the first group tended to be defendants in a single court case (or in a series of cases within one court session) or individuals identified as artisans when selling a piece of property. In the latter case, these men appear to have recently turned twenty-one, thus to have come into their inheritance, and to be selling the land to raise capital needed to move elsewhere. The remaining short-term artisans consisted primarily of those whose careers were cut short by an early death; although they remained in Talbot until death, those deaths came too soon to place them in the long-term group. For the second group, length of stay is assumed to be the time between first appearance (or the known or estimated date of twenty-first birthday for the native-born) and last appearance or date of death.

equip orphans with the ability to support themselves and the changing locus of different craft skills.

Between 1690 and 1759, the justices bound out approximately 270 boys, placing them primarily with planters and artisans and requiring training in a craft skill for about two-thirds of the youths. The crafts to which the justices assigned children fulfilled three criteria: they utilized raw materials readily available in the county, they provided for basic needs of the colonists, and they did not as a rule require a large capital expenditure for equipment. Woodworking, leather, and clothing crafts thus accounted for 91 percent of the craft placements. Woodworkers constituted 42 percent, leatherworkers another 36 percent, and weavers and tailors an additional 13 percent. Carpenters and coopers formed the bulk of the woodworking apprentices, while shoemakers accounted for almost all of the leatherworkers and represented the largest single group among the orphans, claiming one-third of the boys. In their provisions for the remaining youths, the justices showed the same concern for practical solutions, apprenticing them to only three additional trades. They placed eight with blacksmiths, two with millwrights, and five with bricklayers, again choosing trades that met basic needs by providing services that had to be performed in the colony.[42]

Looking beyond the crafts to the men charged with supplying the training again reveals the changing character of the rural craft structure. The pattern of assigning children to artisans or to planters differed considerably among individual crafts. No one accepted an apprentice as a smith, millwright, or bricklayer who was not himself a practicing craftsman. In the woodworking fields, however, masters of orphans divided almost evenly between artisans and planters. Only artisans undertook to train children in the most skilled or specialized of the crafts, such as those practiced by wheelwrights, ship carpenters, or chairmakers. However, planters as well as artisans bound themselves to teach the more basic skills of a carpenter, cooper, or sawyer, evidence again of broader diffu-

42. There does not appear to be any correlation between the age of the child and the type of training he was assigned to receive. Children of all ages were placed as shoemakers, tailors, carpenters, and weavers. Of the three placed with blacksmiths whose ages are known, one was 3 years old and the other two were 8. Children under 5 were bound also to tailors, carpenters, shoemakers, and weavers. The oldest boys received training as coopers and shoemakers, suggesting perhaps that those skills could be most quickly acquired by those over 18 or that the boys may already have possessed some knowledge of those crafts.

sion throughout the population of both the tools and the knowledge needed for those trades.

Of the boys to be trained as tailors or weavers prior to 1720,[43] all were placed with artisans. After that date, six—nearly half of the total in those years—entered the homes of planters, suggesting some movement of those skills beyond the purview of specialists. With such a small number of cases, one hesitates to put much emphasis upon an apparent trend. No such caution is needed, however, in identifying the changes taking place in shoemaking. Prior to 1720, the justices placed half of the twenty-three children to trained as shoemakers with artisans and half with planters. After 1720, all but six of the thirty-two boys bound as shoemakers joined the household of a planter, dramatic confirmation of the inventory evidence, which reveals wider distribution of shoemaking equipment and raw materials among households by the second quarter of the century.

The diffusion of some skills, particularly cooperage and shoemaking, throughout the population, the ready availability of imported consumer goods at competitive prices, and the high entry thresholds for certain crafts defined the craft community and shaped patterns of growth within its various sectors. Competition from imported consumer goods exerted the most powerful influence upon the patterns, marking most eighteenth-century crafts as unsuitable for the rural Chesapeake.

The "forced self-sufficiency" model accurately describes the process whereby Chesapeake settlement and trade patterns prevented most crafts from establishing themselves in the region. Competition from imported goods coupled with low population density so severely limited the available market for most crafts that few if any of their practitioners worked in Talbot County. The model errs, however, in linking the process to self-sufficiency. Its proponents argue that planters compensated for the lack of local craftsmen by training bound workers to fill the void, but the crafts most affected by this process were *not* those that planters attempted to incorporate into their plantations. The absence of coachmakers during the first three-quarters of the century offers an admittedly extreme but apt example. The very few planters wealthy enough to own carriages could afford to import them from England and were too few in number to support even one local craftsman. Not surprisingly, however, the absence of local coachmakers never led any planter to purchase or train a bound worker in the craft.

43. Although women did weave, no girl was ever apprenticed as a weaver.

Among the skills that were potentially appropriate for the region, the "voluntary self-sufficiency" model correctly identifies the process that profoundly affected opportunities for coopers and shoemakers and less markedly for carpenters and sawyers. These were the crafts that planters could and did incorporate into their own households, but more commonly through their own efforts than through the use of skilled bound labor. The numbers of independent craftsmen in these trades declined accordingly.

One final comparative perspective allows us to measure the craft sector of Talbot County against those of contemporary communities. Implicit in the self-sufficiency model is the suggestion that the Chesapeake region experienced a shortage of free craftsmen. Such a judgment further suggests the existence of an accepted standard for the ratio of artisans to total population. Lacking such an arbitrary standard, we can only compare the range of skills and numbers of craftsmen present in Talbot with levels in rural England and other regions of colonial America to determine whether or not the county, and by extension other areas of the Chesapeake, did exhibit such a shortage. This comparison will suggest that the rural Chesapeake was not the anomaly so often portrayed.

English villages did not sustain a uniform array of local crafts. Villages with a pastoral economy often included many residents who engaged in seasonal forest-based employment. Chair bodgers, clogmakers, charcoal burners, and laddermakers were just a few of the many woodland craftsmen who flourished in such rural communities. Other pastoral villages had a large population of underemployed agricultural laborers who worked in a variety of rural industries that produced consumer goods for a mass market. Spinners and weavers, stocking knitters, nailmakers, and others who lived and worked in those villages served the needs not of their fellow villagers but of a wider national and international market. Still a third type of pastoral village exhibited a mixture of self-sufficiency and market orientation. Local craftsmen satisfied needs that could be met only locally, as was the case in Talbot, while other goods were supplied by areas specializing in mass production of consumer items. By the eighteenth century, transportation improvements and advances in marketing techniques had combined to draw many towns and villages into a national market, breaking down patterns of regional autonomy and encouraging patterns of regional specialization.[44]

44. Norman Wymer, *English Country Crafts: A Survey of Their Development from Early Times to Present Day* (London, 1946), 53–66; Joan Thirsk, "Industries in the Countryside," in F. J. Fisher, ed., *Essays in the Economic and Social History of Tudor and Stuart*

Villages in the English countryside offered their inhabitants the same resident crafts as those provided by artisans in Talbot County. For the most part, village craftsmen also consisted of carpenters and wheelwrights, tailors and weavers, shoemakers and blacksmiths, although butchers and bakers were found in greater numbers than in Talbot. The Cumberland village of Lupton, for example, in 1695 numbered among its fifty-two householders sixteen craftsmen and tradesmen; the craftsmen included a carpenter, a shoemaker, a tailor, and a blacksmith. Similarly, in nearby Killington nonfarmers included a blacksmith, a tanner, a weaver, a shoemaker, and a millwright. The Nottinghamshire village of Clayworth in 1688 boasted a comparable assortment of three or four weavers, one or two blacksmiths and wheelwrights, as well as a butcher, a tailor, a cooper, a thatcher, and a bricklayer. Bledington, a Gloucestershire parish of 1,500 acres on the slope of the Cotswold ridge, had two to three hundred inhabitants during the eighteenth century, including as craftsmen only weavers and shoemakers, an occasional smith, and a few coopers. The larger (4,600 acres) woodland parish of Myddle, located in Shropshire and with an economy based upon grazing, subsistence farming, and by-industries, still numbered among its residents roughly the same range of artisans as did those villages more dependent upon arable agriculture. Carpenters, coopers, tailors, weavers, shoemakers, masons, and blacksmiths supplied goods and services for the parish, accounting for one-seventh of all male residents by the latter part of the seventeenth century. In a different pastoral region, the sixty-two householders in the Kent village of Goodnastone in 1676 included seven craftsmen: two carpenters, two brickmakers, a weaver, a shoemaker, and a tailor, a pattern that the village shared with its neighbors.[45]

England (Cambridge, 1961), 86; Thirsk, *Economic Policy*, 107–111; J. Geraint Jenkins, *The Craft Industries* (London, 1972), 111; B. A. Holderness, *Pre-industrial England: Economy and Society, 1500–1750* (London, 1976), 48, 83; Eversley, "Home Market," in Jones and Mingay, eds., *Land, Labour, and Population*, 214; A. H. John, "Aspects of English Economic Growth in the First Half of the Eighteenth Century," *Economica*, XXVIII (1961), 183–187; Thirsk, *Economic Policy*, 122; and, for transportation improvements, Holderness, *Pre-industrial England*, 139–146.

45. Alan Macfarlane, Sarah Harrison, and Charles Jardine, *Reconstructing Historical Communities* (London, 1977), 156–157; Peter Laslett, *Family Life and Illicit Love in Earlier Generations: Essays in Historical Sociology* (Cambridge, 1977), 55, 64; M. K. Ashby, *The Changing English Village: A History of Bledington, Gloucestershire in Its Setting, 1066–1914* (Kineton, Warwick, 1974), 124, 224, 240; David G. Hey, *An English Rural Community: Myddle under the Tudors and Stuarts* (Leicester, 1974), 4, 143–144, 155; Peter Laslett, *The World We Have Lost*, 2d ed. (London, 1971), 66.

The craft mix characteristic of rural English villages prevailed in many parts of British America. Outside of cities and larger market towns, silversmiths, clockmakers, and the like did not set up shop any more frequently in New England or the Middle Atlantic colonies than they did in the Chesapeake region.[46] The occupational structure of Dedham, Massachusetts, during the eighteenth century was unremarkable enough for Kenneth Lockridge to characterize it simply as including "always a miller or two, a blacksmith, a cordwainer or other artisan . . . to supply the specialized needs of the economy." Bruce Daniels, in his study of eighteenth-century Connecticut towns, described the artisan communities of most country towns, although equal in size on a per capita basis to those of the few urban and secondary centers, as catering only to the needs of local farmers rather than engaging in the specialized, luxury-oriented trades found in urban centers. Artisans in a Sharon village, for example, consisted of a blacksmith, a brickmaker, and a tanner rather than a hatter, a barber, or a silversmith. The pattern repeated itself in the rural settlements of Lancaster County, Pennsylvania, where craftsmen worked as coopers, blacksmiths, weavers, itinerant tailors, and shoemakers.[47] Most community studies of towns in these regions, despite their attention to town functions and institutional growth, generational change and population mobility, farming patterns and land use, pay scant heed to occupational structures. If the dominant role of agriculture absolves the historian of the need to look extensively beyond the farmers, it then assures us of the substantial similarity of their craft networks to those of the Chesapeake.

Not only a restricted range of callings, but also a relatively small craft sector characterized most Anglo-American rural communities. In Leicestershire, late-seventeenth-century Wigston had more craftsmen than most, but only 30 percent of its population were artisans *and* tradesmen. Artisans comprised 11 percent of Goodnastone's sixty-two householders in 1695, 14 percent of the adult men in the parish of Myddle

46. Rita Susswein Gottesman, comp., *The Arts and Crafts in New York: Advertisements and News Items from New York City Newspapers, 1726–1776* (New York, 1938), xiii–xiv; Bridenbaugh, *Colonial Craftsman,* 64; Bruce C. Daniels, *The Connecticut Town: Growth and Development, 1635–1790* (Middletown, Conn., 1979), 148.

47. Kenneth A. Lockridge, *A New England Town, the First Hundred Years: Dedham, Massachusetts, 1636–1736* (New York, 1970), 69; Daniels, *Connecticut Town,* 156, 159; James T. Lemon, *The Best Poor Man's Country: A Geographical Study of Early Southeastern Pennsylvania* (Baltimore, 1972), 147.

early in the eighteenth century, and 16 percent of the householders in late-seventeenth-century Clayworth.[48] Speaking broadly of the whole colonial economy, Edwin Perkins argues that artisans—"men who worked with their hands and earned over 50 percent of their income from nonfarm pursuits"—constituted 7 to 10 percent of the heads of colonial households. Carl Bridenbaugh places the figure for craftsmen at 18 percent, while Jackson Turner Main found that artisans accounted for 10 percent of the inventoried Connecticut population (both urban and rural) around 1700 and for 25 percent about 1750, but Main cautions that the percentage was lower for the living population.[49]

By a number of different measures, the proportion of artisans in the Talbot population fell within these ranges. Although the percentage of artisans among the decedent population dropped over the course of the century, even at midcentury craftsmen constituted 10 percent of all decedents and 11 percent of those who were heads of households. Their decline, then, consisted of a falling away from the unusually high levels earlier in the century, when they represented 20 percent of all decedents and between 20 and 40 percent of householders (see table 6). Among the living population, about 30 percent of the estimated 470 householders in 1707 were artisans, while a generation later only one of every five householders was a craftsman. The percentage continued to fall, yet at 10 percent in 1755 still remained at the level cited by Perkins.

What was unusual, then, about rural Chesapeake artisans was not their numbers in relation to total population but rather their diffusion throughout the county. Lacking towns, the region appeared to lack craftsmen as well. In the one survey written of colonial craftsmen, Carl Bridenbaugh argues that "where a village could emerge, there the crafts could take hold and grow; there artisans might dwell together and specialize, each in his trade, certain of a demand for his wares." The southern colonies, because their inhabitants did not group themselves in towns but instead settled on geographically dispersed plantations, could therefore never

48. W. G. Hoskins, *The Midland Peasant: The Economic and Social History of a Leicestershire Village* (London, 1957), 212; Laslett, *World We Have Lost*, 66; Hey, *Myddle*, 143; Laslett, *Family Life*, 55.

49. Edwin J. Perkins, *The Economy of Colonial America* (New York, 1980), 81; Bridenbaugh, *Colonial Craftsman*, 1; Jackson Turner Main, "The Distribution of Property in Colonial Connecticut," in James Kirby Martin, ed., *The Human Dimensions of Nation Making: Essays on Colonial and Revolutionary America* (Madison, Wis., 1976), 89.

TABLE 6. *Relative Presence of Talbot Artisans in Total Population, 1690–1759 (in Percents)*

Decade	Artisans among Male Decedents	Artisans among Male Heads of Households
1690–1699	2	2
1700–1709	20	21
1710–1719	20	22
1720–1729	21	40
1730–1739	19	22
1740–1749	14	15
1750–1759	10	11

Source: Talbot Inventories, Maryland State Archives, Annapolis.

develop an artisan class. Even in the few southern towns that did evolve, Bridenbaugh asserts, the deleterious influence of a plantation economy outweighed the potential benefits of urbanization. "These southern communities are definite exceptions to any generalization about the favorable influence of urban conditions on the growth of native craftsmanship. The factors mentioned . . . as militating against the arts and crafts in the rural South for the most part also frustrated a full flowering in the villages and towns of the region."[50]

While artisans did settle in Oxford, the county's one town, the port never served as a magnet for all craftsmen working in the region. A walk along the town's few streets would have revealed the presence of a smith or a wheelwright or a ship carpenter but would never have indicated the full range of services available to county residents. As in other regions of the Chesapeake, the county's craftsmen could be found only by traveling along the roads and rivers, crisscrossing the landscape to discover the individual plantations and tenements on which the men lived and worked. As in Surry County, Virginia, on the south side of the James River across from Jamestown, "in the absence of urban centers, artisans lived among the planters they served" and were "scattered throughout the county." A similar pattern inscribed itself on All Hallow's Parish in Anne Arundel

50. Bridenbaugh, *Colonial Craftsman*, 63–64, 120.

County, across the Bay from Talbot. Craftsmen located themselves on separate sites throughout the parish, with no greater concentration of services in Londontown than occurred in Oxford.[51]

During the colonial period, the services of smiths and carpenters, weavers and shoemakers, coopers and tailors were readily available to Talbot residents. Although Talbot's artisans did not congregate in towns, neither did their customers; the shops scattered throughout the countryside thus placed their occupants among the planters who needed their products and facilitated the personal contact between manufacturer and buyer required for the conduct of local trade in a preindustrial economy. The range of services the artisans thereby provided, despite its limited contours, reflected a rational adjustment of potential scope to local needs and corresponded to that offered by artisans working in comparable communities in both England and other colonies.

THE ANALYSIS of Talbot's artisan community indicates that networks of local exchange, rather than self-sufficient plantations, provide the key to understanding the position of free artisans within Chesapeake society. The self-sufficiency model posits a community whose economic links consisted of a set of chains extending from individual plantations to tobacco merchants in Great Britain. As "societies in miniature," the plantations depended upon European markets, but not upon their neighbors. In actuality, the community was linked together by nets woven of strands that extended throughout the county, tying its residents together in a multitude of reciprocal bonds. No plantation enjoyed complete self-sufficiency, no matter how large the labor force; all relied to some degree upon the services of specialists within the local community. Ordinary planters, who might build their own barrels or repair their own shoes, nevertheless turned to their neighbors when they needed a tobacco barn built, a piece of furniture repaired, a supply of woolen yarn woven into cloth, or a new pair of boots. At the same time, their ability to mend shoes or make barrels gave those planters a potential source of income in addition to the returns from their crops. Craftsmen worked for their neighbors and, in an economy dependent upon book credit, used their

51. Kevin P. Kelly, "'In dispers'd Country Plantations': Settlement Patterns in Seventeenth-Century Surry County, Virginia," in Thad W. Tate and David L. Ammerman, eds., *The Chesapeake in the Seventeenth Century: Essays on Anglo-American Society* (Chapel Hill, N.C., 1979), 203; Earle, *Tidewater Settlement System*, 78–96.

skills as a form of currency, exchanging the products of their craft for merchandise or services.[52] The artisanal skills of the county's residents thus provided a measure of resiliency for the local economy far greater than a collection of autonomous plantations could have supplied.

To illustrate the extent of those reciprocal ties, consider the experience of Robert Goldsborough. Goldsborough was not a craftsman, but an attorney and one of Talbot's most prominent citizens. He served the county and province as sheriff, justice of the peace, delegate, associate justice, and (from 1719 to 1740) chief justice of the provincial court. In 1690, Goldsborough purchased the property of Ashby on the St. Michael's River, his home for the remainder of his life. In addition to acquiring property in land (1,800 acres in all), Goldsborough purchased bound labor, both servants and slaves. In the early 1700s, Goldsborough's hands, four or five at each location, cultivated his crops of tobacco and grains on both the home plantation and at least one additional quarter. Thirty years later, his slave force numbered eighteen above the age of sixteen and undoubtedly continued to increase in size. As the wealthy owner of a large landed estate and an above-average force of laborers, Robert Goldsborough thus represents the group within colonial society most likely to have satisfied its needs for goods and services through the combination of a trained bound labor force and merchandise imported from England. Goldsborough's ledger books, however, reveal that he depended heavily upon the skills of free artisans working in the local community.[53]

Goldsborough placed his greatest reliance upon the county's carpen-

52. For example, in 1716 tanner Richard Sawer received credit with a storekeeper for five sides of leather, and in 1723 John Oldham's credits on his account with merchant Richard Coward included mending a watch and a gunlock. In the 1740s and 1750s merchants credited cooper William Shieres for trimming 21 pork barrels and a washtub as well as making a well bucket; carpenter John Cowley for 20 days' work plus supplying 600 shingles; sawyer John Connoway for sawing 300 feet of walnut plank; shipwright Abraham Bromwell for work on a sloop being built for the firm; and weaver Benjamin Kinsley for weaving 50 yards of cloth. Judgments, FT 2:101 (6/18 court), PF 3:88 (8/23 court); Civil Judgments, 1747–1748, n.p. (3/48 and 8/48 courts); Judgments, JL 6:111 (3/43 court); Civil Judgments, 1751–1752, n.p. (11/51 court); Civil Judgments, 1750–1751, n.p. (3/51 court). See also Russo, "Free Workers," chaps. 4–7, for further evidence.

53. Roberta Bolling Henry, ed., "Robert Goldsborough of Ashby, and His Six Sons," *Md. Hist. Mag.*, XXXVI (1941), 316–319; Rent Roll, 1707; Debt Books, 1734,

ters, from Ambrose Ford, who built a canoe for him in 1688, to Nicholas Bartlett, who made a flat in 1739. In the intervening years, woodworkers shaped the material world of Ashby, Goldsborough's estate, providing the physical expression of his material success and cultural self-image. Goldsborough first employed James Sandford, a carpenter who worked for him from the early 1690s until 1704, to build an addition to his home and for other work on the house. Prior to 1709, however, Goldsborough contracted to have a new home built, for in that year he paid William Salsbery £60 for "building my house." Because Salsbery directed the construction project, there is no record of how many people shared this payment, but Salsbery must have been assisted by other workers. In addition, Peter Harwood laid the plank in the house and John Stacy supplied a table and other work space for the bricklayers. While the plantation house served as the most elegant symbol of Goldsborough's status and wealth, the numerous outbuildings that surrounded the "great house" and dotted the adjacent quarters offered testimony as well to their owner's position. Slightly more than a dozen carpenters shared responsibility for constructing nearly three dozen outbuildings, from hen houses and beehives to tobacco houses, barns, and a windmill.[54]

William Register, a carpenter who lived in Talbot in the early 1700s until he moved to Pennsylvania sometime prior to 1707 and who owned 150 acres in the neighborhood of Ashby, erected a number of those buildings. Between 1701 and 1704 he built a hen house, a tobacco house, and three larger structures, one with a shed. When Register moved to Pennsylvania, he sold part of his Talbot land to his neighbor Peter Harwood, a fellow carpenter and Quaker (the native-born son of one of the first Quaker families to settle in the county) with whom Register occasionally worked. Harwood, who lived in Talbot until his death at the age of eighty-eight in 1756, worked for Goldsborough from the first decade of the century, building him a shed, two cornhouses, a kitchen loft, a hen house, and five other large outbuildings. These buildings and those constructed by other carpenters served to give the plantation its

---

1738, 1744; "Tobacco Shipments, 1696–1771," M1338; "List of Taxables, 1733." No Goldsborough inventory (which would give the size of his slave force when he died) is recorded in either the provincial or the Talbot County inventories libers.

54. Robert Goldsborough Ledgers, M1338. Unless otherwise noted, the discussion of Goldsborough's employment of artisans is based upon the ledgers.

appearance of a "small village" and the planter the image of being "like one of the Patriarchs."[55]

The contributions of Register, Harwood, and the others to Golds-borough's estate were not limited simply to supplying its buildings, and the diversity of goods that they provided reveals the extent to which even the elite did not, in fact, live "in a kind of Independence on everyone but Providence." Register also made for Goldsborough a mast, four gates, a plow beam, two weeding plows, a sword for a cider press, a harrow, four tobacco hogsheads, and a chair, in addition to hanging two gates, fencing a yard, repairing a cart, and making repairs on the main house. Harwood worked on Goldsborough's boat, erected a partition within the house, covered a shed with weatherboards, made a powdering tub, a pail, a plow, a canoe, a sled, sheepfolds, a furrow plow, forty-six hogsheads, and cider casks, and worked on the cellar and the sheephouse. In the 1720s, two decades later, another carpenter built a large outbuilding at each of two quarters and also made a beehive, a cart, and a cheese press, repaired a gate, and fenced in a grave.

Blacksmiths constituted another group of artisans whose presence contributed goods and services vital to the operation of a successful plantation. The nature of smith's work, however, consisting as it did of numerous small jobs such as repairing tools and shoeing horses, rather than a lengthy building project, meant that one blacksmith could gener-ally satisfy the needs of the plantation. Loughlin McDaniel worked for Goldsborough in the 1690s, making horseshoes, shoeing horses, and performing such tasks as making a key for a stock lock and mending a froe, a weeding hoe, and a pestle. In 1701, Thomas Bartlett, a Yorkshire-man who had settled not far from Ashby ten years earlier, supplied similar services: mending and plating a sidesaddle, making three hoes and three weeding irons, hardening the steel on two axes, putting a new steel blade on another ax, and mending a plow and a pair of snuffers. Following after Bartlett, Oxford blacksmith John Oldham performed smith's work for Goldsborough for at least a dozen years, from supplying a set of weeding-plow irons in 1705 to mending a mill spindle, sharpening a plowshare, and mending a coulter in 1716. In all, Oldham's work consisted of repairs (including that of a watch), replacing the metal portions of old tools, and making new tools.

55. Land Records, MW 1:15, for Register's purchase of land, 1699, RF 11:21, for his sale, 1707; William Byrd II to the earl of Orrery, 1726, as quoted in Mullin, *Flight and Rebellion*, vii.

Just as the plantation required buildings for storage and housing, and workers needed tools with which to cultivate and process crops and raw materials, so too did the Goldsboroughs and their laborers need to be clothed and shod. William Dixon, a neighbor of Goldsborough's, provided a few pairs of gloves and a pair of stockings. Marmaduke Harrison made for the family three gowns and a petticoat, a coat for Goldsborough's daughter Mary, coats for two of the boys, two sets each of vest, breeches, and coat, a greatcoat, and a pair of breeches. Tailor John Carslake supplied various members of the family with clothing from the 1730s to the 1740s. Carslake made vests, breeches, suits, waistcoats, and coats for Goldsborough and three of his six sons. During the 1730s, a second tailor, John Osmont, provided similar items of clothing for the children. At the same time, a half-dozen shoemakers furnished the household with shoes, slippers, and boots. The volume of production—as many as fifty pairs a year from a single shoemaker—and explicit references to "Negro shoes" indicate that most of the articles were intended for Goldsborough's slaves, but some of the shoes were clearly ordered for Goldsborough himself or for his sons, just as the slippers and boots were purchased exclusively for family members.

In all, Robert Goldsborough utilized the skills of almost four dozen Talbot craftsmen: twenty carpenters, six blacksmiths, five shoemakers, four tailors, three coopers, a blockmaker, a bricklayer, a joiner, a plasterer, a glover, a silversmith, a weaver, and a sawyer. The ledgers reveal not just the numbers and types of artisans employed but also most strikingly the extensive and reciprocal ties that bound Goldsborough to a variety of the county's artisans. Goldsborough acted for them as an attorney, sold them merchandise, and offered them opportunities for employment. They in turn enabled him to build up the capital stock of his plantations, to clothe his family and workers, to keep his tools repaired and his horses shod. Goldsborough's preeminent position in Talbot's society thus rested upon the skills of many of his fellow colonists, rather than exclusively upon those of the servants and slaves that he owned. Goldsborough concentrated the efforts of his bound workers upon agricultural production, while free artisans exchanged their services and skills with those of Goldsborough to their mutual benefit.

TALBOT COUNTY was never without a sizable community of artisans, although the crafts represented and their relative numbers did change over the course of the colonial period in response to changes in the structure of the county's economy and evolving practices of plantation management. Some of the craftsmen were indeed temporary residents, whether free immigrants, newly freed servants, or young native-born sons, who worked briefly at a trade before moving elsewhere or acquiring land on which to rely exclusively for their livelihood. Nevertheless, two-thirds of the artisans who came to the county or who learned their skills there worked in the county for all or most of their adult lives. They trained other workers in their craft, including their children and kin, often leaving them tools and equipment as a legacy. As a result, many of the late-eighteenth-century artisans in the county were descendants of those earlier men, still working in the same trades that their fathers and grandfathers had pursued.

Craftsmen settled and remained in Talbot County within a framework of opportunity shaped by the tobacco economy of the region and its place in the broader Atlantic economy. Artisans could not establish themselves in the Talbot marketplace in defiance of that framework. A coachmaker, for example, skilled in making handsome carriages and desirous of serving the elite who purchased such items, would not have enough customers who could afford his wares until late in the century. A glover, on the other hand, could find many potential customers but could not sell his product at prices competitive with imported goods. Almost inevitably, he would soon try his hand at planting tobacco.

All crafts can be divided into two major groups, each with its individual components. The first is composed of those crafts that would not find a place within the county during the period of this study. Most were specialized luxury trades, which never had a presence in the county but were always restricted to urban centers with a wealthy clientele. A few of these would eventually find their way to Annapolis during its "Golden Age" or to Williamsburg, but Talbot never enjoyed a golden age, even during Oxford's most prosperous years (the dancing master and goldsmith who settled there in the 1720s may have been anticipating a golden age but they were soon discouraged and moved on). Other craftsmen made an early appearance, but could not survive in a market so easily supplied from overseas: glovers and hatters serve as the clearest examples. A final group consisted of those who needed a more concentrated market of prosperous customers than the county could offer until late in the century: the coachmakers and watchmakers of the late eighteenth century, for example.

Crafts that can be followed throughout the years from 1690 (and earlier) until 1760 (and later) represent the second group. Uniformly, these crafts offered products or services that had to be supplied locally or could rely on an abundant supply of locally produced raw materials. Although similar in that respect, patterns of growth or decline were not uniform. Coopering and shoemaking represented declining trades for free craftsmen. Low costs for equipment, steady demand within individual plantations, and readily acquired skills meant that planters intent upon pursuing self-sufficiency generally incorporated those two activities first into the routines of their plantations. By contrast, some crafts enjoyed a steady supply of workmen. Wheelwrights, for example, had a limited but secure market, unlikely to be threatened either by imports or by self-sufficiency. Blacksmiths and tanners enjoyed the most favorable position of all artisans, protected by the high entry thresholds both from competition and from incorporation into all but the largest plantations. Finally, some craft groups expanded during these years in response to economic changes. One facet of the efforts to diversify production for external markets (the other side of attempts to introduce internal self-sufficiency) stimulated trade with markets that lay outside the control of British merchants. Local men commissioned ships to sail to the West Indies and New England and hired local ship carpenters to build those vessels. At the same time, planters already established by the 1720s profited from the rise in tobacco prices, with those profits reflected in the clear improvement in the standard of living that began no later than the 1730s. New buildings and new furnishings represented part of that improvement, with more employment for house carpenters, bricklayers, and joiners as a result.

The continued presence of a substantial group of free artisans with strong and durable ties to the local community speaks eloquently of the continued importance of their role in the local economy. Furthermore, their presence testifies to the significance of local economic transactions within the broader regional economy. While the overseas market for tobacco may have exerted the strongest influence upon the Chesapeake economy, there remained a substantial local sector as well. Planters exchanged grain, flour, dairy products, livestock, and lumber with local merchants, who in turn sold these goods to other county residents. Local men, particularly young adults, hired themselves out to planters as overseers and as short-term agricultural workers, while women worked as housekeepers. Craftsmen constructed houses and tobacco sheds, mended tools, wove cloth, tanned leather, and built wagons for neighboring planters and for one another. Chesapeake residents did not inhabit a collection of self-contained, self-sufficient "villages in miniature"; rather, they lived in an interdependent community linked together by a network of local exchange.

Philip D. Morgan

Slave Life in Piedmont Virginia, 1720–1800

SLAVERY FIRST expanded into the Virginia piedmont in the 1720s. The institution took root rapidly. By the middle of the eighteenth century—just about a generation after its introduction—forty thousand slaves, one-third of the colony's total, resided in the piedmont's rolling hills. Within a further generation, a remarkable transformation took place. The piedmont slave population almost trebled in size; Virginia emerged from the Revolutionary War with more slaves living beyond, than within, the fall line. The center of black life had shifted extraordinarily rapidly from tidewater to piedmont. The remaining decades of the eighteenth (and early nineteenth) century maintained the trend. By 1800 the tidewater's share of Virginia's slaves had sunk close to a third, whereas the piedmont's stood at over half.[1]

An understanding of the slave experience in eighteenth-century Virginia, therefore, must come to terms with life in the piedmont. As a preliminary attempt, this essay will first consider the sources of the remarkable growth of the piedmont slave population in the critical third quarter of the eighteenth century. Since African and creole immigrants were important to piedmont population growth, attention will then turn to the presence and interrelationship of these two groups. Because an immigrant society might be expected to place severe obstacles in the way of family formation, an exploration of family life among piedmont slaves follows. Considerations of family raise the broader issue of the existence and character of Afro-American community life, the subject of a subsequent section. An investigation of the internal structure of slave life cannot proceed in a vacuum, for the unfree were locked into an intimate interdependence with the free. The distinctive character of black-white

1. Richard S. Dunn, "Black Society in the Chesapeake, 1776–1810," in Ira Berlin and Ronald Hoffman, eds., *Slavery and Freedom in the Age of the American Revolution* (Charlottesville, Va., 1983), 49–82; Philip D. Morgan and Michael L. Nicholls, "Slaves in Piedmont Virginia, 1720–1790" (*William and Mary Quarterly*, forthcoming); U.S. Bureau of the Census, *Return of the Whole Number of Persons . . . for the Second Census* (Washington, D.C., 1802).

relations in the piedmont is, therefore, singled out for separate analysis. Chronological changes will be kept firmly in view throughout, but last of all, some brief observations are offered on late-eighteenth-century developments.

If the aim is to provide a rounded, though necessarily sketchy, portrait of slave life in the piedmont region, the search for an answer to a single question ties together many of the essay's varied themes. Allan Kulikoff, who has, to date, done more than anyone to investigate the nature of slave life in the Chesapeake tidewater, puts it this way: "How much of the history of tidewater was repeated in the piedmont? If the population of the piedmont was heavily African, perhaps the characteristics of slave society in tidewater in the 1720s and 1730s were replicated in the piedmont in the 1750s and 1760s. But if enough black migrants from tidewater entered the piedmont, the story of the 1750s and 1760s may have been much the same in the two regions."[2] Should, then, the expansion of slavery into the piedmont be conceived in terms of replication or extension? Where appropriate, this essay will attempt to answer that question, while providing an outline of slave life in one region.

I

That the period between 1755 and 1782 marked a significant turning point in Virginia's slave experience is evident from the regional growth rates of the colony's slave population. During that quarter-century the slave populations of tidewater, piedmont, and Shenandoah Valley grew at an average annual rate of around 1, 7, and 30 percent respectively (see table 1). Quite obviously, a massive number of tidewater slaves had been transferred into the other two regions. Wartime developments compounded this trend because the tidewater, particularly the Peninsula (the area between the James and York rivers), lost more slaves than either of the other two regions. In the 1780s, the tidewater again lagged behind its sister regions, even though the slave populations of all three grew rapidly. In the 1790s, the floodgates opened once more—so much so, that the tidewater slave population stood at a virtual standstill,

2. Kulikoff, "The Origins of Afro-American Society in Tidewater Maryland and Virginia, 1700 to 1790," *WMQ*, 3d Ser., XXXV (1978), 259.

marking the beginnings of another, and ultimately more consequential, out-migration.[3]

Because the third quarter of the eighteenth century saw a significant shift in the center of gravity of Virginia's black population, we must ask how this was accomplished. How many tidewater slaves were transferred west of the fall line during the key period, 1755 to 1782? The slave population of Virginia increased naturally over this quarter-century at an annual rate of about 3 percent. Assuming that the slave population of each region increased uniformly at this rate, the tidewater's slave population in 1782 was in deficit to the tune of 36,000 people, while the piedmont and valley registered a combined surplus of around 51,000 slaves (see table 2). Since approximately 4,000 of the tidewater's displaced slaves went neither to piedmont nor valley but left Virginia altogether with the British, this region should be credited with directly increasing the slave populations of piedmont and valley by about 32,000 people.[4]

The shortfall between the tidewater deficit and the piedmont and valley surplus, amounting to 19,000 slaves, can be explained in two ways. First, the piedmont received virtually all the African immigrants—some 15,000—who came to Virginia between 1755 and 1774. The number of Africans still alive in 1782, together with their surviving children, I estimate at about 14,000. Second, the remaining 5,000 can probably be attributed to a rate of natural increase among piedmont and valley slaves slightly in excess of 3 percent a year, since both regions were healthier environments than tidewater. This is all the more likely when we consider that many of the piedmont immigrants from tidewater must have been

3. On the later migration, see Allan Kulikoff, "Uprooted Peoples: Black Migrants in the Age of the American Revolution, 1790–1820," in Berlin and Hoffman, eds., *Slavery and Freedom*, 143–171.

4. The slave population of Virginia grew by 109,092 between 1755 and 1782. My estimate is that just over 15,000 Africans were imported into the colony in that period. Even if one assumes that there were no African survivors from this 15,000 influx (an impossibility), the slave population would have grown naturally at the rate of 2.9% a year. Assuming a few thousand African survivors, the natural rate of increase must have been just over 3%. In order to assume the lowest possible rate of natural increase, I have used the 2.9 figure. For the number of slaves lost to the British, see Kulikoff, "Uprooted Peoples," in Berlin and Hoffman, eds., *Slavery and Freedom*, 144. Compare Sylvia R. Frey, "Between Slavery and Freedom: Virginia Blacks in the American Revolution," *Journal of Southern History*, XLIX (1983), 374.

TABLE I. *Growth of Virginia's Slave Population, 1755–1800*

Region	Population Increase and Average Annual Growth Rates		
	1755–1782	1782–1790	1790–1800
Tidewater	25,978	22,972	4,457
	1.2%	2.7%	0.3%
Piedmont	76,690	32,687	39,603
	7.1%	3.5%	2.6%
Valley	6,424	5,728	8,419
	30.3%	13.8%	5.5%

Sources: Evarts B. Greene and Virginia D. Harrington, *American Population before the Federal Census of 1790* (New York, 1937), 150–155; R. A. Brock, ed., *The Official Records of Robert Dinwiddie, Lieutenant-Governor of the Colony of Virginia, 1751–1758* (Virginia Historical Society, *Collections*, IV [Richmond, Va., 1884]), II, 352–353; personal property assessments for individual counties, 1782, Virginia State Library, Richmond; *Heads of Families at the First Census of the United States Taken in the Year 1790: Reviews of the State Enumerations, 1782 to 1785. Virginia* (Baltimore, 1966), 9–10; U.S. Bureau of the Census, *Return of the Whole Number of Persons . . . for the Second Census* (Washington, D.C., 1802).

creoles, who undoubtedly contributed children to the population quickly and regularly. Moreover, there were a surprising number of girls in African cargoes in the late colonial period—and perhaps women as well. Finally, the proportion of children in the piedmont slave population certainly supports the notion of a relatively high rate of natural increase among that region's slaves.[5]

Viewed, then, from the perspective of both supplying and receiving regions, a 32,000 tidewater deficit seems plausible. Since the newcomers probably produced children at the colony-wide rate, the piedmont must have received over 17,000 tidewater slaves and the valley the other 3,000

5. Morgan and Nicholls, "Slaves in Piedmont Virginia." I estimate surviving immigrants using the African survivor schedule in Allan Kulikoff, "A 'Prolifick' People: Black Population Growth in the Chesapeake Colonies, 1700–1790," *Southern Studies*, XVI (1977), 393 (with a minor modification to allow for a slightly higher survival rate). The estimate of 7,000 surviving children of Africans is nothing more than an educated guess, but I would be surprised if the number of African survivors of 1782 was not matched by a similar number of first-generation children.

TABLE 2. *How the Slave Population Grew in Virginia, 1755–1782*

	By Region		
	Tidewater	Piedmont	Valley
	Gross Deficits and Surpluses		
Actual increase	25,978	76,690	6,424
Natural increase of			
1755 population	61,922	31,421	614
Balance	− 35,944	+ 45,269	+ 5,810
	Adjusted Deficits and Surpluses		
Slaves who left			
Virginia in war	4,000		
Surviving Africans		6,801	
Surviving children of			
Africans		c. 7,000	
Balance	− 31,944	+ 31,468	+ 5,810
Discrepancy		4,499	832
	Intraregional Movements		
Arrivals from tidewater		17,366	3,206
Natural increase of			
newcomers		9,600	1,772
Total	− 31,944	+ 26,966	+ 4,978

Note: See text and n. 4.

between 1775 and 1782. In other words, almost one in five tidewater slaves was transferred west of the fall line during that period.[6]

We are now in a position to assess the sources of slave population

6. This proportion rests on my estimate of the tidewater slave population as it would have been in 1768 (the midpoint) had there been no out-migration, i.e., about 119,000.

growth in the Virginia piedmont between 1755 and 1782. During that quarter-century, the number of slaves increased by about 77,000. The addition of immigrants accounted for almost a third of this increase; the other two-thirds can be attributed to the natural increase of the slaves already resident in the region in 1755 and to the children born to the creole and African newcomers. What this analysis strongly suggests is that the piedmont experience of the 1760s and 1770s was more an extension of contemporary tidewater than a replication of an earlier phase in tidewater history.

II

Turning from the technicalities of population growth to its implications, we need to investigate the changing balance of Africans and creoles among the piedmont slave population. Two contrasting facts immediately command attention. First, although African immigration was not central to slave population growth in the piedmont, more Africans resided beyond the fall line than in tidewater in the late colonial era. In terms of the relative proportions of Africans and creoles, in other words, the late colonial piedmont did replicate to some degree an earlier tidewater experience. Even more notable, however, was the speed at which the piedmont slave population approximated the contemporary, rather than an earlier, tidewater pattern. Native-born slaves soon came to dominate the piedmont slave population, much as they did in contemporary tidewater. Once again, extension rather than replication seems the dominant story.

Still, in certain piedmont counties at particular times the adult population was heavily African. In Amelia County, which probably received more Africans than any other Chesapeake county in the forty years before Independence, about 60 percent of the adult slaves in 1755 were Africans. In 1782, although the proportion had dropped considerably, it still stood at around one-fifth. Even by the late 1760s and early 1770s, the demand for Africans was relatively brisk in certain piedmont counties. In July 1769 Richard Adams considered himself fortunate to have eighty slaves to sell on the upper James. Two years later, another James River merchant informed a correspondent who had proposed an "African Scheme" that "Negroes will always sell well here." As if to prove the point, in 1772 Paul Carrington bought fifty slaves at Bermuda Hundred in order to sell them to eager southside purchasers.[7]

Once Africans reached the plantations, their presence was not always documented. An occasional name or ethnic designation in an inventory, as in Angola Jack, Ebo Sam, Malagawyou Bess, and Gambia James, often provides the only clue to an African identity.[8] Somewhat more exceptional were the quarters of Mrs. Mayo and those of Philip Mayo of Goochland County. On the former estate, seven of seventeen tithables had African names (Jolloff, Quaw, Fatima, Congo, Cudjo, Shantee, and Cudjee), as did four of thirteen on the latter (Bussee, Jallapa, Jubah, and Abanah). Or it might take an unusual event for Africans to come to our notice. The deaths of "two new Negroes" in Goochland County in 1762 prompted the county court to order an inquest. In Prince Edward County, an African influence might explain the extraordinary action of Jacob, who when cornered by six whites, defended himself with "sharp pointed darts of a sufficient length and size to kill a man at a great distance." Or, even more indirectly, we might infer an African presence from place-names. Eighteenth-century Cumberland County, for instance, had its Angola and Guinea roads, its Little Guinea Neck, and its Great Guinea and Angola creeks.[9]

The prominence of Africans among the piedmont runaway population, particularly in the earliest years, provides the most direct evidence of their widespread presence. The residences of two slave runaways captured in

7. Morgan and Nicholls, "Slaves in Piedmont Virginia"; Richard Adams to his brother, July 5, 1769, Adams Family Papers, Virginia Historical Society, Richmond; Roger Atkinson to Samuel Gist, Jan. 10, 1771, Atkinson Letter Book, University of Virginia Library, Charlottesville; "Deposition given between Gordon v. Lockhead, Mar. 5, 1801," Paul Carrington Papers, Va. Hist. Soc.

8. William Ellis inventory, Sept. 1766, Spotsylvania County Will Book D, 261; Jeremiah Merers inventory, Apr. 1772, Spotsylvania Will Book E, 18; Joseph Wilkinson inventory, Jan. 18, 1753, Chesterfield County Will Book 1, 112; Rev. George Fraser inventory, Aug. 9, 1762, *ibid.*, 366. All county records are on microfilm at the Virginia State Library, Richmond. Occasionally, "new" slaves are mentioned in inventories, as in those of William Thornton Smith, Nov. 1749, Amelia County Will Book 1, 61, and John Bibb, Oct. 3, 1769, Goochland County Deed, Will Book 10, 30.

9. "Tithables in Southam Parish in the County of Goochland for the Year 1746 taken by George Carrington," Goochland County Tithable Lists, Va. State Lib.; Goochland County Court Order Book 9, 41; trial of Jacob, Prince Edward County Court Order Book, 1754–1758, 78; Cumberland County Court Order Book, 1758–1762, 286, 1774–1778, 483, 524, 1779–1784, 21, 166.

Louisa County in the mid-1740s could not be determined because neither spoke English. Presumably, it was the slave himself who gave his name to a capturer in Spotsylvania County in 1744: he called himself "Angola Tom."[10] In the following year Sambo, Aaron, and Berwick ran away from their quarter in Orange County eight months after their arrival in the colony; two slaves imported from Senegambia ran away within a month of being brought to Hanover County; and in 1751 David ran from his quarter on Willis Creek in Albemarle County less than a month after arriving on the ship *Williamsburg* with 294 other Africans.[11] These aliens in the piedmont, like their compatriots throughout the New World, took to flight to express their detestation of their new surroundings and situation.

Also typical of Africans throughout the New World, these piedmont immigrants formed strong attachments to fellow shipmates. The snow *Yanimarew* imported 240 Africans in the summer of 1770. One month after being purchased and taken to Amherst County, Charles ran away. Meanwhile, in Richmond three other African men, imported in the same slaver, fled their master. They apparently sought out the companionship of their former shipmates (perhaps Charles was among them), for their master reported "it is imagined that they were seen some time ago (along with three others of the same cargo) on Chickahominy, and it is supposed they are still lurking about the skirts of that swamp." A similar venture occurred the following year when a twenty-year-old man and a twelve-year-old girl, recently purchased by the same master from an African slaver, "went off with several others, being persuaded that they could find the way back to their own Country."[12]

10. Court of Public Claims, Aug. 24, 1744, and Court for Assessing Public Levy, Nov. 25, 1746, Louisa County Court Order Book, 1742–1748, 117, 212; Court of Public Claims, Aug. 1744, Spotsylvania County Court Order Book, 1738–1749, 281. There are few advertised runaways in Virginia newspapers before 1760. Of the 31 from the piedmont before that date, 13 were Africans, 9 creoles, and 9 unidentified. Of those runaways with known birthplaces after 1760, 20% were Africans in the 1760s, rising to 31% in the 1770s (sample size: 219).

11. William Hunter, *Virginia Gazette* (Parks), May 16, 1745; Aaron Truehart, *ibid.*, Sept. 26, 1745; Archibald Cary, *ibid.* (Hunter), Nov. 14, 1751. On the sale of the *Williamsburg*'s cargo, see Walter Minchinton, Celia King, and Peter Waite, eds., *Virginia Slave-Trade Statistics, 1698–1775* (Richmond, Va., 1984), 147. For sheer persistence, the medal must go to Will, a Chesterfield County African, who made four attempts, "as he said, to get to his country." Jordan Anderson, *Va. Gaz.*, Oct. 20, 1768.

12. John Jacob, *Va. Gaz.* (Rind), Feb. 7, 1771; James Buchanan, *ibid.* (Purdie &

The presence of restive Africans may help account for the heavy concentration of "poisoning" cases that appeared in piedmont county courts in the second half of the eighteenth century. Of about 180 slaves tried for "poisoning" in colonial Virginia county courts, two-thirds resided in the piedmont. Rarely can alleged poisoners be proven to have been Africans, but the high concentrations of such cases in counties where large numbers of Africans lived, together with information such as the African names of some alleged poisoners, make the connection plausible. Furthermore, an offhand remark by Edmund Pendleton, a resident of Caroline County (adjoining the piedmont), suggests such a connection in the contemporary mind. In 1777, when referring to the atrocities perpetrated by the British army, Pendleton exclaimed that they had descended to the "low, mean, petiful, skulking, perfidious, wicked Italian & African business of Poisoning."[13]

Even though an African influence was noticeable in the late-eighteenth-century piedmont, it was a constantly dwindling one. The proportion of Africans in the piedmont slave population quickly assumed a profile similar to that of tidewater. In 1755 perhaps as many as one-third of adult slaves throughout the piedmont were Africans. By 1782, in spite of the importation of around 15,000 Africans, almost all of whom went to various piedmont counties, the proportion had dropped to about one in ten.[14] Moreover, by the late colonial period, many Africans were longtime residents of the piedmont region and no longer easily distinguished from creoles. In 1777, Aberdeen, a thirty-five-year-old blacksmith, resided on

---

Dixon), Dec. 13, 1770; the sale of the *Yanimarew* is detailed in Minchinton, King, and Waite, eds., *Virginia Slave-Trade Statistics*, 176–177; George Robertson, *Va. Gaz.* (Purdie & Dixon), Sept. 12, 1771. In 1773 14 "NEW NEGROES," probably part of a group awaiting sale, "went away" from Hanovertown. John Burnley, *ibid.*, Aug. 19, 1773.

13. Philip J. Schwarz, "Hanging in Chains: Slaves and Crime in Virginia, 1619–1865" (unpublished MS), chap. 6; trial of Obee, July 29, 1778, Spotsylvania Order Book, 1774–1782, 94 (this name seems remarkably like *obi* or *obeah*, the term for Jamaican sorcery); trial of Okie, May 3, 1756, Cumberland Order Book, 1752–1758, 389–390; trial of Mustapha, Dec. 7, 1762, *ibid.*, 1762–1764, 114–115; Edmund Pendleton to Brigadier General Woodford, July 11, 1777, Edmund Pendleton Papers, Southern Historical Collection, University of North Carolina at Chapel Hill.

14. The 1755 figure is simply a high estimate based on Kulikoff, "A 'Prolifick' People," *So. Studies*, XVI (1977), 423. See also Morgan and Nicholls, "Slaves in Piedmont Virginia." Note in table 2 that I estimate about 7,000 African adult survivors in 1782.

the Falls Plantation in Chesterfield County. He "came into the country young," his master noted, and therefore spoke "very good English." In the same year, a Fauquier County African was described as "affect[ing] to pronounce the English language very fine, or rather to clip it." He could also read and write.[15]

An African named Bacchus best personifies the speed with which these immigrants adjusted to their new surroundings. In the space of about three years in the early 1770s, Bacchus left a dizzying trail of crime across both tidewater and piedmont. In that time, he ran away at least four times, faced four separate criminal charges, was branded in the hand, heard himself pronounced guilty and sentenced to hang in two county courts, but evaded the hangman's noose on both occasions. In 1771 this "thick set, and well made," seventeen-year-old lad spoke "broken English," but two years later his proficiency had improved so that his master described his speech as only "somewhat broken." His assimilation was never total, however, for he retained his African name, Juba, while also employing the English names Jemmy and James. Nevertheless, he was sufficiently conversant with white ways to pass as a free black in Chesterfield County. In that capacity, it seems, Bacchus got wind of the Somerset Case (a famous legal decision of 1772 that was widely but erroneously perceived to outlaw slavery in England) and imagined he would be free if only he could get to that country. This was, according to his master, "a Notion now too prevalent among the Negroes." Indeed, Bacchus was thought to be in the company of another of his master's fugitives, a twenty-seven-year-old "very black" woman who had since passed herself as free, using the name Sukey Jones. That news of the Somerset Case had reached the ears of a humble African like Bacchus in piedmont Virginia, some three thousand miles away, speaks well of his initiative and resolve, but more particularly of his political education.[16]

Piedmont Africans creolized quickly, one might conjecture, precisely because they came into contact with large numbers of accomplished and

15. William Black, *Va. Gaz.* (Dixon & Hunter), Dec. 5, 1777; Thomas Lawson, *ibid.*, Jan. 23, 1778. See also Samuel Calland, *ibid.* (Dixon & Nicolson), Dec. 18, 1779.

16. Trials of Bacchus, Jan. 15, 1771, Jan. 1, 1772, Mar. 17, 1773, Surry County Criminal Proceedings against People of Color, Surry Courthouse, Surry, Va. (information kindly supplied by Philip J. Schwarz and Kevin Kelly); trials of same, July 21, Sept. 18, 1773, Chesterfield County Court Order Book 5, 305, 347; John Austin Finnie, *Va. Gaz.* (Purdie & Dixon), July 4, 1771, Sept. 30, 1773.

assimilated slaves. By the late colonial era, the African newcomer could regularly encounter slaves like painter Peter Brown, raised in Petersburg, who was "fond of Singing," or thirty-year-old Jacob from Louisa County, who could read and write, spoke "in the Scotch-Irish dialect, and in conversation frequently use[d] the words moreover and likewise," or twenty-eight-year-old Sam from Amelia County, a carpenter and cooper, who could "read print, pretends to a deal of religion, has been a good fiddler, and is acquainted with many parts of Virginia." If an African ran away in a group after midcentury, he usually accompanied creoles, not fellow Africans. Three men ran away from Archibald Cary's forge in Chesterfield County in 1766. One was a Virginia-born carpenter, another a Virginia-born foreman, and the third a Gold Coast native, now a fireman. Nine years later, two Africans who spoke only a rudimentary English ran away with a Jamaica-born black and a Virginian mulatto from their Prince Edward County quarter.[17]

Masters must have been reduced to hoping that their African slaves would fail to emulate the examples set by their creoles. An incident involving a highly assimilated slave belonging to Peter Nunnery of Goochland County illustrates the problems with which masters had to contend. In 1747, Nunnery's runaway slave was thought to have stolen a horse's bell. He was pursued and eventually overtaken in Henrico County by three whites. When confronted, the slave at first denied the charge, then under some duress confessed to the theft, and finally promised to reveal the bell's hiding place. He first took the group to a pile of logs, pretended to search for the missing item, then "s[ai]d with a Laughter that he made [a] fool of them and that the Bell was not there." Not surprisingly, this charade angered his captors, who proceeded to beat him, whereupon the slave promised to reveal the true whereabouts of the bell. But he repeated the performance at a fodder stack. By now the whites were livid with rage and began cutting switches in order to whip the impudent black, but the slave attempted to convince them to follow him one more time to a hollow tree stump by the river's edge where all would be revealed. At this point, one of his captors declared that "he would . . . follow [the] son of a bitch no more for he could make a bell sooner," but the slave won his reprieve from the other two. On their way

17. Peterfield Trent, *Va. Gaz.* (Purdie & Dixon), June 16, 1774; David Hoops, *ibid.* (Dixon & Hunter), Mar. 30, 1776; William Green, *ibid.* (Purdie), May 9, 1772; Archibald Cary, *ibid.*, Feb. 24, 1766; Robert Donald, *ibid.* (Dixon & Hunter), Nov. 25, 1775. See also Richard Eggleston, *ibid.* (Purdie), May 2, 1766.

to the river, the bondman managed to slip away, get ahead of his captors, and jump into the river. When urged to come out, he began "laughing at [them and] Sunk in their sight & they saw him no more." If, as seems likely, this self-assured slave went to his death making a fool of whites, no doubt he would have wanted it no other way.[18]

Creoles soon dominated slave life in the piedmont. Although almost all Africans who reached Virginia from midcentury onward made their home in the piedmont, their numbers were never large enough to put much of an African stamp on the emerging slave society. Piedmont Africans certainly resisted slavery in characteristic ways and seem to have been at the heart of the widespread resort to magic. More noticeable, however, is the speed at which they creolized, evident in everything from their acquisition of English language skills to their running away with native-born slaves. Creoles set the standard and tone of this regional society remarkably quickly.

III

Since the piedmont received many immigrants in the colonial era, the region's slaves did not find it easy to establish a measure of family life. In this sense, black life in the piedmont replicated an earlier phase of the tidewater slave experience. At the same time, there were important differences between the two experiences. Piedmont immigrants were primarily creoles, not Africans. Not surprisingly, therefore, the adult sex ratios among piedmont slaves rapidly approached equality. Taking the region as a whole, adult male slaves outnumbered females heavily during the first decade or so of piedmont settlement. But these imbalanced sex ratios were relatively short-lived. By the late 1730s and early 1740s, there were fewer than 120 men for every 100 slave women in the piedmont. More-skewed imbalances periodically reoccurred as waves of immigrants moved into the region, but the overall trend was a rapid downward one. By the late 1760s and 1770s there were almost as many women as men.[19]

Even more striking is the proportion of children to be found in the

18. Action of trespass of Peter Nunnery against Thomas Williamson, May 1747, Goochland Order Book 6, 320–321.
19. Morgan and Nicholls, "Slaves in Piedmont Virginia."

piedmont slave population. In part this can be attributed to the composition of both migration streams, since young slaves predominated among creole and African newcomers. In any case, from the first years of piedmont settlement, and for much of the colonial period, children outnumbered women by at least two to one. Individual plantation holdings illustrate the broad trend. When William Byrd's 603 slaves, resident at Westover in the tidewater and at the falls of the James River and on the Roanoke River in the interior, were enumerated in 1757, children outnumbered women by well over two to one in the piedmont locations, but by less than two to one in tidewater. Between 1761 and 1771, the slave women belonging to Edward Ambler's plantations in Hanover and Louisa counties produced so many children that the child-woman ratio went from 103 to 236. A detailed listing of Samuel Gist's 149 slaves, distributed over six quarters in Goochland, Hanover, and Louisa counties in 1783, reveals that females outnumbered males heavily (the sex ratio was 86) and that children outnumbered women by well over 200. The age pyramid of this group of slaves was relatively symmetrical (see figure 1).[20] In sum, the youthfulness of the piedmont slave population was striking.

The available measures of the fecundity of female slaves—such indicators as age at first birth, length of intervals between births, and completed family size—support and help account for this youthfulness. Some piedmont slave women were remarkably young when they conceived their first child. Lilly, a Jerdone slave, was not even fifteen when she first conceived. The average age of conception in the late colonial period was 18.2 years, dropping slightly to 17.7 years in the late eighteenth century. Piedmont slave mothers bore children regularly and rapidly—one every twenty-eight months on average, not taking into account early infant mortality.[21]

---

20. *Ibid.*; list of Negroes belonging to William Byrd, July 7–26, 1757, Miscellaneous Manuscript Collection, Library of Congress; the Ambler material was assembled from yearly listings, which extend in some places from 1755 to 1777, in the Dabney Family Papers (microfilm, Colonial Williamsburg Foundation Library, Williamsburg, Va., hereafter CW), and a 1761 listing, Box 6, Slavery Collection, New-York Historical Society, New York City. In an age profile for 39 slaves belonging to another piedmont master, two-thirds were under 24 years of age. Joseph Bass inventory, Mar. 4, 1779, Chesterfield Will Book 3, 218–220.

21. Age at conception data are not readily available. I have used only cases where the precise birthdates of the mother and her presumed first child were known. I found 14 such cases for the 1750s–1770s and 9 for the 1780s–1790s in the William Bolling Register, 1752–1890, the Paul Carrington Account Book, 1755–1775, the Stephen Cocke Account Book, 1772–1847, all in the Va. Hist. Soc., and in the Slave Book of

FIGURE I . *Age Profile of Slaves Belonging to Samuel Gist, 1783*

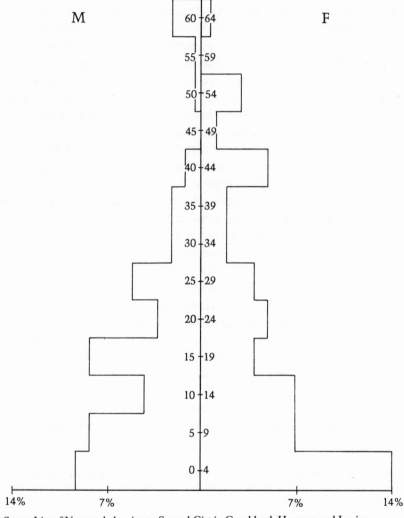

Source: List of Negroes belonging to Samuel Gist in Goochland, Hanover, and Louisa counties, November 12, 1783, Virginia Historical Society, Richmond.

Finally, piedmont slave women probably lived longer than their tidewater counterparts. Robert Rose thought the death of his slave woman Judith sufficiently noteworthy to put in his diary because she was "the first Slave of Mine that has died in Albemarle." This was almost a decade after Rose first set up quarters there. Not surprisingly, therefore, completed family sizes were generally larger for piedmont, than for tidewater, slaves.[22]

Truncated family structures inevitably characterized such a youthful immigrant population. In the late 1750s Peyton Randolph, like many another tidewater planter, established a new plantation in the piedmont. He transferred a number of his young slaves to a quarter in what became Charlotte County, over a hundred miles away from his home plantation. No doubt these teenagers and young adults left kin behind when they moved west. Moreover, the imbalance between men and women meant that large age differentials (of about ten years) separated spouses, when they were fortunate enough to marry. Just over twenty years later, however, some of the children of the original immigrants had reached maturity and established families of their own. Nanny, for instance, certainly left kin behind when she came to the piedmont as a twenty-five-year-old mother of four children. But by 1784, at least two of her three daughters had given birth themselves and Nanny was a grandmother to four children, one of whom bore her name. Sarah, another Randolph slave, was about twenty years of age when she was moved to the piedmont and already the mother of three children, including twins; she gave birth to at least three more children in her new home. By 1784 two of her daughters had married and each had one child apiece. Nanny and Sarah were therefore matriarchs of rapidly growing slave clans.[23]

Struggling to re-create a semblance of an ordered family life, Nanny,

---

the Jerdone Family, Va. State Lib. For comparable tidewater ages, see Kulikoff, "A 'Prolifick' People," *So. Studies*, XVI (1977), 407. The length of interval between births is based on 181 birth intervals (omitting any intervals longer than 60 months) from 1755–1799 in the above sources.

22. Robert Rose diary, Dec. 24, 1749 (microfilm, CW). On the healthiness of piedmont slaves in general, see James Mercer to Battaile Muse, July 10, 1771, and Hugh Nelson to Muse, Mar. 28, 1779, Battaile Muse Papers, Duke University Library, Durham, N.C. For completed family size, see Kulikoff, "A 'Prolifick' People," *So. Studies*, XVI (1977), 409.

23. Inventory of the estate of Peyton Randolph, 1776, and a list of Negroes belonging to Edmund Randolph in Charlotte, Albemarle, and James City counties, Sept. 23, 1784, Randolph Family Papers (microfilm, CW).

Sarah, and their fellow Randolph slaves were at least more fortunate than the slaves of Francis Willis, a planter who made his home in Gloucester County, but who had quarters in the piedmont. In 1766 Willis died and the majority of his slaves in Cumberland and Hanover counties were sold. Few piedmont planters could afford to purchase large lots of slaves. Indeed, most could buy no more than a single slave, so the sale scattered 101 slaves among sixty-one purchasers. Only occasionally can we be certain that families were separated (the couple Butcher Will and his wife Venus were sold with their "sucking child," also named Venus, but their two sons Sam and Lewis were sold separately). However, since three-quarters of the men were sold singly, while almost half of the women were sold with at least one child, it seems a fair assumption that these sales broke many husband-wife, not to mention parent-child, relationships.[24]

A firsthand description of one slave sale is sufficiently interesting to be explored in depth. It took place in the winter of 1787 in Powhatan County, the very heart of the piedmont. Mr. Gay, a Powhatan resident, was apparently in deep debt, particularly to Robert Hare of Philadelphia, who employed the local planter Benjamin Harrison to look after his interests. Gay was forced to put up every one of his slaves, fifty-seven in all, for public auction at the Powhatan County Courthouse. Six slaves who were already mortgaged were immediately claimed. Of those remaining, twelve were not even "set up," owing to their advanced ages and general unsuitability. Their fate is unknown. The sale itself went slowly; as night fell, only twelve slaves had been purchased. In order to protect Mr. Hare's interest, Harrison bought the remaining twenty-seven slaves at £40 apiece. Harrison showed a measure of compassion by allowing his acquisitions to return to Gay that night in order to "collect their little effects together." However, within a few days, Harrison had sold six at £70 each, making a tidy profit. He then advertised his willingness to sell the others privately and set another date for a second public auction. Noting that his purchases had not been clothed that year, he proposed remedying the omission so that they might "sell better." He explained to Hare that "the plan of carrying them from Court to Court will not do at this season of the year for so many [are] small negroes." No mention was made of keeping families together; rather, business decisions ruled this, and presumably many another, slave sale.[25]

24. "Account of Sales of Slaves belonging to Francis Willis, Esq., Dec. 4–22, 1766," Jerdone Memorandum Book, Va. State Lib.

25. Benjamin Harrison to Robert Hare, Dec. 25, 1787, Benjamin Harrison Letter Book, 50–51 (microfilm, CW).

The arbitrariness with which slave family members could be dispersed is revealed in a number of cases concerning a father's verbal gift of a slave to one of his children. In the early 1750s George Thompson of Goochland County gave a slave to his daughter Joyce "as soon as the said [slave] Girl was born." He told Joyce "to take care of her for that he had no more to do with the said Girl." In 1769 a lodger in the Cumberland County household of William Angela, Sr., remembered a conversation between Angela and his daughter Betty some fifteen years previous. The father promised to give his daughter a slave infant named Biddy, provided Betty take care of the child. His action was largely a response to the "grumblings" of his son Benjamin, who as overseer on his father's plantation objected to Biddy's mother "coming in to tend the negro child." In this way, Betty acquired her own slave, and a slave mother was deprived of the care of her own daughter.[26]

Small holdings, constant sales and mortgages, and distribution of property among large numbers of heirs, not to mention the heartlessness displayed by men like Angela, must have exacerbated the chances of separation facing many piedmont slave families. An elderly couple, Tony and his wife, Phillis, were perhaps typical. Both had been born in Lancaster County around the 1720s, but were sold to a Culpeper master, who in turn sold them to an adjacent Fauquier County planter. With each sale, Tony and Phillis had been separated from progressively more of their "several children," so that almost a half-century later they had children "dispersed through Culpeper, Frederick and Augusta Counties." When they ran away in 1770, their master had trouble predicting their whereabouts, in part because they might be harbored by any one of their many progeny. Later in the century, when riding the Hanover circuit, the Methodist minister James Meacham was distraught to see a black couple's children torn from them because they were "legacy'd" to widely scattered heirs. "The crys of the poor Captive Woman . . . on her Taking leave of her children," were, in Meacham's opinion, "enough to move the heart of the most obdurate."[27]

Yet many slaves like Tony and Phillis struggled to maintain kin ties; some, particularly those belonging to the larger planters, managed to create a remarkably robust family life. As early as 1733, two-parent

26. Goochland Order Book 11, July 1768, 230; Cumberland Order Book, 1767–1770, 274. See also Orange County Court Order Book 6, 535–536, 540, 627–629.

27. Cuthburt Bullit, *Va. Gaz.* (Rind), Nov. 8, 1770; "The Meditation and Exercises of James Meacham Upon the Entry of Hanover Circuit," Jan. 12, 1789, Meacham journal, Duke Univ. Lib., Durham, N.C.

families were the norm on Robert "King" Carter's two quarters in Spotsylvania County. At Norman's Ford, a white overseer and a foreman supervised three nuclear families (comprising ten slaves) and four solitaries. At Mount Quarter, two whites had charge of twenty-two slaves, grouped in just four two-parent families, with no child older than nine years of age. In 1758 about 70 percent of the slaves belonging to John Bolling in Chesterfield County were part of two-parent families (and remained so even when divided among his five heirs); in 1770 about three-quarters of Francis Jerdone's slaves were part of families headed by a single parent or a married couple (see table 3). Most notable among the Jerdone slaves on his Louisa County home plantation were Aaron and Winifred. Their oldest surviving child, a boy named Peter, was born on May 8, 1754. Winifred then gave birth to another seven children in just fifteen years, with three more over the following ten years. As if to celebrate their good fortune and offer due recognition to the patriarchal head of this large family, the couple named their second son and sixth surviving child, born in 1765, after his father.[28]

Larger planters could more readily afford to be respectful of slave kin ties. In 1776, when John Blair offered to exchange his slaves in Hanover County for Thomas Adams's land in Albemarle County, he acknowledged that the predominantly youthful character of his slaves "might not suit," but stressed that he "could not think of separating them from their mothers." Thirteen years later, in an action that must have been repeated on many a piedmont plantation, a slave named Frank "asked leave" of his master, Col. Francis Taylor of Orange County, to "have Miss M. Conway's Pat for a Wife." Taylor employed Frank as his messenger and errand runner, a valuable slave whose wishes ought to be respected if possible and who already traveled off the plantation. Thus Taylor "did not object," particularly when Frank told him that he "had the necessary consent."

28. Robert "King" Carter inventory, Nov. 1733, Va. Hist. Soc.; *Thomas Bolling v. John, Robert, Edward, and Archibald Bolling*, June 1758, Chesterfield Order Book 2, 432–434; the Jerdone slave family structures are based on the slave lists for Louisa, Spotsylvania, and Albemarle counties, Jan. 1, 1770, in the Jerdone Slave Book. The distribution of the Bolling slaves seems not to have disrupted many immediate families, although with older children it is not always easy to tell. In any case, only four children were clearly separated from parents, although in two of these cases the extended family was hit hard. An elderly couple named Harry and Sue were kept together with their daughter Charity and devised to John Bolling. But their daughter Betty, married to Solomon, became the property of Archibald Bolling, while their son Jacob and two of Betty's children were allocated to Edward Bolling.

TABLE 3. *Slave Household Structures on Two Piedmont Plantations, 1758 and 1770 (in Percents)*

Family Type	Bolling Plantations				Jerdone Plantations			
	Men $N=36$	Wom-en $N=34$	Chil-dren $N=66$	Total $N=136$	Men $N=46$	Wom-en $N=29$	Chil-dren $N=69$	Total $N=144$
Husband-wife	22	23	0	12	7	10	0	4
Husband-wife-children	42	44	73	57	28	38	46	39
Mother-children	—	12	11	8	—	28	28	19
Father-children	0	—	—	—	13	—	17	12
Solitaries	36	21	17	23	52	24	9	26

Sources: Thomas Bolling v. John, Robert, Edward, and Archibald Bolling, June 1758, Chesterfield County Court Order Book 2, 432–434; slave lists for Louisa, Spotsylvania, and Albemarle counties, Jan. 1, 1770, in the Slave Book of the Jerdone Family, Virginia State Library, Richmond.

Frank must have anticipated his master's approval, because he had already set the time of the wedding for the following evening.[29]

Some slaves—those who became Baptists in the late eighteenth century—were exposed most directly to white views on family morality. Indeed, the most common disciplinary offense brought against black Baptist church members involved a transgression of family norms—whether adultery, fornication, attempted rape, even in one case "attempting to bead with a white woman."[30] At the same time, white Baptists at least recognized slave marriages. In 1793 a slave member of the Boar Swamp

29. James Blair to Thomas Adams, Sept. 16, 1776, Adams Papers; Col. Francis Taylor diary, Jan. 30, 1789, Va. State Lib.

30. In eight piedmont Baptist churches during the period 1774–1800, there were 10 disciplinary actions against slaves on matters of family morality, 6 for theft, lying, or disobedience, 3 for nonattendance at church, and 2 cases of fighting among slaves (as well as many unspecified offenses, such as "disorderly walking" or "unchristian behaviour"). The Baptist church records used were those of Broad Run and Thumb Run in Fauquier County; Boar Swamp, Hanover County; Meherrin and Tussekiah in Lunenburg County; Chestnut Grove, Albemarle County; Occoquan, Prince William County; and Tomahawk, Chesterfield County, all at the Virginia Baptist Historical Society, Richmond, and on microfilm/photostat at the Va. State Lib. The quotation comes from the Tussekiah Baptist Church Records, May 28, 1791.

Baptist Church in Hanover County was excommunicated for leaving "his lawful wife" and taking up "with another woman." Some black Baptists took these strictures to heart and assumed the initiative. In 1772 two "Black Brethren" of the Meherrin Baptist Church of Lunenburg County accused a white woman of "parting . . . a Black Bror & sister (Man & Wife)." Five years later, black Sister Dinah of Chestnut Grove Baptist Church in Albemarle County accused another slave, York, of "attempting her chastity." York was excommunicated. And in 1800 Brother Steven of the same church complained of the "lasciviousness" of a free black preacher, Ben Colley.[31]

Slave families also took the initiative in naming their children. Two patterns are particularly noticeable. Naming after extended kin was perhaps the most common. Tamar, born on April 20, 1770, to Breechy and Beck, both Jerdone slaves, gave birth to her first child in July 1786, whom she named after her own mother. Similarly, Jenny, the daughter of Nanny, a Randolph slave, named one of her children after her mother, as did Belinda, a slave belonging to Paul Carrington. Belinda also named another of her children after a younger sister who had died, while Belinda's sister Mary named her first child after her youngest brother. Another common pattern was naming sons after fathers, while daughters were almost never named for mothers. Four Jerdone slave families named sons after fathers (as did three slave families belonging to John Bolling). Most interesting perhaps is again the family of Breechy and Beck. In January 1779, Breechy died; Beck was presumably carrying his child, for she gave birth later that fall to a son whom she named after her deceased husband. Only one slave family in many piedmont slave lists named a daughter after a mother.[32]

Just as naming patterns indicate the emergence of strong nuclear families and extended kin among piedmont slaves, so do the actions of runaway slaves. By the late colonial period, more and more runaway slaves were attempting to reunite with separated spouses and parents; in some cases, kin networks were thought to be supporting the absentee.

31. Baptist church records of Boar Swamp, fourth Saturday in July 1793, Meherrin, Feb. 22, 1772, Chestnut Grove, May 18, 1770, and third Sunday in August 1800.

32. Naming patterns were deduced from the four registers mentioned in note 21, above. For similar Chesapeake work, see Mary Beth Norton, Herbert G. Gutman, and Ira Berlin, "The Afro-American Family in the Age of Revolution," in Berlin and Hoffman, eds., *Slavery and Freedom*, 175–191.

Sall, a twenty-five-year-old mulatto woman who ran away from an Amherst County quarter in 1774, was said to be "of a numerous Family of Mulattoes, formerly belonging to a Gentleman of the Name of Howard in York County . . . and where probably she may attempt to go again, or perhaps into Cumberland, or Amelia, where . . . many of her kindred live." Abraham, who ran away from his Chesterfield County master in 1777, was said to have "a Wife at a Quarter of the Hon. William Nelson's, Esq. in king William; several Relations at Mr. Claiborne's, in the same county; some at Mr. William Dandridge's and Mr. Sherwood Tinsley's, in Hanover County, at some of which Places," his master conjectured, "he is harboured." Cuthie from Mecklenburg County was supposed to have gone toward York County, where she had "several relations"; Sye from Chesterfield County was thought to be "lurking" in Gloucester County, where he had "many Relations." A wide range of "connections," as contemporary masters termed them, supported some piedmont runaways in the late colonial period.[33]

By the end of the eighteenth century, the building and rebuilding of kin ties had produced dense social networks for some piedmont slaves, in both town and countryside. Thus a Petersburg slave, sentenced to die in 1793 for robbery, gained the support of many of the town's white residents because of the effect that they calculated his death would have on his large family. The petitioners referred to the criminal's "numerous . . . relatives . . . , many of them reputable, some of them respectable, for persons in their humble sphere . . . , all of whom, and particularly his weeping broken hearted parents, now in an advanced age, are anxiously looking . . . for a pardon." In deepest Bedford County, in the southwestern part of the piedmont, an old couple belonging to Thomas Jefferson was surrounded by a bevy of grown children, in-laws, and grandchildren. The quarter was almost one extended family.[34]

Although the obstacles placed in the way of family formation and maintenance were formidable, many piedmont slaves overcame them. It is impossible to say how many of the region's slaves enjoyed a measure of family life, but the surviving evidence, overrepresentative as it may be of

33. Gabriel Penn, *Va. Gaz.* (Purdie & Dixon), Aug. 4, 1774; Edward Johnson, *ibid.* (Dixon & Hunter), May 23, 1777; Robert Munford, *ibid.*, Oct. 12, 1778; Benjamin Branch, *ibid.* (Dixon & Nicolson), Mar. 12, 1779.

34. Petition of 31 Petersburg residents, n.d., Executive Papers, June–Aug. 1793, Va. State Lib.; Norton, Gutman, and Berlin, "Afro-American Family," in Berlin and Hoffman, eds., *Slavery and Freedom*, 182.

the larger plantations, suggests a surprisingly high number, at least after midcentury. An extension of contemporary tidewater, rather than a replication of an earlier experience, best characterizes family patterns among piedmont slaves in the second half of the eighteenth century.

IV

The development of a robust family life went hand in hand with the emergence of an Afro-American society in the piedmont. In part, this was a function of demographic and economic forces. As Richard Dunn has recently observed, the number of piedmont counties with black majorities expanded rapidly over the last half of the eighteenth century. In 1755, only three of the fourteen counties that contained black majorities were in the piedmont region; in 1782 the number had increased to ten out of twenty-four, and by 1800 was sixteen out of thirty-eight. The increasing size of plantation units also created greater opportunities for piedmont slaves to develop a social life of their own. Generally speaking, within one or two decades after the formation of a piedmont county, a majority of its slaves resided on plantations with more than ten slaves. Indeed, by the early 1780s about 40 percent of slaves in most piedmont counties resided on plantations of more than twenty slaves. The rapidity with which plantation sizes in the piedmont caught up with—and, in some cases, surpassed—those in the tidewater is remarkable. Finally, by the 1780s at least, the density of the slave population in many piedmont counties approached tidewater levels, thereby facilitating contacts and communication among slaves.[35]

Black actions, not just impersonal forces, made vital contributions to the development of an Afro-American society in the piedmont. A prime example of the black community ministering to its own needs is the widespread resort to magic, something that contemporary whites pejoratively labeled a propensity for poisoning. At any rate, the dispenser of medicines, charms, or poisons clearly was a person of influence within the slave community. Indeed, even whites recognized the power of such slaves. Thus seventy-six Spotsylvania County residents sought a pardon

35. Dunn, "Black Society in the Chesapeake," in Berlin and Hoffman, eds., *Slavery and Freedom*, 56–58; U.S. Census Bureau, *Return of the Whole Number*; Morgan and Nicholls, "Slaves in Piedmont Virginia."

for two slave blacksmiths who had allegedly attempted to poison their master. These white neighbors mobilized in support of the "Orderly well behaved Fellows" because they believed that "a Negro wench, or Conjurer," was the prime mover in the scheme. Similarly, a Fauquier County slave who burned down a white man's house drew the support of neighboring whites because his chief accuser was "a notorious Villan," a slave named Ben, who "pretend[ed] to be a conjourer or fortune teller." Finally, the murder of a white overseer in Powhatan County disclosed the important role of Pompey, "who is reputed among the Negroes as a Conjurer." The two slaves who plotted the murder "relied much on the art of Pompey to prevent detection." A conjurer's "art" was a powerful weapon.[36]

On the other hand, a large number of alleged poisonings appear to have been little more than one slave administering roots, powders, or charms to others. Court judgments reflect the harmlessness of many "poisoning" cases. In Chesterfield County, for example, eleven slaves were tried as poisoners between 1749 and 1783; eight were acquitted, two were found guilty but received benefit of clergy, and the only one sentenced to hang was recommended for a pardon. Typical was the case of Dinah of Cumberland County, who was arraigned for administering "medicines" to her fellow slave Amey, probably to help with the latter's pregnancy. Dinah was acquitted on the grounds that she administered the substances with no ill intent. Similarly, a number of Fauquier County whites petitioned for a pardon for a slave man, Joe, on the grounds that it was Joe's father who "compounded and administered medicines," which were not, so far as anybody knew, poisonous. Apparently, the son had once "informed his father who was very Deaf that physic was wanted stronger than some he had given before." Indeed Joe had "cautioned his Father to beware and take care not to take life." Furthermore, Joe's "crime" appeared less heinous to many of his white neighbors because part of the evidence against him lay merely in his prediction that sick people would die on the return of warm weather. At worst, this was little more than harmless fortune-telling. Some slaves used "poisons" as charms to influence their masters. Peg of Louisa County administered a

36. Petition of Spotsylvania County residents, Dec. 20, 1795, Executive Papers, Dec. 1795; depositions of Epaphroditus Timberlake, June 6, 1791, and William Pickett, June 30, 1791 (also see that of Charles Marshall, n.d., *ibid.*, May–Aug. 1791); petition of Bentley Crump *et al.*, n.d., *ibid.*, May–June 1794.

substance procured from a slave man in the neighborhood "to keep peace in the family, and to make her Master kind to her." Sarah of Prince Edward County put black seeds "resembling Jaucestor seeds" into the peas she prepared for her white family "for the purpose of making her mistress love her."[37]

Although the widespread resort to magic bound piedmont slaves together, the practice also reflected serious internal tensions within the slave community. In fact, many poisoning incidents that came before piedmont county courts were as much inwardly directed at blacks as outwardly targeted against whites. Intrablack conflict, perhaps stemming from frictions between different African ethnic groups or between Africans and creoles, or from the natural stresses to which all slave communities were subject, lay at the heart of many of these cases. In Cumberland County between 1756 and 1792, of seventeen slaves who stood trial for poisoning offenses, only three were accused of attempting to poison whites. Charged with whipping to death a bondman named Will, Mathew Farley attributed his "immoderate behaviour" to the slave's "Fellow Servants urg[ing] him . . . to encrease his punishment by Alledging that the said Slave Will had just before administered a strong and deadly poison to a Negro Wench named Doll . . . of which she died." Several Louisa County whites petitioned for a pardon of a slave named Peter because, in their opinion, his preparation of substances was an "Ostentatious charade to increase his Credit with Those Negroes who had Pressed him to

37. Trial of Dinah, May 19, 1792, Cumberland Order Book, 1788–1792, 504; petitions of Thomas Maddux, Obadiah Pettit, John Green, Jr., and F. Brooke, Sept. 1790, Executive Papers, Aug.–Nov. 1790 (trial of Joe); petition of John Poindexter, Jr., *et al.*, n.d., and letter of W. O. Callis, Jan. 11, 1794, *ibid.*, Jan.–Feb. 1794 (trial of Peg); depositions of Elizabeth Young and William Keeling, n.d., *ibid.*, Aug.–Sept. 1794 (trial of Sarah). See also trial of James and Rachel, May 12, 1767, Louisa Order Book, 1766–1772, 37. In 45 poisoning cases that I have analyzed for Amherst, Chesterfield, Cumberland, Goochland, Louisa, Orange, Prince William, and Spotsylvania counties (based on the colonial and, to a lesser extent, early national county court order books), only 13% of the 65 slaves tried were sentenced to hang; 29% were found guilty but were granted benefit of clergy (usually requiring a branding of the hand and perhaps the removal of ears), 20% were whipped (either as guilty of a misdemeanor, or found not guilty but whipped for some suspicious activity), and 37% were found not guilty and discharged without punishment. Even a slave found guilty of poisoning a white man could find whites in the neighborhood prepared to intercede on his behalf. For a good example, see petition of 22 Chesterfield County residents, n.d., and letter from Thomas Worsham, Blackman Moseley, and David Pattison, Nov. 19, 1784, Executive Papers, Sept.–Nov. 1784.

Destroy . . . their enemies, for the purpose of Betraying him as a person Guilty of poisoning and conjuring."[38]

An intricate and tangled web of intrablack conflict enmeshed a Pittsylvania County slave named Roger, who was sentenced to hang for poisoning two whites. Three fellow slaves and a white woman testified on his behalf, largely by questioning the motives of Roger's chief accuser, a slave named Matt. Mary Brown, the white witness, cast aspersions on Matt's character, testifying that he had claimed his owner "was the greatest Drunkard in this County and that if the Sea was Brandy she would Drink it up." Chiner, a slave woman, reported hearing Matt say "he would Take a false Oath or sware to a ly to Hang Roger." Jack, another slave, provided a motive for this malice in Roger's uncovering of a theft committed by Matt. For this reason, Matt had boasted that he "would make a Rope" of lies to hang Roger. To complicate the picture even further, a Mr. Williams strongly asserted Roger's guilt. He claimed that Roger had a long history as a poisoner, extending back to Dinwiddie County "near Twenty years ago." Williams also alleged that Roger had poisoned several of his own slaves, and recalled hearing Roger's "master and mistress [say] at several times as he has poison'd as they believe 18 or 20 Slaves for them."[39] Wherever the truth lay, Roger and Matt seem to have aroused strong and contrasting feelings from their fellow slaves, not to mention whites.

Exciting much less controversy, slaves turned to black doctors, as well as black conjurers, though they may have made less of this distinction than did their masters. In 1752, William Dabney of Goochland County paid 11s. 3d. to John Bates "for the use of his negroe Doctor" among his slaves. Over two decades later, Charles Yates bought a slave in Culpeper County only to find that he had been long "distempered" and under the hands of "Negro Doctors" for years. Benjamin Harrison employed a slave doctor on his plantation, while a Chesterfield County master disap-

38. Petition of Mathew Farley, Jr., Dec. 26, 1788, Executive Papers, Jan.–Feb. 1789; petition of Thomas Johnson, Jr., *et al.*, Aug. 11, 1783, *ibid.*, Aug.–Oct. 1783. In the 45 cases mentioned in the preceding note, the victims were evenly split between whites and blacks (with 10 unidentified). The Cumberland cases were the most numerous.

39. Depositions of Mary Brown, Chiner, Jack, and Dall, May 9, 1787, and letters of Mr. S. Williams and Jeremiah White (Roger's owner), May 1787, *ibid.*, Apr.–May 1787. Roger's history as a poisoner can be traced at least to 1782, for in that year he received 39 lashes and had his ears cut off for a poisoning offense. Pittsylvania County Court Order Book 4, 406 (my thanks to Michael L. Nicholls for this reference).

proved of his slave Sambo's doctoring. Black midwives often delivered slave women. Francis Taylor noted that "Granny Venus" attended at the delivery of his slave woman Milly. Blacks turned to other blacks for physical as well as psychological support.[40]

The growth of intercounty and cooperative networks in the actions of slave runaways also provides evidence of an emergent cohesiveness within the black community. As the century proceeded, slaves ran away over greater distances and often remained at large for extensive periods. In the 1740s almost two-thirds of slave runaways captured in the piedmont were from nearby tidewater counties, but by the 1760s 60 percent were piedmont slaves and a third were resident in more westerly counties.[41] Perhaps the most dramatic example of slaves supporting runaways involved Billy and Lucy, who left their Cumberland County plantation in early 1771. Harbored by John Walker's slaves in Albemarle, the couple seemed to have run out of luck when Walker's overseer apprehended them. But the overseer was no match for his supposed charges when they rose up and "violently" rescued the fugitives. The couple remained at large three months later. Group actions were also characteristic of runaways themselves. About a third of the piedmont runaways advertised in Virginia newspapers during the 1760s and 1770s absconded in groups of two or more.[42]

Cooperative actions were common in the committing of crimes. Just over 40 percent of the four hundred or more slaves prosecuted in a

40. Executorship of the estate of Armistead Lightfoot, William Dabney Account Book (1749–1757), 1752, Va. Hist. Soc.; Charles Yates Letter Book, Jan. 11, 1774, CW; Benjamin Harrison to William Benjamin, July 31, 1781, Harrison Letter Book; Alexander Marshall, *Va. Gaz.* (Royle), Nov. 4, 1763; Taylor diary, Mar. 4, 1788.

41. This analysis is based on claims for capturing 179 runaway slaves entered in the county court order books of 10 piedmont counties in the years 1740–1769. The relaxed attitude of masters and officials to running away must be recognized. For instance, in December 1789, the Spotsylvania jailer wrote to a Lunenburg master about his slave Isaac, who had run away in July and been captured in November. Isaac had been caught with a horse that he had stolen a few days before. He merited no runaway advertisement or court case. His master had merely to pay the workhouse charges to retrieve his slave. John Frazer to Lodowick Farmer, Dec. 15, 1789, Hollyday Papers, Va. Hist. Soc.

42. Joseph Calland, *Va. Gaz.* (Rind), May 23, 1771. In the 1760s I count 13 groups, numbering 33 slaves, representing 35% of all runaways; in the 1770s, there were 35 groups, numbering 91 slaves, representing 29% of all runaways.

number of piedmont county courts committed their alleged crimes in groups of two or more persons.[43] Early in the eighteenth century, the groups were already large. In 1733 six slaves belonging to three separate planters in Goochland County were charged with murdering a white man. Two of the men, belonging to different masters, were found guilty and hanged (with heads and quarters "set up in several parts of the county"). Fourteen years later, eight slaves from Orange County belonging to seven masters were charged with "conspiring against Christian White People." Three were whipped and the others discharged.[44] As these cases suggest, a large proportion of the group crimes involved slaves belonging to separate masters. Indeed, this was true of 60 percent of the crimes committed by groups. Cross-plantation alliances were the norm.

Cooperative actions were particularly noticeable in the most common slave crime, theft. In 1743 four slaves, two of them a married couple, belonging to three separate masters in Orange County were found guilty of a burglary. The husband, Frank, was thought to be the ringleader, while his wife, Deborah, proved to be an accessory when part of the stolen goods were "found in her Husbands Chest which was in her Possession." Slaves no doubt traded in stolen goods among themselves.

43. This number is based on all court of oyer and terminer cases in the counties of Albemarle (1744–1748), Amherst (1766–1769, 1773–1775), Chesterfield (1749–1784), Culpeper (1763–1764), Cumberland (1749–1792), Fauquier (1759–1775), Goochland (1728–1775), Loudoun (1757–1775), Louisa (1742–1748, 1766–1781), Orange (1734–1775), Prince William (1752–1757, 1759–1763, 1766–1769), and Spotsylvania (1724–1775). The total number of cases was 313, involving 414 slaves (378 men, 36 women). Of these 414, 169, or 41%, committed a crime in a group. A similar analysis of a number of tidewater counties (Caroline, 1732–1785, Charles City, 1737–1757, Elizabeth City, 1715–1769, Essex, 1721–1783, Middlesex, 1711–1783, Richmond, 1715–1753, and York, 1710–1783) has produced 394 cases involving 567 slaves (521 men, 46 women), with 48% committing crimes in groups. Group crime was therefore of approximately the same dimensions in both regions.

44. Trial of Champion, Lucy, Sampson, Harry, George, and Valentine, June 25, 1733, Goochland Order Book 3, 199–200; trial of Sambo, Frank, Peter, Tom, Tom, Jack, Simon, and Frank, May 31, 1747, Orange Order Book 4A, 65. For "a Company of Negros" visiting an adjoining plantation and allegedly committing a crime, see "Order issued to Thomas Bose or James Lever to bring Negroes of Mary Hill Read before Thomas Bedford," Nov. 21, 1763, Lunenburg County, Bouldin Family Papers, Va. Hist. Soc. In Powhatan County in 1782 an Amelia County slave was "charged with assembleing with sundry other persons" on a plantation at night and burning down a barn. Auditor's Item, Box 1, Condemned Slaves, Oct. 1, 1782, Va. State Lib.

For obvious reasons, this practice rarely came to light. However, in Amelia County at midcentury the slave Lymas offered to sell stolen goods to fellow bondman Ceaser.[45]

The most revealing cooperative crime took place in Brunswick County in 1752. Peter, Harry Cain, and James all stood trial for insurrection and conspiracy to commit murder. The justices targeted Peter as the instigator, sentencing him to hang on July 6, and let off the other two slaves with misdemeanor convictions of thirty-nine lashes apiece. In explaining this lesser sentence, the clerk noted that Harry Cain and James had been "privy to an Opinion entertained among many Negroes of their having a Right to their Freedom and not making a Discovery thereof." Almost twenty years before Bacchus had acted upon the supposedly widespread belief among slaves that freedom could be secured in England, other piedmont slaves apparently thought it could be gained at home. The emergence of a cohesive Afro-American community in the piedmont may well have rested ultimately on this generally shared belief in the "Right to . . . Freedom."[46]

As with the resort to magic, not all aspects of slave crime suggest the development of a cohesive slave community. Just as slave poisoning victims were relatively equally divided between whites and blacks, so were the victims of slave murders. Some of these tensions between slaves may have arisen from the extreme fluidity of the region's population. Recently established estates, often with absentee owners, did not provide a settled environment. In 1745, for instance, the Louisa County Court tried a slave belonging to a Hanover County master for murdering another Hanover master's slave and a Louisa slave. Other conflicts exploded within the confines of a single absentee estate. In 1741 in Goochland County, a slave named Davy and two women were the only working slaves on a plantation owned by Joseph Anthony. One of the women, Pender, "was so badly used by . . . Negro Davy that she endeavoured to go from the plantation where she liv'd to a Quarter belonging to the honble John Carter Esq. of which her master Joseph Anthony was Overseer to Complain to him of the abuse" she had received from Davy. She lost her way in the woods, suffered from exposure, and later died. Meanwhile, Davy directed his

45. Trial of Little Jack, Frank, Coffey, and Deborah, Nov. 23, 1743, Orange Order Book 4, 22–23; trial of Lymas, Nov. 15, 17, 1750, Amelia County Court Order Book 2, 281–282 (information kindly supplied by Michael L. Nicholls).

46. Trial of Peter, Harry Cain, and James, Brunswick County Court Order Book 4, 242–244 (information kindly supplied by Michael L. Nicholls).

anger against the only available object, the other woman, Nanny, and murdered her.[47]

Whites also encouraged blacks to turn on one another. An unwritten but consistently pursued policy of divide and rule put considerable pressure on black cohesiveness. Sometimes slaves served as prosecution witnesses against other bondmen. In cooperative crimes, one slave might be induced to secure his freedom by incriminating his comrades. In Cumberland County in 1765, Toby was found guilty of hog stealing when his partner in crime, Charles, turned King's evidence. It later transpired that Charles had been "a false witness"; for his pains, he was nailed to a pillory for an hour by his ears, which were then cut off. Though the white community encouraged slaves to act as turncoats, they had to be reliable ones. Pecuniary incentives also induced divisiveness, as when slaves or free blacks secured rewards for capturing runaways or conveying them back to their masters.[48] In these and other ways, whites encouraged divisions among slaves.

Another division among blacks arose from the simple fact that not all blacks were slaves. Apart from all the obvious and distinguishing advantages of freedom, skin color usually demarcated free blacks from slaves. Unlike the vast majority of slaves, most pre-Revolutionary free blacks were mulattoes. A "parcel of free Mulattoes" was sufficiently notable in Albemarle County in the 1770s for a Fredericksburg master to be sure that his mulatto servant Hankey had been "protected and harboured" by them for at least two years. Few slaves would have dared to replicate the

47. Trial of Boatswain, Mar. 19, 1745, Louisa Order Book, 1742–1748, 180; trial of Davy, Dec. 15, 1741, Goochland Order Book 5, 17–18. For violence among slaves with absentee masters, see also trial of Joe, Feb. 8, 1773, Louisa Order Book, 1760(72)–1774, 78, and trial of Will, June 25, 1772, Orange Order Book 8, 197. For a particularly good example of an explosive incident, arising from sexual jealousy between two male slaves, see deposition of James Johnson of Pittsylvania County, Dec. 1792, Executive Papers. See also trial of Cudjo, Sept. 10, 1753, Cumberland Order Book, 1752–1758, 19–20. Based on the sources in n. 43, I count 12 white murder victims and 10 blacks, 20 white poisoning victims and 17 blacks.

48. Trial of Charles and Toby, Feb. 26, 1765, Cumberland Order Book, 1764–1767, 83. For another example, see investigation of Adam, Mar. 2, 1761, Spotsylvania County Court Minute Book, 1755–1765, 194. For slaves as prosecution witnesses, see, for example, trials of Ned and James, June 6, 1758, of Humphrey, Apr. 3, 1759, of Pompey, July 9, 1759, of Sampson, Sept. 17, 1759, of Will, Aug. 5, 1760, *ibid.*, 112, 132, 142, 145, 170. For rewards for capturing runaways, see, for example, accounts of Edmund Wilcox, vol. 11, June 1, July 7, 1772, April and Aug. 1777, Hubard Papers (microfilm, CW).

actions of two free mulattoes of Orange County, Reuben and Peter Lanter, self-styled "Planters." On a Saturday night, the Lanters "met a person in the main road who [they] thought was a runaway and after some discourse they had a scrimage & fight." The suspected runaway was none other than John Lynch, a white planter. The Lanters seem to have stood their ground in court; certainly, they made no apologies. Indeed, Peter was sufficiently well-to-do that he could enter a bond of £100 in order to remain at liberty until a second court appearance in Williamsburg.[49]

However, whatever their complexion, most free blacks were not far removed from slaves—either in station or residence. Most lived for a large part of their lives as bound servants, presumably alongside slaves. A list of forty-seven blacks on Hugh Nelson's estate in Fauquier County taken in 1778 lumped together "old Nell a free Negro" and the forty-six slaves. The ever-present threat of sale and eventual reenslavement made a free black's lot particularly precarious. The few court cases involving free blacks indicate how precarious. In 1743, Moll, a twenty-eight-year-old mulatto of Orange County, brought a formal complaint against her master for "claiming her as a slave and Threatning to carry her out of the colony." Ten years later, the churchwardens of St. Thomas Parish in the same county charged Andrew Mannon with "misusage of a mulatto servant girl named Winny Burwell." In 1756 Rose Severally and her son George were arrested, when passing through Orange County, on suspicion of being runaway slaves. Although Moll was eventually freed, Winny Burwell apparently unharmed, and Rose Severally released, such actions eloquently suggest the harsh climate facing free blacks. A number of freedom suits, it is true, were brought by free blacks before piedmont county courts in the late colonial period. One can be impressed that the courts often decided in the blacks' favor, but more significant surely is that free blacks had to bring the suits in the first place. Their prior incarceration—being "kept and detained as a slave," as one petitioner put it—is the most noteworthy feature of these cases.[50]

49. William Smith, *Va. Gaz.* (Dixon & Hunter), Dec. 26, 1777; investigation of Reuben and Peter Lanter, Oct. 11, 1755, Orange Order Book 6, 178. For another free black accused of "threatening to beat & prejudice" a white man, see investigation of John Cousins, Goochland Order Book 7, 512.

50. "List of Negroes . . . belonging to the Estate of Hugh Nelson, Esq. in Fauquier County," Dec. 9, 1778, Muse Papers; complaint of Moll, Jan. 23, 28, 1743, Orange Order Book 3, 312, 323; complaint of churchwardens, June 28, 1753, Orange Order Book 5, 456; investigation of Rose Severally, Aug. 27, 1756, Orange Order Book 6,

Indeed, occasional evidence indicates that free blacks were closely allied to slaves. In 1754 two slaves belonging to the estate of Col. William Randolph in Goochland County were accused of poisoning Obadiah Smith and his wife, Mary. Also accused was Frank Cousens, a free mulatto. All three were acquitted, but Smith swore before the court that he went "in danger of his life from Cousens." The free man had to enter a security of £50 before being released. Similarly, in Chesterfield County thirteen years later, two slaves were acquitted of a felony, but William Bowman, a free mulatto, was sent to the General Court for further trial for the same offense. Gabriel, a mulatto slave in Albemarle County, had close links to free blacks: he was married to one. In 1776 he ran away to visit his free wife, Betty Baines, or so his master assumed. According to a recent article on free blacks in the early southside, families composed of slave men and free black (usually mulatto) women were becoming increasingly common.[51]

A small Afro-Indian community also emerged in the piedmont. Like the free black community, it lived in a twilight zone between slavery and freedom. Thus, a Cumberland County slave, a "Mulatto" named Jim, ran away from his master in 1772 seeking the "Right to his Freedom," as his master put it. His father "was an Indian of the Name of Cheshire," so his master guessed he would "call himself JAMES Cheshire or Chink." Another mulatto runaway slave, from Dinwiddie County, was thought to be joining his brother, who had been "several Times brought from among the Indians on Pamunkey River." A third mulatto slave, also from Dinwiddie, was said to be "of the Indian breed"; he sought his freedom from the General Court in 1773. Again, like free blacks, Afro-Indians lived in close proximity to slaves. In 1762 two quarters in Chesterfield County

---

260; Michael L. Nicholls, "Passing Through This Troublesome World: Free Blacks in the Early Southside," *Virginia Magazine of History and Biography*, XCII (1984), 59. For other freedom suits, see Goochland Order Book 8, 175; Louisa Order Book, 1760(72)–1774, 95; Chesterfield Order Book 6, 264; and John Fleming Ledger, 1754–1766, Aug. 1756 (microfilm, CW). See also Wade Netherland, *Va. Gaz.* (Purdie), May 2, 1766; William Holt, *ibid.* (Purdie & Dixon), Supplement, Sept. 5, 1766; Mathew Mayes, *ibid.*, Oct. 25, 1770; and John Hardaway, *ibid.* (Rind), May 31, 1770.

51. Trial of Squire, Myrtilla, and Frank Cousens, Apr. 1, 1754, Goochland Order Book 7, 380–381, 409, 489; trial of Natt, Cuff, and William Bowman, Oct. 10, 1767, Chesterfield Order Book 4, 146; John Hudson, *Va. Gaz.* (Pinkney), Jan. 20, 1776; Nicholls, "Passing Through This Troublesome World," *VMHB*, XCII (1984), 55. See also Marianne Buroff Sheldon, "Black-White Relations in Richmond, Virginia, 1782–1820," *Jour. So. Hist.*, XLV (1979), 31.

contained thirty "Negroes," fourteen mulattoes, and four Indians. Indians and blacks inevitably married one another. Patrick Rose of Amherst County assumed that his runaway slave Ben had joined his Indian wife, because "she sold off, and moved from her late Dwelling Place in Albemarle, a few Days before the Fellow ran away."[52]

In sum, although serious divisions existed within the Afro-American community of the piedmont, a voluntary cohesiveness, not to mention the cohesion forced on blacks by white hostility, developed quickly. From the actions of runaways and rebels to the more mundane activities of black conjurers and doctors, the black community attempted to stand together. Not always successful, the black community appeared resilient in the face of formidable odds. There were always casualties, ranging from a slave like Ralph who, piqued at being given a mule to ride rather than a horse, beat "the poor Jack without mercy" until it died, to "old Caesar," who was charged with the attempted rape and buggery of a four-year-old white girl.[53] Nobody escaped the effects of slavery no matter where they lived. But the pathology of slavery does not seem to have been any more developed in the piedmont than in the tidewater.

V

Black-white relations assumed a special character in the piedmont. Generally speaking, as plantation units increased in size throughout tidewater, more Afro-Americans lived on quarters beyond their masters' direct supervision. In the piedmont, however, a reverse trend was evident—at least in the short run. In the earliest years of a piedmont county, large numbers of slaves resided on quarters with overseers. In Amelia in 1740 at least a third of the county's slaves lived on units where masters were absent. In 1760 just over half of the slaves in

52. Paul Michaux, *Va. Gaz.* (Purdie & Dixon), Nov. 26, 1772; James Walker, *ibid.*, Mar. 5, 1772; William Cuszens, *ibid.*, July 15, 1773; John Clay and Henry Clay, Sr., inventory, c. 1762, Chesterfield Will Book 1, 344, 351; Patrick Rose, *Va. Gaz.* (Dixon & Hunter), Aug. 3, 1776. See also Daniel Hardaway, *ibid.*, Aug. 1, 1777; Dorothy Jones, *ibid.* (Rind), Nov. 11, 1773; freedom suit of Phillis, Phebe, Eaton, Patt, and Sarah in Petersburg District Court, Sept. 18, 1798, Box 6, Slavery Collection, N.-Y. Hist. Soc.; and Chesterfield Order Book 1, 523, and Order Book 4, 4.

53. Philip Mazzei to Thomas Adams, June 2, 1777, Adams Papers; trial of "old Caesar," Nov. 3–4, 18, 1724, Spotsylvania Order Book, 1724–1730, 29, 36–37.

recently created Loudoun County lived on quarters supervised by over-seers. As more piedmont whites became slaveholders and as some tide-water masters transferred their residences into the piedmont, the propor-tion of slaves under the direct purview of a master increased. By the late 1770s, the vast majority of slaves in Amelia County, and other piedmont counties, resided on plantations with a resident master, although a signifi-cant minority occupied satellite quarters some distance from the home estate.[54]

The more-distanced relationship with a master, which was a promi-nent feature of the slave experience particularly in the early piedmont, had obvious advantages. Some piedmont slaves no doubt enjoyed the relative autonomy inherent in absentee estates. Others may have valued the opportunities for traveling back and forth between piedmont quarter and tidewater home plantation, driving livestock, or taking crops to mar-ket. Some piedmont slaves rode horses on their trips east. Ned, a Spotsylvania slave, abused the privilege by committing highway robbery on a lady traveler from Albemarle. Few piedmont slaves, however, could have matched the stately progress of "Negro Bobb Coachman and Negro George Postillion," who were granted a permit to pass from Fredericks-burg to Williamsburg "without molestation" and with a coach and six horses. The "several Inn Keepers" along the route were requested to furnish them "agreeable to the usual custom of victualling of negroes."[55]

Yet from the perspective of the slaves' material well-being, the draw-backs of a more-distanced relationship with masters probably outweighed the advantages. Many piedmont slaves depended on distant tidewater owners for supplies. Winter clothes, shoes, and bedding could be late in arriving, as Archibald Cary learned when two of his slaves in Buckingham County suffered frostbite. When three female slaves on an Amherst County quarter requested blankets and baby clothes from their absentee

54. Morgan and Nicholls, "Slaves in Piedmont Virginia."

55. Trial of Ned, June 7, 1773, Spotsylvania Order Book, 1768–1774, 256; Thomas Oliver's permit to Bobb and George, Oct. 29, 1771 [with notations by innkeepers on costs] (photostat, CW). See also Rose diary, June 27, 1750, and *passim*; Dudley Digges to William Dabney, Dec. 18, 1758, Mar. 5, 1759, and Mary Ambler to Charles Dabney, Dec. 20, 1769, Dabney Papers (microfilm, CW); accounts of Peyton Randolph's estate with A. Cary, Jan. 14, 1770 (microfilm, CW); John Howard to Dr. William Cabell, June 6, 1771, N. F. Cabell Collection, Va. State Lib.; and William Burtt to William Cocke, Dec. 20, 1788, Miscellaneous MSS, Va. Hist. Soc. The Taylor diary and the Muse correspondence also report much traveling between piedmont and elsewhere.

master, the overseer supported their appeal by asking the owner "to Remember them in [their] Distress."[56]

Although this overseer offered support, many others did not. In 1769, a slave named Maximus journeyed the distance from Louisa County to Jamestown in order to "complain that his overseer was going to whip him." Four years later, Robert C. Nicholas, then resident in Williamsburg, heard a "terrible Complaint" against an overseer from his slave Ben, who also traveled down from a Louisa quarter. Nor was there any doubt where Nicholas stood on the matter. "I am [a] stranger to [this] Overseer," he admitted, "but know very well that few common Overseers are to be trusted." In the same year William Cabell dismissed an overseer in Amherst County just one month after engaging him because he had heard "shocking acc[oun]ts of his Cruelty to Slaves."[57]

The poor opinion in which piedmont overseers were generally held was undoubtedly small compensation to the slaves for the cruelties they suffered, but at least it provided them with opportunities to redress grievances. Maximus, for example, was not punished for leaving his Louisa County quarter at a particularly urgent time in the agricultural year; rather, his owner wished him "excuse[d]" from blame, particularly in light of the slave's promises of future good behavior. James Mercer of Fredericksburg was certainly prepared to listen to his slaves' complaints. After one of his overseers in Loudoun County had made what he considered excessive demands, Mercer "inquired of the Negroes as to his conduct." Acknowledging that his slaves were "not legal Evidences," Mercer nevertheless took their side, noting that he had "allmost constantly found negroes tell Truth enough of distant overseers." John Norton, though less emphatic, followed much the same line when complaints surfaced against his overseer in Fauquier County. Noting that "it is not altogether proper to attend to the Tales of Negroes," he did so anyway, finding that there "may be too just grounds of Complaint."[58]

Piedmont slaves could, then, occasionally exploit the tenuous position

56. Archibald Cary to Anthony Mullins, n.d., Misc. MS Coll., Mullins, Lib. Cong.; Burtt to Cocke, Dec. 20, 1788, Misc. MSS, Va. Hist. Soc.

57. John Blair, Jr., to [Charles Dabney], Apr. 1, 1769, and Robert C. Nicholas to Charles Dabney, Sept. 4, 1773, Dabney Papers; William Cabell, Sr., diary, Aug. 28, 1773, Va. State Lib.

58. Blair to [Dabney], Apr. 1, 1769, Dabney Papers; James Mercer to Battaile Muse, Dec. 6, 1778, and John H. Norton to Muse, June 30, 1786, Muse Papers.

occupied by many a white overseer. Most piedmont overseers averaged only a year or two in the employ of a single planter. A particularly revealing incident occurred on one of Edward Ambler's piedmont quarters in 1770, with the hiring of a new overseer, John Smith. He immediately incurred the opposition of the fourteen adult slaves put under him. According to the plantation steward, the problem lay in the attitude of Smith's predecessor, Thomas Wingfield, who "was so good natured to the Negroes under him that he suffered them to Impose on him very much." In the last year of Wingfield's incumbency, the steward continued, "the Negroes were almost free." As a result, they were "very unwilling to give up the privileges they [had been] allowed." Indeed, "they seem," noted the steward, "to be determined to Maintain them" and tried to get Smith "turned off." The slaves prevailed on George, the oldest bondman on the plantation, to visit their master, thinking that "a complaint from him wou'd be listened to." Although Smith apparently had the backing of his superiors at this time, he was replaced the following year.[59]

The example of Thomas Wingfield suggests that some overseers, only too well aware of the precariousness of their position, took the line of least resistance and sided with the slaves. An overseer employed by Hugh Nelson in Fauquier County seems to have adopted this strategy, for he was said to "suffer the Negroes to go to the Corn house at will." Similarly, Battaile Muse, a steward and resident of Loudoun County, complained of the prior management of a parcel of slaves he had agreed to supervise. They were, he noted, "very difficult to manage owing to the Great Indulgence as they have had." He was convinced that the "old ones" among the group would "never be Broke to Labour." As for the rest, he described them as "high fed and well clothed," willing to work only "at their own discretion," and "given to complaints which they are too much

59. Charles Dabney to [?], 1770, Dabney Papers. See also James Allen to Philip King, c. 1757, Spragins Family Papers, Va. Hist. Soc. Between 1762 and 1773, Francis Jerdone employed 21 overseers, most of whom served no more than two years; Paul Carrington's turnover of overseers was even more marked, most lasting only one year, while between 1786 and 1800, Thomas Jefferson's 10 overseers generally served either one or two years. See Jerdone Slave Book, Carrington Account Books, and Edwin Morris Betts, ed., *Thomas Jefferson's Farm Book: With Commentary and Relevant Extracts from Other Writings* (Princeton, N.J., 1953), 149–150. See also overseer turnover on the Ambler quarters in the early 1760s (Dabney Papers) and on A. Lightfoot's Goochland quarters in the early 1750s (William Dabney Account Book).

Indulged in to make them Either happy to themselves or Invisible to their Master."[60]

As a last resort, slaves occasionally took direct and violent action against their overseers. In Goochland County in 1742, a slave woman was found guilty of persuading two male slaves to kill their overseer. A generation later, three Loudoun County slaves struck down their overseer with "axes and hoes." Such actions must have sent ripples of concern throughout the white community. We catch a glimpse of the effect when, in 1786, Francis Taylor entered the following note in his otherwise humdrum diary: "heard a negro of Capt. C. Conways yesterday wounded his overseer . . . with an ax, in a dangerous manner." Although such actions were rare, slaves committed enough murders of whites for distinctive tidewater and piedmont patterns to be discerned. According to a study of slave crime in colonial Virginia, the slaves' murder victims tended to be overseers in the piedmont and masters in the tidewater, presumably a function of the greater absenteeism in the former region.[61]

By the late colonial era, many more piedmont slaves resided on plantations headed by masters and, particularly on the larger estates, became subject to a more patriarchal planter style. The Frederick Hall Plantation books kept in the 1740s and 1750s by a Louisa County proprietor record small payments or sales of cloth in exchange for the slaves' chickens. The late colonial accounts of Dr. Edmund Wilcox, an Amherst County resident, reveal remittances to slaves for their ducks, chickens, fish, picked cotton, even hogsheads of shells. Charles Dabney reimbursed Edward Ambler's slaves for picked cotton in Louisa County in the late 1760s. In 1779 James Mercer proposed exchanging bacon for "Chickens & other fresh meat" obtained from the "Negroes who are the general Chicken Merchants." William Cabell paid a slave 40 shillings for finding his two stray horses. Thomas Jefferson allowed his slaves to plant their own "peculiam," objecting only when they "planted considerable crops of tobacco."[62]

Patriarchs prided themselves on their responsiveness to the human, as

60. Hugh Nelson to Battaile Muse, Dec. 22, 1778, and Muse to George William Fairfax, c. 1784, Muse Papers.

61. Trial of Jack, Yorkshire, and Lucy, June 30, 1742, Goochland Order Book 5, 83; trial of Joe, Sam, and Pendoe, Feb. 21, 1767, Loudoun County Court Order Book C, 236–237; Taylor diary, Jan. 11, 1786; Schwarz, "Hanging in Chains," chap. 4.

62. Smith Ledger, 1746, and Merchandise Day Book, vol. 8 (1755–1756), Frederick Hall Plantation Account Books (microfilm, CW); Wilcox accounts, vol. 6 (1761–

well as the material, needs of their slaves. Erasmus Gill of Stirling Castle in Dinwiddie County allowed his slave Aggy and her youngest children to go to Petersburg because Aggy was "desirous of living with her Husband." Gill arranged for her eldest child, Page, to be "brought up by some genteel Lady to learn how to soe, and attend to other domestic duties" in a three-year apprenticeship "for good Cloaths &c. provided she is treated with tenderness." A Fredericksburg master permitted his "old & faithful family slave" Charles to "see for the last time" his "other old acquaintances" in Stafford County.[63] Patriarchal benevolence was not confined to the tidewater gentry.

Indeed, as the eighteenth century proceeded, the rough edges of life in the interior were gradually smoothed away. Harsh sentences for slaves seem to have become less common over time. A good indication of the changing temper of the times comes from an anonymous letter to the *Virginia Gazette* in 1773. In it, a man known by the initials R. M. (almost undoubtedly Robert Munford of Amelia County) is said to have practiced barbaric cruelties upon his slaves, including the slaughter of at least fifty and the castration and dismemberment of a captured runaway. Presumably, the claims were exaggerated, but most notable is that one piedmonter would criticize the inhumanity of another.[64] Whatever the reality, slavery was not *meant* to be barbaric any longer.

1764), fols. 18, 23, 26, 32, vol. 11, July 1771, Mar. 26, 1775, Dec. 22, 27, 1777, Hubard Papers; Dabney Account Book, vol. 6, "memo of money to be paid Mr. Ambler's Negroes for Sam Sexton," CW (see also Charles Dabney Commonplace Book, 1791–1805, Jan. 8, 1799, Dabney Papers, Va. Hist. Soc.); James Mercer to Battaile Muse, Apr. 8, 1779 (see also Jan. 6, 1782), Muse Papers; Cabell diary, Jan. 24, 1778 (see also Jan. 22, 1775); Betts, ed., *Jefferson's Farm Book*, 268–269. See also Taylor diary, Aug. 15, Dec. 16, 1787.

63. Erasmus Gill to Duncas Rose, Jan. 24, 1801, Haxall Family Papers, Va. Hist. Soc.; James Mercer to Battaile Muse, Jan. 9, 1779, Muse Papers.

64. *Va. Gaz.* (Purdie & Dixon), Dec. 23, 1773. Michael L. Nicholls has kindly informed me that a slave named Hamshear is listed on Munford's plantation in the Amelia County tithable list of 1767. The slave who was castrated and later committed suicide was named Hampshire. Hangings were much more frequent before 1750 than after. In actions against property before midcentury, almost a third of all slaves were hanged; only 13% were hanged after that date. For actions against persons, the proportions were 44% and 29% respectively. Moreover, the most brutal sentences tended to come early in the century. See, for example, trial of Peter, June 23, 1737 (head severed from body and put on pole), Orange Order Book 1, 180–181, and trial of Eve, Jan. 23, 1746 (drawn upon a hurdle to place of execution and burned), Orange Order Book 4, 454–455.

Smaller planters were, of course, less able to afford the liberality of their more prosperous neighbors. It is they, for example, who were occasionally hauled into court, as was Thomas Dickinson of Goochland County in 1731, for "learning his Negro Boy to profain the Lord's Prayer." It is they who faced charges, as did John Nelson of Cumberland County and Joseph Price of Orange County, for "dealing" with or buying tobacco from slaves.[65] And it is they who invariably stood in the dock when masters were accused of either killing or wounding one of their own slaves. In most of these cases, the gentlemen justices discharged their less affluent neighbors without further trial—confirming the gentry's magnanimity toward fellow whites. Humble yeomen, however, were often incorrigible. When Daniel McPherson, a veteran of the Royal Highland Company Regiment that had fought in Quebec, confronted a slave suspected of theft, he acted in the classic small slaveholder manner. Rather than resorting to the courts, he whipped the man. Later, the same slave was incautious enough to jeer at McPherson, using "scurrilous language" to boot. McPherson was on his schooner at the time, but waded into the water intent on beating the slave a second time. The two men fought in the river, oblivious to the larger dangers they faced, were swept away, and drowned.[66] This sort of confrontation was a far cry from the patriarchal ideal.

Not all small planters were devoid of benevolent feelings. In July 1773 Toby, a slave belonging to James Wimbish of Halifax County, disappeared for over twelve years. When Wimbish discovered his bondman, he found that Toby had fought for his country in the Revolutionary War by enlisting

65. Presentments of the grand jury, May 1731, Goochland Order Book 2, 107 (see also presentments of the grand jury, May 27, 1746, Louisa Order Book, 1742–1748, 189); Fleming Ledger, 1754–1766, Jan. 1756, fol. 10; Taylor diary, Feb. 13, 1786. For other cases of trading with slaves, see James C. Bradford, "Society and Government in Loudoun County, Virginia, 1790–1800" (Ph.D. diss., University of Virginia, 1976), 203, 211.

66. *Va. Gaz.* (Purdie & Dixon), Aug. 6, 1772. For accusations of wounding or murdering slaves, see Cumberland Order Book, 1758–1762, 348, 1762–1764, 177 (case involving a free black), 1788–1792, 52; Orange Order Book 7, 168; Loudoun Order Book E, 410, F, 552–553; Spotsylvania Minute Book, 1755–1765, 354; Goochland Order Book 5, 339; and Chesterfield Order Book 4, 55, 382. In virtually all these cases, the charge was dismissed. See n. 87, below, for a case in the late 18th century with a different outcome. See also Mecklenburg County Court Order Book, 1779–1784, 530, for dismissal of a case against a small planter charged with castrating one of his slaves.

in the 14th Virginia Regiment under a fictitious name. Upon his retirement, he had married a white woman, by whom he had several children. Wimbish, in his words, felt "compassion" toward his slave and "subscribed a considerable sum toward obtaining his freedom, which was effected by several Gentlemen who bore part of the loss."[67] Even here, then, gentlemen aided a small planter.

Toby's marriage to a white woman raises the question of how much interracial sexual contact occurred in the piedmont. It is almost impossible to say. The indications are that it was not widespread—certainly not as widespread as seems to have been the case in seventeenth-century tidewater. In part, this can be explained by the decline in the numbers of white female servants over the course of the eighteenth century. Some piedmont women, invariably white servants, were the subjects of grand jury presentments for giving birth to mulatto children, but the numbers were small and apparently declining over time. Elizabeth Gallemore, a white resident of Amelia County, is the exception that proves the rule. She was charged in 1759 with "unlawfully cohabiting with a negro slave . . . and having several mulatto children."[68]

Of course, sexual contacts between whites and blacks continued to occur, primarily between white men and black women. Unfortunately, little direct evidence as to the dimensions of this practice survives. The number of mulattoes might be one indirect measure of its extent, but no census of the colonial Virginia population tallied them. We can count mulattoes in runaway advertisements (there were seventy-nine from the 1730s through the 1770s, forming just under one-fifth of the total), but we know that the runaway population was heavily weighted toward the assimilated. We can also count mulattoes in inventories (just under sixty were listed in the estates of five piedmont counties, representing only 1 percent of the appraised total), but we can never be sure that appraisers consistently noted their presence.[69] In sum, while the evidence is certainly inconclusive, interracial sexual contact does not seem to have been

67. Petition of James Wimbish, Oct. 22, 1789, Legislative Petitions, 1776–1791, Va. State Lib.

68. From all the county court order books searched, I count only 9 white servant women cited by grand juries for having a "mulatto bastard" before 1755. After this date, the number drops to 2. For Gallemore, see Nicholls, "Passing Through This Troublesome World," *VMHB*, XCII (1984), 50.

69. This number is based on the inventories of Chesterfield, Goochland, Loudoun, Orange, and Spotsylvania counties from 1734–1775.

rampant. Rather than replicating an earlier tidewater experience, the piedmont probably was an extension of the contemporary tidewater pattern.

Indeed, the sense of shame attached to sexual liaisons with blacks seems to have been felt more strongly in piedmont than in tidewater. Consider the proceedings of the Meherrin Baptist Church in Lunenburg County in the fall of 1775. Brother Sherwood Walton was accused by some of his fellow brethren of "offering the Act of uncleaness to a Mulatto Girl of his own." While in her pregnancy, the girl had often hinted to Walton's daughters that her master was the father. She claimed more directly that she knew "not that any person had carnal knowledge of her but supposed it might be done while she was asleep but that she knew of [Walton's] coming & offering such things at times to her." When delivering the child, the midwives had pressed the girl to tell the truth, "and as her extremity was more than common, they told her it might be a Judgment of God upon her, & that she might die." But the girl confidently kept to her story. However, when the child was born, "it proved to be a remarkable black child, a negro without any doubt." Even then, four members of the church at first refused to "give satisfaction" to Walton. That the matter had gone so far indicates the potentially explosive character of a charge of sexual misconduct, particularly when it involved a slave.[70]

This involvement of a Baptist church in relations between blacks and whites is hardly accidental, for the piedmont was the center of the evangelical revival that swept Virginia in the late colonial era. In this respect, the piedmont was hardly replicating or extending a tidewater experience; it was leading the way. A number of Virginia slaves, it is true, from both tidewater and piedmont, had been exposed to Christianity in the early eighteenth century. In 1738, for instance, the new incumbent of a parish in Goochland County baptized almost two hundred slaves on his first trip through his domain. However, the first sustained proselytization of slaves took place in neighboring Hanover County at midcentury, under the inspired leadership of the charismatic Presbyterian Samuel Davies. In 1751 Davies reported that one hundred slaves attended his services and that forty had been baptized in the previous three years. Four years later, the numbers had increased to three hundred and one hundred, respectively. His efforts then gained momentum, for in 1757 he claimed to have

70. Meherrin Baptist Church Records, Lunenburg County, second Saturday in September 1775 (photostat, Va. State Lib.).

baptized one hundred and fifty black adults in the previous eighteen months and to have sixty black communicants in attendance. The influence of this revival radiated outward to other piedmont counties. Slaves who had been converted by Davies but transferred to Charlotte County proselytized other slaves in their new home.[71]

What is perhaps most surprising about this Presbyterian success was its conservative and bookish nature. Davies and his disciples thought it part of their mission to teach the slaves to read. In the middle of the nineteenth century, one Virginian recalled seeing African slaves clasping the books given to them by their eminent preacher. Davies was also demanding of his converts. He acknowledged that he was "affraid of discouraging them . . . by imposing high Forms of Admission to Baptism," but equally he underlined his caution at not "swelling the number of proselites with only nominal Christians." He excluded many blacks from baptism because they thought it either a fashionable communal rite or, more ominously, a means to "be upon an Equality with their Masters." Davies strenuously opposed these misinterpretations of his message. Indeed, he reported that planters were impressed "by the visiable Reformation wrought by his preaching among the Slaves, whose Sobriety and diligence excited their Curiosity."[72]

Evangelical successes among the slaves gained impetus as less conservative groups—first the New Light Baptists and then the Methodists—began to make their influence felt. The New Lights established their first beachhead in Virginia in the southside. The earliest Baptist church records report small black memberships (see table 4). In 1759 the

71. Anthony Gavin to Bishop Gibson, Aug. 5, 1738, Fulham Papers, XII, 273–274, Lambeth Palace Library, London; *Letters from the Rev. Samuel Davies &c., Shewing the State of Religion in Virginia; Particularly among the Negroes* . . . (London, 1757), 10, 12, 27–31, 41; Rev. William Henry Foote, *Sketches of Virginia: Historical and Biographical* (Philadelphia, 1855), 302–303. See also Samuel Davies, *The Duty of Christians to Propagate Their Religion among Heathens, Earnestly Recommended to the Masters of Negroe Slaves in Virginia: A Sermon Preached in Hanover, January 8, 1757* (London, 1758); George William Pilcher, "Samuel Davies and the Instruction of Negroes in Virginia," *VMHB*, LXXIV (1966), 293–300; and Michael Greenberg, "Revival, Reform, Revolution: Samuel Davies and the Great Awakening in Virginia," *Marxist Perspectives*, III, no. 2 (1980), 102–119.

72. Anonymous review of *The Religious Instruction of Negroes in the United States*, by Charles C. Jones, in *Biblical Repertory and Princeton Review*, XV (1843), 26–27, as quoted in Pilcher, "Samuel Davies," *VMHB*, LXXIV (1966), 294; *Letters from Rev. Davies*, 30–31; "An Extract from Mr. Davies's letter," n.d., New College, London, L61/4, SR 7749 (photostat, CW).

TABLE 4. *Black Membership in Piedmont Baptist Churches, 1758–1808*

Church	Year of Membership List	% Black	Total Members
Dan River (Pittsylvania)	1758	26	42
Birchcreek (Pittsylvania)	1769	10	20
Rapidan (Orange)	1769	4	53
Fall Creek (Pittsylvania)	1770	11	37
Goochland (Goochland)	1771	12	88
Meherrin (Lunenburg)	1771	10	100
Buckingham (Buckingham)	1772	11	36
Chesterfield (Chesterfield)	1786	15	48
Lower Banister (Pittsylvania)	1798	28	43
Tussekiah (Lunenburg)	1798	43	95
Chestnut Grove (Albemarle)	1799	54	128
Bear Swamp (Hanover)	1787–1808	55	164

Sources: Morgan Edwards, "Materials towards a History of the Baptists in the Provinces of Maryland, Virginia, North Carolina, South Carolina, Georgia," MS, 1772 (microfilm, Duke University Library, Durham, N.C.); manuscript church records at the Virginia Baptist Historical Society, Richmond, and photostats and microfilm at the Virginia State Library, Richmond.

Note: Almost all the black members were slaves.

Lunenburg County Anglican minister spoke of the "spectre of dissenters" hovering around him. He singled out for particular notice their opening up of the ministry to all, "whether he be a slave or a free Person." Piedmont slaves were certainly preaching. In 1772 a twenty-year-old mulatto from Chesterfield County had "been a Preacher ever since he was sixteen Years of Age"; another mulatto, who ran away from Dinwiddie County three years later, was "very fond of singing hymns and preaching"; and in 1778 a Brunswick County slave formerly belonging to an Anglican minister had shown enough independence to become "a Baptist teacher."[73]

73. Rev. James Craig to Thomas Dawson, Sept. 8, 1759, William Dawson Papers, Lib. Cong.; Seth Ward, *Va. Gaz.* (Purdie & Dixon), Feb. 27, 1772; David Walker, *ibid.* (Purdie), Sept. 8, 1775; Turner Bynam, *ibid.*, May 1, 1778. For the geography of evangelical progress in Virginia, see Robert B. Semple, *A History of the Rise and*

Indeed, Baptist slaves had to be independent, for masters openly scorned their slaves' religious sincerity. In 1767 a Buckingham County master referred to his slave woman "pretend[ing] much to the religion the Negroes of late have practised." Ten years later a Prince Edward County master described his mulatto runaway as "pretend[ing] to know something of religious matters, and misses no opportunity of holding forth on that subject." Slaves faced more than derision for their beliefs. In 1769 James Ireland noted that the "poor negroes have been stripped and subjected to stripes" in Culpeper County for listening to the Baptists. Nine years later, Cumberland County masters petitioned the governor to put a halt to their slaves' attendance at night meetings. They cited two reasons: first, the "fruits of disobedience and insolence to Masters," but even more significant, the slaves' "glorying in what they are taught to believe to be the persecution for Conscience's Sake."[74]

In the 1770s the Methodists too began to make inroads in the piedmont, particularly in the southside. In June 1776, at a chapel near Petersburg, Methodist circuit rider Thomas Rankin had "a powerful meeting" with a large number of whites and blacks. "What was peculiarly affecting to him," he noted, were the blacks in the gallery, "almost every one of them upon their knees; some for themselves, and others for their distressed companions." In the following month, Rankin, now joined by Francis Asbury, attended a number of extremely emotional meetings in this area. On one occasion, Asbury had to stop a meeting "again and again, and beg of the people to compose themselves." In the congregation were "Hundreds of Negroes . . . with tears streaming down their faces." Two years later, Nelson Reed preached in a piedmont chapel in the morning, witnessed a funeral service in the afternoon, and returned to the chapel to find "a Negro woman lying on the ground as if she was all but dead, and had been there all the while."[75] Such responsiveness made a strong impression on Reed and other Methodist preachers.

Progress of the Baptists in Virginia (Richmond, Va., 1810) and Wesley M. Gewehr, *The Great Awakening in Virginia, 1740–1790* (Durham, N.C., 1930).

74. Stephen Dence, *Va. Gaz.* (Purdie & Dixon), Mar. 26, 1767; John Murchie, *ibid.* (Purdie), June 13, 1777; Lewis Peyton Little, *Imprisoned Preachers and Religious Liberty in Virginia* . . . (Lynchburg, Va., 1938), 163; petition of sundry inhabitants of Cumberland County, Nov. 6, 1778, Legislative Petitions (see also petition from sundry inhabitants of the county of Cumberland, May 21, 1777, Religious Petitions, Va. State Lib.).

75. Rev. Thomas Rankin diary, June 30, July 7, 14, 1776, typescript, 172–177, Garrett Biblical Institute Library, Evanston, Ill.; Elmer T. Clark *et al.*, eds., *The*

Why were the Baptists, Methodists, and to a lesser extent, Presbyterians so successful among piedmont slaves? Part of the reason lay in the evangelicals' emphasis on an untutored, spontaneous religious response. As William Spencer on the southside circuit put it, "My Soul is happy when I preach to people that are engaged but when I get among formalists, or half-hearted Christians, my Soul is troubled, and I am bowed down." Spencer went on to draw a direct comparison between the "engaged" and the "half-hearted" in racial terms: "in general the dear black people, that profess Religion are much more engaged than the whites." Similarly, James Meacham "thought that [he] could get more blacks to hear [him] preach of a night than whites in the day." The minister of Cub Creek Presbyterian Church in Charlotte County described his lay exhorter, "Old Harry," as "one of the most fervently devout men I ever met with." Harry's "soul appeared to be all on fire with love to Jesus Christ." Some evangelicals owed their conversion to their slaves. Edward Baptist's "deep religious impressions" had their origins in the teachings of a slave who kept him "looking out for voices and visions"; Anne Randolph Page's spiritual rebirth came through contact with "an old blind negro woman . . . who was a dear child of God."[76]

The musical and emotional responsiveness of slaves encouraged and impressed evangelical preachers. Samuel Davies spoke of the "torrent of sacred harmony" of which blacks were capable. "The Negroes above all the human species that ever I knew," he declared, "have an ear for Music, and a Kind of extatic delight in Psalmody." One evening in Mecklenburg County, the singing of blacks in a nearby cottage inspired James Meacham to pray with them. He was so moved as to feel that "Heaven was just

Journal and Letters of Francis Asbury, 3 vols. (London, 1958), I, 219–222; Nelson Reed diary, Aug. 9, 1778, typescript, 12, Lovely Lane Museum, Baltimore, Md.

76. William Spencer diary, Jan. 1790, Va. Hist. Soc.; Spencer diary, July 27, 1790, CW; "A Journal and Travel of James Meacham: Part II, 1784–1797," *Trinity College Historical Society Papers*, X (1914), 88; James W. Alexander, *The Life of Archibald Alexander . . .* (New York, 1854), 525; Edward Baptist diary, typescript, 1 (event took place c. 1798–1800), Va. Hist. Soc.; Charles Wesley Andrews, *Memoir of Mrs. Anne R. Page* (Philadelphia, 1844), 10, 17–19, 24. For examples of the spirited black response, see Philip Cox, *Arminian Magazine* (Philadelphia), II (1790), 91–92; Freeborn Garrettson, "An Account of the Revival of the Work of God at Petersburg in Virginia, Feb. 1788," *Magazine of the Wesleyan Methodist Church . . .* (London), XIII (1790), 300–307; and Robert H. Bishop, *An Outline of the History of the Church in the State of Kentucky, during a Period of Forty Years: Containing the Memoirs of Rev. David Rice . . .* (Lexington, Ky., 1824), 57.

then at hand." A month later, at another home, Meacham "awaked in raptures of Heaven by the sweet Echo of Singing in the Kitchen among the dear Black people (who my Soul loves)." Scarcely had he "ever heard anything to equal it upon earth." The "hollering" of slaves impressed John Kobler when on the Bedford circuit, while Thomas Morrell observed at Lanes Chapel near Petersburg that "the people in Virginia are fond of noisy meetings particularly the blacks." If the "noise" made by blacks appeared "too mechanical" to Morrell, he was nevertheless impressed by its "power." By mechanical, Morrell may have been suggesting a choreographed response, a characteristic feature of the Afro-American religious tradition.[77]

The evangelicals' success among slaves also owed much to their initial willingness to adopt a radical stance toward the white opponents of black conversion. Until the 1790s many Baptist and Methodist preachers actively opposed slavery. Perhaps none matched James Meacham, who spoke of his "burning fury" at the "blood and oppression" faced by blacks. Nevertheless, there were others, like Reverend Kobler, who remonstrated with a master for burning his slave on each cheek and forehead and noted in his diary that masters "will be sick of hot irons in a coming day"; or Samuel Watson, who in 1790 interceded with the governor on behalf of a Fauquier County slave condemned to death for "compounding or administering medicines." Even the relatively conservative Hanover presbytery, meeting in Amherst County in 1774, took a stand on the liberty of conscience possessed by all human beings. "When a servant appears to be penitent and makes a profession of his faith in Christ," declared the presbytery, "it is our indispensable duty to admit him into our Church," with or without the master's permission.[78]

Another indication of the radical stance of evangelicalism—at least in

77. *Letters from Rev. Davies*, 12, 16; "A Journal and Travel of James Meacham: Part I, May 19 to Aug. 31, 1789," *Trinity Coll. Hist. Soc. Papers*, IX (1912), 79, 88; Rev. John Kobler journal, 1789–1792, July 7, 1791, 101–102, Lovely Lane Museum, Baltimore; Thomas Morrell journal, 1789–1809, Dec. 23, 1791, Drew University, Madison, N.J.

78. "Meditation and Exercises of James Meacham," Nov. 24, 1788, Jan. 12, 1789, Meacham journal; "Journal of James Meacham," *Trinity Coll. Hist. Soc. Papers*, IX (1912), 68, 78–79, *passim*; Kobler journal, July 15, 1791, 108–109; petition of Samuel Watson, c. 1790, Executive Papers, Aug.–Nov. 1790; petition of the presbytery of Hanover, Nov. 11, 1774, Religious Petitions. See also W. Harrison Daniel, "Virginia Baptists and the Negro in the Early Republic," *VMHB*, LXXX (1972), 64–68, and Albert Matthews, "Notes on the Proposed Abolition of Slavery in Virginia in 1785," Colonial Society of Massachusetts, *Publications*, VI (1904), 370–380.

the context of late-eighteenth-century Chesapeake society—was the implicit or even explicit egalitarianism that characterized their disciplinary proceedings. Although evangelical church discipline certainly served to buttress the master's authority over his slave, disciplinary meetings rarely served to rubber-stamp a master's whim. In 1786 Tussekiah Baptist Church in Lunenburg County resolved to "deal" with black members just as with whites. At the Boar Swamp Baptist Church in Hanover County, five years later, a disciplinary action followed precisely this procedure: two women, one a slave and the other a free white, were together brought before the church, accused of adultery, and excommunicated. The Meherrin Baptist Church of Lunenburg County disciplined whites for their transgressions against slaves. Brother Charles Cook "acknowledged his sin in unlawfully burning one of his negroes." In another case, two blacks accused a white woman of "the sin of anger & unchristian language."[79]

Who among the slaves responded to the evangelical message? Creoles were probably the most likely converts, but Africans were not to be discounted. Samuel Davies described his efforts to teach a forty-year-old African, "a very stupid lubberly Fellow in appearance and but [in]differently acquainted with our Language." Despairing of his own abilities, Davies was later amazed to find the slave succeeding on his own. Simply passing on further books to him, Davies discovered that his former pupil could "read English almost as intelligibly as he can speak it." This African's description of his conversion and beliefs was "a very broken account," but his life was a model of piety. John Wright, a disciple of Davies and a minister in Cumberland County, was "transported" by the "exercises of the most savage boy" among his black converts. In 1793, when on the Bedford circuit, Jeremiah Norman heard the experiences of "an out Landish Black woman" who "seemed wonderfully transported, ah said she, my Blessed God I see you coming." A slave known as Uncle Jack, kidnapped in Africa at the age of seven and brought to the piedmont before the American Revolution, converted at the age of forty in Nottoway County. He soon received a license to preach from plantation to plantation.[80]

79. Tussekiah Baptist Church Recs., Aug. 26, 1786; Boar Swamp Baptist Church Recs., fourth Saturday in July 1791; Meherrin Baptist Church Recs., July 5, Feb. 22, 1772, Va. Baptist Hist. Soc.

80. *Letters from Rev. Davies*, 29, 11; Jeremiah Norman diary, Aug. 1793, V, 10, Stephen B. Weeks Collection, Univ. of North Carolina, Chapel Hill; William S. White, *The African Preacher: An Authentic Narrative* (Philadelphia, 1849), 1–12.

Most significant of all, perhaps, is the occasional suggestion of a distinctive black religiosity, owing something no doubt to these African roots. On June 8, 1787, Francis Taylor noted that an old slave woman named Judy belonging to a neighbor had died. A month later, Taylor's slave Betty died after a long illness. On July 29, a Sunday, Taylor observed that "the Negroes had a Funeral over Old Judy & Betty." Perhaps the funeral took the form described by the Reverend John Holt Rice of Charlotte County, who was impressed by the "great numbers of negro preachers" presiding over these events. Writing in 1809, Rice believed that these ceremonies exhibited "many remains, I suppose, of the savage customs of Africa. They cry and bawl and howl around the grave and roll in the dirt, and make many expressions of the most frantic grief. This is when they are unrestrained by the presence of the whites. Sometimes the noise that they make may be heard as far as one or two miles."[81]

The story of black-white relations in eighteenth-century piedmont Virginia is a complex one. There was certainly a measure of replication of an earlier tidewater experience. For instance, Africans, a significant minority in the colonial piedmont (as they had been earlier in tidewater), made their presence felt in everything from the general instability of plantation life to the fashioning of distinctive burial practices. At the same time, the piedmont soon assumed many of the characteristics of contemporary tidewater: most slaves worked under the eye of a resident master; a patriarchal planter style emerged; and sexual contacts between the races seem to have been uncommon. Even more interesting, perhaps, the piedmont anticipated developments that would eventually reach tidewater. In the early piedmont, slaves often experienced a distanced relationship with a master, something tidewater slaves would undergo as plantations increased in size. Moreover, the piedmont represented the heart of a religious revival that only later radiated outward into parts of tidewater.

VI

By the very end of the eighteenth century, as some of the foregoing evidence has indicated, the question of replication or extension becomes somewhat redundant. There were certainly still dif-

81. Taylor diary, June 8, July 7, 29, 1787; John H. Rice, "Report to the General Assembly's Committee on Missions, 1809," *Evangelical Intelligencer*, III (1809), 390–391.

ferences between the experiences of slaves in tidewater and piedmont. For one thing, tobacco production was still expanding rapidly in parts of the piedmont. Consequently, it is no surprise to learn that the heart of the opposition to the increase in manumissions that occurred in late-eighteenth-century Virginia centered in this region, particularly the southern piedmont.[82] However, by the late eighteenth century the similarities between piedmont and tidewater were far greater than their differences. A full exploration of this phenomenon is not possible here, but a few remarks are in order.

One fundamental area of convergence between piedmont and tidewater lay in religion. As growing numbers of piedmont Baptists and Methodists became slave owners, inevitably their outspokenness against Virginia's primary institution grew more muted. By the 1790s it had dwindled to insignificance. The antislavery zealousness of many an evangelical preacher either waned in the face of increasingly hostile audiences or impelled their departure from the state. These developments paved the way for a readier acceptance of the evangelical message by all white Virginians. An evangelical counterculture that had once been regionally based now became part of establishment culture throughout the state.[83]

Another area of convergence, surprisingly, concerned the war. It might be thought that the Revolutionary War affected only tidewater slaves directly. Certainly, it affected them the most directly. Perhaps four thousand tidewater slaves left Virginia permanently as a result of the war, whereas very few piedmont slaves escaped. However, piedmont slaves faced their own somewhat lesser disruptions. Some fought in the war: of one hundred and fifty blacks who served as soldiers or sailors, over a quarter were from piedmont counties. A runaway slave from Amelia County passed himself off as a free black in Goochland County and substituted for a white man in the local militia force. Billy, a mulatto slave, served the British forces so well that he was tried for "traiterously wag-

82. Fredrika Teute Schmidt and Barbara Ripel Wilhelm, "Early Proslavery Petitions in Virginia," *WMQ*, 3d Ser., XXX (1973), 133–146.

83. James David Essig, "A Very Wintry Season: Virginia Baptists and Slavery, 1785–1797," *VMHB*, LXXXVIII (1980), 170–185; Richard R. Beeman, *The Evolution of the Southern Backcountry: A Case Study of Lunenburg County, Virginia, 1746–1832* (Philadelphia, 1984), 190–191, 208–209, 218–221; Donald G. Mathews, "The Second Great Awakening as an Organizing Process, 1780–1830: An Hypothesis," *American Quarterly*, XXI (1969), 23–43; Albert J. Raboteau, "The Slave Church in the Era of the American Revolution," in Berlin and Hoffman, eds., *Slavery and Freedom*, 193–213.

[ing] and levy[ing] war" against the commonwealth.[84] Piedmont slaves were moved further inland to be far away from the action, and many other slaves were brought into their midst, even from as far away as South Carolina and Georgia. Not all slaves were willing to move. The "greatest part" of John Norton's "People" refused to leave Hanover County for a new quarter in Fauquier County in April 1782. A month later, Norton continued to hope that his overseer would "be able to prevail upon most of them to set out." Masters could never be sure that their slaves were completely isolated from the action. In August 1782 a nervous James Mercer wrote to his Loudoun County steward pointing out that it would be "highly prudent" to make life tolerable for his slaves in order "to engage [them] to stay." Unless the "situation of these poor devils is rendered at least supportable," he declared, "the natural consequence will be that we shall be left without."[85]

This wartime experience, together with many shifting social and intellectual currents—a more affectionate family environment, the extension of evangelicalism, the growth of Romanticism and humanitarianism—softened some of the sterner features of slavery in the piedmont, just as much as in tidewater. The changing tenor of the times can be glimpsed in a variety of forms. When Anne Peachey petitioned for the pardon of her slave convicted of a burglary, she declared her belief that he was "the Workmanship of the same Being with myself." Ninety-two residents of Dinwiddie and two other southside counties begged a pardon for two

84. Luther P. Jackson, "Virginia Negro Soldiers and Seamen in the American Revolution," *Journal of Negro History*, XXVII (1942), 257–261 (discounting unknowns); depositions and letter from Lt. Col. Jolly Parish, Mar. 10, 1781, letters from Cuthbert Bullitt, Mann Page, H. Lee, and William Carr, May 11–13, 1781, Executive Papers. See Frey, "Between Slavery and Freedom," *Jour. So. Hist.*, XLIX (1983), 382–383, for the war's penetration of the piedmont. The largest known group of Virginia runaways, nine men and four women, left Goochland County in April 1780. John Payne, *Maryland Journal and Baltimore Advertiser*, June 27, 1780, Supplement.

85. John H. Norton to Battaile Muse, Apr. 21, May 11, 1782, and James Mercer to Muse, Aug. 9, 1782, Muse Papers. The Executive Papers series contains lists, often by name and age, of those slaves brought into various piedmont counties (mostly Amherst, Charlotte, and Halifax counties) by South Carolina and Georgia planters. Between June 1780 and August 1781, I count 267 slaves (90 men, 72 women, 50 boys, and 55 girls) belonging to 13 separate masters. Another planter brought in 63 slaves (not enumerated), and the marquis de Chastellux noted in 1782 that a Carolinian named Stephen Bull had brought 200 slaves into Virginia (Chastellux, *Travels in North America in the Years 1780, 1781, and 1782*, trans. and ed. Howard C. Rice, Jr., 2 vols. [Chapel Hill, N.C., 1963], II, 425). No doubt there were more such cases.

slaves on the grounds that the bondmen had expressed "the most sincere penitence" and were motivated to steal only from hunger.[86] When two patrollers from Dinwiddie County attempted to capture a slave whom they had been led to believe was a runaway, they were brought before the Petersburg District Court and fined for infringing the rights of the black man, who was in the process of suing for his freedom. Mathew Farley of Cumberland County was even sentenced to death for killing his father's slave. Most instructive are the sentiments of his and his neighbors' petitions seeking mercy. Farley claimed to treat "Slaves with Humanity," spoke of the "Tenderness which we owe our Fellow Creatures," and begged forgiveness for one moment's aberration. His neighbors were "shock'd and distressed at the horrid tho' perhaps *just* sentence pass'd on their friend and countryman," who was clerk of the church, singing master, constable, and patroller. They did not dispute the justice of the verdict, but claimed that Farley was "still capable of becoming a good member of society."[87]

Even the aggressive proslavery sentiments of many piedmont residents did not preclude the extension of manumission to numbers of piedmont slaves. In fact, by 1800 free blacks in the piedmont almost equaled in number those in tidewater, excluding those on the Eastern Shore (a special case due to the large presence of freedmen dating back to the seventeenth century). By the end of the century, free blacks made up at least 5 percent of the black population in eleven piedmont counties and in all the region's major towns.[88] As in tidewater, three influences account

86. Anne Peachey to the governor, Dec. 26, 1793, Executive Papers, Nov.–Dec. 1793; petition of sundry inhabitants of Dinwiddie, Prince George, and Surry counties, July 24, 1787, *ibid.*, July–Aug. 1787. See also Henry Lee to the mayor of Fredericksburg, Jan. 20, 1794, Executive Letter Book, 1792–1794, 336, Va. State Lib. On the "softening" of slavery in the late-18th-century tidewater, see Gerald W. Mullin, *Flight and Rebellion: Slave Resistance in Eighteenth-Century Virginia* (New York, 1972), 127 and *passim*, and Robert McColley, *Slavery and Jeffersonian Virginia*, 2d ed. (Urbana, Ill., 1973), 57 and *passim*.

87. Petition of Gabriel Burnett and Richard Townsend, n.d. (c. 1790), Legislative Petitions; petition of inhabitants of Chesterfield and Powhatan counties, n.d., and petition of Mathew Farley, Jr., Dec. 26, 1788, Executive Papers, Jan.–Feb. 1789.

88. In 1800 there were 7,688 free blacks in the piedmont, 8,311 in tidewater (Western Shore only), and 2,195 on the Eastern Shore. The black populations of 10 piedmont counties were 5–9% free: Bedford, Campbell, Goochland, Greensville, Henry, Loudoun, Mecklenburg, Powhatan, Prince William, and Spotsylvania. One piedmont county (Patrick) was in the 10–19% range, and the black populations of Petersburg and Richmond were over 20% free.

for the rising numbers of free blacks. First, many evangelicals freed their slaves. Second, urban masters seem to have been particularly responsive to emancipationist sentiment. Finally, the piedmont had its patriarchs just like tidewater, some of whom manumitted all their slaves. For instance, many of Joseph Mayo's 180 slaves resident in Chesterfield, Cumberland, Goochland, Henrico, and Mecklenburg counties were freed in the 1780s. The executors of Mayo's will spoke of granting "that liberty natural to all Men, and which [the slaves'] humane late Master was anxiously desirous to grant them."[89]

VII

In most respects, the expansion of slavery into the piedmont should be conceived in terms of extension, not replication. What is most impressive is the way in which the social and demographic constraints that had existed in the oldest tidewater counties for generations disappeared in a matter of decades on the frontier. The stages of development through which tidewater slave society passed were often compressed, skipped altogether, or simply extended in the piedmont. From some perspectives, particularly the religious aspirations of its slaves, the piedmont was even in advance of the tidewater. By the end of the century, there was little to distinguish the slave experiences of the two regions.

Perhaps no better testimonial exists to some of the dominant themes of slave life in the piedmont than the prayer said to have been written by a slave in "the lower part of Virginia" in the year 1790 and recorded by the Quaker Joshua Evans. It speaks to the formidable odds slaves faced; to their resilience of spirit; to their familiarity with white ways; to their religious faith; and, above all, to their desire and hopes for freedom.

89. Petition of Paul Carrington, Miles Selden, and Joseph Carrington, administrators of the will of Joseph Mayo, Oct. 28, 1786, Legislative Petitions. On evangelical manumissions, see Arthur Dicken Thomas, Jr., "The Second Great Awakening in Virginia and Slavery Reform, 1785–1837" (Th.D. diss., Union Theological Seminary, 1981), 17–18, 36–37, 60–62, 84, and Luther P. Jackson, "Religious Development of the Negro in Virginia from 1760 to 1860," *Jour. Negro Hist.*, XVI (1931), 177–179. On urban manumission, see Suzanne Lebsock, *The Free Women of Petersburg: Status and Culture in a Southern Town, 1784–1860* (New York, 1984), 94–96. Whether a shift toward mixed farming also encouraged manumissions in the piedmont has yet to be explored.

Lord, if thou dost with equal eye,
See all the sons of Adam rise,
Why dost thou hide thy face from slaves,
Confin'd by fate to serve such knaves?
Stolen and sold in Africa,
Transported to America,
Like hogs and sheep in market sold,
To stand the heat, and bear the cold,

. . . .

When will Jehovah hear our cries?
When will the sun of freedom rise?
When will a Moses for us stand,
And free us all from Pharoah's hand?
What tho' our skin be black as jet,
Our hair be curl'd our noses flat,
Must we for this, no freedom have
until we find it in the grave?

. . . . . .

Contentment, Lord, on me bestow,
While I remain a slave below,
And whilst I suffer grief and wrong;
May thy Salvation be my song.[90]

90. Joshua Evans diary, July 3, 1797, 263–265, Southern Hist. Coll., Univ. of North Carolina, Chapel Hill.

Acknowledgments

All of the essays in this volume were initially presented at two conferences, one organized by Lois Green Carr of Historic St. Mary's City and David Beers Quinn and J. Frederick Fausz of St. Mary's College of Maryland, the other by Jack P. Greene and Jean B. Russo of the Johns Hopkins University. We would particularly like to thank Jack P. Greene, without whose sponsorship this volume would not have appeared, as well as the Maryland Humanities Council, the Maryland State Archives, and the St. Maries Citty Foundation, for their generous subsidies. The contributions of many people at the conferences—whether as formal commentators, presenters of papers, or discussants from the floor—also deserve recognition. Many essays in this volume benefited from suggestions made in Baltimore and St. Mary's City. James Henretta undertook to read all the papers delivered at one of the conferences, and his stimulating critique provided further assistance.

As the Introduction took shape, a number of scholars supplied us with valuable suggestions. Philip Morgan thanks James Horn for many hours spent discussing Chesapeake history and for some particularly constructive remarks on a then prospective Introduction. Drew McCoy was equally supportive at a much later stage.

The maps for Lorena Walsh's essay were computer generated, using the AutoCAD system, at the Department of Geography at the University of Maryland. This new process allows the author to revise and correct maps as they are being produced. We thank Robert D. Mitchell and Allen Eney for their interest and help in bringing these maps into being.

Finally, it is a pleasure to acknowledge the invaluable assistance of the staff at the Institute of Early American History and Culture. To the late Stephen Botein, who acted as a patient and astute broker when relations became strained among the Chesapeakers (as he termed them), we register our continuing sense of loss. To the Institute's wise director, we dedicate the volume as a token of our appreciation and gratitude for his outstanding contributions to early American history. To its unsung heroine, Cynthia Carter Ayres, we owe more than we can express for the care and consideration bestowed on all aspects of this volume.

Notes on the Contributors

Lois Green Carr, the Historian at Historic St. Mary's City, is the coauthor (with David W. Jordan) of *Maryland's Revolution of Government, 1689–1692* and the author and coauthor of numerous articles on colonial Chesapeake history.

Douglas Deal, Associate Professor of History at the State University of New York, College at Oswego, is working on a study of race relations and slavery on the Eastern Shore of Virginia during the colonial period.

J. Frederick Fausz, Professor of History at St. Mary's College of Maryland, has published extensively on ethnohistory of the seventeenth-century Chesapeake.

Michael Graham is Assistant Professor of History at Xavier University.

James Horn, Principal Lecturer at Brighton Polytechnic, Sussex, England, is completing a comparative study of local society in England, and the Chesapeake in the seventeenth century.

Jean Butenhoff Lee, Assistant Professor of History at the University of Wisconsin–Madison, is completing a study of Charles County, Maryland, in the Revolutionary period.

Russell R. Menard, Professor of History at the University of Minnesota, is the coauthor (with John J. McCusker) of *The Economy of British America, 1607–1789*.

Henry M. Miller, Director of Research at Historic St. Mary's City, is a historical archaeologist with research interests in the evolution of vernacular landscape, consumer behavior, and the interaction between culture and environment.

Philip D. Morgan, Associate Professor of History at Florida State University, is completing a comparative study of black culture in the low country and the Chesapeake in the eighteenth century.

Jean B. Russo, Research Director for Historic Annapolis, Inc., and Research Associate at Historic St. Mary's City, is working on a study of the social history of the Chesapeake in the early national period.

Lorena S. Walsh, Research Fellow at the Colonial Williamsburg Foundation, is completing a study of plantation management in the colonial Chesapeake.

Index

Absentee planters: and slaves, 465–468, 479, 481
Accomac Indians, 54
Accomack County, Va., 63, 92, 259, 275, 280, 286, 288, 299
Accomack County Court, 80, 286
Adams, Mary, 338
Adams, Richard, 438
Adams, Thomas, 450
Adams, William Godfrey, 338
African slaves, 11, 99, 456; adjustment of, in Virginia, 30, 434, 442–444; importation of, 129, 435–436, 438–439, 441; runaway, 439–440, 442; and poisoning, 441; religion of, 478–479. *See also* Slaves
Afro-Americans: political perspective of, 302–303; and rebellion, 303
Afro-American society, 30, 433; effects of Africans on, 444; emergence of, in Virginia piedmont, 454–464; and religion, 472–479. *See also* Slaves
Afro-Indians, 30, 463–464
Age of majority, 318, 331n
Albemarle County, Va., 440, 447, 450, 452, 458, 461, 463, 464, 465
Alexander, Sir William, 61–62, 92
Algonquian Indians, 50, 51, 60, 68, 69, 74
All Hallow's Parish, Md., 424
Ambler, Edward, 445, 467, 468
Amelia County, Va., 438, 443, 453, 460, 464, 465, 469, 471, 480
Amenities scores, 379–380
Amherst County, Va., 440, 453, 464, 465, 466, 477
Angela, Benjamin, 449
Angela, Betty, 449
Angela, William, Sr., 449
Anglican church. *See* Church of England

Anglicization, 8; and Indians, 50–52
Anglo-Indian alliances, 18, 28, 47–79, 83–84, 87–91
Anglo-Indian wars. *See* Powhatan Uprising; *individual wars*
Anglo-Powhatan War, First, 51, 57
Anglo-Powhatan War, Second, 54–55, 59, 81
Anglo-Powhatan War, Third, 78, 85–86
Angola Creek, 439
Angola Road, 439
Animal remains, 176; excavated, 181–192
Annamessex Hundred, Md., 344, 364
Annapolis, Md., 9, 430
Anne Arundel County, Md., 81, 227, 242, 247, 254, 259, 263, 357, 362, 424; diversification in, 343, 358–362; inventoried wealth of, 350; inventory reporting rates in, 383, 385, 386; inventory coding practices for, 387
Anthony, Joseph, 460
Apprenticeship. *See* Artisans; Free craftsmen
Archaeology: and housing, 20; and diet, 21–22, 176–199; methods, 181, 198–199; sites of, 196–197
Architecture: impermanent, 4, 20; of planter mansions, 10
Argall, Samuel, 51, 59
Ark, 246, 259
Artisans: and variations in resources, 32–33; lack of, in 17th-century Chesapeake, 147, 350–351; free black, 289–290, 291, 298; and crop mixes, 342, 357–362, 365–371; increase of, 351, 353–355, 357–362; in Talbot County, Md., 391–432; in England, 420–425; in Pennsylvania, 422; in New England, 422–423. *See also* Free craftsmen